SELLING YOUR COINS & BANKNOTES?

Warwick and Warwick have an expanding requirement for coin and banknote collections, British and worldwide and for coins and notes of individual value. Our customer base is increasing dramatically and we need an ever larger supply of quality material to keep pace with demand. The market has never been stronger and if you are considering the sale of your collection, now is the time to act.

FREE VALUATIONS

We will provide a free, professional and without obligation valuation of your collection. Either we will make you a fair, binding private treaty offer, or we will recommend inclusion of your property in our next specialist public auction.

FREE TRANSPORTATION

We can arrange insured transportation of your collection to our Warwick offices completely free of charge. If you decline our offer, we ask you to cover the return carriage costs only.

FREE VISITS

Visits by our valuers are possible anywhere in the country or abroad, usually within 48 hours, in order to value larger collections. Please telephone for details.

VALUATION DAYS

We are staging a series of valuation days and will be visiting all areas of England, Scotland, Wales and Ireland during the coming months. Please visit our website or telephone for further details.

EXCELLENT PRICES

Because of the strength of our customer base we are in a position to offer prices that we feel sure will exceed your expectations.

ACT NOW

Telephone or email Richard Beale today with details of your property.

THE

COIN
Yearbook
2016

Edited by
John W. Mussell
and the Editorial Team of COIN NEWS

ISBN 978 1 908828 26 2

Published by
TOKEN PUBLISHING LIMITED
Orchard House, Duchy Road, Heathpark, Honiton, EX14 1YD
Telephone: 01404 46972   Fax: 01404 44788
e-mail: info@tokenpublishing.com. Website: http://www.tokenpublishing.com

Printed in Great Britain by Latimer Trend & Company Ltd., Plymouth

CONTENTS

FOREWORD

WELCOME to the 2016 edition of the COIN YEARBOOK, the UK's bestselling coin price-guide and collectors' handbook. Many of you will be repeat buyers of the YEARBOOK and will already know how useful it can be; others will be new to the work, indeed new to the fascinating world of coin collecting (numismatics to the uninitiated) and still more of you will be reading this because you have come across some coins and want to know more—specifically what they are worth. Many of you who are coming to coins anew will be eager to know the value of your new acquisitions, of course you are—after all, television shows such as Flog It and the Antiques Roadshow, and newspaper and internet headlines about miraculous "treasure" being unearthed from farmers' fields or dug out from attics, have convinced you that every old coin is worth a fortune. Sadly it isn't and as you go through this book you will realise that much of what you have is worth no more than a few pence—pounds if you are lucky—and that's a good thing too. After all, if every coin was worth thousands of pounds we wouldn't have a hobby as no one would be able to afford to collect. However, do not despair, for whilst not every coin is worth a king's ransom there are undoubtedly those that are, and who knows you may have one of them…!

The key to value is very much rarity, followed by condition—after all, coins were minted to be used every day and as such any given coin from any given year will, usually, have had hundreds of thousands, if not millions, just like it in circulation. There is no doubt that over the years many of these coins have disappeared, they've been recalled to banks or melted down but, certainly for the later issues (Victoria and onwards) the chances are there are still a fair few thousands in existence. However, that isn't always the case. In some instances, usually where there were already enough of that denomination in circulation, the Royal Mint either didn't strike any circulating coins for a particular year (the 1933 penny is the best example, where only a handful were struck to be placed in cornerstones of civic buildings) or struck very few (the 1905 shilling is a good example where less than 500,000 were struck—a large number but far fewer than in 1904 or 1906!). It is these coins that command a premium. For coins with higher mintages then condition is king. As they were all struck to be used, finding them in EF (extremely fine) condition, looking as if they'd come direct from the bank even after a hundred or more years, is very difficult and so collectors will pay more for them.

As you work through this book and check your own collections, bear these things in mind. Of course there are other factors that affect price too and even modern, decimal coins can be worth far more than face value. Take the example of the 1983 2p piece inadvertently struck with an old reverse showing "New Pence" instead of "Two Pence", that will fetch you over £750. Or the recent 2008 20p "without the date", a result of the mint using an early obverse "muled" with the new design reverse—they retail at about £50. The latest rarity is the "drowning swimmer": the Olympic 50p with the swimmer's face obscured by the lines of water—later coins had the face clear. The original minting will make you around £500. Do you have one of those in your pocket?

Many of you will be buying this book because you have found something with your metal detector and are hoping for riches—well, hammered coins are always sought after, again the better condition ones fetching the most money and whilst true riches will come if you discover a hoard you will see that even single coins can be worth some serious money. If you were the lucky treasure seeker who unearthed the Edward III "double leopard" you would have seen your coin fetch £460,000 at auction!

Not everyone that is buying the book is doing so solely with a view to "making it big". Hopefully some of you will learn enough from these pages to realise that numismatics is a fascinating hobby—not every coin is worth a fortune but just about every coin is interesting in its own way. You only have to look at the beauty of the Gothic crown or the design of the 12-sided threepenny bit to see that. However, the primary purpose of this book is to reflect the current market and to do that we look at auction prices and dealers' lists, taking an average to put in the book (the key thing to note with both is that quality is going up and up in price and value). We also have a number of specialists who have worked tirelessly to ensure our pricing is accurate across the coin spectrum and to them we owe our thanks. These include: Elizabeth Cottam and Chris Rudd for sharing their expertise in the Celtic section, Mike Vosper for his hard work on the Roman, Stephen Mitchell of Studio Coins for help with the Hammered, Roy Norbury of West Essex Coins, for revising the Milled section, Patrick Mackenzie for his intimate knowledge of the Royal Mint issues for up-dating the Decimal section, Nick Swabey for expanding the Maundy coins and Charles Riley for assisting with the commemorative medals. In addition we would like to acknowledge our indebtedness to David Stuart who helped with the Scottish section, Del Parker who advised on the Irish and David Fletcher who assisted with the modern issues. We would also like to thank the numerous other individuals, both collectors and dealers, who have freely offered advice and the many auction houses who have allowed us to use images from their archives.

If you have any queries regarding this publication or need assistance or advice with any aspect of the hobby please feel free to email or write to the address to be found on page 9 and we will do our best to help. If you not familiar with our monthly magazine COIN NEWS, or if you need any accessories to help you with your collection, then please visit our user-friendly website at www.tokenpublishing.com. For a free sample issue of the magazine simply email or telephone us and we will be happy to send you a copy with our compliments.

Finally, because of the present volatility of the prices of precious metal, which, of course, affects the coin market in many ways, particularly when buying and selling gold coins such as sovereigns, it is impossible to publish accurate prices for bullion-related coins as they can change from day to day. Therefore the prices given for these are a guide only.

Britannia, Rule the Waves

The eagerly anticipated annual release of the Britannia Proof Collection has arrived, with a design for 2015 that nods to Britannia's nautical heritage. This comprehensive range in fine gold and fine silver includes individual coins, such as the grand Five-Ounce, and exceptional sets of three or six coins, all finished to pristine Proof standard. Britannia coins will be in great demand this year, as they will bear the fifth definitive portrait of The Queen – two British icons united.

Treasure for Life™

The Britannia Collection 2015, prices start from £50

The Queen's *Coinage*

The first coins bearing the portrait of Her Majesty Queen Elizabeth II were issued in 1953, her Coronation year, for the UK, the Dominions and the dependent territories (the new term for "colonies") of Jamaica, Mauritius, the Seychelles, and Malaya and British Borneo. Mary Gillick's attractive uncrowned effigy was well received, though the laurel wreath looks old-fashioned nowadays. Cecil Thomas created the elegant crowned effigy. Imperial coinage was still hierarchical: Britain and the Dominions (Australia, New Zealand, Canada and South Africa) used the uncrowned effigy of the monarch, whilst those crowned dependencies (in practice only Jersey) and dependent territories that portrayed the monarch were required to use the crowned effigy. Upon independence in 1948, India, Pakistan and Ceylon (now Sri Lanka) had become the first Dominions that were not white-ruled to freely retain the British monarch as head of state, though only Ceylon chose to use the monarch's portrait on its coins. India became a republic in 1950, but Elizabeth automatically became Queen of Pakistan and Ceylon when she ascended the throne. During her reign, Ceylon issued only a scalloped 2 cents coin (in 1955 and 1957): the only coin of a non-white-ruled Dominion to portray the Queen uncrowned. Ceylon replaced the Queen's portrait with the coat of arms in 1963. Nowadays the "Dominions" are called Commonwealth realms.

The obverse legend on the UK coins of 1953, "ELIZABETH II DEI GRATIA BRITT.OMN REGINA" was Latin for "Elizabeth II, by the grace of God Queen of all Britains". "BRITT.OMN " was added in 1902, honouring Britain's Imperial allies in the Boer War as "other Britains"; now considered patronisingly outdated, it was dropped from the coins in 1954.

Jersey and Guernsey in predecimal times issued only low denominations but otherwise used British coinage. According to William Exley's 1968 monograph, entitled "Guernsey Coinage", silver coinage was not introduced due to fears of forgery. "In the spacious times before 1914, silver was worth two shillings to two shillings and sixpence per ounce, and each ounce could be coined to give five shillings." However, Guernsey issued its first threepence coin in 1956, and Jersey followed suit in 1957 with its "one fourth of a shilling", equivalent to threepence.

The Guernsey piece was scalloped and in copper-nickel, while the Jersey coin was round and made of nickel-brass. Below the denomination of one shilling, the related predecimal coins of the Empire and Commonwealth rarely matched the format of their UK counterparts. Guernsey's coins did not carry the Queen's portrait until 1985, despite being a crown dependency. It is these small anomalies that make the Queen's coinage so fascinating.

In 1963 Arnold Machin created his now famous numismatic effigy of the Queen wearing a tiara, and Britain reluctantly allowed it to be used on Rhodesia's new coinage, which was released in 1964 and denominated both in shillings and pence and in Rhodesian cents. The Queen now made the portrait available to any Commonwealth country or territory wishing to use it: the old crowned/uncrowned numismatic hierarchy would no longer hold sway.

In 1968 Britain issued the first 5p and 10p decimal coins, followed in 1969 by the 50p, the world's first heptagonal coin. Machin's new effigy allowed immediate visual identification of the new coins. These phased introductions, which occurred also in Jersey and Guernsey, were the first steps in a familiarisation campaign, leading to full decimalisation in 1971. For the first time, Guernsey and Jersey each had a full set of circulation coins to match their UK counterparts. The Isle of Man, which lacked its own coinage, waited until 1971 to release its own full decimal series. Nonetheless, British coinage still co-circulated in all three Crown dependencies. Guernsey retained its state arms instead of the Queen's portrait, but Jersey and the Isle of Man now both used the Machin portrait. With the demise of the crowned/uncrowned hierarchy, Jersey was at last allowed to use the same portrait as the UK, and the Machin effigy became synonymous with decimalisation.

Mary Gillick's classical portrait was the first to appear on Her Majesty's coinage (image courtesy the Royal Mint).

Arnold Machin's regal effigy was used on the UK's first decimal coinage.

In the UK, the Gillick portrait still rubbed shoulders with the Machin effigy, since the sixpence, shilling and florin were retained in circulation as 2½p, 5p and 10p respectively, a situation that often puzzled foreign tourists. In the 1960s Victorian bronze coins and Edwardian silver coins had still been commonly found in circulation. However, the pre-1947 silver coins quickly disappeared in the 1970s, resulting in an ever higher proportion of coins with the Queen's portrait, whilst a decreasing proportion bore her father's portrait. In 1973, this loss of numismatic diversity was alleviated slightly when Prime Minister Edward Heath authorised a 50 pence

coin that commemorated Britain's entry into the EEC (now the EU). Readily found in change, it was Britain's first circulating commemorative coin, and the human element of the design, showing linked hands, added to its charm and popularity. Though the 50p coin proved the perfect vehicle for a commemorative, nineteen years were to elapse before its next appearance in that role. The Royal Mint's overseas customers also coveted the elegant heptagonal shape, and as the 1970s progressed, seven-sided coins were issued as far afield as Mexico, Sri Lanka, the Solomon Islands and the Seychelles.

After Mrs Thatcher became UK Prime Minister in 1979, unemployment soared as she administered harsh economic medicine, but the wedding of Prince Charles and Lady Diana Spencer in 1981 provided a romantic interlude; the event was commemorated on a UK collector coin, the last to be denominated as 25 pence. The issue of a 20 pence coin to fill the gap between the 10p and 50p was the UK's main numismatic event of 1982, along with the removal of the now redundant word "NEW" from the legends. To accommodate the amended legend, significant changes were made to the thistle on the 5p and Britannia on the 50p, but these were noticed only by those with keen eyes. High inflation necessitated the introduction of a circulating pound in 1983. Its reverse design was changed annually, honouring separately the UK and each of its four constituent nations on a five year basis. Britain's decimal coinage was rapidly gaining in variety. Meanwhile Jersey ditched its heraldic coins for a new set profiling the island's landmarks, reflecting the growing trend for thematic designs.

Raphael Maklouf's portrait which replaced that by Arnold Machin.

In 1985 a new portrait of the Queen, created by Raphael Maklouf, replaced the long-serving Machin portrait in Britain and related countries and territories. Maklouf also provided various uncouped versions of the effigy for use on special coins, such as the 1985 Royal Visit commemoratives of Antigua, Dominica and Grenada. Guernsey, whose coins had previously featured the Queen only on commemoratives, now replaced the state arms with the new effigy, aiming to increase the coinage's collector appeal, and also introduced new reverse designs. The Isle of Man was also now catering to collectors by regularly replacing its design series and issuing numerous commemorative coins. In 1986, Britain's first commemorative coin since 1981 celebrated the Commonwealth Games held in Scotland. The first in a series of nickel-brass two pound coins, it reflected the march of inflation and ousted the long-traditional collector crown (25p).

In 1989 Alderney, a dependency of Guernsey, issued its first coin, a 2 pound collector coin commemorating the Queen's visit. In 1990 Canada became the first Commonwealth country to use its own portrait of the Queen on its circulation coinage. Designed by Dora de Pédery-Hunt, it replaced the widely used Maklouf portrait. In the 1990s various territories, such as the Turks and Caicos, began using new non-standard portraits of the Queen on their collector coins.

Britain still had relatively large coins, but in 1990 a radically smaller 5 pence replaced the larger version, followed by a smaller 10 pence in 1992. The older versions were demonetised, along with the old shillings and florins; the familiar portrait of George VI disappeared from circulation, while that of the Queen now reigned supreme. Also in 1992 the UK issued its first commemorative 50 pence since 1973, to mark Britain's presidency of the EU, and the commemorative 50p now became something of a fixture.

A smaller 50 pence was issued in 1997, along with a circulating bimetallic 2 pound coin, which was slightly thinner than the old nickel-brass collector coin, last minted in 1996. From 1999 the new bimetallic coin also usurped its predecessor's function as a commemorative coin. Ian Rank-Broadley's daringly realistic new effigy was introduced in 1998, showing the Queen as old, regal and dignified. The Noughties saw the first collector coins issued for South Georgia and the South Sandwich Islands, British Antarctic Territory, and British Indian Ocean Territory. The coins, carrying an elegant uncouped version of Rank-Broadley's effigy, proclaim Britain's possession of these territories, which are used for research and/or military purposes and have no permanent human inhabitants.

In 2013 Fiji, a republic since 1987, became the first country in many years to remove the Queen's portrait from its coinage. This may become a trend, since other Commonwealth realms are considering becoming republics. However, some Commonwealth republics, such as Malawi, Uganda and Nauru, use the Queen's portrait on collector coins to increase their appeal.

In this new millennium, Britain's circulating commemoratives have become more frequent and more adventurously designed too, encompassing numerous themes and far less heraldry. However, in 2008 Britain's new circulation design series straddled the traditional and the post-modern, by splitting the royal shield of arms into conceptual jigsaw pieces. In 2015 Jody Clark's new portrait of a smiling Queen appeared on Britain's circulation coins. Yet throughout the Queen's long reign, one category of coins has remained unchanged: Maundy money. The Maundy coins retain the original Gillick effigy, while their face values, in numerals only, have catered for predecimal and decimal times alike.

2015 is the year in which Her Majesty surpasses Queen Victoria's length of reign. Since Victoria's day, economic growth has facilitated a huge increase in global wealth and population, meaning that Elizabeth has appeared on billions more coins than any other person, and it is unlikely that this record will ever be matched.

Ian Rank-Broadley, uncouped portrait featured on collector coins (image courtesy Pobjoy Mint).

Ian Rank Broadley's portrait was introduced in 1998 (image courtesy the Royal Mint).

The latest portrait by Jody Clark (image courtesy the Royal Mint).

This is a shortened version of an article by Phil McLoughlin that appeared in COIN NEWS, September 2015.

PUBLIC AUCTIONS
IN THE NORTH OF ENGLAND
Coins, Medals & Banknotes

MUSEUM

archive

Every month in **COIN NEWS** we are privileged to feature one of the rare items from the Royal Mint's Museum at Llanstrisant. The collection represents one of the most impressive numismatic collections in the world, featuring outstanding rarities alongside the currency we all use in our every day lives. Here we have chosen a few of the items we have featured, as a "snap shot" of the Museum's treasures.

Waterloo Bridge Medal

The Royal Mint Museum has a number of accessions registers, recording the details of items coming into the collection. One of the most handsome is that opened for medals in 1816, leather bound, embossed with gold leaf and entries filled out in the elegant scribe's hand of the day on heavyweight paper. It is a volume established with a long future in mind but the total number of items listed in the entire volume comes to the intriguing total of three. One of the three is the Waterloo

Bridge Medal of 1817, a beautiful silver piece with incuse edge lettering, commemorating the opening of Waterloo Bridge over the Thames. Other medals from the first half of the 19th century did find their way into the collection but the small number noted in the original volume reflects the quantity of official medals made at the time by the Royal Mint. Much of the rest of the medal work passed through the hands of the engravers as private commissions and therefore did not always formally justify specimens being set aside for the Museum.

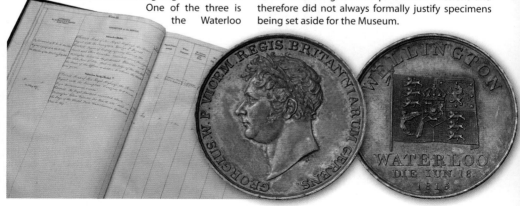

Coinage tools of James I

While the Royal Mint Museum has an unrivalled collection of coinage tools from the 1650s, the survival of minting equipment of an earlier date is much less strong. The few medieval tools that are present in the collection were acquired from the Pyx Chapel, Westminster Abbey, in the 1840s but the James I shilling dies illustrated here were not part of that group and, although W. J. Hocking's catalogue from the early 20th century records them as genuine, their authenticity has been called into question. What is immediately apparent is the square form of the sleeve that surrounds the dies. It is thought a restraining sleeve could have been used in the striking of hammered coins but one of this type is not readily encountered elsewhere. In addition, the royal style and titles on the obverse includes the letters RX, an abbreviation not known from surviving coins. It is not at all clear how the tools came into the collection and their odd appearance, combined with suspect design details, must leave a good deal of doubt hanging over their status as genuine dies of the period.

Nicholas Briot's gold coins

Experimentation with machinery at the Royal Mint had been explored by Eloy Mestrell in the 1560s and although his coins were beautifully made he encountered resistance from within the organisation. Another attempt was initiated in the 1630s by the French engraver Nicholas Briot who had tried but failed to persuade the mint in Paris of the virtues of his techniques and in moving to England was allowed to set up his own operation within the bounds of the Tower of London.

The gold coins he produced under Charles I, struck between 1631 and 1632, conformed to the regular standards of the time and included unites, double-crowns and crowns. As with the unite illustrated, they are delicately engraved and highly refined pieces, not only demonstrating Briot's technical mastery but also his ability as an artist to capture the subtle character of the king. It would be another 30 years before hammer-struck coins finally gave way to the screw press but Briot's experiments made a lasting contribution and are evidence of the desire Charles had to improve the standard to which the coinage was made.

Thomas Stanley Medal

Medals struck in honour of Royal Mint officials are a particular strength of the Museum's collection but the series is by no means complete and consequently when one is offered at auction efforts are almost always made to fill the gaps. One such opportunity arose recently in relation to the silver medal for the 16th-century Mint official Thomas Stanley. He was successively Assay Master, Comptroller and Under-Treasurer at the Mint in the Tower between 1545 and 1571, and therefore a key figure in the organisation during the troubled times of the mid-Tudor period. The medal, handsome in proportions, shows Stanley in profile wearing a fashionable high ruffed collar and bonnet. The reverse displays an armorial shield and the quality of striking is extremely high. Dating from the 1560s it is one of the earliest medals known to have been struck for a Mint official and its acquisition represents a welcome addition to the early part of the medal collection.

Spectacular gift

Royal portraits are in the news at the moment. With this in mind, the item pictured above from the Royal Mint Museum is a pattern gold crown of Edward VI which came into the Museum in 1818 as part of the spectacular gift of coins from the collection put together by Sarah Sophia Banks. Despite many rivals for affection, the coin has long been a particular favourite of Museum staff.

The charm of the coin lies in the remarkable success of the engraver in capturing the youthful appearance of the boy-king, who was not yet ten years old when he came to the throne in 1547 following the death of his father Henry VIII. In its features, highlighted perhaps by the cropped hair, the portrait represents a major step in the progress towards realistic portraiture begun a couple of generations earlier with the profile or "half-face" coins of Henry VII. Edward's bare-headed coins received high praise from Dr Humphrey Sutherland in his *Art in Coinage* published in 1955, writing with his customary elegance of "the boy-king's bare-headed portrait conveying all the simple, unemotional pathos of the finest coin-portraiture of any age". The compliment is all the greater when we reflect that, young as he was, Edward VI is known to have taken an intelligent interest in the coins of his brief reign.

Bronze plaque of Sir William Chandler Roberts-Austen

About 1900 the Royal Mint's engraver George William De Saulles prepared a portrait plaque in bronze of the Chemist and Assayer, Sir William Chandler Roberts-Austen. It was one of a group of plaques, two of the other senior figures chosen being the Deputy Master Horace Seymour and the Superintendent of the Operative Department Edward Rigg, each accorded accomplished and dignified profiles by De Saulles.

Roberts-Austen had entered the Royal Mint some 30 years previously and had become a key figure within the hierarchy as a result of his work on improving several aspects of the minting process, including the manufacture of dies, the assaying of precious metals and the melting of bullion. In the wider world of science he rose to prominence through his pioneering work on the nature of steel which was itself an important contribution to the study of metallurgy and helped establish the Royal Mint for a time as one of the country's leading scientific institutions. Striking or casting medals in honour of Royal Mint officials goes back certainly to the 16th century and, in creating the plaques, De Saulles was in a very real sense continuing that tradition, albeit in a slightly different form.

James I Unite

When James I came to the throne in 1603 it was as king of England and Scotland, but within about 18 months, on October 20, 1604, he proclaimed himself king of Great Britain, France and Ireland. Aside from such edicts he had the coinage at his disposal to help him redefine the identity of the monarchy and in less than a month the 20-shilling gold sovereign had been renamed the unite, an explicit reference to his achievement of bringing the crowns of England and Scotland together. The politicisation of the coinage carried on down to the five-shilling piece being referred to as a Britain crown and a new four-shilling coin as the thistle crown.

The Royal Mint Museum is well served with gold coins of the Tudor and Stuart periods but it has a particularly strong collection of gold of James I. A good run of mintmarks on unites is represented, the earliest being the lis, from the period of initial transition at the end of 1604. His new status was reflected on the coinage in changed titles, revised heraldry and, demonstrating a little more subtlety, gold unites from their first issue carried in Latin the quotation from Ezekiel 37: 22 "I will make them one nation". It is clear James was making a concerted effort to change the iconography of the monarchy and his political ambitions found one of their most prominent expressions through his new gold coins.

MONARCHS *of England*

Here we list the Kings and Queens from Anglo-Saxon times to the present, with the dates of their rule. Before Eadgar became the King of all England the country had been divided up into small kingdoms, each with their own ruler.

ANGLO-SAXON KINGS

The Anglo-Saxon monarchs ruled over the various kingdoms which existed in England following the withdrawal of the Romans in the 5th century AD. The most prominent kingdoms in the land were Kent, Sussex, Wessex, Mercia and Northumbria. Each kingdom produced its own coinage but in 973 Eadgar introduced a new coinage that became the standard for the whole of the country.

Eadgar (959–975)
Edward the Martyr (975–978)
Aethelred II (978–1016)
Cnut (1016–1035)
Harold I (1035–1040)
Harthacanut (1035–1042)
Edward the Confessor (1042–1066)
Harold II (1066)

NORMAN KINGS

The Normans came to Britain from their native France following the establishment of a kingdom in Sicily and southern Italy. An expedition led by the powerful Duke William of Normandy culminated in the battle of Hastings in 1066 where he defeated Harold II and was proclaimed King of All England. Their influence spread from these new centres to the Crusader States in the Near East and to Scotland and Wales in Great Britain, and to Ireland. Today their influence can be seen in their typical Romanesque style of architecture.

William I (1066–1087)
William II (1087–1100)
Henry I (1100–1135)
Stephen (1135–1154)

PLANTAGENETS

The Plantagenet kings of England were descended from the first House of Anjou who were established as rulers of England through the Treaty of Wallingford, which passed over the claims of Eustace and William, Stephen of Blois's sons, in favour of Henry of Anjou, son of the Empress Matilda and Geoffrey V, Count of Anjou.

Henry II (1154–1189)
Richard I (1189–1199)
John (1199–1216)
Henry III (1216–1272)
Edward I (1272–1307)
Edward II (1307–1327)
Edward III (1327–1377)
Richard II (1377–1399)

HOUSE OF LANCASTER

The House of Lancaster, a branch of the English royal House of Plantagenet, was one of the opposing factions involved in the Wars of the Roses, the civil war which dominated England and Wales during the 15th century. Lancaster provided England with three Kings

Henry IV (1399–1413)
Henry V (1413–1422)
Henry VI (1422–1461) and again 1470

HOUSE OF YORK

The House of York was the other branch of the House of Plantagenet involved in the disastrous Wars of the Roses. Edward IV was descended from Edmund of Langley, 1st Duke of York, the fourth surviving son of Edward III.

Edward IV (1461–1483 and again 1471–83)
Richard III (1483–1485)

TUDORS

The House of Tudor was an English royal dynasty that lasted 118 years, from 1485 to 1603. The family descended from the Welsh courtier Owen Tudor (Tewdwr). Following the defeat of Richard III at Bosworth, the battle that ended the Wars of the Roses, Henry Tudor, 2nd Earl of Richmond, took the throne as Henry VII.

Henry VII (1485–1509)
Henry VIII (1509–1547)
Edward VI (1547–1553)
Mary (1553–1558)
Philip & Mary (1554–1558)
Elizabeth I (1558–1603)

STUARTS

The House of Stuart ruled Scotland for 336 years, between 1371 and 1707. Elizabeth I of England's closest heir was James VI of Scotland via her grandfather Henry VII of England, who was founder of the Tudor dynasty. On Elizabeth's death, James Stuart ascended the thrones of England and Ireland and inherited the English claims to the French throne. The Stuarts styled themselves "Kings and Queens of Great Britain", although there was no parliamentary union until the reign of Queen Anne, the last monarch of the House of Stuart.

James I (1603–1625)
Charles I (1625–1649)
The Commonwealth (1653–1658)
Charles II (1660–1685)
James II (1685–1688)
William III & Mary (1688–1694)
William III (1694–1702)
Anne (1702–1714)

HOUSE OF HANOVER

The House of Hanover was a Germanic royal dynasty which ruled the Duchy of Brunswick-Lüneburg and the Kingdom of Hanover. George Ludwig ascended to the throne of the Kingdom of Great Britain and Ireland through the female line from Princess Elizabeth, sister of Charles I.

George I (1714–1727)
George II (1727–1760)
George III (1760–1820)
George IV (1820–1830)
William IV (1830–1837)
Victoria (1837–1901)

HOUSES OF SAXE-COBURG-GOTHA AND WINDSOR

The name Saxe-Coburg-Gotha was inherited by Edward VII from his father Prince Albert, the second son of the Duke of Saxe-Coburg-Gotha and husband of Victoria. During World War I the name was changed to Windsor to avoid the Germanic connotatiion.

Edward VII (1901–1910)
George V (1910–1936)
Edward VIII (1936)
George VI (1936–1952)
Elizabeth II (1952–)

VIEW *of the Bay*

Here is some timely advice for those thinking of bidding on-line

When I registered with eBay UK 17 years ago the grand total of items for sale in *all* categories was 850,000 which I thought at the time was an enormous amount of listings but that now looks tiny. Seventeen years later the "coins" category alone contains over 250,000 items, "banknotes" almost 53,000, over 6,000 in "tokens" and 6,500 in "historical medals/medallions". This gives a grand total of about 315,500 numismatic items to choose from and there are still collectors who don't have internet access at home—they are missing out massively as this is an increase of 115,500 items in one year.

At the time of writing the number of British items listed on eBay.co.uk in each category was as follows: coins almost 111,000, banknotes 8,500, tokens 4,000 and also 4,000 in historical medals/medallions. Sellers have moved away from auction type listings, with around 66 per cent now preferring to list under "Buy It Now" with a fixed price which is sometimes open to offers. The prices range from one penny to £80,000.

When selling on eBay make full use of the title rather than putting off potential bidders by just having "coin" in the title as some sellers do. If a seller can't be bothered to write an informative title then why should bidders be bother to bid? The title of any numismatic item should include as much relevant information as there is space for, i.e. country of origin, denomination, date, metal, size, condition. It's acceptable to have a title in all capitals but not the actual listing as this might put bidders off. If a bidder is visually impaired they will have adjusted their PC's font size accordingly, so a huge font size is unnecessary. Some sellers have minimum information about their item on offer but have several paragraphs of terms and conditions, this is not required as all that happens is, the buyer pays and the seller posts the well-packed item. It's a good idea to search eBay for completed similar items before creating a listing as it's pointless asking £100 for a coin if a similar one sold recently for £9.99. Try to use the most appropriate numismatic category to maximise the selling price and avoid spelling errors in order to appear in the maximum number of buyer's search results.

When buying on eBay beware of sellers who sell coins using US grading terms or whose coins have been graded by US grading companies and then quote UK catalogue prices, as a US EF is miles away from a UK EF. Few collectors would claim to be an expert on coin grading so compare eBay grading with similar coins on offer by long established UK dealers on their web sites before deciding on a maximum bid. A dealer's VF coin at £200 might be a better buy than the same coin at £100 graded as being EF on eBay. Read coin descriptions very carefully especially that of gold coins. If a coin is described as weighing .2gr. don't misread this as 2gr as sometimes happens, most sellers will use "0.2" and not ".2" to make it clear.

To snipe or not to snipe is a subject often under consideration by bidders. Not bidding until the final few seconds has advantages as it denies competitors from placing any more bids but it also does likewise for the sniper. Another benefit is that rival collectors who regularly battle for items are prevented from searching for current items bid on by competing collectors if sniping is used, it also prevents drawing attention to that once-in-a-decade eBay super bargain. As some coin dealers recommend not sniping then it's definitely the best tactic for a collector to get an item for the lowest possible price. It also removes the possibility of a bidding war breaking out with the victim of auction fever paying over the odds just to win at all costs and beat the opposition.

eBay listings can be entertaining when looking at silly sellers listing items at silly high prices, many of whom sell just a very small percentage of their overpriced and often over graded offerings. A search for "unknown" or "mystery" can sometimes bring up interesting or valuable items but some sellers sell only "unknown" items regardless of how easy they are to identify. A search using spelling errors can find items that the majority of collectors

might miss, e.g. "soveren", "Scotish" or if local tokens are the item of interest, try a few town name spelling errors.

Unfortunately as it now seems possible to fool many of the people most of the time 100 per cent feedback is no longer a true indication of a seller's honesty. Some unscrupulous eBayers will list a penny for sale at one penny with collection only, with no option to have it posted and of course the penny is never collected, so every time they do this they and each buyer receives a positive feedback. They are in effect selling feedback for 1p and they get to build up a lot of positive feedback for themselves, presumably to make it easier to defraud buyers later when they have a reasonable amount of feedback.

For young collectors or for those on a limited budget eBay shops can be worth a browse, but the better coins tend to be listed as an auction or a "Buy It Now". The categories are well laid out, so finding a specific area of interest is

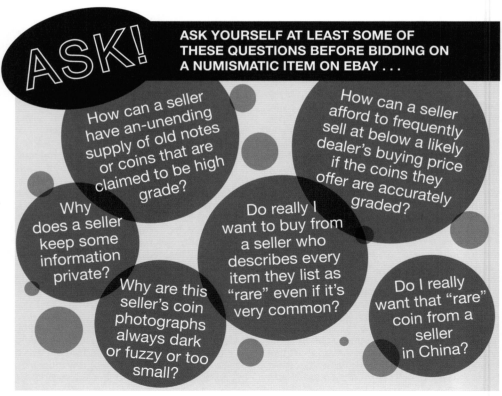

ASK YOURSELF AT LEAST SOME OF THESE QUESTIONS BEFORE BIDDING ON A NUMISMATIC ITEM ON EBAY . . .

How can a seller have an-unending supply of old notes or coins that are claimed to be high grade?

How can a seller afford to frequently sell at below a likely dealer's buying price if the coins they offer are accurately graded?

Why does a seller keep some information private?

Do really I want to buy from a seller who describes every item they list as "rare" even if it's very common?

Why are this seller's coin photographs always dark or fuzzy or too small?

Do I really want that "rare" coin from a seller in China?

easy. Shop items tend to be low grade and priced at full retail, so a bargain buy will require a lot of time-consuming luck to find. A seller can be offering several thousand UK coins with some priced at hundreds of pounds each, but a look at their feedback reveals that the majority of their sales are for coins priced at under £10. For a seller this is a way of getting a lot of traffic which would be very difficult to achieve otherwise.

As a few banknote collectors might be reading this, a few words of warning will not go wrong. There are very large numbers of ironed notes on eBay with some sellers selling only ironed notes to gullible collectors. Some collectors have yet to work out that to be able to offer an unlimited supply of older "uncirculated" notes the seller must be selling ironed notes that they themselves have probably ironed. Look at a seller's buying feedback as their "unc" note may have been VF if bought a few weeks previously. USA and Canada grading of bank notes is similar to their grading of coins—very optimistic, so look at the pictures very carefully and ignore the claimed grade before bidding. If a note has been slabbed it's probably best to assume that the note will grade in the UK at least one full grade below the grade on the slab. Overgrading of notes is also rife on eBay with many notes that appear from the scans to be in no better than fine condition claimed to be "gVF", if a note arrives in the post that is of lower grade than claimed then send it back and give at least a neutral feedback to warn other

collectors. As it's now easier to get unc money for an ironed note than it is to get VF money for a genuine VF note, overgrading can only get worse as more sellers adopt the view "if you can't beat them join them". Unfortunately if a seller claims to grade to IBNS standards this is not a guarantee that they accurately grade their notes as notes claimed to be "EF" can have many creases. When a banknote has been sold and placed in a sleeve and encased in cardboard it's a good idea to place the complete package inside a waterproof bag and seal it with tape, most of us will have experienced a soggy envelope coming through the letterbox so a note should be sent in waterproof packaging.

Entering an eBay seller's ID into google can be a way of avoiding expensive buying mistakes as it can sometimes reveal information that a bad seller would rather be kept quiet. They might have sold forgeries, have a history of selling over-graded coins or have had legal problems for example. Regular readers of COIN NEWS are probably savvy enough not to be fooled by bad eBay sellers but the less experienced collector must bid with extreme caution. Regular browsing can be time well spent as a few astute buys can produce a greater profit when resold than twelve months of small time selling, with no time-consuming scanning and listing to do and no ever-increasing fees to pay.

DATES *on coins*

The vast majority of modern coins bear the date prominently on one side. In most cases dates are expressed in modified Arabic numerals according to the Christian calendar and present no problem in identification. There have been a few notable exceptions to this general rule, however. Morocco, for example, has used European numerals to express dates according to the Moslem calendar, so that a coin dated 1321 actually signifies 1903. Dates are almost invariably written from left to right—even in Arabic script which writes words from right to left. An exception, however, occurred in the Philippines quarto of 1822 where the date appeared as 2281, and the "2"s back to front for good measure.

	ARABIC-TURKISH	CHINESE, JAPANESE KOREAN, ANNAMESE (ORDINARY)	CHINESE, JAPANESE KOREAN, ANNAMESE (OFFICIAL)	INDIAN	SIAMESE	BURMESE
1	١	一	壹	٩	๑	၁
2	٢	二	貳	٦	๒	၂
3	٣	三	叁	٣	๓	၃
4	٤	四	肆	٨	๔	၄
5	٥	五	伍	٤	๕	၅
6	٦	六	陸	٦	๖	၆
7	٧	七	柒	٧	๗	၇
8	٨	八	捌	٢	๘	၈
9	٩	九	玖	٩	๙	၉
0	٠			٠	๐	၀
10	١٠	十	拾		๑๐	
100	١٠٠	百			๑๐๐	
1000	١٠٠٠	千				

Dates in Roman numerals have been used since 1234 when this practice was adopted by the Danish town of Roskilde. Such Roman numerals were used sporadically throughout the Middle Ages and in later centuries and survive fitfully to this day. This was the system used in England for the first dated coins, the gold half-sovereigns of Edward VI struck at Durham House in 1548 (MDXLVIII). This continued till 1550 (MDL) but thereafter Arabic numerals were used, beginning with the half-crown of 1551. Notable exceptions of more recent times include the Gothic coinage of Queen Victoria (1847–87).

The first coin with the date in European numerals was a plappart of St Gallen, Switzerland dated 1424, but this was an isolated case. In 1477 Maria of Burgundy issued a guldiner which bore a date on the reverse, in the form of two pairs of digits flanking the crown at the top. The numerals in this instance were true Gothic, an interesting transition between true Arabic numerals and the modified Arabic figures now used in Europe. The Tyrolese guldengroschen of 1484–6 were the first coins to be regularly dated in European numerals and thereafter this custom spread rapidly.

For the numismatist, the problem arises when coins bear a date in the numerals of a different alphabet or computed according to a different era. Opposite is a table showing the basic numerals used in different scripts. The various eras which may be found in coin dates are as listed and explained opposite.

Hijra

The era used on Moslem coins dates from the flight of Mohammed from Mecca to Medina on July 15, 622 and is often expressed as digits followed by AH (Anno Hegirae). Moslems employ a lunar calendar of twelve months comprising 354 11/30 days. Tipu Sultan of Mysore in 1201 AH (the fifth year of his reign) introduced a new era dating from the birth of Mohammed in AD 570 and using a luni-solar system. Tipu also adopted the Hindu cycle of sixty years (the Tamil Brihaspate Cycle), but changed this two or three years later, from Hijra to Muludi.

Afghan coins used the lunar calendar until 1920 and during 1929–31, but at other times have used the solar calendar. Thus the Democratic Republic began issuing its coins in SH 1358 (1979).

To convert an AH date to the Christian calendar you must translate the Arabic into European numerals. Taking an Arabic coin dated 1320, for example, first deduct 3% (to convert from the Moslem lunar year to our solar year). This gives 39.6 which, rounded up to the nearest whole number, is 40. Deduct 40 from 1320 (1280), then add 622. The answer is 1902.

There have been a few notable exceptions. Thus the Khanian era of Ilkhan Ghazan Mahmud began on 1st Rajab 701 AH (1301). This era used a solar calendar, but was shortlived, being confined to coins of Mahmud and his nephew Abu Said down to year 34 (1333).

The era of Tarikh Ilahi was adopted by the Mughal emperor Akbar in the thirteenth year of his reign (922 AH). This era dated from his accession on 5th Rabi al-Sani 963 AH (February 19, 1556). The calendar had solar months and days but no weeks, so each day of the month had a different name. This system was used by Akbar, Jahangir and Shah Jahan, often with a Hijra date as well.

Saphar

The era of the Caesars began on January 1, 38 BC and dated from the conquest of Spain by Augustus. Its use on coinage, however, seems to have been confined to the marabotins of Alfonso VIII of Castile and was expressed in both Latin and Arabic.

Samvat

The era of Vikramaditya began in 57 BC and was a luni-solar system used in some Indian states. Coins may be found with both Samvat and Hijra dates. Conversion to the Christian date is simple; merely subtract 57 from the Samvat to arrive at the AD date.

Saka

This originated in the southwestern district of Northern India and began in AD 78. As it used the luni-solar system it converts easily by adding 78 to the Saka date.

Nepal

Nepalese coins have used four different date systems. All coins of the Malla kings were dated in Nepal Samvat (NS) era, year 1 beginning in 881. This system was also used briefly by the state of Cooch Behar. Until 1888 all coins of the Gurkha dynasty were dated in the Saka era (SE) which began in AD 78. After 1888 most copper coins were dated in the Vikram Samvat (VS) era from 57 BC. With the exception of some gold coins struck in 1890 and 1892, silver and gold coins only changed to the VS era in 1911, but now this system is used for all coins struck in Nepal. Finally, dates in the Christian era have appeared on some commemorative coins of recent years.

Ethiopian

This era dates from August AD 7, so that EE 1885 is AD 1892. Ethiopian dates are expressed in five digits using Amharic numerals. The first two are the digits of the centuries, the third is the character for 100, while the fourth and fifth are the digits representing the decade and year. On modern coins dates are rendered in Amharic numerals using the Christian era.

Thailand

Thai coins mainly use the Buddhist era (BE) which dates from 543 BC, but some coins have used dates from the Chula-Sakarat calendar (CS) which began in AD 638, while others use a Ratanakosind Sok (RS) date from the foundation of the Chakri dynasty in AD 1781.

Hebrew

The coins of Israel use the Jewish calendar dating from the beginning of the world (Adam and Eve in the Garden of Eden) in 3760 BC. Thus the year 1993 is rendered as 5753. The five millennia are assumed in dates, so that only the last three digits are expressed. 735 therefore equates with AD 1975. Dates are written in Hebrew letters, reading from right to left. The first two characters signify 400 and 300 respectively, totalling 700. The third letter denotes the decades (lamedh = 30) and the fourth letter, following the separation mark (") represents the final digit (heh = 5). The Jewish year runs from September or October in the Christian calendar.

Dates from the creation of the world

This system was also used in Russia under Ivan IV. The dating system Anno Mundi (AM) was established by the Council of Constantinople in AD 680 which determined that the birth of Christ had occurred in 5508 AM. Ivan's coins expressed the date as 7055 (1447).

Dynastic dates

The system of dating coinage according to regnal years is a feature of Chinese and Japanese coins. Chinese coins normally have an inscription stating that they are coins of such and such a reign period (not the emperor's name), and during the Southern Sung dynasty this was joined by the numeral of the year of the reign. This system was continued under the republic and survives in Taiwan to this day, although the coins of the Chinese Peoples Republic are dated in western numerals using the Christian calendar.

Early Japanese coins bore a reference to the era (the title assumed by each emperor on his accession) but, like Chinese coins, could not be dated accurately. From the beginning of the Meiji era (1867), however, coins have included a regnal number. The Showa era, beginning in 1926 with the accession of Hirohito, eventually ran to sixty-three (expressed in western numerals on some denominations, in Japanese ideograms on others) to denote 1988, although the rest of the inscription was in Japanese characters.

Dynastic dates were used on Korean milled coins introduced in 1888. These bore two characters at the top Kae Kuk (founding of the dynasty) followed by quantitative numerals. The system dated from the founding of the Yi dynasty in 1392. Curiously enough, some Korean banknotes have borne dates from the foundation of the first dynasty in 2333 BC.

Iran adopted a similar system in 1975, celebrating the 15th anniversary of the Pahlavi regime by harking back to the glories of Darius. The new calendar dated from the foundation of the Persian Empire 2535 years earlier, and was abolished only three years later when the Shah was overthrown.

Political eras

France adopted a republican calendar in 1793 when the monarchy was abolished. Coins were then inscribed L'AN (the year) followed by Roman numerals, but later Arabic numerals were substituted. This continued to the year 14 (1806) but in that year the Emperor Napoleon restored the Christian calendar. The French system was emulated by Haiti whose coins dated from the revolution of 1803. The date appeared as AN followed by a number until AN 31 (1834) on some coins; others had both the evolutionary year and the Christian date from 1828 until 1850 (AN 47). Coins with a date in the Christian calendar appeared only in 1807–9 and then from 1850 onwards.

Mussolini introduced the Fascist calendar to Italy, dating from the seizure of power in October 1922. This system was widely employed on documents and memorials, but was first used on silver 20 lire coins of 1927 and then only in addition to the Christian date and appearing discreetly as Roman numerals. Subsequently it was extended to gold 50 lire and 100 lire coins in 1931 and the subsidiary coinage in 1936, being last used in the year XXI (1943).

BALDWIN'S
The Name for Numismatics
Established 1872

AUCTIONS AROUND THE WORLD

Sell your collection in the best place possible
and achieve the highest prices

New York ~ London ~ Hong Kong

AUCTION ADVANCES

up to 50% pre-auction payment to you
for your coins and medals,
so no need to wait for six months

LOWEST CHARGES

we can charge less
than all other UK coin auctioneers
no hidden fees for photography,
insurance or unsold lots

For more information:
contact Seth Freeman, seth@baldwin.co.uk
or Sam Weedall, sam@baldwin.co.uk
or call our London showroom on +44 (0)207 930 9808
to make an appointment with our specialists.

399 Strand, London, WC2R 0LX
tel: +44 (0)20 7930 6879   fax: +44 (0)20 7930 9450

Follow us on Twitter @BaldwinsCoins Facebook.com/BaldwinsCoins

For a free guide to coin collecting email auctions@baldwin.co.uk and quote this advertisement

www.baldwin.co.uk

ssociation 诚信
ccredited 拍卖行
uctioneers 协会

Part of The Stanley Gibbons Group plc

BNTA

COIN TERMS *glossary*

In this section we list all the terms commonly encountered in numismatics or in the production of coins.

Abbey Coins Medieval coins struck in the abbeys, convents and other great religious houses which were granted coinage rights. These coins were often used also by pilgrims journeying from one monastery to another.

German restrikes or abschlag of a kreuzer of the Archbishops of Mainz: Friedrich Karl Joseph von Erthal (1774–1802). Dated 1795. (Image courtesy of CNG/Wikipedia)

Abschlag (German for "discount") A *restrike* from an original die.

Accolated Synonym for *conjoined* or *jugate* and signifying two or more profiles overlapping.

Acmonital Acronym from *Aciaio Monetario Italiano*, a stainless steel alloy used for Italian coins since 1939.

Adjustment Reduction of metal in a *flan* or *blank* to the specified weight prior to striking, accomplished by filing down the face. Such file marks often survived the coining process and are occasionally met with in coins, especially of the 18th century.

Ae Abbreviation for the Latin *Aes* (bronze), used for coins made of brass, bronze or other copper alloys.

Aes Grave (Latin for heavy bronze) Heavy circular coins first minted at Rome in 269 BC.

Aes Rude (Latin for rough bronze) Irregular lumps of bronze which gradually developed into ingots of uniform shape and were the precursors of coins in Rome.

Aes Signatum (Latin for signed bronze) Bronze ingots of regular size and weight, bearing marks of authority to guarantee their weight (289–269 BC).

Agonistic (Greek) Term for coins issued to commemorate, or pertaining to, sporting events.

Alliance Coinage struck by two or more states acting together and having common features of design or inscription.

Alloy Coinage metal composed of two or more metallic elements.

Altered Deliberately changed, usually unofficially, with the aim of increasing the numismatic value of a coin, medal or note. This applies particularly to dates, where a common date may be altered to a rare date by filing or re-engraving one of the digits.

Aluminium (American *Aluminum*) Silvery lightweight metal, developed commercially in the late 19th century for commemorative medals, but used for tokens and emergency money during the First World War and since 1940 widely used in subsidiary coinage.

Aluminium-bronze Alloy of aluminium and copper. Hard-wearing and gold-coloured, it is now widely used in tokens and subsidiary coinage.

Amulet Coin or medal believed to have talismanic qualities, such as warding off disease and bad luck. Many Chinese and Korean pieces come into this category. See also *Touchpiece*.

Androcephalous Heraldic term for creatures with a human head.

Anepigraphic Coins or medals without a legend.

Annealing Process of heating and cooling applied to metal to relieve stresses and prepare it for striking into coins.

Annulet Small circle often used as an ornament or spacing device in coin inscriptions.

Antimony Brittle white metal, chemical symbol *Sb*, virtually impractical as a coinage metal but used for the Chinese 10 cents of Kweichow, 1931. Alloyed with tin, copper or lead, it produces the white metal popular as a medallic medium.

Antoniniani Silver coins minted in Imperial Rome. The name derives from the Emperor Caracalla (Marcus Aurelius Antoninus) in whose reign they were first struck. The silver content was progressively reduced and by the last issue (AD 295) they were reduced to *billon*.

Ar Abbreviation for Latin *Argentum* (silver), used for coins struck in this metal.

Assay Mark Mark applied to a medal struck in precious metal by an assayer or assay office as a guarantee of the fineness of the metal.

Assignat Type of paper money used in France 1789–96, representing the land assigned to the holders.

Attribution Identification of a coin by characteristics such as issuing authority, date or reign, mint, denomination, metal, and by a standard reference.

Au Abbreviation for *aurum* (Latin for gold), denoting coins of this metal.

AU Abbreviation for "About Uncirculated", often found in catalogues and dealers' lists to describe the condition of a numismatic piece.

Autodollar Name given to the silver yuan issued by Kweichow, 1928, and having a contemporary motor car as the obverse motif.

Auxiliary Payment Certificate Form of paper money intended for use by American military personnel stationed in overseas countries. See also *Baf* and *Scrip*.

Babel Note Nickname given to the paper money of the Russian Socialist Federated Soviet Republic (1919) because it bore the slogan "workers of the world unite" in seven languages, a reference to the biblical tower of Babel.

Baf Acronym from British Armed Forces, the popular name for the vouchers which could only be exchanged for goods in service canteens from 1945 onwards.

Bag Mark Minor scratch or abrasion on an otherwise uncirculated coin, caused by coins in mint bags knocking together.

Banknote Form of paper money issued by banks and usually promising to pay the bearer on demand in coin of the realm.

Barbarous Imitation of Greek or Roman coins by the Celtic and Germanic tribes who lived beyond the frontiers of the civilised world.

Base Non-precious metals or alloys.

Bath Metal Inferior bronze alloy, named after the English city where it was used for casting cannon. Used by William Wood of Bristol for Irish and American tokens and by Amos Topping for Manx coins of 1733/4.

Beading Ornamental border found on the raised rim of a coin.

Behalfszahlungsmittel German term for auxiliary payment certificates used in occupied Europe from 1939 to 1945.

Bell Metal Alloy of copper and tin normally used for casting bells, but employed for the subsidiary coinage of the French Revolutionary period.

Billon Silver alloy containing less than 50 per cent fine silver, usually mixed with copper. In Spain this alloy was known as *vellon*.

Bi-metallic Coins struck in two separate metals or alloys. Patterns for such coins exist from the 19th century but actual coins with a centre of one metal surrounded by a ring of another did not appear till 1982 (Italy, San Marino and Vatican). Canada introduced coins with a tiny plaque inset in a second metal (1990). See also *Clad, Plugged* and *Sandwich*.

Bi-metallism Monetary system in which two metals are in simultaneous use and equally available as legal tender, implying a definite ratio between the two. A double standard of gold and silver, with a ratio of 16:1, existed till the mid-19th century.

Bingle American term for a trade token, more specifically the US government issue of tokens for the Matacuska, Alaska colonization project, 1935.

Birthday Coins Coins celebrating the birthday of a ruler originated in Roman Imperial times, notably the reigns of Maximianus (286–305) and Constantinus I (307–37). Birthday talers were issued by many German states, and among recent examples may be cited coins marking the 70th, 80th and 90th birthdays of Gustaf Adolf VI of Sweden, 80th and 90th birthday coins from the British Commonwealth for the Queen Mother, and coins honouring Queen Elizabeth, the Duke of Edinburgh and the Prince of Wales.

Bit Term denoting fragments of large silver coins, cut up and circulating as fractional values.

Spanish dollars were frequently broken up for circulation in the American colonies and the West indies. Long bits and short bits circulated at 15 and 10 cents respectively, but the term came to be equated with the Spanish real or eighth peso, hence the American colloquialism "two-bit" signifying a quarter dollar.

Black Money English term for the debased silver deniers minted in France which circulated freely in England until they were banned by government decree in 1351.

Blank Piece of metal, cut or punched out of a roller bar or strip, and prepared for striking to produce coins. Alternate terms are *flan* and *planchet*.

Blundered Inscription Legend in which the lettering is jumbled or meaningless, indicating the illiteracy of the tribes who copied Greek and Roman coins.

Bonnet Piece Scottish gold coin, minted in 1539–40. The name is derived from the obverse portraying King James V in a large, flat bonnet.

Bon Pour French for "good for", inscribed on Chamber of Commerce brass tokens issued in 1920–7 during a shortage of legal tender coinage.

Bouquet Sou Canadian copper token halfpenny of 1837 deriving its name from the nosegay of heraldic flowers on the obverse.

Box Coin Small container formed by *obverse* and *reverse* of two coins, hollowed out and screwed together.

Bracteate (Latin *bractea*, a thin piece of metal) Coins struck on blanks so thin that the image applied to one side appears in reverse on the other. First minted in Erfurt and Thuringia in the 12th century, and later produced elsewhere in Germany, Switzerland and Poland till the 14th century.

Victoria Young or "Bun" head bronze penny.

Brass Alloy of copper and zinc, widely used for subsidiary coinage. The term was also formerly used for bronze Roman coins, known numismatically as first, second or third brass.

Breeches Money Derisive term given by the Royalists to the coinage of the Commonwealth, 1651, the conjoined elongated oval shields on the reverse resembling a pair of breeches.

Brockage Mis-struck coin with only one design, normal on one side and *incuse* on the other. This occurs when a coin previously struck adheres to the die and strikes the next blank to pass through the press.

Broken Bank-note Note issued by a bank which has failed, but this is often applied more generally to banknotes which have actually been demonetised.

Bronze Alloy of copper and tin, first used as a coinage metal by the Chinese c. 1000 BC. Often used synonymously with copper, though it should be noted that bronze only superseded copper as the constituent of the base metal British coins in 1860.

Bull Neck Popular term for the coins of King George III, 1816–17.

Bullet Money Pieces of silver, *globular* in shape, bearing various *countermarks* and used as coins in Siam (Thailand) in the 18th and 19th centuries.

Bullion Precious metal in bars, ingots, strip or scrap (i.e. broken jewellery mounts, watch-cases and plate), its weight reckoned solely by weight and fineness, before being converted into coin.

Bullion Coin A coin struck in platinum, gold or silver, whose value is determined solely by the prevailing market price for the metal as a commodity. Such coins do not generally have a nominal face value, but include in their inscriptions their weight and fineness. Good examples of recent times include the Krugerrand (South Africa), the Britannia (UK), the Maple Leaf (Canada), Libertad (Mexico), the Nugget (Australia) and the Eagle (USA).

Bun Coinage British coins of 1860–94 showing Queen Victoria with her hair in a bun.

Bungtown Coppers Derisive term (from Anglo-American slang *bung*, to swindle or bribe) for halfpence of English or Irish origin, often counterfeit, which circulated in North America towards the end of the colonial period.

Carat (American *Karat*) Originally a unit of weight for precious stones, based on carob seeds (ceratia), it also denotes the fineness or purity of gold, being 1/24th part of the whole. Thus 9 carat gold is .375 fine and 22 carat, the English sovereign standard, is .916 fine. Abbreviated as ct or kt.

Cartwheel Popular term for the large and cumbersome penny and twopenny pieces of 1797 weighing one and two ounces, struck by Matthew Boulton at the Soho Mint, Birmingham.

Cased Set Set of coins in mint condition, housed in the official case issued by the mint. Formerly leather cases with blue plush or velvet lining were used, but nowadays many sets are encapsulated in plastic to facilitate handling.

Cash (from Portuguese *caixa*, Hindi *kasu*). Round piece of bronze or brass with a square hole in the centre, used as subsidiary coinage in China for almost 2000 years, till the early 12th century. In Chinese these pieces were known as *Ch'ien* or *Li* and strung together in groups of 1000 were equivalent to a silver tael.

Cast Coins Coins cast from molten metals in moulds. This technique, widespread in the case of early commemorative medals, has been used infrequently in coins, the vast majority of which are struck from *dies*. Examples include the Chinese cash and the Manx coins of 1709.

Check A form of *token* given as a means of identification, or issued for small amounts of money or for services of a specific nature.

Cheque (American *Check*) A written order directing a bank to pay money.

Chop (Hindi, to seal). Countermark, usually consisting of a single character, applied by Chinese merchants to precious metal coins and ingots as a guarantee of their weight and fineness. Coins may be found with a wide variety of chop marks and the presence of several different marks on the same coin enhances its interest and value. See also *Shroff mark*.

Christmas Coins issued as Christmas gifts date from the Middle Ages when the Venetian Doges struck *Osselle* as presents for their courtiers. In modern times, however, the custom has developed only since the late 1970s and several countries having issued them since then.

Siliquae of Constantine II from the Hoxne Hoard, showing heavy clipping. (Photograph courtesy Wikipedia).

Cistophori (Greek for chest bearing) a generic term for the coins of Pergamum with an obverse motif of a chest showing a serpent crawling out of the half-opened lid. Cistophori became very popular all over Asia Minor in the 3rd and 2nd centuries BC and were struck also at mints in Ionia, Phrygia, Lydia and Mysia.

Clad Coins Coins with a core of one alloy, covered with a layer or coating of another. US half dollars from 1965 to 1970, for example, had a core of 21 per cent silver and 79 per cent copper, bonded to outer layers of 80 per cent silver and 20 per cent copper. More recently, however, coins usually have a body in a cheap alloy, with only a thin cladding of a more expensive material, such as the British 1p and 2p coins of stainless steel with a copper cladding, introduced late in 1992.

Clash Marks Mirror image traces found on a coin which has been struck from a pair of dies, themselves damaged by having been struck together without a blank between.

Clipped Coins Precious metal coins from which small amounts have been removed by clipping the edges. It was to prevent this that *graining* and *edge inscriptions* were adopted.

Cob Crude, irregularly shaped silver piece, often with little more than a vestige of die impressions, produced in the Spanish American mints in the 16th–18th centuries.

Coin Piece of metal, marked with a device, issued by government authority and intended for use as money.

Collar Retaining ring within which the *dies* for the *obverse* and *reverse* operate. When the *blank* is struck under high pressure between the dies the metal flows sideways and is formed by the collar, taking up the impression of *reeding* or *edge inscription* from it.

Commemorative Coin, medal, token or paper note issued to celebrate a current event or the anniversary of a historic event or personality.

Communion Token Token, cast in lead, but later struck in pewter, brass, bronze or white metal, issued to members of a congregation to permit them to partake of the annual communion service in the Calvinist and Presbyterian churches. John Calvin himself is said to have invented the communion token in 1561 but they were actually referred to in the minutes of the Scottish General Assembly in 1560. Later they were adopted by the Reformed churches in many parts of Europe. They survived in Scotland till the early years of this century. Each parish had its own tokens, often bearing the names or initials of individual ministers, with dates, symbols and biblical texts.

Conjoined Term denoting overlapped profiles of two or more rulers (e.g. William and Mary).

Contorniate (from Italian *contorno*, edge). Late 4th and 5th century Roman bronze piece whose name alludes to the characteristic grooving on the edges.

Contribution Coins Coins struck by Bamberg, Eichstatt, Fulda and other German cities in the 1790s during the First Coalition War against the French Republic. The name alludes to the fact that the bullion used to produce the coins necessary to pay troops was raised by contribution from the Church and the public.

Convention Money Any system of coinage agreed by neighbouring countries for mutual acceptance and interchange. Examples include the Amphictyonic coins of ancient Greece, and the Austrian and Bavarian talers and gulden of

1753–1857 which were copied by other south German states and paved the way for the German Monetary union.

Copper Metallic element, chemical symbol *Cu*, widely used as a coinage medium for 2,500 years. Pure or almost pure copper was used for subsidiary coinage in many countries till the mid-19th century, but has since been superseded by copper alloys which are cheaper and more durable: *bronze* (copper and tin), *brass* (copper and zinc), *Bath metal* or *bell metal* (low-grade copper and tin), *aluminium-bronze* (copper and aluminium), *potin* (copper, tin, lead and silver) or *cupro-nickel* (copper and nickel). Copper is also alloyed with gold to give it its reddish hue, and is normally alloyed with silver in coinage metals. When the copper exceeds the silver content the alloy is known as *billon*.

Copperhead Popular term for a copper *token* about the size and weight of an American cent which circulated in the USA during the Civil War (1861–65) during a shortage of subsidiary coinage. Many different types were produced, often of a political or patriotic nature.

Coppernose Popular name for the debased silver shillings of Henry VIII. Many of them were struck in copper with little more than a silver wash which tended to wear off at the highest point of the obverse, the nose on the full-face portrait of the king.

Counter A piece resembling a coin but intended for use on a medieval accountancy board or in gambling. See also *jeton*.

Counterfeit Imitation of a coin, token or banknote intended for circulation to deceive the public and defraud the state.

Countermark Punch mark applied to a coin some time after its original issue, either to alter its nominal value, or to authorise its circulation in some other country.

Cowrie Small shell (*Cypraea moneta*) circulating as a form of primitive currency from 1000 BC (China) to the present century (East and West Africa) and also used in the islands of the Indian and Pacific Oceans.

Crockard Debased silver imitation of English pennies produced in the Netherlands and imported into England in the late 13th century. Edward I tried to prevent their import then, in 1299, allowed them to pass current as halfpennies. As they contained more than a halfpennyworth of silver this encouraged their trading in to be melted down and they disappeared from circulation within a year. Sometimes known as *pollards*. See also *Lushbourne*.

Crown Gold Gold of 22 carat (.916) fineness, so

called on account of its adoption in 1526 for the English gold crown. It has remained the British standard gold fineness ever since.

"To Hanover" token or "Cumberland Jack", marking the Duke of Cumberland's departure from Britain. These pieces were struck through much of the 19th century as whist counters and were sometimes passed as real gold coins to the unwary. (Image courtesy Wikipedia).

Cumberland Jack Popular name for a counter or medalet of sovereign size, struck unofficially in 1837 in brass. The figure of St George was replaced by the Duke of Cumberland on horseback with the inscription "To Hanover" a reference to the unpopular Duke of Cumberland, uncle of Queen Victoria, who succeeded to the Hanoverian throne since Victoria, as a female, was debarred by Salic law from inheritance.

Cupellation (Latin *cupella*, a little cup). Process by which gold and silver were separated from lead and other impurities in their ores. A cupel is a shallow cup of bone-ash or other absorbent material which, when hot, absorbs any molten material that wets its surface. Lead melts and oxidises with impurities into the cupel, whereas gold and silver remain on the cupel. Cupellation is also used in assaying the fineness of these precious metals.

Cupro-nickel Coinage alloy of 75 per cent copper and 25 per cent nickel, now widely used as a base metal substitute for silver. A small amount of zinc is added to the alloy in modern Russian coins.

Currency Coins, tokens, paper notes and other articles intended to pass current in general circulation as money.

Current Coins and paper money still in circulation.

Cut Money Coins cut into smaller pieces to provide correspondingly smaller denominations. The cross on many medieval coins assisted the division of silver pennies into halfpence and farthings. Spanish dollars were frequently divided into *bits* which themselves became units of currency in America and the West Indies.

Darlehnskassen (German for "state loan notes"). Paper money issued during the First World War in an abortive bid to fill the shortage of coinage in circulation. These low-denomination notes failed to meet demand and were superseded by local issues of small *Notgeld* in 1916.

Debasement The reduction in the precious metal content of the coinage, widely practised since time immemorial by governments for economic reasons. British coins, for example, were debased from sterling (.925 fine) silver to .500 in 1920 and from silver to cupro-nickel in 1947.

Decimalisation A currency system in which the principal unit is subdivided into ten, a hundred, or a thousand fractions. Russia was the first country to decimalise, in 1534 when the rouble of 100 kopeks was introduced, but it was not till 1792 that France adopted the franc of 100 centimes and 1793 when the USA introduced the dollar of 100 cents. Most European countries decimalised their currency in the 19th century. Britain toyed with the idea, introducing the florin or tenth of a pound in 1849 as the first step, but did not complete the process till 1971. The last countries to decimalise were Malta and Nigeria, in 1972 and 1973 respectively.

Demidiated Heraldic term to describe the junction of two armorial devices, in which only half of each is shown.

Demonetisation The withdrawal of coins or paper money from circulation and declaring them to be worthless.

Device Heraldic term for the pattern or emblem on coins or paper notes.

Die Hardened piece of metal bearing a mirror image of the device to be struck on one side of a coin or medal.

Die Proof An impression, usually pulled on soft carton or India paper, of an *intaglio* engraving of a banknote, usually taken during the progress of the engraving to check the detail. Banknote proofs of this nature usually consist of the portrait or some detail of the design, such as the border, rather than the complete motif.

Dodecagonal Twelve-sided, a term applied to the nickel-brass threepence of Great Britain, 1937–67.

Dump Any primitive coin struck on a very thick *flan*, but more specifically applied to the circular pieces cut from the centre of Spanish dollars, countermarked with the name of the colony, a crown and the value, and circulated in New South Wales at 15 pence in 1813. See *Holey Dollar*.

Duodecimal Currency system based on units of twelve, i.e. medieval money of account (12 denarii = 1 soldo) which survived in Britain as 12 pence to the shilling as late as 1971.

Punches used at different stages in making the die (bottom right). Image courtesy of the Royal Mint.

Ecclesiastical Coins   Coins struck by a religious authority, such as an archbishop, bishop, abbot, prior or the canons of a religious order. Such coins were common in medieval times but survived as late as the early 19th century, the bishops of Breslau (1817) and Gurk (1823) being the last prelates to exercise coinage rights. Coins were always struck by authority of the Pope at Rome till 1870 but since 1929 coinage has been struck at the Italian state mint on behalf of the Vatican.

Edge Inscription   Lettering on the edge of a coin or medal to prevent clipping. Alluding to this, the Latin motto *Decus et Tutamen* (an ornament and a safeguard) was applied to the edge of English milled coins in the reign of Charles II.

Edge Ornament   An elaboration of the *graining* found on many milled coins to prevent clipping, taking the form of tiny leaves, florets, interlocking rings, pellets and zigzag patterns. In some cases the ornament appears between layers of more conventional reeding.

EF   Abbreviation for Extremely Fine.

Effigy   An image or representation of a person, normally the head of state, a historical personage, or an allegorical figure, usually on the *obverse* or "heads" side of a coin or medal.

Electrotype   A reproduction of a coin or medal made by an electrolytic process.

Electrum   Alloy of gold and silver, sometimes called white gold, used for minting the staters of Lydia, 7th century BC, and other early European coins.

Elongated Coin   An oval *medalet* created by passing a coin, such as an American cent, between rollers under pressure with the effect of squeezing it out and impressing on it a souvenir or commemorative motif.

Emergency Money   Any form of money used in times of economic and political upheaval, when traditional kinds of currency are not available. Examples include the comparatively crude silver coins issued by the Royalists during the *Civil War* (1642–49), *obsidional* money, issued in time of siege, from Tyre (1122) to Mafeking (1900), the *Notgeld* issued by many German towns (1916–23), *encased money, fractional currency, guerrilla notes, invasion, liberation* and *occupation money* from the two World Wars and minor campaigns. Among the more recent examples may be cited the use of sweets and cheques in Italy (1976–77) and the issue of coupons and vouchers in many of the countries of the former Soviet Union pending the introduction of their own coins and notes.

Enamelled Coins   Coins decorated by enamelling the obverse and reverse motifs in contrasting colours was an art practised by many jewellers in Birmingham and Paris in the 19th century, and revived in Europe and America in the 1970s.

Encased Money   Postage and revenue stamps enclosed in small metal and mica-faced discs, circulated as small change in times of emergency. The practice was invented by John Gault, a Boston sewing-machine salesman, during the American Civil War (1862). The face of the stamp was visible through the transparent window, while the back of the disc was embossed with firms' advertisements. This practice was revived during and after the First World War when there was again a shortage of small coins. Encased stamps have also been recorded from France, Austria, Norway, Germany and Monaco. See also under *Stamp Money*.

Engrailing   Technical term for the close serrations or vertical bars round the edge of a coin, applied as a security device.

Engraving   The art of cutting lines or grooves in plates, blocks or dies. Numismatically this takes the form of engraving images into the face of the dies used in striking coins, a process which has now been almost completely superseded by *hubbing* and the use of *reducing machinery*. In the production of paper money, *intaglio* engraving is still commonly practised. In this process the engraver cuts the design into a steel die and the printing ink lies in the grooves. The paper is forced under great pressure into the grooves and picks up the ink, and this gives banknotes their characteristic ridged feeling to the touch. Nowadays many banknotes combine traditional intaglio engraving with multicolour lithography or photogravure to defeat the would-be counterfeiter.

Epigraphy   The study of inscriptions, involving the classification and interpretation of coin legends, an invaluable adjunct to the study of a coin series, particularly the classical and medieval coins which, in the absence of dates and mintmarks, would otherwise be difficult to arrange in chronological sequence.

Erasion   The removal of the title or effigy of a ruler from the coinage issued after his or her death. This process was practised in imperial Rome, and applied to the coins of Caligula, Nero and Geta, as part of the more general practice of *damnatio memoriae* (damnation of the memory) ordered by the Senate.

Error   Mistakes on coins and paper money may be either caused at the design or engraving stage, or as a result of a fault in the production processes. In the first category come mis-spellings in legends causing, in extreme cases, *blundered inscriptions*, or anachronisms or inaccuracies in details of the design. In the second, the most glaring error is the mule caused by marrying the wrong dies. Faulty alignment of dies can cause obverse and reverse to be out of true. Although many coins are issued with obverse and reverse upside down in relation to each other, this can also occur as an error in coins where both sides should normally be facing the same way up. Other errors caused at the production stage include striking coins in the wrong metal or with the wrong *collar* thus creating a different edge from the normal.

Essay (From the French *essai*, a trial piece). The term is applied to any piece struck for the purposes of examination, by parliamentary or financial bodies, prior to the authorisation of an issue of coins or paper money. The official nature of these items distinguishes them from *patterns*, which denote trial pieces often produced by mints or even private individuals bidding for coinage contracts.

Evasion Close copy or imitation of a coin, with sufficient deliberate differences in the design or inscription to avoid infringing counterfeit legislation. A good example is the imitation of Sumatran coins by European merchants, inscribed SULTANA instead of SUMATRA.

Exergue Lower segment of a coin or medal, usually divided from the rest of the *field* by a horizontal line, and often containing the date, value, ornament or identification symbols.

Exonumia Generic term for numismatic items not authorised by a government, e.g. *patterns*, *tokens*, *medalets* or *model coins*.

F Fine

Face The surface of a coin, medal or token, referred to as the *obverse* or the *reverse*. The corresponding faces of a paper note are more correctly termed *verso* and *recto*, but the coin terms are often used instead.

Facing Term for the portrait, usually on the obverse, which faces to the front instead of to the side (profile).

Fantasy Piece of metal purporting to be the coinage of a country which does not exist. Recent examples include the money of Atlantis and the Hutt River Province which declared its independence of Western Australia.

FDC Abbreviation for *Fleur de Coin*, a term denoting the finest possible condition of a coin.

Fiat Money Paper notes issued by a government but not redeemable in coin or bullion.

Field Flat part of the surface of a coin or medal, between the *legend*, the *effigy* and other raised parts of the design.

Fillet Heraldic term for the ribbon or headband on the effigy of a ruler or allegorical figure.

Find Term applied to an archaeological discovery of one or more coins. A large quantity of such material is described as a *hoard*.

Flan Alternative name for *blank* or *planchet*, the piece of metal struck between dies to produce a coin or medal.

Forgery An unauthorised copy or imitation, made with the intention of deceiving collectors. Forgeries intended to pass current for real coins or notes are more properly called *counterfeits*.

Fractional Currency Emergency issue of small-denominaton notes by the USA in 1863–5, following a shortage of coins caused by the Civil War. This issue superseded the *Postage Currency* notes, but bore the inscription "Receivable for all US stamps", alluding to the most popular medium of small change at that time. Denominations ranged from 3c to 50c.

Franklinium Cupro-nickel alloy developed by the Franklin Mint of Philadelphia and used for coins, medals and gaming tokens since 1967.

Freak An *error* or *variety* of a non-recurring type, usually caused accidentally during production.

Frosting Matt surface used for the high relief areas of many proof coins and medals, for greater contrast with the mirrored surface of the field.

Funeral Money Imitations of banknotes, used in China and Latin America in funeral ceremonies.

Geat (Git) Channel through which molten metal is ducted to the mould. Cast coins often show tiny protrusions known as geat marks.

Ghost Faint image of the design on one side of a coin visible on the other. Good examples were the British penny and halfpenny of George V, 1911–27, the ghosting being eliminated by the introduction of a smaller effigy in 1928.

Globular Coins struck on very thick *dumps* with convex faces. Examples include some Byzantine coins, and the *bullet money* of Siam (Thailand)

Godless (or *Graceless*) Epithet applied to any coin which omits the traditional reference to the deity, e.g. the British florin of 1849 which omitted D.G. (*Dei Gratia*, "by the Grace of God").

Gold Precious metal, chemical symbol and numismatic abbreviation *Au*, from the *Latin Aurum*, used as a coinage medium from the 7th century BC till the present day. The purity of gold is reckoned in *carats* or a decimal system. Thus British gold sovereigns are 22 carat or .916 fine. Medieval coins were 23.5 carat or .995 fine, and some modern bullion coins are virtually pure gold, denoted by the inscription .999. Canadian maple leaves are now struck in "four nines" gold and bear the inscription .9999.

Goodfor Popular name for token coins and

emergency money made of paper or card, from the inscription "Good for" or its equivalent in other languages (e.g. French *Bon pour* or Dutch *Goed voor*) followed by a monetary value. They have been recorded from Europe, Africa and America during times of economic crises or shortage of more traditional coinage.

Gothic Crown   Popular name for the silver crown issued by the United Kingdom (1847–53), so-called on account of its script (more properly Old English, rather than Gothic).

Grain   The weight of a single grain of wheat was taken as the smallest unit of weight in England. The troy grain was 1/5760 of a pound, while the avoirdupois grain was 1/7000 pound, the former being used in the weighing of precious metals and thus employed by numismatists in weighing coins. A grain is 1/480 troy ounce or 0.066 gram in the metric system.

Graining   Term sometimes used as a synonym for the *reeding* on the edge of milled coins.

Gun money.

Gripped Edge   Pattern of indentations found on the majority of American cents of 1797, caused by the milling process. Coins of the same date with a plain edge are rather scarcer.

Guerrilla Money   Money issued in areas under the control of guerrillas and partisans during wartime range from the *veld ponds* of the Boers (1900–2) to the notes issued by the Garibaldi Brigade in Italy and the anti-fascist notes of Tito's forces in Yugoslavia. The most prolific issues were those produced in Luzon, Mindanao and Negros Occidental by the Filipino resistance during the Japanese occupation (1942–5).

Guilloche   French term signifying the intricate pattern of curved lines produced by the rose engine and used as a security feature in the production of banknote, cheques, stocks and share certificates.

Gun Money   Emergency coinage of Ireland (1689–91) minted from gunmetal, a type of bronze used in the casting of cannon. All denominations of James II, from the sixpence to the crown, normally struck in silver, were produced in this base metal.

Gutschein   German word for voucher or coupon, denoting the paper money used aboard ships of the Imperial Navy during the First World War. The last issue was made at Scapa Flow, 1918–19, during the internment of the High Seas Fleet.

Hammered   Term denoting coins produce by the traditional method of striking a *flan* laid on an anvil with a hammer. A characteristic of hammered coins is their uneven shape which tended to encourage *clipping*. This abuse was gradually eliminated by the introduction of the screw press in the 15th century and the mechanisation of coining processes in the course of the 16th and 17th centuries.

Hard Times Token   Copper piece the size of the large cent, issued in the USA, 1834–44, during a shortage of coins caused by the collapse of the Bank of the United States, the panic of 1837 and the economic crisis of 1839, the landmarks in the period known as the Hard Times. Banks suspended *specie* payments and the shortage of coinage was filled by tradesmen's tokens. Many of these were more in the nature of satirical *medalets* than circulating pieces.

Hat Piece   Alternative name for the *bonnet piece* of James VI of Scotland, 1591.

Hell Notes   Imitation paper money used in Chinese funeral ceremonies and buried with the dead to pay for services in the next world.

Hoard   Accumulation of coins concealed in times of economic or political upheaval and discovered, often centuries later. Under English common law, such hoards are subject to th law of *treasure trove* if they contain precious metal.

Hog Money   Popular name for the early coinage of Bermuda, issued about 1616. The coins were minted in brass with a silver wash and circulated at various values from twopence to a shilling. They derived their name from the hog depicted on the obverse, an allusion to the pigs introduced to the island in 1515 by Juan Bermudez.

Holed   Term denoting two different categories: (a) coins which have been pierced for suspension as a form of jewellery or talisman, and (b) coins which have a hole as part of their design. In the latter category come the Chinese *cash* with a square hole, and numerous issues of the 19th and 20th centuries from many countries, with the object of reducing weight and metal without sacrificing overall diameter.

Holey Dollar   Spanish silver peso of 8 reales with the centre removed. The resultant ring was counter-marked "New South Wales" and dated 1813, with "Five Shillings" on the reverse, and placed into circulation during a shortage of British coin. The centre, known as a *dump*, was circulated at 15 pence.

Hub   Heavy circular piece of steel on which the *die* for a coin or medal is engraved. The process of cutting the die and transferring the master die, by means of intermediary *punches*, to the die from which the coins will be struck, is known as hubbing. Soft steel is used in the preliminary process, and after the design has been transferred, the hub is hardened by chemical action.

Hybrid   Alternative name for a *mule*.

Imitation Money   Also known as play money or toy money, it consists of coins and notes produced for games of chance (like Monopoly), children's toy shops and post offices, as tourist souvenirs, or for political satire (e.g. the shrinking pound or dollar). See also *funeral money*, *hell notes*, *model coins* and *skit notes*.

Imprint   Inscription on a paper note giving the name of the printer.

Incuse   Impression which cuts into the surface of a coin or medal, as opposed to the more usual raised relief. Many of the earliest coins, especially those with a device on one side only, bear an incuse impression often in a geometric pattern. An incuse impression appears on one side of the coins, reflecting the image on the other side. Few modern coins have had an incuse design, notable examples being the American half and quarter eagle gold coins of 1908–29 designed by Bela Pratt. Incuse inscriptions on a raised rim, however, are more common, and include the British *Cartwheel* coins of 1797 and the 20p coins since 1982.

Inflation Money   Coins produced as a result of inflation date back to Roman times when bronze minimi, little bigger than a pinhead, circulated as denarii. Nearer the present day inflation has had devastating effects on the coinge and banknotes of Germany (1921–3), Austria (1923), Poland (1923), Hungary (1945–6), Greece (1946) and many Latin American countries since the 1980s. Hungary holds the record for the highest value of any note ever issued — one thousand million adopengos, which is written as 20,000,000,000,000,000, 000,000,000,000 pengos.

Ingot   Piece of precious metal, usually cast in a mould, and stamped with the weight and fineness. A convenient method of storing bullion, ingots have been used as currency in many countries, notably Russia and Japan.

Inlay   Insertion into the surface of a coin or medal of another substance for decorative effect. e.g. Poland Amber Trade Routes 20zl (amber), Isle of Man Queen Mother centenery (pearl) and various coins incorporating rubies or diamonds.

Intaglio   Form of *engraving* in which lines are cut into a steel die for the recess-printing of banknotes.

Intrinsic   The net metallic value of a coin, as distinguished from the nominal or face value.

Iron   Metal, chemical symbol Fe (from Latin *Ferrum*), used as a primitive form of currency from classical times onwards. Iron spits (obeliskoi) preceded the obol as the lowest unit of Greek coinage, a handful of six spits being worth a drachma (from *drassomai*, "I grasp"). Cast iron coins were issued in China as a substitute for copper *cash*. Many of the emergency token issues of Germany during the First World War were struck in iron. Iron coins were issued by Bulgaria in 1943. See also *Steel*.

Ithyphallic   (Greek for "erect penis"). Term descriptive of coins of classical Greece showing a satyr.

Janiform   Double profiles back to back, after the Roman god Janus.

Jeton from Dordrecht 1588: the Armada destroyed.

Jeton   (From French *jeter*, to throw). Alternative term for *counter*, and used originally on the chequerboard employed by medieval accountants. Nuremberg was the most important centre for the production of medieval jetons, often issued in lengthy portrait series. In modern parlance the term is often synonymous with *token*, though more specifically confined to pieces used in vending equipment, parking meters, laundromats, telephones and urban transport systems in many European countries. Apart from security, removing the temptation of vandals to break into the receptacles, the main advantage of such pieces is that they can be retariffed as charges increase, without any alteration in their design or composition, a method that is far cheaper than altering costly equipment to take larger coins.

Jubilee Head The effigy of Queen Victoria by Joseph Boehm adopted for British coinage after the 1887 Golden Jubilee.

Jugate (From Latin *jugum*, a yoke). Alternative to *accolated* or *conjoined* to denote overlapping profiles of rulers.

Key Date Term describing the rarest in a long-running series of coins with the dates changed at annual intervals.

Kipperzeit German term meaning the time of clipped money, denoting the period during and after the Thirty Years War (1618–48) in which debased and clipped money was in circulation.

Klippe Rectangular or square pieces of metal bearing the impression of a coin. Coins of this type were first struck in Sweden in the 16th century and were subsequently produced in many of the German states. The idea has been revived in recent years as a medium for striking commemorative pieces.

Knife Money Cast bronze pieces, with an elongated blade and a ring at one end to facilitate stringing together in bunches, were used as currency in China from the 9th century BC until the 19th century.

Kreditivsedlar (Swedish for "credit notes"). The name given to the first issue of paper money made in the western world. Paper money of this type was the brainchild of Johan Palmstruch at Riga in 1652, but nine years elapsed before it was implemented by the Stockholm Bank. The notes were redeemable in copper *platmynt*.

Laureate Heraldic term for a laurel wreath, often framing a state emblem or shown, in the Roman fashion, as a crown on the ruler's forehead.

Leather Money Pieces of leather embossed with an official device have been used as money on various occasions, including the sieges of Faenza and Leiden and in the Isle of Man in the 15th and 16th centuries. Several towns in Austria and Germany produced leather tokens during and after the First World War.

Legal Tender Coins or paper money which are declared by law to be current money and which tradesmen and shopkeers are obliged to accept in payment for goods or services. (See *Money and the Law*).

Legend The inscription on a coin or medal.

Liberation Money Paper money prepared for use in parts of Europe and Asia, formerly under Axis occupation. Liberation notes were used in France, Belgium and the Netherlands in 1944–5, while various different Japanese and Chinese notes were overprinted for use in Hong Kong when it was liberated in 1945. Indian notes overprinted for use in Burma were issued in 1945–6 when that country was freed from Japanese occupation.

Ligature (From Latin *ligatus*, bound together). Term denoting the linking of two letters in a *legend*, e.g. Æ and Œ.

Long Cross Coinage Type of coinage introduced by King Henry III in 1247, deriving its name from the reverse which bore a cross whose arms extended right to the edge to help safeguard the coins against *clipping*. This remained the style of the silver penny, its fractions and multiples, till the reign of Henry VII, and vestiges of the long cross theme is seen in the silver coins throughout the remaining years of the Tudor period.

Love Token A coin which has been altered by smoothing one or both surfaces and engraving initials, dates, scenes, symbols of affection and messages thereon.

Lushbourne English word for base pennies made of inferior silver, said to have emanated from Luxembourg, from which the name derived. These coins were first minted under John the Blind who adopted the curious spelling of his name EIWANES in the hope that illiterate English merchants might confuse it with EDWARDVS and thus be accepted as coin issued in the name of Edward III. Lushbournes were also minted by Robert of Bethune, William I of Namur and the bishops of Toul during the mid-14th century.

Lustre The sheen or bloom on the surface of an uncirculated coin resulting from the centrifugal flow of metal caused by striking.

Magnimat Trade name used by VDM (*Verein Deutscher Metallwerke*) for a high-security alloy containing copper, nickel and magnetised steel. First used for the 5 deutschemark coin of 1975, it has since been adopted for other high-value coins in Germany and other countries.

Manilla Copper, bronze or brass rings, sometimes shaped like horseshoes and sometimes open, with flattened terminals, used as currency in West Africa until recent years.

Matrix Secondary die for a coin or medal, produced from the master die by means of an intermediate punch. In this way dies can be duplicated from the original cut on the reducing machine.

Matt or Matte Finely granulated surface or overall satin finish to proof coins, a style which was briefly fashionable at the turn of the century. The Edward VII proof set of 1902 is a notable example. In more recent years many issues produced by the Franklin Mint have been issued with this finish.

Maundy Money Set of small silver coins, in denominations of 1, 2, 3 and 4 pence, distributed by the reigning British monarch to the poor and needy on Maundy Thursday. The custom dates back to the Middle Ages, but in its present form, of distributing pence to as many men and women as the years in the monarch's age, it dates from 1666. At first ordinary silver pennies and multiples were used but after they went out of everyday use distinctive silver coins were produced specifically for the purpose from the reign of George II (1727–60) onwards. For centuries the ceremony took place in Westminster Abbey but since 1955 other venues have been used in alternate years.

Medal (French *medaille*, Italian *medaglia*, from Latin *metallum*). A piece of metal bearing devices and legends commemorating an event or person, or given as an award. Military medals date from the 16th and 17th centuries, but were not generally awarded to all ranks till the 19th century. Commemora-tive medals can be traced back to Roman times, but in their present form they date from the Italian Renaissance when there was a fashion for large cast portrait medals.

Medalet A small medal, generally 25mm or less in diameter.

Medallion Synonym for medal, but usually confined to those with a diameter of 50mm or more.

Milling Process denoting the mechanical production of coins, as opposed to the handmade technique implied in *hammering*. It alludes to the use of watermills to drive the machinery of the screw presses and blank rollers developed in the 16th century. As the even thickness and diameter of milled coins permitted a security edge, the term milling is popularly, though erroneously, used as a synonym for *graining* or *reeding*.

Mint The place in which coins and medals are produced. Mint condition is a term sometimes used to denote pieces in an uncirculated state.

Mint Set A set of coins or medals in the package or case issued by the mint. See also *year set*.

Mintmark A device appearing on a coin to denote the place of minting. Athenian coins of classical times have been recorded with up to 40 different marks, denoting individual workshops. In the 4th century AD the Romans adopted this system to identify coins struck in provincial mints. This system was widely used in the Middle Ages and survives in France and Germany to this day. Initials and symbols are also used to identify mints, especially where the production of a coin is shared between several different mints.

Maundy money.

From 1351 onwards symbols were adopted in England to denote periods between trials of the *Pyx*, and thus assist the proper chronological sequence of coins, in an era prior to the adoption of dating. These mintmarks continued into the 17th century, but gradually died out as the use of dates became more widespread. See also *countermark* and *privy mark*.

Mionnet Scale Scale of nineteen diameters covering all sizes of coins belonging to the classical period, devised by the French numismatist, Theodore-Edme Mionnet (1770–1842) during the compilation of his fifteen-volume catalogue of the numismatic collection in the Bibliotheque Nationale in Paris.

Mirror Finish The highly polished surface of proof coins.

Misstrike A coin or medal on which the impression has been struck off-centre.

Model Coin Tiny pieces of metal, either reproducing the designs of existing coins (used as play money by children) or, more specifically, denoting patterns produced by Joseph Moore and Hyam Hyams in their attempts to promote an improved subsidiary coinage in 19th century Britain. These small coins were struck in bronze with a brass or silver centre and were designed to reduce the size of the existing cumbersome range of pence, halfpence and farthings.

Modified Effigy Any coin in which the profile on the obverse has been subtly altered. Examples include minor changes in the Victorian Young Head and Old Head effigies and the George V profile by Sir Bertram Mackennal.

Money Order Certificate for a specified amount of money, which may be transmitted by post and encashed at a money order office or post office. This system was pioneered by Britain and the United States in the early 19th century and is now virtually worldwide. The term is now confined to certificates above a certain value, the terms *postal order* and *postal note* being used for similar certificates covering small amounts.

Mule Coin whose obverse is not matched with its official or regular reverse. Mules include the erroneous combination of dies from different reigns, but in recent years such hybrids have arisen in mints where coins for several countries are struck. Examples include the Coronation Anniversary crowns combining Ascension and Isle of Man dies and the 2 cent coins with Bahamas and New Zealand dies. *Restrikes* of rare American coins have been detected in which the dated die has been paired with the wrong reverse die, e.g. the 1860 restrike of the rare 1804 large cent.

Mute An *anepigraphic* coin, identifiable only by the devices struck on it.

Nail Mark Small indentation on ancient coins. The earliest coins of Asia Minor developed from the electrum *dumps* which merchants marked with a broken nail as their personal guarantee of value, the ancient counterpart of the *chop* marks used in China and Japan.

NCLT Coins Abbreviation for "Non Circulating Legal Tender", a term devised by modern coin catalogues to denote coins which, though declared *legal tender*, are not intended for general circulation on account of their precious metal content or superior finish.

Nicked Coin Coin bearing a tiny cut or nick in its edge. Silver coins were tested by this method, especially in the reign of Henry I (1100–35) when so many base silver pennies were in circulation. Eventually people refused to accept these nicked coins a problem which was only overcome when the state decreed that all coins should have a nick in them.

Nickel Metallic element, chemical symbol *Ni*, a hard white metal relatively resistant to tarnish, and extensively used as a cheap substitute for silver. It was first used for the American 5 cent coin in 1866, hence its popular name which has stuck ever since, although nowadays the higher denominations are minted in an alloy of copper and nickel. Although best known as a silver substitute, nickel was widely used in Jamaica (1869–1969) for halfpence and pennies and in British West Africa for the tiny 1/10th pennies (1908–57). Pure nickel was used for French francs and German marks, but usually it is alloyed with copper or zinc to produce *cupro-nickel* or nickel brass.

Notaphily Hybrid word from Latin *nota* (note) and Greek *philos* (love), coined about 1970 to denote the branch of numismatics devoted to the study of paper money.

Notgeld German word meaning emergency money, applied to the *tokens*, in metals, wood, leather and even ceramic materials, issued during the First World War when coinage disappeared from circulation. These tokens were soon superseded by low-denomination paper money issued by shops and businessmen in denominations from 10 to 50 pfennige and known as *kleine Notgeld* (small emergency money). These notes were prohibited in September 1922 but by that time some 50,000 varieties are thought to have been issued. Inflation raced out of control and the government permitted a second issue of local notes, known as *large Notgeld*, as the denomi-nations were in thousands, and latterly millions, of marks. Some 3,600 types appeared in 1922 and over 60,000 in 1923 alone. These mementoes of the German hyperinflation ceased to circulate in 1924 when the currency was reformed.

Numismatics The study of coins, medals and other related fields, a term derived from the Latin *numisma* and Greek *nomisma* (money).

Obsidional Currency (From Latin *obsidium*, a siege). Term for *emergency money* produced by the defenders of besieged towns and cities. These usually took the form of pieces of silver plate, commandeered for the purpose, crudely marked with an official device and the value. Instances of such seige coinage have been recorded from the 12th to the 19th centuries.

Obverse The "heads" side of a coin or medal, generally bearing the effigy of the head of state or an allegorical figure.

Off Metal Term denoting a piece struck in a metal other than the officially authorisied or issued alloy. This originally applied to *patterns* which were often struck in lead or copper instead of gold and silver as trial pieces or to test the dies; but in recent years it has applied to collectors' versions, e.g. proofs in platinum, gold or silver of coins normally issued in bronze or cupro-nickel.

Overdate One or more digits in a date altered by superimposing another figure. Alterations of this kind, by means of small hand punches, were made to dated dies so that they could be used in years other than that of the original manufacture. Coins with overdates invariably show traces of the original digit.

Overstrike Coin, token or medal produced by using a previously struck pieces as a flan. The Bank of England dollar of 1804 was overstruck on Spanish pieces of eight, and examples showing traces of the original coins are worth a good premium.

Paduan Name given to imitations of medals and bogus coins produced in Italy in the 16th century, and deriving from the city of Padua where forgeries of bronze sculpture were produced for the antique market.

Patina Oxidation forming on the surface of metallic objects. So far as coins and medals are concerned, this applies mainly to silver, brass, bronze and copper pieces which may acquire oxidation from the atmosphere, or spectacular patination from salts in the ground in which they have been buried. In extreme forms patina leads to verdigris and other forms of rust which corrode the surface, but in uncirculated coins it may be little more than a mellowing of the original *lustre*. Coins preserved in blue velvet presentation cases often acquire a subtle toning from the dyes in the material.

Pattern Piece resembling a coin or medal, prepared by the mint to the specifications or on the authorisation of the coin-issuing authority, but also applied to pieces produced by mints when tendering for coinage or medal contracts. Patterns may differ from the final coins as issued in the type of alloy used (*off metal*) but more often they differ in details of the design.

Pellet Raised circular ornament used as a spacing device between words and abbreviations in the *legend* of coins and medals. Groups of pellets were also used as ornaments in the angles of the cross on the reverse of English silver pennies.

Piece de Plaisir (French for "fancy piece"). Term given to coins struck in a superior precious metal, or to a superior finish, or on a much thicker flan than usual. See *off metal*, *piedfort* and *proof*.

Piedfort (Piefort) Piece struck with coinage dies on a *flan* of much more than normal thickness. This practice originated in France in the late 16th century and continues to the present day. In recent years it has been adopted by mints in Britain and other countries as a medium for collectors' pieces.

Pile Lower die incorporating the obverse motif, used in striking coins and medals. See also *trussel*.

Planchet French term used as an alternative for *blank* or *flan*.

Plaque or **Plaquette** Terms sometimes used for medals struck on a square or rectangular flan.

Plaster Cast taken from the original model for a coin or medal sculpted by an artist, and used in modern reducing machines in the manufacture of the master *die*.

Plated Coins Coins stuck in base metal but given a wash of silver or some other precious metal. This expedient was adopted in inflationary times, from the Roman Republic (91 BC) till the Tudor period. American cents of 1943 were struck in steel with a zinc coating, and more recently *clad* coins have produced similar results.

Platinum The noblest of all precious metals, platinum has a higher specific gravity than gold and a harder, brighter surface than silver. Until an industrial application was discovered in the mid-19th century, it was regarded as of little value, and was popular with counterfeiters as a cheap substitute for gold in their forgeries which, with a light gold wash, could be passed off as genuine. It was first used for circulating coins in Russia (the chief source of the metal since 1819) and 3, 6 and 12 rouble coins were mined at various times between 1828 and 1845. In recent years platinum has been a popular metal for limited-edition proof coins.

Platmynt (Swedish for "plate money"). Large copper plates bearing royal cyphers and values from half to ten dalers produced in Sweden between 1643 and 1768. They represented laudable attempts by a country rich in copper to produce a coinage in terms of its silver value, but the net result was far too cumbersome to be practical. The weight of the daler plate, for example, ranged from 766 grams to 1.1kg, and special carts had to be devised to transport them!

Plugged Coins Coins struck predominantly in one metal, but containing a small plug of another. This curious practice may be found in the farthings of Charles II (1684–85) and the halfpence or farthings of James II (1685–87), which were struck in tin, with a copper plug, to defeat forgers.

Porcelain Money Tokens made of porcelain circulated in Thailand from the late 18th century till 1868. The Meissen pottery struck tokens in 1920–22 as a form of small *Notgeld*, using reddish-brown Bottger stoneware and white *bisque* porcelain. These ceramic tokens circulated in various towns of Saxony.

Postage Currency Small paper notes in denominations of 5, 10, 25 and 50 cents, issued by the US federal government in 1862–63, were thus inscribed and had reproductions of postage stamps engraved on them — five 5c stamps on the 25c and five 10c stamps on the 50c notes. The earliest issue even had perforations in the manner of stamps, but this unnecessary device was soon done away with. See also *stamp money*.

Postal Notes or Orders Low-value notes intended for transmission by post and encashable at post offices. Introduced by Britain in 1883, they were an extension of the earlier *money order* system, and are now issued by virtually every country.

Potin (French for pewter). Alloy of copper, tin, lead and silver used as a coinage metal by the Celtic tribes of eastern Gaul at the beginning of the Christian era.

Privy Mark Secret mark incorporated in the design of a coin or medal to identify the minter, or even the particular die used. The term is also used more loosely to denote any small symbol or initials appearing on a coin other than a *mint mark*, and is sometimes applied to the symbols associated with the trial of the *Pyx* found on English coins.

Prize Coins Coins of large size and value struck primarily as prizes in sporting contests. this principle dates from the late 5th century BC when Syracuse minted decadrachms as prizes in the Demareteian Games. The most notable example in modern times is the lengthy series of talers and five-franc coins issued by the Swiss cantons since 1842 as prizes in the annual shooting festivals, the last of which honoured the Lucerne contest of 1939.

Profile A side view of the human face, widely used as a coinage effigy.

Proof Originally a trial strike testing the *dies*, but now denoting a special collectors' version struck with dies that have been specially polished on *flans* with a mirror finish. Presses operating at a very slow speed, or multi-striking processes, are also used.

Propaganda Notes Paper money containing a political slogan or a didactic element. During the Second World War forgeries of German and Japanese notes were produced by the Allies and additionally inscribed or overprinted with slogans such as "Co-Prosperity Sphere — What is it worth?" (a reference to the Japanese occupied areas of SE Asia). Forged dollars with anti-American propaganda were airdropped over Sicily by the Germans in 1943 and counterfeit pounds with Arabic propaganda over Egypt in 1942–43. Various anti-communist organisations liberated propaganda forgeries of paper money by balloon over Eastern Europe during the Cold War period.

Provenance Mark Form of *privy mark* denoting the source of the metal used in coins. Examples include the plumes or roses on English coins denoting silver from Welsh or West of England mines, and the elephant or elephant and castle on gold coins denoting bullion imported by the African Company. Coins inscribed VIGO (1702–03) or LIMA (1745–46) denote bullion seized from the Spaniards by Anglo-Dutch privateers and Admiral Anson respectively. Other provenance marks on English coins include the letters EIC and SSC, denoting bullion imported by the East India Company or the South Sea Company.

Pseudo Coins Derisory term coined in recent years to signify pieces of precious metal, often struck in *proof* versions only, aimed at the international investment market. Many of these pieces, though bearing a nominal face value, are not *legal tender* in the countries purporting to issue them and in many cases they go straight from the overseas mint where they are produced to coin dealers in America and western Europe, without ever appearing in the so-called country of origin. See also *NCLT coins*.

Punch or Puncheon Intermediate *die* whereby working dies can be duplicated from the master die, prior to the striking of coins and medals.

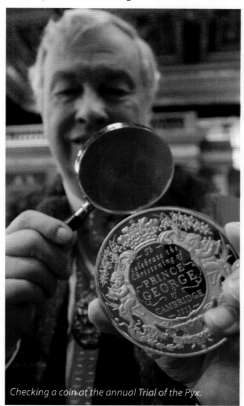
Checking a coin at the annual Trial of the Pyx.

Pyx Box in which a specimen from every 15 pounds troy weight of gold and every 60 pounds of silver minted in England is kept for annual trial by weight and assay. Many of the *mintmarks* on English coins of the 14th–17th centuries were in use from one trial to the next and still exist today and can therefore be used to date them.

Reducing Machinery Equipment designed on the pantographic principle for transferring the image from a *plaster* to a *hub* and reducing it to the size of the actual coin or medal. The image is transferred by means of a stylus operating rather like a gramophone needle, but working from the centre to the outer edge.

Reeding Security edging on coins, consisting of close vertical ridges. As a rule, this appears all round the edge but some coins, e.g. New Zealand's 50c (1967) and the Isle of Man's £1 (1978) have segments of reeding alternating with a plain edge, to help blind and partially sighted persons to identify these coins.

Re-issue A coin or note issued again after an extended lapse of time.

Relief Raised parts of the *obverse* and *reverse* of coins and medals, the opposite of *incuse*.

Remainder A note from a bank or issuing authority which has never been circulated, due to inflation, political changes or bank failure. Such notes, some-times in partial or unfinished state (e.g. missing serial numbers or signatures), are generally unloaded on to the numismatic market at a nominal sum and provide a good source of inexpensive material for the beginner.

Restrike Coin, medal or token produced from *dies* subsequent to the original use. Usually restrikes are made long after the original and can often be identified by marks caused by damage, pitting or corrosion of the dies after they were taken out of service.

Retrograde Term describing inscriptions running from right to left, or with the letters in a mirror image, thought to arise from unskilled die-cutters failing to realise that inscriptions have to be engraved in negative form to achieve a positive impression. Retrograde inscriptions are common on ancient Greek coins, but also found on Roman and Byzantine coins.

Reverse The side of a coin or medal regarded as of lesser importance; in colloquial parlance, the "tails" side.

Saltire Heraldic term for a cross in the shape of an X.

Sandwich Coin *blank* consisting of thin outer layers in one alloy bonded to a core in another. See *clad coins*.

Sceat (Anglo-Saxon for "treasure", or German *Schatz*). Money of account in Kent early in the 7th century as the twelfth part of a shilling or Merovingian gold tremissis. As a silver coin, it dates from about AD 680–700 and weighed about 20 grains, putting it on par with the Merovingian denier or penny. Sceats spread to other parts of England in the 8th century but tended to decline in weight and value, but from about 760 it was gradually superseded by the silver penny minted under Offa and his successors.

Anglo-Saxon sceat from a mint in east Kent. (Image courtesy CNG/Wikipedia).

Scissel The clippings of metal left after a *blank* has been cut. Occasionally one of these clippings accidentally adheres to the blank during the striking process, producing characteristic crescent-shaped flaws which are present on the finished coin.

Scrip Paper money of restricted validity or circulation, e.g. *Bafs* and other military scrip used in canteens and post exchanges.

Scyphate (Greek *scypha*, a skiff or small boat). Byzantine coin with a concave *flan*.

Sede Vacante (Latin for "Vacant See"). Coins struck at *ecclesiastical mints* between the death of a prelate and the election of his successor are often thus inscribed. This practice originated at Rome in the 13th century.

Seignorage or Seigneurage Royalty or percentage paid by persons bringing *bullion* to a mint for conversion into coin, but nowadays synonymous with the royalty paid by mints in respect of the precious metal versions of coins sold direct to collectors. It arises from the medieval right of the king to a small portion of the proceeds of a mint, and amounted to a tax on moneying. It has also been applied to the money accruing to the state when the coinage is re-issued in an alloy of lesser fineness, as, for example, the debased sovereigns of Henry VIII in 20 instead of 23 carat gold, the king's treasury collecting the difference.

Series Term applied to sets of medals of a thematic character, which first became fashionable in the early 18th century. Jean Dassier pioneered the medallic series in the 1720s with his set of 72 medals portraying the rulers of France till Louis XV. The idea was developed by J. Kirk, Sir Edward Thomason, J. Mudie and A. J. Stothard in Britain, and by Moritz Fuerst and Amedee Durand in Europe. The fashion died out in the 19th century, but has been revived in America and Europe since 1964.

Serrated Having a notched or toothed edge,

rather like a cogwheel. Coins of this type, struck in *electrum*, an alloy of silver and gold, are known from Carthage in the 2nd century BC, and some silver denarii of Rome in the 2nd century AD also come into this category.

Sexagesimal System Monetary system in which the principal unit is divided into 60 parts. The oldest system in the Western world was based on the gold talent of 60 minae and the mina of 60 shekels. In medieval Europe 60 groschen were worth a fine mark; in England from 1551, the silver coinage was based on the crown of 60 pence, and in the south German states till 1873 the gulden was worth 60 kreuzers.

Shin Plasters Derisory term originally applied to the Continental currency notes issued during the American War of Independence, the fractional currency of the Civil War period and also the low-denomination notes of Canada between 1870 and 1935, but often applied indiscriminately to any other low-denomination, small-format notes.

Short Cross Coinage Term for the silver coinage introduced by Henry II in 1180 and minted till 1247 at which time it was replaced by the *Long Cross* type. The termination of the arms of the cross on the reverse well within the circumference encouraged the dishonest practice of *clipping*.

Shroff Mark A *countermark* applied by Indian bankers or merchants to attest the full weight and purity of coins. See also *chop*.

Siege Money See *Obsidional Currency*

Silver Precious metal, chemical symbol *Ag*, numismatic abbreviation *Ar*, from Latin *Argentum*, widely used as a coinage metal from the 6th century BC to the present day.

Sterling silver denotes an alloy of .925 fine silver with .075 copper. Fine silver alloys used over the past 2,500 years have ranged from .880 to .960 fine, but base silver has also been all too common. British coins from 1920 to 1946 were struck in .500 fine silver, while alloys of lesser fineness are known as *billon* or *vellon*. Silver alloyed with gold produces a metal called *electrum*, used for the earliest coinage of the western world, the staters of Lydia in the 7th century BC. Since 1970 silver as a medium for circulating coinage has almost virtually disappeared, yet the volume of silver coins for sale to collectors has risen considerably in recent years.

Skit Note Piece of paper masquerading as a banknote. It differs from a *counterfeit* in that its design parodies that of a genuine note, often for political, satirical or advertising reasons. Others were produced as April Fools' Day jokes or a form

of Valentine (e.g. the Bank of Lovers). In recent years they have been produced as advertising gimmicks, or as coupons permitting a discount off the list price of goods.

Slug Popular name for the $50 gold pieces produced by private mints in California in the mid-19th century. The term is also applied nowadays to *tokens* intended for use in gaming machines.

Spade Guinea Name given to the guineas of George III issued between 1787 and 1799 because the shield on the reverse design resembled the shape of a spade. In Victorian times the spade guinea was extensively copied in brass for gaming counters.

Spade Money Cast bronze pieces resembling miniature spades and other agricultural implements, used as money and derived from the actual implements which had previously been used in barter. Often referred to as *Pu* or *Boo* money.

Specie Financial term denoting money in the form of precious metals (silver and gold), usually struck as coin, as opposed to money in the form of paper notes and bills of exchange. It occurs in the name of some European coins (e.g. *speciedaler*, *speciestaler* and *speciesducat*) to denote the use of fine silver or gold.

Specimen Generally used to denote a single piece, but more specifically applying to a coin in a special finish, less than *proof* in quality but superior to the general circulating version. It also denotes paper notes intended for circulation between banks or for press publicity and distinguished from the generally issued version by zero serial numbers, punch holes or a security endorsement.

Spintriae Metal tokens produced in Roman imperial times, with erotic motifs, thought to have been tickets of admission to brothels.

Spit Copper or iron rod used as a primitive form of currency in the Mediterranean area. The Greek word *belos* meant a spit, dart or bolt, and from this came the word *obolos* used for a coin worth a 6th of a drachma.

Stamp Money Both postage and revenue (fiscal) stamps have circulated as money during shortages of coins, from the American Civil War onwards. *Encased postage stamps* were used in the USA, 1861–62, before they were superseded by *Postage Currency* notes, but the same expedient was adopted by many countries during and immediately after the First World War. Stamps affixed to special cards have circulated as money in Rhodesia (now Zimbabwe) in 1900, the French colonies and Turkey during the First World War, in Spain during the Civil War

(1936–39) and the Philippines during the Second World War. Stamps printed on thick card, with an inscription on the reverse signifying their parity with silver coins, were issued in Russia (1917–18) and also in Armenia, the Crimea and the Ukraine (1918–20). During the Second World War Ceylon (now Sri Lanka) and several Indian states issued small money cards with contemporary stamps printed on them.

Steel   Refined and tempered from *iron*, and used in chromed or stainless versions as a coinage metal in the 20th century. Zinc-coated steel cents were issued by the USA (1943) but in the form known as *acmonital* (nickel steel) it has been extensively used by Italy since 1939. Other alloys of nickel and steel have been used for coins of the Philippines (1944–45) and Roumania since 1963. Chrome steel was used by France for 5 centime coins in 1961–64. Copper-clad steel is now extensively used for subsidiary coins formerly struck in bronze.

Sterling   Word of uncertain origin denoting money of a standard weight and fineness, and hence the more general meaning of recognised worth. The traditionally accepted derivation from the Easterlings, north German merchants who settled in London in the 13th century and produced silver pennies of uniform fineness, is unlikely as the term has been found in documents a century earlier. A more plausible explanation is from Old English *steorling* ("little coin with a star"), alluding to Viking pennies with this device, or even as a diminutive of *stater*. Sterling silver denotes silver of .925 fineness.

Stone Money   Primitive currency in the form of large stone discs, used in West Africa in the pre-colonial period, and in the Pacific island of Yap (now Micronesia) as recently as 1940.

Striation   A pattern of alternate light and dark parallel marks or minute grooves on the surface of a coin or medal. In the latter case it is sometimes done for textural effect, but in coins it may result from faulty *annealing*. Deliberate ridging of the surface, however, was a distinctive feature of Japanese *koban* and *goryoban* coins of 1736–1862.

Styca   Name given to the debased silver *sceats* of Northumbria in the 8th century.

Tael   Chinese unit of weight corresponding to the European ounce and sometimes referred to as a liang. It was a measure of silver varying between 32 and 39 grams. In the 19th century it served as *money of account*, 100 British or Mexican trade dollars being worth 72 tael. The term has also been loosely applied to the Chinese silver yuan, although this was worth only .72 tael, or 7 mace and 2 candareens (10 candareens = 1 mace; 10 mace = 1 tael).

Thrymsa   Early Anglo-Saxon gold coin based on the Merovingian tremissis or third-solidus, current in Kent, London and York around AD 63–75.

Tical   Unit of weight in Thailand, first appearing as coins in the form of crudely shaped *bullet money* current from the 14th till the late 19th centuries. When European-style coins were introduced in 1860 the word was retained as a denomination (32 solot = 16 atts = 8 peinung or sio = 4 songpy or sik = 2 fuang= 1 salung or quarter-tical. The currency was decimalised in 1909 (100 satangs = 1 tical), and the tical was superseded by the baht about 1950.

Tin   Metallic element, chemical symbol *Sn* (from Latin *Stannum*). Because of its unstable nature and tendency to oxidise badly when exposed to the atmosphere, it is unsatisfactory as a coinage metal, but has been used on several occasions, notably in Malaya, Thailand and the East Indies. In was also used for British halfpence and farthings, 1672–92.

Token   Any piece of money whose nominal value is greater than its intrinsic value is, strictly speaking, a token or promise. Thus most of the coins issued since 1964 can be regarded in this light, but numismatists reserve the term for a piece of limited validity and circulation, produced by tradesmen, chambers of commerce and other organisations during times of a shortage of government coinage. The term is also loosely applied to metal tickets of admission, such as *communion tokens*, or *jetons* and *counters* intended for games of chance. Tokens with a nominal value may be produced for security reasons to lessen the possibility of theft from milk bottles, vending machines, telephones, parking meters and transport facilities. Tokens exchangeable for goods have been issued by co-operative societies and used in prisons and internment camps in wartime. In addition to the traditional coinage alloys, tokens have been produced in ceramics, plastics, wood, stout card, leather and even rubber, in circular, square or polygonal shapes.

Tombac   Type of brass alloy with a high copper content, used in coinage requiring a rich golden colour. It is, in fact, a modern version of the *aurichalcum* used by the Romans. It was used for the Canadian 5-cent coins of 1942–43, while 5- and 10-pfennig coins of Germany have a tombac cladding on a steel core.

Touchpiece   Coin kept as a lucky charm, but more specifically the medieval gold angel of England which was worn round the neck as an antidote to scrofula, otherwise known as king's evil, from the belief that the reigning monarch

Trial plate.

possessed the power of healing by touch. The ceremony of touching for king's evil involved the suspension of an angel round the victim's neck, hence the prevalence of these coins pierced for suspension.

Trade Coins Coins widely used as a medium of international trade, often far beyond the boundaries of the country issuing them. The earliest examples were the Aiginetan turtles and Athenian tetrdrachms of the classical period. In the Middle Ages the English *sterling* was widely prized on account of its silver purity. Arab dinars and Italian florins were popular as gold coins in late-medieval times, while the British gold sovereign has been the preferred gold coin of modern times. The Maria Theresa silver thaler of Austria, with its date frozen at 1782, has been minted widely down to the present time for circulation in the Near and Middle East as a trade coin. Trade dollars were minted by Britain, the USA, the Netherlands and Japan to compete with the Spanish, and later the Mexican, peso or 8-reales coins as a trading medium in the Far East.

Transport Tokens Coin-like pieces of metal, plastic or card, issued by companies and corporations to employees and exchangeable for rides on municipal transport systems, date from the mid-19th century. In more recent times similar tokens have been used in many countries to activate turnstiles in buses, trams and rapid-transit railway systems.

Treasury Note Paper money worth 10 shillings or one pound, issued by the British Treasury on the outbreak of the First World War when *specie* payments were suspended, and continuing till 1928 when the Bank of England took over responsibility for note-issuing.

Treasure Trove Articles of precious metal concealed in times of economic or political upheaval and discovered years (often centuries) later are deemed by law to be treasure trove (from the French word *trouve*, found). For further details see *Money and the Law*.

Trial Plate Plate of the same metal as the current coinage against which the fineness and quality of the coins produced are compared and tested.

Troy Weight System of weights derived from the French town of Troyes whose standard pound was adopted in England in 1526. It continued in Britain till 1879 when it was abolished, with the exception of the troy ounce and its decimal parts and multiples, which were retained for gold, silver, platinum and precious stones. The troy ounce of 480 grains is used for weighing coins.

Truncation Stylised cut at the base of a coinage effigy, sometimes containing a die number, engraver's initials or *mintmark*.

Trussel Reverse die in *hammered* coinage, the opposite of the *pile*.

Type Principal motif on a coin or medal, enabling numismatists to identify the issue.

Type Set A set of coins comprising one of each coin in a particular series, regardless of the actual date of issue.

Uncirculated Term used in grading coins to denote specimens in perfect condition, with original mint lustre. In recent years the term "Brilliant Uncirculated" has been adopted (abbreviated as BUnc or BU) both to indicate the condition of a coin, and, by The Royal Mint, to indicate the standard to which some coins are minted, being a standard between Circulation and Proof.

Uniface Coin with a device on one side only.

Vecture Term (mainly used in the US) for a *transport token*.

Veiled Head The effigy of Queen Victoria by Thomas Brock adopted for British coinage after 1893 — often referred to as the "Old Head" coinage.

Veld Pond (Dutch for "field pound"). Gold coin struck by the Boer guerrillas at Pilgrims Rest in 1902, in imitation of the British sovereign.

VF Abbreviation for Very Fine, used to describe the state of a coin or medal.

VG Abbreviation for Very Good, used to describe the state of a coin or medal.

Vignette Strictly speaking the pictorial element of a paper note shading off into the surrounding unprinted paper rather than having a clearly defined border or frame; but nowadays applied generally to the picture portion of a banknote, as opposed to portrait, armorial or numeral elements.

Vis-à-Vis (French for "face to face"). Term describing coins with double portraits of rulers, their profiles or busts facing each other. A good example is the English coinage of Philip and Mary, 1554–58.

Wampum Barter currency of the North American Indians, composed of shells of *Venus mercenaria* strung together to form belts or "fathoms" worth 5 shillings. Wampum were tariffed variously from three to six to the English penny in the American colonies till 1704.

Wire Money Primitive currency of the Maldive Islands in the form of lengths of silver wire known as lari, from which the modern currency unit *laree* is derived. The term was also applied to English coins of the 18th century in which the numerals of value were exceptionally thin, resembling wire. Many Russian coins of the 17th/18th century were also made from pieces of wire cut from strips which were then roughly flattened, often in an oval shape. These blanks were then struck with round dies which often meant that parts of the wording and design was missed off.

Wooden Coins Thin pieces of wood used as tokens are known from many parts of China and Africa, and as small *Notgeld* from Austria and Germany during World War I. Wooden nickels is the name given to tokens of a commemorative nature, widely popular in the USA since 1930.

Young Head Profile of Queen Victoria sculpted by William Wyon for the Guildhall Medal of 1837 and subsequently utilised for British coins struck from 1837 to 1860 (copper) and 1887 (silver and gold).

Zinc Metallic element, chemical symbol *Zn*, widely used, with copper, as a constituent of brass. Alloyed with copper to form *tombac*, it was used for Canadian 5-cent coins (1942–43) and, coated on steel, it was used for American cents (1943). Zinc was used for *emergency coinage* in Austria, Belgium, Luxembourg and Germany (1915–18) and in Germany and German-occupied countries during World War II. Since then alloys of copper, nickel and zinc have been used for coinage in Eastern Europe.

MINTMARKS *of the world*

The following is a list of the initials and symbols denoting mints. In many cases, notably the Royal Mint, no mintmark was used on either British coins or those struck on behalf of other countries. Conversely many countries have only used one mintmark, that of one or other of the leading private mints.

It should be noted that the mintmarks of the main private mints have been recorded on the coins of the following countries:

H (Heaton, later the Birmingham Mint): Australia, Bolivia, British Honduras, British North Borneo, British West Africa, Bulgaria, Canada, Ceylon, Chile, Colombia, Costa Rica, Cyprus, Dominican Republic, East Africa, Ecuador, Egypt, El Salvador, Finland, French Indochina, Great Britain, Greece, Guatemala, Guernsey, Haiti, Hong Kong, Iran, Israel, Italy, Jamaica, Jersey, Liberia, Malaya and British Borneo, Mauritius, Mombasa, Mozambique, Newfoundland, Nicaragua, Poland, Roumania, Sarawak, Serbia, Siam, Straits Settlements, Uruguay and Venezuela.

FM (Franklin Mint, Philadelphia): Bahamas, Belize, British Virgin Islands, Cayman Islands, Cook Islands, Guyana, Jamaica, Liberia, Malaysia, Malta, Panama, Papua New Guinea, Philippines, Solomon Islands, Trinidad and Tobago.

PM (Pobjoy Mint, Sutton, Surrey): Ascension, Bosnia, Cook Islands, Gibraltar, Isle of Man, Liberia, Macau, Niue, Philippines, St Helena, Senegal, Seychelles, Tonga and Tristan da Cunha.

ALBANIA
L	London
R	Rome
V	Valona

ARGENTINA
BA	Buenos Aires
Bs	Buenos Aires
B.AS	Buenos Aires
JPP	Jose Policarpo Patino
M	Mendoza
PNP	Pedro Nolasco Pizarro
PP	Pedro Nolasco Pizarro
PTS	Potosi
R	Rioja
RA	Rioja
SE	Santiago del Estero
SoEo	Santiago del Estero
TN	Tucuman

AUSTRALIA
A	Perth
D	Denver
H	Heaton (1912–16)
I	Bombay (1942–43)
I	Calcutta (1916–18)
M	Melbourne
P	Perth
PL	Royal Mint, London
S	Sydney
S	San Francisco (1942–43)
Dot before and after PENNY and I on obverse	Bombay (1942–43)
Dot before and after HALFPENNY and I on obverse	Bombay (1942–43)
Dot before and after PENNY	Bombay (1942–43)
Dot after HALFPENNY	Perth
Dot before SHILLING	Perth (1946)
Dot above scroll on reverse	Sydney (1920)
Dot below scroll on reverse	Melbourne (1919–20)
Dot between designer's initials KG	Perth (1940–41)
Dot after AUSTRALIA	Perth (1952–53)

AUSTRIA

A	Vienna (1765–1872)
AH–AG	Carlsburg, Transylvania (1765–76)
AH–GS	Carlsburg (1776–80)
A–S	Hall, Tyrol (1765–74)
AS–IE	Vienna (1745)
AW	Vienna (1764, 1768)
B	Kremnitz (1765–1857)
B–L	Nagybanya (1765–71)
B–V	Nagybanya (1772–80)
C	Carlsburg (1762–64)
C	Prague (1766–1855)
C–A	Carlsburg (1746–66)
C–A	Vienna (1774–80)
CG–AK	Graz (1767–72)
CG–AR	Graz (1767)
C–K	Vienna (1765–73)
CM	Kremnitz (1779)
CVG–AK	Graz (1767–72)
CVG–AR	Graz (1767)
D	Graz (1765–72), Salzburg (1800–09)
E	Carlsburg (1765–1867)
EC–SK	Vienna (1766)
EvM–D	Kremnitz (1765–74)
EvS–AS	Prague (1765–73)
EvS–IK	Prague (1774–80)
F	Hall (1765–1807)
FH	Hall
G	Graz (1761–63)
G	Gunzburg (1764–79)
G	Nagybanya (1766–1851)
G–K	Graz (1767–72)
G–R	Graz (1746–67)
GTK	Vienna (1761)
H	Hall (1760–80)
H	Gunzburg (1765–1805)
H–A	Hall (1746–65)
H–G	Carlsburg (1765–77)
H–S	Carlsburg (1777–80)
IB–FL	Nagybanya (1765–71)
IB–IV	Nagybanya (1772–80)
IC–FA	Vienna (1774–80)
IC–IA	Vienna (1780)
IC–SK	Vienna (1765–73)
I–K	Graz (1765-67)
I–K	Vienna (1767)
IZV	Vienna (1763–65)
K	Kremnitz (1760–63)
K–B	Kremnitz (1619–1765)
K–D	Kremnitz (1765)
K–M	Kremnitz (1763–65)
M	Milan (1780–1859)
N	Nagybanya (1780)
N–B	Nagybanya (1630–1777, 1849)
O	Oravicza (1783–1816)
P	Prague (1760–63)
P–R	Prague (1746–67)
PS–IK	Prague (1774–80)
S	Hall (1765–80), Schmollnitz (1763–1816)
S–C	Gunzburg (1765–74)
SC–G	Gunzburg (1765)

S–F	Gunzburg (1775–80)
S–G	Gunzburg (1764–65)
S–IE	Vienna (1745)
SK–PD	Kremnitz (1774–80)
TS	Gunzburg (1762–88)
V	Venice (1805–66)
VC–S	Hall (1774–80)
VS–K	Prague (1774–80)
VS–S	Prague (1765–73)
W	Vienna (1748–63)
W–I	Vienna (1746–71)

BAHAMAS

FM	Franklin Mint
JP	John Pinches

BELGIUM

A	Vienna
B	Kremnitz
C	Prague
E	Carlsburg
F	Hall
G	Nagybanya
H	Gunzburg
hand	Antwerp
lion	Bruges

BELIZE (British Honduras)

FM	Franklin Mint
H	Heaton (1912–16)

BOLIVIA

H	Heaton (1892–1953)
P, PTR, PTS	Potosi

BRAZIL

A	Berlin (1913)
B	Bahia (1714–1831)
C	Cuiaba (1823–33)
G	Goias (1823–33)
M	Minas Gerais (1823–28)
P	Pernambuco
R	Rio de Janeiro (1703–1834)
RS	Rio de Janeiro (1869)
SP	Sao Paulo (1825–32)

BRITISH NORTH BORNEO (Sabah)

H	Heaton (1882–1941)

BRITISH WEST AFRICA

G	JR Gaunt, Birmingham
H	Heaton, Birmingham (1911–57)
K	King's Norton
KN	King's Norton
SA	Pretoria

BULGARIA

A	Berlin
BP	Budapest
Heaton	Heaton, Birmingham (1881–1923)
KB	Kormoczbanya
cornucopia	Paris
thunderbolt	Poissy

CANADA
C	Ottawa
H	Heaton (1871–1907)
maple leaf	Ottawa (on coins struck after the year inscribed on them)

CENTRAL AMERICAN REPUBLIC
CR	San Jose (Costa Rica)
G	Guatemala
NG	Guatemala
T	Tegucigalpa (Honduras)

CEYLON
H	Heaton (1912)

CHILE
A	Agustin de Infante y Prado (1768–72)
AJ	The above and Jose Maria de Bobadilla (1800–01)
D	Domingo Eizaguirre
DA	Domingo Eizaguirre and Agustin de Infante (1772–99)
BFF	Francisco Rodriguez Brochero
FJJF	Brochero and Jose Maria de Bobadilla (1803–17)
H	Heaton (1851)
J	Jose Larraneta (1749–67)
So	Santiago
VA	Val Distra

COLOMBIA
A	Paris
B	Bogota
BA	Bogota
B.B	Bogota
H	Heaton (1912)
M	Medellin
NR	Nuevo Reino
NoRo	Nuevo Reino
P	Popayan
PN, Pn	Popayan
SM	Santa Marta

COSTA RICA
CR	San Jose (1825–1947)
HBM	Heaton (1889–93)
S	San Domingo
SD	San Domingo

COURLAND
ICS	Justin Carl Schroder
IFS	Johan Friedrich Schmickert

CYPRUS
H	Heaton (1881–2)

DENMARK
FF	Altona
KM	Copenhagen Altona (1842)
crown	Copenhagen
heart	Copenhagen

orb	Altona (1839–48)

Other letters are the initials of mintmasters and moneyers

DOMINICAN REPUBLIC
HH	Heaton (1888–1919)

EAST AFRICA
A	Ackroyd & Best, Morley
H	Heaton (1910–64)
I	Bombay
K	Kynoch (IMI)
KN	King's Norton
SA	Pretoria

ECUADOR
BIRM^MH	Heaton (1915)
BIRMING-HAM	Heaton (1899–1900, 1928)
D	Denver
H	Heaton (1890, 1909, 1924–5)
HEATON BIRMING-HAM	Heaton (1872–95)
HF	Le Locle
LIMA	Lima
Mo	Mexico
PHILA	Philadelphia
QUITO	Quito
SANTIAGO	Santiago de Chile

EGYPT
H	Heaton (1904–37)

EL SALVADOR
CAM	Central American Mint, San Salvador
H	Heaton (1889–1913)
Mo	Mexico
S	San Francisco

FIJI
S	San Francisco

FINLAND
H	Heaton (1921)
heart	Copenhagen (1922). Since then coins have been struck at Helsinki without a mintmark.

Initials of mintmasters:
S	August Soldan (1864–85)
L	Johan Lihr (1885–1912)
S	Isaac Sundell (1915–47)
L	V. U. Liuhto (1948)
H	Uolevi Helle (1948–58)
S	Allan Soiniemi (1958–75)
SH	Soiniemi & Heikki Halvaoja (1967–71)
K	Timo Koivuranta (1977, 1979)
KN	Koivuranta and Antti Neuvonen (1978)
KT	Koivuranta and Erja Tielinen (1982)
KM	Koivuranta and Pertti Makinen (1983)
N	Reino Nevalainen (1983)

FRANCE

A	Paris (1768)
AA	Metz (1775–98)
B	Rouen (1786–1857)
B	Beaumont le Roger (1943–58)
BB	Strasbourg (1743–1870)
C	Castelsarrasin (1914, 1942–46)
CC	Genoa (1805)
CL	Genoa (1813–14)
D	Lyons (1771–1857)
G	Geneva (1796–1805)
H	La Rochelle (1770–1837)
L	Limoges (1766–1837)
K	Bordeaux (1759–1878)
L	Bayonne (1761–1837)
M	Toulouse (1766–1837)
MA	Marseilles (1787–1857)
N	Montpellier (1766–93)
O	Riom
P	Dijon
Q	Perpignan (1777–1837)
R	Royal Mint, London (1815)
R	Orleans (1780–92)
T	Nantes (1739–1835)
U	Turin (1814)
V	Troyes
W	Lille (1759–1857)
X	Amiens (1740)
&	Aix en Provence (1775)
9	Rennes
cow	Pau (1746–93)
flag	Utrecht (1811–14)
crowned R	Rome (1811–14)
thunderbolt	Poissy (1922-24)
star	Madrid (1916)

In addition, French coins include symbols denoting the privy marks of Engravers General (Chief Engravers since 1880) and Mint Directors.

GERMANY

The first name gives the location of the mint, and the second the name of the country or state issuing the coins.

A	Amberg, Bavaria (1763–94)
A	Berlin (1850)
A	Clausthal, Hannover (1832–49)
AE	Breslau, Silesia (1743–51)
AGP	Cleve, Rhineland (1742–43)
AK	Dusseldorf, Julich-Berg (1749–66)
ALS	Berlin (1749)
B	Bayreuth, Franconia (1796–1804)
B	Breslau, Silesia (1750–1826)
B	Brunswick, Brunswick (1850–60)
B	Brunswick, Westphalia (1809–13)
B	Dresden, Saxony (1861–72)
B	Hannover, Brunswick (1860–71)
B	Hannover, East Friesland (1823–25)
B	Hannover, Hannover (1821–66)
B	Hannover, Germany (1866-78)
B	Regensburg, Regensburg (1809)
B	Vienna, Germany (1938–45)

BH	Frankfurt (1808)
B–H	Regensburg, Rhenish Confederation (1802–12)
C	Cassel, Westphalia (1810–13)
C	Clausthal, Brunswick
C	Clausthal, Westphalia (1810–11)
C	Dresden, Saxony (1779–1804)
C	Frankfurt, Germany (1866–79)
CHI	Berlin (1749–63)
CLS	Dusseldorf, Julich-Berg (1767–70)
D	Aurich, East Friesland (1750–1806)
D	Dusseldorf, Rhineland (1816–48)
D	Munich, Germany (1872)
E	Dresden, Germany (1872–87)
E	Koenigberg, East Prussia (1750–98)
E	Muldenhutte, Germany (1887–1953)
EC	Leipzig, Saxony (1753–63)
EGN	Berlin (1725–49)
F	Dresden, Saxony (1845–58)
F	Magdeburg, Lower Saxony (1740–1806)
F	Cassel, Hesse-Cassel (1803–07)
F	Stuttgart, Germany (1872)
FW	Dresden, Saxony (1734–63)
G	Dresden, Saxony (1833–44, 1850–54)
G	Glatz, Silesia (1807–09)
G	Karlsruhe, Germany (1872)
G	Stettin, Pomerania (1750–1806)
GK	Cleve (1740–55)
GN	Bamberg, Bamberg
H	Darmstadt, Germany (1872–82)
H	Dresden, Saxony (1804–12)
HK	Rostock, Rostock (1862–64)
I	Hamburg, Germany (1872)
IDB	Dresden, Prussian occupation (1756–59)
IEC	Dresden, Saxony (1779–1804)
IF	Leipzig, Saxony (1763–65)
IGG	Leipzig, Saxony (1716–34, 1813–32)
J	Hamburg, Germany (1873)
J	Paris, Westphalia (1808–09)
L	Leipzig, Saxony (1761–62)
MC	Brunswick, Brunswick (1813–14, 1820)
PM	Dusseldorf, Julich-Berg (1771–83)
PR	Dusseldorf, Julich-Berg (1783–1804)
S	Dresden, Saxony (1813–32)
S	Hannover, Hannover (1839–44)
S	Schwabach, Franconia (1792–94)
SGH	Dresden, Saxony (1804–12)
ST	Strickling, Blomberg (1820–40)

GREAT BRITAIN

A	Ashby (1645)
B	Nicolas Briot (1631–39)
B	Bridgnorth (1646)
B	Bristol (1696)
Br	Bristol (1643–45)
C	Chester (1696)
CARL	Carlisle (1644–45)
CC	Corfe Castle (1644)
CHST	Chester (1644)
CR	Chester (1644)
E	Southwark (1547–49)

E	Exeter (1696)
E	Edinburgh (1707–13)
E*	Edinburgh (1707–09)
H	Heaton, Birmingham (1874–1919)
HC	Hartlebury Castle (1646)
K	London (1547–49)
KN	King's Norton
N	Norwich (1696)
OX	Oxford (1644–45)
OXON	Oxford (1644)
PC	Pontefract (1648–49)
SC	Scarborough (1644–45)
SOHO	Birmingham (1797–1806)
T	Canterbury (1549)
TC	Bristol (1549)
WS	Bristol (1547–49)
Y	Southwark (1551)
boar	Shrewsbury (1643–44)
book	Aberystwyth (1638–42)
bow	Durham House (1548–49)
castle	Exeter (1644–45)
crown	Aberystwyth Furnace (1648–49)
plume	Shrewsbury (1642)
plume	Oxford (1642–46)
plume	Bristol (1643–46)

Other symbols and marks on the hammered coins of Great Britain are usually referred to as Initial Marks. Complete listings of these marks appear in a number of specialist publications.

GREECE

A	Paris
B	Vienna
BB	Strasbourg
H	Heaton (1921)
K	Bordeaux
KN	King's Norton
owl	Aegina (1828–32)
owl	Athens (1838-55)
thunderbolt	Poissy

GUATEMALA

CG	Guatemala City (1733-76)
G	Guatemala City (1776)
H	Heaton (1894–1901)
NG	Nueva Guatemala (1777)

GUERNSEY

H	Heaton (1855–1949)

HAITI

A	Paris
HEATON	Heaton (1863)

HONDURAS

A	Paris (1869–71)
T	Tegucigalpa (1825–62)

HONG KONG

H	Heaton (1872–1971)
KN	King's Norton

HUNGARY

A	Vienna
B	Kremnitz
BP	Budapest
CA	Vienna
G	Nagybanya
GN	Nagybanya
GYF	Carlsburg
HA	Hall
K	Kremnitz
KB	Kremnitz
NB	Nagybanya
S	Schmollnitz
WI	Vienna

INDIA

B	Bombay (1835-1947)	
C	Calcutta (1835-1947)	
I	Bombay (1918)	
L	Lahore (1943-45)	
M	Madras (1869)	
P	Pretoria (1943-44)	
diamond	Bombay	
dot in diamond		Hyderabad
split diamond		Hyderabad
star	Hyderabad	

IRAN

H	Heaton (1928–29)

IRAQ

I	Bombay

ISRAEL

H	Heaton (1951–52)
star of David	Jerusalem

ITALY AND STATES

B	Bologna
B/I	Birmingham (1893–4)
FIRENZE	Florence
H	Heaton (1866–67)
KB	Berlin
M	Milan
N	Naples
OM	Strasbourg
R	Rome
T	Turin
V	Venice
ZV	Venice
anchor	Genoa
eagle head	Turin

JAMAICA

C	Ottawa
FM	Franklin Mint
H	Heaton (1882–1916)

JERSEY

H	Heaton (1877)

KENYA

C/M	Calcutta
H	Heaton (1911–64)

LIBERIA

B	Berne
FM	Franklin Mint
H	Heaton (1896–1906)
PM	Pobjoy Mint

LIECHTENSTEIN

A	Vienna
B	Berne
M	Munich

LUXEMBOURG

A	Paris
H	Gunzburg
anchor	Paris
angel	Brussels
caduceus	Utrecht
double eagle	Brussels
sword	Utrecht

MALAYSIA

B	Bombay
FM	Franklin Mint
H	Heaton (1955–61)
I	Calcutta (1941)
I	Bombay (1945)
KN	King's Norton
W	James Watt, Birmingham

MAURITIUS

H	Heaton (1877–90)
SA	Pretoria

MEXICO

A, As	Alamos
C, CN	Culiacan
CA, CH	Chihuahua
Ce	Real del Catorce
D, Do	Durango
Eo	Tlalpam
GA	Guadalajara
GC	Guadelupe y Calvo
Go	Guanajuato
Ho	Hermosillo
M, Mo	Mexico City
Mo	Morelos
MX	Mexico City
O, OA, OKA	Oaxaca
Pi	San Luis Potosi
SLPi	San Luis Potosi
TC	Tierra Caliente
Z, Zs	Zacatecas

MONACO

A	Paris
M	Monte Carlo
clasped hands	Cabanis
thunderbolt	Poissy

MOZAMBIQUE

H	Heaton (1894)
R	Rio

NETHERLANDS AND COLONIES
Austrian Netherlands (1700-93)

H	Amsterdam
S	Utrecht
W	Vienna
hand	Antwerp
head	Brussels
lion	Bruges

Kingdom of the Netherlands

B	Brussels (1821–30)
D	Denver (1943–45)
P	Philadelphia (1941–45)
S	Utrecht (1816–36)
S	San Francisco (1944–45)
Sa	Surabaya
caduceus	Utrecht

NICARAGUA

H	Heaton (1880–1916)
NR	Leon de Nicaragua

NORWAY

hammers	Kongsberg

PANAMA

CHI	Valcambi
FM	Franklin Mint

PERU

AREQ, AREQUIPA	Arequipa
AYACUCHO	Ayacucho
CUZCO, Co	Cuzco
L, LM, LR	Lima
LIMAE	Lima
PASCO	Pasco
Paz, Po	Pasco
P	Lima (1568-70)
P	Philadelphia
S	San Francisco

PHILIPPINES

BSP	Bangko Sentral Pilipinas
D	Denver (1944–45)
FM	Franklin Mint
M, MA	Manila
PM	Pobjoy Mint
S	San Francisco (1903–47)
5 point star	Manila

POLAND

AP	Warsaw (1772–74)
CI	Cracow (1765–68)
EB	Warsaw (1774–92)
EC	Leipzig (1758–63)
FF	Stuttgart (1916–17)
FH	Warsaw (1815–27)
FS	Warsaw (1765–68)
FWoF	Dresden (1734–64)
G	Cracow (1765–72)

H	Heaton (1924)
IB	Warsaw (1811–27)
IGS	Dresden (1716–34)
IP	Warsaw (1834–43)
IS	Warsaw (1768–74)
JGG	Leipzig (1750–53)
JS	Warsaw (1810–11)
KG	Warsaw (1829–34)
MV, MW	Warsaw
arrow	Warsaw (1925–39)
Dot after date	Royal Mint (1925)
8 torches	Paris (1924)

ROUMANIA

B	Bucharest (1879–85)
C	Bucharest (1886)
H	Heaton (1867–1930)
HUGUENIN	Le Locle
J	Hamburg
KN	King's Norton
V	Vienna
W	Watt, Birmingham
thunderbolt	Poissy

RUSSIA

AM	Annensk (1762–96)
BM	Warsaw (1825–55)
bM	St Petersburg (1796)
C–M	Sestroretsk (1762–96)
CM	Souzan (1825–55)
E–M	Ekaterinburg (1762–1810)
KM	Kolpina (1810)
K–M	Kolyvan (1762–1810)
MM, M–M	Moscow (1730–96)
MMD	Moscow (1730–96)
MW	Warsaw (1842–54)
NM	Izhorsk (1811–21)
SP	St Petersburg (1798–1800)
SPB	St Petersburg (1724–1915)
SPM	St Petersburg (1825–55)
T–M	Feodosia (1762–96)

SAN MARINO

M	Milan
R	Rome
SIAM (Thailand)	H Heaton (1898)

SOUTH AFRICA

SA	Pretoria

SPAIN

B	Burgos
B, BA	Barcelona
Bo	Bilbao
C	Catalonia
C	Cuenca
C	Reus
CA	Zaragoza
G	Granada
GNA	Gerona
LD	Lerida

J, JA	Jubia
M, MD	Madrid
P	Palma de Majorca
PpP, PL, PA	Pamplona
S, S/L	Seville
Sr	Santander
T, To, Tole	Toledo
TOR:SA	Tortosa
V, VA, VAL	Valencia
crowned C	Cadiz
crowned M	Madrid
aqueduct	Segovia
crowned shield	Tarragona
pomegranate	Granada
quartered shield	Palma
scallop	Coruna
stars:	
3 points	Segovia
4 points	Jubia
5 points	Manila
6 points	Madrid
7 points	Seville (1833)
8 points	Barcelona (1838)
wavy lines	Valladolid

SURINAM

P	Philadelphia
S	Sydney
caduceus	Utrecht

SWITZERLAND

A	Paris
AB	Strasbourg
B	Berne
B	Brussels (1874)
BA	Basle
BB	Strasbourg
S	Solothurn

URUGUAY

H	Heaton (1869)

UNITED STATES OF AMERICA

C	Charlotte, North Carolina
Cc	Carson City, Nevada
D	Dahlonega, Georgia (1838–61)
D	Denver, Colorado (1906)
O	New Orleans
P	Philadelphia
S	San Francisco
W	West Point

VENEZUELA

A	Paris
H	Heaton (1852)
HEATON	Heaton (1852–63)

YUGOSLAVIA (including former Serbia)

A	Paris
H	Heaton (1883–84)
KOBHNUA, A.D.	Kovnica
V	Vienna
thunderbolt	Poissy

Where money talks

COIN *inscriptions*

This alphabetical listing is confined to inscriptions found on coins, mainly in the form of mottoes or of a commemorative nature. Names of rulers are, for the most part, excluded. Where the inscription is in a language other than English a translation is given, followed by the name of the issuing country or authority in parentheses.

A Deo et Caesare   From God and the Emperor (Frankfurt).

A Domino Factum est Istud et est Mirabile in Oculis Nostris   This is the Lord's doing and it is marvellous in our eyes (England, Mary).

A Solo Iehova Sapientia   From God alone comes true wisdom (Wittgenstein).

Ab Inimicis Meis Libera Me Deus   Free me from enemies (Burgundy).

Ad Legem Conventionis   According to the law of the Convention (Furstenberg).

Ad Normam Conventionis   According to the standard of the Convention (Prussia).

Ad Palmam Pressa Laeturo Resurgo   Pressed to the palm I rise more joyfully (Wittgenstein).

Ad Usam Luxemburgi CC Vallati   For the use of the besieged Luxembourgers (Luxembourg siege coins).

Adiuva Nos Deus Salutaris Noster   Help us, O God, our Saviour (Lorraine).

Adventus Optimi Principis   The coming of the noblest prince (Papacy).

Aes Usibus Aptius Auro   Bronze in its uses is more suitable than gold (Brazil).

Aeternum Meditans Decus   An ornament intended for all time (Alencon).

Aliis Inserviendo Consumor   I spend my life devoted to others (Brunswick-Wolfenbuttel).

Alles Mit Bedacht   All with reflection (Brunswick).

Amor Populi Praesidium Regis   The love of the people is the king's protection (England, Charles I).

Ang Fra Dom Hib & Aquit   (King) of England and France, Lord of Ireland and Aquitaine (England, Edward III).

Anno Regni Primo   In the first year of the reign (Britain, edge inscription on crowns).

Apres les Tenebres la Lumiere   After the shadows, the light (Geneva).

Archangelus Michael   Archangel Michael (Italy, Grimoald IV).

Ardua ad Gloriam Via   Struggles are the way to glory (Waldeck).

Arte Mea Bis Iustus Moneta Lud Iust   By my art I am twice the just coin of King Louis (France, 1641).

Aspera Oblectant   Wild places delight (Nassau-Weilburg).

Aspice Pisas Sup Omnes Specio   Behold the coin of Pisa, superior to all (Pisa).

Audiatur Altera Pars   Let the other part be heard (Stavelot).

Auf Gott Trawe Ich   In God I trust (Brunswick).

Ausen Gefaesen der Kirchen und Burger   From the vessels of the Church and citizens (Frankfurt siege, 1796).

Auspicio Regis et Senatus Angliae   By authority of the king and parliament of England (East India Company).

Auxilio fortissimo Dei   With the strongest help of God (Mecklenburg).

Auxilium de Sanctio   Aid from the sanctuary (Papacy).

Auxilium Meum a Dno Qui Fecit Celum e Terram   My help comes from God who made heaven and earth (Portugal).

Beata Tranquillatis   Blessed tranquillity (Rome, Licinius II).

Beatus Qui Speravit in dom   Blessed is he who has hoped in the Lord (Mansfeld).

Benedic Haereditati Tuae   Blessings on your inheritance (Savoy).

Benedicta Sit Sancta Trinitas   Blessed be the Holy Trinity (Albon).

Benedictio Domini Divites Facit   The blessing of the Lord makes the rich (Teschen).

Benedictus Qui Venit in Nomine Domini   Blessed is he who comes in the name of the Lord (Flanders).

Beschaw das Ziel Sage Nicht Viel   Consider the matter but say little (Quedlinburg).

Besser Land und Lud Verloren als ein Falscher Aid Geschworn   Better to lose land and wealth than swear a false oath (Hesse).

Bey Gott ist Rath und That   With God is counsel and deed (Mansfeld).

Britanniarum Regina   Queen of the Britains (Britain, Victoria).

Britt Omn Rex   King of all the Britains (i.e. Britain and the overseas dominions) (Britain, 1902–52).

Cal et Car Com de Fugger in Zin et Norn Sen & Adm Fam   Cajetan and Carl, Counts of Fugger in Zinnenberg and Nordendorf, Lords and Administrators of the Family (Empire, Fugger).

Candide et Constanter   Sincerely and steadfastly (Hesse-Cassel).

Candide sed Provide   Clearly but cautiously (Osterwitz).

Candore et Amore   With sincerity and love (Fulda).

Candore et Constantia   With sincerity and constancy (Bavaria).

Capit Cath Ecclesia Monasteriensis   Chapter of the Cathedral Church of Munster (Munster).

Capit Eccle Metropolit Colon   Chapter of the Metropolitan Church of Cologne (Cologne).

Capitulum Regnans Sede Vacante   Chapter governing, the See being vacant (Eichstadt).

Carola Magna Ducissa Feliciter Regnante   Grand Duchess Charlotte, happily reigning (Luxembourg).

Carolus a Carolo   Charles (I) to Charles (II) (England).

Cedunt Prementi Fata   The fates yield to him who presses (Ploen, Hese-Cassel).

Charitate et Candore   With charity and sincerity (East Frisia).

Charta Magna Bavariae   The Great Charter of Bavaria (Bavaria).

Christo Auspice Regno   I reign under the auspices of Christ (England, Charles I).

Christus Spes Una Salutis   Christ is our one hope of salvation (Cleve).

Chur Mainz   Electoral Principality of Mainz (Mainz).

Circumeundo Servat et Ornat   It serves and decorates by going around (Sweden).

Civibus Quorum Pietas Coniuratione Die III Mai MDCCXCI Obrutam et Deletam Libertate Polona Tueri Conabatur Respublica Resurgens   To the citizens whose piety the resurgent commonwealth tried to protect Poland overturned and deprived of liberty by the conspiracy of the third day of May 1791 (Poland).

Civitas Lucemborgiensis Millesimum Ovans Expletannum   Completing the celebration of a thousand years of the city of Luxembourg (Luxembourg).

Civium Industria Floret Civitas   By the industry of its people the state flourishes (Festival of Britain crown, 1951).

Cluniaco Cenobio Petrus et Paulus   Peter and Paul from the Abbey of Cluny (Cluny).

Comes Provincie Fili Regis Francie   Court of Provence and son of the King of France (Provence).

Communitas et Senatus Bonon   City and senate of Bologna (Bologna).

Concordia Fratrum   The harmony of the brothers (Iever).

Concordia Patriae Nutrix   Peace, the nurse of the fatherland (Waldeck).

Concordia Res Parvae Crescunt   Little things increase through harmony (Batavian Republic).

Concordia Res Parvae Crescunt, Discordia Dilabuntur   By harmony little things increase, by discord they fall apart (Lowenstein-Wertheim-Virneburg).

Concordia Stabili   With lasting peace (Hildesheim).

Confidens Dno Non Movetur   He who trusts in God is unmoved (Spanish Netherlands).

Confidentia in Deo et Vigilantia   Trust in God and vigilance (Prussian Asiatic Company).

Confoederato Helvetica   Swiss Confederation (Switzerland)

Conjuncto Felix   Fortunate in his connections (Solms).

Conservator Urbis Suae   Saviour of his city (Rome, 4th century).

Consilio et Aequitate   With deliberation and justice (Fulda).

Consilio et Virtutis   With deliberation and valour (Hesse-Cassel).

Constanter et Sincere   Steadfastly and sincerely (Lautern).

Crescite et Multiplicamini   Increase and multiply (Maryland).

Cristiana Religio   Christian religion (Germany, 11th century).

Crux Benedicat   May the cross bless you (Oldenburg).

Cuius Cruore Sanati Sumus   By His sacrifice are we healed (Reggio).

Cultores Sui Deus Protegit   God protects His followers (England, Charles I).

Cum Deo et Die (Jure)   With God and the day (Wurttemberg).

Cum Deo et Jure   With God and the law (Wurttemberg).

Cum Deo et Labore   With God and work (Wittgenstein).

Cum His Qui Orderant Pacem Eram Pacificus   With those who order peace I was peaceful (Zug).

Curie Bonthon to so Doulo   Protect his servant, o Lord (Byzantine Empire).

Custos Regni Deus   God is the guardian of the kingdom (Naples and Sicily).

Da Gloriam Deo et Eius Genitrici Marie   Give glory to God and His mother Mary (Wurttemberg).

Da Mihi Virtutem Contra Hostes Tuos   Give me valour against mine enemies (Netherlands, Charles V).

Dat Wort is Fleis Gworden   The word is made flesh (Muster).

Date Caesaris Caesari et Quae Sunt Dei Deo   Render unto Caesar the things that are Caesar's and unto God the things that are God's (Stralsund).

De Oficina . . .   From the mint of . . . (France, medieval).

Decreto Reipublicae Nexu Confoederationis Iunctae Die V Xbris MDCCXCII Stanislao Augusto Regnante   By decree of the state in conjunction with the joint federation on the fifth day of December 1792, Stanislaus Augustus ruling (Poland).

Decus et Tutamen   An ornament and a safeguard (Britain, pound).

Deducet Nos Mirabiliter Dextera Tua   Thy right hand will guide us miraculously (Savoy).

Denarium Terrae Mariae   Penny of Maryland (Maryland).

Deo Conservatori Pacis   To God, preserver of peace (Brandenburg-Ansbach).

Deo OM Auspice Suaviter et Fortiter sed Luste nec Sibi sed Suis   Under the auspices of God, greatest and best, pleasantly and bravely but justly, not for himself but for his people (Speyer).

Deo Patriae et Subditio   For God, fatherland and neighbourhood (Mainz).

Der Recht Glaubt In Ewig Lebt   Who believes in right will live in eternity (Linange-Westerburg).

Der Rhein ist Deutschlands Strom Nicht Deutschlands Grenze   The Rhine is Germany's River not Germany's Frontier.

Deum Solum Adorabis   You will venerate God alone (Hesse).

Deus Constituit Regna   God establishes kingdoms (Ni jmegen).

Deus Dat Qui Vult   God gives to him who wishes (Hanau-Munzenberg).

Deus et Dominus   God and Lord (Rome, 3rd century).

Deus in Adiutorium Meum Intende   God stretch out in my assistance (France).

Deus Providebit   God will provide (Lowenstein-Wertheim-Virneburg).

Deus Refugium Meum   God is my refuge (Cleve).

Deus Solatium Meum   God is my comfort (Sweden).

Dextera Domini Exaltavit Me   The right hand of God has raised me up (Modena, Spain).

Dextra Dei Exalta Me   The right hand of God exalts me (Denmark).

Dieu et Mon Droit   God and my right (Britain, George IV).

Dilexit Dns Andream   The Lord delights in St Andrew (Holstein).

Dilexit Dominus Decorem Iustitiae   The Lord is pleased with the beauty of justice (Unterwalden).

Dirige Deus Gressus Meos   O God, direct my steps (Tuscany, Britain, Una £5).

Discerne Causam Meam   Distinguish my cause (Savoy).

Divina Benedictiae et Caesarea Iustitia   Sacrifice of blessings and imperial justice (Coblenz).

Dn Ihs Chs Rex Regnantium   Lord Jesus Christ, King of Kings (Rome, Justinian II).

Dns Ptetor Ms Z Lib'ator Ms   The Lord is my protector and liberator (Scotland, David II).

Dominabitur Gentium et Ipse   He himself will also be lord of the nations (Austrian Netherlands).

Domine Conserva Nos in Pace   O Lord preserve us in peace (Basle, Mulhausen).

Domine Elegisti Lilium Tibi   O Lord Thou hast chosen the lily for Thyself (France, Louis XIV).

Domine ne in Furore Tuo Arguas Me   O Lord rebuke me not in Thine anger (England, Edward III).

Domine Probasti Me et Congnovisti Me   O Lord Thou hast tested me and recognised me (Mantua).

Domini est Regnum   The Kingdom is the Lord's (Austrian Netherlands).

Dominus Deus Omnipotens Rex   Lord God, almighty King (Viking coins).

Dominus Mihi Adiutor   The Lord is my helper (Spanish Netherlands).

Dominus Providebit   The Lord will provide (Berne).

Dominus Spes Populi Sui   The Lord is the hope of his people (Lucerne).

Donum Dei ex Fodinis Vilmariens   A gift of God from the Vilmar mines (Coblenz).

Duce Deo Fide et Justicia   By faith and justice lead us to God (Ragusa).

Dum Praemor Amplior   I increase while I die prematurely (Savoy).

Dum Spiro Spero   While I live, I hope (Pontefract siege coins).

Dum Totum Compleat Orbem   Until it fills the world (France, Henri II).

Dura Pati Virtus   Valour endures hardships (Saxe-Lauenburg).

Durae Necessitatis   Through force of necessity (Bommel siege, 1599).

Durum Telum Necessitas   Hardship is a weapon of necessity (Minden).

Dux et Gubernatores Reip Genu   Duke and governors of the republic of Genoa (Genoa).

E Pluribus Unum   One out of more (USA).

Eccl S. Barbarae Patronae Fodin Kuttenbergensium Duo Flor Arg Puri   The church of St Barbara, patron of the Kuttensberg mines, two florins of pure silver (Hungary).

Een en Ondelbaer Sterk   One and indivisible (Batavian Republic).

Eendracht Mag Macht   Unity makes strength (Belgium, South African Republic).

Einigkeit Recht und Freiheit   Union, right and freedom (Germany).

Electorus Saxoniae Administrator   Elector and administrator of Saxony (Saxony).

Elimosina   Alms (France, Pepin).

Ep Fris & Ratisb Ad Prum Pp Coad Aug   Bishop of Freising and Regensburg, administrator of Pruem, prince-provost, co-adjutant bishop of Augsburg (Trier).

Equa Libertas Deo Gratia Frat Pax in Virtute Tua et in Domino Confido   I believe in equal liberty by the grace of God, brotherly love in Thy valour and in the Lord (Burgundy).

Equitas Iudicia Tua Dom   Equity and Thy judgments O Lord (Gelderland).

Espoir Me Conforte   Hope comforts me (Mansfeld).

Espreuve Faicto Par Lexpres Commandement du Roy   Proof made by the express commandment of the King (France, piedforts).

Et in Minimis Integer   Faithful even in the smallest things (Olmutz).

Ex Auro Argentes Resurgit   From gold it arises, silver again (Sicily).

Ex Auro Sinico   From Chinese gold (Denmark).

Ex Flammis Orior   I arise from the flames (Hohenlohe-Neuenstein-Ohringen).

Ex Fodinis Bipontio Seelbergensibus   From the Seelberg mines of Zweibrucken (Pfalz-Birkenfeld).

Ex Metallo Novo   From new metal (Spain).

Ex Uno Omnis Nostra Salus   From one is all our salvation (Eichstadt, Mulhouse).

Ex Vasis Argent Cleri Mogunt Pro Aris et Focis   From the silver vessels of the clergy of Mainz for altars and for hearths (Mainz).

Ex Visceribus Fodinse Bieber   From the bowels of the Bieber mine (Hanau-Munzenberg).

Exaltabitur in Gloria   He shall be exalted in glory (England, quarter nobles).

Exemplum Probati Numismatis   An example of a proof coin (France, Louis XIII piedforts).

Exemtae Eccle Passau Episc et SRI Princ   Prince Bishop of the freed church of Passau, prince of the Holy Roman Empire (Passau).

Expectate Veni   Come, o expected one (Roman Britain, Carausius).

Extremum Subidium Campen   Kampen under extreme siege (Kampen, 1578).

Exurgat Deus et Dissipentur Inimici Eius   Let God arise and let His enemies be scattered (England, James I).

Faciam Eos in Gentem Unam   I will make them one nation (England, unites and laurels).

Faith and Truth I will Bear unto You   (UK £5, 1993).

Fata Consiliis Potiora   The fates are more powerful than councils (Hesse-Cassel).

Fata Viam Invenient   The fates will find a way (Gelderland).

Fecit Potentiam in Brachio Suo   He put power in your forearm (Lorraine).

Fecunditas   Fertility (Naples and Sicily).

Fel Temp Reparatio   The restoration of lucky times (Rome, AD 348).

Felicitas Perpetua   Everlasting good fortune (Rome, Constantius II).

Felix coniunctio   Happy Union (Brandenburg-Ansbach).

Fiat Misericordia Tua Dne   Let Thy mercy be O Lord (Gelderland).

Fiat Voluntas Domini Perpetuo   Let the goodwill of the Lord last for ever (Fulda).

Fidei Defensor   Defender of the Faith (Britain).

Fidelitate et Fortitudine   With fidelity and fortitude (Batthanyi).

Fideliter et Constanter   Faithfully and steadfastly (Saxe-Coburg-Gotha).

Fidem Servando Patriam Tuendo   By keeping faith and protecting the fatherland (Savoy).

Filius Augustorum   Son of emperors (Rome, 4th century).

Fisci Iudaici Calumnia Sublata   The false accusation of the Jewish tax lifted (Rome, Nerva).

Florent Concordia Regna   Through harmony kingdoms flourish (England, Charles I and II).

Fortitudo et Laus Mea Dominu   Fortitude and my praise in the Lord (Sardinia).

Free Trade to Africa by Act of Parliment (*Sic*) (Gold Coast).

Friedt Ernehrt Unfriedt Verzehrt   Peace nourishes, unrest wastes (Brunswick).

Fulgent Sic Littora Rheni   Thus shine the banks of the Rhine (Mannheim).

Fundator Pacis   Founder of peace (Rome, Severus).

Gaudium Populi Romani   The joy of the Roman people (Rome, 4th century).

Gen C Mar VI Dim Col USC & RAMAI Cons & S Conf M   General field marshal, colonel of the only dragoon regiment, present privy councillor of both their sacred imperial and royal apostolic majesties, and state conference minister (Batthanyi).

Gerecht und Beharrlich   Just and steadfast (Bavaria).

Germ Hun Boh Rex AAD Loth Ven Sal   King of Germany, Hungary and Bohemia, Archduke of Austria, Duke of Lorraine, Venice and Salzburg (Austria).

Germ Jero Rex Loth Bar Mag Het Dux   King of Germany, Jerusalem, Lorraine and Bar, Grand Duke of Tuscany (Austrian Netherlands).

Germania Voti Compos   Germany sharing the vows (Brandenburg-Ansbach).

Gloria ex Amore Patriae   Glory from love of country (Denmark).

Gloria in Excelsis Deo   Glory to God in the highest (France, Sweden).

Gloria Novi Saeculi   The glory of a new century (Rome, Gratian).

God With Us   (England, Commonwealth).

Godt Met Ons   God with us (Oudewater).

Gottes Freundt der Pfaffen Feindt   God's friend, the Pope's enemy (Brunswick, Christian).

Gratia Dei Sum Id Quod Sum By the grace of God, I am what I am (Navarre).

Gratia Di Rex By the grace of God, king (France, 8th century).

Gratitudo Concivibus Exemplum Posteritati Gratitude to fellow Citizens, an example to posterity (Poland).

Gud och Folket God and the people (Sweden).

Hac Nitimur Hanc Tuemur With this we strive, this we shall defend (Batavian Republic).

Hac Sub Tutela Under this protection (Eichstadt).

Haec Sunt Munera Minerae S Antony Eremitae These are the rewards of the mine of St Antony the hermit (Hildesheim).

Hanc Deus Dedit God has given this (Pontefract siege coins).

Hanc Tuemur Hac Nitimur This we defend, by this we strive (Batavian Republic).

Has Nisi Periturus Mihi Adimat Nemo Let no one remove these (Letters) from me under penalty of death (Commonwealth, edge inscription).

Henricus Rosas Regna Jacobus Henry (united) the roses, James the kingdoms (England and Scotland, James VI and I).

Herculeo Vincta Nodo Bound by a Herculean fetter (Savoy).

Herr Nach Deinem Willen O Lord Thy will be done (Palatinate, Erbach).

Herre Gott Verleich Uns Gnade Lord God grant us grace (Brunswick).

Hic Est Qui Multum Orat Pro Populo Here is he who prays a lot for the people (Paderborn).

Hir Steid te Biscop Here is represented the bishop (Gittelde).

His Ventis Vela Levantur By these winds the sails are raised up (Hesse-Cassel).

Hispaniarum Infans Infante of Spain and its dominions (Spain).

Hispaniarum et Ind Rex King of Spain and the Indies.

Hispaniarum Rex King of Spain (Spain).

Hoc Signo Victor Eris With this sign you will be victor (Rome, Vetranio).

Honeste et Decenter Honestly and decently (Nassau-Idstein).

Honi Soit Qui Mal y Pense Evil to him who evil thinks (Britain, George III).

Honni Soit Qui Mal y Pense (Hesse-Cassel).

Hospitalis et S Sepul Hierusal Hospital and Holy Sepulchre of Jerusalem (Malta).

Hun Boh Gal Rex AA Lo Wi et in Fr Dux King of Hungary, Bohemia and Galicia, Archduke of Austria, Dalmatia, Lodomeria, Wurzburg and Duke in Franconia (Austria).

Hung Boh Lomb et Ven Gal Lod III Rex Aa King of Hungary, Bohemia, Lombardo-Venezia, Galicia, Lodomeria and Illyria, Archduke of Austria (Austria).

Ich Dien I serve (Aberystwyth 2d, UK 2p).

Ich Getrawe Got in Aller Noth I trust in God in all my needs (Hesse-Marburg).

Ich Habe Nur Ein Vaterland und das Heisst Deutschland I have only one fatherland and that is called Germany (Germany).

Ielithes Penniae Penny of Gittelde (Gittelde, 11th century).

Iesus Autem Transiens Per Medium Illorum Ibat But Jesus, passing through the midst of them, went His way (England, Scotland, Anglo-Gallic).

Iesus Rex Noster et Deus Noster Jesus is our king and our God (Florence).

Ihs Xs Rex Regnantium Jesus Christ, King of Kings (Byzantine Empire).

Ihsus Xristus Basileu Baslie Jesus Christ, King of Kings (Byzantine Empire).

Imago Sanch Regis Illustris Castelle Legionis e Toleto The image of Sancho the illustrious king of Castile, Leon and Toledo.

In Casus Per Vigil Omnes In all seasons through vigil (Wertheim).

In Deo Meo Transgrediar Murum In my God I shall pass through walls (Teschen).

In Deo Spes Mea In God is my hope (Gelderland).

In Domino Fiducia Nostra In the Lord is our trust (Iever).

In Equitate Tua Vivificasti Me In thy equity Thou hast vivified me (Gelderland).

In God We Trust (USA).

In Hoc Signo Vinces In this sign shalt thou conquer (Portugal).

In Honore Sci Mavrici Marti In honour of the martyr St Maurice (St Maurice, 8th century).

In Manibus Domini sortes Meae In the hands of the Lord are my fates (Mainz siege, 1688–9).

In Memor Vindicatae Libere ac Relig In memory of the establishment of freedom and religion (Sweden).

In Memoriam Conjunctionis Utriusque Burgraviatus Norice In memory of the union of both burgraviates in peace (Brandenburg-Ansbach).

In Memorian Connub Feliciaes Inter Princ Her Frider Carol et Dub Sax August Louis Frider Rodas D 28 Nov 1780 Celebrati In memory of the most happy marriage between the hereditary prince Friedrich Karl and the Duchess of Saxony Augusta Louisa Frederika, celebrated on 28 Nov 1780 (Schwarzburg-Rudolstadt).

In Memorian Felicisssimi Matrimonii In memory of the most happy marriage (Wied).

In Memoriam Pacis Teschinensis Commemorating the Treaty of Teschen (Brandenburg-Ansbach).

In Nomine Domini Amen In the name of the Lord amen (Zaltbommel).

In Omnem Terram Sonus Eorum In to all the land their shall go sound (Chateau Renault, Papal States).

In Silencio et Spe Fortitudo Mea In silence and hope is my fortitude (Brandenburg-Kustrin).

In Spe et Silentio Fortitudo Mea   In hope and silence is my fortitude (Vianen).

In Te Domine Confido   In you O Lord I place my trust (Hesse).

In Te Domine Speravi   In You, O Lord, I have hoped (Gurk).

In Terra Pax   Peace in the land (Papacy).

In Via Virtuti Nulla Via   There is no way for virtue on the way. (Veldenz).

Ind Imp, Indiae Imperator, Imperatrix   Emperor (Empress) of India (Britain).

India Tibi Cessit   India has yielded to thee (Portuguese India).

Infestus Infestis   Hostile to the troublesome (Savoy).

Inimicos Eius Induam Confusione   As for his enemies, I shall clothe them in shame (Sardinia, England, Edward VI).

Insignia Capituli Brixensis   The badge of the chapter of Brixen (Brixen).

Isti Sunt Patres Tui Verique Pastores   These are your fathers and true shepherds (Papacy).

Iudicium Melius Posteritatis Erit   Posterity's judgment will be better (Paderborn).

Iure et Tempore   By right and time (Groningen).

Iusques a Sa Plenitude   As far as your plenitude (France, Henri II).

Iuste et Constanter   Justly and constantly (Paderborn).

Iustirt   Adjusted (Hesse-Cassel).

Iustitia et Concordia   Justice and harmony (Zurich).

Iustitia et Mansuetudine   By justice and mildness (Bavaria, Cologne).

Iustitia Regnorum Fundamentum   Justice is the foundation of kingdoms (Austria).

Iustitia Thronum Firmat   Justice strengthens the throne (England, Charles I).

Iustus Non Derelinquitur   The just person is not deserted (Brandenburg-Calenberg).

Iustus Ut Palma Florebit   The just will flourish like the palm (Portugal).

L Mun Planco Rauracorum Illustratori Vetustis-simo   To L Municius Plancus the most ancient and celebrated of the Rauraci (Basle).

Landgr in Cleggov Com in Sulz Dux Crum   Landgrave of Klettgau, count of Sulz, duke of Krumlau (Schwarzburg-Sonderhausen).

Latina Emeri Munita   Latin money of Merida (Suevi).

Lege et Fide   By law and faith (Austria).

Lex Tua Veritas   Thy law is the truth (Tuscany).

Liberta Eguaglianza   Freedom and equality (Venice)

Libertad en la Ley   Freedom within the law (Mexico).

Libertas Carior Auro   Freedom is dearer than gold (St Gall).

Libertas Vita Carior   Freedom is dearer than life (Kulenberg).

Libertas Xpo Firmata   Freedom strengthened by Christ (Genoa).

Liberte, Egalite, Fraternite   Liberty, equality, fraternity (France).

Lucerna Pedibus Meis Verbum Est   Thy word is a lamp unto mine feet (England, Edward VI).

Lumen ad Revelationem Gentium   Light to enlighten the nations (Papacy).

L'Union Fait la Force   The union makes strength (Belgium)

Macula Non Est in Te   There is no sin in Thee (Essen).

Magnus ab Integro Saeculorum Nascitur Ordo   The great order of the centuries is born anew (Bavaria).

Mandavit Dominus Palatie hanc Monetam Fiert   The lord of the Palatine ordained this coin to be made (Balath).

Manibus Ne Laedar Avaris   Lest I be injured by greedy hands (Sweden).

Mar Bran Sac Rom Imp Arcam et Elec Sup Dux Siles   Margrave of Brandenburg, archchamberlain of the Holy Roman Empire and elector, senior duke of Silesia (Prussia).

Maria Mater Domini Xpi   Mary mother of Christ the Lord (Teutonic Knights).

Maria Unxit Pedes Xpisti   Mary washes the feet of Christ (France, Rene d'Anjou).

Mater Castrorum   Mother of fortresses (Rome, Marcus Aurelius).

Matrimonio Conjuncti   Joined in wedlock (Austria).

Me Coniunctio Servat Dum Scinditur Frangor   The relationship serves me while I am being torn to pieces (Lowenstein-Wertheim).

Mediolani Dux   Duke of Milan (Milan).

Mediolani et Man   Duke of Mantua and Milan (Milan).

Memor Ero Tui Iustina Virgo   I shall remember you, o maiden Justina (Venice).

Merces Laborum   Wages of work (Wurzburg).

Mirabilia Fecit   He wrought marvels (Viking coinage).

Misericordia Di Rex   King by the mercy of God (France, Louis II).

Mo Arg Ord Foe Belg D Gel & CZ   Silver coin of the order of the Belgian Federation, duchy of Guelder-land, county of Zutphen (Guelderland).

Moneta Abbatis   Coin of the abbey (German ecclesiastical coins, 13th–14th centuries).

Moneta Argentiae Ord Foed Belgii Holl   Silver coin of the federated union of Belgium and Holland (Batavian Republic).

Mo No Arg Con Foe Belg Pro Hol   New silver coin of the Belgian Federation, province of Holland (Holland).

Mo No Arg Pro Confoe Belg Trai Holl   New silver coin of the confederated Belgian provinces, Utrecht and Holland (Batavian Republic).

Mon Lib Reip Bremens   Coin of the free state of Bremen (Bremen).

Mon Nova Arg Duc Curl Ad Norma Tal Alb   New silver coin of the duchy of Courland, according to the standard of the Albert thaler (Courland).

Mon Nov Castri Imp   New coin of the Imperial free city of . . . (Friedberg).

Moneta Bipont   Coin of Zweibrucken (Pfalz-Birkenfeld-Zweibrucken).

Monet Capit Cathedr Fuld Sede Vacante   Coin of the cathedral chapter of Fulda, the see being vacant (Fulda).

Moneta in Obsidione Tornacensi Cusa   Coin struck during the siege of Tournai (Tournai, 1709).

Moneta Livosesthonica   Coin of Livonia (Estonia).

Moneta Nov Arg Regis Daniae   New silver coin of the king of Denmark (Denmark).

Moneta Nova Ad Norman Conventionis   New coin according to the Convention standard (Orsini-Rosenberg).

Moneta Nova Domini Imperatoris   New coin of the lord emperor (Brunswick, 13th century).

Moneta Nova Lubecensis   New coin of Lubeck.

Moneta Nova Reipublicae Halae Suevicae   New coin of the republic of Hall in Swabia.

Moneta Reipublicae Ratisbonensis   Coin of the republic of Regensburg.

Nach Alt Reichs Schrot und Korn   According to the old empire's grits and grain (Hesse).

Nach dem Conventions Fusse   According to the Convention's basis (German Conventionsthalers).

Nach dem Frankf Schlus   According to the Frankfurt standard (Solms).

Nach dem Schlus der V Staend   According to the standard of the union (Hesse).

Navigare Necesse Est   It is necessary to navigate (Germany).

Nec Aspera Terrent   Nor do difficulties terrify (Brunswick).

Nec Cito Nec Temere   Neither hastily nor rashlly (Cambrai).

Nec Numina Desunt   Nor is the divine will absent (Savoy).

Nec Temere Nec Timide   Neither rashly nor timidly (Danzig, Lippe).

Necessitas Legem Non Habet   Necessity has no law (Magdeburg).

Nemo Me Impune Lacessit   No one touches me with impunity (UK, Scottish pound edge inscription).

Nihil Restat Reliqui   No relic remains (Ypres).

Nil Ultra Aras   Nothing beyond the rocks (Franque-mont).

No Nobis Dne Sed Noi Tuo Da Gloriam   Not to us, o Lord but to Thy name be glory given (France, Francis I).

Nobilissimum Dom Ac Com in Lipp & St   Most noble lord and count in Lippe and Sternberg (Schaumburg-Lippe).

Nomen Domini Turris Fortissima   The name of the Lord is the strongest tower (Frankfurt).

Non Aes Sed Fides   Not bronze but trust (Malta).

Non Est Mortale Quod Opto   What I desire is not mortal. (Mecklenburg).

Non Mihi Sed Populo   Not to me but to the people (Bavaria).

Non Relinquam Vos Orphanos   I shall not leave you as orphans (Papacy).

Non Surrexit Major   None greater has arisen (Genoa, Malta).

Nullum Simulatum Diuturnum Tandem   Nothing that is feigned lasts long (Wittgenstein).

Nummorum Famulus   The servant of the coinage (England, tin halfpence and farthings).

Nunquam Retrorsum   Never backwards (Brunswick-Wolfenbuttel).

O Crux Ave Spes Unica   Hail, o Cross, our only hope (England half-angels, France, Rene d'Anjou).

O Maria Ora Pro Me   O Mary pray for me (Bavaria).

Ob Cives Servatos   On account of the rescued citizens (Rome, Augustus).

Oculi Domini Super Iustos   The eyes of the Lord look down on the just (Neuchatel).

Omnia Auxiliante Maria   Mary helping everything (Schwyz).

Omnia Cum Deo   Everything with God (Reuss-Greiz).

Omnia cum Deo et Nihil Sine Eo   Everthing with God and nothing without Him (Erbach).

Omnis Potestas a Deo Est   All power comes from God (Sweden).

Opp & Carn Dux Comm Rittb SCM Cons Int & Compi Mareschal   Duke of Troppau and Carniola, count of Rietberg, privy councillor of his sacred imperial majesty, field marshal (Liechtenstein).

Opp & Carn . . . Aur Velleris Eques   Duke of Troppau . . . knight of the Golden Fleece (Liechtenstein).

Opportune   Conveniently (Savoy).

Optimus Princeps   Best prince (Rome, Trajan).

Opulentia Salerno   Wealthy Salerno (Siculo-Norman kingdom).

Pace et Iustitia   With peace and justice (Spanish Netherlands).

Pacator Orbis   Pacifier of the world (Rome, Aurelian).

Palma Sub Pondere Crescit   The palm grows under its weight (Waldeck).

Pater Noster   Our Father (Flanders, 14th century).

Pater Patriae   Farther of his country (Rome, Caligula).

Patria Si Dreptul Meu   The country and my right (Roumania).

Patrimon Henr Frid Sorte Divisum   The heritage of Heinrich Friedrich divided by lot (Hohenlohe-Langenberg).

Patrimonia Beati Petri   The inheritance of the blessed Peter (Papacy).

Patrona Franconiae   Patron of Franconia (Wurzburg).

Pax Aeterna   Eternal peace (Rome, Marcus Aurelius).

Pax et Abundantia   Peace and plenty (Burgundy, Gelderland).

Pax Missa Per Orbem   Peace sent throughout the world (England, Anne).

Pax Petrus   Peace Peter (Trier, 10th century).

Pax Praevalet Armis   May peace prevail by force of arms (Mainz).

Pax Quaeritur Bello   Peace is sought by war (Commonwealth, Cromwell).

Pecunia Totum Circumit Orbem   Money goes round the whole world (Brazil).

Per Aspera Ad Astra   Through difficulties to the stars (Mecklenburg-Schwerin).

Per Angusta ad Augusta   Through precarious times to the majestic (Solms-Roedelheim, a pun on the name of the ruler Johan August).

Per Crucem Tuam Salva Nos Christe Redemptor   By Thy cross save us, O Christ our Redeemer (England, angels).

Per Crucem Tuam Salva Nos Xpe Redemt   By Thy cross save us, O Christ our Redeemer (Portugal, 15th century).

Perdam Babillonis Nomen   May the name of Babylon perish (Naples).

Perennitati Iustissimi Regis   For the duration of the most just king (France, Louis XIII).

Perennitati Principis Galliae Restitutionis   For the duration of the restoration of the prince of the Gauls (France, Henri IV).

Perfer et Obdura Bruxella   Carry on and stick it out, Brussels (Brussels siege, 1579–80).

Perpetuus in Nemet Vivar   Hereditary count in Nemt-Ujvar (Batthanyi).

Pietate et Constantia   By piety and constancy (Fulda).

Pietate et Iustitia   By piety and justice (Denmark).

Plebei Urbanae Frumento Constituto   Free distribu-tion of grain to the urban working-class established (Rome, Nerva).

Pleidio Wyf Im Gwlad   True am I to my country (UK, Welsh pound edge inscription).

Plus Ultra   Beyond (the Pillars of Hercules) (Spanish America).

Point du Couronne sans Peine   Point of the crown without penalty (Coburg).

Pons Civit Castellana   The bridge of the town of Castellana (Papacy).

Populus et Senatus Bonon   The people and senate of Bologna (Bologna).

Post Mortem Patris Pro Filio   For the son after his father's death (Pontefract siege coins).

Post Tenebras Lux   After darkness light (Geneva).

Post Tenebras Spero Lucem   After darkness I hope for light (Geneva).

Posui Deum Adiutorem Meum   I have made God my helper (England, Ireland, 1351–1603).

Praesidium et Decus   Protection and ornament (Bologna).

Prima Sedes Galliarum   First see of the Gauls (Lyon).

Primitiae Fodin Kuttenb ab Aerari Iterum Susceptarum   First results dug from the Kuttenberg mines in a renewed undertaking (Austria).

Princps Iuventutis   Prince of youth (Roman Empire).

Pro Defensione Urbis et Patriae   For the defence of city and country (France, Louis XIV).

Pro Deo et Patria   For God and the fatherland (Fulda).

Pro Deo et Populo   For God and the people (Bavaria).

Pro Ecclesia et Pro Patria   For the church and the fatherland (Constance).

Pro Fausio PP Reitur VS   For happy returns of the princes of the Two Sicilies (Naples and Sicily).

Pro Lege et Grege   For law and the flock (Fulda).

Pro maximo Dei Gloria et Bono Publico   For the greatest glory of God and the good of the people (Wurttemberg).

Pro Patria   For the fatherland (Wurzburg).

Propitio Deo Secura Ago   With God's favour I lead a secure life. (Saxe-Lauenburg).

Protector Literis Literae Nummis Corona et Salus   A protection to the letters (on the face of the coin), the letters (on the edge) are a garland and a safeguard to the coinage (Commonwealth, Cromwell broad).

Protege Virgo Pisas   Protect Pisa, O Virgin (Pisa).

Provide et Constanter   Wisely and firmly (Wurttem-berg).

Providentia et Pactis   Through foresight and pacts (Brandenburg-Ansbach).

Providentia Optimi Principis   With the foresight of the best prince (Naples and Sicily).

Proxima Fisica Finis   Nearest to natural end (Orciano).

Proxima Soli   Nearest to the sun (Modena).

Pulcra Virtutis Imago   The beautiful image of virtue (Genoa).

Pupillum et Viduam Suscipiat   May he support the orphan and the widow (Savoy).

Quae Deus Conjunxit Nemo Separet   What God hath joined let no man put asunder (England, James I).

Quem Quadragesies et Semel Patriae Natum Esse Gratulamur   Whom we congratulate for the forty-first time for being born for the fatherland (Lippe-Detmold).

Qui Dat Pauperi Non Indigebit   Who gives to the poor will never be in need (Munster).

Quid Non Cogit Necessitas   To what does Necessity not drive. (Ypres).

Quin Matrimonii Lustrum Celebrant   They celebrate their silver wedding (Austria, 1879).

Quocunque Gesseris (Jeceris) Stabit   Whichever way you throw it it will stand (Isle of Man).

Quod Deus Vult Hoc Semper Fit What God wishes always occurs. (Saxe-Weimar).

Reconduntur, non Retonduntur They are laid up in store, not thundered back (Savoy).

Recta Tueri Defend the right (Austria).

Recte Constanter et Fortiter Rightly, constantly and bravely (Bavaria).

Recte Faciendo Neminem Timeas May you fear no one in doing right. (Solms-Laubach).

Rector Orbis Ruler of the world (Rome, Didius Julianus).

Rectus et Immotus Right and immovable (Hesse).

Redde Cuique Quod Suum Est Render to each that which is his own (England, Henry VIII).

Redeunt antiqui Gaudia Moris There return the joys of ancient custom (Regensburg).

Reg Pr Pol et Lith Saxon Dux Royal prince of Poland and Lithuania and duke of Saxony (Trier).

Regia Boruss Societas Asiat Embdae Royal Prussian Asiatic Society of Emden (Prussia).

Regier Mich Her Nach Deinen Wort Govern me here according to Thy word (Palatinate).

Regnans Capitulum Ecclesiae Cathedralis Ratisbonensis Sede Vacante Administering the chapter of the cathedral church at Regensburg, the see being vacant (Regensburg).

Regni Utr Sic et Hier Of the kingdom of the Two Sicilies and of Jerusalem (Naples and Sicily).

Religio Protestantium Leges Angliae Libertas Parliamenti The religion of the Protestants, the laws of England and the freedom of Parliament (England, Royalists, 1642).

Relinquo Vos Liberos ab Utroque Homine I leave you as children of each man (San Marino).

Restauracao da Independencia Restoration of inde-pendence (Portugal, 1990).

Restitutor Exercitus Restorer of the army (Rome, Aurelian).

Restitutor Galliarum Restorer of the Gauls (Rome, Gallienus).

Restitutor Generis Humani Restorer of mankind (Rome, Valerian).

Restitutor Libertatis Restorer of freedom (Rome, Constantine).

Restitutor Orbis Restorer of the world (Rome, Valerian).

Restitutor Orientis Restorer of the east (Rome, Valerian).

Restitutor Saeculi Restorer of the century (Rome, Valerian).

Restitutor Urbis Restorer of the city (Rome, Severus).

Rosa Americana Utile Dulci The American rose, useful and sweet (American colonies).

Rosa Sine Spina A rose without a thorn (England, Tudor coins).

Rutilans Rosa Sine Spina A dazzling rose without a thorn (England, Tudor gold coins).

S Annae Fundgruben Ausb Tha in N Oe Mining thaler of the St Anne mine in Lower Austria (Austria).

S Ap S Leg Nat Germ Primas Legate of the Holy Apostolic See, born Primate of Germany (Salzburg).

S Carolus Magnus Fundator Charlemagne founder (Munster).

S. Gertrudis Virgo Prudens Niviella St Gertrude the wise virgin of Nivelles (Nivelles).

Sl Aul Reg Her & P Ge H Post Mag General hereditary postmaster, supreme of the imperial court of the hereditary kingdom and provinces (Paar).

S. Ian Bapt F. Zachari St John the Baptist, son of Zachary (Florence).

S. Kilianus Cum Sociis Francorum Apostoli St Kilian and his companions, apostles to the Franks (Wurzburg).

S. Lambertus Patronus Leodiensis St Lambert, patron of Liege (Liege).

Sac Nupt Celeb Berol For the holy matrimony celebrated at Berlin (Brandenburg-Ansbach).

Sac Rom Imp Holy Roman Empire (German states).

Sac Rom Imp Provisor Iterum Administrator of the Holy Roman Empire for the second time (Saxony).

Salus Generis Humani Safety of mankind (Rome, Vindex).

Salus Patriae Safety of the fatherland (Italy).

Salus Populi The safety of the people (Spain).

Salus Provinciarum Safety of the provinces (Rome, Postumus).

Salus Publica Salus Mea Public safety is my safety (Sweden).

Salus Reipublicae The safety of the republic (Rome, Theodosius II).

Salus Reipublicae Suprema Lex The safety of the republic is the supreme law (Poland).

Salvam Fac Rempublicam Tuam Make your state safe (San Marino).

Sanctus Iohannes Innoce St John the harmless (Gandersheim).

Sans Changer Without changing (Isle of Man).

Sans Eclat Without pomp (Bouchain siege, 1711).

Sapiente Diffidentia Wise distrust (Teschen).

Scutum Fidei Proteget Eum / Eam The shield of faith shall protect him / her (England, Edward VI and Elizabeth I).

Secundum Voluntatem Tuam Domine Your favourable will o Lord (Hesse).

Securitati Publicae For the public safety (Brandenburg-Ansbach).

Sede Vacante The see being vacant (Papal states, Vatican and ecclesiastical coinage).

Sena Vetus Alpha et W Principum et Finis Old Siena alpha and omega, the beginning and the end (Siena).

Senatus Populus QR Senate and people of Rome (Rome, 1188).

Si Deus Nobiscum Quis Contra Nos If God is with us who can oppose us (Hesse).

Si Deus Pro Nobis Quis Contra Nos   If God is for us who can oppose us (Roemhild).

Sieh Deine Seeligkeit Steht Fest Ins Vaters Liebe   Behold thy salvation stands surely in thy Father's love (Gotha).

Signis Receptis   When the standards had been recovered (Rome, Augustus).

Signum Crucis   The sign of the cross (Groningen).

Sincere et Constanter   Truthfully and steadfastly (Hesse-Darmstadt).

Sit Nomen Domini Benedictum   Blessed be the name of the Lord (Burgundy, Strasbourg).

St T X Adiuto Reg Iste Domba   Let it be to you, o Christ, the assistant to the king of Dombes (Dombes).

Sit Tibi Xpe Dat q'tu Regis Iste Ducat   May this duchy which Thou rulest be given to Thee, O Christ (Venice, ducat).

Sit Unio Haec Perennis   May this union last for ever (Hohenlohe-Langenberg).

Sola Bona Quae Honesta   The only good things are those which are honest (Brunswick).

Sola Facta Deum Sequor   Through deeds alone I strive to follow God (Milan).

Soli Deo Honor et Gloria   To God alone be honour and glory (Nassau).

Soli Reduci   To him, the only one restored (Naples and Sicily).

Solius Virtutis Flos Perpetuus   The flower of Virtue alone is perpetual (Strasbourg).

Spes Confisa Deo Nunquam Confusa Recedit   Hope entrusted in God never retreats in a disorderly fashion (Lippe).

Spes Nr Deus   God is our hope (Oudenarde siege, 1582).

Spes Rei Publicae   The hope of the republic (Rome, Valens).

Strena ex Argyrocopeo Vallis S Christoph   A New Year's gift from the silver-bearing valley of St Christopher (Wurttemberg, 1625).

Sub His Secura Spes Clupeus Omnibus in Te Sperantibus   Under these hope is safe, a shield for all who reside hope in Thee (Bavaria).

Sub Pondere   Under weight (Fulda).

Sub Protectione Caesarea   Under imperial protection (Soragna).

Sub Tuum Praesidium Confug   We flee to Thy protection (Salzburg).

Sub Umbra Alarum Tuarum   Under the shadow of Thy wings (Iever, Scotland, James V).

Subditorum Salus Felicitas Summa   The safety of the subjects is the highest happiness (Lubeck).

Sufficit Mihi Gratia Tua Domine   Sufficient to me is Thy grace, o Lord (Ploen).

Supra Firmam Petram   Upon a firm rock (Papacy).

Susceptor Noster Deus   God is our defence (Tuscany).

Sydera Favent Industriae   The stars favour industry (Furstenberg).

Sylvarum Culturae Praemium   Prize for the culture of the forest (Brandenburg-Ansbach).

Tali Dicata Signo Mens Fluctuari Nequit   Consecrated by such a sign the mind cannot waver (England, Henry VIII George noble).

Tandem Bona Caus Triumphat   A good cause eventually triumphs (Dillenburg).

Tandem Fortuna Obstetrice   With good luck ultimately as the midwife (Wittgenstein).

Te Stante Virebo   With you at my side I shall be strong (Moravia).

Tene Mensuram et Respice Finem   Hold the measure and look to the end (Burgundy).

Tert Ducat Secular   Tercentenary of the duchy (Wurttemberg).

Thu Recht Schev Niemand   Go with right and fear no one (Saxe-Lauenburg).

Tibi Laus et Gloria   To Thee be praise and glory (Venice).

Timor Domini Fons Vitae   The fear of the Lord is a fountain of life (England, Edward VI shillings).

Tout Avec Dieu   Everything with God (Brunswick, 1626).

Traiectum ad Mosam   The crossing of the Maas (Maastricht).

Transvolat Nubila Virtus   Marriageable virtue soon flies past (Grueyeres).

Travail, Famille, Patrie   Work, family, country (Vichy France).

Triumphator Gent Barb   Victor over the barbarian people (Byzantine Empire, Arcadius).

Tueatur Unita Deus   May God guard these united (Kingdoms) (England, James I; Britain, 1847).

Turck Blegert Wien   Vienna besieged by the Turks (Vienna, 1531).

Tut Mar Gab Pr Vid de Lobk Nat Pr Sab Car et Aug Pr de Lobk   Regency of Maria Gabriela, widow of the prince of Lobkowitz, born princess of Savoy-Carignan, and August prince of Lobkowitz (Lobkowitz).

Tutela Italiae   The guardianship of Italy (Rome, Nerva).

Ubi Vult Spirat   He breathes where he will (Papacy).

Ubique Pax   Peace everywhere (Rome, Gallienus).

Union et Force   Union and strength (France).

Urbe Obsessa   The city under siege (Maastricht).

Urbem Virgo Tuam Serva   Protects thy city o virgin (Mary) (Strasbourg).

USC & RAM Cons Int Gen C Mar & Nob Praet H Turmae Capit   Privy councillor of both their holy imperial and royal apostolic majesties, general field marshal and captain of the noble praetorian Hungarian squadrons (Eszterhazy).

Veni Luumen Cordium   Come light of hearts (Vatican).

Veni Sancte Spiritus   Come Holy Ghost (Vatican).

Verbum Domini Manet in Aeternum   The word of the Lord abides forever (Hesse-Darmstadt, Veldenz).

Veritas Lex Tua   The truth is your law (Salzburg).
Veritas Temporis Filia   Truth is the daughter of time (England and Ireland, Mary Tudor).
Veritate et Labore   By truth and work (Wittgenstein).
Veritate et Iustitia   By truth and justice (German states).
Victoria Principum   The victory of princes (Ostrogoths).
Videant Pauperes et Laetentur   Let the poor see and rejoice (Tuscany).
Virgo Maria Protege Civitatem Savonae   Virgin Mary Protect the city of Savona (Savona).
Viribus Unitis   With united strength (Austria).
Virtute et Fidelitate   By virtue and faithfulness (Hesse-Cassel).
Virtute et Prudentia   With virtue and prudence (Auersperg).
Virtute Viam Dimetiar   I shall mark the way with valour (Waldeck).
Virtutis Gloria Merces   Glory is the reward of valour (Holstein-Gottorp).
Vis Unita Concordia Fratrum Fortior   United power is the stronger harmony of brothers (Mansfeld).

Visitavit Nos Oriens ex Alto   He has visited us arising on high (Luneburg).
Vivit Post Funera   He lives after death (Bremen).
Vota Optata Romae Fel   Vows taken for the luck of Rome (Rome, Maxentius).
Vox de Throno   A voice from the throne (Papacy).
Was Got Beschert Bleibet Unerwert   What God hath endowed leave undisturbed
Wider macht und List Mein Fels Gott Ist   Against might and trickery God is my rock (Hesse-Cassel).
Xpc Vincit Xpc Regnat   Christ conquers, Christ reigns (Scotland, Spain).
Xpc Vivet Xpc Regnat Xpc Impat   Christ lives, Christ reigns, Christ commands (Cambrai).
Xpe Resurescit   Christ lives again (Venice).
Xpistiana Religio   Christian religion (Carolingian Empire).
Xps Ihs Elegit me Regem Populo   Jesus Christ chose me as king to the people (Norway).
Zelator Fidei Usque ad Montem   An upholder of the faith through and through (Portugal).
Zum Besten des Vaterlands   To the best of the fatherland (Bamberg).

ABBREVIATIONS COMMONLY USED TO DENOTE METALLIC COMPOSITION	
Cu	Copper
Cu/Steel	Copper plated Steel
Ag/Cu	Silver plated copper
Ae	Bronze
Cu-Ni	Cupro-Nickel
Ni-Ag	Nickel Silver (note-does not contain silver)
Brass/Cu-Ni	Brass outer, Cupro-Nickel inner
Ni-Brass	Nickel-Brass
Ag	Silver
Au/Ag	Gold plated silver
Au	Gold
Pl	Platinum

CARE *of coins*

There is no point in going to a great deal of trouble and expense in selecting the best coins you can afford, only to let them deteriorate in value by neglect and mishandling. Unless you give some thought to the proper care of your coins, your collection is unlikely to make a profit for you if and when you come to sell it. Housing your coins is the biggest problem of all, so it is important to give a lot of attention to this.

Storage

The ideal, but admittedly the most expensive, method is the coin cabinet, constructed of air-dried mahogany, walnut or rosewood *(never* oak, cedar or any highly resinous timber likely to cause chemical tarnish). These cabinets have banks of shallow drawers containing trays made of the same wood, with half-drilled holes of various sizes to accommodate the different denominations of coins. Such cabinets are handsome pieces of furniture but, being largely handmade, tend to be rather expensive. Occasionally good specimens can be picked up in secondhand furniture shops, or at the dispersal of house contents by auction, but the best bet is still to purchase a new cabinet, tailored to your own requirements. These collectors cabinets are hand-made using certified solid mahogany, as specified by leading museums, as mahogany does not contain any chemicals or resins that could result in the discolouration of the collection inside the cabinet. The polish used on the outside of the cabinets is based on natural oils and hand applied then finished with bees wax. The trays are left as untreated mahogany so as not to introduce any harmful contaminants. The coin trays are available as single thickness or double thickness for holding thicker coins, capsules or artifacts.

Peter Nichols Cabinets (telephone 0115 9224149, www.coincabinets.com) was established in 1967. In October 2010 Peter retired and passed the cabinet making business on to Geoff Skinner, Shirley Watts and Ben Skinner-Watts. Now based in Nottingham, the family run business continues to provide specialist and bespoke display and storage systems to suit every need from the seven-tray Pheon all the way up to the massive 40-tray specials supplied to the British Museum. All cabinets are fitted with double doors. Prices start at around £80 and go up to about £350 for the thirty-tray Coronet. They are not cheap, but you have the satisfaction of acquiring exquisite examples of the cabinet maker's craft.

An excellent storage option is provided by a number of firms who manufacture coin trays in durable, felt-lined materials with shallow compartments to suit the various sizes of coins. Most of these trays interlock so that they build up into a cabinet of the desired size, and there are also versions designed as carrying cases, which are ideal for transporting coins.

The Mascle Classic—the ideal "entry-level" coin cabinet for collectors and just one of a range of hand-made pieces for those seeking practical as well as beautiful storage solutions.

The popular and extensive **Lighthouse** range is available from The Duncannon Partnership, 4 Beaufort Road, Reigate, RH2 9DJ (telephone 01737 244222, www.duncannon.co.uk) or Token Publishing Ltd (telephone 01404 44167, www.tokenpublishing.com). This range includes a wide variety of cases and albums for the general collector in basic or de luxe styles as required, as well as printed albums for the specialist. Their cases, including the popular aluminium range, are manufactured to the highest standards, lined with blue plush which displays any coin to its best advantage. The red-lined single trays come in deep or standard size and make an ideal cabinet when stacked together or housed in their attractive aluminium case, which is available separately. The trays themselves come with a variety of compartments for every size of coin. Their complete range can be viewed on-line.

The extensive **Lindner** range is supplied in the UK by Prinz Publications of 3A Hayle Industrial Park, Hayle, Cornwall TR27 5JR (telephone 01736 751914, www.prinz.co.uk) or from Token Publishing Ltd (telephone 01404 44167, www.tokenpublishing.com). Well-known for their wide range of philatelic and numismatic accessories, but these include a full array of coin boxes, capsules, carrying cases and trays. The basic Lindner coin box is, in fact, a shallow tray available in a standard version or a smoked glass version. These trays have a crystal clear frame, red felt inserts and holes for various diameters of coins and medals. A novel feature of these trays is the rounded insert which facilitates the removal of coins from their spaces with the minimum

Adding on to the stacking Lindner range is easy.

of handling. These boxes are designed in such a manner that they interlock and can be built up into banks of trays, each fitted with a draw-handle and sliding in and out easily. Various types of chemically inert plastic capsules and envelopes have been designed for use in combination with plain shallow trays, without holes drilled. Lindner also manufacture a range of luxury cases lined in velvet and Atlas silk with padded covers and gold embossing on the spines, producing a most tasteful and elegant appearance.

Safe Albums of 16 Falcon Business Park, 38 Ivanhoe Road, Finchampstead, Berkshire RG40 4QQ (telephone 0118 932 8976, www.safealbums.co.uk) are the UK agents for the German Stapel-Element, a drawer-stacking system with clear plasticiser-free trays that fit into standard bookshelves. The sliding coin compartments, lined with blue velvet, can be angled for display to best advantage. Stackable drawers can be built up to any height desired. A wide range of drawer sizes is available, with compartments suitable for the smallest coins right up to four-compartment trays designed for very large artefacts such as card-cases or cigarette cases. The Mobel-Element cabinet is a superb specialised cabinet constructed of the finest timber with a steel frame and steel grip bars which can be securely locked. It thus combines elegance with security and is the ideal medium for the most valuable coins and medals.

There are also various storage systems, such as **Coindex**, which operate on the principle of narrow drawers in which the coins are stored in envelopes of chemically-inert plastic. A strip across the top holds a little slip giving a brief description, catalogue number and the price of each coin.

The Sydney Museum in Australia, for example, keeps its coins in manila envelopes stored in plastic lunch-boxes which seems to do the job pretty well!

Coin Albums

When coin collecting became a popular hobby in the 1960s, several firms marketed ranges of coin albums. They had clear plastic sleeves divided into tiny compartments of various sizes and had the merit of being cheap and taking up little room on a bookshelf.

They had several drawbacks, however, not the least being the tendency of the pages to sag with the weight of the coins, or even, in extreme cases, to pull away from the pegs or rings holding them on to the spine. They required very careful handling as the coins could easily fall out of the top row as the pages were turned. The more expensive albums had little flaps that folded over the top of the coin to overcome this problem.

Arguably the worst aspect of these albums was the use of polyvinyl chloride (PVC) in the construction of the sleeves. Collectors soon discovered to their horror that this reacted chemically with their coins, especially those made of silver, causing a rather disgusting yellow slime to adhere to the coins' surface. I shudder to think how many fine collections were ruined as a result, or of the countless coins that required highly expert treatment in a bid to restore them to as near the original condition as possible.

Fortunately the lesson has been learned and the coin albums now on the market are quite safe. Lighthouse and Lindner offer a wide range of albums designed to house coins, medals or banknotes. The old problem about sagging pages is overcome by the use of a multi-ring binding welded to a very stout spine, while the sleeves contain neither Styrol nor PVC and will not affect any metals at all. In addition to pages with pockets of uniform size, the Karat range of albums operates on a slide principle which enables the user to insert vertical strips of different sizes on the same page, so that the coins of one country or series, or perhaps a thematic display of coins from different countries, can be displayed side by side.

Safe Albums offer a wide range of albums in the Coinholder System and Coin-Combi ranges. These, too, offer the choice of fixed pages with uniform-sized pockets, or interchangeable sliding inserts for different sizes side by side.

In the United States in the past few decades one of the preferred methods for keeping coins in pristine condition is the use of "slabs"—these tough plastic rectangles cannot be easily broken into meaning that the coin inside remains in exactly the same condition as when it was placed in there. This has led to the rise of professional grading and encapsulation companies who not only "slab" your coin but also grade it and guarantee that grade. This allows coins to be bought and sold with both vendor and purchaser knowing exactly what the grade is thus taking out the subjectivity of dealer or collector—an issue that can mean hundreds of pounds difference in the value of the coin. Slabbing in this way is essentially a tool to help a coin maintain a grade and thus more easily guarantee its value, however, many collectors prefer it as a method of protecting their coins as it allows them to be stored and transported easily with no fear of damage. The biggest companies in the United States for the encapsulation of coins are **PCGS** and **NGC**, they have been in business for some years and in America the "slabbed" coin is a common sight. It is less common over here, with many collectors still unsure about the look of the slabs and uncertain whether or not they would prefer to be able to handle their coins directly; British company **CGS** aims to change that and is confident that the benefits of the slab outweigh any disadvantages and they are hoping that the encapsulation and consequent grade guarantee

The Lighthouse range includes a wide selection of de luxe and printed albums.

and protection of the coin will soon be as popular in the UK as it is "over the pond".

Token Publishing Ltd stock a varied range of coin accessories from magnifying glasses to coin albums. To find out more, simply log onto **www.tokenpublishing.com** or call 01404 44166 for an up-to-date illustrated, colour catalogue.

CLEANING *coins*

This is like matrimony—it should not be embarked on lightly. Indeed, the advice given by the magazine *Punch* in regard to marriage is equally sound in this case—don't do it! It is far better to have a dirty coin than an irretrievably damaged one. Every dealer has horror stories of handling coins that previous owners have cleaned, to their detriment. The worst example I ever saw was a display of coins found by a metal detectorist who "improved" his finds by abrading them in the kind of rotary drum used by lapidarists to polish gemstones. If you really must remove the dirt and grease from coins, it is advisable to practise on coins of little value.

Warm water containing a mild household detergent or washing-up liquid will work wonders in removing surface dirt and grease from most coins, but silver is best washed in a weak solution of ammonia and warm water—one part ammonia to ten parts water. Gold coins can be cleaned with diluted citric acid, such as lemon juice. Copper or bronze coins present more of a problem, but patches of verdigris can usually be removed by careful washing in a 20 per cent solution of sodium sesquicarbonate. Wartime coins made of tin, zinc, iron or steel can be cleaned in a 5 per cent solution of caustic soda containing some aluminium or zinc foil or filings, but they must be rinsed afterwards in clean water and carefully dried. Cotton buds are ideal for gently prising dirt out of coin legends and crevices in the designs. Soft brushes (with animal bristles—*never* nylon or other artificial bristles) designed for cleaning silver are most suitable for gently cleaning coins.

Coins recovered from the soil or the sea bed present special problems, due to chemical reaction between the metals and the salts in the earth or sea water. In such cases, the best advice is to take them to the nearest museum and let the professional experts decide on what can or should be done.

Both Lindner and Safe Albums offer a range of coin-cleaning kits and materials suitable for gold, silver, copper and other base alloys respectively. Safe (living up to their name) also provide a stern warning that rubber gloves should be worn and care taken to avoid breathing fumes or getting splashes of liquid in your eyes or on your skin. Obviously, the whole business of cleaning is a matter that should not be entered into without the utmost care and forethought.

POLISHING: A WARNING

If cleaning should only be approached with the greatest trepidation, polishing is definitely OUT! Beginners sometimes fall into the appalling error of thinking that a smart rub with metal polish might improve the appearance of their coins. Short of actually punching a hole through it, there can hardly be a more destructive act. Polishing a coin may improve its superficial appearance for a few days, but such abrasive action will destroy the patina and reduce the fineness of the high points of the surface.

Even if a coin is only polished once, it will never be quite the same again, and an expert can tell this a mile off.

CELTIC *coinage of Britain*

Pritanic coins were the first coins made in Britain. They were issued for a century and a half before the Roman invasion, and possibly a little later in some areas. They were minted by the rulers of thirteen tribal groups or administrative authorities situated on the southeast of a line from the Humber to the Severn. In this short article Pritanic specialist CHRIS RUDD introduces this increasingly popular series.

Most folk call them British Celtic or Celtic coins of Britain. But I'll begin by letting you into a little known secret: most folk may be wrong. You see, there is no ancient textual evidence—none whatsoever—that anyone in iron age Britain called themselves a Celt. Neither is there a hint—not a whisper—that anyone else in the ancient world ever referred to the Brits as Celts. The Greeks didn't, the Gauls didn't, the Romans didn't. The correct name for iron age Britons is Pritani—well formed people or people of the forms. How do we know? Because a sailor from Marseilles said so.

Many Gaulish coins were imported to Britain, like this silver stater of the Coriosolites (ABC 70), typical of many in the huge Jersey hoard found in June 2012, containing an estimated 50,000 coins.

The first coins made in Britain were made like this

Molten tin-rich bronze was poured into clay moulds.

Coin designs were scribed onto clay strip-moulds with a stylus prior to firing. Tentative reconstruction.

and look like this

Cast bronze
c.120-100 BC

Cast potin
c.80-50 BC

Around 330 BC an explorer, Pytheas of Marseilles, sailed to Britain in search of tin. His visit indicates early trade links with southern Gaul and that the Britons were called Pritani. Marseilles inspired Britain's first homemade coinage: potin coins cast in clay strip-moulds, with Apollo on one side and a bull on the other, plus MA for Massalia (Marseilles). Made in Kent c. 120–100 BC, these cast potins circulated alongside gold coins imported from Gaul. During the Gallic Wars (58–51 BC) many other Gaulish coins—gold, silver and bronze—came to Britain, some brought by refugees, others by British mercenaries, others by trade.

The most famous Gallic migrant was Commios "friend", a former ally of Caesar, who became king of the Regini and Atrebates in the south of England c. 50–25 BC. Commios was the first British ruler to place his name on coins. His three sons—Tincomarus (great in peace), Eppillus (little horse) and Verica (the high one), made the Commian dynasty one of the wealthiest and most powerful in Britain. Most of their coins adopted Roman imagery and archaeology indicates that they imported Roman luxury goods, especially Italian wine. Many coins of Verica show grapes, vine leaves and wine cups.

The main rivals of the Regini and Atrebates were the Catuvellauni of Hertfordshire. Their first known ruler was probably Cassivellaunos "bronze commander", leader of the British coalition against Caesar in 54 BC. Many of Britain's earliest gold coins were probably struck to fund resistance to Caesar and then to pay tribute to him. Cassivellaunos may have organised this war money. Addedomaros "great in chariots" (c. 45–25 BC) was the first ruler north of the Thames to inscribe his coins, perhaps copying Commios.

Thirteen possible tribal groups which were producing coins by c.50-40 BC (Cantiaci much earlier). By c.30 BC the Belgae, East Wiltshire and Berkshire group had apparently stopped minting independently.

Gold stater of Commios (ABC 1022) the first British king to place his name on coins. There are two hidden faces on the obverse.

Verica silver minim with wine cup (ABC 1331) and Verica gold stater with vine leaf (ABC 1193)—evidence of Britain's thirst for fine Italian wine and Roman silverware.

Catuvellaunian expansion continued under Tasciovanos "killer of badgers" whose coins became increasingly Roman in style. His son Cunobelinus "hound of Belenus"—Shakespeare's *Cymbeline*) was the most potent tribal king in Atlantic Europe. Suetonius called him "king of the Britons". During his thirty-year reign (c. AD 8–41) Cunobelinus may have minted well over a million gold staters, most of them displaying a corn ear and CAMV— short for *Camulodunon* (Colchester). When his brother Epaticcus "leader of horsemen" and his son Caratacus "the beloved"—both clad as Hercules on their silver coins—crossed the Thames and attacked the Atrebates, Verica fled to Claudius who invaded Britain in AD 43. The minting of tribal coins ceased shortly afterwards.

Other tribes that issued coins included the Cantiaci of Kent, the Belgae of Hampshire, the Durotriges of Dorset, the Dobunni of the West Midlands, the Trinovantes of Essex, the Iceni of East Anglia and the Corieltavi of Lincolnshire. However, only a minority of people in the British Isles used coins regularly—the moneyed minority in southeast England. Cornwall, Devon, Wales, northern England, Scotland and Ireland remained coinless. Which is why ancient British coins are relatively rare. For example, whereas Greek coins were minted for about 600 years, Roman for about 800 years and Gaulish for about 250 years, ancient British coins were produced for little more than 150 years, and often in much smaller runs.

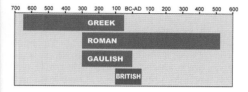

Ancient British coins weren't minted for as long as Greek, Roman or Gaulish coins were. That's one of the reasons they are so scarce.

This century and a half of Pritanic (not Celtic) coin production generated a remarkable flowering of insular creativity and insular technology, unmatched by any other northern European nation of the period. Though initially influenced by Gallic minting techniques and Gallic iconography, ancient British coinage rapidly developed its own denominational systems, its own gold standards and its own highly distinctive coin designs—often inspired by Roman prototypes, but invariably modified to suit local needs. Between c. 110 BC and c. AD 45 around a thousand different coin types were minted in Britain. Many if not most of these thousand types displayed what might loosely be described as "religious" imagery. Not surprising, really, when one recalls that Caesar says that Druidism originated in Britain. Moreover, Tasciovanos struck coins in no fewer than five different denominations, whereas most Gaulish rulers issued no more than two or three.

The history of late iron age Britain, particularly the century prior to the Claudian conquest, has largely been rewritten with the help of ancient British coins. Most of the recent advances in our knowledge of this period have been due to amateur metal detecting. As a direct result of coin finds made by metal detectorists since the 1970s four new coin-issuing groups and maybe ten new rulers, previously unknown or unrecognised, have been identified. Not bad for barely forty years of

Unlike Gaul, most of the British Isles was virtually coinless throughout the late iron age (and later). Coin production was confined to south-east Britain. That's why, overall, ancient British coins are much rarer than Gaulish coins.

unfunded, unofficial fieldwork.

What is it about ancient British coins that is making them increasingly popular with collectors all over the world? Having been involved with them for many years (I excavated my first in 1952) I'll tell you why they appeal to me.

I love the *primal antiquity* of Pritanic coins. They were the first coins made in Britain over two thousand years ago. When you see the flamboyant freedom of their designs you realise that they are the most boisterously British coins ever minted, unlike the unsmiling Roman, Anglo-Saxon and Norman series that marched soberly in their dancing footsteps.

I love the *anarchic regality* of Pritanic coins. Like the rumbustious tribal kings that issued them, their personality is wild, strong and highly irregular. These coins were made by the first British rulers known by name to us—unruly, quarrelsome, beer-swilling, tribal warlords such as Cassivellaunos who fought Julius Caesar in 54 BC and Caratacus, the British resistance leader who opposed Claudius in AD 43.

I love the *imaginative imagery* you find on Pritanic coins: all the different gods and goddesses, armed warriors, chariot wheels, hidden faces, decapitated heads, suns, moons, stars, thunderbolts, floral motifs, magic signs and phallic symbols. Plus an amazing menagerie of wild animals, birds and mythical beasts.

I love the *myths, mystery and mysticism* behind Pritanic coins. Look closely at this late iron

Ancient British denominations

There was no national currency in pre-Roman Britain and little consistency from region to region. Different tribes issued different mixtures of low, medium and high value coins. Here are the most common denominations used by the ancient Brits. The names are ours, not theirs. We've no idea what they called their coins, shown here actual size.

GOLD STATERS
Can also be silver, billon or bronze

Norfolk Wolf, ABC 1393

GOLD QUARTER STATERS
Can also be silver or billon

Irstead Smiler, ABC 1480

SILVER UNITS

Norfolk God, ABC 1567

SILVER HALF UNITS

Aunt Cost Half, ABC 1953

SILVER MINIMS

Verica Sphinx, ABC 1340

BRONZE UNITS

Cunobelinus Centaur, ABC 2957

BRONZE HALF UNITS

Tasciovanos Goat, ABC 2709

CAST POTIN UNITS

Nipples, ABC 174

age money of Albion and you'll catch glimpses of long-lost legends and ancient pagan rituals such as head-hunting, bull sacrificing and shape-shifting. You'll marvel at the plethora of occult signs and arcane symbols and you may even feel the secret power of the Druids.

I love the *palpitating unpredictability* of Pritanic coins. Even after sixty years of heart-racing intimacy they are constantly and delightfully surprising me. Attributions, names and dates are always being revised. Not long ago the Coritani were renamed Corieltavi and Tincommios was rechristened Tincomarus. Almost every month exciting new types and new variants keep leaping out of the ground, thanks to metal detectorists.

Bronze units of Cunobelinus, son of Tasciovanos, showing a bull being sacrificed (ABC 2972) and a man—perhaps a Druid priest?—carrying a severed human head (ABC 2987).

For example, on September 4, 2010 the late Danny Baldock discovered the first recorded coin of Anarevitos, a Kentish ruler previously unknown to history.

I love the *uncommon scarcity* of Pritanic coins. Ask any metdet how many so-called Celtic coins he or she has found and you'll immediately realise that they are rarer than Roman coins—at least a thousand times rarer on average—for the reasons stated above.

Finally I love the *galloping good value* of this horsey money (some Pritanic horses have three tails, some breathe fire, others have a human

Silver unit of freedom-fighter Caratacus (ABC 1376) who defied the Roman invaders for eight years until he was betrayed by Cartimandua, queen of the Brigantes.

torso). Their greater rarity doesn't mean they are costlier than other ancient coins. In fact, they are often cheaper because demand determines price and because there are far fewer collectors of ancient British coins than there are, say, of Greek or Roman coins. For example, a very fine British gold stater typically costs less than half the price—sometimes even a third the price of a Roman aureus or English gold noble of comparable quality and rarity. But the disparity is gradually diminishing as more and more canny collectors are appreciating the untamed beauty and undervalued scarcity of Pritanic coins.

Coin Yearbook provides a great guide to current prices of commoner Pritanic types, but because new types keep turning up and because big hoards are sometimes found (causing values to fluctuate temporarily) you'd be well advised to also keep an eye on dealers' catalogues and prices realised at auction. If you're buying in Britain, buy from people who are members of the BNTA (British Numismatic Trade Association). If you're buying overseas, check that your suppliers belong to the IAPN (International Association of Professional Numismatists). And, if you're a beginner, beware of dodgy traders on the internet, or you could end up with a fistful of fakes and no refund.

I'd also counsel you to spend a day at the British Museum. Its collection of almost 7,000 ancient British coins is the most comprehensive, publicly accessible collection of its kind in the world. As their curator, Ian Leins, says: "They're public coins . . . your coins, and they're here for you to see. So come and see them. We'll be pleased to show them to you". Access to the collection is free for everyone. But you'll need to make an appointment before you go, and take some photo ID and proof of address. Email: coins@thebritishmuseum.ac.uk or telephone: 020 7323 8607.

Before you buy coins—any coins of any period—it always pays to read about them first. As an old adman I'm not shy about blowing my own trumpet. The best little introduction to Pritanic coins is *Britain's First Coins* by Chris Rudd (expected late 2012) and the most comprehensive catalogue of the series is *Ancient British Coins* also by Chris Rudd (2010), known in the trade as ABC. If you have even half the fun I've had with ancient British coins (and am still having)—I can promise you that you'll be a very happy person indeed. Never bored, and never with a complete collection.

A unique gold stater of Anarevitos, a previously unknown ruler of the Cantiaci, probably a son of Eppillus, king of Calleva (Silchester). Sold by Elizabeth Cottam of Chris Rudd for £21,000, a record price for an ancient British coin (Coin News, December 2010).

Chris Rudd started studying ancient British coins sixty years ago and has written a hundred articles about them, many published by COIN NEWS. "I've still got a lot to learn" he says.

COLLECTING *ancient coins*

Ancient coins differ from most other series which are collected in Britain in that every piece has spent the major part of the last two thousand years in the ground. As JOHN CUMMINGS, dealer in ancient coins and antiquities explains here, the effect that burial has had on the surface of the coin determines more than anything else the value of a particular piece. With more modern coins, the only things which affect price are rarity and grade. There may be a premium for coins exhibiting particularly fine tone, or with outstanding pedigrees, but an 1887 crown in "extremely fine" condition has virtually the same value as every other piece with the same grade and of the same date. With ancient coins the story is very different.

A large number of different criteria affect the price of an ancient coin. Factors affecting prices can be broken down into several categories:

Condition

The most important factor by far in determining price. Ancient coins were struck by hand and can exhibit striking faults. Value suffers if the coin is struck with the designs off-centre, is weakly struck, or if the flan is irregular in shape. Many of the Celtic tribes issued coins of varying fineness and those made from low quality gold or silver are worth less than similar specimens where the metal quality is better. Conversely, coins on exceptional flans, particularly well struck, or with fine patinas command a premium.

Many ancient coins have suffered during their stay in the ground. It must be borne in mind that the prices given in the price guide are for uncorroded, undamaged examples. A Roman denarius should be graded using the same criteria as those used for grading modern coins. The surfaces must be good, and the coin intact. The fact that the coin is 2,000 years old is irrelevant as far as grading is concerned. Coins which are not perfectly preserved are certainly not without value, however, the value for a given grade decreases with the degree of fault.

Rarity

As with all other series, rare coins usually command higher prices than common ones. A unique variety of a small fourth century Roman bronze coin, even in perfect condition, can be worth much less than a more worn and common piece from an earlier part of the empire. In the Celtic series, there is an almost infinite variety of minor types and a unique variety of an uninscribed type will rarely outbid an inscribed issue of a known king.

Historical and local significance

Types which have historical or local interest can command a price far above their scarcity value. Denarii of the emperor Tiberius are believed to have been referred to in the New Testament and command a far higher price than a less interesting piece of similar rarity. Similarly, pieces which have British reverse types such as the "VICT BRIT" reverse of the third century AD are more expensive than their scarcity would indicate. The 12 Caesars remain ever popular especially in the American market and this affects prices throughout the world. In the Celtic series, coins of Cunobelin or Boudicca are far more popular than pieces which have no historical interest but which may be far scarcer.

Reverse types

All Roman emperors who survived for a reasonable time issued coins with many different reverse types. The most common of these usually show various Roman gods. When a coin has an unusual reverse it always enhances the value. Particularly popular are architectural scenes, animals, references to Judaism, and legionary types.

Artistic merit

The Roman coinage is blessed with a large number of bust varieties and these can have a startling effect on price. For example, a common coin with the bust facing left instead of right can be worth several times the price of a normal specimen. Like many of the emperors, the coinage of Hadrian has a large number of bust varieties, some of which are extremely artistic and these, too, can command a premium.

> **The coinage used in Britain from the time of the invasion in AD 43 was the same as that introduced throughout the Empire by the emperor Augustus around 20 BC. The simple divisions of 2 asses equal to one dupondius, 2 dupondii equal to 1 sestertius, 4 sestertii equal to one denarius and 25 denarii equal to one aureus continued in use until the reformation of the coinage by Caracalla in AD 214.**

Aureus (gold)

Denarius (silver)

Sestertius (bronze)

Dupondius (copper)

As (copper)

HAMMERED *coinage*

The hammered currency of medieval Britain is among some of the most interesting coinage in the world. The turbulent history of these islands is reflected in the fascinating changes in size, design, fineness and workmanship, culminating in the many strange examples that emanated from the strife of the Civil War.

The Norman Conquest of England in 1066 and succeeding years had far-reaching effects on all aspects of life. Surprisingly, however, it had little impact on the coinage. William the Conqueror was anxious to emphasise the continuity of his reign, so far as the ordinary people were concerned, and therefore he retained the fabric, size and general design pattern of the silver penny. Almost 70 mints were in operation during this reign, but by the middle of the 12th century the number was reduced to 55 and under Henry II (1154–89) it fell to 30 and latterly to only eleven. By the early 14th century the production of coins had been centralised on London and Canterbury, together with the ecclesiastical mints at York and Canterbury. The silver penny was the principal denomination throughout the Norman period, pieces cut along the lines of the cross on the reverse continuing to serve as halfpence and farthings.

Eight types of penny were struck under William I and five under his son William Rufus, both profiles (left and right) and facing portraits being used in both reigns allied to crosses of various types. Fifteen types were minted under Henry I (1100–35), portraiture having now degenerated to crude caricature, the lines engraved on the coinage dies being built up by means of various punches. Halfpence modelled on the same pattern were also struck, but very sparingly and are very rare.

On Henry's death the succession was contested by his daughter Matilda and his nephew Stephen of Blois. Civil war broke out in 1138 and continued till 1153. Stephen controlled London and its mint, but Matilda and her supporters occupied the West Country and struck their own coins at Bristol. Several of the powerful barons struck their own coins, and there were distinct regional variants of the regal coinage. Of particular interest are the coins

Silver pennies of, from left to right, William I, William Rufus, Henry I and Stephen.

struck from obverse dies with Stephen's portrait erased or defaced, believed to date from 1148 when the usurper was under papal interdict.

Peace was restored in 1153 when it was agreed that Matilda's son Henry should succeed Stephen. On the latter's death the following year, Henry II ascended the throne. Coins of Stephen's last type continued to be minted till 1158, but Henry then took the opportunity to overhaul the coinage which had become irregular and sub-standard during the civil war. The new "Cross Crosslet" coins, usually known as the Tealby coinage (from the hoard of over 5,000 pennies found at Tealby, Lincolnshire in 1807), were produced at 30 mints, but when the recoinage was completed this number was reduced to a dozen. The design of Henry's coins remained virtually the same throughout more than two decades, apart from minor variants. Then, in 1180, a new type, known as the Short Cross coinage, was introduced. This was a vast improvement over the poorly struck Cross Crosslet coins and continued without alteration, not only to the end of the reign of Henry II in 1189, but throughout the reigns of his sons Richard (1189–99) and John (1199–1216) and the first half of the reign of his grandson Henry III (1216–46). Throughout that 66 year period, however, there were minor variations in portraits and lettering which enable numismatists to attribute the HENRICUS coins to specific reigns and periods.

"Tealby" type penny (top), and
"Short Cross" penny of Henry II.

The style and workmanship of the Short Cross coinage deteriorated in the reign of Henry III. By the 1220s coin production was confined to the regal mints at London and Canterbury, the sole exception being the ecclesiastical mint maintained by the Abbot of Bury St Edmunds.

Halfpence and farthings were briefly struck in 1221–30, though halfpence are now extremely rare and so far only a solitary farthing has been discovered.

By the middle of this reign the coinage was in a deplorable state, being poorly struck, badly worn and often ruthlessly clipped. In 1247 Henry ordered a new coinage and in this the arms of the cross on the reverse were extended to the rim as a safeguard against clipping. This established a pattern of facing portrait and long cross on obverse and reverse respectively that was to continue till the beginning of the 16th century. Several provincial mints were re-activated to assist with the recoinage but they were all closed down again by 1250, only the regal mints at London and Canterbury and the ecclesiastical mints at Durham and Bury St Edmunds remaining active.

"Long Cross" pennies of Henry III (top),
and Edward I.

In 1257 Henry tentatively introduced a gold penny (worth 20 silver pence and twice the weight of a silver penny). The coin was undervalued and soon disappeared from circulation.

The Long Cross coinage of Henry III continued under Edward I till 1279 when the king introduced a new coinage in his own name. The penny continued the style of its predecessors, though much better designed and executed; but new denominations were now added. Henceforward halfpence and farthings became a regular issue and, at the same time, a fourpenny coin known as the groat (from French *gros*) was briefly introduced (minting ceased in 1282 and was not revived till 1351). Due to the centralisation of coin production the name of the moneyer was now generally dropped, although it lingered on a few years at Bury St Edmunds. The provincial mints were again revived in 1299–1302 to recoin the lightweight foreign imitations of pennies which had flooded in from the Continent.

The coinage of Edward II (1307–27) differed only in minor respects from that of his father, and a similar pattern prevailed in the first years of Edward III. In 1335 halfpence and farthings below the sterling fineness were struck. More importantly, further attempts were made to introduce gold coins. In 1344 the florin or double

Pre-Treaty Noble of Edward III which contained reference to France in the legend.

leopard of six shillings was introduced, along with its half and quarter. This coinage was not successful and was soon replaced by a heavier series based on the noble of 80 pence (6s. 8d.), half a mark or one third of a pound. The noble originally weighed 138.5 grains but it was successively reduced to 120 grains, at which weight it continued from 1351. During this reign the protracted conflict with France known as the Hundred Years' War erupted. Edward III, through his mother, claimed the French throne and inscribed this title on his coins. By the Treaty of Bretigny (1361) Edward temporarily gave up his claim and the reference to France

Noble of Edward IV, issued before he was forced to abandon the throne of England.

was dropped from the coins, but when war was renewed in 1369 the title was resumed, and remained on many English coins until the end of the 18th century. The silver coinage followed the pattern of the previous reign, but in 1351 the groat was re-introduced and with it came the twopence or half-groat. Another innovation was the use of mintmarks at the beginning of the inscriptions. Seven types of cross and one crown were employed from 1334 onwards and their sequence enables numismatists to date coins fairly accurately.

The full range of gold (noble, half-noble and quarter-noble) and silver (groat, half-groat, penny, halfpenny and farthing) continued under Richard II (1377–99). Little attempt was made to alter the facing portrait on the silver coins, by now little more than a stylised caricature anyway.

Noble of Henry IV which was reduced in weight due to the shortage of gold.

Under Henry IV (1399–1413) the pattern of previous reigns prevailed, but in 1412 the weights of the coinage were reduced due to a shortage of bullion. The noble was reduced to 108 grains and its sub-divisions lightened proportionately. The penny was reduced by 3 grains, and its multiples and sub-divisions correspondingly reduced. One interesting change was the reduction of the fleur de lis of France from four to three in the heraldic shield on the reverse of the noble; this change corresponded with the alteration in the arms used in France itself. The Calais mint, opened by Edward III in 1363, was closed in 1411. There was no change in the designs used for the coins of Henry V (1413–22) but greater use was now made of mintmarks to distinguish the various periods of production. Coins were by now produced mainly at London, although the episcopal mints at Durham and York were permitted to strike pennies.

The supply of gold dwindled early in the reign of Henry VI and few nobles were struck after 1426. The Calais mint was re-opened in 1424 and struck a large amount of gold before closing finally in 1440. A regal mint briefly operated at York in 1423–24. Mintmarks were now much more widely used and tended to correspond more closely to the annual trials of the Pyx. The series of civil upheavals known as the Wars of the Roses erupted in this period.

In 1461 Henry VI was deposed by the Yorkist Earl of March after he defeated the Lancastrians at Mortimer's Cross. The Yorkists advanced on London where the victor was crowned Edward IV. At first he continued the gold series of his predecessor, issuing nobles and quarter-nobles, but in 1464 the weight of the penny was reduced to 12 grains and the value of the noble was raised to 100 pence (8s. 4d.).The ryal or rose-

Groat of Richard III (1483–85).

noble of 120 grains, together with its half and quarter, was introduced in 1465 and tariffed at ten shillings or half a pound. The need for a coin worth a third of a pound, however, led to the issue of the angel of 80 grains, worth 6s. 8d., but this was initially unsuccessful and very few examples are now extant. The angel derived its name from the figure of the Archangel Michael on the obverse; a cross surmounting a shield appeared on the reverse.

In 1470 Edward was forced to flee to Holland and Henry VI was briefly restored. During this brief period (to April 1471) the ryal was discontinued but a substantial issue of angels and half-angels was made both at London and Bristol. Silver coins were struck at York as well as London and Bristol, the issues of the provincial mints being identified by the initials B or E (Eboracum, Latin for York). Edward defeated the Lancastrians at Tewkesbury and deposed the luckless Henry once more. In his

second reign Edward struck only angels and half-angels as well as silver from the groat to halfpenny. In addition to the three existing mints, silver coins were struck at Canterbury, Durham and the archiepiscopal mint at York. Mintmarks were now much more frequent and varied. Coins with a mark of a halved sun and rose are usually assigned to the reign of Edward IV, but they were probably also struck in the nominal reign of Edward V, the twelve-year-old prince held in the Tower of London under the protection of his uncle Richard, Duke of Gloucester. Coins with this mark on the reverse had an obverse mark of a boar's head, Richard's personal emblem. The brief reign of Richard III (1483–5) came to an end with his defeat at Bosworth and the relatively scarce coins of this period followed the pattern of the previous reigns, distinguished by the sequence of mint marks and the inscription RICAD or RICARD.

In the early years of Henry VII's reign the coinage likewise followed the previous patterns, but in 1489 the first of several radical changes was effected, with the introduction of the gold sovereign of 20 shillings showing a full-length portrait of the monarch seated on an elaborate throne. For reverse, this coin depicted a Tudor rose surmounted by a heraldic shield. A similar reverse appeared on the ryal of 10 shillings, but the angel and angelet retained previous motifs. The silver coins at first adhered to the medieval pattern, with the stylised facing portrait and long cross, but at the beginning of the 16th century a large silver coin, the testoon or shilling of 12 pence, was introduced and adopted a realistic profile of the king, allied to a reverse showing a cross surmounted by the royal arms. The same design was also used for the later issue of groat and half groat.

First coinage Angel of Henry VIII which retained the traditional 23.5 carat fineness.

This established a pattern which was to continue till the reign of Charles I. In the reign of Henry VIII, however, the coinage was subject to considerable debasement. This led to the eventual introduction of 22 carat (.916 fine) gold for the crown while the traditional 23 1/2 carat gold was retained for the angel and ryal. This dual system continued until the angel was discontinued at the outset of the Civil War in 1642; latterly it had been associated with the ceremony of touching for "King's Evil" or scrofula, a ritual used by the early Stuart monarchs to bolster their belief in the divine right of kings.

Under the Tudors and Stuarts the range and complexity of the gold coinage increased, but it was not until the reign of Edward VI that the silver series was expanded. In 1551 he introduced the silver crown of five shillings, the first English coin to bear a clear date on the obverse. Under Mary dates were extended to the shilling and sixpence.

The mixture of dated and undated coins continued under Elizabeth I, a reign remarkable for the range of denominations—nine gold and

eight silver. The latter included the sixpence, threepence, threehalfpence and threefarthings, distinguished by the rose which appeared behind the Queen's head.

The coinage of James I was even more complex, reflecting the king's attempts to unite his dominions. The first issue bore the legend ANG: SCO (England and Scotland), but from 1604 this was altered to MAG: BRIT (Great Britain). This period witnessed new denominations, such as the rose-ryal and spur-ryal, the unite, the Britain crown and the thistle crown, and finally the laurel of 20 shillings and its sub-divisions.

In the reign of Elizabeth experiments began with milled coinage under Eloi Mestrell. These continued sporadically in the 17th century, culminating in the beautiful coins struck by Nicholas Briot (1631–39). A branch mint was established at Aberystwyth in 1637 to refine and coin silver from the Welsh mines. Relations between King and Parliament deteriorated in the reign of Charles I and led to the Civil War (1642). Parliament controlled London but continued to strike coins in the King's name. The Royalists struck coins, both in pre-war and new types, at Shrewsbury, Oxford, Bristol, Worcester, Exeter, Chester, Hereford and other Royalist strongholds, while curious siege pieces were pressed into service at Newark, Pontefract and Scarborough.

After the execution of Charles I in 1649 the Commonwealth was proclaimed and gold and silver coins were now inscribed in English instead of Latin. Patterns portraying Cromwell and a crowned shield restored Latin in 1656. Plans for milled coinage were already being considered before the Restoration of the monarchy in 1660. Hammered coinage appeared initially, resuming the style of coins under Charles I, but in 1662 the hand-hammering of coins was abandoned in favour of coins struck on the mill and screw press. The hammered coins of 1660–62 were undated and bore a crown mintmark, the last vestiges of medievalism in British coinage.

The magnificent second coinage Rose-Ryal of James I (1603–25).

Images courtesy of Spink.

COIN *grading*

Condition is the secret to the value of virtually anything, whether it be antiques, jewellery, horses or second-hand cars—and coins are certainly no exception. When collecting coins it is vital to understand the recognised standard British system of grading, i.e. accurately assessing a coin's condition or state of wear. Grading is an art which can only be learned by experience and so often it remains one person's opinion against another's, therefore it is important for the beginner or inexperienced collector to seek assistance from a reputable dealer or knowledgeable numismatist when making major purchases.

The standard grades as used in the Price Guide are as follows:	
UNC	**Uncirculated** A coin that has never been in circulation, although it may show signs of contact with other coins during the minting process.
EF	**Extremely Fine** A coin in this grade may appear uncirculated to the naked eye but on closer examination will show signs of minor friction on the highest surface.
VF	**Very Fine** A coin that has had very little use, but shows signs of wear on the high surfaces.
F	**Fine** A coin that has been in circulation and shows general signs of wear, but with all legends and date clearly visible.
Other grades used in the normal grading system are:	
BU	**Brilliant Uncirculated** As the name implies, a coin retaining its mint lustre.
Fair	A coin extensively worn but still quite recognisable and legends readable.
Poor	A coin very worn and only just recognisable.
Other abbreviations used in the Price Guide are:	
Obv	**Obverse**
Rev	**Reverse**
Other abbreviations, mintmarks, etc. can be identified under the appropriate section of this Yearbook.	

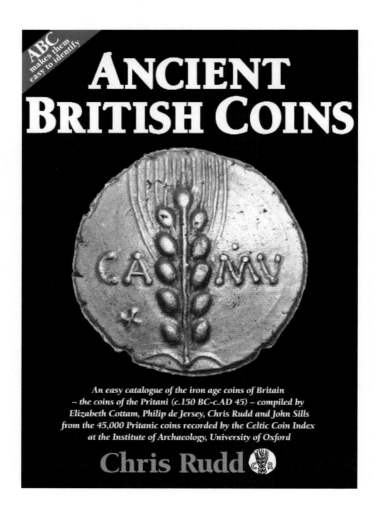

A SIMPLIFIED PRICE GUIDE TO

ANCIENT COINS USED IN BRITAIN

PART I
Ancient British

The prices given in this section are those that you would expect to pay from a reputable dealer and not the prices at which you could expect to sell coins.

The list below, which has been generously provided by Celtic coin dealer Elizabeth Cottam of Chris Rudd, contains most of the commonly available types: a full comprehensive guide is beyond the scope of this book. Prices are for coins with good surfaces which are not weakly struck or struck from worn dies. Examples which are struck from worn or damaged dies can be worth considerably less. Particularly attractive examples of bronze Celtic coins command a very high premium. Where a price is given for an issue of which there are many varieties, the price is for the most common type. The illustrations are representative examples only and are not shown actual size.

	F	VF	EF

UNINSCRIBED COINAGE

GOLD STATERS

	F	VF	EF
Broad Flan	£700	£1750	£5500
Gallic War Uniface	£225	£300	£600
Remic types	£250	£400	£775
Wonersh types	£250	£450	£1800
Chute	£200	£300	£600
Cheriton	£250	£450	£895
Iceni (various types)	£300	£500	£1300
Norfolk "wolf" type			
fine gold	£250	£450	£1300
brassy gold	£175	£300	£675
very debased	£120	£200	£425
Corieltavi (various types)	£200	£400	£850
Dobunni	£250	£500	£1300
Whaddon Chase types	£275	£450	£1250

Cheriton Smiler gold stater

GOLD QUARTER STATERS

	F	VF	EF
Gallic Imported Types	£80	£150	£375
Kent types	£200	£300	£500
Southern types	£125	£200	£350
Iceni	£150	£250	£425
Corieltavi	£125	£200	£450
Dobunni	£175	£300	£550
East Wiltshire	£300	£500	£900
Durotriges	£120	£200	£375
North Thames types	£220	£300	£500

Cranborne Chase silver stater

SILVER COINAGE

	F	VF	EF
Armorican billion staters	£80	£150	£425
Kent Types	£150	£300	£650
South Thames types	£120	£175	£350

	F	VF	EF
Iceni ('crescent' types)...........................	£35	£75	£175
Iceni ('Norfolk God' types)...................	£60	£100	£275
Corieltavi..	£50	£100	£200
Dobunni...	£80	£125	£275
Durotriges full stater			
fine silver.......................................	£80	£175	£320
base silver......................................	£30	£55	£160
Durotriges quarter silver.......................	£25	£35	£80

(Note—most examples are for base coins as better quality items are appreciably higher)

	F	VF	EF
North Thames types	£110	£185	£350

Hengistbury cast bronze

POTIN COINAGE

	F	VF	EF
Kent	£25	£50	£125

BRONZE COINAGE

	F	VF	EF
Durotriges debased stater....................	£30	£60	£110
Durotriges cast bronze	£65	£125	£220
North Thames types. Various issues from:	£45	£110	£420

INSCRIBED CELTIC COINAGE

CANTIACI
Dubnovellaunos

	F	VF	EF
stater...	£320	£595	£1300
silver unit.......................................	£135	£220	£550
bronze unit	£55	£175	£375

Vosenos

	F	VF	EF
stater...	£1100	£2500	£5100
quarter stater	£295	£585	£1200
silver unit.......................................	£140	£295	£650

Sam

	F	VF	EF
silver unit.......................................	£185	£350	£785
bronze unit	£110	£260	£500

Eppillus

Vosenos gold quarter stater

	F	VF	EF
stater...	£1100	£2000	£4300
quarter stater	£150	£255	£550
silver unit.......................................	£75	£145	£375
bronze unit	£65	£125	£475
bronze minim..................................	£85	£165	£295

Anarevitos

	F	VF	EF
stater (unique)			—

Touto

	F	VF	EF
silver unit.......................................	£200	£450	£850

Verica...

	F	VF	EF
silver unit.......................................	£200	£350	£675
bronze unit	£165	£300	£625

Sego

	F	VF	EF
stater...	£525	£1000	£3200
quarter stater	£220	£500	£1200
silver unit.......................................	£150	£350	£650
silver minim....................................	£80	£200	£425
bronze unit	£80	£165	£475

Amminus

	F	VF	EF
silver unit.......................................	£165	£325	£675
silver minim....................................	£110	£215	£450
bronze unit	£85	£160	£525

Solidus

	F	VF	EF
silver unit.......................................	£525	£1100	£2300
silver minim....................................	£525	£1100	£1550

Verica gold stater

	F	VF	EF

REGINI & ATREBATES
Commios

stater	£575	£1550	£2900
silver unit	£80	£160	£325
silver minim	£65	£125	£275

Tincomarus

stater	£450	£875	£2000
quarter stater	£150	£250	£450
silver unit	£75	£145	£295
silver minim	£65	£125	£195

Eppillus

quarter stater	£160	£245	£550
silver unit	£80	£145	£320

Tincomarus gold stater

Verica

stater	£275	£550	£1250
quarter stater	£155	£275	£425
silver unit	£55	£150	£250
silver minim	£50	£120	£225

Epaticcus

stater	£1000	£2000	£4000
silver unit	£50	£100	£265
silver minim	£55	£110	£275

Caratacus

silver unit	£165	£320	£465
silver minim	£110	£220	£325

VECTUARII
Crab

silver unit	£165	£325	£675
silver minim	£110	£295	£420

Ale Scavo silver unit

ICENI
Cani Duro

silver unit	£115	£275	£575

Antedios

stater	£425	£1000	£2500
silver unit	£40	£65	£195
silver half unit	£45	£100	£150

Ecen

stater	£425	£1000	£2500
silver unit	£45	£85	£185
silver half unit	£50	£100	£165

Saenu

silver unit	£65	£125	£295

Aesu

silver unit	£65	£125	£295

Ale Scavo

silver unit	£250	£500	£1200

Esuprasto

silver unit	£425	£1000	£1900

CORIELTAVI
Cat

silver unit	£400	£1000	£2000
silver half unit (unique)			—

Vep CorF gold stater

VEPO

stater	£450	£1000	£2500
silver unit	£85	£150	£320

Esuprasu

stater	£350	£675	£1250
silver unit	£165	£310	£565

	F	VF	EF
Aunt Cost			
stater	£275	£575	£1200
silver unit	£90	£195	£325
silver half unit	£90	£165	£320
Lat Ison			
stater	£1000	£2000	£4000
silver unit	£165	£425	£1150
silver half unit	£160	£300	£550
Dumnocoveros Tigirseno			
stater	£850	£2000	£3575
silver unit	£100	£195	£500
silver half unit	£100	£200	£600
Volisios Dumnocoveros			
stater	£350	£675	£1250
silver unit	£100	£185	£495
silver half unit	£100	£195	£475
Volisios Cartivellaunos			
stater	£1000	£2000	£4000
silver half unit	£300	£675	£1150
Volisios Dumnovellaunos			
stater	£320	£745	£1575
silver half unit	£150	£325	£650

Catti gold stater

DOBUNNI

	F	VF	EF
Bodvoc			
stater	£1000	£2250	£3000
quarter stater (unique)			—
silver unit	£200	£500	£875
Corio			
stater	£275	£550	£1500
quarter stater	£200	£350	£650
Comux			
stater	£285	£550	£1500
Catti			
stater	£285	£555	£1500
Inamn			
plated stater (unique)			—
silver unit (unique)			—
Anted			
stater	£350	£700	£1500
silver unit	£60	£125	£300
Eisu			
stater	£450	£750	£1575
silver unit	£75	£125	£325

Dumno Tigir Seno gold stater

TRINOVANTES

	F	VF	EF
Dubnovellaunos			
stater	£275	£475	£1250
quarter stater	£175	£350	£600
silver unit	£75	£150	£350
silver half unit	£100	£200	£450
bronze unit	£65	£130	£275

CATUVELLAUNI

	F	VF	EF
Addedomaros			
stater	£300	£450	£1250
quarter stater	£300	£550	£1250
silver unit	£100	£200	£400
silver half unit	£100	£200	£450
bronze unit	£35	£75	£275

Addedomaros gold stater

	F	VF	EF
Tasciovanos			
stater..................................	£250	£450	£1500
quarter stater	£165	£250	£495
silver unit...........................	£85	£165	£375
bronze unit.........................	£60	£135	£250
bronze half unit	£60	£135	£275
Andoco			
stater.................................	£350	£550	£1575
quarter stater	£200	£420	£750
silver unit...........................	£155	£400	£750
bronze unit.........................	£85	£220	£350
Dias			
silver unit...........................	£100	£200	£400
bronze unit.........................	£50	£150	£400
Rues			
bronze unit.........................	£50	£150	£400
Cat			
plated silver unit (unique)................			—

Tasciovanos gold stater

CATUVELLAUNI & TRINOVANTES

	F	VF	EF
Cunobelinus			
stater.................................	£250	£450	£1575
quarter stater	£150	£250	£475
silver unit...........................	£85	£165	£475
bronze unit.........................	£60	£135	£375
bronze half	£60	£135	£275
Trocc			
bronze unit.........................	£50	£150	£500
Agr			
quarter stater	£125	£250	£850
silver unit...........................	£100	£200	£500
bronze unit (only two).......................		(too rare to price)	
Dubn			
quarter stater (only three).................		(too rare to price)	

Cunobelinus gold stater

Illustrations by courtesy of Chris Rudd

An important hoard of 20 Iron Age gold staters was unearthed Over the weekend of March 6–7, 2015, near Fakenham, north Norfolk, in the former territory of the Iceni. (Image by Steve Llewellyn, The Searcher, June 2015.)

Coincraft

Coincraft Needs to Buy

Coincraft is a family owned and family run business that has been helping collectors for over 60 years. We buy and sell British and world coins, British and world banknotes, ancient coins, antiquities, medallions and most things numismatic.

We need to buy single items, collections, accumulations, hoards, you name it and we want it. Remember, that we offer instant payment, no waiting six months for your lots to be auctioned only to have half of them returned unsold. Quantities do not frighten us, the more the merrier, we know how to buy and sell large lots, after all we have had more than sixty years experience.

If you have something to sell, please give us a try, I think that you will be pleasantly surprised at how easy it is to sell to Coincraft. And don't forget, we offer instant payment on all purchases.

A SIMPLIFIED PRICE GUIDE TO
ANCIENT COINS USED IN BRITAIN

PART II
Roman Britain

The list below has been generously provided by coin dealer Mike Vosper. These prices are for the most common types unless otherwise noted. In most cases, especially with large bronze coins, the price for coins in extremely fine condition will be <u>much</u> higher than the price for the same coin in very fine condition as early bronze coins are seldom found in hoards and perfect, undamaged examples are rarely available.

The illustrations provided are a representative guide to assist with identification only.

REPUBLICAN COINAGE 280–41 BC

	FROM F	VF	EF
Republican			
Quadrigatus (or Didrachm) (Janus/Quadriga) £135		£450	£1750
Victoriatus (Jupiter/Victory)	£35	£100	£450
+Denarius (Roma/Biga)	£20	£75	£375
+Denarius (other types)	£30	£85	£425
Denarius (Gallic warrior—L.Hostilius			
Saserna)..	£400	£1100	£5950
Quinarius	£25	£80	£400
Cast Aes Grave, As	£400	£1100	—
Struck As/Semis/Litra	£60	£200	—
Struck Triens/Quadrands	£50	£150	—

Gnaeus Pompey Junior

IMPERATORIAL COINAGE 49–27 BC

Pompey the Great			
Denarius (Hd. of Pompilius/Prow)	£150	£450	£2250
Scipio			
Denarius (Jupiter/Elephant...............	£100	£280	£1400
Cato Uticensis			
Quinarius (Bacchus/Victory)	£45	£125	£600
Gnaeus Pompey Junior			
Denarius (Roma/Hispania)	£110	£325	£1500
Sextus Pompey			
Denarius (his bust)	£275	£750	£3700
Denarius (other types)......................	£180	£550	£2700
As	£160	£550	—
Julius Caesar			
Aureus	£1200	£3300	£20,000
Denarius ("elephant" type)	£150	£475	£2000
Denarius (Ceasar portrait)	£450	£1400	£6900
Denarius (heads of godesses)..........	£115	£360	£1750

Julius Caesar

	FROM F	VF	EF
Brutus			
Denarius (his portrait/EID MAR)	£25,000	£70,000	£295,000
Denarius (others)..............................	£150	£450	£2200
Cassius			
Denarius..	£125	£400	£1700
Ahenobarbus			
Denarius	£400	£1200	£5700
Mark Antony			
Denarius ("Galley" type)	£75	£260	£1550
Denarius (with portrait)	£100	£375	£1900
Denarius (other types)	£70	£295	£1750
Mark Antony & Lepidus			
AR quinarius	£65	£185	£950
Mark Antony & Octavian			
AR denarius	£175	£595	£2500
Quninarius	£55	£165	£800
Mark Antony & Lucius Antony			
AR denarius	£335	£850	£4000
Mark Antony & Octavia			
AR Cistophorus	£225	£650	£3000
Cleopatra VII & Mark Antony			
AR denarius	£1400	£4000	£28,000
Fulvia			
AR quinarius	£125	£350	£1700
Octavian (later known as Augustus)			
Gold Aureus	£1200	£3900	£20,000
Denarius	£125	£350	£2000
Quinarius (ASIA RECEPTA)	£45	£120	£650
Octavian & Divos Julius Caesar			
AE sestertius	£275	£1500	—

Brutus

Mark Antony & Octavian

IMPERIAL COINAGE—Julio-Claudian Dynasty 27BC–AD 69

	FROM F	VF	EF
Augustus			
Gold Aureus (Caius & Lucius Caesar)	£1200	£3000	£15,000
AR Cistophorus.................................	£200	£600	£3000
Denarius (Caius & Lucius Caesar)	£60	£175	£750
Denarius (other types)	£65	£215	£1100
AR quinarius	£50	£150	£750
Sestertius (large SC)	£135	£395	£1850
Dupondius or as (large SC)..............	£55	£160	£700
Quadrans	£18	£50	£220
Divus Augustus (struck under Tiberius)			
As	£70	£200	£1100
Augustus & Agrippa			
Dupondius (Crocodile rev)	£70	£200	£1100
Livia			
Sestertius or Dupondius	£195	£595	£3750
Gaius Caesar			
AR denarius	£375	£1350	£3550
Tiberius			
Aureus (Tribute penny)	£1000	£2750	£9000
Denarius (Tribute penny)	£80	£225	£900
Sestertius	£195	£595	£3000
Dupondius	£160	£550	£2500
As	£70	£200	£900
Drusus			
Sestertius...	£275	£900	£4250
As (Large S C)..................................	£75	£200	£1000
Caligula			
Denarius (rev. portrait)	£450	£1300	£6500
Sestertius (PIETAS & Temple)	£300	£1750	£8000
As (VESTA).......................................	£80	£275	£1350

Augustus

Tiberius

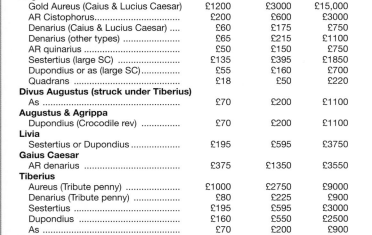

	FROM F	VF	EF
Agrippa (struck under Caligula)			
As.......................................	£55	£170	£850
Germanicus (struck under Caligula or Claudius)			
As (Large S C)	£65	£190	£950
Agrippina Senior (struck under Caligula)			
Sestertius (Carpentum).....................	£500	£1450	£8000
Nero & Drusus (struck under Caligula)			
Dupondius (On horseback, galloping)	£180	£600	£3300
Claudius			
Aureus ("DE BRITANN" type)	£1650	£5000	£30,000
Denarius as above	£400	£1700	£8000
Didrachm as above	£375	£1100	£5500
Denarius other types	£360	£950	£5000
Sestertius	£165	£500	£3300
Dupondius	£60	£200	£1250
As	£45	£140	£900
Quadrans	£18	£50	£265
Irregular British Sestertius...............	£30	£85	£450
Irregular British As	£20	£60	£300
Claudius & Agrippina Junior or Nero			
Denarius	£450	£1350	£6750
Nero Cludius Drusus (struck under Claudius)			
Sestertius	£250	£850	£5500
Antonia (struck under Claudius)			
Dupondius	£130	£450	£2350
Britannicus			
Sestertius	£6500	£28000	—
Nero			
Aureus	£1000	£3200	£16000
Denarius	£95	£260	£1500
Sestertius	£135	£550	£3300
Sestertius (Port of Ostia)	£1800	£6000	£45000
Dupondius	£85	£250	£1300
As	£50	£165	£1000
Semis...	£42	£115	£575
Quadrans	£20	£55	£275
Civil War			
Denarius	£190	£550	£2750
Galba			
Denarius	£110	£350	£1900
Sestertius	£170	£475	£2800
Dupondius	£180	£500	£2500
As	£110	£325	£1750
Otho			
Denarius	£190	£575	£3300
Vitellius			
Denarius	£90	£265	£1350
Sestertius	£1000	£2800	£17000
Dupondius	£350	£900	£5175
As	£195	£500	£2750

Caligula

Agrippina Senior

Claudius

Nero

IMPERIAL COINAGE—Flavian Dynasty AD 69–96

Vespasian			
Aureus	£850	£2500	£12500
Denarius	£30	£80	£450
Denarius (IVDAEA)	£80	£200	£1100
Sestertius	£190	£595	£4000
Dupondius	£70	£210	£1200
As	£55	£180	£1100
Titus			
Aureus	£900	£2650	£13500
Denarius as Caesar	£40	£115	£650
Denarius as Augustus	£45	£130	£750

Galba

	FROM F	VF	EF
Sestertius	£135	£450	£3000
Dupondius	£50	£175	£1150
As	£45	£160	£1150
As (IVDAEA CAPTA)	£170	£500	£2750
Julia Titi			
Denarious	£190	£565	£2800
Domitian			
Aureus	£950	£2400	£12000
Cistophorus	£115	£400	£1800
Denarius as Caesar	£35	£85	£425
Denarius as Augustus	£25	£70	£350
Sestertius	£95	£340	£1500
Dupondius	£35	£120	£1000
As	£35	£110	£600
Ae Semis	£30	£90	£450
Ae Quadrands.................................	£25	£70	£295
Domitia			
Cistophorus	£235	£695	£3000

Titus

Domitian

IMPERIAL COINAGE—Adoptive Emperors AD 96–138

Nerva

Aureus	£1850	£5600	£28,000
Denarius	£50	£120	£650
Sestertius	£140	£500	£2950
Sestertius (Palm-tree)	£500	£1600	£9500
Dupondius	£70	£215	£1100
As	£55	£160	£900
Trajan			
Aureus	£950	£2400	£12000
Denarius	£25	£60	£350
Denarius (Trajan's Column)	£40	£130	£700
Sestertius	£65	£215	£1250
Sestertius (Dacian rev.)	£75	£250	£1450
Dupondius or as	£35	£100	£550
Ae Quadrands	£25	£65	£325
Plotina, Marciana or Matidia			
Denarius	£425	£1300	£4000
Hadrian			
Aureus	£950	£2600	£13000
Cistophourus	£120	£450	£1800
Denarius (Provinces)	£45	£135	£750
Denarius other types	£25	£75	£450
Sestertius	£75	£230	£1350
Sestertius (RETITVTORI province types)	£135	£420	£2500
Sestertius (Britannia std)	£3000	£10000	—
Dupondius or As	£35	£120	£650
As (Britannia std)	£210	£650	—
Ae Semiis or Quadrands	£30	£90	£450
Eygpt, Alexandrian Billon Tetradrachm	£30	£85	£475
Sabina			
Denarius	£30	£85	£475
Sestertius	£115	£365	£2000
As or Dupondius	£70	£195	£1000
Aelius Ceasar			
Denarius	£70	£200	£1100
Sestertius	£145	£450	£2500
As or Dupondius	£65	£190	£1000

Nerva

Trajan

Hadrian

	FROM F	VF	EF

IMPERIAL COINAGE—The Antonines AD 138–193

Antoninus Pius

	FROM F	VF	EF
Aureus	£750	£2000	£9500
Denarius	£18	£45	£225
Sestertius Britannia seated	£500	£1400	£10000
Sestertius other types	£40	£135	£750
As - Britannia rev.	£65	£200	£1350
Dupondius or As other types	£25	£75	£375

Antoninus Pius & Marcus Aurelius

Denarius (bust each side)	£30	£100	£500

Diva Faustina Senior

Denarius	£18	£45	£250
Sestertius	£45	£145	£775
As or Dupondius	£25	£80	£425

Antoninus Pius

Marcus Aurelius

Aureus	£850	£2400	£12000
Denarius as Caesar	£18	£55	£325
Denarius as Augustus	£17	£50	£275
Sestertius	£45	£160	£900
As or Dupondius	£25	£75	£400

Faustina Junior

Denarius	£18	£60	£350
Sestertius	£40	£175	£1100
As or Dupondius	£28	£85	£450

Marcus Aurelius

Lucius Verus

Denarius	£25	£75	£425
Sestertius	£45	£200	£1100
As or Dupondius	£30	£90	£500

Lucilla

Denarius	£20	£65	£350
Sestertius	£55	£180	£1000
As or Dupondius	£30	£95	£500

Commodus

Aureus	£1050	£2800	£14000
Denarius as Caesar	£28	£75	£400
Denarius as Augustus	£18	£50	£300
Sestertius	£45	£160	£900
Sestertius (VICT BRIT)	£150	£500	£3000
As or Dupondius	£22	£85	£475

Faustina Junior

Crispina

Denarius	£25	£75	£400
Sestertius	£70	£225	£1250
As or Dupondius	£32	£110	£600

IMPERIAL COINAGE—The Severan Dynasty AD 193–235

Pertinax

Denarius	£225	£645	£3300
Sestertius	£500	£1750	£11500

Didius Julianus

Denarius	£395	£1250	£7300
Sestertius or Dupondius	£325	£1000	£7500

Manlia Scantilla or Didia Clara

Denarius	£395	£1250	£8000

Pescennius Niger

Denarius	£270	£750	£4500

Clodius Albinus

Denarius as Caesar	£45	£130	£650
Denarius as Augustus	£85	£260	£1350
Sestertius	£275	£800	£4500
As	£80	£250	£1250

Lucius Verus

Commodus

	FROM F	VF	EF
Septimius Severus			
Aureus	£900	£2500	£12,500
Aureus (VICT BRIT)	£1200	£3500	£20,000
+Denarius (Mint of Rome)	£12	£35	£195
+Denarius (Mints of Emesa & Laodicea)	£15	£45	£225
Denarius (LEG XIIII)	£30	£85	£450
Denarius (VICT BRIT)	£25	£90	£400
Sestertius other types	£75	£240	£1500
Sestertius (VICT BRIT).....................	£350	£1000	£6000
Dupondius or as	£50	£160	£900
Dupondius or As (VICT BRIT)	£125	£365	£2000
Julia Domna			
Denarius	£15	£40	£225
Sestertius	£75	£230	£1300
As or Dupondius	£50	£160	£850
Caracalla			
Aureus (VICT BRIT)	£1350	£3500	£20,000
Denarius as Caesar	£15	£45	£250
Denarius as Augustus	£14	£40	£225
Denarius (VICT BRIT)	£30	£90	£475
Antoninianus	£25	£75	£400
Sestertius	£100	£295	£1600
Sestertius (VICT BRIT).....................	£300	£860	£5500
Dupondius or As	£50	£165	£850
Dupondius or As (VICT BRIT)	£100	£300	£1600
Plautilla			
Denarius	£25	£75	£400
Geta			
Denarius as Caesar	£16	£45	£250
Denarius as Augustus	£25	£70	£400
Denarius (VICT BRIT)	£30	£95	£500
Sestertius	£125	£350	£2000
Sestertius (VICT BRIT).....................	£250	£770	£4500
Dupondius or as	£75	£230	£1150
As (VICT BRIT)	£120	£340	£2000
Macrinus			
Antoninianus	£90	£275	£1500
Denarius	£40	£125	£650
Sestertius	£175	£400	£3000
Diadumenian			
Denarius	£65	£195	£950
Dupondius or As	£135	£395	£2300
Elagabalus			
Aureus	£1200	£3500	£16000
Antoninianus	£20	£65	£395
Denarius	£12	£35	£195
Sestertius	£100	£320	£1700
Dupondius or As	£60	£175	£950
Julia Paula			
Denarius	£30	£110	£550
Aquilla Severa			
Denarius	£55	£185	£1000
Julia Soaemias			
Denarius	£28	£75	£400
Dupondius or As	£65	£225	£1250
Julia Maesa			
Denarius	£15	£45	£250
Sestertius	£80	£240	£1600
Severus Alexander			
Aureus	£900	£2400	£12000
Denarius as Caesar	£65	£200	£1100
Denarius as Augustus	£12	£35	£200
Sestertius	£35	£100	£550
Dupondius or As	£25	£90	£450

Septimus Severus

Julia Domna

Geta

Macrinus

Elagabalus

Julia Maesa

	FROM F	VF	EF
Orbiana			
Denarius	£60	£195	£1000
As	£90	£325	£1700
Julia Mamaea			
Denarius	£14	£40	£225
Sestertius	£35	£110	£595

Orbiana

IMPERIAL COINAGE—Military Anarchy AD 235–270

	FROM F	VF	EF
Maximinus I			
Denarius	£15	£45	£250
Sestertius, Dupondius or As	£35	£125	£675
Diva Paula			
Denarius	£150	£450	£2250
Maximus Caesar			
Denarius	£70	£200	£1000
Sestertius	£55	£165	£1000
Gordian I & II, Africanus			
Denarius	£500	£1500	£6000
Sestertius	£550	£1650	£8000
Balbinus & Pupienus			
Antoninanus	£90	£250	£1250
Denarius	£80	£260	£1300
Gordian III			
Antoninianus	£8	£22	£130
Denarius	£12	£35	£175
Sestertius or As	£22	£85	£450
Tranquillina			
Common Colonial	£30	£110	£550
Philip I			
Antoninianus "Animal"			
Lion, stag, antelope, wolf & twins ...	£20	£60	£325
Other Antoninianus	£8	£22	£130
Sestertius, Dupondius or As	£25	£80	£450
Otacilla Severa			
Antoninianus	£9	£25	£150
Antoninianus "Hipo"	£25	£80	£450
Sestertius	£25	£85	£450
Philip II			
Antoninianus	£8	£22	£125
Antoninianus "Goat"	£20	£65	£350
Sestertius, Dupondius or As	£27	£85	£475
Pacatian			
Antoninianus	£1500	£4700	—
Trajan Decius			
Antoninianus	£8	£22	£125
Antoninianus (DIVI series Augustus, Trajan etc)	£40	£125	£625
Double Sestertius	£260	£900	£4500
Sestertius, Dupondius or As	£27	£85	£475
Herennius Etruscilla			
Antoninianus	£9	£27	£150
Sestertius, Dupondius or As.............	£30	£110	£600
Herennius Etruscus			
Antoninianus	£16	£55	£300
Sesterius, Dupondius or As	£55	£185	£1000
Hostilian			
Antoninianus as Caesar	£30	£110	£550
Antoninianus as Augustus	£70	£220	£1125
Trebonianus Gallus			
Antoninianus	£9	£26	£140
Sestertius or As	£30	£100	£550
Volusian			
Antoninianus....................................	£10	£35	£195
Sestertius..	£30	£110	£575

Julia Mamaea

Diva Paula

Gordian III

Trajan Decius

Hostilian

119

	FROM F	VF	EF
Aemilian			
Antoninianus	£45	£140	£700
Valerian I			
Antoninianus	£8	£25	£135
Sestertius & As.................	£45	£150	£800
Diva Mariniana			
Antoninianus	£35	£125	£650
Gallienus			
Silver Antoninianus	£8	£22	£110
AE Antoninianus	£4	£18	£90
Ae Antoninianus (Military bust)	£8	£25	£150
AE Antoninianus (Legionary)	£70	£220	—
Ae Sestertius	£40	£140	£900
Ae Denarius	£45	£125	£650
Saloninus			
Ae Antoninianus	£6	£20	£110
Valerian II			
Billon Antoninianus	£10	£35	£180
Saloninus			
Antoninianus	£12	£45	£225
Macrianus & Quietus			
Billon Antoninianus	£45	£130	£675
Regalianus or Dryantilla			
Billon Antoninianus	£1850	£7000	—
Postumus			
Silver Antoninianus	£7	£22	£125
Ae Antoninianus	£5	£18	£100
Radiated sestertius.............	£45	£175	£1100
Laelianus			
Ae Antoninianus	£250	£750	£3000
Marius			
Ae Antoninianus	£40	£125	£650
Victorinus			
Ae Antoninianus	£5	£16	£90
Tetricus I & II			
Ae Antoninianus	£5	£18	£100
Claudius II Gothicus			
Ae Antoninianus	£4	£20	£100
Egypt, Alexandrian Billon tetradrachm	£5	£25	£110
DIVO Ae Antoninianus	£5	£25	£135
Quintillus			
Ae Antoninianus	£10	£30	£175

Postumus

Aurelian

Severina

IMPERIAL COINAGE—The Illyrian Emperors—AD 270–285

Aurelian			
Ae Antoninianus	£6	£20	£110
Ae Denarius	£18	£65	£350
Vabalathus & Aurelian			
Ae Antoninianus (bust both sides) ...	£20	£65	£350
Vabalathus			
Ae Antoninianus	£350	£950	—
Severina			
Ae Antoninianus	£12	£35	£200
Ae As.................	£35	£100	£575
Zenobia			
Eygpt, Alexandrian Billon Tetradrachm	£700	£2500	—
Tacitus			
Ae Antoninianus	£12	£30	£175
Florian			
Ae Antoninianus	£25	£85	£450
Probus			
Gold Aureus	£1150	£3200	£15,000
Ae Antoninianus	£6	£20	£125

Tacitus

Florian

	FROM F	VF	EF
Antoninianus (military or imp. Busts RIC G or H)	£10	£35	£185
Antoninianus			
(Other military or imp NOT BUSTS G or H)	£20	£65	£350
Antoninianus (VICTOR GERM rev.) ..	£11	£32	£160
Egypt, Alexandrian Billon tetradrachm	£5	£15	£75
Carus			
Ae Antoninianus	£13	£40	£210
Numerian			
Ae Antoninianus	£12	£38	£195
Carinus			
Ae Antoninianus	£11	£35	£185
Magna Urbica			
Ae Antoninianus	£90	£250	£1350
Julian of Pannonia			
Ae Antoninianus	£600	£2300	-

Diocletian

IMPERIAL COINAGE—The Tetrarchy AD 285–307

Diocletian

Gold Aureus	£1000	£2750	£13,500
AR Argenteus	£90	£275	£1000
Ae Antoninianus & Radiates	£7	£22	£135
Ae Follis (London Mint)	£12	£45	£225
As above with LON mint mark	£100	£300	£1500
Ae Follis (other mints)	£10	£27	£140
Ae Follis (Imperial bust)....................	£23	£75	£375

Maximianus

Maximianus

AR Argenteus	£90	£275	£1000
Ae Follis (London mint)	£12	£40	£200
Ae Follis (other mints)	£8	£27	£140
Ae Follis (MONETA rev.)	£10	£35	£175

Carausius

Aureus	£8000	£25,000	—
Denarius	£400	£1100	£6000
Ae Antoninianus (PAX)......................	£22	£80	£450
As above but full silvering	£35	£115	£650
Legionary Antoninianus	£70	£200	£1500
Expectate Veni Antoninianus	£100	£300	—
In the name of Diocletian or Maximian	£35	£105	£735

Carausius

Allectus

Aureus...	£11000	£32000	—
Ae Antoninianus	£25	£90	£550
As above but full silvering	£45	£145	£800
Quinarius	£25	£90	£550

Constantius I

AR Argenteus	£95	£285	£1200
Ae Follis (London Mint)	£15	£45	£225
Ae Follis (other mints)	£8	£27	£140
Ae Follis (SALVS rev.)	£11	£40	£210
Ae 4 (Lion or Eagle)	£9	£30	£150

Galerius

Ae Follis (London mint)	£12	£35	£175
Ae Follis (other mints)	£7	£22	£120

Severus II

Galeria Valeria

Ae Follis	£28	£80	£400

Severus II

Ae Follis (London mint)	£33	£100	£500
Ae Follis (other mints)	£27	£85	£425
Ae Radiate	£15	£50	£225
Ae Denarius	£25	£85	£400

Maximinus II

Ae Follis (London mint)	£12	£40	£200
Ae Follis (other mints)	£5	£17	£90
Ae Radiate	£8	£28	£130

Maximinus II

	FROM F	VF	EF
Maxentius			
Ae Follis	£8	£27	£150
Romulus			
Ae Follis	£40	£135	£1200
Licinius I			
Billon Argenteus	£45	£150	£750
Ae Follis (London mint)	£7	£25	£125
Ae Follis (other mints)	£6	£18	£90
AE3	£5	£15	£75
Licinius II			
AE3	£7	£22	£115
Alexander or Martinian			
AE	£1500	£4000	—

Licinius II

IMPERIAL COINAGE—Family of Constantine AD 307–350

Constantine I			
Billon Argenteus	£50	£160	£750
Ae Follis (London mint)	£7	£22	£115
As above—helmeted bust	£13	£42	£200
Ae Follis (other mints) as Caesar ...	£16	£50	£250
Ae Follis (other mints) as Augustus	£4	£15	£75
AE3	£4	£15	£75
AE3 (London mint)	£7	£25	£125
AE3 (SARMATIA rev)	£10	£35	£175
Urbs Roma / Wolf & twins AE3/4.........	£4	£18	£90
Constantinopolis AE3/4	£3	£15	£75
Fausta & Helena			
AE3 (London mint)	£50	£155	£775
AE3 (other mints)	£14	£55	£225
Theodora			
AE4	£7	£25	£125
Crispus			
AE3 (London mint)	£8	£28	£125
AE3	£7	£18	£95
Delmatius			
AE3/4	£12	£40	£175
Hannibalianus Rex			
AE4	£75	£225	£1000
Constantine II			
AE3 (London mint)	£8	£25	£125
AE3	£5	£18	£95
AE3/4	£2	£10	£50
Constans			
AE2 (centenionalis)	£9	£28	£145
AE3 (half centenionalis)	£5	£20	£100
AE4	£2	£10	£50
Constantius II			
Gold Solidus	£300	£750	£3750
Siliqua	£25	£85	£450
AE2 (or centenionalis)	£7	£25	£125
AE3 (or half centenionalis)	£4	£15	£75
AE3 (London mint)..........................	£16	£45	£200
AE3..	£2	£8	£40

Constantine I

Constantine II

Magnentius

IMPERIAL COINAGE—Late period to the collapse of the Empire AD 350 to end

Magnentius			
Gold Solidus..................................	£800	£2200	£11,000
Silver Siliqua	£250	£790	£3750
Double centenionalis	£45	£185	£1100
Centenionalis	£15	£50	£275
Decentius			
Double centenionalis.......................	£70	£225	£1250
Centenionalis	£20	£60	£300
Vetranio			
AE2 (centenionalis)	£40	£125	£650
AE3 (half centenionalis)	£30	£100	£500

Vetranio

	FROM F	VF	EF
Nepotian			
AE2 (centenionalis)	£1950	£6500	—
Constantius Gallus			
AE2 (centenionalis)	£11	£32	£165
AE3 (half centenionalis)	£5	£15	£75
Julian II			
Siliqua	£28	£85	£450
AE1	£40	£125	£650
AE3 (helmeted bust)	£8	£28	£140
Anonymous, Serapis + Jupiter AE3	£195	£550	—
Jovian			
AE1	£65	£210	£1000
AE3	£12	£38	£180
Valentinian I			
Sold Solidus	£200	£510	£2000
Silver Milliarense.............................	£165	£550	£2750
Siliqua	£25	£90	£450
AE3	£5	£15	£75
Valens			
Gold Solidus	£200	£500	£2000
Silver Milliarense.............................	£190	£600	£3000
Siliqua	£25	£85	£450
AE3	£5	£15	£75
Procopius			
AE3	£45	£140	£700
Gratian			
Silver Milliarense.............................	£165	£520	£2000
Siliqua	£24	£80	£400
AE3	£4	£15	£75
AE4	£3	£12	£60
Valentinian II			
Solidus	£220	£550	£2250
Siliqua	£25	£85	£425
AE2	£10	£28	£135
AE4	£2	£10	£50
Theodosius I			
Solidus	£225	£550	£2300
Siliqua	£30	£100	£500
AE2	£10	£35	£150
AE3	£8	£30	£140
Aelia Flaccilla			
AE2	£30	£110	£550
AE4...	£15	£50	£250
Magnus Maximus			
Solidus (AVGOB)	£4800	£13,000	—
Solidus	£800	£2300	£12,000
Siliqua	£40	£125	£600
Siliqua (AVGPS)	£730	£2200	—
AE2	£18	£65	£300
Flavius Victor			
Silver Sliqua	£140	£450	£2000
AE4	£27	£75	£375
Eugenius			
Silver Siliqua	£150	£475	£2100
Arcadius			
Gold Solidus....................................	£200	£500	£2000
Silver Siliqua	£25	£90	£450
Silver Half-siliqua	£150	£450	£2200
AE2	£9	£38	£125
AE4	£2	£10	£50

Julian II

Jovian

Valentinian I

Valens

Theodosius I

Arcadius

	FROM F	VF	EF
Eudoxia			
AE3	£25	£70	£375
Honorius			
Gold Solidus	£200	£475	£1900
Silver Siliqua	£30	£95	£475
AE4	£4	£15	£75
Constantine III			
Silver Siliqua	£140	£475	£2200
Theodosius II			
Gold Solidus	£200	£475	£1900
Johannes			
AE4	£110	£450	—
Valentinian III			
Gold Soldius.................................	£200	£495	£1900
AE4	£25	£80	£375

Honorius

Theodosius II

Ae = bronze; AE 1, 2, 3, 4 = bronze coins in descending order of size.

Illustrations by courtesy of Classical Numismatic Group/Seaby Coins.

A typical Roman fortification built on the borders of the empire and comprising of a ditch, steep ramparts and palisade (a public domain image courtesy Wikimedia Commons).

ENGLISH HAMMERED COINS

PART I

959-1485

INTRODUCTION

We have taken our starting point for hammered coin prices back to the Anglo-Saxon reign of Edgar; who could reasonably claim to be the first king of All England. Also it is from this time onwards that we start to get regular "portraits" as well as moneyers and mints on most issues. This gives a total of eight rulers to the list of kings prior to the Norman Conquest and most of these have coin issues that can be purchased quite reasonably. It is also worth pointing out here that of course coins had previously been struck in England for approximately 1000 years prior to our listings by Celtic, Roman and earlier Saxon rulers, details of which can be found in more specific publications.

PRICING

The prices given in the following pages are intended to be used as a "Pocket book guide" to the values of the *most common* coins within any denomination of any one reign. The price quoted is what a collector may expect to pay for such a piece in the condition indicated. For more detailed information we recommend the reader to one of the many specialist publications.

GRADING

The prices quoted are for three different grades of condition: Fine (F), Very Fine (VF) and Extremely Fine (EF). A "Fine" coin is assumed to be a fairly worn, circulated, piece but with all or most of the main features and lettering still clear. "Very Fine" is a middle grade with a small amount of wear and most details fairly clear. For this edition we have included the prices for coins in Extremely Fine condition where appropriate, although very few hammered coins actually turn up in this grade (i.e. nearly mint state with hardly any wear). In some instances the prices quoted are theoretically based and are only included to provide a guide. It is important to note that on all hammered coins the very nature of striking, i.e. individually, by hand, means hammered coinage is rarely a straight grade and when listed by a dealer the overall condition will often be qualified by terms such as: *weak in parts, struck off-centre, cracked or chipped flan, double struck,* etc. When applicable the price should be adjusted accordingly.

HISTORY

Below the heading for each monarch we have given a few historical notes as and when they apply to significant changes in the coinage.

EDGAR (First King of All England)
(959–975)

	F	VF	EF
Edgar Penny, non portrait (2 line inscription)............................	£300	£575	£1400

EDWARD THE MARTYR
(975–978)

	F	VF	EF
Edward, Penny, Portrait.......................	£1600	£4750	—

AETHELRED II
(978–1016)

	F	VF	EF
Aethelred II, Penny, last small cross type (First hand type illustrated)	£160	£275	£700

CNUT
(1016–1035)

	F	VF	EF
Cnut, Penny (short cross type).............. *(Quatrefoil type illustrated)*	£140	£260	£600

HAROLD I
(1035–40)

	F	VF	EF
Harold I, Penny	£375	£900	£2000

HARTHACANUTE
(1035–42)

	F	VF	EF
Harthacanute, Penny, English Mint (in his own name)	£1400	£4500	—
Harthacanute, Penny, Danish type	£350	£750	—

Danish type

EDWARD THE CONFESSOR
(1042–66)

	F	VF	EF
Edward the Confessor, Penny	£175	£325	£900

HAROLD II
(1066)

	F	VF	EF
Harold II, Penny	£1500	£3250	—

WILLIAM I
(1066–87)

The Norman Conquest had very little immediate effect on the coinage of England. The Anglo-Saxon standard of minting silver pennies was very high and the practice of the moneyer putting his name and mint town on the reverse continued as before, except with William's portrait of course. It is worth noting here that non-realistic, stylised portraits were used until the reign of Henry VII.
There are eight major types of pennies of which the last, the PAXS type, is by far the commonest.

	F	VF	EF
William I, Penny............................	£275	£550	£1200

WILLIAM II
(1087–1100)

Very little change from his father's reign except that five new types were issued, most of which were much more crudely designed than previous, all are scarce.

	F	VF	EF
William II, Penny....................................	£900	£2400	—

HENRY I
(1100–35)

There are fifteen different types of penny for this reign of which the last two are the most common. Most issues are of a very poor standard both in workmanship and metal, the prices reflect a poor quality of issue.

	F	VF	EF
Henry I, Penny...	£175	£500	—
Halfpenny	£1750	£5500	—

STEPHEN
(1135–54)

This is historically a very complicated time for the coinage, mainly due to civil war and a consequential lack of central control in the country which resulted in very poor quality and deliberately damaged pieces. Coins were struck not only in the name of Stephen and his main rival claimant Matilda but also by their supporters. The commonest issue is the "Watford" type; so named, as are many issues, after the area in which a hoard was found.

	F	VF	EF
Stephen, Penny	£275	£750	—

HENRY II
(1154–89)

There were two distinct issues struck during this reign. The first, Cross and Crosslets or "Tealby" coinage (named after Tealby in Lincolnshire), continued to be very poorly made and lasted 20 years. However, in 1180 the new and superior "Short Cross" issue commenced, being issued from only twelve major towns.

	F	VF	EF
Henry II, Penny, Tealby	£120	£350	—

	F	VF	EF
Henry II, Penny, Short Cross	£50	£150	—

RICHARD I
(1189–1199)

There were no major changes during this reign, in fact pennies continued to be struck with his father Henry's name throughout the reign. The coins struck under Richard tend to be rather crude in style.

	F	VF	EF
Richard I, Penny	£75	£220	—

JOHN
(1199–1216)

As with his brother before him, there were no major changes during the reign of King John, and pennies with his father's name were struck throughout the reign, although they tended to be somewhat neater in style than those struck during the reign of Richard I.

	F	VF	EF
John, Penny.......................................	£55	£140	£300

HENRY III
(1216–72)

The coinage during Henry III's reign continued as before with the short cross issue. However, in 1247 a new long cross design was introduced to prevent clipping. This design was to last in one form or another for many centuries. A gold penny is known with a throned monarch on the obverse.

	F	VF	EF
Henry III, Penny, Short Cross	£25	£75	£225
Henry III, Penny, Long Cross..................	£25	£60	£160

EDWARD I
(1272–1307)

After a few years of issuing similar pieces to his father, in 1279 Edward I ordered a major re-coinage. This consisted of well-made pennies, halfpennies and farthings in relatively large quantities, and for a brief period a groat (four pence) was produced. These were often mounted and gilded, price is for an undamaged peice.The pennies are amongst the most common of all hammered coins.

	F	VF	EF
Edward I (and Edward II)			
Groat (often damaged).....................	£4000	£9000	—
Penny..	£20	£55	—
Halfpenny...	£20	£70	—
Farthing..	£20	£60	—

Edward I penny

EDWARD II
(1307–1327)

The coinage of Edward II differs in only a very few minor details from that of Edward I and are of similar value for the common types.

EDWARD III
(1327–77)

This was a long reign which saw major changes in the coinage, the most significant being the introduction of a gold coinage (based on the Noble, valued at 6s 8d, and its fractions) and a regular issue of a large silver groat (and half groat). The mints were limited to a few episcopal cities but coins of English type were also struck in the newly-acquired Calais.

	F	VF	EF
Gold			
Noble	£825	£2250	£4750
Half Noble	£575	£1750	£3500
Quarter Noble	£325	£625	£1200
Silver			
Groat	£40	£140	£750
Half Groat	£25	£100	£375
Penny	£20	£85	£300
Half Penny	£20	£70	£250
Farthing	£25	£90	£300

Gold Noble

RICHARD II
(1377–1399)

The denominations continued during this reign much as before. However, coins are quite rare mainly due to the lack of bullion gold and silver going into the mints, mainly because of an inbalance with European weights and fineness.

	F	VF	EF
Gold			
Noble	£1250	£3500	—
Half Noble	£1250	£4200	—
Quarter Noble	£400	£1100	—
Silver			
Groat	£500	£1850	—
Half Groat	£235	£800	—
Penny	£70	£275	—
Half Penny	£30	£100	—
Farthing	£125	£425	—

Gold Noble

HENRY IV
(1399–1413)

Because of the continuing problems with the scarcity of gold and silver the coinage was reduced in weight in 1412, towards the end of the reign. All coins of this reign are quite scarce.

	F	VF
Gold		
Noble	£2000	£6000
Half Noble	£2250	£7250
Quarter Noble	£750	£2100
Silver		
Groat	£3000	£8500
Half Groat	£800	£2350
Penny	£450	£1250
Half Penny	£350	£850
Farthing	£750	£2250

Noble

HENRY V
(1413–22)

Monetary reform introduced towards the end of his father's reign in 1412 improved the supply of bullion and hence coins of Henry V are far more common. All of the main denominations continued as before.

	F	VF	EF
Gold			
Noble	£1000	£3000	£5500
Half Noble	£850	£2750	—
Quarter Noble	£375	£775	£1650
Silver			
Groat	£175	£525	—
Half Groat	£130	£375	—
Penny	£30	£125	—
Half Penny	£25	£85	—
Farthing	£350	£850	—

Groat

HENRY VI
(1422–61 and again 1470–71)

Although there were no new denominations during these reigns (see Edward IV below), Henry's first reign saw eleven different issues, each for a few years and distinguished by privy marks, i.e. crosses, pellets, annulets, etc.

HENRY VI *continued*

Gold	F	VF	EF
First reign—			
Noble	£900	£2750	£5000
Half Noble	£700	£2000	£4000
Quarter Noble	£325	£750	£1400
2nd reign—			
Angel	£1850	£5000	—
Half Angel	£4500	£13500	—

Silver			
Groat	£40	£125	£300
Half Groat	£30	£90	£265
Penny	£25	£80	£325
Half Penny	£20	£70	£175
Farthing	£100	£300	—

Noble

EDWARD IV
(1461–70 and again 1471–83)

The significant changes during these reigns were the replacement of the noble by the rose ryal (and revalued at 10 shillings) and the introduction of the angel at the old noble value. We also start to see mint-marks or initial marks appearing, usually at the top of the coin, they were used to denote the period of issue for dating purposes and often lasted for two to three years.

Gold	F	VF	EF
Ryal	£850	£2400	£4000
Half Ryal	£750	£2000	£3500
Quarter Ryal	£450	£1150	£2000
Angel	£800	£2250	£3500
Half Angel	£750	£2160	—

Silver			
Groat	£40	£130	£450
Half Groat	£45	£140	£400
Penny	£25	£120	£350
Half Penny	£20	£90	—
Farthing	£200	£700	—

Angel

RICHARD III
(1483–85)

The close of the Yorkist Plantagenet and Medieval period come together at this time. There are no new significant numismatic changes but most coins of Richard whilst not really rare, continue to be very popular and priced quite high.

Gold	F	VF	EF
Angel	£5500	£16000	—
Half Angel	£8000	£24000	—

Silver			
Groat	£800	£2200	—
Half Groat	£1500	£4350	—
Penny	£450	£1200	—
Half Penny	£325	£900	—
Farthing	£1500	£4250	—

Groat

PART II
1485–1663

Among the more significant features of the post-Renaissance period as it affected coinage is the introduction of realistic portraiture during the reign of Henry VII. We also have a much wider and varied number of new and revised denominations, for example eleven different gold denominations of Henry VIII and the same number of silver for Elizabeth I. Here we only mention the introduction or changes in the main denominations, giving a value for all of them, once again listing the commonest type.

HENRY VII
(1485–1509)

The gold sovereign of 20 shillings makes its first appearance in 1489 as does the testoon (later shilling) in about 1500. The silver penny was re-designed to a rather crude likeness of the sovereign.

	F	VF	EF
Gold			
Sovereign	£30000	£100,000	—
Ryal	£35000	£135,000	—
Angel	£775	£2000	—
Half Angel	£675	£1800	—
Silver			
Testoon 1/-	£20000	£40,000	—
Groat	£70	£180	£650
Half Groat	£30	£110	£325
Penny	£30	£100	£300
Half Penny	£20	£75	—
Farthing	£450	£1350	—

Profile Groat

HENRY VIII
(1509–47)

After a long initial period of very little change in the coinage, in 1526 there were many, with an attempt to bring the gold/silver ratio in line with the continental currencies. Some gold coins only lasted a short time and are very rare. The crown (in gold) makes its first appearance. Towards the end of the reign we see large issues of debased silver coins (with a high copper content) bearing the well-known facing portrait of the ageing King. These tend to turn up in poor condition.

Gold			
Sovereign	£6000	£22000	—
Half Sovereign	£900	£3000	—
Angel	£750	£1850	£3350
Half Angel	£700	£1750	£2750
Quarter Angel	£775	£2200	—
George Noble	£11000	£36000	—
Half George Noble	£10000	£32000	—
Crown of the rose	£7250	£26500	—
Crown of the double rose	£750	£2350	—
Half Crown of the double rose	£575	£1500	—
Silver			
Testoon 1/-	£900	£4500	—
Groat	£90	£250	£1000
Half Groat	£50	£160	£650
Penny	£35	£120	£425
Half Penny	£25	£90	—
Farthing	£350	£1000	—

Gold Sovereign

EDWARD VI
(1547–53)

Some of the coins struck in the first few years of this short reign could really be called Henry VIII posthumous issues as there is continuity in both name and style from his father's last issue. However, overlapping this period are portrait issues of the boy King, particularly shillings (usually poor quality coins). This period also sees the first dated English coin (shown in Roman numerals). In 1551 however, a new coinage was introduced with a restored silver quality from the Crown (dated 1551) down to the new sixpence and threepence.

	F	VF	EF
Gold			
Sovereign (30s)	£7500	£27500	—
Half Sovereign	£1700	£6500	—
Crown	£2000	£6650	—
Half Crown	£1600	£5250	—
Angel	£14000	£40000	—
Half Angel	—	£45000	—
Sovereign (20s)	£5500	£17500	—
Silver			
Crown	£900	£2500	—
Half Crown	£650	£1750	—
Shilling	£100	£400	—
Sixpence	£110	£475	—
Groat	£775	£3750	—
Threepence	£225	£1000	—
Half Groat	£400	£1300	—
Penny	£60	£225	—
Half Penny	£200	£800	—
Farthing	£1250	£4000	—

*Crowned bust half
sovereign*

MARY
(1553–54)

The early coins of Mary's sole reign are limited and continue to use the same denominations as Edward, except that the gold ryal was reintroduced.

	F	VF
Gold		
Sovereign (30s)	£7500	£25000
Ryal	£35000	—
Angel	£2250	£6500
Half Angel	£5500	£15000
Silver		
Groat	£160	£500
Half Groat	£700	£2250
Penny	£600	£2150

Groat

PHILIP & MARY
(1554–58)

After a very short reign alone, Mary married Philip of Spain and they technically ruled jointly (although not for very long in practise) until her death. After her marriage we see both her and Philip on the shillings and sixpences.

	F	VF
Gold		
Angel	£6000	£20000
Half Angel	£14000	—
Silver		
Shilling	£450	£2000
Sixpence	£450	£1750
Groat	£175	£600
Half Groat	£475	£1700
Penny	£70	£235

Shilling

ELIZABETH I
(1558–1603)

As might be expected with a long reign there are a number of significant changes in the coinage which include several new denominations—so many in silver that every value from the shilling downwards was marked and dated to distinguish them. Early on we have old base Edward VI shillings countermarked to a new reduced value (not priced here). Also due to a lack of small change and the expense of making a miniscule farthing we have a new threehalfpence and threefarthings. Finally we see the beginnings of a milled (machine produced) coinage for a brief period from 1561–71.

	F	VF	EF
Gold			
Sovereign (30s)	£6000	£18500	—
Ryal (15s)	£25000	£75000	—
Angel	£1200	£3300	—
Half Angel	£1000	£3000	—
Quarter Angel	£900	£2800	—
Pound (20s)	£3250	£10000	—
Half Pound	£1600	£4600	—
Crown	£1200	£3400	—
Half Crown	£1250	£3350	—
Silver			
Crown	£1500	£4750	—
Half Crown	£1100	£2600	—
Shilling	£100	£450	£1500
Sixpence	£50	£200	£850
Groat	£70	£275	£750
Threepence	£35	£170	£465
Half Groat	£30	£85	£250
Threehalfpence	£45	£185	—
Penny	£25	£80	£225
Threefarthings	£80	£235	—
Half Penny	£40	£130	£185

Shilling

JAMES I
(1603–25)

Although the size of the gold coinage remains much the same as Elizabeth's reign, the name and weight or value of the denominations have several changes, i.e. Pound = Sovereign = Unite = Laurel. A new four shilling gold coin (thistle crown) was introduced. A number of the silver coins now have their value in Roman numerals on the coin. Relatively few angels were made from this period onwards and they are usually found pierced.

	F	VF	EF
Gold			
Sovereign (20s)	£2650	£11000	—
Unite	£700	£1700	£3500
Double crown/half unite	£450	£1200	£2600
Crown	£300	£650	£1750
Thistle Crown	£325	£700	£1750
Half Crown	£260	£525	—
Rose Ryal (30s)	£3100	£10000	—
Spur Ryal (15s)	£8000	£30000	—
Angel (pierced)	£800	£2300	—
Half Angel (Unpierced)	£3250	£11500	—
Laurel	£700	£1750	£3500
Half Laurel	£500	£1425	£2800
Quarter Laurel	£280	£650	£1500
Silver			
Crown	£750	£1900	—
Half Crown	£300	£750	—
Shilling	£65	£235	—
Sixpence	£55	£200	—
Half Groat	£15	£55	£120
Penny	£15	£45	£110
Half Penny	£15	£35	£80

Gold Unite, second bust

Silver Halfcrown

CHARLES I
(1625–49)

This reign is probably the most difficult to simplify as there are so many different issues and whole books have been produced on this period alone. From the beginning of the King's reign and throughout the Civil War, a number of mints operated for varying lengths of time, producing both regular and irregular issues. The Tower mint was taken over by Parliament in 1642 but before this a small quantity of milled coinage was produced alongside the regular hammered issues. The Court then moved to Oxford from where, for the next three years, large quantities of gold and silver were struck (including rare triple unites and large silver pounds). The most prolific of the provincial mints were those situated at Aberystwyth, York, Oxford, Shrewsbury, Bristol, Exeter, Truro, Chester and Worcester as well as some smaller mints mainly situated in the West Country. Among the more interesting coins of the period are the pieces struck on unusually-shaped flans at Newark and Pontefract whilst those towns were under siege. As many of the coins struck during the Civil War were crudely struck on hastily gathered bullion and plate, they provide a fascinating area of study. The prices indicated below are the minimum for the commonest examples of each denomination irrespective of town of origin.

	F	VF	EF
Gold			
Triple Unite (£3)	£17500	£50000	—
Unite	£700	£1750	—
Double crown/Half unite	£500	£1300	—
Crown	£300	£650	—
Angel (pierced)	£850	£2750	—
Angel (unpierced)	£2750	£8500	—
Silver			
Pound (20 shillings—Oxford)	£3000	£8000	—
Half Pound (Shrewsbury)	£1400	£3500	—
Crown (Truro, Exeter)	£500	£1250	—
Half Crown	£55	£215	—
Shilling	£40	£170	£900
Sixpence	£40	£150	£800
Groat	£70	£220	£550
Threepence	£55	£200	£475
Half Groat	£20	£60	£175
Penny	£20	£60	£160
Half Penny	£15	£30	£65

Triple unite

Oxford Halfcrown

Above: Newark siege shilling.

THE COMMONWEALTH
(1649–60)

After the execution of Charles I, Parliament changed the design of the coinage. They are simple non- portrait pieces with an English legend.

	F	VF	EF
Gold			
Unite	£2400	£5500	—
Double crown/Half unite	£1500	£4000	—
Crown	£1250	£3500	—
Silver			
Crown	£1000	£2400	£6750
Half Crown	£350	£775	£3500
Shilling	£230	£600	£2350
Sixpence	£225	£550	£1750
Half Groat	£40	£120	£300
Penny	£45	£135	£325
Halfpenny	£35	£90	£175

Crown

CHARLES II
(1660–85)

Although milled coins had been produced for Oliver Cromwell in 1656–58, after the Restoration of the monarchy hammered coins continued to be produced until 1663, when the machinery was ready to manufacture large quantities of good milled pieces.

	F	VF	EF
Gold			
Unite	£1850	£5250	—
Double crown/Half unite	£1400	£4000	—
Crown	£1800	£5350	—
Silver			
Half Crown	£260	£750	—
Shilling	£150	£550	—
Sixpence	£135	£450	—
Fourpence	£40	£125	£250
Threepence	£35	£115	£225
Twopence	£25	£60	£160
Penny	£35	£80	£180

Halfcrown

141

A COMPREHENSIVE PRICE GUIDE
TO THE COINS OF

THE
UNITED KINGDOM
1656–2015
including

England, Scotland,
Isle of Man,
Guernsey, Jersey, Alderney,
also Ireland

When referring to this price guide one must bear a number of important points in mind. The points listed here have been taken into consideration during the preparation of this guide and we hope that the prices given will provide a true reflection of the market at the time of going to press. Nevertheless, the publishers can accept no liability for the accuracy of the prices quoted.

1. "As struck" examples with flaws will be worth less than the indicated price.
2. Any coin which is particularly outstanding, with an attractive natural toning or in superb state will command a much *higher* price than that shown.
3. These prices refer strictly to the British market, and do not reflect outside opinions.
4. Some prices given for coins not seen in recent years are estimates based on a knowledge of the market.
5. In the case of coins of high rarity, prices are not generally given.
6. In the listing, "—" indicates, where applicable, one of the following:
    a. Metal or bullion value only
    b. Not usually found in this grade
    c. Not collected in this condition
7. Proof coins are listed in FDC under the UNC column.
8. All prices are quoted in £ sterling, exclusive of VAT (where applicable).

FIFTY SHILLINGS

	F	VF	EF

OLIVER CROMWELL (1656–58)

	F	VF	EF
1656..	£18,000	£44,000	£130,000

Opinions differ as to whether the portrait coinage of Oliver Cromwell was ever meant for circulation but for the sake of completeness it has been decided to include it in this Yearbook. The fifty shillings gold coin is unique as it was only struck during Cromwell's time using the same dies that were used for the broad or 20 shillings coin but with a weight of approximately 2.5 times that of the broad.

FIVE GUINEAS

CHARLES II (1660–85)

	F	VF	EF
1668 First bust	£3000	£6000	£22000
1668 — Elephant below bust	£2700	£6000	£22000
1669 —	£2700	£6000	—
1669 — Elephant....................................	£3000	£6500	—
1670 —	£2750	£6000	£22000
1670 Proof...	—	—	£13500
1671 —	£3000	£6500	£22000
1672 —	£2750	£6000	£22000
1673 —	£2750	£6000	£22000
1674 —	£3500	£7000	£24000
1675 —	£3000	£6500	£24000
1675 — Elephant....................................	£3200	£7000	—
1675 — Elephant & Castle below bust...	£3500	£7000	£25000
1676 —	£3000	£6000	£22000
1676 — Elephant & Castle	£3000	£6500	£23000
1677 —	£2500	£6000	£21500
1677/5 — Elephant.................................	£3000	£7500	£25000
1677 — Elephant & Castle	£3200	£6500	£24000
1678/7 — 8 over 7	£2700	£6000	£22000
1678/7 — Elephant & Castle	£3250	£7000	£24000
1678/7 Second Bust...............................	£2800	£6000	£22000
1679 —	£2700	£6000	£22000
1680 —	£2750	£6000	£22000
1680 — Elephant & Castle	£3000	£7000	£24000
1681 —	£3000	£6500	£24000
1681 — Elephant & Castle	£3000	£6500	£24000
1682 —	£2600	£6000	£21500
1682 — Elephant & Castle	£2750	£6250	£21500
1683 —	£2600	£6000	£21500
1683 — Elephant & Castle	£3000	£6500	£22000
1684 —	£2600	£6500	£22000
1684 — Elephant & Castle	£2600	£6000	£22000

Charles II

JAMES II (1685–88)

	F	VF	EF
1686..	£3500	£8000	£28000
1687..	£3250	£8000	£22000
1687 Elephant & Castle...........................	£3300	£7000	£22000
1688	£3300	£7500	£22000
1688 Elephant & Castle...........................	£3500	£8000	£25000

	F	VF	EF

WILLIAM AND MARY (1688–94)

	F	VF	EF
1691	£2750	£6000	£20000
1691 Elephant & Castle	£2800	£6000	£20000
1692	£2800	£6000	£20000
1692 Elephant & Castle	£3000	£6000	£21000
1693	£2800	£6000	£20000
1693 Elephant & Castle	£2800	£6000	£21000
1694	£2800	£6000	£20000
1694 Elephant & Castle	£2800	£6000	£21000

WILLIAM III (1694–1702)

	F	VF	EF
1699 First bust	£3000	£7500	£24000
1699 — Elephant & Castle	£3200	£7000	£25000
1700 —	£3000	£6500	£23000
1701 Second bust "fine work"	£3000	£7000	£22000

(1701 "fine work"—beware recent forgeries)

ANNE (1702–14)

Pre-Union with Scotland

	F	VF	EF
1703 VIGO below bust	£35000	£90000	£270000
1705	£4500	£10000	£40000
1706	£4200	£9000	£35000

Post-Union (different shields)

	F	VF	EF
1706	£3000	£7000	£21000
1709 Narrow shields	£3000	£6500	£22000
1711 Broader shields	£3200	£6500	£22000
1713 —	£3200	£6500	£22000
1714 —	£3200	£6500	£23000
1714/3	£3200	£6500	£22000

William & Mary

GEORGE I (1714–27)

	F	VF	EF
1716	£4000	£9000	£28000
1717	£4000	£8500	£28000
1720	£3800	£8500	£28000
1726	£3500	£7500	£27000

GEORGE II (1727–60)

	F	VF	EF
1729 Young head	£2750	£6000	£20000
1729 — E.I.C. below head	£2700	£6000	£18500
1731 —	£3250	£6500	£23000
1735 —	£2500	£6500	£23000
1738 —	£2500	£5500	£20000
1741	£2500	£5000	£20000
1741/38 41 over 38	£2500	£5000	£20000
1746 Old head, LIMA	£2750	£5000	£19000
1748 —	£2750	£5000	£19000
1753 —	£2750	£5000	£19000

GEORGE III (1760–1820)

	F	VF	EF
1770 Patterns	—	—	£200000
1773	—	—	£200000
1777	—	—	£180000

Anne

145

TWO GUINEAS

	F	VF	EF

CHARLES II (1660–85)

	F	VF	EF
1664 First bust	£1600	£4000	£10000
1664 — Elephant	£1500	£3500	£9000
1665 —		Extremely rare	
1669 —		Extremely rare	
1671 —	£1800	£5000	£15000
1673 First bust		Extremely rare	
1675 Second bust	£1600	£4000	£10000
1676 —	£1600	£4000	£10000
1676 — Elephant & Castle	£1650	£4000	£10000
1677 —	£1600	£3750	£9000
1677 — Elephant & Castle		Extremely rare	
1678/7 —	£1400	£3250	£8500
1678 — Elephant	£1600	£3500	£9500
1678 — Elephant & Castle	£1600	£3500	£9000
1679 —	£1600	£4000	£9500
1680 —	£1800	£4500	£12000
1681 —	£1600	£3250	£8500
1682 — Elephant & Castle	£1600	£3250	£8500
1683 —	£1500	£3200	£8500
1683 — Elephant & Castle	£1800	£4250	£12000
1684 —	£1600	£3500	£8500
1684 — Elephant & Castle	£1600	£4000	£10000

Charles II

JAMES II (1685–88)

	F	VF	EF
1687	£2000	£4750	£14000
1688/7	£2200	£4800	£15000

WILLIAM AND MARY (1688–94)

	F	VF	EF
1691 Elephant & Castle		Extremely rare	
1693	£1600	£3750	£9000
1693 Elephant & Castle	£1800	£4000	£13000
1694 — 4 over 3	£1600	£4000	£11500
1694/3 Elephant & Castle	£1600	£4000	£11500

James II

WILLIAM III (1694–1702)

	F	VF	EF
1701 "fine work"	£1850	£4200	£12000

ANNE (1702–14)

	F	VF	EF
1709 Post Union	£1500	£3200	£9000
1711	£1400	£3200	£8000
1713	£1400	£3250	£8000
1714/3	£1600	£3750	£9250

GEORGE I (1714–27)

	F	VF	EF
1717	£1400	£2500	£7500
1720	£1400	£2500	£7200
1720/17	£1400	£2750	£7500
1726	£1200	£2500	£7250

Anne

	F	VF	EF

GEORGE II (1727–60)

	F	VF	EF
1733 Proof only FDC		Extremely Rare	
1734 Young head 4 over 3	£1500	£4000	—
1735 —	£1000	£2200	£6500
1738 —	£850	£1600	£3000
1739 —	£850	£1600	£3000
1739 Intermediate head	£850	£1600	£3000
1740 —	£850	£1600	£3100
1748 Old head	£800	£1700	£3800
1753 —	£800	£1850	£5000

GEORGE III (1760–1820)

1768 Patterns only	—	Extremely Rare
1773 Patterns only	—	Extremely Rare
1777 Patterns only	—	Extremely Rare

George II

GUINEAS

	F	VF	EF

CHARLES II (1660–85)

	F	VF	EF
1663 First bust	£3000	£8000	£37500
1663 — Elephant below	£2500	£7500	—
1664 Second bust	£3000	£8500	—
1664 — Elephant	£3500	£10000	£35000
1664 Third bust	£900	£3000	£11000
1664 — Elephant	£1500	£4000	£13000
1665 —	£850	£2500	£10000
1665 — Elephant	£1500	£4000	£15000
1666 —	£850	£2500	£9000
1667 —	£850	£2500	£9000
1668 —	£850	£2500	£9000
1668 — Elephant		Extremely rare	
1669 —	£850	£2750	£10000
1670 —	£850	£2500	£9500
1671 —	£850	£2500	£10000
1672 —	£800	£2800	£10000
1672 Fourth bust	£800	£2200	£5500
1673 Third bust	£900	£3000	£11000
1673 Fourth bust	£700	£2000	£6500
1674 —	£700	£2000	£6500
1674 — Elephant & Castle		Extremely rare	
1675 —	£700	£2200	£7000
1675 — CRAOLVS Error		Extremely rare	
1675 — Elephant & Castle	£800	£2500	£9000
1676 —	£700	£2200	£6500
1676 — Elephant & Castle	£800	£2500	£8500
1677 —	£600	£2000	£6500
1677/5 — Elephant 7 over 5		Extremely rare	
1677 — Elephant & Castle	£700	£2000	£7000
1678 —	£700	£1800	£6000
1678 — Elephant		Extremely rare	
1678 — Elephant & Castle	£800	£2500	£10000

Charles II, third bust

Charles II, fourth bust, elephant & castle below

	F	VF	EF
1679 —	£700	£1800	£6500
1679 — Elephant & Castle	£800	£2500	£9000
1680 —	£700	£1800	£6500
1680 — Elephant & Castle	£800	£2500	£9000
1681 —	£750	£2000	£6500
1681 — Elephant & Castle	£750	£2500	£9000
1682 —	£700	£2000	£6500
1682 — Elephant & Castle	£800	£2800	£9500
1683 —	£650	£1800	£6500
1683 — Elephant & Castle	£800	£2500	£9000
1684 —	£700	£2200	£6500
1684 — Elephant & Castle	£800	£2500	£10000

James II, first bust, elephant & castle below

JAMES II (1685–1688)

	F	VF	EF
1685 First bust	£700	£2200	£8000
1685 — Elephant & Castle	£800	£2600	£9000
1686 —	£800	£2600	£9000
1686 — Elephant & Castle		Extremely rare	
1686 Second bust	£650	£2000	£6750
1686 — Elephant & Castle	£800	£2500	£8000
1687 —	£700	£2000	£6500
1687 —Elephant & Castle	£750	£2500	£8500
1688 —	£600	£2200	£6500
1688 — Elephant & Castle	£700	£2500	£8000

WILLIAM AND MARY (1688–94)

	F	VF	EF
1689	£600	£2000	£7000
1689 Elephant & Castle	£600	£2000	£7000
1690	£600	£2200	£7500
1690 GVLIFLMVS	£700	£2200	£8000
1690 Elephant & Castle	£800	£2400	£8000
1691	£600	£2200	£7000
1691 Elephant & Castle	£650	£2200	£7000
1692	£600	£2000	£7250
1692 Elephant	£900	£3000	£9000
1692 Elephant & Castle	£650	£2400	£7250
1693	£600	£2000	£7250
1693 Elephant		Extremely rare	
1693 Elephant & Castle		Extremely rare	
1694	£650	£2000	£6500
1694/3	£650	£2000	£6500
1694 Elephant & Castle	£675	£2200	£6700
1694/3 Elephant & Castle	£675	£2200	£6700

James II, second bust

WILLIAM III (1694–1702)

	F	VF	EF
1695 First bust	£600	£1800	£6000
1695 — Elephant & Castle	£1000	£2800	£11000
1696 —	£600	£2000	£6500
1696 — Elephant & Castle		Extremely rare	
1697 —	£600	£1800	£6250
1697 Second bust	£525	£1800	£7250
1697 — Elephant & Castle	£1400	£4250	—
1698 —	£525	£1800	£5500
1698 — Elephant & Castle	£525	£2000	£5500
1699 —	£550	£1750	£6000
1699 — Elephant & Castle		Extremely rare	
1700 —	£550	£1750	£5750
1700 — Elephant & Castle	£1100	£4250	—
1701 —	£550	£1750	£5250
1701 — Elephant & Castle		Extremely rare	
1701 Third bust "fine work"	£900	£3000	£10000

William III, second bust

	F	VF	EF

ANNE (1702–1714)

	F	VF	EF
1702 (Pre-Union) First bust	£900	£3000	£10000
1703 — VIGO below	£14000	£35000	£90000
1705 —	£1000	£3000	£10000
1706 —	£1000	£3000	£10000
1707 —	£1000	£3000	£10000
1707 — (Post-Union)	£650	£2500	£8250
1707 — Elephant & Castle	£750	£3000	£10000
1707 Second bust	£600	£2000	£7250
1708 First bust	£650	£2500	£8000
1708 Second bust	£500	£1800	£6000
1708 — Elephant & Castle	£800	£3000	£9000
1709 —	£500	£1800	£6000
1709 — Elephant & Castle	£800	£2800	£7500
1710 Third bust	£625	£1500	£4500
1711 —	£625	£1500	£4500
1712 —	£600	£1500	£4500
1713 —	£500	£1300	£4000
1714 —	£550	£1300	£4000
1714 GRΛTIΛ	£700	£1700	£4000

Anne, second bust

GEORGE I (1714–27)

	F	VF	EF
1714 First bust (Prince Elector)	£1300	£3250	£9000
1715 Second bust	£600	£1500	£3500
1715 Third bust	£500	£1500	£4000
1716 —	£500	£1500	£3500
1716 Fourth bust	£475	£1300	£3500
1717 —	£475	£1300	£3500
1718 —		Extremely rare	
1719 —	£500	£1400	£3750
1720 —	£500	£1400	£3800
1721 —	£500	£1400	£3800
1721 — Elephant & Castle		Extremely rare	
1722 —	£500	£1300	£3750
1722 — Elephant & Castle		Extremely rare	
1723 —	£525	£1400	£3750
1723 Fifth bust	£525	£1400	£3800
1724 —	£525	£1300	£3750
1725 —	£525	£1300	£3750
1726 —	£500	£1300	£3500
1726 — Elephant & Castle	£1750	£5000	£16000
1727 —	£600	£1800	£5000

George I, third bust

GEORGE II (1727–60)

	F	VF	EF
1727 First young head, early large shield	£800	£2500	£8000
1727 — Larger lettering, early small shield	£800	£2500	£8000
1728 — —	£900	£2750	£8500
1729 2nd young head E.I.C. below	£1000	£3000	£10000
1729 — Proof		Very Rare	
1730 —	£600	£1500	£5000
1731 —	£500	£1500	£4500
1731 — E.I.C. below	£900	£2750	£8000
1732 —	£700	£2500	£7500
1732 — E.I.C. below	£800	£2500	£8000
1732 — Larger lettering obverse	£550	£1500	£4500
1732 — — E.I.C. below	£900	£1800	£8000
1733 — —	£500	£1300	£3400
1734 — —	£500	£1300	£3400
1735 — —	£500	£1300	£3400
1736 — —	£500	£1500	£3250
1737 — —	£500	£1500	£3250

George II, 1759, old head, larger lettering

	F	VF	EF
1738 — —	£500	£1400	£3500
1739 Intermediate head	£500	£1100	£3000
1739 — E.I.C. below	£1100	£2800	£8000
1740 —	£500	£1400	£5000
1741/39 —	£800	£2400	£6250
1743 —	£800	£2400	£6250
1745 — Larger lettering obv. Older bust	£500	£1300	£4250
1745 — LIMA below	£1200	£3500	£11000
1746 — (GEORGIVS) Larger lettering obv.	£500	£1500	£3750
1747 Old head, large lettering	£400	£1000	£3000
1748 —	£400	£1000	£3200
1749 —	£450	£1100	£3300
1750 —	£400	£1000	£3400
1751 — small lettering	£400	£1000	£3400
1753 —	£400	£1000	£3400
1755 —	£400	£1000	£3200
1756 —	£400	£1000	£3300
1758 —	£400	£1000	£3300
1759 —	£400	£1000	£3000
1760 —	£400	£1000	£2800

George III first head

GEORGE III (1760–1820)

	F	VF	EF
1761 First head	£1750	£5000	£9000
1763 Second head	£1400	£3750	£7500
1764 —	£1000	£3500	£7000
1765 Third head	£350	£600	£1750
1766 —	£350	£600	£1750
1767 —	£500	£800	£2200
1768 —	£400	£700	£1800
1769 —	£400	£700	£2000
1770 —	£800	£1800	£3500
1771 —	£400	£500	£1250
1772 —	£400	£500	£1250
1773 —	£400	£550	£1500
1774 Fourth head	£375	£575	£1000
1775 —	£350	£550	£900
1776 —	£350	£550	£900
1777 —	£350	£550	£900
1778 —	£500	£900	£2350
1779 —	£400	£700	£1250
1781 —	£350	£550	£1100
1782 —	£350	£550	£1100
1783 —	£350	£550	£1100
1784 —	£350	£600	£1150
1785 —	£350	£600	£1100
1786 —	£400	£650	£1150
1787 Fifth head, "Spade" reverse	£325	£525	£950
1788 —	£325	£525	£950
1789 —	£325	£525	£950
1790 —	£325	£525	£950
1791 —	£325	£525	£950
1792 —	£325	£525	£950
1793 —	£325	£525	£975
1794 —	£325	£525	£950
1795 —	£325	£525	£950
1796 —	£325	£525	£950
1797 —	£325	£525	£950
1798 —	£325	£525	£950
1799 —	£375	£650	£1250
1813 Sixth head, "Military" reverse	£800	£1900	£4000

(Beware of counterfeits of this series—many dangerous copies exist)

Fourth head

Fifth head, Spade reverse

Sixth "Military" head

HALF GUINEAS

	F	VF	EF
### CHARLES II (1660–85)			
1669 First bust	£350	£1000	£3750
1670 —	£350	£1000	£3250
1671 —	£450	£1300	£4750
1672 —	£400	£1100	£4000
1672 Second bust	£400	£950	£3500
1673 —	£450	£1300	£4000
1674 —	£500	£1600	£4000
1675 —	£500	£1600	£4000
1676 —	£350	£1000	£3500
1676 — Elephant & Castle	£675	£2500	—
1677 —	£350	£1000	£3250
1677 — Elephant & Castle	£600	£1800	—
1678 —	£400	£1100	£3500
1678 — Elephant & Castle	£500	£1500	£5000
1679 —	£400	£1100	£3250
1680 —	£400	£1800	—
1680 — Elephant & Castle	£600	£1750	£5500
1681 —	£400	£1600	—
1682 —	£400	£1300	£3500
1682 — Elephant & Castle	£600	£1800	—
1683 —	£375	£1000	£3500
1683 — Elephant & Castle		Extremely rare	
1684 —	£350	£900	£3500
1684 — Elephant & Castle	£600	£1500	£5750

Charles II, first bust

	F	VF	EF
### JAMES II (1685–88)			
1686	£450	£1100	£3500
1686 Elephant & Castle	£800	£3750	£7000
1687	£450	£1400	£4200
1688	£450	£1400	£4200

	F	VF	EF
### WILLIAM AND MARY (1688–94)			
1689 First busts	£500	£1800	£4000
1690 Second busts	£500	£1850	£4200
1691 —	£500	£1800	£4000
1691 — Elephant & Castle	£500	£1700	£4200
1692 —	£450	£1500	£3500
1692 — Elephant		Extremely rare	
1692 — Elephant & Castle	£450	£1600	£4000
1693 —		Extremely rare	
1694 —	£450	£1600	£3850

William & Mary, first busts

	F	VF	EF
### WILLIAM III (1694–1702)			
1695	£350	£825	£3000
1695 Elephant & Castle	£600	£1500	£4500
1696 —	£400	£1000	£3250
1697 Larger Harp rev.	£500	£1400	£4500
1698	£500	£1200	£4000
1698 Elephant & Castle	£600	£1500	£3250
1699		Extremely rare	
1700	£325	£850	£3000
1701	£300	£800	£3000

William III, elephant & castle below bust

	F	VF	EF

ANNE (1702–14)

	F	VF	EF
1702 (Pre-Union)	£700	£2200	£6500
1703 VIGO below bust	£5000	£12000	£30000
1705	£600	£2000	£6000
1707 (Post-Union)	£300	£900	£2500
1708	£325	£900	£2500
1709	£350	£900	£2500
1710	£300	£750	£2300
1711	£300	£750	£2300
1712	£325	£800	£2750
1713	£300	£750	£2200
1714	£300	£750	£2200

Anne

GEORGE I (1714–27)

	F	VF	EF
1715 First bust	£700	£1250	£4250
1717 —	£300	£700	£2500
1718 —	£300	£700	£2500
1719 —	£300	£700	£2500
1720 —	£325	£700	£2750
1721 —			Extremely rare
1721 — Elephant & Castle			Extremely rare
1722 —	£300	£700	£2700
1723 —	£400	£800	£3000
1724 —	£325	£800	£2850
1725 Second bust	£300	£600	£2400
1726 —	£300	£600	£2500
1727 —	£300	£600	£2750

*George I,
second bust*

GEORGE II (1727–60)

	F	VF	EF
1728 Young head	£500	£1250	£3750
1729 —	£500	£1250	£3500
1729 — E.I.C.	£600	£1500	£4500
1730 —	£700	£2000	—
1730 — E.I.C.	£675	£2000	—
1731 —	£300	£950	£3000
1731 — E.I.C.			Extremely rare
1732 —	£300	£900	£3000
1732 — E.I.C.			Extremely rare
1733 —			Unknown
1734 —	£300	£800	£2500
1735 —			Extremely rare
1736 —	£300	£800	£3000
1737 —	£400	£800	£3000
1738 —	£300	£750	£2500
1739 —	£300	£750	£2500
1739 — E.I.C.			Extremely rare
1740 Intermediate head	£375	£1000	£3000
1743 —			Extremely rare
1745 —	£300	£900	£3000
1745 — LIMA	£1100	£3500	£7000
1746 —	£275	£700	£2200
1747 Old head	£300	£700	£2200
1748 —	£275	£800	£2200
1749 —	£300	£650	£2000
1750 —	£300	£650	£1950
1751 —	£275	£600	£1900
1752 —	£275	£600	£1900
1753 —	£275	£600	£1900
1755 —	£275	£600	£1800
1756 —	£260	£800	£2000
1758 —	£300	£700	£2000
1759 —	£260	£650	£1800
1760 —	£260	£650	£1800

*George I,
second bust*

*George II,
young head*

*George II,
old head*

GEORGE III (1760–1820)

	F	VF	EF
1762 First head	£650	£1750	£4000
1763 —	£700	£2000	£3750
1764 Second head	£250	£500	£1100
1765 —	£500	£1200	£3000
1766 —	£250	£500	£1300
1768 —	£250	£550	£1300
1769 —	£225	£550	£1400
1772 —		Extremely rare	
1773 —	£300	£600	£1500
1774 —	£350	£700	£1800
1774 Third head		Extremely rare	
1775 —	£1000	£2500	£6000
1775 Fourth head	£200	£275	£550
1775 — Proof		Extremely rare	
1776 —	£225	£400	£1000
1777 —	£225	£400	£800
1778 —	£225	£400	£800
1779 —	£225	£400	£900
1781 —	£225	£400	£975
1783 —	£500	£1600	—
1784 —	£220	£375	£800
1785 —	£220	£375	£700
1786 —	£220	£375	£700
1787 Fifth head, "Spade" rev.	£220	£375	£700
1788 —	£220	£375	£700
1789 —	£220	£375	£750
1790 —	£220	£375	£650
1791 —	£220	£375	£650
1792 —	£1000	£3000	—
1793 —	£200	£400	£700
1794 —	£200	£400	£700
1795 —	£200	£500	£850
1796 —	£200	£400	£700
1797 —	£200	£400	£700
1798 —	£200	£400	£700
1800 —	£300	£800	£2000
1801 Sixth head, Shield in Garter rev.	£200	£300	£550
1802 —	£200	£300	£550
1803 —	£200	£300	£550
1804 Seventh head	£200	£300	£550
1805		Extremely rare	
1806 —	£200	£300	£625
1808 —	£200	£300	£625
1899 —	£200	£300	£625
1810 —	£200	£300	£650
1811 —	£300	£600	£1100
1813 —	£300	£600	£950

George III, second head

George III, fifth head, "spade" reverse

THIRD GUINEAS

GEORGE III (1760–1820)

DATE	F	VF	EF
1797 First head, date in legend	£140	£220	£500
1798 — —	£140	£220	£500
1799 — —	£140	£260	£525
1800 — —	£140	£220	£525
1801 Date under crown	£140	£220	£525
1802 —	£140	£220	£525
1803 —	£140	£220	£525
1804 Second head	£95	£160	£500
1806 —	£100	£240	£500
1808 —	£125	£300	£500
1809 —	£125	£300	£500
1810 —	£125	£300	£500
1811 —	£450	£1200	£2500
1813 —	£275	£450	£850

George III, date in legend

George III, date under crown

QUARTER GUINEAS

GEORGE I (1714–27)

	F	VF	EF
1718	£150	£275	£600

GEORGE III (1760–1820)

	F	VF	EF
1762	£200	£400	£725

George I

FIVE POUNDS

DATE	Mintage	F	VF	EF	UNC

GEORGE III (1760–1820)

DATE	Mintage	F	VF	EF	UNC
1820 (pattern only)	—				Extremely rare

GEORGE IV (1820–30)

1826 proof only	—	—	—	£26,500

VICTORIA (1837–1901)

1839 Proof Only (Una & The Lion) Many Varieties FDC £40,000 upwards

DATE	Mintage	F	VF	EF	UNC
1887	53,844	£1200	£1400	£1800	£2800
1887 Proof	797	—	—	—	£5000
1887 S on ground on rev. (Sydney Mint)					Excessively rare
1893	20,405	£1400	£2000	£2500	£4000
1893 Proof	773	—	—	—	£6000

EDWARD VII (1902–10)

1902	34,910	£1250	£1600	£2200	£2750
1902 Matt proof	8,066	—	—	—	£2500

DATE	MINTAGE	F	VF	EF	UNC

GEORGE V (1911–36)
1911 Proof only	2,812	—	—	—	£4000

GEORGE VI (1937–52)
1937 Proof only	5,501	—	—	—	£2250

Later issues are listed in the Decimal section.

TWO POUNDS

GEORGE III (1760–1820)
1820 (pattern only).............	—	—	—	Extremely rare

GEORGE IV (1820–30)
1823 St George reverse.....	—	£750	£1000	£1750	£2750
1826 Proof only, shield reverse	—	—	—	—	£12000

WILLIAM IV (1830–37)
1831 Proof only	225	—	—	—	£10000

VICTORIA (1837–1901)
1887...................................	91,345	£450	£550	£700	£850
1887 Proof.........................	797	—	—	—	£1750
1887 S on ground of rev. (Sydney Mint)				Excessively rare	
1893...................................	52,212	£500	£650	£900	£1700
1893 Proof.........................	773	—	—	—	£2500

EDWARD VII (1902–10)
1902...................................	45,807	£400	£500	£575	£800
1902 Matt proof.................	8,066	—	—	—	£800

GEORGE V (1911–36)
1911 Proof only	2,812	—	—	—	£1250

GEORGE VI (1937–52)
1937 Proof only	5,501	—	—	—	£1000

Later issues are listed in the Decimal section.

BROAD or GOLD 20 SHILLINGS

	F	VF	EF

OLIVER CROMWELL (1656–58)
	F	VF	EF
1656..	£5,500	£13,500	£28,000

SOVEREIGNS

DATE	MINTAGE	F	VF	EF	UNC

GEORGE III (1760–1820)

DATE	MINTAGE	F	VF	EF	UNC
1817	3,235,239	£500	£800	£1800	£3250
1818	2,347,230	£500	£800	£1800	£3500
1819	3,574		Exceedingly rare		
1820	931,994	£500	£775	£1750	£3200

George III

GEORGE IV (1820–30)

DATE	MINTAGE	F	VF	EF	UNC
1821 First bust, St George reverse	9,405,114	£450	£750	£1500	£2400
1821 — Proof	incl. above	—	—	—	£6250
1822 —	5,356,787	£450	£750	£1500	£2700
1823 —	616,770	£1000	£2750	£7000	—
1824 —	3,767,904	£500	£900	£2000	£3000
1825 —	4,200,343	£700	£2000	£5000	£8000
1825 Second bust, shield reverse	incl. above	£425	£700	£1200	£2350
1826 —	5,724,046	£425	£700	£1200	£2350
1826 — Proof	—	—	—	—	£5000
1827 —	2,266,629	£475	£750	£1500	£2700
1828 —	386,182	£5000	£10000	£25000	—
1829 —	2,444,652	£475	£800	£1800	£2850
1830 —	2,387,881	£475	£800	£1800	£2850

George IV, shield reverse

WILLIAM IV (1830–37)

DATE	MINTAGE	F	VF	EF	UNC
1831	598,547	£600	£1000	£2200	£3800
1831 Proof, plain edge	—	—	—	—	£6250
1832	3,737,065	£500	£900	£2000	£3500
1833	1,225,269	£500	£900	£2000	£3500
1835	723,441	£500	£900	£2000	£3500
1836	1,714,349	£500	£900	£2000	£3500
1837	1,172,984	£525	£950	£2000	£3600

Note—from the Victoria reign onwards, the prices of coins in lower grade will be subject to the bullion price of gold.

VICTORIA (1837–1901)

Many of the gold coins struck at the colonial mints found their way into circulation in Britain, for the sake of completeness these coins are listed here. These can easily be identified by a tiny initial letter for the appropriate mint which can be found below the base of the reverse shield or, in the case of the St George reverse, below the bust on the obverse of the Young Head issues, or on the "ground" below the horse's hoof on the later issues.

William IV

YOUNG HEAD ISSUES

Shield reverse

(Note—Shield back sovereigns in Fine/VF condition, common dates, are normally traded as bullion + a percentage)

DATE	MINTAGE	F	VF	EF	UNC
1838	2,718,694	£700	£1200	£2500	£4500
1839	503,695	£1000	£2750	£5000	£6500
1839 Proof, plain edge	—	—	—	—	£6000
1841	124,054	£3250	£8000	£20000	—
1842	4,865,375	£250	£270	£500	£1200
1843	5,981,968	£250	£270	£500	£1200
1843 "Narrow shield" variety	incl. above	£4000	£10000		
1843 Roman I in date not 1841	—	£750	£1500	—	—
1844	3,000,445	£250	£270	£600	£1200
1845	3,800,845	£250	£270	£600	£1300
1846	3,802,947	£250	£270	£600	£1300

DATE	MINTAGE	F	VF	EF	UNC
1847	4,667,126	£225	£250	£500	£1100
1848	2,246,701	£225	£250	£500	£1100
1849	1,755,399	£225	£250	£500	£1100
1850	1,402,039	£225	£250	£500	£1100
1851	4,013,624	£225	£250	£500	£1100
1852	8,053,435	£225	£250	£500	£1100
1853	10,597,993	£225	£250	£500	£1100
1853 Proof	—	—	—	—	£15000
1854 Incuse WW	3,589,611	£225	£250	£500	£1100
1854 Surface raised WW	3,589,611	£225	£250	£500	£1600
1855	4,806,160	£225	£250	£500	£1000
1856	8,448,482	£225	£250	£500	£1000
1857	4,495,748	£225	£250	£500	£1000
1858	803,234	£225	£250	£500	£1000
1859	1,547,603	£225	£250	£500	£1000
1859 "Ansell" (additional line on lower part of hair ribbon)	—	£700	£1600	£7000	—
1860	2,555,958	£225	£250	£500	£1000
1861	7,624,736	£225	£250	£500	£1000
1862	7,836,413	£225	£250	£500	£1000
1863	5,921,669	£225	£250	£500	£1000
1863 Die No 827 on Truncation				Extremely rare	
1863 with Die number below shield	incl. above	£225	£250	£500	£1000
1864 —	8,656,352	£225	£250	£500	£1000
1865 —	1,450,238	£225	£250	£500	£1000
1866 —	4,047,288	£225	£250	£500	£1000
1868 —	1,653,384	£225	£250	£500	£1000
1869 —	6,441,322	£225	£250	£500	£1000
1870 —	2,189,960	£225	£250	£500	£1000
1871 —	8,767,250	£225	£250	£500	£1000
1872 —	8,767,250	£225	£250	£500	£1000
1872 no Die number	incl. above	£225	£250	£500	£1000
1873 with Die number	2,368,215	£225	£250	£500	£1000
1874 —	520,713	£1700	£4000	£9000	—

M below reverse shield (Melbourne Mint)

1872	748,180	£225	£250	£500	£1000
1873	—			Extremely rare	
1874	1,373,298	£225	£250	£500	£1100
1879				Extremely rare	
1880	3,053,454	£600	£1500	£3500	£9500
1881	2,325,303	£225	£250	£500	£1500
1882	2,465,781	£225	£250	£500	£1000
1883	2,050,450	£225	£250	£500	—
1884	2,942,630	£225	£250	£500	£900
1885	2,967,143	£225	£250	£500	£900
1886	2,902,131	£1800	£4000	£6000	£20000
1887	1,916,424	£600	£1350	£4500	£12000

The mint initial appears below the shield, i.e. "S" indicates that the coin was struck at the Sydney Mint

S below reverse shield (Sydney Mint)

1871	2,814,000	£225	£250	£500	£1300
1872	1,815,000	£225	£250	£500	£1500
1873	1,478,000	£225	£250	£500	£1300
1875	2,122,000	£225	£250	£500	£1300
1877	1,590,000	£225	£250	£500	£1300
1878	1,259,000	£225	£250	£500	£1300
1879	1,366,000	£225	£250	£500	£1300
1880	1,459,000	£225	£250	£500	£2000
1881	1,360,000	£225	£250	£500	£1700
1882	1,298,000	£225	£250	£500	£1500
1883	1,108,000	£225	£250	£500	£1100
1884	1,595,000	£225	£250	£500	£1100
1885	1,486,000	£225	£250	£500	£1100
1886	1,667,000	£225	£250	£500	£1100
1887	1,000,000	£225	£250	£500	£1500

IMPORTANT NOTE: The prices quoted in this guide are set at August 2015 with the price of gold at £726 per ounce and silver £9 per ounce—market fluctuations can have a marked effect on the values of modern precious metal coins.

DATE	MINTAGE	F	VF	EF	UNC
St George & Dragon reverse					
1871	incl. above	£185	£200	£240	£500
1872	incl. above	£185	£200	£240	£500
1873	incl. above	£185	£200	£240	£500
1874	incl. above	£185	£200	£240	£500
1876	3,318,866	£185	£200	£240	£500
1878	1,091,275	£185	£200	£240	£500
1879	20,013	£500	£1100	£4250	—
1880	3,650,080	£185	£200	£240	£500
1884	1,769,635	£185	£200	£240	£500
1885	717,723	£185	£200	£240	£500
M below bust on obverse (Melbourne Mint)					
1872	incl. above	£300	£500	£1100	£4000
1873	752,199	£185	£200	£240	£500
1874	incl. above	£185	£200	£240	£500
1875	incl. above	£185	£200	£240	£500
1876	2,124,445	£185	£200	£240	£500
1877	1,487,316	£185	£200	£240	£500
1878	2,171,457	£185	£200	£240	£500
1879	2,740,594	£185	£200	£240	£500
1880	incl. above	£185	£200	£240	£500
1881	incl. above	£185	£200	£240	£500
1882	incl. above	£185	£200	£240	£500
1883	incl. above	£185	£200	£240	£500
1884	incl. above	£185	£200	£240	£500
1885	incl. above	£185	£200	£240	£500
1886	incl. above	£185	£200	£240	£500
1887	incl. above	£185	£200	£240	£500
S below bust on obverse (Sydney Mint)					
1871	2,814,000	£185	£200	£240	£500
1872	incl. above	£185	£200	£240	£650
1873	incl. above	£185	£200	£240	£500
1874	1,899,000	£185	£200	£240	£500
1875	inc above	£185	£200	£240	£500
1876	1,613,000	£185	£200	£240	£500
1877	—			Unknown	
1879	incl. above	£185	£200	£240	£500
1880	incl. above	£185	£200	£240	£500
1881	incl. above	£185	£200	£240	£500
1882	incl. above	£185	£200	£240	£550
1883	incl. above	£185	£200	£240	£500
1884	incl. above	£185	£200	£240	£500
1885	incl. above	£185	£200	£240	£500
1886	incl. above	£185	£200	£240	£500
1887	incl. above	£185	£200	£240	£500
JUBILEE HEAD ISSUES					
1887	1,111,280	£185	£200	£240	£350
1887 Proof	797	—	—	—	£1850
1888	2,717,424	£185	£200	£240	£350
1889	7,257,455	£185	£200	£240	£350
1890	6,529.887	£185	£200	£240	£350
1891	6,329,476	£185	£200	£240	£350
1892	7,104,720	£185	£200	£240	£350
M on ground on reverse (Melbourne Mint)					
1887	940,000	£185	£200	£240	£350
1888	2,830,612	£185	£200	£240	£350
1889	2,732,590	£185	£200	£240	£350
1890	2,473,537	£185	£200	£240	£350
1891	2,749,592	£185	£200	£240	£350
1892	3,488,750	£185	£200	£240	£350
1893	1,649,352	£185	£200	£240	£350

"M" below the horse's hoof above the date indicates that the coin was struck at the Melbourne Mint

Jubilee head type

DATE	MINTAGE	F	VF	EF	UNC

S on ground on reverse (Sydney Mint)

1887	1,002,000	£185	£400	£1000	£2500
1888	2,187,000	£185	£200	£240	£300
1889	3,262,000	£185	£200	£240	£300
1890	2,808,000	£185	£200	£240	£300
1891	2,596,000	£185	£200	£240	£300
1892	2,837,000	£185	£200	£240	£300
1893	1,498,000	£185	£200	£240	£300

OLD HEAD ISSUES

1893	6,898,260	£185	£200	£240	£300
1893 Proof	773	—	—	—	£2000
1894	3,782,611	£185	£200	£240	£300
1895	2,285,317	£185	£200	£240	£300
1896	3,334,065	£185	£200	£240	£300
1898	4,361,347	£185	£200	£240	£300
1899	7,515,978	£185	£200	£240	£300
1900	10,846,741	£185	£200	£240	£300
1901	1,578,948	£185	£200	£240	£300

M on ground on reverse (Melbourne Mint)

1893	1,914,000	£185	£200	£240	£300
1894	4,166,874	£185	£200	£240	£300
1895	4,165,869	£185	£200	£240	£300
1896	4,456,932	£185	£200	£240	£300
1897	5,130,565	£185	£200	£240	£300
1898	5,509,138	£185	£200	£240	£300
1899	5,579,157	£185	£200	£240	£300
1900	4,305,904	£185	£200	£240	£300
1901	3,987,701	£185	£200	£240	£300

P on ground on reverse (Perth Mint)

1899	690,992	£220	£225	£500	£1850
1900	1,886,089	£185	£200	£240	£300
1901	2,889,333	£185	£200	£240	£300

S on ground on reverse (Sydney Mint)

1893	1,346,000	£185	£200	£300	£450
1894	3,067,000	£185	£200	£240	£300
1895	2,758,000	£185	£200	£240	£300
1896	2,544,000	£185	£200	£240	£300
1897	2,532,000	£185	£200	£240	£300
1898	2,548,000	£185	£200	£240	£300
1899	3,259,000	£185	£200	£240	£300
1900	3,586,000	£185	£200	£240	£300
1901	3,012,000	£185	£200	£240	£300

Old head type

EDWARD VII (1902–10)

1902	4,737,796	£185	£200	£240	£300
1902 Matt proof	15,123	—	—	—	£500
1903	8,888,627	£185	£200	£240	£300
1904	10,041,369	£185	£200	£240	£300
1905	5,910,403	£185	£200	£240	£300
1906	10,466,981	£185	£200	£240	£300
1907	18,458,663	£185	£200	£240	£300
1908	11,729,006	£185	£200	£240	£300
1909	12,157,099	£185	£200	£240	£300
1910	22,379,624	£185	£200	£240	£300

C on ground on reverse (Ottawa Mint)

1908 Satin finish Proof only	633			Extremely rare	
1909	16,300	£220	£225	£325	£600
1910	28,020	£220	£225	£325	£600

DATE	MINTAGE	F	VF	EF	UNC
M on ground on reverse (Melbourne Mint)					
1902..................................	4,267,157	£185	£200	£240	£300
1903..................................	3,521,780	£185	£200	£240	£300
1904..................................	3,743,897	£185	£200	£240	£300
1905..................................	3,633,838	£185	£200	£240	£300
1906..................................	3,657,853	£185	£200	£240	£300
1907..................................	3,332,691	£185	£200	£240	£300
1908..................................	3,080,148	£185	£200	£240	£300
1909..................................	3,029,538	£185	£200	£240	£300
1910..................................	3,054,547	£185	£200	£240	£300
P on ground on reverse (Perth Mint)					
1902	3,289,122	£185	£200	£240	£300
1903..................................	4,674,783	£185	£200	£240	£300
1904..................................	4,506,756	£185	£200	£240	£300
1905..................................	4,876,193	£185	£200	£240	£300
1906..................................	4,829,817	£185	£200	£240	£300
1907..................................	4,972,289	£185	£200	£240	£300
1908..................................	4,875,617	£185	£200	£240	£300
1909..................................	4,524,241	£185	£200	£240	£300
1910..................................	4,690,625	£185	£200	£240	£300
S on ground on reverse (Sydney Mint)					
1902	2,813,000	£185	£200	£240	£280
1902 Proof..........................	incl. above		Extremely rare		
1903..................................	2,806,000	£185	£200	£240	£300
1904..................................	2,986,000	£185	£200	£240	£300
1905..................................	2,778,000	£185	£200	£240	£300
1906..................................	2,792,000	£185	£200	£240	£300
1907..................................	2,539,000	£185	£200	£240	£300
1908..................................	2,017,000	£185	£200	£240	£300
1909..................................	2,057,000	£185	£200	£240	£300
1910..................................	2,135,000	£185	£200	£240	£300

> **IMPORTANT NOTE:** The prices quoted in this guide are set at August 2015 with the price of gold at £726 per ounce and silver £9 per ounce—market fluctuations can have a marked effect on the values of modern precious metal coins.

GEORGE V (1911–36)

(Extra care should be exercised when purchasing as good quality forgeries exist of virtually all dates and mintmarks)

DATE	MINTAGE	F	VF	EF	UNC
1911..................................	30,044,105	£185	£200	£240	£300
1911 Proof..........................	3,764	—	—	—	£700
1912..................................	30,317,921	£185	£200	£240	£300
1913..................................	24,539,672	£185	£200	£240	£300
1914..................................	11,501,117	£185	£200	£240	£300
1915..................................	20,295,280	£185	£200	£240	£300
1916..................................	1,554,120	£185	£200	£240	£300
1917..................................	1,014,714	£1500	£4000	£11000	—
1925..................................	4,406,431	£185	£200	£240	£300
C on ground on reverse (Ottawa Mint)					
1911..................................	256,946	£185	£200	£240	£400
1913..................................	3,715	£275	£300	£1400	—
1914..................................	14,891	£185	£200	£700	—
1916..................................	6,111		Extremely rare		
1917..................................	58,845	£185	£200	£240	£400
1918..................................	106,516	£185	£200	£240	£400
1919..................................	135,889	£185	£200	£240	£400
I on ground on reverse (Bombay Mint)					
1918..................................	1,295,372	£185	£200	£240	—
M on ground on reverse (Melbourne Mint)					
1911..................................	2,851,451	£185	£200	£240	£300
1912..................................	2,469,257	£185	£200	£240	£300
1913..................................	2,323,180	£185	£200	£240	£300
1914..................................	2,012,029	£185	£200	£240	£300
1915..................................	1,637,839	£185	£200	£240	£300
1916..................................	1,273,643	£185	£200	£240	£300
1917..................................	934,469	£185	£200	£240	£300
1918..................................	4,969,493	£185	£200	£240	£300
1919..................................	514,257	£185	£200	£240	£425

DATE	MINTAGE	F	VF	EF	UNC
1920	530,266	£1200	£2000	£4000	£6500
1921	240,121	£4000	£7000	£10000	£20000
1922	608,306	£4000	£7000	£10000	£18500
1923	510,870	£185	£200	£240	£300
1924	278,140	£185	£200	£240	£300
1925	3,311,622	£185	£200	£240	£300
1926	211,107	£185	£200	£240	£300
1928	413,208	£500	£900	£1500	£3000
1929	436,719	£900	£1500	£2500	£4750
1930	77,547	£185	£200	£240	£300
1931	57,779	£185	£200	£400	£700

P on ground on reverse (Perth Mint)

1911	4,373,165	£185	£200	£240	£300
1912	4,278,144	£185	£200	£240	£300
1913	4,635,287	£185	£200	£240	£300
1914	4,815,996	£185	£200	£240	£300
1915	4,373,596	£185	£200	£240	£300
1916	4,096,771	£185	£200	£240	£300
1917	4,110,286	£185	£200	£240	£300
1918	3,812,884	£185	£200	£240	£300
1919	2,995,216	£185	£200	£240	£300
1920	2,421,196	£185	£200	£240	£300
1921	2,134,360	£185	£200	£240	£300
1922	2,298,884	£185	£200	£240	£300
1923	2,124,154	£185	£200	£240	£300
1924	1,464,416	£185	£200	£240	£300
1925	1,837,901	£185	£200	£400	£600
1926	1,313,578	£400	£750	£1500	£3000
1927	1,383,544	£185	£200	£240	£500
1928	1,333,417	£185	£200	£240	£375
1929	1,606,625	£185	£200	£240	£375
1930	1,915,352	£185	£200	£240	£375
1931	1,173,568	£185	£200	£240	£375

S on ground on reverse (Sydney Mint)

1911	2,519,000	£185	£200	£240	£300
1912	2,227,000	£185	£200	£240	£300
1913	2,249,000	£185	£200	£240	£300
1914	1,774,000	£185	£200	£240	£300
1915	1,346,000	£185	£200	£240	£300
1916	1,242,000	£185	£200	£240	£300
1917	1,666,000	£185	£200	£240	£300
1918	3,716,000	£185	£200	£240	£300
1919	1,835,000	£185	£200	£240	£300

DATE	MINTAGE	F	VF	EF	UNC
1920	—		Excessively rare		
1921	839,000	£500	£750	£1850	£2600
1922	578,000		Extremely rare		
1923	416,000		Extremely rare		
1924	394,000	£500	£800	£1500	£2500
1925	5,632,000	£185	£200	£240	£300
1926	1,031,050		Extremely rare		

SA on ground on reverse (Pretoria Mint)

1923	719	£800	£1850	£4000	£7000
1923 Proof	655		Extremely rare		
1924	3,184	—	£2500	£5000	—
1925	6,086,264	£185	£200	£240	£300
1926	11,107,611	£185	£200	£240	£300
1927	16,379,704	£185	£200	£240	£300
1928	18,235,057	£185	£200	£240	£300
1929	12,024,107	£185	£200	£240	£300
1930	10,027,756	£185	£200	£240	£300
1931	8,511,792	£185	£200	£240	£300
1932	1,066,680	£185	£200	£240	£300

GEORGE VI (1937–52)

1937 Proof only	5,501	—	—	£1500	£2100

ELIZABETH II (1952–   )

Pre Decimal Issues

1957	2,072,000	£185	£200	£240	£300
1958	8,700,140	£185	£200	£240	£300
1959	1,358,228	£185	£200	£240	£300
1962	3,000,000	£185	£200	£240	£300
1963	7,400,000	£185	£200	£240	£300
1964	3,000,000	£185	£200	£240	£300
1965	3,800,000	£185	£200	£240	£300
1966	7,050,000	£185	£200	£240	£300
1967	5,000,000	£185	£200	£240	£300
1968	4,203,000	£185	£200	£240	£300

Later issues are included in the Decimal section.

HALF SOVEREIGNS

GEORGE III (1760–1820)

1817	2,080,197	£200	£370	£600	£1000
1818	1,030,286	£220	£400	£700	£1200
1820	35,043	£220	£400	£650	£1200

GEORGE IV (1820–30)

1821 First bust, ornate shield reverse	231,288	£600	£1600	£3200	£5000
1821 — Proof	unrecorded	—	—	—	£5500
1823 First bust, Plain shield rev.	224,280	£200	£280	£700	£1100
1824 —	591,538	£200	£280	£700	£1100
1825 —	761,150	£200	£280	£700	£1000
1826 bare head, shield with full legend reverse	344,830	£200	£320	£700	£1000
1826 — Proof	unrecorded	—	—	—	£2250
1827 —	492,014	£200	£340	£750	£1000
1828 —	1,224,754	£200	£350	£750	£1200

DATE	MINTAGE	F	VF	EF	UNC

WILLIAM IV (1830–37)

DATE	MINTAGE	F	VF	EF	UNC
1831 Proof only	unrecorded	—	—	—	£3200
1834	133,899	£275	£550	£1100	£1800
1835	772,554	£225	£550	£800	£1500
1836	146,865	£200	£400	£800	£1600
1836 obverse from 6d die	incl. above	£1600	£3500	£7000	—
1837	160,207	£220	£475	£850	£1500

VICTORIA (1837–1901)

YOUNG HEAD ISSUES

Shield reverse

DATE	MINTAGE	F	VF	EF	UNC
1838	273,341	£130	£190	£700	£1350
1839 Proof only	1,230	—	—	—	£3000
1841	508,835	£140	£225	£700	£1500
1842	2,223,352	£130	£180	£600	£950
1843	1,251,762	£130	£180	£600	£1000
1844	1,127,007	£130	£180	£600	£900
1845	887,526	£300	£600	£1800	£3500
1846	1,063,928	£140	£180	£600	£900
1847	982,636	£140	£180	£600	£900
1848	410,595	£140	£180	£600	£900
1849	845,112	£140	£180	£600	£900
1850	179,595	£180	£400	£1100	£2500
1851	773,573	£140	£180	£600	£700
1852	1,377,671	£140	£180	£600	£700
1853	2,708,796	£140	£180	£600	£700
1853 Proof	unrecorded	—	—	—	£7500
1854	1,125,144		Extremely rare		
1855	1,120,362	£140	£180	£600	£850
1856	2,391,909	£140	£180	£600	£850
1857	728,223	£140	£180	£600	£850
1858	855,578	£140	£180	£600	£850
1859	2,203,813	£140	£180	£600	£850
1860	1,131,500	£140	£180	£600	£850
1861	1,130,867	£140	£180	£600	£850
1862	unrecorded	£700	£1800	£8000	—
1863	1,571,574	£140	£180	£600	£800
1863 with Die number	incl. above	£140	£180	£600	£850
1864 —	1,758,490	£140	£180	£600	£850
1865 —	1,834,750	£140	£180	£600	£850
1866 —	2,058,776	£140	£180	£600	£850
1867 —	992,795	£140	£180	£600	£750
1869 —	1,861,764	£140	£180	£600	£850
1870 —	1,159,544	£140	£180	£600	£700
1871 —	2,062,970	£140	£180	£600	£850
1872 —	3,248,627	£140	£180	£600	£850
1873 —	1,927,050	£140	£180	£600	£850
1874 —	1,884,432	£140	£180	£600	£850
1875 —	516,240	£140	£180	£600	£850
1876 —	2,785,187	£140	£180	£600	£850
1877 —	2,197,482	£140	£180	£600	£850
1878 —	2,081,941	£140	£180	£600	£850
1879 —	35,201	£140	£180	£600	£850
1880 —	1,009,049	£140	£180	£600	£850
1880 no Die number	incl. above	£140	£180	£600	£600
1883 —	2,870,457	£140	£180	£600	£600
1884 —	1,113,756	£140	£180	£600	£850
1885 —	4,468,871	£140	£180	£600	£850

M below shield (Melbourne Mint)

DATE	MINTAGE	F	VF	EF	UNC
1873	165,034	£120	£195	£1000	—
1877	80,016	£120	£195	£900	—
1881	42,009	£120	£300	£950	—
1882	107,522	£120	£195	£950	—
1884	48,009	£120	£195	£900	—

Date	Mintage	F	VF	EF	UNC
1885..	11,003	£115	£300	£1500	—
1886..	38,008	£115	£140	£1500	—
1887..	64,013	£115	£400	£1500	£4500

S below shield (Sydney Mint)

1871	180,000 (?)	£115	£140	£700	—
1872..	356,000	£115	£140	£700	—
1875..	unrecorded	£115	£140	£700	—
1879..	94,000	£115	£140	£1000	—
1880..	80,000	£115	£400	£1000	—
1881..	62,000	£115	£140	£1000	—
1882..	52,000			Extremely rare	
1883..	220,000	£115	£140	£900	—
1886..	82,000	£115	£140	£900	—
1887..	134,000	£115	£140	£1100	£3750

JUBILEE HEAD ISSUES

1887..	871,770	£115	£125	£150	£175
1887 Proof..................................	797	£115	£125	—	£800
1890..	2.266,023	£115	£125	£150	£175
1891..	1,079,286	£115	£125	£150	£175
1892..	13,680,486	£115	£125	£150	£175
1893..	4,426,625	£115	£125	£150	£175

M below shield (Melbourne Mint)

1887	incl. above	£115	£130	£300	£600
1893..	110,024	£115	£130	£550	—

S below shield (Sydney Mint)

1887..	incl. above	£115	£130	£280	£500
1889..	64,000	£115	£130	£280	—
1891..	154,000	£115	£130	£280	—

OLD HEAD ISSUES

1893..	incl. above	£115	£125	£150	£175
1893 Proof..................................	773	—	—	—	£900
1894..	3,794,591	£115	£125	£150	£175
1895..	2,869,183	£115	£125	£150	£175
1896..	2,946,605	£115	£125	£150	£175
1897..	3,568,156	£115	£125	£150	£175
1898..	2,868,527	£115	£125	£150	£175
1899..	3,361,881	£115	£125	£150	£175
1900..	4,307,372	£115	£125	£150	£175
1901..	2,037,664	£115	£125	£150	£175

M on ground on reverse (Melbourne Mint)

1893	unrecorded			Extremely rare	
1896..	218,946	£115	£125	£450	—
1899..	97,221	£115	£125	£450	—
1900..	112,920	£115	£125	£450	—

P on ground on reverse (Perth Mint)

1899..				Proof Unique	
1900	119,376	£115	£300	£550	—

S on ground on reverse (Sydney Mint)

1893..	250,000	£115	£125	£375	—
1897..	unrecorded	£115	£125	£350	—
1900..	260,00	£115	£125	£350	—

EDWARD VII (1902–10)

1902..	4,244,457	£100	£115	£140	£150
1902 Matt proof..........................	15,123	—	—	—	£375
1903..	2,522,057	£100	£115	£140	£150
1904..	1,717,440	£100	£115	£140	£150
1905..	3,023,993	£100	£115	£140	£150
1906..	4,245,437	£100	£115	£140	£150
1907..	4,233,421	£100	£115	£140	£150
1908..	3,996,992	£100	£115	£140	£150
1909..	4,010,715	£100	£115	£140	£150
1910..	5,023,881	£100	£115	£140	£150

DATE		F	VF	EF	UNC
M on ground on reverse (Melbourne Mint)					
1906	82,042	£100	£115	£150	£350
1907	405,034	£100	£115	£150	£325
1908	incl. above	£100	£115	£150	£350
1909	186,094	£100	£115	£150	£325
P on ground on reverse (Perth Mint)					
1904	60,030	£100	£115	£500	—
1908	24,668	£100	£115	£500	—
1909	44,022	£100	£115	£500	—
S on ground on reverse (Sydney Mint)					
1902	84,000	£100	£115	£140	£325
1902 Proof			Extremely rare		
1903	231,000				£300
1906	308,00	£100	£115	£140	£300
1908	538,000	£100	£115	£140	£300
1910	474,000	£100	£115	£140	£300

GEORGE V (1911–36)

		F	VF	EF	UNC
1911	6,104,106	£100	£115	£140	£150
1911 Proof	3,764	—	—	—	£425
1912	6,224,316	£100	£115	£140	£150
1913	6,094,290	£100	£115	£140	£150
1914	7,251,124	£100	£115	£140	£150
1915	2,042,747	£100	£115	£140	£150
M on ground on reverse (Melbourne Mint)					
1915	125,664	£100	£115	£140	£150
P on ground on reverse (Perth Mint)					
1911	130,373	£100	£115	£140	£225
1915	136,219	£100	£115	£140	£225
1918	unrecorded	£175	£500	£1000	£2000
S on ground on reverse (Sydney Mint)					
1911	252,000	£100	£115	£140	£150
1912	278,000	£100	£115	£140	£150
1914	322,000	£100	£115	£140	£150
1915	892,000	£100	£115	£140	£150
1916	448,000	£100	£115	£140	£150
SA on ground on reverse (Pretoria Mint)					
1923 Proof only	655	—	—	—	£900
1925	946,615	£100	£115	£140	£150
1926	806,540	£100	£115	£140	£150

GEORGE VI (1937–52)

		F	VF	EF	UNC
1937 Proof only	5,501	—	—	—	£550

Later issues are included in the Decimal section.

The reference books used by collectors and dealers throughout the world

WORLD COIN CATALOG® PRICES:

1601–1700	£61.99+p&p
1701–1800	£57.99+p&p
1801–1900	£58.99+p&p
1901–2000	£47.99+p&p
2001–Date	£37.99+p&p
South Asia Coin & Paper	£41.99+p&p

These excellent books are essential references, however they are heavy. Postage costs are: £8* for 1 volume. For bulk orders of these books, please call for details.

*These prices are UK only.
Europe / Worldwide (surface) £10
Worldwide (airmail) £18

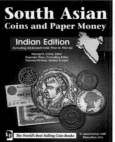

To world coin collectors the Krause series certainly needs no introduction. The *Standard Catalog® of World Coins* is now divided into five comprehensive volumes covering the 17th, 18th, 19th, 20th and 21st centuries, along with a companion volume detailing the 'unusual world coins' that are becoming popular amongst collectors. The Krause series is unique inasmuch that in these volumes just about every conceivable coin ever minted worldwide since 1601 has been catalogued and valued (in US$). These huge books are essential references for any coin collector.

Order your copies today and take advantage of our great postage rates if you order one volume or more.

Krause Paper Money

The catalogues comprise three volumes—Specialised Issues, General Issues and Modern Issues. All volumes contain thousands of illustrations and every item is catalogued and valued in various grades, making these publications the essential collectors' guides.

Vol. I. Specialised Issues £61.99,
Vol. II. General Issues £61.99,
Vol. III. Modern Issues £51.99

(Plus postage as above)

TO ORDER CALL 01404 44166

log on to www.tokenpublishing.com
or write to Token Publishing Ltd, Orchard House, Duchy Road, Heathpark, Honiton, Devon, EX14 1YD

CROWNS

DATE	F	VF	EF	UNC

OLIVER CROMWELL

1658 8 over 7 (always)	£1800	£3500	£6500	—
1658 Dutch Copy		Extremely rare		
1658 Patterns. In Various Metals		Extremely rare		

CHARLES II (1660–85)

1662 First bust, rose (2 varieties)	£250	£800	£4500	—
1662 — no rose (2 varieties)	£250	£800	£4500	—
1663 —	£250	£800	£4250	—
1664 Second bust	£200	£800	£4000	—
1665 —	£1500	£4000	—	—
1666 —	£300	£900	£4750	—
1666 — error RE.X for REX		Extremely rare		
1666 — Elephant below bust	£700	£2500	£15000	—
1667 —	£160	£500	£3000	—
1668/7 — 8 over 7	£170	£550		—
1668 —	£170	£550	£3500	—
1669/8 — 9 over 8	£350	£800	—	—
1669 —	£300	£1000	£4750	—
1670/69 — 70 over 69	£200	£1000		—
1670 —	£175	£600	£3500	—
1671	£170	£600	£3000	—
1671 Third bust	£170	£600	£3000	—
1672 —	£170	£500	£3000	—
1673 —	£170	£500	£3000	—
1674 —		Extremely rare		
1675 —	£700	£2200	—	—
1675/3 —	£700	£2200	—	—
1676 —	£175	£550	£3000	—
1677 —	£180	£550	£3000	—
1677/6 — 7 over 6	£200	£900	—	—
1678/7 —	£200	£900	—	—
1678/7 — 8 over 7	£275	£850	—	—
1679 —	£180	£600	£3000	—
1679 Fourth bust	£180	£600	£3000	—
1680 Third bust	£180	£800	£3500	—
1680/79 — 80 over 79	£200	£800	—	—
1680 Fourth bust	£180	£750	£4000	—
1680/79 — 80 over 79	£200	£1000	—	—
1681 —	£180	£600	£3500	—
1681 — Elephant & Castle below bust	£3000	£10000	—	—
1682/1 —	£180	£700	£3250	—
1682 — edge error QVRRTO for QVARTO	£400	—	—	—
1683 —	£400	£1000	£4000	—
1684 —	£400	£1300	—	—

JAMES II (1685–88)

1686 First bust	£325	£950	£5000	—
1686 — No stops on obv	£400	£1500	—	—
1687 Second bust	£275	£700	£3500	—
1688/7 — 8 over 7	£280	£800	—	—
1688 —	£275	£800	£3500	—

WILLIAM AND MARY (1688–94)

1691	£600	£1600	£4800	—
1692	£600	£1600	£4750	—
1692 2 over upside down 2	£600	£1600	£4750	—

DATE	F	VF	EF	UNC

WILLIAM III (1694–1702)

DATE	F	VF	EF	UNC
1695 First bust	£100	£300	£1900	—
1696 —	£90	£275	£1700	—
1696 — no stops on obv.	£225	£400	—	—
1996 — no stops obv./rev.	£250	£400	—	—
1696 — GEI for DEI	£750	£1800	—	—
1696 Second bust				Unique
1696 Third bust	£90	£275	£1700	—
1697 —	£1500	£5000	£18500	—
1700 Third bust variety edge year DUODECIMO	£140	£550	£1800	—
1700 — edge year DUODECIMO TERTIO..	£140	£550	£1800	—

ANNE (1702–14)

DATE	F	VF	EF	UNC
1703 First bust, VIGO	£350	£1000	£4000	—
1705 — Plumes in angles on rev.	£500	£1500	£6000	—
1706 — Roses & Plumes in angles on rev...	£160	£600	£2200	—
1707 — —	£160	£600	£2200	—
1707 Second bust, E below	£160	£500	£2100	—
1707 — Plain	£160	£500	£2100	—
1708 — E below	£160	£500	£2100	—
1708/7 — 8 over 7	£160	£800	—	—
1708 — Plain	£160	£600	£2100	—
1708 — — error BR for BRI.......................			Extremely rare	
1708 — Plumes in angles on rev.	£180	£700	£2500	—
1713 Third bust, Roses & Plumes in angles on rev..	£180	£700	£2500	—

GEORGE I (1714–27)

DATE	F	VF	EF	UNC
1716...	£600	£1600	£6000	—
1718 8 over 6...	£600	£1600	£5000	—
1720 20 over 18...	£600	£1600	£5000	—
1723 SSC in angles on rev. (South Sea Co.)	£600	£1600	£5000	—
1726	£600	£1600	£5500	—

GEORGE II (1727–60)

DATE	F	VF	EF	UNC
1732 Young head, Plain, Proof	—	—	£12,000	—
1732 — Roses & Plumes in angles on rev ..	£325	£700	£2750	—
1734 — —	£325	£700	£2750	—
1735 — —	£325	£700	£2750	—
1736 — —	£325	£700	£2750	—
1739 — Roses in angles on rev..................	£325	£600	£2750	—
1741 — —	£325	£600	£2500	—
1743 Old head, Roses in angles on rev.......	£225	£600	£2250	—
1746 — — LIMA below bust	£225	£600	£2250	—
1746 — Plain, Proof	—	—	£7500	—
1750 — —	£400	£1100	£3500	—
1751 — —	£500	£1400	£3800	—

GEORGE III (1760–1820)

DATE	F	VF	EF	UNC
Dollar with oval counterstamp....................	£175	£650	£1000	—
Dollar with octagonal counterstamp	£200	£600	£850	—
1804 Bank of England Dollar, Britannia rev.	£120	£275	£550	—
1818 LVIII...	£40	£100	£250	£800
1818 LIX	£40	£100	£250	£800
1819 LIX	£40	£100	£250	£800
1819 LIX 9 over 8	£45	£150	£400	—
1819 LIX no stops on edge	£60	£150	£400	£1000
1819 LX	£40	£100	£325	£900
1820 LX	£35	£100	£300	£800
1820 LX 20 over 19	£35	£200	£500	—

DATE	MINTAGE	F	VF	EF	UNC

GEORGE IV (1820–30)

1821 First bust, St George rev.

	MINTAGE	F	VF	EF	UNC
SECUNDO on edge	437,976	£40	£180	£700	£1500
1821 — — Proof......................... Incl. above		£40	£180	—	£5000
1821 — — Proof TERTIO (error edge)Incl above		£40	£180	—	£4000
1822 — — SECUNDO.................. 124,929		£40	£180	£700	£1500
1822 — — TERTIO .... Incl above		£40	£180	£700	£1500
1823 — — Proof only				Extremely rare	
1826 Second bust, shield rev, SEPTIMO					
Proof only.................................		—	—	£2200	£8500

WILLIAM IV (1830–37)

					UNC
1831 Proof only W.W. on truncation............		—	—		£15000
1831 Proof only W. WYON on truncation....		—	—		£17500
1834 Proof only		—	—		—£30000

VICTORIA (1837–1901)

YOUNG HEAD ISSUES

	MINTAGE	F	VF	EF	UNC
1839 Proof only	—	—	—		—£10000
1844 Star stops on edge.............	94,248	£50	£260	£1200	£3000
1844 Cinquefoil stops on edge ...	incl. above	£50	£260	£1200	£3000
1845 Star stops on edge.............	159,192	£50	£260	£1200	£3000
1845 Cinquefoil stops on edge ...	incl. above	£50	£260	£1200	£3000
1847..	140,976	£60	£280	£1300	£4000

GOTHIC HEAD ISSUES (Proof only)

	MINTAGE	F	VF	EF	UNC
1847 mdcccxlvii UNDECIMO on edge	8,000	£650	£1100	£1900	£3200
1847 — Plain edge......................		—	—	—	£3800
1853 mdcccliii SEPTIMO on edge	460	—	—	—	£9000
1853 — Plain edge......................		—	—	—	—£15000

JUBILEE HEAD ISSUES

	MINTAGE	F	VF	EF	UNC
1887	173,581	£20	£30	£60	£150
1887 Proof..................................	1,084	—	—	—	£1000
1888 Narrow date........................	131,899	£20	£35	£90	£240
1888 Wide date	incl above	£25	£60	£300	—
1889..	1,807,224	£20	£30	£60	£150
1890..	997,862	£20	£30	£70	£225
1891..	556,394	£20	£30	£70	£225
1892..	451,334	£20	£30	£80	£250

OLD HEAD ISSUES (Regnal date on edge in Roman numerals)

	MINTAGE	F	VF	EF	UNC
1893 LVI......................................	497,845	£20	£45	£150	£375
1893 LVII.....................................	incl. above	£20	£45	£200	£425
1893 Proof..................................	1,312	—	—	—	£1250
1894 LVII.....................................	144,906	£20	£45	£175	£400
1894 LVIII....................................	incl. above	£20	£45	£175	£400
1895 LVIII	252,862	£20	£45	£175	£400
1895 LIX	incl. above	£20	£45	£175	£400
1896 LIX	317,599	£20	£45	£175	£450
1896 LX	incl. above	£20	£45	£175	£400
1897 LX	262,118	£20	£45	£175	£400
1897 LXI	incl. above	£20	£45	£175	£450
1898 LXI	166,150	£20	£45	£175	£500
1898 LXII	incl. above	£20	£45	£175	£400
1899 LXII	166,300	£20	£45	£175	£400
1899 LXIII	incl. above	£20	£45	£175	£400
1900 LXIII	353,356	£20	£45	£175	£400
1900 LXIV	incl. above	£20	£45	£175	£400

Victoria, Jubilee head

DATE	MINTAGE	F	VF	EF	UNC

EDWARD VII (1901–10)

1902..	256,020	£65	£120	£190	£275
1902 "Matt Proof"	15,123	—	—	—	£275

GEORGE V (1910–36)

1927 Proof only	15,030	—	£100	£170	£350
1928..	9,034	£110	£160	£300	£500
1929..	4,994	£110	£160	£300	£500
1930..	4,847	£110	£160	£300	£525
1931..	4,056	£110	£160	£300	£500
1932..	2,395	£200	£400	£800	£1250
1933..	7,132	£110	£160	£300	£525
1934..	932	£800	£1600	£3500	£5500
1935 Jubilee issue. Incuse edge inscription	714,769	£15	£20	£30	£45
1935 — — error edge inscription	incl. above	—	—	—	£1500
1935 — Specimen in box	incl. above	—	—	—	£60
1935 — Proof	incl. above	—	—	—	£200
1935 — Proof. Raised edge inscription	2,500	—	—	£175	£300
1935 — — fine lettering..............	incl. above	—	—	—	£1000
1935 — — error edge inscription	incl. above	—	—	—	£1500
1935 — Gold proof......................	30	—	—	Extremely rare	
1936..	2,473	£180	£350	£600	£1000

GEORGE VI (1936–52)

1937 Coronation..........................	418,699	£18	£24	£38	£55
1937 Proof...................................	26,402	—	—	—	£65
1951 Festival of Britain, Proof-like	1,983,540	—	—	£4	£7

ELIZABETH II (1952–   )

Pre-Decimal issues (Five Shillings)

1953	5,962,621	—	—	£3	£6
1953 Proof...................................	40,000	—	—	—	£25
1960..	1,024,038	—	—	£3	£6
1960 Polished dies	70,000	—	—	—	£9
1965 Churchill	19,640,000	—	—	—	£1

Later issues are listed in the Decimal section.

DOUBLE FLORINS

VICTORIA (1837–1901)

1887 Roman I	483,347	£15	£30	£50	£110
1887 Roman I Proof	incl. above	—	—	—	£550
1887 Arabic 1	incl. above	£15	£30	£50	£110
1887 Arabic 1 Proof....................	incl. above	—	—	—	£550
1888..	243,340	£15	£40	£80	£130
1888 Second I in VICTORIA an inverted 1	incl. above	£22	£45	£90	£350
1889..	1,185,111	£18	£30	£45	£130
1889 inverted 1...........................	incl. above	£25	£45	£90	£350
1890..	782,146	£15	£40	£60	£130

Patterns were also produced in 1911, 1914 and 1950 and are all extremely rare.

HALFCROWNS

DATE	MINTAGE	F	VF	EF	UNC

OLIVER CROMWELL

DATE	MINTAGE	F	VF	EF	UNC
1656				Extremely rare	
1658		£1200	£2250	£4700	—
1658 Proof in Gold				Extremely rare	

CHARLES II (1660–1685)

DATE	MINTAGE	F	VF	EF	UNC
1663 First bust		£160	£600	£3500	—
1663 — no stops on obv.		£200	£800	—	—
1664 Second bust		£250	£1200	£5000	—
1666 Third bust		£900	—	—	—
1666 — Elephant		£800	£3300	—	—
1667/4 — 7 over 4				Extremely rare	
1668/4 — 8 over 4		£300	£1500	—	—
1669 —		£400	£1600	—	—
1669/4 — 9 over 4		£250	£900	—	—
1670 —		£125	£500	£2500	—
1670 — MRG for MAG		£300	£1000	—	—
1671 —		£140	£450	£2500	—
1671/0 — 1 over 0		£150	£600	£3000	—
1672 — Third bust				Extremely rare	
1672 Fourth bust		£140	£500	£2750	—
1673 —		£140	£500	£2500	—
1673 — Plumes both sides				Extremely rare	
1673 — Plume below bust		£6500	£18,000	—	—
1674 —		£150	£650	—	—
1675 —		£140	£400	£2000	—
1676 —		£140	£400	£2000	—
1676 — inverted 1 in date		£140	£400	£2000	—
1677 —		£140	£400	£1800	—
1678 —		£200	£800	—	—
1679 — GRATTA error				Extremely rare	
1679 —		£140	£400	£1800	—
1680 —		£175	£750	—	—
1681/0 — 1 over 0		£250	—	—	—
1681 —		£145	£500	£2350	—
1681 — Elephant & Castle		£3500	£10000	—	—
1682 —		£140	£475	£3000	—
1683 —		£140	£500	£2750	—
1683 — Plume below bust				Extremely rare	
1684/3 — 4 over 3		£325	£900	£4200	—

JAMES II (1685–1688)

DATE	MINTAGE	F	VF	EF	UNC
1685 First bust		£220	£600	£3200	—
1686 —		£220	£600	£3500	—
1686/5 — 6 over 5		£220	£700	—	—
1686 — V over S		£225	£750	—	—
1687 —		£220	£650	£3300	—
1687/6 — 7 over 6		£300	£850	—	—
1687 Second bust		£200	£600	£3200	—
1688 —		£200	£600	£3000	—

WILLIAM AND MARY (1688–1694)

DATE	MINTAGE	F	VF	EF	UNC
1689 First busts; first shield		£100	£350	£1600	—
1689 — — no pearls in crown		£100	£350	£1600	—
1689 — — FRA for FR		£160	£600	£2000	—
1689 — — No stop on obv		£100	£500	£1850	—
1689 — Second shield		£100	£350	£1600	—
1689 — — no pearls in crown		£100	£350	£1600	—
1690 — —		£160	£700	£2600	—
1690 — — error GRETIA for GRATIA		£500	£1500	£5000	—
1691 Second busts		£150	£450	£2200	—
1692 —		£150	£450	£2200	—

DATE	MINTAGE	F	VF	EF	UNC
1693 —		£170	£450	£2200	—
1693 — 3 over inverted 3		£180	£650	£2750	—

WILLIAM III (1694–1702)

DATE	MINTAGE	F	VF	EF	UNC
1696 First bust, large shields, early harp		£70	£240	£900	—
1696 — — — B (Bristol) below bust		£70	£240	£1000	—
1696 — — — C (Chester)..................................		£80	£325	£1100	—
1696 — — — E (Exeter)		£100	£400	£1300	—
1696 — — — N (Norwich)		£90	£400	£1300	—
1696 — — — y (York)		£80	£350	£1500	—
1696 — — — — Scottish arms at date............				Extremely rare	
1696 — — ordinary harp		£80	£275	£1400	—
1696 — — — C		£110	£500	£1100	
1696 — — — E..		£100	£500	£1100	—
1696 — — — N		£150	£600	£2250	—
1696 — Small shields, ordinary harp		£70	£250	£1000	—
1696 — — — B		£90	£300	£1100	—
1696 — — — C		£90	£300	£1300	—
1696 — — — E..		£100	£450	£2000	—
1696 — — — N		£110	£450	£1500	—
1696 — — — y		£100	£500	£1600	—
1696 Second bust				Only one known	
1697 First bust, large shields, ordinary harp		£75	£300	£1100	—
1697 — — — GRR for GRA				Extremely rare	
1697 — — — B		£80	£300	£1200	—
1697 — — — C		£80	£350	£1250	—
1697 — — — E..		£90	£350	£1250	—
1697 — — — N		£100	£350	£1250	—
1697 — — — y		£90	£350	£1300	—
1698 —		£100	£350	£1300	—
1698/7 — — 8 over 7				Extremely rare	
1699 — —		£140	£450	£1800	—
1699 — — Scottish arms at date.....................				Extremely rare	
1700 — —		£120	£375	£1600	—
1701 — —		£125	£400	£1700	—
1701 — — No stops on rev.............................		£150	£600	—	—
1701 — — Elephant & Castle below .... Fair £2200					
1701 — — Plumes in angles on rev.		£230	£650	£3000	—

ANNE (1702–1714)

DATE	MINTAGE	F	VF	EF	UNC
1703 Plain (pre-Union)......................................		£600	£2200	—	—
1703 VIGO below bust		£100	£340	£1100	—
1704 Plumes in angles on rev...........................		£150	£500	£1600	—
1705 —		£120	£500	£1750	—
1706 Roses & Plumes in angles on rev.		£90	£350	£1400	—
1707 —		£80	£300	£1100	—
1707 Plain (post-Union)...................................		£80	£200	£900	—
1707 E below bust...		£80	£200	£900	—
1707 — SEPTIMO edge				Extremely rare	
1708 Plain..		£80	£250	£1000	—
1708 E below bust...		£80	£250	£1000	—
1708 Plumes in angles on rev...........................		£90	£275	£1100	—
1709 Plain..		£75	£275	£900	—
1709 E below bust...		£220	£900	—	—
1710 Roses & Plumes in angles on rev.		£80	£325	£1000	—
1712 —		£80	£325	£1000	—
1713 Plain..		£80	£325	£1000	—
1713 Roses & Plumes in angles on rev.		£80	£325	£1000	—
1714 —		£80	£325	£1000	—
1714/3 4 over 3		£125	£500	—	—

GEORGE I (1714–1727)

DATE	MINTAGE	F	VF	EF	UNC
1715 Roses & Plumes in angles on rev.		£450	£900	£3200	—
1715 Plain edge...				Extremely rare	
1717 —		£450	£900	£3200	—
1720 —		£425	£900	£3200	—
1720/17 20 over 17		£400	£800	£3000	—
1723 SSC in angles on rev.		£400	£800	£2750	—
1726 Small Roses & Plumes in angles on rev... .		£4000	£11,500	—	—

DATE	MINTAGE	F	VF	EF	UNC

GEORGE II (1727–1760)

DATE	MINTAGE	F	VF	EF	UNC
1731 Young head, Plain, proof only	—	—	—	£5500	—
1731 — Roses & Plumes in angles on rev.	—	£160	£400	£1500	—
1732 — —	—	£160	£400	£1500	—
1734 — —	—	£160	£400	£1550	—
1735 — —	—	£160	£400	£1550	—
1736 — —	—	£160	£400	£1550	—
1739 — Roses in angles on rev.	—	£150	£380	£1450	—
1741/39 — — 41 over 30	—	£160	£550	—	—
1741 — —	—	£150	£400	£1450	—
1743 Old head, Roses in angles on rev.	—	£85	£225	£1000	—
1745 — —	—	£85	£225	£1000	—
1745 — LIMA below bust	—	£70	£175	£650	—
1746 — —	—	£70	£175	£650	—
1746/5 — — 6 over 5	—	£80	£220	£800	—
1746 — Plain, Proof	—	—	—	£3500	—
1750 — —	—	£200	£500	£1800	—
1751 — —	—	£240	£700	£2000	—

GEORGE III (1760–1820)

DATE	MINTAGE	F	VF	EF	UNC
1816 "Bull head"	—	£25	£80	£250	£500
1817 —	8,092,656	£25	£80	£250	£500
1817 "Small head"	incl. above	£25	£80	£250	£500
1818 —	2,905,056	£25	£80	£250	£500
1819/8 — 9 over 8	incl. above			Extremely rare	
1819 —	4,790,016	£25	£80	£250	£525
1820 —	2,396,592	£50	£140	£500	£1000

GEORGE IV (1820–30)

DATE	MINTAGE	F	VF	EF	UNC
1820 First bust, first reverse	incl. above	£30	£80	£300	£600
1821 — —	1,435,104	£30	£80	£300	£600
1821 — — Proof	incl. above	—	—	—	£2500
1823 — —	2,003,760	£1000	£3000	—	—
1823 — Second reverse	incl. above	£30	£80	£300	£600
1824 — —	465,696	£30	£90	£275	£650
1824 Second bust, third reverse .	incl. above			Extremely rare	
1825 — —	2,258,784	£30	£80	£200	£450
1826 — —	2,189,088	£30	£80	£200	£450
1826 — — Proof	incl. above	—	—	—	£1500
1828 — —	49,890	£80	£200	£600	£1100
1829 — —	508,464	£60	£150	£450	£900

WILLIAM IV (1830–37)

DATE	MINTAGE	F	VF	EF	UNC
1831	—	—	—	Extremely rare	
1831 Proof (W.W. in script & block)	—	—	—	—	£2200
1834 W.W. in block	993,168	£30	£80	£300	£700
1834 W.W. in script	incl. above	£30	£80	£300	£700
1835	281,952	£35	£90	£300	£750
1836	1,588,752	£30	£70	£275	£650
1836/5 6 over 5	incl. above	£60	£125	£600	—
1837	150,526	£45	£160	£550	£1150

VICTORIA (1837–1901)

YOUNG HEAD ISSUES

DATE	MINTAGE	F	VF	EF	UNC
1839 (two varieties)	—	£1100	£3500	£8500	—
1839 Proof	—	—	—	—	£5000
1840	386,496	£60	£200	£700	£1800
1841	42,768	£900	£2000	£4000	£7500
1842	486,288	£55	£150	£700	£1500
1843	454,608	£140	£450	£1100	£3200
1844	1,999,008	£45	£110	£550	£1400
1845	2,231,856	£45	£110	£550	£1400
1846	1,539,668	£55	£140	£600	£1400
1848 Plain 8	367,488	£150	£450	£1400	£3750
1848/6	incl. above	£120	£300	£800	£2800
1849	261,360	£70	£160	£600	£1600
1849 Small date	incl. above	£90	£220	£850	£1900

DATE	MINTAGE	F	VF	EF	UNC
1850	484,613	£70	£200	£600	£2000
1853 Proof only	—	—	—	—	£4250
1874	2,188,599	£25	£70	£250	£600
1875	1,113,483	£25	£70	£250	£550
1876	633,221	£30	£80	£280	£650
1876/5 6 over 5	incl. above	£35	£80	£280	£650
1877	447,059	£25	£70	£250	£550
1878	1,466,323	£25	£70	£250	£550
1879	901,356	£35	£80	£280	£650
1880	1,346,350	£25	£70	£250	£500
1881	2,301,495	£25	£70	£250	£475
1882	808,227	£30	£70	£250	£475
1883	2,982,779	£25	£70	£250	£450
1884	1,569,175	£25	£70	£250	£450
1885	1,628,438	£25	£70	£250	£440
1886	891,767	£25	£70	£250	£440
1887	1,438,046	£25	£65	£240	£440
JUBILEE HEAD ISSUES					
1887	incl. above	£8	£14	£30	£75
1887 Proof	1,084	—	—	—	£350
1888	1,428,787	£12	£25	£50	£160
1889	4,811,954	£10	£20	£50	£140
1890	3,228,111	£12	£22	£70	£160
1891	2,284,632	£12	£22	£70	£160
1892	1,710,946	£12	£22	£75	£175
OLD HEAD ISSUES					
1893	1,792,600	£12	£25	£60	£100
1893 Proof	1,312	—	—	—	£600
1894	1,524,960	£15	£35	£90	£240
1895	1,772,662	£12	£30	£70	£170
1896	2,148,505	£12	£22	£65	£180
1897	1,678,643	£12	£22	£65	£160
1898	1,870,055	£12	£22	£65	£160
1899	2,865,872	£12	£22	£65	£160
1900	4,479,128	£12	£22	£65	£160
1901	1,516,570	£12	£22	£65	£160

DATE	MINTAGE	F	VF	EF	UNC

EDWARD VII (1901–10)

DATE	MINTAGE	F	VF	EF	UNC
1902	1,316,008	£12	£30	£80	£160
1902 "Matt Proof"	15,123	—	—	—	£200
1903	274,840	£175	£550	£2200	£4500
1904	709,652	£60	£225	£500	£1500
1905	166,008	£500	£1400	£5000	£9000
1906	2,886,206	£12	£50	£200	£800
1907	3,693,930	£12	£50	£200	£800
1908	1,758,889	£20	£80	£400	£1200
1909	3,051,592	£12	£60	£340	£700
1910	2,557,685	£12	£45	£120	£450

GEORGE V (1910–36)

First issue

DATE	MINTAGE	F	VF	EF	UNC
1911	2,914,573	£12	£30	£70	£160
1911 Proof	6,007	—	—	—	£240
1912	4,700,789	£10	£22	£50	£175
1913	4,090,169	£10	£24	£75	£185
1914	18,333,003	£7	£12	£40	£65
1915	32,433,066	£7	£12	£35	£60
1916	29,530,020	£7	£12	£35	£60
1917	11,172,052	£8	£15	£45	£95
1918	29,079,592	£7	£12	£35	£70
1919	10,266,737	£7	£15	£45	£95

Second issue—debased silver

DATE	MINTAGE	F	VF	EF	UNC
1920	17,982,077	£4	£8	£22	£70
1921	23,677,889	£4	£8	£22	£60
1922	16,396,724	£5	£9	£24	£70
1923	26,308,526	£6	£8	£20	£45
1924	5,866,294	£15	£35	£90	£200
1925	1,413,461	£30	£75	£300	£900
1926	4,473,516	£10	£25	£45	£175

Third issue —Modified effigy

DATE	MINTAGE	F	VF	EF	UNC
1926	incl. above	£6	£14	£40	£100
1927	6,837,872	£6	£12	£35	£70

Fourth issue—New shield reverse

DATE	MINTAGE	F	VF	EF	UNC
1927 Proof	15,000	—	—	—	£90
1928	18,762,727	£5	£8	£20	£35
1929	17,632,636	£5	£8	£20	£35
1930	809,051	£15	£60	£300	£850
1931	11,264,468	£5	£8	£20	£35
1932	4,793,643	£6	£10	£25	£90
1933	10,311,494	£5	£8	£20	£40
1934	2,422,399	£7	£12	£65	£185
1935	7,022,216	£5	£8	£18	£25
1936	7,039,423	£5	£8	£18	£20

George V, fourth issue, new shield reverse

GEORGE VI (1936–52)

DATE	MINTAGE	F	VF	EF	UNC
1937	9,106,440	—	£6	£9	£14
1937 Proof	26,402	—	—	—	£20
1938	6,426,478	£5	£6	£15	£25
1939	15,478,635	£5	£6	£9	£10
1940	17,948,439	£5	£6	£9	£10
1941	15,773,984	£5	£6	£9	£10
1942	31,220,090	£5	£6	£9	£10
1943	15,462,875	£5	£6	£9	£10
1944	15,255,165	£5	£6	£9	£10
1945	19,849,242	£5	£6	£9	£10
1946	22,724,873	£5	£6	£9	£10

Cupro-nickel

DATE	MINTAGE	F	VF	EF	UNC
1947	21,911,484	—	£1	£2	£4
1948	71,164,703	—	£1	£2	£4
1949	28,272,512	—	£1	£2	£6
1950	28,335,500	—	£1	£2	£6
1950 Proof	17,513	—	£1	£2	£10
1951	9,003,520	—	£1	£2	£6
1951 Proof	20,000	—	—	—	£10
1952				Only one known	

DATE	MINTAGE	F	VF	EF	UNC

ELIZABETH II (1952–   )

1953	4,333,214	—	—	£1	£3
1953 Proof....................................	40,000	—	—	—	£8
1954..	11,614,953	—	£1	£6	£35
1955..	23,628,726	—	—	£1	£6
1956..	33,934,909	—	—	£1	£6
1957..	34,200,563	—	—	£1	£6
1958..	15,745,668	—	£1	£6	£28
1959..	9,028,844	—	£1	£9	£32
1960..	19,929,191	—	—	£1	£2
1961..	25,887,897	—	—	—	£2
1961 Polished dies	incl. above	—	—	£1	£2
1962..	24,013,312	—	—	—	£1
1963..	17,625,200	—	—	—	£1
1964..	5,973,600	—	—	—	£1
1965..	9,778,440	—	—	—	£1
1966..	13,375,200	—	—	—	£1
1967..	33,058,400	—	—	—	£1
1970 Proof....................................	—	—	—	—	£8

FLORINS

VICTORIA (1837–1901)

YOUNG (CROWNED) HEAD ISSUES
"Godless" type (without D.G.—"Dei Gratia")

1848 "Godless" Pattern only plain edge	—			Very rare	
1848 "Godless" Pattern only milled edge	—			Extremely rare	
1849	413,820	£25	£60	£200	£400

(Beware of recent forgeries)

"Gothic" type i.e. date in Roman numerals in obverse legend
"brit." in legend. No die no.

1851 mdcccli Proof	1,540			Extremely rare	
1852 mdccclii	1,014,552	£22	£60	£200	£500
1853 mdcccliii	3,919,950	£22	£55	£200	£550
1853 — Proof	incl. above	—	—	—	£3500
1854 mdcccliv	550,413	£500	£1500	—	—
1855 mdccclv	831,017	£25	£70	£225	£550
1856 mdccclvi	2,201,760	£25	£70	£225	£550
1857 mdccclvii	1,671,120	£25	£55	£225	£550
1858 mdccclviii	2,239,380	£24	£55	£225	£550
1859 mdccclix	2,568,060	£24	£55	£200	£550
1860 mdccclx	1,475,100	£35	£80	£250	£700
1862 mdccclxii	594,000	£240	£600	£1200	£3000
1863 mdccclxiii	938,520	£900	£1800	£3500	£7000

"brit" in legend. Die no. below bust

1864 mdccclxiv	1,861,200	£24	£55	£220	£550
1864 Gothic Piedfort flan	incl. above			Extremely rare	
1865 mdccclxv	1,580,044	£35	£70	£275	£625
1866 mdccclxvi	914,760	£35	£70	£275	£550
1867 mdccclxvii	423,720	£40	£100	£350	£750
1867 — only 42 arcs in border	incl. above			Extremely rare	

"britt" in legend. Die no. below bust

1868 mdccclxviii........................	896,940	£30	£75	£300	£700
1869 mdccclxix	297,000	£30	£75	£300	£800
1870 mdccclxx	1,080,648	£20	£55	£200	£500
1871 mdccclxxi	3,425,605	£22	£55	£200	£500
1872 mdccclxxii	7,199,690	£22	£55	£185	£450
1873 mdccclxxiii.........................	5,921,839	£22	£55	£200	£450
1874 mdccclxxiv	1,642,630	£22	£55	£200	£450
1874 — iv over iii in date	incl. above	£30	£70	£300	£625
1875 mdccclxxv	1,117,030	£20	£55	£200	£475
1876 mdccclxxvi	580,034	£40	£110	£425	£850
1877 mdccclxxvii.........................	682,292	£25	£60	£200	£450
1877 — 48 arcs in border no W.W.	incl. above	£25	£60	£200	£450
1877 — 42 arcs	incl. above	£25	£60	£200	£450
1877 — — no die number	incl. above			Extremely rare	
1878 mdccclxxviii with die number	1,786,680	£20	£55	£200	£425

"Gothic" florin

DATE	MINTAGE	F	VF	EF	UNC
1879 mdccclxxix no die no	1,512,247			Extremely rare	
1879 — 48 arcs in border	incl. above	£25	£60	£220	£450
1879 — no die number	incl. above			Extremely rare	
1879 — 38 arcs, no W.W..	incl. above	£20	£55	£200	£450
1880 mdccclxxx Younger portrait	—			Extremely rare	
1880 — 34 arcs, Older portrait ...	2,167,170	£25	£60	£200	£425
1881 mdccclxxxi — —	2,570,337	£20	£55	£200	£525
1881 — xxΓ̄i broken puncheon...	incl. above	£30	£70	£200	£450
1883 mdccclxxxiii — —	3,555,667	£20	£50	£180	£400
1884 mdccclxxxiv — —	1,447,379	£20	£50	£180	£400
1885 mdccclxxxv — —	1,758,210	£20	£50	£180	£400
1886 mdccclxxxvi — —	591,773	£20	£50	£180	£400
1887 mdccclxxxvii — —	1,776,903	£50	£120	£300	£650
1887 — 46 arcs........................	incl. above	£50	£120	£350	£700

JUBILEE HEAD ISSUES

1887	incl. above	£6	£15	£30	£55
1887 Proof	1,084	—	—	—	£300
1888..	1,547,540	£7	£15	£45	£120
1889..	2,973,561	£8	£18	£50	£140
1890..	1,684,737	£10	£25	£80	£250
1891..	836,438	£20	£60	£200	£500
1892..	283,401	£30	£100	£325	£800

VICTORIA — OLD HEAD ISSUES

1893..	1,666,103	£7	£16	£40	£85
1893 Proof	1,312	—	—	—	£300
1894..	1,952,842	£10	£20	£70	£220
1895..	2,182,968	£9	£25	£70	£200
1896..	2,944,416	£7	£20	£55	£150
1897..	1,699,921	£7	£20	£55	£140
1898..	3,061,343	£7	£20	£55	£140
1899..	3,966,953	£7	£20	£55	£140
1900..	5,528,630	£7	£20	£55	£140
1901..	2,648,870	£7	£20	£55	£140

EDWARD VII (1901–10)

1902..	2,189,575	£10	£22	£60	£100
1902 "Matt Proof"	15,123	—	—	—	£140
1903..	1,995,298	£10	£35	£120	£550
1904..	2,769,932	£12	£40	£150	£500
1905..	1,187,596	£65	£175	£600	£1600
1906..	6,910,128	£10	£35	£130	£500
1907..	5,947,895	£11	£35	£130	£500
1908..	3,280,010	£18	£55	£350	£900
1909..	3,482,829	£15	£50	£240	£700
1910..	5,650,713	£14	£35	£100	£300

GEORGE V (1910–36)

First issue

1911..	5,951,284	£6	£12	£40	£85
1911 Proof	6,007	—	—	—	£150
1912	8,571,731	£6	£15	£35	£125
1913..	4,545,278	£10	£25	£50	£170
1914..	21,252,701	£6	£18	£28	£60
1915..	12,367,939	£7	£18	£26	£60
1916..	21,064,337	£6	£18	£25	£60
1917..	11,181,617	£7	£22	£35	£90
1918..	29,211,792	£6	£18	£28	£90
1919..	9,469,292	£8	£20	£40	£90

Second issue —debased silver

1920..	15,387,833	£4	£12	£40	£85
1921..	34,863,895	£4	£12	£40	£65
1922..	23,861,044	£4	£12	£40	£65
1923..	21,546,533	£4	£10	£30	£60
1924..	4,582,372	£12	£35	£95	£240
1925..	1,404,136	£30	£75	£300	£800
1926..	5,125,410	£7	£22	£50	£145

Fourth issue—new reverse

1927 Proof only........................	101,497	—	—	—	£100
1928..	11,087,186	£4	£7	£15	£40

DATE	MINTAGE	F	VF	EF	UNC
1929	16,397,279	£4	£7	£16	£35
1930	5,753,568	£4	£7	£20	£50
1931	6,556,331	£4	£7	£18	£35
1932	717,041	£12	£30	£225	£600
1933	8,685,303	£4	£7	£18	£40
1935	7,540,546	£4	£7	£14	£30
1936	9,897,448	£4	£7	£14	£30

GEORGE VI (1936–52)

1937	13,006,781	£4	£5	£7	£12
1937 Proof	26,402	—	—	—	£15
1938	7,909,388	£6	£8	£15	£30
1939	20,850,607	£4	£5	£8	£10
1940	18,700,338	£4	£5	£7	£12
1941	24,451,079	£4	£5	£7	£9
1942	39,895,243	£4	£5	£7	£9
1943	26,711,987	£4	£5	£7	£9
1944	27,560,005	£4	£5	£7	£9
1945	25,858,049	£4	£5	£7	£9
1946	22,300,254	£4	£5	£7	£9

Cupro-nickel

1947	22,910,085	—	—	£1	£3
1948	67,553,636	—	—	£1	£3
1949	28,614,939	—	—	£1	£5
1950	24,357,490	—	—	£2	£7
1950 Proof	17,513	—	—	£1	£9
1951	27,411,747	—	—	£2	£8
1951 Proof	20,000	—	—	—	£9

ELIZABETH II (1952–   )

1953	11,958,710	—	—	—	£2
1953 Proof	40,000	—	—	—	£6
1954	13,085,422	—	—	£6	£30
1955	25,887,253	—	—	£1	£3
1956	47,824,500	—	—	£1	£3
1957	33,071,282	—	—	£4	£25
1958	9,564,580	—	—	£3	£25
1959	14,080,319	—	—	£4	£30
1960	13,831,782	—	—	£1	£4
1961	37,735,315	—	—	£1	£2
1962	35,147,903	—	—	£1	£2
1963	26,471,000	—	—	£1	£2
1964	16,539,000	—	—	£1	£2
1965	48,163,000	—	—	—	£1.50
1966	83,999,000	—	—	—	£1.50
1967	39,718,000	—	—	—	£1.50
1970 Proof	—	—	—	—	£10

SHILLINGS

OLIVER CROMWELL

1658	£850	£1800	£4000	—
1658 Dutch Copy			Extremely rare	

CHARLES II (1660–85)

1663 First bust	£125	£500	£1500	—
1663 — GARTIA error			Extremely rare	
1663 — Irish & Scottish shields transposed	£250	£800	—	—
1666 — Elephant below bust	£500	£1500	£6000	—
1666 "Guinea" head, elephant	£1800	£4500	—	—
1666 Second bust			Extremely rare	
1668 —	£120	£400	£1400	—
1668/3 — 8 over 3	£150	£500	—	—
1668 Second bust	£120	£450	£1400	—
1669/6 First bust variety			Extremely rare	
1669			Extremely rare	

DATE	F	VF	EF	UNC
1669 Second bust			Extremely rare	
1670 —	£150	£500	£1800	—
1671 —	£150	£500	£1800	—
1671 — Plume below, plume in centre rev.	£400	£1000	£3750	—
1672 —	£150	£550	£1800	—
1673 —	£150	£550	£1800	—
1673 — Plume below, plume in centre rev.	£450	£1100	£4750	—
1673/2 — 3 over 2...	£175	£600	—	—
1674/3 — 4 over 3...	£150	£550	—	—
1674 —	£150	£500	£2000	—
1674 — Plume below bust, plume in centre rev.	£350	£1100	£4250	—
1674 — Plume rev. only...................................	£700	£2000	£4400	—
1674 Third bust	£450	£1600	—	—
1675 Second bust	£200	£800	—	—
1675/4 — 5 over 4...	£220	£850	—	—
1675 — Plume below bust, plume in centre rev.	£400	£1100	£4500	—
1675 Third bust	£350	£1250	—	—
1675/3 — 5 over 3...	£300	£1100	—	—
1676 Second bust..	£125	£450	£1700	—
1676/5 — 6 over 5...	£160	£550	—	—
1676 — Plume below bust, plume in centre rev.	£400	£1500	£4700	—
1677 —	£120	£500	£1900	—
1677 — Plume below bust	£900	£2500	£7500	—
1678 —	£140	£500	£1750	—
1678/7 — 8 over 7...	£160	£700	—	—
1679 —	£140	£500	£2000	—
1679 — Plume below bust, plume in centre rev.	£400	£1100	£4500	—
1679 — Plume below bust	£700	£2500	£5500	—
1679 — 9 over 7..	£160	£600	—	—
1680 —			Extremely rare	
1680 — Plume below bust, plume in centre rev.	£900	£2500	£5300	—
1680/79 — — 80 over 79	£850	£2500	—	—
1681 —	£300	£850	£3000	—
1681 — 1 over 0...	£375	£900	£3250	—
1681/0 Elephant & Castle below bust	£3000	£9000	—	—
1682/1 — 2 over 1	£1000	£3300	—	—
1683 —			Extremely rare	
1683 Fourth (Larger) bust.................................	£220	£700	£2250	—
1684 —	£220	£700	£2250	—

JAMES II (1685–88)

1685...	£200	£500	£2000	—
1685 Plume in centre rev. rev			Extremely rare	
1685 No stops on rev.	£220	£650	—	—
1686...	£220	£550	£2200	—
1686/5 6 over 5	£225	£600	£2250	—
1687...	£200	£600	£2200	—
1687/6 7 over 6	£200	£550	£2300	—
1688...	£200	£600	£2300	—
1688/7 last 8 over 7...	£220	£550	£2250	—

WILLIAM & MARY (1688–94)

1692	£180	£500	£2250	—
1692 inverted 1..	£210	£550	£2300	—
1693...	£180	£500	£2250	—

WILLIAM III (1694–1702)

Provincially produced shillings carry privy marks or initials below the bust:
B: Bristol. C: Chester. E: Exeter. N: Norwich. Y or y: York.

1695 First bust	£40	£120	£600	—
1696 —	£40	£100	£450	—
1696 — no stops on rev.	£60	£140	£750	—
1696 — MAB for MAG......................................			Extremely rare	
1696 — 1669 error			Extremely rare	
1696 — 1669 various GVLELMVS errors			Extremely rare	
1696 — B below bust	£60	£150	£800	—
1696 — C	£55	£150	£800	—
1696 — E...	£60	£160	£850	—

DATE	F	VF	EF	UNC
1696 — N	£55	£150	£750	—
1696 — y	£55	£150	£750	—
1696 — Y	£50	£150	£750	—
1696 Second bust			Only one known	
1696 Third bust C below	£160	£400	£1500	—
1696 — Y			Extremely rare	
1697 First bust	£50	£110	£400	—
1697 — GRI for GRA error			Extremely rare	
1697 — Scottish & Irish shields transposed			Extremely rare	
1697 — Irish arms at date			Extremely rare	
1697 — no stops on rev	£60	£180	£700	—
1697 — GVLELMVS error			Extremely rare	
1697 — B	£60	£150	£800	—
1697 — C	£60	£150	£800	—
1697 — E	£60	£150	£800	—
1697 — N	£60	£140	£750	—
1697 — — no stops on obv			Extremely rare	
1697 — y	£60	£150	£700	—
1697 — — arms of France & Ireland transposed			Extremely rare	
1697 — Y	£50	£150	£650	—
1697 Third bust	£50	£125	£550	—
1697 — B	£60	£150	£650	—
1697 — C	£60	£150	£700	—
1697 — — Fr.a error	£150	£500	—	—
1697 — — no stops on obv	£90	£300	—	—
1697 — — arms of Scotland at date			Extremely rare	
1697 — E	£60	£150	£700	—
1697 — N	£60	£150	£750	—
1697 — y	£60	£150	£725	—
1697 Third bust variety	£60	£140	£500	—
1697 — B	£60	£150	£800	—
1697 — C	£120	£550	—	—
1698 —	£80	£250	£950	—
1698 — Plumes in angles of rev.	£200	£500	£2000	—
1698 Fourth bust "Flaming hair"	£150	£500	£2000	—
1699 —	£110	£400	£1400	—
1699 Fifth bust	£100	£300	£1100	—
1699 — Plumes in angles on rev.	£150	£450	£1800	—
1699 — Roses in angles on rev.	£160	£500	£1800	—
1700 —	£65	£120	£550	—
1700 — Small round oo in date	£65	£120	£550	—
1700 — no stop after DEI			Extremely rare	
1700 — Plume below bust	£2500	£9000	—	—
1701 —	£80	£250	£850	—
1701 — Plumes in angles on rev.	£160	£600	£1800	—

William III First bust

ANNE (1702–14)

1702 First bust (pre-Union with Scotland)	£80	£300	£700	—
1702 — Plumes in angles on rev.	£90	£275	£800	—
1702 — VIGO below bust	£70	£220	£650	—
1702 — — colon before ANNA			Extremely rare	
1703 Second bust, VIGO below	£65	£180	£700	—
1704 — Plain	£500	£1800	—	—
1704 — Plumes in angles on rev.	£80	£200	£800	—
1705 — Plain	£75	£200	£650	—
1705 — Plumes in angles on rev.	£70	£200	£700	—
1705 — Roses & Plumes in angles on rev.	£70	£200	£650	—
1707 —	£60	£180	£600	—
1707 Second bust (post-Union) E below bust	£50	£125	£500	—
1707 — E* below bust	£70	£200	£750	—
1707 Third bust, Plain	£35	£100	£425	—
1707 — Plumes in angles on rev.	£50	£160	£750	—
1707 — E below bust	£40	£90	£475	—
1707 "Edinburgh" bust, E* below			Extremely rare	
1708 Second bust, E below	£50	£100	£450	—
1708 — E* below bust	£55	£165	£700	—
1708/7 — — 8 over 7			Extremely rare	

Anne, VIGO below bust

DATE	MINTAGE	F	VF	EF	UNC
1708 — Roses & Plumes in angles on rev.........		£80	£275	£650	—
1708 Third bust, Plain		£40	£120	£400	—
1708 — Plumes in angles on rev.		£70	£200	£600	—
1708 Third bust, E below bust		£60	£175	£650	—
1708/7 — — 8 over 7		£200	£450	—	—
1708 — Roses & Plumes in angles on rev.		£70	£180	£550	—
1708 "Edinburgh" bust, E* below.....................		£60	£170	£525	—
1709 Third bust, Plain		£50	£140	£500	—
1709 "Edinburgh" bust, E* below.....................		£50	£170	£650	—
1709 — E no star (filled in die?)......................		£70	£160	£550	—
1710 Third bust, Roses & Plumes in angles......		£60	£140	£625	—
1710 Fourth bust, Roses & Plumes in angles ...		£60	£150	£600	—
1711 Third bust, Plain		£70	£160	£425	—
1711 Fourth bust, Plain		£30	£75	£240	—
1712 — Roses & Plumes in angles on rev.........		£60	£120	£400	—
1713 — —		£60	£120	£375	—
1713/2 — 3 over 2..		£60	£200	—	—
1714 — —		£60	£100	£325	—
1714/3 —..				Extremely rare	

GEORGE I (1714–27)

	MINTAGE	F	VF	EF	UNC
1715 First bust, Roses & Plumes in angles on rev.		£80	£200	£850	—
1716 — —		£150	£500	£2000	—
1717 — —		£90	£300	£1350	—
1718 — —		£70	£225	£800	—
1719 — —		£120	£400	£1800	—
1720 — —		£70	£175	£450	—
1720/18 — —		£150	£500	£1400	—
1720 — Plain		£40	£100	£450	—
1721 — Roses & Plumes in angles on rev.........		£100	£350	£1500	—
1721/0 — — 1 over 0		£70	£220	£900	—
1721 — Plain		£120	£450	£1400	—
1721/19 — — 21 over 19		£125	£400	—	—
1721/18 21 over 18 error, Plumes & Roses.......		£500	£1800	—	—
1722 — Roses & Plumes in angles on rev.........		£80	£220	£950	—
1723 — —		£90	£240	£1000	—
1723 — SSC rev., Arms of France at date		£100	£275	£750	—
1723 — SSC in angles on rev		£35	£110	£250	—
1723 Second bust, SSC in angles on rev.		£50	£160	£525	—
1723 — Roses & Plumes in angles		£90	£240	£1000	—
1723 — WCC (Welsh Copper Co) below bust ..		£600	£1800	£5500	—
1724 — Roses & Plumes in angles on rev.........		£80	£200	£750	—
1724 — WCC below bust...................................		£600	£1800	£5500	—
1725 — Roses & Plumes in angles on rev.........		£80	£200	£1000	—
1725 — — no stops on obv...............................		£90	£225	£1100	—
1725 — WCC below bust...................................		£650	£1850	£6000	—
1726 — — Roses & Plumes		£650	£1750	£6500	—
1726 — WCC below bust...................................		£650	£1850	£6000	—
1727 — —				Extremely rare	
1727 — — no stops on obv...............................				Extremely rare	

GEORGE II (1727–60)

	MINTAGE	F	VF	EF	UNC
1727 Young head, Plumes in angles on rev.......		£75	£300	£950	—
1727 — Roses & Plumes in angles on rev.........		£60	£180	£650	—
1728 — —		£65	£180	£650	—
1728 — Plain		£75	£220	£700	—
1729 — Roses & Plumes in angles on rev.........		£60	£200	£700	—
1731 — —		£70	£200	£700	—
1731 — Plumes in angles on rev.		£100	£400	£1250	—
1732 — Roses & Plumes in angles on rev.........		£65	£200	£750	—
1734 — —		£65	£200	£700	—
1735 — —		£65	£200	£700	—
1736 — —		£65	£200	£700	—
1736/5 — — 6 over 5		£70	£200	£800	—
1737 — —		£65	£200	£650	—
1739 — Roses in angles on rev.		£50	£160	£450	—
1739/7 — — 9 over 7				Extremely rare	
1741 — —		£50	£160	£450	—
1741/39 — — 41 over 39				Extremely rare	
1743 Old head, Roses in angles on rev.............		£30	£80	£325	—
1745 — —		£30	£80	£325	—

George II
Young head

George II
Old head

DATE	MINTAGE	F	VF	EF	UNC
1745 — — LIMA below bust		£30	£90	£325	—
1745/3 — — — 5 over 3		£60	£175	£400	—
1746 — — —		£50	£175	£650	—
1746/5 — — — 6 over 5		£100	£300	—	—
1746 — Plain, Proof		—	—	£3000	—
1747 — Roses in angles on rev.		£45	£100	£375	—
1750 — Plain		£40	£140	£400	—
1750/6 — — 0 over 6		£60	£150	£500	—
1751 — —		£125	£400	£1100	—
1758 — —		£20	£50	£140	—

GEORGE III (1760–1820)

1763 "Northumberland" bust		£450	£800	£1600	—
(Beware recent counterfeits)					
1787 rev. no semée of hearts in 4th shield		£20	£35	£100	—
1787 — No stop over head		£25	£40	£120	—
1787 — No stop at date		£45	£75	£150	—
1787 — No stops on obv		£100	£250	£850	—
1787 rev. with semée of hearts in shield		£35	£65	£125	—
1798 "Dorrien Magens" bust		—	—	—	£25,000

NEW COINAGE — shield in garter reverse

1816	—	£12	£25	£75	£150
1817	3,031,360	£12	£35	£85	£175
1817 GEOE for GEOR	incl. above	£120	£250	£600	—
1818	1,342,440	£25	£45	£150	£400
1819	7,595,280	£15	£35	£100	£200
1819/8 9 over 8	incl. above	£20	£50	£150	—
1820	7,975,440	£12	£25	£100	£200

GEORGE IV (1820–30)

1821 First bust, first reverse	2,463,120	£15	£40	£150	£450
1821 — — Proof	incl. above	—	—	—	£1200
1823 — Second reverse	693,000	£50	£90	£250	£600
1824 — —	4,158,000	£12	£40	£150	£375
1825 — —	2,459,160	£20	£50	£150	£500
1825/3 — — 5 over 3	incl. above			Extremely rare	
1825 Second bust, third reverse	incl. above	£10	£25	£60	£200
1825 — — Roman I	incl. above			Extremely rare	
1826 — —	6,351,840	£10	£25	£60	£200
1826 — — Proof	incl. above	—	—	—	£600
1827 — —	574,200	£30	£70	£200	£475
1829 — —	879,120	£20	£60	£175	£425

WILLIAM IV (1830–37)

1831 Proof only		—	—	—	£1000
1834	3,223,440	£15	£35	£170	£400
1835	1,449,360	£15	£35	£170	£400
1836	3,567,960	£15	£35	£170	£400
1837	478,160	£20	£60	£200	£525

VICTORIA (1837–1901)

YOUNG HEAD ISSUES
First head

1838 WW on truncation	1,956,240	£20	£50	£200	£450
1839 —	5,666,760	£20	£50	£200	£450

Second head

1839 WW on truncation, Proof only	incl. above	—	—	—	£900
1839 no WW	incl. above	£20	£50	£180	£450
1840	1,639,440	£20	£50	£180	£450
1841	875,160	£22	£50	£180	£450
1842	2,094,840	£20	£45	£170	£450
1843	1,465,200	£20	£50	£180	£475
1844	4,466,880	£15	£40	£150	£400
1845	4,082,760	£15	£40	£150	£400
1846	4,031,280	£15	£40	£150	£400
1848 last 8 of date over 6	1,041,480	£80	£160	£600	£1200

DATE	MINTAGE	F	VF	EF	UNC
1849	845,480	£25	£60	£200	£625
1850	685,080	£700	£1400	£3000	£6000
1850/49	incl. above	£700	£1500	£4000	—
1851	470,071	£40	£110	£400	£850
1852	1,306,574	£15	£35	£125	£400
1853	4,256,188	£15	£35	£125	£400
1853 Proof................................	incl. above	—	—	—	£1500
1854	552,414	£200	£550	£1200	£3200
1854/1 4 over 1	incl. above	£200	£900	—	—
1855	1,368,400	£12	£30	£110	£300
1856	3,168,000	£12	£30	£110	£300
1857	2,562,120	£12	£30	£110	£300
1857 error F:G with inverted G ...	incl. above	£200	£600	—	—
1858	3,108,600	£12	£30	£110	£300
1859	4,561,920	£12	£30	£110	£300
1860	1,671,120	£12	£30	£110	£350
1861	1,382,040	£14	£40	£150	£500
1862	954,360	£60	£150	£400	£1200
1863	859,320	£125	£375	£850	£1800
1863/1 3 over 1				Extremely rare	

Die no. added above date up to 1879

1864	4,518,360	£10	£30	£110	£250
1865	5,619,240	£10	£30	£110	£250
1866	4,984,600	£10	£30	£110	£250
1866 error BBITANNIAR	incl. above	£80	£250	£800	—
1867	2,166,120	£10	£35	£110	£275

Third head—with die no

1867	incl. above	£100	£450	—	—
1868	3,330,360	£12	£40	£110	£275
1869	736,560	£18	£50	£120	£350
1870	1,467,471	£12	£40	£100	£275
1871	4,910,010	£10	£40	£100	£250
1872	8,897,781	£10	£40	£100	£250
1873	6,489,598	£10	£40	£100	£250
1874	5,503,747	£12	£40	£100	£250
1875	4,353,983	£10	£40	£100	£250
1876	1,057,487	£10	£40	£100	£375
1877	2,989,703	£10	£40	£100	£275
1878	3,127,131	£10	£40	£100	£275
1879	3,611,507	£20	£60	£200	£550

Fourth head—no die no

1879 no Die no.	incl. above	£10	£28	£75	£190
1880	4,842,786	£10	£28	£75	£190
1881	5,255,332	£10	£28	£75	£190
1882	1,611,786	£22	£75	£200	£450
1883	7,281,450	£10	£28	£65	£180
1884	3,923,993	£10	£28	£65	£180
1885	3,336,526	£10	£28	£65	£180
1886	2,086,819	£10	£28	£65	£180
1887	4,034,133	£10	£28	£65	£180

JUBILEE HEAD ISSUES

1887	incl. above	£4	£8	£15	£40
1887 Proof................................	1,084	—	—	—	£250
1888..	4,526,856	£6	£10	£25	£60
1889..	7,039,628	£35	£90	£300	—
1889 Large bust (until 1892)........	incl. above	£6	£12	£45	£75
1890..	8,794,042	£6	£12	£45	£75
1891..	5,665,348	£6	£12	£45	£80
1892..	4,591,622	£6	£12	£45	£100

OLD HEAD ISSUES

1893..	7,039,074	£5	£10	£30	£65
1893 small lettering	incl. above	£5	£10	£30	£65
1893 Proof................................	1,312	—	—	—	£200
1894..	5,953,152	£9	£25	£60	£150
1895..	8,880,651	£9	£25	£55	£145
1896..	9,264,551	£7	£15	£40	£80
1897..	6,270,364	£7	£12	£40	£75
1898..	9,768,703	£7	£12	£40	£70
1899..	10,965,382	£7	£12	£40	£70
1900..	10,937,590	£7	£12	£40	£75
1901..	3,426,294	£7	£12	£40	£70

Victoria Jubilee head

Victoria Old or Veiled head

DATE	MINTAGE	F	VF	EF	UNC

EDWARD VII (1901–10)

DATE	MINTAGE	F	VF	EF	UNC
1902	7,809,481	£5	£15	£45	£80
1902 Proof matt	13,123	—	—	—	£100
1903	2,061,823	£10	£35	£140	£475
1904	2,040,161	£8	£35	£130	£440
1905	488,390	£110	£300	£1100	£3500
1906	10,791,025	£5	£12	£40	£120
1907	14,083,418	£5	£12	£40	£130
1908	3,806,969	£10	£25	£150	£500
1909	5,664,982	£9	£22	£110	£375
1910	26,547,236	£5	£10	£45	£100

GEORGE V (1910–36)

First issue

DATE	MINTAGE	F	VF	EF	UNC
1911	20,065,901	£4	£8	£20	£55
1911 Proof	6,007	—	—	—	£125
1912	15,594,009	£5	£10	£25	£80
1913	9,011,509	£7	£20	£50	£150
1914	23,415,843	£4	£7	£25	£55
1915	39,279,024	£4	£7	£25	£55
1916	35,862,015	£4	£7	£25	£55
1917	22,202,608	£4	£7	£25	£60
1918	34,915,934	£4	£7	£25	£55
1919	10,823,824	£5	£8	£30	£65

Second issue — debased silver

DATE	MINTAGE	F	VF	EF	UNC
1920	22,825,142	£2	£4	£20	£45
1921	22,648,763	£2	£4	£20	£45
1922	27,215,738	£2	£4	£20	£45
1923	14,575,243	£2	£4	£20	£45
1924	9,250,095	£7	£15	£50	£150
1925	5,418,764	£6	£10	£40	£110
1926	22,516,453	£3	£8	£30	£110

George V First obverse

Third issue — Modified bust

DATE	MINTAGE	F	VF	EF	UNC
1926	incl. above	£2	£4	£25	£55
1927 —	9,247,344	£2	£4	£25	£55

Fourth issue — large lion and crown on rev., date in legend

DATE	MINTAGE	F	VF	EF	UNC
1927	incl. above	£2	£4	£20	£40
1927 Proof	15,000	—	—	—	£60
1928	18,136,778	£2	£4	£15	£40
1929	19,343,006	£2	£4	£15	£40
1930	3,172,092	£2	£4	£20	£50
1931	6,993,926	£2	£4	£15	£40
1932	12,168,101	£2	£4	£15	£45
1933	11,511,624	£2	£4	£15	£35
1934	6,138,463	£2	£4	£18	£50
1935	9,183,462	—	£4	£10	£22
1936	11,910,613	—	£4	£9	£20

GEORGE VI (1936–52)

George V Second obverse

E = England rev. (lion standing on large crown). S = Scotland rev. (lion seated on small crown holding sword and mace)

DATE	MINTAGE	F	VF	EF	UNC
1937 E	8,359,122	—	£2	£4	£6
1937 E Proof	26,402	—	—	—	£18
1937 S	6,748,875	—	£2	£4	£6
1937 S Proof	26,402	—	—	—	£18
1938 E	4,833,436	—	£3	£10	£20
1938 S	4,797,852	—	£3	£10	£20
1939 E	11,052,677	—	£2	£4	£6
1939 S	10,263,892	—	£2	£4	£6
1940 E	11,099,126	—	—	£4	£7
1940 S	9,913,089	—	—	£4	£7

DATE	MINTAGE	F	VF	EF	UNC
1941 E	11,391,883	—	—	£4	£6
1941 S	8,086,030	—	—	£4	£5
1942 E	17,453,643	—	—	£4	£5
1942 S	13,676,759	—	—	£4	£5
1943 E	11,404,213	—	—	£4	£6
1943 S	9,824,214	—	—	£4	£5
1944 E	11,586,751	—	—	£4	£5
1944 S	10,990,167	—	—	£4	£5
1945 E	15,143,404	—	—	£4	£6
1945 S	15,106,270	—	—	£4	£5
1946 E	16,663,797	—	—	£4	£5
1946 S	16,381,501	—	—	£4	£5
Cupro-nickel					
1947 E	12,120,611	—	—	—	£2
1947 S	12,283,223	—	—	—	£2
1948 E	45,576,923	—	—	—	£2
1948 S	45,351,937	—	—	—	£2
1949 E	19,328,405	—	—	—	£5
1949 S	21,243,074	—	—	—	£5
1950 E	19,243,872	—	—	—	£5
1950 E Proof	17,513	—	—	—	£20
1950 S	14,299,601	—	—	—	£5
1950 S Proof	17,513	—	—	—	£20
1951 E	9,956,930	—	—	—	£5
1951 E Proof	20,000	—	—	—	£20
1951 S	10,961,174	—	—	—	£6
1951 S Proof	20,000	—	—	—	£20

English reverse

Scottish reverse

ELIZABETH II (1952–   )

E = England rev. (shield with three lions). S = Scotland rev. (shield with one lion).

DATE	MINTAGE	F	VF	EF	UNC
1953 E	41,942,894	—	—	—	£1
1953 E Proof	40,000	—	—	—	£4
1953 S	20,663,528	—	—	—	£1
1953 S Proof	40,000	—	—	—	£4
1954 E	30,262,032	—	—	—	£2
1954 S	26,771,735	—	—	—	£2
1955 E	45,259,908	—	—	—	£2
1955 S	27,950,906	—	—	—	£2
1956 E	44,907,008	—	—	—	£10
1956 S	42,853,639	—	—	—	£10
1957 E	42,774,217	—	—	—	£1
1957 S	17,959,988	—	—	—	£10
1958 E	14,392,305	—	—	—	£10
1958 S	40,822,557	—	—	—	£1
1959 E	19,442,778	—	—	—	£1
1959 S	1,012,988	£1	£3	£10	£40
1960 E	27,027,914	—	—	—	£1
1960 S	14,376,932	—	—	—	£1
1961 E	39,816,907	—	—	—	£1
1961 S	2,762,558	—	—	—	£3
1962 E	36,704,379	—	—	—	£1
1962 S	17,475,310	—	—	—	£1
1963 E	49,433,607	—	—	—	£1
1963 S	32,300,000	—	—	—	£1
1964 E	8,590,900	—	—	—	£1
1964 S	5,239,100	—	—	—	£1
1965 E	9,216,000	—	—	—	£1
1965 S	2,774,000	—	—	—	£2
1966 E	15,002,000	—	—	—	£1
1966 S	15,604,000	—	—	—	£1
1970 E Proof	—				£10
1970 S Proof	—				£10

English reverse

Scottish reverse

SIXPENCES

DATE	F	VF	EF	UNC

OLIVER CROMWELL
1658 Patterns by Thos. Simon & Tanner
Four varieties .... Extremely rare

CHARLES II (1660–85)

	F	VF	EF	UNC
1674	£70	£300	£900	—
1675	£70	£300	£900	—
1675/4 5 over 4	£80	£300	£950	—
1676	£80	£300	£900	—
1676/5 6 over 5	£85	£300	£900	—
1677	£70	£300	£900	—
1678/7	£70	£300	£925	—
1679	£75	£300	£900	—
1680	£90	£500	£1000	—
1681	£80	£300	£900	—
1682/1	£80	£300	£1000	—
1682	£100	£320	£1000	—
1683	£70	£300	£925	—
1684	£80	£300	£900	—

JAMES II (1685–88)

	F	VF	EF	UNC
1686 Early shields	£140	£425	£1000	—
1687 Ealy Shields	£150	£475	£1200	—
1687/6 — 7 over 6	£150	£450	£1100	—
1687 Late shields	£150	£450	£1300	—
1687/6 — 7 over 6	£150	£475	£1150	—
1688 —	£150	£450	£1150	—

WILLIAM & MARY (1688–94)

	F	VF	EF	UNC
1693	£130	£425	£975	—
1693 error inverted 3	£200	£500	£1350	—
1694	£130	£450	£1100	—

WILLIAM III (1694–1702)
Provincially produced sixpences carry privy marks or initials below the bust:
B: Bristol. C: Chester. E: Exeter. N: Norwich. Y or y: York.

	F	VF	EF	UNC
1695 First bust, early harp in 4th shield on rev.	£35	£100	£400	—
1696 — —	£35	£100	£325	—
1696 — — French arms at date		Extremely rare		
1696 — — Scottish arms at date		Extremely rare		
1696 — — DFI for DEI		Extremely rare		
1696 — — No stops on obv.	£50	£140	£500	—
1696 — — B	£40	£100	£400	—
1696 — — — B over E		Extremely rare		
1696 — — C	£35	£100	£440	—
1696 — — E	£50	£110	£440	—
1696 — — N	£45	£100	£440	—
1696 — — y	£40	£110	£500	—
1696 — — Y	£50	£200	£525	—
1696 — Later harp	£50	£175	£400	—
1696 — — B	£70	£225	£550	—
1696 — — — no stops on obv	£80	£275	£550	—
1696 — — C	£80	£350	£850	—
1696 — — N	£70	£325	—	—
1696 Second bust	£300	£800	£2200	—
1697 First bust, later harp	£30	£75	£300	—
1697 — — Arms of France & Ireland transposed		Extremely rare		

DATE	MINTAGE	F	VF	EF	UNC
1697 — — B		£50	£110	£450	—
1697 — — C		£70	£200	£500	—
1697 — — — Irish shield at date			Extremely rare		
1697 — — E		£70	£200	£475	—
1697 — — — error GVLIEMVS			Extremely rare		
1697 — — y		£60	£125	£475	—
1697 — — — Irish shield at date			Extremely rare		
1697 Second bust		£175	£500	£1500	—
1697 Third bust		£25	£70	£275	—
1697 — error GVLIEIMVS			Extremely rare		
1697 — B		£50	£110	£450	—
1697 — — IRA for FRA			Extremely rare		
1697 — C		£75	£220	£500	—
1697 — E		£75	£200	£550	—
1697 — Y		£60	£200	£500	—
1698 —		£60	£190	£475	—
1698 — Plumes in angles on rev.		£75	£200	£700	—
1699 —		£90	£250	£800	—
1699 — Plumes in angles on rev.		£70	£250	£750	—
1699 — Roses in angles on rev.		£70	£250	£750	—
1699 — — error GⱯLIELMVS			Extremely rare		
1700 —		£45	£100	£375	—
1700 — Plume below bust		£2000	—	—	—
1701 —		£65	£160	£500	—

ANNE (1702–14)

1703 VIGO below bust Before Union with Scotland	£40	£130	£400	—
1705 Plain		£60	£170	£500	—
1705 Plumes in angles on rev.		£45	£150	£450	—
1705 Roses & Plumes in angles on rev.		£60	£150	£450	—
1707 Roses & Plumes in angles on rev.		£50	£150	£425	—
1707 (Post-Union), Plain		£40	£80	£300	—
1707 E (Edinburgh) below bust		£40	£80	£300	—
1707 Plumes in angles on rev.		£45	£120	£325	—
1708 Plain		£45	£100	£400	—
1708 E below bust		£50	£100	£350	—
1708 E* below bust		£60	£140	£400	—
1708 "Edinburgh" bust E* below		£50	£140	£400	—
1708 Plumes in angles on rev.		£55	£140	£450	—
1710 Roses & Plumes in angles on rev.		£35	£110	£450	—
1711 Plain		£25	£70	£240	—

GEORGE I (1714–27)

1717 Roses & Plumes in angles on rev.		£90	£270	£750	—
1717 Plain edge			Extremely rare		
1720 —		£90	£270	£675	—
1723 SSC in angles on rev.		£30	£70	£200	—
1723 Larger lettering		£30	£70	£200	—
1726 Small Roses & Plumes in angles on rev.	£80	£225	£650	—

GEORGE II (1727–60)

1728 Young head, Plain		£70	£240	£525	—
1728 — Proof		—	—	£3500	—
1728 — Plumes in angles on rev.		£40	£140	£400	—
1728 — Roses & Plumes in angles on rev.		£35	£125	£350	—
1731 — —		£40	£140	£375	—
1732 — —		£35	£125	£350	—
1734 — —		£40	£140	£375	—
1735 — —		£35	£140	£375	—
1735/4 5 over 4		£45	£150	£425	—
1736 — —		£45	£150	£400	—
1739 — Roses in angles on rev.		£30	£100	£320	—
1741 — —		£30	£100	£300	—
1743 Old head, Roses in angles on rev.		£25	£75	£250	—
1745 — —		£25	£75	£250	—

DATE	MINTAGE	F	VF	EF	UNC
1745 — — 5 over 3		£30	£85	£275	—
1745 — Plain, LIMA below bust		£30	£80	£260	—
1746 — — —		£30	£80	£260	—
1746 — — Proof	—	—	£1500	—
1750 — —		£30	£120	£325	—
1751 — —		£35	£150	£350	—
1757 — —		£15	£30	£85	—
1758 — —		£15	£30	£85	—

GEORGE III (1760–1820)

1787 rev. no semée of hearts on 4th shield		£15	£35	£80	£110
1787 rev. with semée of hearts		£15	£35	£80	£110

NEW COINAGE

1816	—	£7	£15	£40	£100
1817	10,921,680	£7	£15	£40	£100
1818	4,284,720	£10	£25	£80	£175
1819	4,712,400	£8	£15	£40	£90
1819 very small 8 in date	incl. above	£12	£22	£60	£140
1820	1,488,960	£8	£15	£50	£120

GEORGE IV (1820–30)

1821 First bust, first reverse	863,280	£12	£30	£120	£350
1821 error BBRITANNIAR		£100	£300	£950	—
1821 — — Proof	incl. above	—	—	—	£900
1824 — Second (garter) reverse	633,600	£10	£30	£100	£325
1825 — —	483,120	£12	£30	£100	£300
1826 — —	689,040	£40	£100	£250	£550
1826 Second bust, third (lion on crown) reverse	incl. above	£10	£30	£100	£220
1826 — — Proof	incl. above	—	—	—	£500
1827 — —	166,320	£40	£100	£300	£600
1828 — —	15,840	£20	£50	£150	£325
1829 — —	403,290	£15	£45	£125	£350

WILLIAM IV (1830–37)

1831	1,340,195	£15	£40	£125	£300
1831 Proof, milled edge	incl. above	—	—	—	£600
1834	5,892,480	£15	£40	£125	£300
1835	1,552,320	£15	£40	£125	£300
1836	1,987,920	£15	£45	£250	£350
1837	506,880	£20	£45	£220	£500

VICTORIA (1837–1901)

YOUNG HEAD ISSUES
First head

1838	1,607,760	£15	£40	£130	£350
1839	3,310,560	£15	£40	£130	£350
1839 Proof	incl. above	—	—	—	£850
1840	2,098,800	£15	£40	£130	£350
1841	1,386,000	£18	£40	£130	£350
1842	601,920	£15	£40	£130	£350
1843	3,160,080	£15	£40	£130	£350
1844	3,975,840	£15	£30	£140	£350
1844 Large 44 in date	incl. above	£18	£40	£130	£400
1845	3,714,480	£15	£35	£90	£350
1846	4,226,880	£15	£35	£90	£350
1848	586,080	£50	£100	£300	£100
1848/6 final 8 over 6	incl. above	£50	£120	£400	—
1850	498,960	£12	£35	£100	£350
1850/3 0 over 3	incl. above	£18	£40	£110	£400
1851	2,288,107	£10	£30	£100	£350
1852	904,586	£10	£30	£150	£360
1853	3,837,930	£10	£30	£150	£360

DATE	MINTAGE	F	VF	EF	UNC
1853 Proof	incl above	—	—	—	£1000
1854	840,116	£175	£500	£1000	£2500
1855	1,129,684	£10	£30	£120	£250
1855/3 last 5 over 3	incl. above	£15	£45	£140	£300
1856	2,779,920	£10	£40	£120	£270
1857	2,233,440	£10	£40	£120	£270
1858	1,932,480	£10	£40	£120	£270
1859	4,688,640	£10	£40	£120	£270
1859/8 9 over 8	incl. above	£12	£40	£120	£375
1860	1,100,880	£10	£35	£120	£300
1862	990,000	£100	£200	£600	£1500
1863	491,040	£70	£150	£475	£1100

Die no. added above date from 1864 to 1879

DATE	MINTAGE	F	VF	EF	UNC
1864	4,253,040	£10	£25	£110	£250
1865	1,631,520	£10	£25	£100	£250
1866	4,140,080	£10	£25	£100	£250
1866 no Die no.	incl. above		Extremely Rare		

Jubilee head, shield reverse

Second head

DATE	MINTAGE	F	VF	EF	UNC
1867	1,362,240	£10	£30	£120	£300
1868	1,069,200	£10	£30	£110	£270
1869	388,080	£10	£30	£110	£270
1870	479,613	£10	£30	£110	£270
1871	3,662,684	£8	£30	£75	£200
1871 no Die no.	incl. above	£8	£30	£75	£220
1872	3,382,048	£8	£30	£75	£200
1873	4,594,733	£8	£30	£75	£200
1874	4,225,726	£8	£30	£75	£220
1875	3,256,545	£8	£30	£75	£220
1876	841,435	£8	£30	£75	£220
1877	4,066,486	£8	£30	£75	£220
1877 no Die no	incl. above	£8	£30	£75	£220
1878	2,624,525	£8	£30	£75	£225
1878 Dritanniar Error	incl. above	£125	£300	£1000	—
1879	3,326,313	£8	£25	£80	£220
1879 no Die no	incl. above	£8	£25	£80	£220
1880 no Die no	3,892,501	£8	£25	£75	£220

Jubilee head, wreath reverse

Third head

DATE	MINTAGE	F	VF	EF	UNC
1880	incl above	£8	£20	£80	£175
1881	6,239,447	£8	£20	£80	£175
1882	759,809	£15	£50	£150	£425
1883	4,986,558	£8	£20	£70	£150
1884	3,422,565	£8	£20	£70	£150
1885	4,652,771	£8	£20	£70	£150
1886	2,728,249	£8	£20	£70	£140
1887	3,675,607	£8	£20	£70	£150

JUBILEE HEAD ISSUES

DATE	MINTAGE	F	VF	EF	UNC
1887 Shield reverse	incl. above	£6	£10	£15	£30
1887 — Proof	incl. above	—	—	—	£160
1887 Six Pence in wreath reverse	incl. above	£6	£8	£18	£35
1888	4,197,698	£8	£12	£35	£60
1889 —	8,738,928	£8	£12	£35	£70
1890 —	9,386,955	£8	£12	£35	£70
1891 —	7,022,734	£8	£12	£35	£70
1892 —	6,245,746	£8	£12	£35	£80
1893 —	7,350,619	£650	£1200	£3500	—

OLD HEAD ISSUES

DATE	MINTAGE	F	VF	EF	UNC
1893	incl. above	£7	£12	£22	£50
1893 Proof	1,312	—	—	—	£175
1894	3,467,704	£8	£18	£50	£130
1895	7,024,631	£8	£18	£45	£100
1896	6,651,699	£7	£15	£35	£65
1897	5,031,498	£7	£15	£35	£65
1898	5,914,100	£7	£15	£35	£65
1899	7,996,80	£7	£15	£35	£55
1900	8,984,354	£7	£15	£35	£55
1901	5,108,757	£7	£15	£35	£55

DATE	MINTAGE	F	VF	EF	UNC

EDWARD VII (1901–10)

DATE	MINTAGE	F	VF	EF	UNC
1902	6,367,378	£5	£10	£30	£60
1902 "Matt Proof"	15,123	—	—	—	£110
1903	5,410,096	£7	£20	£50	£160
1904	4,487,098	£15	£50	£175	£500
1905	4,235,556	£8	£20	£70	£200
1906	7,641,146	£7	£12	£40	£110
1907	8,733,673	£7	£12	£45	£120
1908	6,739,491	£10	£30	£110	£350
1909	6,584,017	£7	£18	£50	£175
1910	12,490,724	£5	£8	£25	£50

Edward VII

GEORGE V (1910–36)

First issue

DATE	MINTAGE	F	VF	EF	UNC
1911	9,155,310	£3	£7	£15	£40
1911 Proof	6,007	—	—	—	£90
1912	10,984,129	£3	£7	£20	£65
1913	7,499,833	£3	£8	£22	£75
1914	22,714,602	£3	£7	£10	£35
1915	15,694,597	£3	£7	£12	£45
1916	22,207,178	£3	£7	£10	£35
1917	7,725,475	£8	£24	£60	£140
1918	27,553,743	£3	£7	£12	£30
1919	13,375,447	£3	£7	£12	£40
1920	14,136,287	£3	£7	£10	£35

George V, first reverse above and second reverse below

Second issue—debased silver

DATE	MINTAGE	F	VF	EF	UNC
1920	incl. above	£1	£3	£10	£40
1921	30,339,741	£1	£3	£10	£40
1922	16,878,890	£1	£3	£10	£30
1923	6,382,793	£4	£10	£45	£110
1924	17,444,218	£1	£5	£10	£35
1925	12,720,558	£1	£3	£10	£35
1925 Broad rim	incl. above	£1	£3	£10	£35
1926 —	21,809,621	£1	£3	£10	£35

Third issue—Modified bust

DATE	MINTAGE	F	VF	EF	UNC
1926	incl. above	£1	£2	£10	£35
1927	8,924,873	—	£2	£10	£35

Fourth issue—New design (oakleaves)

DATE	MINTAGE	F	VF	EF	UNC
1927 Proof only	15,000	£1	£2	£10	£35
1928	23,123,384	£1	£2	£8	£25
1929	28,319,326	£1	£2	£8	£25
1930	16,990,289	£1	£2	£8	£30
1931	16,873,268	£1	£2	£8	£30
1932	9,406,117	£1	£2	£8	£40
1933	22,185,083	£1	£2	£8	£25
1934	9,304,009	£1	£2	£12	£35
1935	13,995,621	£1	£2	£6	£15
1936	24,380,171	£1	£2	£6	£15

GEORGE VI (1936–52)

First type

DATE	MINTAGE	F	VF	EF	UNC
1937	22,302,524	—	—	£1	£5
1937 Proof	26,402	—	—	—	£10
1938	13,402,701	—	£2	£5	£18
1939	28,670,304	—	—	£1	£5
1940	20,875,196	—	—	£1	£5
1941	23,086,616	—	—	£1	£5
1942	44,942,785	—	—	£1	£4
1943	46,927,111	—	—	£1	£4
1944	36,952,600	—	—	£1	£4
1945	39,939,259	—	—	£1	£3
1946	43,466,407	—	—	£1	£3

George VI first reverse

Cupro-nickel

DATE	MINTAGE	F	VF	EF	UNC
1947	29,993,263	—	—	£1	£3
1948	88,323,540	—	—	£1	£3

Second type—new cypher on rev.

DATE	MINTAGE	F	VF	EF	UNC
1949	41,335,515	—	—	£1	£3

George VI second reverse

193

DATE	MINTAGE	F	VF	EF	UNC
1950	32,741,955	—	—	£1	£3
1950 Proof	17,513	—	—	—	£7
1951	40,399,491	—	—	£1	£3
1951 Proof	20,000	—	—	—	£7
1952	1,013,477	£5	£18	£45	£120

ELIZABETH II (1952–   )

1953	70,323,876	—	—	—	£2
1953 Proof	40,000	—	—	—	£4
1954	105,241,150	—	—	—	£3
1955	109,929,554	—	—	—	£1
1956	109,841,555	—	—	—	£1
1957	105,654,290	—	—	—	£1
1958	123,518,527	—	—	—	£3
1959	93,089,441	—	—	—	£1
1960	103,283,346	—	—	—	£3
1961	115,052,017	—	—	—	£3
1962	166,483,637	—	—	—	25p
1963	120,056,000	—	—	—	25p
1964	152,336,000	—	—	—	25p
1965	129,644,000	—	—	—	25p
1966	175,676,000	—	—	—	25p
1967	240,788,000	—	—	—	25p
1970 Proof	—				£8

GROATS OR FOURPENCES

DATE	MINTAGE	F	VF	EF	UNC

The earlier fourpences are included in the Maundy oddments section as they are generally considered to have been issued for the Maundy ceremony.

WILLIAM IV (1831–37)

1836	—	£8	£18	£40	£85
1837	962,280	£8	£18	£40	£90

VICTORIA (1838–1901)

1837	Extremely Rare Proofs or Patterns only				
1838	2,150,280	£7	£15	£40	£90
1838 over last 8 on its side		£10	£20	£60	£120
1839	1,461,240	£7	£16	£50	£100
1839 Proof	incl. above				Rare
1840	1,496,880	£7	£15	£50	£100
1840 Small 0 in date	incl. above	£7	£15	£50	£100
1841	344,520	£7	£15	£50	£100
1842/1 2 over 1	incl. above	£7	£15	£50	£100
1842	724,680	£7	£15	£45	£100
1843	1,817640	£8	£16	£50	£120
1843 4 over 5	incl. above	£7	£15	£50	£120
1844	855,360	£7	£15	£50	£110
1845	914,760	£7	£15	£50	£110
1846	1,366,200	£7	£15	£50	£100
1847 7 over 6	225,720	£15	£35	£125	—
1848	712,800	£7	£15	£50	£90
1848/6 8 over 6	incl. above	£30	£110	—	—
1848/7 8 over 7	incl. above	£8	£20	£60	£110
1849	380,160	£7	£15	£50	£100
1849/8 9 over 8	incl. above	£8	£20	£70	£135
1851	594,000	£30	£80	£250	£400
1852	31,300	£50	£120	£400	—
1853	11,880	£80	£170	£550	—
1853 Proof Milled Rim	incl. above	—	—	—	£1000
1853 Plain edge Proof				Extremely rare	
1854	1,096,613	£7	£15	£40	£90
1855	646,041	£7	£15	£40	£90
1857 Proofs only				Extremely rare	
1862 Proofs only				Extremely rare	
1888 Jubilee Head	—	£10	£20	£45	£100

THREEPENCES

DATE	MINTAGE	F	VF	EF	UNC

The earlier threepences are included in the Maundy oddments section.

WILLIAM IV (1830–37)
(issued for use in the West Indies)

DATE	MINTAGE	F	VF	EF	UNC
1834		£8	£20	£80	£200
1835		£8	£20	£80	£200
1836		£8	£20	£80	£200
1837		£8	£25	£100	£220

VICTORIA (1837–1901)

DATE	MINTAGE	F	VF	EF	UNC
1838 BRITANNIAB error				Extremely rare	
1838	—	£10	£25	£80	£200
1839	—	£10	£25	£80	£200
1840	—	£10	£25	£80	£200
1841	—	£10	£25	£70	£210
1842	—	£10	£25	£70	£200
1843	—	£10	£25	£60	£180
1843/34 43 over 34	—	£10	£25	£90	£220
1844	—	£12	£25	£80	£190
1845	1,319,208	£12	£25	£70	£180
1846	52,008	£15	£35	£150	£340
1847	4,488			Extremely rare	
1848	incl. above			Extremely rare	
1849	131,208	£12	£25	£80	£220
1850	954,888	£12	£24	£50	£175
1851	479,065	£12	£26	£60	£185
1851 5 over 8	incl. above	£25	£45	£175	—
1852	4,488			Extremely rare	
1853	36,168	£35	£100	£220	£550
1854	1,467,246	£8	£22	£60	£175
1855	383,350	£12	£26	£60	£175
1856	1,013,760	£8	£22	£60	£160
1857	1,758,240	£8	£22	£70	£180
1858	1,441,440	£8	£22	£60	£170
1858 BRITANNIAB error	incl. above			Extremely rare	
1858/6 final 8 over 6	incl. above	£10	£30	£125	—
1858/5 final 8 over 5	incl. above	£10	£30	£125	—
1859	3,579,840	£7	£20	£50	£150
1860	3,405,600	£8	£22	£50	£170
1861	3,294,720	£8	£22	£50	£150
1862	1,156,320	£8	£22	£50	£150
1863	950,400	£20	£55	£110	£250
1864	1,330,560	£7	£22	£50	£150
1865	1,742,400	£7	£22	£50	£150
1866	1,900,800	£7	£22	£50	£150
1867	712,800	£7	£22	£50	£150
1868	1,457,280	£7	£22	£50	£150
1868 RRITANNIAR error	incl. above			Extremely rare	
1869	—	£40	£75	£175	£350
1870	1,283,218	£5	£16	£45	£90
1871	999,633	£5	£16	£40	£90
1872	1,293,271	£5	£16	£40	£90
1873	4,055,550	£5	£16	£40	£90
1874	4,427,031	£5	£16	£40	£90
1875	3,306,500	£5	£16	£40	£90
1876	1,834,389	£5	£16	£40	£90
1877	2,622,393	£5	£16	£40	£90
1878	2,419,975	£5	£16	£40	£110
1879	3,140,265	£5	£16	£40	£90
1880	1,610,069	£5	£16	£40	£80
1881	3,248,265	£5	£16	£40	£80
1882	472,965	£8	£25	£70	£170
1883	4,369,971	£5	£10	£30	£60

Victoria first type

DATE	MINTAGE	F	VF	EF	UNC
1884..	3,322,424	£5	£12	£30	£60
1885..	5,183,653	£5	£12	£30	£60
1886..	6,152,669	£5	£12	£30	£60
1887..	2,780,761	£5	£12	£30	£60
JUBILEE HEAD ISSUES					
1887	incl. above	£2	£4	£11	£24
1887 Proof.................................	incl. above	—	—	—	£130
1888..	518,199	£2	£5	£20	£40
1889..	4,587,010	£2	£5	£20	£45
1890..	4,465,834	£2	£5	£20	£45
1891..	6,323,027	£2	£5	£20	£45
1892..	2,578,226	£2	£5	£20	£45
1893..	3,067,243	£10	£40	£125	£275
OLD HEAD ISSUES					
1893..	incl. above	£2	£4	£15	£30
1893 Proof.................................	incl. above	—	—	—	£80
1894..	1,608,603	£3	£6	£25	£55
1895..	4,788,609	£2	£5	£22	£50
1896..	4,598,442	£2	£5	£18	£35
1897..	4,541,294	£2	£5	£18	£35
1898..	4,567,177	£2	£5	£18	£35
1899..	6,246,281	£2	£5	£18	£35
1900..	10,644,480	£2	£5	£18	£35
1901..	6,098,400	£2	£5	£14	£30

Victoria Jubilee head

Victoria Old or Veiled head

EDWARD VII (1901–10)

	MINTAGE	F	VF	EF	UNC
1902..	8,268,480	£2	£2	£7	£15
1902 "Matt Proof"	incl. above	—	—	—	£40
1903..	5,227,200	£2	£4	£20	£50
1904..	3,627,360	£3	£10	£45	£100
1905..	3,548,160	£2	£4	£25	£60
1906..	3,152,160	£2	£6	£25	£60
1907..	4,831,200	£2	£4	£20	£50
1908..	8,157,600	£2	£3	£20	£50
1909..	4,055,040	£2	£4	£20	£50
1910..	4,563,380	£2	£4	£18	£35

GEORGE V (1910–36)

First issue

	MINTAGE	F	VF	EF	UNC
1911..	5,841,084	—	—	£3	£10
1911 Proof.................................	incl. above	—	—	—	£45
1912	8,932,825	—	—	£3	£12
1913..	7,143,242	—	—	£3	£12
1914..	6,733,584	—	—	£3	£12
1915..	5,450,617	—	—	£3	£15
1916..	18,555,201	—	—	£3	£10
1917..	21,662,490	—	—	£3	£10
1918..	20,630,909	—	—	£3	£10
1919	16,845,687	—	—	£3	£10
1920	16,703,597	—	—	£3	£10
Second issue—debased silver					
1920	incl. above	—	—	£3	£12
1921..	8,749,301	—	—	£3	£12
1922..	7,979,998	—	—	£3	£40
1925..	3,731,859	—	—	£5	£25
1926	4,107,910	—	—	£7	£30
Third issue—Modified bust					
1926..	incl. above	—	—	£8	£22
Fourth issue—new design (oakleaves)					
1927 Proof only	15,022	—	—	—	£90
1928..	1,302,106	£4	£9	£30	£65
1930..	1,319,412	£2	£4	£10	£40
1931..	6,251,936	—	—	£2	£7
1932..	5,887,325	—	—	£2	£7
1933..	5,578,541	—	—	£2	£7
1934..	7,405,954	—	—	£2	£7
1935..	7,027,654	—	—	£2	£7
1936..	3,328,670	—	—	£2	£7

George V second issue

George V, fourth issue oak leaves design reverse

DATE	MINTAGE	F	VF	EF	UNC

GEORGE VI (1936–52)

Silver

DATE	MINTAGE	F	VF	EF	UNC
1937	8,148,156	—	—	£1	£4
1937 Proof	26,402	—	—	—	£15
1938	6,402,473	—	—	£1	£4
1939	1,355,860	—	—	£4	£15
1940	7,914,401	—	—	£1	£3
1941	7,979,411	—	—	£1	£3
1942	4,144,051	£2	£5	£12	£35
1943	1,397,220	£2	£5	£12	£35
1944	2,005,553	£7	£15	£40	£90
1945				Only one known	

Nickel brass

DATE	MINTAGE	F	VF	EF	UNC
1937	45,707,957	—	—	£1	£4
1937 Proof	26,402	—	—	—	£10
1938	14,532,332	—	—	£1	£18
1939	5,603,021	—	—	£3	£40
1940	12,636,018	—	—	£3	£30
1941	60,239,489	—	—	£1	£8
1942	103,214,400	—	—	£1	£8
1943	101,702,400	—	—	£1	£8
1944	69,760,000	—	—	£1	£8
1945	33,942,466	—	—	£3	£20
1946	620,734	£6	£25	£175	£700
1948	4,230,400	—	—	£7	£50
1949	464,000	£5	£25	£200	£750
1950	1,600,000	—	£2	£20	£110
1950 Proof	17,513	—	—	—	£15
1951	1,184,000	—	£2	£25	£100
1951 Proof	20,000	—	—	—	£20
1952	25,494,400	—	—	—	£10

George VI "Thrift" design of the brass 3d

ELIZABETH II (1952–   )

DATE	MINTAGE	F	VF	EF	UNC
1953	30,618,000	—	—	—	£1
1953 Proof	40,000	—	—	—	£6
1954	41,720,000	—	—	—	£5
1955	41,075,200	—	—	—	£5
1956	36,801,600	—	—	—	£6
1957	24,294,500	—	—	—	£6
1958	20,504,000	—	—	—	£9
1959	28,499,200	—	—	—	£6
1960	83,078,400	—	—	—	£2
1961	41,102,400	—	—	—	£1
1962	51,545,600	—	—	—	£1
1963	39,482,866	—	—	—	£1
1964	44,867,200	—	—	—	—
1965	27,160,000	—	—	—	—
1966	53,160,000	—	—	—	—
1967	151,780,800	—	—	—	—
1970 Proof	—				£8

TWO PENCES

GEORGE III (1760–1820)

	F	VF	EF	UNC
1797 "Cartwheel"	£30	£60	£350	£900
1797 Copper Proofs	Many types from £500+			

VICTORIA (1837–1901)

For use in the Colonies

	F	VF	EF	UNC
1838	£4	£10	£18	£35
1848	£4	£12	£20	£40

Earlier issues of the small silver two pences are listed in the Maundy section.

THREE-HALFPENCES

DATE		F	VF	EF	UNC

WILLIAM IV (1830–37)

For use in the Colonies

		F	VF	EF	UNC
1834		£6	£16	£35	£80
1835		£10	£25	£75	£200
1835 over 4		£6	£16	£40	£90
1836		£8	£18	£40	£95
1837		£15	£35	£110	£300

VICTORIA (1837–1901)

For use in the Colonies

		F	VF	EF	UNC
1838		£6	£15	£35	£75
1839		£6	£15	£35	£75
1840		£8	£20	£60	£125
1841		£6	£15	£35	£80
1842		£6	£18	£40	£90
1843		£6	£15	£30	£70
1860		£10	£24	£75	£160
1862		£10	£24	£75	£160

PENNIES

DATE	MINTAGE	F	VF	EF	UNC

The earlier small silver pennies are included in the Maundy oddments section.

GEORGE III (1760–1820)

	MINTAGE	F	VF	EF	UNC
1797 "Cartwheel", 10 laurel leaves	8,601,600	£25	£60	£300	£900
1797 — 11 laurel leaves	incl. above	£25	£60	£300	£900
1806 Third type	—	£7	£18	£70	£300
1807	—	£7	£18	£70	£300
1808					Unique

GEORGE IV (1820–30)

	MINTAGE	F	VF	EF	UNC
1825	1,075,200	£12	£45	£250	£600
1826 (varieties)	5,913,600	£12	£45	£250	£600
1826 Proof	—	—	—	—	£650
1827	1,451,520	£220	£800	£3000	—

WILLIAM IV (1830–37)

	MINTAGE	F	VF	EF	UNC
1831 (varieties)	806,400	£25	£70	£425	£1100
1831 Proof	—	—	—	—	£800
1834	322,560	£30	£70	£400	£1250
1837	174,720	£65	£200	£800	£2800

VICTORIA (1837–1901)

YOUNG HEAD ISSUES
Copper

	MINTAGE	F	VF	EF	UNC
1839 Proof	unrecorded	—	—	—	£1700
1841	913,920	£10	£50	£300	£750
1841 No colon after REG	incl. above	£8	£20	£175	£550
1843	483,840	£90	£350	£2000	£5000
1844	215,040	£12	£25	£160	£550
1845	322,560	£15	£35	£220	£750
1846	483,840	£15	£25	£200	£700
1846 FID: DEF colon spaced	incl. above	£15	£25	£200	£700
1846 FID:DEF colon close	incl. above	£16	£25	£210	£725
1847	430,080	£12	£25	£180	£550
1848	161,280	£10	£25	£160	£500
1848/7 final 8 over 7	incl. above	£8	£20	£150	£450

George III "Cartwheel" penny

DATE	MINTAGE	F	VF	EF	UNC
1848/6 final 8 over 6	incl. above £20	£120	£525	—
1849	268,800 £225	£600	£2200	—
1851	268,800 £15	£45	£200	£800
1853	1,021,440 £7	£15	£100	£180
1853 Proof	— —	—	—	£2000
1854	6,720,000 £8	£20	£100	£180
1854/3 4 over 3	incl. above £14	£45	£180	—
1855	5,273,856 £8	£20	£100	£250
1856	1,212,288 £100	£250	£700	£2700
1857 Plain trident	752,640 £7	£18	£80	£280
1857 Ornamental trident	incl. above £6	£18	£70	£280
1858/7 final 8 over 7	incl. above £7	£18	£80	£300
1858/6 final 8 over 6	— £40	£120	£500	—
1858/3 final 8 over 3	incl. above £25	£90	£400	—
1858	1,599,040 £7	£16	£90	£250
1859	1,075,200 £8	£25	£150	£350
1860/59	32,256 £600	£1500	£3750	£6500

Bronze

Prices of bronze Victoria Young "bun" head pennies are for the common types. There are many known varieties which are listed in detail in other more specialised publications. Prices for coins in mint with full lustre will be considerably higher.

Victoria copper penny

DATE	MINTAGE	F	VF	EF	UNC
1860 Beaded border	5,053,440 £25	£50	£170	£700
1860 Toothed border	incl. above £6	£20	£60	£3000
1860 — Piedfort flan	—	Extremely rare		
1861	36,449,280 £5	£12	£50	£275
1862	50,534,400 £5	£12	£50	£275
1862 8 over 6	incl. above	Extremely rare		
1863	28,062,720 £5	£12	£45	£250
1863 Die no below date	incl. above	Extremely rare		
1864 Plain 4	3,440,640 £25	£140	£600	£3000
1864 Crosslet 4	incl. above £30	£150	£600	£3200
1865	8,601,600 £7	£16	£55	£350
1865/3 5 over 3	incl. above £40	£125	£450	—
1866	9,999,360 £6	£20	£80	£475
1867	5,483,520 £7	£20	£95	£800
1868	1,182,720 £15	£70	£200	£1800
1869	2,580,480 £130	£450	£1700	£5500
1870	5,695,022 £12	£40	£140	£725
1871	1,290,318 £35	£120	£450	£2000
1872	8,494,572 £6	£20	£60	£270
1873	8,494,200 £6	£20	£60	£270
1874	5,621,865 £7	£20	£60	£270
1874 H	6,666,240 £7	£22	£60	£270
1874 Later (older) bust	incl. above £14	£35	£90	£450

Victoria Young or "Bun" head bronze penny

DATE	MINTAGE	F	VF	EF	UNC
1875	10,691,040	£7	£22	£75	£325
1875 H	752,640	£35	£110	£800	£2500
1876 H	11,074,560	£5	£12	£60	£275
1877	9,624,747	£5	£14	£55	£275
1878	2,764,470	£5	£14	£55	£275
1879	7,666,476	£4	£15	£55	£275
1880	3,000,831	£4	£15	£55	£280
1881	2,302,362	£5	£15	£55	£275
1881 H	3,763,200	£5	£15	£55	£275
1882 H	7,526,400	£5	£15	£55	£275
1882 no H	—		Extremely Rare		
1883	6,237,438	£5	£15	£55	£250
1884	11,702,802	£5	£15	£55	£250
1885	7,145,862	£5	£15	£55	£250
1886	6,087,759	£5	£15	£55	£250
1887	5,315,085	£5	£15	£55	£250
1888	5,125,020	£5	£15	£55	£250
1889	12,559,737	£5	£15	£50	£325
1890	15,330,840	£5	£15	£50	£200
1891	17,885,961	£5	£12	£50	£200
1892	10,501,671	£6	£15	£70	£235
1893	8,161,737	£5	£12	£55	£230
1894	3,883,452	£10	£35	£140	£420

OLD HEAD ISSUES

1895 Trident 2mm from P(ENNY)	5,395,830	£20	£90	£280	£800
1895 Trident 1mm from P	incl. above	—	£2	£18	£75
1896	24,147,156	—	£2	£18	£65
1897	20,756,620	—	£2	£15	£60
1897 Raised dot after One (O·NE)		£125	£225	£800	—
1898	14,296,836	—	£3	£18	£60
1899	26,441,069	—	£3	£16	£50
1900	31,778,109	—	£3	£16	£40
1901	22,205,568	—	£3	£10	£30

EDWARD VII (1901–10)

1902	26,976,768	—	£1	£8	£30
1902 "Low tide" to sea line	incl. above	£4	£15	£60	£200
1903	21,415,296	—	£3	£15	£80
1904	12,913,152	—	£4	£25	£185
1905	17,783,808	—	£3	£15	£80
1906	37,989,504	—	£3	£15	£70
1907	47,322,240	—	£3	£15	£70
1908	31,506,048	—	£3	£18	£120
1909	19,617,024	—	£3	£20	£150
1910	29,549,184	—	£3	£15	£60

GEORGE V (1910–36)

1911	23,079,168	—	£3	£12	£60
1912	48,306,048	—	£3	£12	£50
1912 H	16,800,000	—	£4	£40	£220
1913	65,497,812	—	£3	£15	£70
1914	50,820,997	—	£3	£18	£70
1915	47,310,807	—	£3	£20	£80
1916	86,411,165	—	£3	£15	£60
1917	107,905,436	—	£3	£15	£50
1918	84,227,372	—	£3	£12	£50
1918 H	3,660,800	£1	£15	£100	£450
1918 KN	incl. above	£8	£80	£550	£2200
1919	113,761,090	—	£2	£15	£50
1919 H	5,209,600	£1	£15	£200	£700
1919 KN	incl. above	£15	£110	£750	£2750
1920	124,693,485	—	£2	£12	£30
1921	129,717,693	—	£2	£12	£40
1922	16,346,711	—	£3	£25	£140
1922 with reverse of 1927		£1000	£2500	—	—
1926	4,498,519	—	£6	£25	£140
1926 Modified effigy	incl above	£25	£150	£800	£2500
1927	60,989,561	—	£2	£10	£40

DATE	MINTAGE	F	VF	EF	UNC
1928	50,178,00	—	£2	£10	£35
1929	49,132,800	—	£2	£10	£40
1930	29,097,600	—	£2	£20	£70
1931	19,843,200	—	£2	£10	£50
1932	8,277,600	—	£2	£15	£100
1933			Only 7 examples known		
1934	13,965,600	—	£2	£25	£100
1935	56,070,000	—	—	£2	£12
1936	154,296,000	—	—	£2	£12

GEORGE VI (1936–52)

DATE	MINTAGE	F	VF	EF	UNC
1937	88,896,000	—	—	—	£4
1937 Proof	26,402	—	—	—	£14
1938	121,560,000	—	—	—	£6
1939	55,560,000	—	—	—	£15
1940	42,284,400	—	—	£8	£25
1944 Mint Dark	42,600,000	—	—	—	£8
1945 Mint Dark	79,531,200	—	—	—	£8
1946 Mint Dark	66,855,600	—	—	—	£8
1947	52,220,400	—	—	—	£5
1948	63,961,200	—	—	—	£5
1949	14,324,400	—	—	—	£8
1950	240,000	£7	£15	£30	£50
1950 Proof	17,513	—	—	—	£25
1951	120,000	£20	£24	£50	£75
1951 Proof	20,000	—	—	—	£40

ELIZABETH II (1952–)

DATE	MINTAGE	F	VF	EF	UNC
1953	1,308,400	—	—	£1	£4
1953 Proof	40,000	—	—	—	£7
1954			Only one known		
1961	48,313,400	—	—	—	£2
1962	143,308,600	—	—	—	50p
1963	125,235,600	—	—	—	50p
1964	153,294,000	—	—	—	50p
1965	121,310,400	—	—	—	50p
1966	165,739,200	—	—	—	50p
1967	654,564,000	—	—	—	—
1970 Proof	—				£8

Later issues are included in the Decimal section.

HALFPENNIES

CHARLES II (1660–85)

	F	VF	EF	UNC
1672	£70	£300	£1250	—
1672 CRAOLVS error		Extremely rare		
1673	£70	£300	£1200	—
1673 CRAOLVS error		Extremely rare		
1673 No rev. stop	£100	£600	—	—
1673 No stops on obv.		Extremely rare		
1675	£60	£500	£1400	—
1675 No stops on obv.	£80	£550	—	—
1675/3 5 over 3	£175	£625	—	—

JAMES II (1685–88)

	F	VF	EF	UNC
1685 (tin)	£250	£750	£4000	—
1686 (tin)	£280	£750	£4100	—
1687 (tin)	£320	£800	£4000	—

WILLIAM & MARY (1688–94)

Tin

	F	VF	EF	UNC
1689 Small draped busts, edge dated		Extremely rare		
1690 Large cuirassed busts, edge dated	£200	£750	£3400	—
1691 — date on edge and in exergue	£180	£700	£3200	—
1692 — —	£200	£750	£3200	—

DATE	F	VF	EF	UNC

Copper

	F	VF	EF	UNC
1694 Large cuirassed busts, date in exergue	£80	£300	£1200	—
1694 — — GVLIEMVS error		Extremely rare		
1694 — — MΛRIΛ error		Extremely rare		
1694 — — No stops on rev.		Extremely rare		

WILLIAM III (1694–1702)

	F	VF	EF	UNC
1695 First issue (date in exergue)...................	£50	£200	£1100	—
1695 — No stop after BRITANNIA on rev.		Extremely rare		
1696 —	£40	£180	£1000	—
1696 — TERTVS error		Extremely rare		
1697 —	£45	£170	£1000	—
1697 — No stop after TERTIVS on obv.	£50	£300	—	—
1698 —	£50	£200	£1000	—
1698 Second issue (date in legend)	£50	£180	—	—
1698 — No stop after date............................	£50	£180	—	—
1699 —	£55	£210	£1100	—
1699 — No stop after date............................	£225	—	—	—
1699 Third issue (date in exergue) (Britannia with right hand on knee).......................................	£40	£175	£900	—
1699 — No stop after date............................		Extremely rare		
1699 — BRITΛNNIΛ error	£200	—	—	—
1699 — TERTVS error		Extremely rare		
1699 — No stop on rev.................................		Extremely rare		
1699 — No stops on obv..............................	£90	£375	—	—
1700 —	£45	£190	£950	—
1700 — No stops on obv..............................	£100	£350	—	—
1700 — No stops after GVLIELMUS	£100	£350	—	—
1700 — BRITVANNIA error............................		Extremely rare		
1700 — GVIELMS error..............................	£100	£350	—	—
1700 — GVLIEEMVS error............................	£100	£350	—	—
1701 —	£40	£175	£900	—
1701 — BRITΛNNIΛ error	£80	£300	—	—
1701 — No stops on obv..............................		Extremely rare		
1701 — inverted As for Vs.............................	£80	£320	—	—

GEORGE I (1714–27)

	F	VF	EF	UNC
1717 "Dump" issue	£40	£240	£800	
1718 —	£35	£225	£775	—
1719 "Dump" issue. Patterns.........................				Rare
1719 Second issue....................................	£40	£200	£800	—
1720 —	£35	£160	£600	—
1721 —	£35	£150	£600	—
1721 — Stop after date...............................	£45	£150	—	—
1722 —	£35	£140	£650	—
1722 — inverted A for V on obv.		Extremely rare		
1723 —	£35	£150	£625	—
1723 — No stop on rev.................................	£110	£500	—	—
1724 —	£35	£150	£625	—

GEORGE II (1727–60)

	F	VF	EF	UNC
1729 Young head	£25	£90	£400	—
1729 — No stop on rev.................................	£25	£80	£400	—
1730 —	£20	£90	£400	—
1730 — GEOGIVS error..............................	£70	£225	£650	—
1730 — Stop after date...............................	£25	£120	£400	—
1730 — No stop after REX on obv.	£30	£140	£450	—
1731 —	£20	£110	£400	—
1731 — No rev. stop..................................	£25	£125	£425	—
1732 —	£20	£100	£400	—
1732 — No rev. stop..................................	£25	£125	£450	—
1733 —	£20	£90	£400	—
1734/3 — 4 over 3....................................	£35	£210	—	—
1734 — No stop on obv.	£35	£210	—	—

DATE	MINTAGE	F	VF	EF	UNC
1735 —		£20	£80	£400	—
1736 —		£20	£80	£400	—
1737 —		£20	£85	£400	—
1738 —		£20	£80	£350	—
1739 —		£18	£70	£350	—
1740 Old head		£15	£70	£320	—
1742 —		£15	£70	£320	—
1742/0 — 2 over 0		£25	£150	£450	—
1743 —		£15	£70	£320	—
1744 —		£15	£70	£320	—
1745 —		£15	£70	£330	—
1746 —		£15	£70	£320	—
1747 —		£15	£70	£320	—
1748 —		£15	£70	£330	—
1749 —		£15	£70	£330	—
1750 —		£15	£70	£330	—
1751 —		£15	£70	£330	—
1752 —		£15	£70	£330	—
1753 —		£15	£70	£330	—
1754 —		£15	£70	£330	—

GEORGE III (1760–1820)

First type—Royal Mint

1770		£18	£50	£300	—
1770 No stop on rev.		£25	£65	£350	—
1771		£12	£50	£280	—
1771 No stop on rev.		£20	£65	£300	—
1772 Error GEORIVS		£70	£225	£700	
1772		£12	£50	£225	—
1772 No stop on rev		£20	£65	£280	—
1773		£10	£45	£280	—
1773 No stop after REX		£30	£80	£400	—
1773 No stop on rev.		£20	£70	£300	—
1774		£12	£40	£220	—
1775		£12	£40	£220	—

Second type—Soho Mint

1799		£5	£12	£55	£120

Third type

1806		£5	£11	£60	£110
1807		£5	£11	£60	£110

George III second type

GEORGE IV (1820–30)

1825	215,040	£12	£45	£190	£380
1826 (varieties)	9,031,630	£12	£45	£190	£380
1826 Proof	—	—	—	—	£520
1827	5,376,000	£12	£45	£160	£340

WILLIAM IV (1830–37)

1831	806,400	£12	£30	£130	£325
1831 Proof	—	—	—	—	£500
1834	537,600	£12	£30	£130	£325
1837	349,440	£12	£30	£130	£325

VICTORIA (1837–1901)

Copper

1838	456,960	£8	£18	£80	£310
1839 Proof	268,800	—	—	—	£475
1841	1,075,200	£6	£16	£60	£220
1843	967,680	£30	£50	£200	£725
1844	1,075,200	£12	£40	£180	£375

DATE	MINTAGE	F	VF	EF	UNC
1845...	1,075,200	£200	£450	£1800	—
1846...	860,160	£12	£25	£85	£240
1847...	725,640	£12	£22	£85	£240
1848...	322,560	£12	£22	£80	£240
1848/7 final 8 OVER 7	incl. above	£14	£35	£100	£275
1851...	215,040	£7	£18	£75	£240
1852...	637,056	£10	£22	£80	£240
1853...	1,559,040	£5	£10	£40	£120
1853/2 3 over 2	incl. above	£15	£30	£60	£240
1853 Proof..............................	—	—	—	—	£750
1854...	12,354,048	£5	£9	£40	£130
1855...	1,455,837	£5	£9	£40	£130
1856...	1,942,080	£10	£24	£80	£275
1857...	1,820,720	£6	£18	£50	£130
1858...	2,472,960	£5	£12	£50	£130
1858/7 final 8 over 7................	incl. above	£5	£12	£50	£130
1858/6 final 8 over 6................	incl. above	£5	£12	£50	£130
1859...	1,290,240	£7	£22	£70	£225
1859/8 9 over 8	incl. above	£8	£25	£70	£260
1860...	unrecorded	£1400	£3500	£7000	£12000

Victoria copper halfpenny

Bronze

1860 Beaded border	6,630,400	£3	£10	£50	£190
1860 Toothed border..............		£4	£12	£60	£270
1861...	54,118,400	£4	£10	£40	£185
1862 Die letter A, B or C to left of lighthouse				Extremely rare	
1862...	61,107,200	£3	£9	£40	£160
1863...	15,948,800	£3	£9	£75	£160
1864...	537,600	£3	£10	£45	£175
1865...	8,064,000	£4	£18	£75	£300
1865/3 5 over 3	incl. above	£50	£120	£450	—
1866...	2,508,800	£5	£15	£70	£240
1867...	2,508,800	£5	£15	£60	£220
1868...	3,046,400	£5	£15	£70	£260
1869...	3,225,600	£25	£90	£250	£1400
1870...	4,350,739	£5	£15	£60	£250
1871...	1,075,280	£75	£100	£500	£1500
1872...	4,659,410	£4	£10	£50	£180
1873...	3,404,880	£4	£10	£50	£200
1874...	1,347,655	£6	£25	£110	£300
1874 H	5,017,600	£3	£10	£60	£220
1875...	5,430,815	£3	£8	£60	£200
1875 H	1,254,400	£5	£12	£60	£200
1876 H	5,809,600	£4	£10	£60	£220
1877...	5,209,505	£3	£10	£60	£180
1878...	1,425,535	£6	£20	£100	£350
1878 Wide date		£100	£200	£550	—
1879...	3,582,545	£3	£10	£40	£200
1880...	2,423,465	£4	£12	£60	£210
1881...	2,007,515	£4	£12	£50	£180
1881 H	1,792,000	£3	£10	£50	£200
1882 H	4,480,000	£3	£10	£50	£210
1883...	3,000,725	£3	£12	£60	£225
1884...	6,989,580	£3	£10	£45	£160
1885...	8,600,574	£3	£10	£45	£160
1886...	8,586,155	£3	£10	£45	£160
1887...	10,701,305	£3	£10	£45	£160
1888...	6,814,670	£3	£10	£45	£160
1889...	7,748,234	£3	£10	£45	£160
1889/8 9 over 8	incl. above	£30	£60	£250	—
1890...	11,254,235	£3	£10	£40	£120
1891...	13,192,260	£3	£10	£35	£120
1892...	2,478,335	£3	£10	£45	£140

Victoria bronze halfpenny

DATE	MINTAGE	F	VF	EF	UNC
1893	7,229,344	£3	£10	£35	£130
1894	1,767,635	£5	£12	£70	£270

OLD HEAD ISSUES

1895	3,032,154	£2	£7	£20	£65
1896	9,142,500	£1	£4	£10	£45
1897	8,690,315	£1	£4	£10	£45
1898	8,595,180	£1	£5	£12	£55
1899	12,108,001	£1	£4	£10	£45
1900	13,805,190	£1	£4	£10	£35
1901	11,127,360	£1	£3	£8	£25

EDWARD VII (1901–10)

1902	13,672,960	£2	£4	£8	£30
1902 "Low tide"	incl. above	£18	£80	£180	£425
1903	11,450,880	£2	£5	£20	£60
1904	8,131,200	£2	£6	£25	£80
1905	10,124,800	£2	£5	£20	£55
1906	16,849,280	£2	£5	£25	£70
1907	16,849,280	£2	£5	£20	£70
1908	16,620,800	£2	£5	£20	£70
1909	8,279,040	£2	£5	£20	£70
1910	10,769,920	£2	£5	£20	£50

GEORGE V (1910–36)

1911	12,570,880	£1	£4	£15	£40
1912	21,185,920	£1	£3	£15	£35
1913	17,476,480	£1	£3	£15	£40
1914	20,289,111	£1	£3	£15	£40
1915	21,563,040	£2	£3	£20	£55
1916	39,386,143	£1	£2	£15	£40
1917	38,245,436	£1	£2	£15	£35
1918	22,321,072	£1	£2	£15	£35
1919	28,104,001	£1	£2	£15	£35
1920	35,146,793	£1	£2	£15	£40
1921	28,027,293	£1	£2	£15	£40
1922	10,734,964	£1	£4	£25	£45
1923	12,266,282	£1	£2	£15	£35
1924	13,971,038	£1	£2	£15	£30
1925	12,216,123	—	£2	£15	£30
1925 Modified effigy	incl. above	£4	£10	£50	£90
1926	6,172,306	—	£2	£10	£40
1927	15,589,622	—	£2	£10	£40
1928	20,935,200	—	£2	£8	£35
1929	25,680,000	—	£2	£8	£35
1930	12,532,800	—	£2	£8	£35
1931	16,137,600	—	£2	£8	£35
1932	14,448,000	—	£2	£8	£35
1933	10,560,000	—	£2	£8	£35
1934	7,704,000	—	£2	£12	£45
1935	12,180,000	—	£1	£6	£20
936	23,008,800	—	£1	£5	£15

GEORGE VI (1936–52)

1937	24,504,000	—	—	£1	£5
1937 Proof	26,402	—	—	—	£18
1938	40,320,000	—	—	£1	£6
1939	28,924,800	—	—	£1	£5
1940	32,162,400	—	—	£2	£10

DATE	MINTAGE	F	VF	EF	UNC
1941	45,120,000	—	—	£1	£8
1942	71,908,800	—	—	£1	£5
1943	76,200,000	—	—	£1	£5
1944	81,840,000	—	—	£1	£5
1945	57,000,000	—	—	£1	£5
1946	22,725,600	—	—	£1	£6
1947	21,266,400	—	—	£1	£6
1948	26,947,200	—	—	£1	£4
1949	24,744,000	—	—	£1	£4
1950	24,153,600	—	—	£1	£5
1950 Proof	17,513	—	—	—	£18
1951	14,868,000	—	—	£1	£6
1951 Proof	20,000	—	—	—	£18
1952	33,784,000	—	—	£1	£4

ELIZABETH II (1952–)

1953	8,926,366	—	—	—	£1
1953 Proof	40,000	—	—	—	£4
1954	19,375,000	—	—	—	£3
1955	18,799,200	—	—	—	£3
1956	21,799,200	—	—	—	£3
1957	43,684,800	—	—	—	£1
1957 Calm sea	incl. above	—	—	£10	£30
1958	62,318,400	—	—	—	£1
1959	79,176,000	—	—	—	£1
1960	41,340,000	—	—	—	£1
1962	41,779,200	—	—	—	£1
1963	45,036,000	—	—	—	20p
1964	78,583,200	—	—	—	20p
1965	98,083,200	—	—	—	20p
1966	95,289,600	—	—	—	20p
1967	146,491,200	—	—	—	10p
1970 Proof	—				£5

Later issues are included in the Decimal section.

FARTHINGS

DATE		F	VF	EF	UNC

OLIVER CROMWELL

Undated (copper) Draped bust, shield rev. Variations — Extremely rare

CHARLES II (1660–85)

Copper

	F	VF	EF	UNC
1672	£40	£225	£725	—
1673	£45	£240	£750	—
1673 CAROLA for CAROLO error	£125	£500	—	—
1673 No stops on obv.			Extremely rare	
1673 No stop on rev.			Extremely rare	
1674	£45	£250	£800	—
1675	£40	£220	£725	—
1675 No stop after CAROLVS			Extremely rare	
1679	£55	£275	£900	—
1679 No stop on rev.	£60	£300	—	—
Tin				
1684 with date on edge	£200	£700	—	—
1685 —			Extremely rare	

DATE	F	VF	EF	UNC

JAMES II (1685–88)

	F	VF	EF	UNC
1684 (tin) Cuirassed bust		Extremely rare		
1685 (tin) —	£170	£600	£2250	—
1686 (tin) —	£180	£600	£2250	—
1687 (tin) —		Extremely rare		
1687 (tin) Draped bust	£220	£800	—	—

WILLIAM & MARY (1688–94)

	F	VF	EF	UNC
1689 (tin) Small draped busts	£650	—	—	—
1689 (tin) — with edge date 1690		Extremely rare		
1690 (tin) Large cuirassed busts	£150	£600	£2750	
1690 (tin) — with edge date 1689		Extremely rare		
1691 (tin) —	£160	£600	—	—
1692 (tin) —	£175	£650	£2750	—
1694 (copper) —	£70	£250	£900	—
1694 No stop after MARIΛ		Extremely rare		
1694 No stop on obv.		Extremely rare		
1694 No stop on rev.		Extremely rare		
1694 Unbarred As in BRITANNIA		Extremely rare		

WILLIAM III (1694–1702)

	F	VF	EF	UNC
1695 First issue (date in exergue)	£40	£200	£800	—
1695 — GVLIELMV error		Extremely rare		
1696 —	£40	£200	£850	—
1697 —	£40	£200	£850	—
1697 — GVLIELMS error		Extremely rare		
1698 —	£200	£750	—	—
1698 Second issue (date in legend)	£50	£250	£850	—
1699 First issue	£40	£200	£800	—
1699 Second issue	£40	£200	£800	—
1699 — No stop after date	£50	£300	—	—
1700 First issue	£35	£140	£675	—
1700 — error RRITANNIA		Extremely rare		

ANNE (1702–14)

	F	VF	EF	UNC
1714	£400	£650	£1400	—

GEORGE I (1714–27)

	F	VF	EF	UNC
1717 First small "Dump" issue	£200	£600	£1200	—
1718 1 Known				—
1719 Second issue	£30	£140	£450	—
1719 — No stop on rev.	£70	£350	—	—
1719 — No stops on obv.	£70	£300	—	—
1720 —	£30	£140	£500	—
1721 —	£25	£140	£500	—
1721/0 — Last 1 over 0	£40	£160	—	—
1722 —	£35	£125	£475	—
1723 —	£35	£125	£500	—
1723 — R over sideways R in REX		Extremely rare		
1724 —	£35	£140	£500	—

George I, first type

GEORGE II (1727–60)

	F	VF	EF	UNC
1730 Young head	£15	£60	£325	—
1731 —	£15	£60	£325	—
1732 —	£15	£75	£375	—
1733 —	£15	£70	£375	—
1734 —	£15	£65	£375	—
1734 — No stop on obv.	£30	£110	£425	—

George I second type

DATE	MINTAGE	F	VF	EF	UNC
1735 —		£15	£60	£340	—
1735 — 3 over 5		£20	£100	£425	—
1736 —		£12	£60	£325	—
1737 —		£12	£60	£300	—
1739 —		£12	£60	£300	—
1741 Old Head		£12	£50	£300	—
1744 —		£12	£50	£300	—
1746 —		£12	£50	£300	—
1746 — V over LL in GEORGIVS				Extremely rare	
1749 —		£15	£60	£300	—
1750 —		£15	£55	£285	—
1754 —		£10	£30	£200	—
1754 — 4 over 0		£25	£100	£325	—

GEORGE III (1760–1820)

	MINTAGE	F	VF	EF	UNC
1771 First (London) issue		£20	£60	£250	—
1773 —		£12	£40	£200	—
1773 — No stop on rev.		£18	£60	£230	—
1773 — No stop after REX		£25	£75	£250	
1774 —		£10	£40	£190	—
1775 —		£10	£40	£190	—
1797 Second (Soho Mint) issue				Patterns only	
1799 Third (Soho Mint) issue		£2	£8	£40	£100
1806 Fourth (Soho Mint) issue		£2	£8	£40	£100
1807 —		£2	£8	£40	£100

George III, third (Soho Mint) issue

GEORGE IV (1820–30)

	MINTAGE	F	VF	EF	UNC
1821 First bust (laureate, draped), first reverse (date in exergue)	2,688,000	£3	£10	£60	£110
1822 —	5,924,350	£3	£10	£60	£110
1823 —	2,365,440	£4	£10	£60	£110
1823 I for 1 in date	incl. above	£20	£70	£300	£600
1825 —	4,300.800	£4	£10	£60	£130
1826 —	6,666,240	£4	£10	£60	£110
1826 Second bust (couped, date below), second reverse (ornament in exergue)	incl. above	£4	£10	£60	£110
1826 — Proof	—	—	—	—	£350
1827 —	2,365,440	£4	£10	£60	£140
1828 —	2,365,440	£4	£12	£60	£140
1829 —	1,505,280	£4	£12	£60	£140
1830 —	2,365,440	£4	£12	£60	£140

George III, fourth (Soho Mint) issue

WILLIAM IV (1830–37)

	MINTAGE	F	VF	EF	UNC
1831	2,688,000	£5	£12	£45	£125
1831 Proof	—	—	—	—	£400
1834	1,935,360	£5	£12	£50	£120
1835	1.720,320	£5	£12	£50	£120
1836	1,290.240	£5	£12	£55	£120
1837	3.010,560	£5	£12	£55	£140

VICTORIA (1837–1901)

FIRST YOUNG HEAD (COPPER) ISSUES

	MINTAGE	F	VF	EF	UNC
1838	591,360	£5	£15	£45	£170
1839	4,300,800	£5	£15	£45	£170
1839 Proof	—	—	—	—	£475
1840	3,010,560	£4	£15	£40	£145
1841	1,720,320	£4	£15	£40	£170
1841 Proof				Extremely rare	
1842	1,290,240	£10	£35	£100	£340
1843	4,085,760	£5	£14	£40	£175

DATE	MINTAGE	F	VF	EF	UNC
1843 I for 1 in date		£90	£425	—	—
1844	430,080	£75	£200	£800	£2200
1845	3,225,600	£6	£10	£40	£150
1846	2,580,480	£7	£20	£55	£200
1847	3,879,720	£5	£12	£50	£150
1848	1,290,240	£5	£12	£50	£150
1849	645,120	£50	£100	£300	£900
1850	430,080	£5	£10	£40	£140
1851	1,935,360	£8	£20	£80	£240
1851 D over sideways D in DEI	incl. above	£80	£110	£450	—
1852	822,528	£10	£20	£70	£220
1853	1,028,628	£4	£7	£30	£65
1853 Proof	—	—	—	—	£900
1854	6,504,960	£4	£10	£35	£70
1855	3,440,640	£4	£10	£35	£70
1856	1,771,392	£10	£22	£70	£240
1856 R over E in VICTORIA	incl. above	£20	£50	£250	—
1857	1,075,200	£4	£10	£35	£80
1858	1,720,320	£4	£10	£35	£80
1859	1,290,240	£10	£25	£70	£300
1860	unrecorded	£1500	£3750	£6750	—

Victoria Young Head first (copper) issue

SECOND YOUNG OR "BUN" HEAD (BRONZE) ISSUES

	MINTAGE	F	VF	EF	UNC
1860 Toothed border	2,867,200	£2	£5	£40	£100
1860 Beaded border	incl. above	£3	£7	£40	£110
1860 Toothed/Beaded border mule	incl. above			Extremely rare	
1861	8,601,600	£2	£5	£35	£100
1862	14,336,000	£1	£5	£35	£100
1862 Large 8 in date	incl. above			Extremely rare	
1863	1,433,600	£35	£70	£300	£650
1864	2,508,800	£1	£5	£30	£100
1865	4,659,200	£1	£5	£30	£90
1865 5 over 2	incl. above	£10	£20	£65	—
1866	3,584,000	£1	£5	£25	£90
1867	5,017,600	£1	£5	£25	£90
1868	4,851,210	£1	£5	£25	£90
1869	3,225,600	£2	£10	£45	£160
1872	2,150,400	£1	£5	£25	£80
1873	3,225,620	£1	£5	£25	£80
1874 H	3,584,000	£1	£5	£25	£100
1874 H both Gs over sideways G	incl. above	£150	£350	£1000	—
1875	712,760	£4	£12	£40	£130
1875 H	6,092,800	£1	£5	£20	£80
1876 H	1,175,200	£3	£12	£50	£150
1878	4,008,540	£1	£4	£20	£75
1879	3,977,180	£1	£4	£20	£75
1880	1,842,710	£1	£4	£20	£75
1881	3,494,670	£1	£4	£20	£75
1881 H	1,792,000	£1	£4	£20	£75
1882 H	1,792,000	£1	£5	£20	£75
1883	1,128,680	£5	£18	£60	£150
1884	5,782,000	£1	£4	£20	£40
1885	5,442,308	£1	£4	£20	£40
1886	7.707,790	£1	£4	£20	£40
1887	1,340,800	£1	£4	£20	£40
1888	1,887,250	£1	£4	£20	£40
1890	2,133,070	£1	£4	£20	£40
1891	4,959,690	£1	£4	£20	£40
1892	887,240	£3	£12	£50	£140
1893	3,904,320	£1	£4	£20	£40
1894	2,396,770	£1	£4	£20	£40
1895	2,852,852	£10	£25	£80	£225

Victoria Young Head second (bronze) issue

DATE	MINTAGE	F	VF	EF	UNC
OLD HEAD ISSUES					
1895 Bright finish	incl. above	£1	£2	£16	£35
1896 —	3,668,610	£1	£2	£16	£25
1897 —	4,579,800	£1	£2	£16	£25
1897 Dark finish	incl. above	£1	£2	£16	£25
1898 —	4,010,080	£1	£2	£16	£25
1899 —	3,864,616	£1	£2	£16	£25
1900 —	5,969,317	£1	£2	£16	£25
1901 —	8,016,460	£1	£2	£10	£20

EDWARD VII (1901–10)

1902..	5,125,120	50p	£1	£10	£15
1903..	5,331,200	50p	£1	£12	£20
1904..	3,628,800	£2	£5	£20	£45
1905..	4,076,800	£1	£2	£12	£30
1906..	5,340,160	50p	£1	£12	£25
1907..	4,399,360	50p	£1	£10	£20
1908..	4,264,960	50p	£1	£10	£20
1909..	8,852,480	50p	£1	£10	£20
1910..	2,298,400	£3	£8	£25	£65

GEORGE V (1910–36)

1911..	5,196,800	50p	£1	£6	£14
1912..	7,669,760	50p	£1	£8	£14
1913..	4,184,320	50p	£1	£6	£14
1914..	6,126,988	50p	£1	£5	£14
1915..	7,129,255	50p	£1	£5	£16
1916..	10,993,325	50p	£1	£5	£14
1917..	21,434,844	25p	50p	£4	£10
1918..	19,362,818	25p	50p	£4	£10
1919..	15,089,425	25p	50p	£4	£10
1920..	11,480,536	25p	50p	£4	£8
1921..	9,469,097	25p	50p	£4	£8
1922..	9,956,983	25p	50p	£4	£8
1923..	8,034,457	25p	50p	£4	£8
1924..	8,733,414	25p	50p	£4	£8
1925..	12,634,697	25p	50p	£4	£8
1926 Modified effigy...................	9,792,397	25p	50p	£4	£8
1927..	7,868,355	25p	50p	£4	£8
1928	11,625,600	25p	50p	£4	£8
1929	8,419,200	25p	50p	£4	£8
1930	4,195,200	25p	50p	£4	£8
1931	6,595,200	25p	50p	£4	£8
1932	9,292,800	25p	50p	£4	£8
1933	4,560,000	25p	50p	£4	£8
1934	3,052,800	25p	50p	£4	£8
1935	2.227,200	£1	£3	£10	£25
1936	9,734,400	25p	50p	£3	£6

GEORGE VI (1936–52)

1937..	8,131,200	—	—	50p	£1
1937 Proof.................................	26,402	—	—	—	£7
1938..	7,449,600	—	—	£1	£6
1939..	31,440,000	—	—	50p	£1
1940..	18,360,000	—	—	50p	£1
1941..	27,312,000	—	—	50p	£1
1942..	28,857,600	—	—	50p	£1
1943..	33,345,600	—	—	50p	£1
1944..	25,137,600	—	—	50p	£1
1945..	23,736,000	—	—	50p	£1

DATE	MINTAGE	F	VF	EF	UNC
1946	24,364,800	—	—	50p	£1
1947	14,745,600	—	—	50p	£1
1948	16,622,400	—	—	50p	£1
1949	8,424,000	—	—	50p	£1
1950	10,324,800	—	—	50p	£1
1950 Proof	17,513	—	—	50p	£8
1951	14,016,000	—	—	50p	£1
1951 Proof	20,000	—	—	50p	£8
1952	5,251,200	—	—	50p	£1

ELIZABETH II (1952–   )

DATE	MINTAGE	F	VF	EF	UNC
1953	6,131,037	—	—	—	£1
1953 Proof	40,000	—	—	—	£7
1954	6,566,400	—	—	—	£2
1955	5,779,200	—	—	—	£1.50
1956	1,996,800	—	£1	£2	£6

HALF FARTHINGS

DATE	MINTAGE	F	VF	EF	UNC

GEORGE IV (1820–30)

	MINTAGE	F	VF	EF	UNC
1828 (two different obverses) (issued for Ceylon)	7,680,000	£10	£20	£50	£150
1830 (large or small date) (issued for Ceylon)	8,766,320	£10	£20	£50	£140

WILLIAM IV (1830–37)

	MINTAGE	F	VF	EF	UNC
1837 (issued for Ceylon)	1,935,360	£20	£55	£140	£250

VICTORIA (1837–1901)

	MINTAGE	F	VF	EF	UNC
1839	2,042,880	£5	£10	£30	£85
1842	unrecorded	£4	£8	£25	£85
1843	3,440,640	£3	£6	£20	£50
1844	6,451,200	£3	£6	£15	£50
1844 E over N in REGINA	incl. above	£10	£45	£100	—
1847	3,010,560	£6	£12	£35	£80
1851	unrecorded	£5	£12	£35	£110
1851 5 over 0	unrecorded	£8	£20	£60	£150
1852	989,184	£5	£12	£40	£120
1853	955,224	£5	£15	£50	£130
1853 Proof	incl. above	—	—	—	£450
1854	677,376	£8	£25	£75	£185
1856	913,920	£8	£25	£75	£185
1868 Proof	unrecorded				£1000

THIRD FARTHINGS

DATE	MINTAGE	F	VF	EF	UNC

GEORGE IV (1820–30)

DATE	MINTAGE	F	VF	EF	UNC
1827 (issued for Malta)	unrecorded	£8	£18	£50	£125

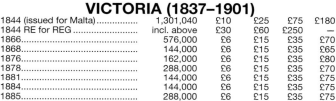

WILLIAM IV (1830–37)

DATE	MINTAGE	F	VF	EF	UNC
1835 (issued for Malta)	unrecorded	£8	£18	£50	£150

VICTORIA (1837–1901)

DATE	MINTAGE	F	VF	EF	UNC
1844 (issued for Malta)	1,301,040	£10	£25	£75	£180
1844 RE for REG	incl. above	£30	£60	£250	—
1866	576,000	£6	£15	£35	£70
1868	144,000	£6	£15	£35	£65
1876	162,000	£6	£15	£35	£80
1878	288,000	£6	£15	£35	£70
1881	144,000	£6	£15	£35	£75
1884	144,000	£6	£15	£35	£75
1885	288,000	£6	£15	£35	£75

EDWARD VII (1902–10)

DATE	MINTAGE	F	VF	EF	UNC
1902 (issued for Malta)	288,000	£5	£10	£25	£45

GEORGE V (1911–36)

DATE	MINTAGE	F	VF	EF	UNC
1913 (issued for Malta)	288,000	£5	£10	£25	£45

QUARTER FARTHINGS

DATE	MINTAGE	F	VF	EF	UNC

VICTORIA (1837–1901)

DATE	MINTAGE	F	VF	EF	UNC
1839 (issued for Ceylon)	3,840,000	£35	£60	£100	£225
1851 (issued for Ceylon)	2,215,680	£35	£60	£100	£225
1852 (issued for Ceylon)	incl. above	£35	£60	£100	£240
1853 (issued for Ceylon)	incl. above	£35	£60	£100	£225
1853 Proof	—	—	—	—	£900

EMERGENCY ISSUES

DATE	F	VF	EF	UNC

GEORGE III (1760–1820)

To alleviate the shortage of circulating coinage during the Napoleonic Wars the Bank of England firstly authorised the countermarking of other countries' coins, enabling them to pass as English currency. The coins, countermarked with punches depicting the head of George III, were mostly Spanish American 8 reales of Charles III. Although this had limited success it was later decided to completely overstrike the coins with a new English design on both sides—specimens that still show traces of the original host coin's date are avidly sought after by collectors. This overstriking continued for a number of years although all the known coins are dated 1804. Finally, in 1811 the Bank of England issued silver tokens which continued up to 1816 when a completely new regal coinage was introduced.

DOLLAR

Oval countermark of George III

	F	VF	EF	UNC
On "Pillar" type 8 reales	£175	£650	£1000	—
*On "Portrait" type.............	£200	£350	£800	—

Octagonal countermark of George III

	F	VF	EF	UNC
On "Portrait" type..............	£200	£600	£850	—

HALF DOLLAR

Oval countermark of George III

	F	VF	EF	UNC
On "Portrait" type 4 reales	£200	£400	£900	—

FIVE SHILLINGS OR ONE DOLLAR

These coins were overstruck on Spanish-American coins

	F	VF	EF	UNC
1804..................................	£120	£275	£550	—

— With details of original coin still visible add from 10%.

BANK OF ENGLAND TOKENS

THREE SHILLINGS

	F	VF	EF	UNC
1811 Draped bust..............	£35	£60	£200	—
1812 —	£35	£60	£220	—
1812 Laureate bust	£35	£60	£150	—
1813 —	£35	£60	£150	—
1814 —	£35	£60	£150	—
1815 —	£35	£60	£150	—
1816 —	£200	£400	£1250	—

ONE SHILLING AND SIXPENCE

	F	VF	EF	UNC
1811 Draped bust..............	£20	£45	£100	£175
1812 —	£20	£45	£100	£175
1812 Laureate bust	£20	£45	£100	£175
1812 Proof in platinum				Unique
1813 —	£20	£40	£75	£175
1813 Proof in platinum				Unique
1814 —	£20	£35	£75	£160
1815 —	£20	£35	£75	£160
1816 —	£20	£35	£75	£160

NINEPENCE

	F	VF	EF	UNC
1812 Pattern only	—	—		Very Rare

MAUNDY SETS

DATE	F	VF	EF	UNC

Sets in contemporary dated boxes are usually worth a higher premium. For example approximately £30 can be added to sets from Victoria to George VI in contemporary undated boxes and above £40 for dated boxes.

CHARLES II (1660–85)

DATE	F	VF	EF	UNC
Undated	£230	£370	£785	—
1670	£220	£360	£735	—
1671	£215	£350	£725	—
1672	£210	£340	£710	—
1673	£210	£320	£705	—
1674	£215	£325	£715	—
1675	£200	£320	£700	—
1676	£225	£360	£725	—
1677	£190	£310	£680	—
1678	£265	£450	£850	—
1679	£220	£355	£735	—
1680	£210	£340	£695	—
1681	£230	£345	£735	—
1682	£220	£350	£705	—
1683	£225	£350	£710	—
1684	£240	£410	£750	—

JAMES II (1685–88)

DATE	F	VF	EF	UNC
1686	£225	£360	£715	—
1687	£225	£360	£725	—
1688	£230	£385	£740	—

WILLIAM & MARY (1688–94)

DATE	F	VF	EF	UNC
1689	£845	£1200	£2000	—
1691	£715	£900	£1800	—
1692	£705	£915	£1700	—
1693	£525	£850	£1700	—
1694	£475	£725	£1250	—

WILLIAM III (1694–1702)

DATE	F	VF	EF	UNC
1698	£240	£475	£880	—
1699	£525	£700	£1600	—
1700	£250	£480	£875	—
1701	£240	£435	£850	—

ANNE (1702–14)

DATE	F	VF	EF	UNC
1703	£220	£425	£750	—
1705	£220	£400	£725	—
1706	£195	£370	£650	—
1708	£575	£875	£2000	—
1709	£245	£450	£825	—
1710	£250	£445	£795	—
1713	£225	£415	£715	—

GEORGE I (1714–27)

DATE	F	VF	EF	UNC
1723	£225	£425	£755	—
1727	£220	£425	£750	—

GEORGE II (1727–60)

DATE	F	VF	EF	UNC
1729	£190	£320	£660	—
1731	£190	£325	£660	—
1732	£185	£315	£625	—
1735	£180	£315	£630	—
1737	£190	£320	£630	—
1739	£180	£315	£600	—
1740	£170	£300	£575	—
1743	£265	£430	£850	—
1746	£165	£290	£550	—
1760	£175	£310	£580	—

GEORGE III (1760–1820)

DATE	F	VF	EF	UNC
1763	£165	£290	£475	—
1763 Proof	—		Extremely rare	
1766	£190	£290	£500	—
1772	£180	£290	£500	—
1780	£190	£300	£525	—
1784	£185	£310	£490	—
1786	£185	£300	£490	—
1792 Wire	£250	£425	£615	£790
1795	£115	£190	£315	£395
1800	£115	£185	£285	£390
New Coinage				
1817	£130	£200	£280	£415
1818	£135	£200	£270	£410
1820	£140	£210	£275	£415

GEORGE IV (1820–30)

DATE	F	VF	EF	UNC
1822	—	£150	£240	£405
1823	—	£150	£250	£395
1824	—	£155	£250	£395
1825	—	£145	£245	£375
1826	—	£140	£240	£375
1827	—	£140	£250	£375
1828	—	£145	£240	£380
1828 Proof	—	—	—	£3500
1829	—	£145	£240	£375
1830	—	£145	£235	£370

WILLIAM IV (1830–37)

DATE	F	VF	EF	UNC
1831	—	£165	£270	£425
1831 Proof	—	—	—	£1600
1831 Proof Gold	—	—	£35000	
1832	—	£175	£275	£425
1833	—	£165	£265	£395
1834	—	£165	£265	£395
1835	—	£155	£260	£400
1836	—	£170	£270	£410
1837	—	£180	£290	£435

DATE	MINTAGE	EF	UNC

VICTORIA (1837–1901)

YOUNG HEAD ISSUES

DATE	MINTAGE	EF	UNC
1838	4,158	£215	£405
1838 Proof	unrecorded		£2800
1838 Proof Gold			£33000
1839	4,125	£250	£450
1839 Proof	unrecorded	£650	£1300
1840	4,125	£300	£435
1841	2,574	£350	£575
1842	4,125	£350	£575
1843	4,158	£240	£400
1844	4,158	£325	£515
1845	4,158	£215	£375
1846	4,158	£525	£850
1847	4,158	£550	£900
1848	4,158	£500	£850
1849	4,158	£350	£515
1850	4,158	£225	£395
1851	4,158	£260	£405
1852	4,158	£550	£875
1853	4,158	£550	£925
1853 Proof	unrecorded		£1700
1854	4,158	£250	£405
1855	4,158	£265	£425
1856	4,158	£225	£350
1857	4,158	£255	£410
1858	4,158	£235	£365
1859	4,158	£210	£315
1860	4,158	£230	£365
1861	4,158	£200	£360
1862	4,158	£240	£370
1863	4,158	£255	£425
1864	4,158	£235	£330
1865	4,158	£230	£335
1866	4,158	£215	£330
1867	4,158	£210	£335
1867 Proof	unrecorded	–	£2750
1868	4,158	£200	£300
1869	4,158	£230	£395
1870	4,458	£180	£280
1871	4,488	£180	£275
1871 Proof	unrecorded	–	£2400
1872	4,328	£175	£270
1873	4,162	£175	£260
1874	4,488	£180	£260
1875	4,154	£175	£260
1876	4,488	£180	£260
1877	4,488	£175	£240
1878	4,488	£180	£245
1878 Proof	unrecorded	–	£2450
1879	4,488	£185	£240
1879 Proof	unrecorded	–	£2700
1880	4,488	£180	£235
1881	4,488	£175	£235
1881 Proof	unrecorded	–	£2200
1882	4,146	£200	£270
1882 Proof	unrecorded	–	£2450
1883	4,488	£150	£215
1884	4,488	£150	£215
1885	4,488	£150	£215
1886	4,488	£150	£215
1887	4,488	£175	£245

JUBILEE HEAD ISSUES

DATE	MINTAGE	EF	UNC
1888	4,488	£160	£225
1888 Proof	unrecorded	–	£2100
1889	4,488	£150	£215
1890	4,488	£160	£225
1891	4,488	£155	£220
1892	4,488	£160	£225

OLD HEAD ISSUES

DATE	MINTAGE	EF	UNC
1893	8,976	£100	£200
1894	8,976	£125	£210
1895	8,976	£110	£185
1896	8,976	£110	£195
1897	8,976	£110	£195
1898	8,976	£110	£200
1899	8,976	£110	£200
1900	8,976	£100	£190
1901	8,976	£100	£190

EDWARD VII (1902–110)

DATE	MINTAGE	EF	UNC
1902	8,976	£90	£185
1902 Matt proof	15,123	–	£200
1903	8,976	£95	£195
1904	8,976	£105	£195
1905	8,976	£115	£200
1906	8,800	£105	£185
1907	8,760	£100	£185
1908	8,769	£95	£185
1909	1,983	£165	£270
1910	1,440	£185	£295

GEORGE V (1911–136)

DATE	MINTAGE	EF	UNC
1911	1,786	£145	£235
1911 Proof	6,007	–	£250
1912	1,246	£155	£245
1913	1,228	£150	£245
1914	982	£165	£260
1915	1,293	£160	£250
1916	1,128	£150	£245
1917	1,237	£155	£245
1918	1,375	£155	£245
1919	1,258	£155	£245
1920	1,399	£155	£245
1921	1,386	£150	£245
1922	1,373	£160	£255
1923	1,430	£160	£255
1924	1,515	£160	£255
1925	1,438	£145	£240
1926	1,504	£145	£240
1927	1,647	£150	£250
1928	1,642	£150	£245
1929	1,761	£155	£245
1930	1,724	£145	£240
1931	1,759	£140	£240
1932	1,835	£140	£240
1933	1,872	£140	£240
1934	1,887	£140	£240
1935	1,928	£150	£250
1936	1,323	£190	£295

GEORGE VI (1936–52)

DATE	MINTAGE	EF	UNC
1937	1,325	£140	£215
1937 Proof	20,900	£140	£215
1938	1,275	£170	£250
1939	1,234	£170	£250
1940	1,277	£170	£250
1941	1,253	£175	£255
1942	1,231	£170	£250
1943	1,239	£170	£250
1944	1,259	£165	£250

DATE	MINTAGE	EF	UNC
1945	1,355	£165	£250
1946	1,365	£170	£250
1947	1,375	£175	£265
1948	1,385	£175	£270
1949	1,395	£180	£275
1950	1,405	£180	£280
1951	1,468	£185	£285
1952	1,012	£195	£300
1952 Proof (copper)			£10,000

ELIZABETH II (1952–)

DATE AND PLACE OF ISSUE	MINTAGE	UNC
1953 St. Paul's Cathedral	1,025	— £925
1953 Proof in gold	unrecorded	Ex. rare
1953 Proof Matt		Very rare
1954 Westminster Abbey	1,020	— £195
1955 Southwark Cathedral	1,036	— £205
1955 Proof Matt		— £3000
1956 Westminster Abbey	1,088	— £205
1957 St. Albans Cathedral	1,094	— £205
1958 Westminster Abbey	1,100	— £205
1959 St. George's Chapel, Windsor	1,106	— £205
1960 Westminster Abbey	1,112	— £205
1961 Rochester Cathedral	1,118	— £205
1962 Westminster Abbey	1,125	— £205
1963 Chelmsford Cathedral	1,131	— £205
1964 Westminster Abbey	1,137	— £205
1965 Canterbury Cathedral	1,143	— £205
1966 Westminster Abbey	1,206	— £205
1967 Durham Cathedral	986	— £215
1968 Westminster Abbey	964	— £225
1969 Selby Cathedral	1,002	— £215
1970 Westminster Abbey	980	— £215
197 Tewkesbury Abbey	1,018	£215
1972 York Minster	1,026	£215
1973 Westminster Abbey	1,004	£215
1974 Salisbury Cathedral	1,042	£215
1975 Peterborough Cathedral	1,050	£215
1976 Hereford Cathedral	1,158	£220
1977 Westminster Abbey	1,138	£220

DATE AND PLACE OF ISSUE	MINTAGE	UNC
1978 Carlisle Cathedral	1,178	£215
1979 Winchester Cathedral	1,188	£215
1980 Worcester Cathedral	1,198	£215
1981 Westminster Abbey	1,178	£215
1982 St David's Cathedral	1,218	£215
1983 Exeter Cathedral	1,228	£215
1984 Southwell Minster	1,238	£215
1985 Ripon Cathedral	1,248	£215
1986 Chichester Cathedral	1,378	£220
1987 Ely Cathedral	1,390	£220
1988 Lichfield Cathedral	1,402	£220
1989 Birmingham Cathedral	1,353	£220
1990 Newcastle Cathedral	1,523	£220
1991 Westminster Abbey	1,384	£220
1992 Chester Cathedral	1,424	£225
1993 Wells Cathedral	1,440	£225
1994 Truro Cathedral	1,433	£225
1995 Coventry Cathedral	1,466	£225
1996 Norwich Cathedral	1,629	£230
1997 Birmingham Cathedral	1,786	£230
1998 Portsmouth Cathedral	1,654	£230
1999 Bristol Cathedral	1,676	£230
2000 Lincoln Cathedral	1,686	£220
2000 Silver Proof	13,180	£200
2001 Westminster Abbey	1,132	£230
2002 Canterbury Cathedral	1,681	£230
2002 Gold Proof	2,002	£2100
2003 Gloucester Cathedral	1,608	£235
2004 Liverpool Cathedral	1,613	£240
2005 Wakefield Cathedral	1,685	£240
2006 Guildford Cathedral	1,937	£240
2006 Silver Proof	6,394	£200
2007 Manchester Cathedral	1,822	£280
2008 St Patrick's Cathedral (Armagh)	1,833	£750
2009 St. Edmundsbury Cathedral	1,602	£700
2010 Derby Cathedral	1,617	£650
2011 Westminster Abbey	1,734	£575
2012 York Minster	1,633	£650
2013 Christ Church Cathedral Oxford	1,627	£575
2014 Blackburn Cathedral	1,693	£600
2015 Sheffield Cathedral		£600

Despite the decimalisation of the coinage in 1971, in keeping with ancient tradition the Royal Maundy sets are still made up of four silver coins (4p, 3p, 2p and 1p). The designs for the reverse of the coins are a crowned numeral in a wreath of oak leaves—basically the same design that has been used for Maundy coins since Charles II.

MAUNDY ODDMENTS
SINGLE COINS

DATE	F	VF	EF

FOUR PENCE
CHARLES II (1660–85)

	F	VF	EF
Undated	£70	£115	£185
1670	£70	£120	£195
1671	£55	£95	£170
1672/1	£65	£105	£175
1673	£60	£100	£170
1674	£60	£100	£165
1674 7 over 6	£70	£120	£205
1675	£60	£100	£165
1675/4	£70	£115	£190
1676	£65	£100	£185
1676 7 over 6	£80	£120	£200
1677	£55	£95	£165
1678	£55	£95	£160
1678 8 over 7	£65	£115	£175
1679	£55	£85	£150
1680	£60	£95	£170
1681	£55	£100	£180
1682	£60	£90	£180
1682/1	£65	£95	£190
1683	£60	£90	£180
1684	£60	£95	£180
1684 4 over 3	£75	£110	£200

JAMES II (1685–88)

	F	VF	EF
1686	£65	£110	£200
1686 Date over crown	£75	£125	£215
1687	£60	£100	£180
1687 7 over 6	£75	£115	£190
1688	£70	£105	£195
1688 1 over 8	£80	£120	£210

WILLIAM & MARY (1688–94)

	F	VF	EF
1689	£60	£110	£175
1689 GV below bust	£70	£120	£190
1689 GVLEELMVS	£135	£215	£325
1690	£60	£115	£210
1690 6 over 5	£90	£130	£230
1691	£80	£120	£225
1691 1 over 0	£90	£140	£230
1692	£120	£170	£260
1692 Maria	£200	£245	£350
1692 2 over 1	£130	£160	£260
1693	£85	£185	£300
1693 3 over 2	£105	£185	£315
1694	£80	£135	£225

WILLIAM III (1694–1702)

	F	VF	EF
1698	£80	£135	£215
1699	£70	£120	£210
1700	£80	£130	£215
1701	£80	£125	£215
1702	£80	£130	£225

ANNE (1702–14)

	F	VF	EF
1703	£75	£125	£210
1704	£60	£105	£185
1705	£90	£160	£245

It is nowadays considered that the early small denomination silver coins 4d–1d were originally struck for the Maundy ceremony although undoubtedly many subsequently circulated as small change—therefore they are listed here under "Maundy silver single coins".

Charles II

William & Mary

Queen Anne

DATE	F	VF	EF	UNC
1706	£70	£115	£175	—
1708	£75	£120	£205	—
1709	£70	£110	£180	—
1710	£60	£100	£165	—
1713	£70	£120	£190	—

GEORGE I (1714–27)

	F	VF	EF	UNC
1717	£65	£110	£180	—
1721	£65	£110	£185	—
1723	£75	£125	£195	—
1727	£75	£120	£190	—

GEORGE II (1727–60)

	F	VF	EF	UNC
1729	£65	£105	£160	—
1731	£60	£105	£160	—
1732	£60	£105	£155	—
1735	£55	£95	£150	—
1737	£65	£105	£160	—
1739	£55	£100	£155	—
1740	£50	£95	£140	—
1743	£130	£180	£290	—
1743 3 over 0	£140	£205	£300	
1746	£55	£85	£135	—
1760	£60	£110	£155	—

George II

GEORGE III (1760–1820)

	F	VF	EF	UNC
1763 Young head	£50	£95	£135	—
1763 Proof	—	—	Extremely rare	
1765	£450	£680	£1175	—
1766	£65	£100	£140	—
1770	£155	£230	£360	—
1772	£80	£130	£190	—
1776	£65	£120	£170	—
1780	£50	£95	£135	—
1784	£50	£95	£130	—
1786	£60	£110	£155	—
1792 Older head, Thin 4	£90	£140	£220	£325
1795	—	£55	£95	£130
1800	—	£50	£90	£125
1817 New coinage	—	£50	£80	£130
1818	—	£50	£80	£125
1820	—	£50	£80	£130

George III

GEORGE IV (1820–30)

	F	VF	EF	UNC
1822	—	—	£70	£130
1823	—	—	£65	£125
1824	—	—	£70	£130
1826	—	—	£65	£120
1827	—	—	£65	£120
1828	—	—	£65	£120
1829	—	—	£60	£115
1830	—	—	£60	£115

WILLIAM IV (1830–37)

	F	VF	EF	UNC
1831–37	—	—	£70	£145
1831 Proof	—	—	£250	£400

VICTORIA (1837–1901)

	F	VF	EF	UNC
1838 Proof	—	—	—	£550
1839 Proof	—	—	—	£450
1853 Proof	—	—	—	£500
1838–87 (Young Head)	—	—	£40	£65
1841	—	—	£50	£75
1888–92 (Jubilee Head)	—	—	£35	£60
1893–1901 (Old Head)	—	—	£30	£50

Victoria

DATE	F	VF	EF	UNC

EDWARD VII (1901–10)

	F	VF	EF	UNC
1902–08	—	—	£30	£50
1909 & 1910	—	—	£60	£90
1902 Proof	—	—	£35	£55

GEORGE V (1910–36)

	F	VF	EF	UNC
1911–36	—	—	£50	£65
1911 Proof	—	—	£55	£75

GEORGE VI (1936–52)

	F	VF	EF	UNC
1937–52	—	—	£55	£75
1937 Proof	—	—	£40	£60

ELIZABETH II (1952–   )

	F	VF	EF	UNC
1953	—	—	£180	£235
1954–85	—	—	£45	£75
1986–2007	—	—	£60	£85
2002 in Gold Proof	—	—	£500	£750
2008	—	—	£90	£190
2009	—	—	£85	£180
2010	—	—	£75	£170
2011	—	—	£60	£145
2012	—	—	£70	£170
2013	—	—	£75	£165
2014	—	—	£75	£160
2015	—	—	£70	£160

Elizabeth II

THREEPENCE
CHARLES II (1660–85)

	F	VF	EF	UNC
Undated	£65	£105	£195	—
1670	£65	£105	£165	—
1671	£55	£100	£165	—
1671 GRVTIA	£75	£115	£230	—
1672	£60	£105	£165	—
1673	£60	£95	£160	—
1674	£65	£100	£165	—
1675	£65	£105	£170	—
1676	£70	£115	£210	—
1676 ERA for FRA	£90	£135	£225	—
1677	£65	£90	£165	—
1678	£50	£80	£135	—
1679	£50	£80	£135	—
1679 O/A in CAROLVS	£105	£140	£240	—
1680	£60	£100	£175	—
1681	£65	£105	£175	—
1682	£60	£100	£170	—
1683	£60	£105	£170	—
1684	£60	£105	£175	—
1684/3	£70	£110	£180	—

James II

JAMES II (1685–88)

	F	VF	EF	UNC
1685	£65	£105	£190	—
1685 Struck on fourpence flan	£130	£175	£290	—
1686	£65	£95	£175	—
1687	£60	£90	£170	—
1687 7 over 6	£65	£95	£175	—
1688	£65	£120	£195	—
1688 8 over 7	£70	£130	£215	—

WILLIAM & MARY (1688–94)

	F	VF	EF	UNC
1689	£55	£100	£180	—
1689 No stop on reverse	£65	£115	£195	—
1689 LMV over MVS (obverse)	£100	£145	£240	—
1690	£75	£120	£195	—
1690 6 over 5	£85	£135	£210	—
1691 First bust	£390	£590	£850	—
1691 Second bust	£260	£420	£570	—

William & Mary

DATE	F	VF	EF	UNC
1692.................................	£85	£140	£240	—
1692 G below bust................	£90	£150	£230	—
1692 GV below bust..............	£90	£140	£225	—
1692 GVL below bust............	£90	£145	£235	—
1693.................................	£120	£195	£270	—
1693 3 over 2.......................	£125	£210	£280	—
1694.........Λ.........................	£80	£115	£200	—
1694 MARI	£130	£170	£265	—

WILLIAM III (1694–1702)

1698.................................	£75	£125	£210	—
1699.................................	£60	£110	£180	—
1700.................................	£70	£135	£210	—
1701.................................	£65	£110	£180	—
1701 GBA instead of GRA......	£80	£140	£205	—

ANNE (1702–14)

1703.................................	£70	£100	£195	—
1703 7 of date above crown...	£80	£130	£210	—
1704.................................	£60	£90	£160	—
1705.................................	£80	£130	£200	—
1706.................................	£65	£100	£170	—
1707.................................	£55	£100	£155	—
1708.................................	£60	£115	£180	—
1709.................................	£65	£120	£180	—
1710.................................	£50	£95	£145	—
1713.................................	£65	£125	£180	—

Queen Anne

GEORGE I (1714–27)

1717.................................	£60	£100	£160	—
1721.................................	£60	£100	£165	—
1723.................................	£75	£115	£190	—
1727.................................	£70	£110	£185	—

GEORGE II (1727–60)

1729.................................	£55	£95	£145	—
1731.................................	£55	£95	£150	—
1731 Small lettering................	£70	£115	£170	—
1732.................................	£55	£95	£145	—
1732 Stop over head..............	£65	£110	£165	—
1735.................................	£65	£105	£160	—
1737.................................	£55	£95	£165	—
1739.................................	£60	£95	£170	—
1740.................................	£55	£90	£145	—
1743 Small and large lettering	£65	£90	£155	—
1743 Stop over head..............	£65	£95	£160	—
1746.................................	£45	£80	£140	—
1746 6 over 3.......................	£50	£85	£150	—
1760.................................	£60	£90	£155	—

George II

GEORGE III (1760–1820)

1762.................................	£30	£50	£70	—
1763.................................	£30	£50	£75	—
1763 Proof............................	—	—	Extremely rare	
1765.................................	£350	£500	£750	—
1766.................................	£60	£95	£155	—
1770.................................	£70	£110	£190	—
1772.................................	£55	£85	£120	—
1780.................................	£55	£85	£120	—
1784.................................	£80	£115	£190	—
1786.................................	£80	£110	£180	—
1792.................................	£95	£135	£215	£325
1795.................................	—	£40	£80	£120
1800.................................	—	£45	£85	£130
1817.................................	—	£50	£90	£155
1818.................................	—	£50	£90	£155
1820.................................	—	£45	£90	£155

DATE	F	VF	EF	UNC
GEORGE IV (1820–30)				
1822	—	—	£85	£165
1823	—	—	£75	£155
1824	—	—	£75	£160
1825–30	—	—	£75	£155
WILLIAM IV (1830–37)				
1831 Proof	—	—	£225	£425
1831–1832	—	—	£125	£250
1833–1836	—	—	£80	£170
1837	—	—	£105	£190
VICTORIA (1837–1901)				
1838	—	—	£115	£200
1839	—	—	£195	£375
1840	—	—	£140	£275
1841	—	—	£275	£475
1842	—	—	£250	£400
1843	—	—	£125	£225
1844	—	—	£175	£300
1845	—	—	£85	£165
1846	—	—	£400	£700
1847	—	—	£425	£800
1848	—	—	£375	£750
1849	—	—	£215	£365
1850	—	—	£115	£225
1851	—	—	£145	£265
1852	—	—	£450	£775
1853	—	—	£475	£825
1854	—	—	£155	£275
1855	—	—	£170	£285
1856	—	—	£100	£220
1857	—	—	£150	£275
1858	—	—	£120	£225
1859	—	—	£100	£195
1860	—	—	£135	£240
1861	—	—	£130	£235
1862	—	—	£135	£255
1863	—	—	£175	£300
1864	—	—	£125	£235
1865	—	—	£130	£250
1866	—	—	£120	£240
1867	—	—	£125	£235
1868	—	—	£115	£215
1869	—	—	£155	£275
1870	—	—	£105	£195
1871	—	—	£100	£185
1872	—	—	£95	£180
1873	—	—	£90	£170
1874	—	—	£90	£175
1875	—	—	£85	£165
1876	—	—	£85	£165
1877	—	—	£80	£160
1878	—	—	£85	£165
1879	—	—	£85	£160
1880	—	—	£80	£150
1881	—	—	£80	£150
1882	—	—	£130	£225
1883	—	—	£75	£145
1884	—	—	£75	£145
1885	—	—	£70	£130
1886	—	—	£70	£125
1887	—	—	£80	£170
1888–1892 (Jubilee Head)	—	—	£50	£110
1893–1901 (Old Head)	—	—	£40	£65

Victoria Jubilee Head

DATE	F	VF	EF	UNC

EDWARD VII (1901–10)

	F	VF	EF	UNC
1902	—	—	£30	£50
1902 Proof	—	—	—	£55
1903	—	—	£40	£85
1904	—	—	£55	£105
1905	—	—	£55	£95
1906	—	—	£45	£90
1907	—	—	£45	£90
1908	—	—	£40	£80
1909	—	—	£70	£120
1910	—	—	£80	£150

GEORGE V (1910–36)

	F	VF	EF	UNC
1911–34	—	—	£55	£85
1911 Proof	—	—	—	£95
1935	—	—	£65	£100
1936	—	—	£75	£135

GEORGE VI (1936–52)

	F	VF	EF	UNC
1937–52	—	—	£55	£100
1937 Proof	—	—	—	£70

ELIZABETH II (1952–)

	F	VF	EF	UNC
1953	—	—	£160	£265
1954–85	—	—	£45	£80
1986–2007	—	—	£55	£85
2002 In gold (proof)	—	—	—	£615
2008	—	—	—	£170
2009	—	—	—	£160
2010	—	—	—	£150
2011	—	—	—	£130
2012	—	—	—	£140
2013	—	—	—	£140
2014	—	—	—	£140
2015	—	—	—	£130

TWOPENCE

CHARLES II (1660–85)

	F	VF	EF	UNC
Undated	£55	£90	£155	—
1668	£65	£90	£170	—
1670	£50	£80	£150	—
1671	£50	£85	£150	—
1672	£50	£85	£150	—
1672/1	£65	£100	£160	—
1673	£50	£85	£155	—
1674	£55	£90	£150	—
1675	£50	£90	£140	—
1676	£55	£95	£155	—
1677	£45	£85	£135	—
1678	£35	£75	£130	—
1679	£40	£70	£125	—
1680	£50	£85	£135	—
1681	£55	£80	£135	—
1682	£60	£85	£155	—
1682/1 ERA for FRA	£70	£100	£200	—
1683	£55	£90	£150	—
1684	£55	£95	£155	—

Charles II

JAMES II (1685–88)

	F	VF	EF	UNC
1686	£60	£95	£160	—
1686 reads IACOBVS	£75	£120	£215	—
1687	£65	£95	£165	—
1687 ERA for FRA	£75	£130	£215	—
1688	£50	£85	£150	—
1688/7	£65	£90	£170	—

James II

DATE	F	VF	EF	UNC

WILLIAM & MARY (1688–94)

DATE	F	VF	EF	UNC
1689	£60	£100	£175	—
1691	£55	£85	£140	—
1692	£75	£130	£190	—
1693	£65	£110	£185	—
1693 GV below bust	£75	£115	£185	—
1693/2	£65	£100	£170	—
1694	£50	£85	£140	—
1694 MARLA error	£80	£130	£250	—
1694 HI for HIB	£75	£120	£210	—
1694 GVLI under bust	£60	£100	£185	—
1694 GVL under bust	£55	£95	£185	—

WILLIAM III (1694–1702)

DATE	F	VF	EF	UNC
1698	£60	£115	£175	—
1699	£50	£90	£145	—
1700	£65	£110	£175	—
1701	£60	£100	£165	—

ANNE (1702–14)

DATE	F	VF	EF	UNC
1703	£65	£100	£180	—
1704	£50	£80	£135	—
1704 No stops on obverse	£60	£90	£170	—
1705	£60	£100	£160	—
1706	£75	£110	£175	—
1707	£50	£85	£150	—
1708	£65	£95	£165	—
1709	£85	£125	£215	—
1710	£45	£80	£115	—
1713	£70	£110	£195	—

Queen Anne

GEORGE I (1714–27)

DATE	F	VF	EF	UNC
1717	£45	£80	£130	—
1721	£50	£85	£125	—
1723	£65	£95	£160	—
1726	£50	£80	£135	—
1727	£60	£85	£150	—

GEORGE II (1727–60)

DATE	F	VF	EF	UNC
1729	£40	£75	£115	—
1731	£35	£75	£120	—
1732	£40	£80	£115	—
1735	£45	£75	£110	·
1737	£40	£80	£115	·
1739	£45	£80	£120	·
1740	£40	£70	£110	·
1743	£35	£65	£105	·
1743/0	£45	£80	£115	·
1746	£35	£70	£95	·
1756	£35	£65	£95	·
1759	£35	£70	£95	·
1760	£50	£75	£100	·

GEORGE III (1760–1820)

DATE	F	VF	EF	UNC
1763	£40	£70	£95	·
1763 Proof			Extremely rare	
1765	£345	£525	£725	—
1766	£45	£75	£95	—
1772	£35	£70	£90	—
1780	£35	£70	£90	—
1784	£40	£70	£90	—
1786	£50	£80	£95	—
1792	—	£80	£125	£190
1795	—	£30	£60	£85
1800	—	£30	£70	£85
1817	—	£35	£70	£90
1818	—	£35	£70	£90
1820	—	£40	£70	£95

George II

DATE	F	VF	EF	UNC

GEORGE IV (1820–30)

	F	VF	EF	UNC
1822–30	—	—	£40	£70
1825 TRITANNIAR	—	—	£60	£115

WILLIAM IV (1830–37)

	F	VF	EF	UNC
1831–37	—	—	£45	£80
1831 Proof	—	—	£95	£225

VICTORIA (1837–1901)

	F	VF	EF	UNC
1838–87 (Young Head)	—	—	£30	£60
1859 BEITANNIAR	—	—	£75	£135
1861 6 over 1	—	—	£40	£80
1888–92 (Jubilee Head)	—	—	£30	£60
1893–1901 (Old Head	—	—	£25	£50
1838 Proof	—	—	—	£395
1839 Proof	—	—	—	£235
1853 Proof	—	—	—	£250

Victoria

EDWARD VII (1901–10)

	F	VF	EF	UNC
1902–08	—	—	£25	£35
1909	—	—	£45	£80
1910	—	—	£50	£90
1902 Proof	—	—	£30	£50

GEORGE V (1910–36)

	F	VF	EF	UNC
1911–34	—	—	£35	£65
1911 Proof	—	—	£40	£70
1935	—	—	£40	£65
1936	—	—	£50	£75

GEORGE VI (1936–52)

	F	VF	EF	UNC
1937–47	—	—	£40	£60
1948–52	—	—	£45	£70
1937 Proof	—	—	£35	£60

ELIZABETH II (1952–)

	F	VF	EF	UNC
1953	—	—	£130	£200
1954–85	—	—	£40	£65
1986–2007	—	—	£40	£70
2002 Gold Proof	—	—	—	£450
2008	—	—	—	£125
2009	—	—	—	£115
2010	—	—	—	£110
2011	—	—	—	£85
2012	—	—	—	£100
2013	—	—	—	£110
2014	—	—	—	£105
2015	—	—	—	£100

PENNY

CHARLES II (1660–85)

	F	VF	EF	UNC
Undated	£70	£110	£200	—
1670	£65	£110	£175	—
1671	£65	£110	£170	—
1672/1	£70	£110	£175	—
1673	£65	£110	£170	—
1674	£70	£110	£175	—
1674 Gratia (error)	£100	£160	£250	—
1675	£65	£115	£170	—
1675 Gratia (error)	£100	£165	£260	—
1676	£80	£120	£185	—
1676 Gratia (error)	£110	£170	£275	—
1677	£60	£100	£165	—
1677 Gratia (error)	£95	£135	£230	—
1678	£150	£265	£380	—
1678 Gratia (error)	£180	£280	£400	—
1679	£85	£125	£210	—
1680	£75	£110	£185	—
1681	£110	£155	£230	—
1682	£75	£115	£195	—
1682 ERA for FRA	£90	£150	£245	—

Charles II

DATE	F	VF	EF	UNC
1683	£80	£115	£195	—
1683/1	£85	£150	£225	—
1684	£175	£265	£330	—
1684/3	£190	£270	£340	—

JAMES II (1685–88)

1685	£65	£100	£165	—
1686	£70	£105	£170	—
1687	£80	£120	£180	—
1687/8	£85	£130	£190	—
1688	£65	£90	£165	—
1688/7	£70	£105	£185	—

James II

WILLIAM & MARY (1688–94)

1689	£450	£675	£950	—
1689 MΛRIΛ	£470	£685	£950	—
1689 GVIELMVS (Error)	£450	£700	£975	—
1690	£75	£145	£230	—
1691	£75	£150	£225	—
1692	£240	£340	£550	—
1692/1	£250	£355	£570	—
1693	£95	£160	£245	—
1694	£75	£130	£230	—
1694 HI for HIB	£110	£170	£275	—
1694 No stops on obverse	£90	£150	£240	—

WILLIAM III (1694–1702)

1698	£85	£135	£200	—
1698 HI. BREX (Error)	£100	£165	£270	—
1699	£290	£425	£650	—
1700	£85	£135	£215	—
1701	£85	£130	£205	—

ANNE (1702–14)

1703	£75	£125	£195	—
1705	£65	£110	£180	—
1706	£70	£95	£165	—
1708	£425	£550	£765	—
1709	£60	£95	£150	—
1710	£135	£200	£300	—
1713/0	£85	£120	£180	—

GEORGE I (1714–27)

1716	£45	£90	£115	—
1718	£45	£90	£115	—
1720	£50	£95	£125	—
1720 HIPEX (Error)	£75	£115	£205	—
1723	£65	£115	£165	—
1725	£50	£85	£130	—
1726	£50	£85	£125	—
1727	£60	£115	£165	—

GEORGE II (1727–60)

1729	£40	£90	£120	—
1731	£45	£90	£125	—
1732	£45	£80	£110	—
1735	£40	£70	£100	—
1737	£40	£70	£105	—
1739	£40	£70	£100	—
1740	£40	£65	£100	—
1743	£35	£70	£95	—
1746	£45	£80	£115	—
1746/3	£50	£80	£120	—
1750	£30	£55	£85	—
1752	£30	£55	£85	—
1753	£30	£55	£85	—
1754	£30	£55	£85	—
1755	£30	£55	£85	—
1756	£30	£55	£80	—
1757	£30	£55	£80	—

George II

DATE	F	VF	EF	UNC
1757 No colon after Gratia	£45	£80	£100	—
1758...	£30	£60	£85	—
1759...	£35	£60	£80	—
1760...	£40	£75	£95	—

GEORGE III (1760–1820)

1763...	£45	£70	£100	—
1763 Proof..............................	—	—	Extremely rare	
1766...	£40	£70	£90	—
1772...	£40	£70	£85	—
1780...	£85	£125	£185	—
1781...	£35	£60	£85	—
1784...	£45	£65	£90	—
1786...	£35	£60	£90	—
1792...	£35	£70	£90	£120
1795...	—	£25	£50	£70
1800...	—	£25	£50	£70
1817...	—	£25	£50	£70
1818...	—	£25	£50	£70
1820...	—	£30	£55	£75

George III

GEORGE IV (1820–30)

1822–30....................................	—	—	£35	£60

WILLIAM IV (1830–37)

1831–37....................................	—	—	£45	£70
1831 Proof..............................	—	—	—	£205

VICTORIA (1837–1901)

1838–87 (Young Head)	—	—	£30	£55
1888–92 (Jubilee Head)..........	—	—	£30	£50
1893–1901 (Old Head)............	—	—	£25	£40
1838 Proof..............................	—	—	—	£250
1839 Proof..............................	—	—	—	£175
1853 Proof..............................	—	—	—	£215

EDWARD VII (1901–10)

1902–08....................................	—	—	£20	£35
1909	—	—	£40	£75
1910...	—	—	£50	£90
1902 Proof..............................	—	—	£25	£40

GEORGE V (1910–36)

1911–14....................................	—	—	£45	£80
1915...	—	—	£50	£85
1916–19....................................	—	—	£45	£80
1920...	—	—	£45	£80
1921–28....................................	—	—	£45	£75
1929...	—	—	£45	£80
1930–34....................................	—	—	£40	£75
1935...	—	—	£45	£80
1936...	—	—	£55	£85
1911 Proof..............................	—	—	£45	£80

GEORGE VI (1936–52)

1937–40....................................	—	—	£50	£80
1941...	—	—	£55	£90
1942–47....................................	—	—	£50	£85
1948–52....................................	—	—	£60	£95
1937 Proof..............................	—	—	£45	£80

ELIZABETH II (1952–   )

1953...	—	—	£285	£400
1965–85....................................	—	—	£45	£80
1986–2007...............................	—	—	£45	£85
2002 Proof in gold	—	—	—	£485
2008...	—	—	£80	£145
2009...	—	—	£80	£140
2010...	—	—	£75	£130
2011...	—	—	£75	£105
2012...	—	—	£80	£120
2013...	—	—	£80	£125
2014...	—	—	£80	£120
2015...	—	—	—	£110

Elizabeth II

DECIMAL COINAGE

Since the introduction of the Decimal system in the UK, many coins have been issued for circulation purposes in vast quantities. In addition, from 1982 sets of coins to non-proof standard, and including examples of each denomination found in circulation, have been issued each year. For 1982 and 1983 they were to "circulation" standard and described as "Uncirculated". Individual coins from these sets are annotated "Unc" on the lists that follow. From 1984 to the present day they were described as "Brilliant Uncirculated" (BU on the lists), and from around 1986 these coins are generally distinguishable from coins intended for circulation. They were from then produced by the Proof Coin Division of the Royal Mint (rather than by the Coin Production Room which produces circulation-standard coins). For completeness however, we have included the annotations Unc and BU back to 1982, the start year for these sets.

It is emphasised that the abbreviations Unc and BU in the left-hand columns adjacent to the date refer to an advertising description or to an engineering production standard, not the preservation condition or grade of the coin concerned. Where no such annotation appears adjacent to the date, the coin is circulation-standard for issue as such.

We have included the "mintage" figures for circulation coins down to Half Penny. The figure given for the 1997 Two Pounds, is considerably less than the actual quantity struck, because many were scrapped before issue due to failing an electrical conductivity test. Where a coin is available in uncirculated grade at, or just above, face value no price has been quoted.

Base metal Proof issues of circulation coinage (£2 or £1 to one or half penny) of the decimal series were only issued, as with Unc or BU, as part of Year Sets, but many of these sets have been broken down into individual coins, hence the appearance of the latter on the market.

The lists do not attempt to give details of die varieties, except where there was an obvious intention to change the appearance of a coin, e.g. 1992 20p.

2008 saw new reverses and modified obverses for all circulation denominations from the One Pound to the One Penny. All seven denominations were put into circulation dated 2008, all with both the old and the new reverses.

The circulation standard mintage figures have mainly been kindly supplied by courtesy of the Head of Historical Services and the Department of UK Circulation Coin Sales, both at the Royal Mint.

KILO COINS
(gold and silver)

The UK's first-ever Kilo coins were struck to commemorate the 2012 Olympic Games in 0.999 fine gold and 0.999 fine silver (pictured above). These and subsequent issues are listed in detail below, and all were struck to proof standard and to similar metallic standards.

DATE	FACE VALUE	AUTH ISSUE QTY.	ISSUE PRICE

2012 Olympic Gold;
    obverse: 1998 Ian Rank-Broadley's Royal Portrait
    reverse: Sir Anthony Caro's "Individual Endeavour" £1,000
		60	£100,000

2012 Olympic Silver;
    obverse: 1998 Rank-Broadley Royal Portrait
    reverse: Tom Phillip's "Team Endeavour".......................................£500
		2012	£3,000

2012 Diamond
Jubilee Gold

DATE	FACE VALUE	AUTH ISSUE QTY.	ISSUE PRICE

2012 Diamond Jubilee Gold;
   obverse: Queen in Garter Robes (Rank-Broadley)
   reverse: Royal Arms (Buckingham Palace Gates) £1,000
		60	£60,000

2012 Diamond Jubilee Silver;
   obverse: Queen in Garter Robes (Rank-Broadley)
   reverse: Royal Arms (Buckingham Palace Gates) £500
		1250	£2,600

2013 Coronation Anniversary Gold;
   obverse: 1998 Rank-Broadley Royal Portrait
   reverse: John Bergdahl's Coronation Regalia £1,000
		27	£50,000

2013 Coronation Anniversary Silver;
   obverse: 1998 Rank-Broadley Royal Portrait
   reverse: John Bergdahl's Coronation Regalia £500
		400	£2,600

2013 Royal Christening Gold;
   obverse: 1998 Rank-Broadley Royal Portrait
   reverse: John Bergdahl's Lily Font £1,000
		22	£48,000

2013 Royal Christening Silver;
   obverse: 1998 Rank-Broadley Royal Portrait
   reverse: John Bergdahl's Lily Font £500
		500	£2,600

2014 First World War Outbreak Gold;
   obverse: 1998 Rank-Broadley Royal Portrait
   reverse: Sandle's Hostile Environment... £1,000
		25	£45,000

2014 First World War Outbreak Silver;
   obverse: 1998 Rank-Broadley Royal Portrait
   reverse: Sandle's Hostile Environment.. £500
		430	£2,000

2015 50th Anniversary of Death of Sir Winston Churchill Gold
   obverse: 1998 Rank-Broadley Royal Portrait
   reverse: Millner's image of Churchill... £1,000
		15	£45,000

2015 50th Anniversary of Death of Sir Winston Churchill Silver
   obverse: 1998 Rank-Broadley Royal Portrait
   reverse: Milner's image of Churchill £500
		170	£2,000

*2013 Royal
Christening Gold*

*2014 First World War
Outbreak Gold*

*2015 Anniversary of
Death of Sir Winston
Churchill Silver*

Illustrations on
this page are not
shown to scale.

FIVE-OUNCE COINS
(gold and silver, including Britannia Coins)

Also appearing for the first time in 2012 were Five-Ounce coins, minted in the same metals and standards as the Kilo Coins. Included here also are Five-Ounce Britannia coins, both gold and silver proofs, which appeared first in 2013. It should be noted that the reverses of these coins, in common with other denominations of Britannias, have a different design from those minted to BU ("bullion") standard.

DATE	FACE VALUE	AUTH ISSUE QTY.	ISSUE PRICE
2012 Olympic Gold;			
obverse: 1998 Rank-Broadley Royal Portrait			
reverse: Pegasus (C. Le Brun) £10		500	£11,500
2012 Olympic Silver;			
obverse: 1998 Rank-Broadley Royal Portrait			
reverse: Pegasus (C. Le Brun) £10		7500	£525
2012 Diamond Jubilee Gold;			
obverse: Queen in Garter Robes (Rank-Broadley)			
reverse: Queen seated (facing) £10		250	£9,500
2012 Diamond Jubilee Silver;			
obverse: Queen in Garter Robes (Rank-Broadley)			
reverse: Queen seated (facing) £10		1952	£450
2013 Coronation Anniversary Gold;			
obverse: 1998 Rank-Broadley Royal Portrait			
reverse: Regalia in Westminster Abbey (J. Olliffe) £10		129	£9,500
2013 Coronation Anniversary Silver;			
obverse: 1998 Rank-Broadley Royal Portrait			
reverse: Regalia in Westminster Abbey (J. Olliffe) £10		1,953	£450
2013 Britannia Gold;			
obverse: 1998 Rank-Broadley Royal Portrait			
reverse: Britannia seated with owl (R. Hunt) £500		125	£8,200

DATE	FACE VALUE	AUTH ISSUE QTY.	ISSUE PRICE
2013 Britannia Silver; obverse: 1998 Rank-Broadley Royal Portrait reverse: Britannia seated with owl (R. Hunt).................................... £10		4,655	£450
2013 Royal Christening Gold; obverse: 1998 Rank-Broadley Royal Portrait reverse: Bergdahl's Lily Font £10		150	£8,200
2013 Royal Christening Silver; obverse: 1998 Rank-Broadley Royal Portrait reverse: Bergdahl's Lily Font £10		1,660	£450
2014 Britannia Gold; obverse: 1998 Rank-Broadley Royal Portrait reverse: Clark's portrayal of Britannia £500		75	£7,500
2014 Britannia Silver; obverse: 1998 Rank-Broadley Royal Portrait reverse: Clark's portrayal of Britannia £10		1,350	£395
2014 First World War Outbreak Gold; obverse: 1998 Rank-Broadley Royal Portrait reverse: Bergdahl's Britannia.. £10		110	£7,500
2014 First World War Outbreak Silver; obverse: 1998 Rank-Broadley Royal Portrait reverse: Bergdahl's Britannia.. £10		1,300	£395
2015 Year of the Sheep Gold obverse: 1998 Rank-Broadley Royal Portrait reverse: Wuon-Gean Ho's Swaledale Sheep £500		38	£7,500
2015 Year of the Sheep Silver obverse: 1998 Rank-Broadley Royal Portrait reverse: Wuon-Gean Ho's Swaledale Sheep £10		1,088	£395
2015 Britannia Gold obverse: Clark Royal Portrait reverse: Dufort's Britannia.. £500		50	£7,500
2015 Britannia Silver obverse: Clark Royal Portrait reverse: Dufort's Britannia.. £10		1,150	£395
2015 50th Anniversary of Death of Sir Winston Churchill Gold obverse: Clark Royal Portrait reverse: Millner's image of Churchill.................................... £10		60	£7,500
2015 50th Anniversary of Death of Sir Winston Churchill Silver obverse: Clark Royal Portrait reverse: Millner's image of Churchill.................................... £10		500	£395

5 ounce silver coin
shown actual size
(65mm)

NOTE: As the BRITANNIA series of coins are
essentially bullion pieces, their values are
usually related to the current price of gold and
silver, therefore no attempt has been made in
this publication to give values for the series. To
ascertain the value of a piece it is necessary to check
with the prevailing price of precious metals.

HUNDRED POUNDS AND BELOW
(including Britannia and Olympic Gold series)

In 1987 the gold £100 coin was introduced, known as the Britannia. It contained one Troy ounce of fine gold, alloyed to 22 carat, and this has continued to the present day. At the same time, and also continuing, coins of face value £50, £25 and £10 appeared, containing a half ounce, quarter ounce and one tenth of an ounce of fine gold respectively. From 1987 to 1989 the alloy was of copper (Red Gold), whereas from 1990 to the present day the alloy has been of silver and copper (yellow gold).

Proof sets of these coins are listed in the "Proof and Specimen Sets" section. In addition, non-proof coins have been minted, it is believed for each of the four coins for every year. The one ounce £100 Britannia is primarily issued as a bullion coin in the non-proof standard, originally in competition with the South African Krugerrand. Its price is quoted daily on the financial pages of some newspapers.

There were five reverse designs by Philip Nathan:- 1987-1996 Standing Britannia, 1997 Chariot, 1998-2000 Standing Britannia, 2001 Una and the Lion, 2002 Standing Britannia, 2003 Britannia's Helmeted Head, 2004 Standing Britannia, 2005 Britannia seated, 2006 Standing Britannia. For 2007 the design is a Seated Britannia with lion at her feet, by Christopher Le Brun. The 2008 design is of Britannia standing and facing left, by John Bergdahl. The 2009 reverse is similar to that of 1997, Britannia on a chariot, while 2010 has Suzie Zamit's Britannia potrait with a Corinthian style helmet. The 2011 design is by David Mach, and portrays a seated Britannia with trident and shield, replicating the design on a 1937 penny, superimposed on a Union Flag. The rotation of the coin from left to right, or vice-versa, creates an illusion of Britannia moving with the ripple of the flag.

In general the proof coins have reverse features frosted, The proofs with Standing Britannia and Una and the Lion reverses include P NATHAN on the reverse, whereas the equivalent bullion coins include NATHAN. The other three reverses have PN on both proofs and bullion coins.

The issue of the second series of three coins in the Olympic Games gold proof coin was in 2011, with the completion of the 9-coin series in 2012. The obverses all have the 1998 Ian Rank-Broadley portrait of the Queen, but a few 2011 £100 coins were issued without his initials IRB under her portrait. Reverses are summarised below:

DATE	FACE VALUE	FINE GOLD WEIGHT	FEATURED GOD	FEATURED PART OF OLYMPIC MOTTO
2010	£100	1 Troy oz	Neptune	CITIUS
	£25	1/4 Troy oz	Diana	
	£25	1/4 Troy oz	Mercury	
2011	£100	1 Troy oz	Jupiter	ALTIUS
	£25	1/4 Troy oz	Juno	
	£25	1/4 Troy oz	Apollo	
2012	£100	1 Troy oz	Mars	FORTIUS
	£25	1/4 Troy oz	Vulcan	
	£25	1/4 Troy oz	Minerva	

2012 was also the 25th anniversary of the Gold Britannia coin series, and the reverse design chosen was that of the 1987 coins, standing Britannia, by Philip Nathan. This was repeated in 2013, but only for Brilliant Uncirculated "Bullion" coins. A separate new series was introduced for Proof coins, a seated Britannia with an owl was featured, the artist being Robert Hunt. The range of Britannia Proofs was increased from 4 to 6, with the addition of a Five-ounce coin (qv) and a one-twentieth of an ounce, curiously denominated at One Pound and with a diameter of 12mm, just larger than a Maundy One Penny. All 2013 Gold Britannias are minted in 0.999 Au alloy.

2014 and 2015 each saw three Reverse designs. The Nathan outstretched arm of Britannia continued as the bullion coin. The Shengxiào Collection by Wuon-Gean Ho saw the Year of the Horse (2014) and the Year of the Sheep (2015). The series by new artists of Britannia designs were of a standing Britannia facing left with lion (2014) by Jody Clark, and a "head and shoulders" Britannia holding the trident on her right shoulder, by Antony Dufont, the latter coin included the Clark portrayal of the Queen on the obverse.

A further new denomination appeared in 2014, the gold one-fortieth of an ounce, diameter 8mm and face value 50 pence.

HUNDRED POUNDS AND BELOW
(Britannia Platinum series)

2007 saw the issue of four-coin proof sets in platinum, 0.9995 fine. The denomination and designs are similar to those of the Gold series of the same year. The issue was repeated in 2008, and again in 2009, above rule applies. It is understood that no bullion coins have been issued.

HUNDRED POUNDS

Following on from the late 2013 introduction of the Twenty Pounds (see below) a "Hundred Pounds for £100" appeared, again a 0.999 Fine Silver coin, of two ounces weight, in early 2015.

DATE	Mintage	UNC
2015 Big Ben, BU	50,000	£100
2015 New Portrait, Buckingham Palace, BU	50,000	£100

TWENTY POUNDS

Another new denomination was added in late 2013. Marketed by the Royal Mint under the slogan "Twenty Pounds for £20", it is a 27mm diameter 0.999 Fine silver coin.

DATE	UNC
2013 Pistrucci St George & Dragon BU	£24
2014 Centenary of the outbreak of the First World War	£24
2015 Sir Winston Churchill	£20

FIVE POUNDS (Sovereign series)

This series is all minted in gold, and, except where stated, have the Pistrucci St George and Dragon reverse. BU coins up to 2001 bear a U in a circle. From 2009 the initials B.P. in the exergue are replaced by PISTRUCCI in small letters on the left. From 2014 the denomination is called the "Five-Sovereign" piece by the Royal Mint in their marketing publications.

DATE	Mintage	UNC
1980 Proof	10,000	£1000
1981 Proof	5,400	£1000
1982 Proof	2,500	£1000
1984 BU	15,104	£1000
1984 Proof	8,000	£1100
1985 New portrait BU	13,626	£1000
1985 — Proof	6,130	£1000
1986 BU	7,723	£1000
1987 Uncouped portrait BU	5,694	£1000
1988 BU	3,315	£1000
1989 500th Anniversary of the Sovereign. Enthroned portrayal obverse and		
Crowned shield reverse BU	2,937	£1400

NOTE: The prices quoted in this guide are set at August 2015 with the price of gold at £726 per ounce and silver £9 per ounce— market fluctuations will have a marked effect on the values of modern precious metal coins.

DATE	Mintage	UNC
1989 — Proof	5,000	£1500
1990 Reverts to couped portrait BU	1,226	£1000
1990 Proof	1,721	£1000
1991 BU	976	£1000
1991 Proof	1,336	£1000
1992 BU	797	£1000
1992 Proof	1,165	£1000
1993 BU	906	£1000
1993 Proof	1,078	£1000
1994 BU	1,000	£1000
1994 Proof	918	£1000
1995 BU	1,000	£1000
1995 Proof	1,250	£1000
1996 BU	901	£1000
1996 Proof	742	£1150
1997 BU	802	£1000
1997 Proof	860	£1000
1998 New portrait BU	825	£1100
1998 Proof	789	£1200
1999 BU	991	£1000
1999 Proof	1,000	£1100
2000 ("Bullion")	10,000	£1000
2000 BU	994	£1150
2000 Proof	3,000	£1200
2001 BU	1,000	£1000
2001 Proof	3,500	£1100
2002 Shield rev. ("Bullion")	—	£1000
2002 BU	—	£1100
2002 Proof	3,000	£1150
2003 BU	—	£1000
2003 Proof	—	£1200
2004 BU	—	£1000
2004 Proof	—	£1100
2005 Noad's heraldic St George and Dragon BU	—	£1150
2005 — Proof	—	£1400
2006 BU	—	£1000
2006 Proof	—	£1100
2007 BU	—	£1000
2007 Proof	—	£1100
2008 BU	—	£1000
2008 Proof	—	£1100
2009 BU	—	£1000
2009 Proof	—	£1150
2010 BU	—	£1000
2010 Proof	—	£1150
2011 BU	—	£1000
2011 Proof	—	£1150
2012 Day's St George and Dragon BU	1,250	£1150
2012 — Proof	—	£1450
2013 BU	—	£1000
2013 Proof	—	£1200
2014 BU	—	£1000
2014 Proof	—	£1200
2015 Proof	—	—
2015 New Portrait BU	—	£1450
2015 — Proof	—	—

The obverse of the 1989 gold coins portray HM the Queen enthroned.

Pistrucci's famous rendering of St George and the Dragon.

FIVE POUNDS (Crown series)

This series commenced in 1990 when the "Crown" was declared legal tender at £5, instead of 25p as all previous issues continued to be. Mintage is in cupro-nickel unless otherwise stated. BU includes those in individual presentation folders, and those in sets sold with stamp covers and/or banknotes.

DATE	Mintage	UNC
1990 Queen Mother's 90th Birthday.	2,761,431	£8
1990 — BU	48,477	£10
1990 — Silver Proof	56,800	£40
1990 — Gold Proof	2,500	£1100
1993 Coronation 40th Anniversary	1,834,655	£8
1993 — BU	—	£10
1993 — Proof	—	£15
1993 — Silver Proof	58,877	£45
1993 — Gold Proof	2,500	£1100
1996 HM the Queen's 70th Birthday	2,396,100	£8
1996 — BU	—	£10
1996 — Proof	—	£15
1996 — Silver Proof	39,336	£45
1996 — Gold Proof	2,127	£1100
1997 Royal Golden Wedding	1,733,000	£8
1997 — BU	—	£10
1997 — — with £5 note	5,000	£75
1997 — Proof	—	£20
1997 — Silver Proof	33,689	£45
1997 — Gold Proof	2,750	£1100
1998 Prince of Wales 50th Birthday	1,407,300	£9
1998 — BU	—	£12
1998 — Proof	—	£20
1998 — Silver Proof	13,379	£50
1998 — Gold Proof	—	£1100
1999 Princess of Wales Memorial.	1,600,000	£10
1999 — BU	—	£14
1999 — Proof	—	£20
1999 — Silver Proof	49,545	£50
1999 — Gold Proof	7,500	£1150
1999 Millennium	3,796,300	£8
1999 — BU	—	£12
1999 — Proof	—	£20
1999 — Silver Proof	49,057	£45
1999 — Gold Proof	2,500	£1150
2000 —	3,147,092*	£12
2000 — BU	—	£20
2000 — — with special Millennium Dome mintmark	—	£30
2000 — Proof	—	£25
2000 — Silver Proof with gold highlight	14,255	£50
2000 — Gold Proof	2,500	£1100
2000 Queen Mother's 100th Birthday	*incl. above**	£8
2000 — BU	—	£12
2000 — Silver Proof	31,316	£45
2000 — — — Piedfort	14,850	£60
2000 — Gold Proof	3,000	£1100
2001 Victorian Era	851,491	£10
2001 — BU	—	£12
2001 — Proof	—	£20
2001 — Silver Proof	19,216	£50
2001 — — with frosted relief	596	£150
2001 — Gold Proof	3,000	£1100
2001 — — with frosted relief	733	£1150
2002 Golden Jubilee	3,687,882*	£9
2002 — BU	—	£12
2002 — Proof	—	£20
2002 — Silver Proof	54,012	£45
2002 — Gold Proof	5,502	£1100

DATE	Mintage	UNC
2002 Queen Mother Memorial.. *incl. above**		£9
2002 — BU..	—	£12
2002 — Silver Proof	16,117	£45
2002 — Gold Proof..	3,000	£1100
2003 Coronation Jubilee	1,307,147	£10
2003 — BU..	—	£13
2003 — Proof..	—	£20
2003 — Silver Proof	28,758	£45
2003 — Gold Proof..	—	£1150
2004 Entente Cordiale Centenary 1,205,594		£10
2004 — Proof Reverse Frosting	—	£15
2004 — Silver Proof	11,295	£50
2004 — — Piedfort..	2,500	£125
2004 — Gold Proof..	—	£1150
2004 — Platinum Proof Piedfort..	501	£4000
2005 Trafalgar Bicentenary..	1,075 516	£12
2005 — BU..	—	£14
2005 — Proof..	—	£25
2005 — Silver Proof	21,448	£50
2005 — — — Piedfort..	2,818	£75
2005 — Gold Proof..	—	£1150
2005 Bicentenary of the Death of Nelson ....*incl. above**		£12
2005 — BU..	—	£14
2005 — Proof..	—	£25
2005 — Silver Proof	12,852	£50
2005 — — — Piedfort..	2,818	£75
2005 — Gold Proof..	—	£1150
2005 — Platinum Proof Piedfort..	200	£4000
2006 Queen's 80th Birthday...	—	£10
2006 — BU..	—	£14
2006 — Proof..	—	£20
2006 — Silver Proof	20,790	£50
2006 — — — Piedfort, selective gold plating on reverse	5,000	£75
2006 — Gold Proof..	—	£1150
2006 — Platinum Proof Piedfort..	250	£4000
2007 Queen's Diamond Wedding	—	£10
2007 — BU..	—	£15
2007 — Proof..	—	£20
2007 — Silver Proof	15,186	£50
2007 — — — Piedfort..	2,000	£80
2007 — Gold Proof..	—	£1150
2007 — Platinum Proof Piedfort..	—	£4000
2008 Prince of Wales 60th Birthday	—	£12
2008 — BU..	—	£15
2008 — Proof..	—	£20
2008 — Silver Proof	7,446	£55
2008 — — — Piedfort..	2,000	£90
2008 — Gold Proof..	—	£1150
2008 Elizabeth I 450th Anniversary of Accession	—	£12
2008 — BU..	—	£15
2008 — Proof..	—	£20
2008 — Silver Proof	10,398	£50
2008 — — Piedfort..	2,000	£90
2008 — Gold Proof..	—	£1150
2008 — Platinum Proof Piedfort..	—	£4000
2009 500th Anniversary of Henry VIII accession........................	30,000	£12
2009 — BU..	—	£15
2009 — Proof..	—	£25
2009 — Silver Proof	10,419	£50
2009 — — — Piedfort..	3,580	£90
2009 — Gold Proof..	1,509	£1150
2009 — Platinum Proof Piedfort..	100	£4250
2009 Olympic Countdown (3 years) BU	—	£12
2009 — Silver Proof	26,645	£55
2009 — — — Piedfort..	4,874	£90
2009 — Gold Proof..	—	£1250
2009 Olympic Celebration of Britain "The Mind" series (incl. green logo):		
Stonehenge Silver Proof	—	£60

DATE	Mintage	UNC
Palace of Westminster/Big Ben Silver Proof	—	£60
— Cu Ni Proof	—	£20
Angel of the North Silver Proof	—	£60
Flying Scotsman Silver Proof	—	£60
Globe Theatre Silver Proof	—	£60
Sir Isaac Newton Silver Proof	—	£60
2010 350th Anniversary of the Restoration of the Monarchy ...	15,000	£12
2010 — BU	—	£15
2010 — Proof	—	£25
2010 — Silver Proof	6,518	£50
2010 — — Piedfort	4,435	£100
2010 — Gold Proof	—	£1250
2010 — Platinum Proof Piedfort	—	£4000
2010 Olympic Countdown (2 years) BU	—	£12
2010 — Silver Proof	20,159	£55
2010 — — Piedfort	2,197	£150
2010 — Gold Proof	—	£1250
2010 Olympic Celebration of Britain, "The Body" series (incl. red logo):		
Coastline of Britain (Rhossili Bay) Silver Proof	—	£60
Giants Causeway Silver Proof	—	£60
River Thames Silver Proof	—	£60
British Fauna (Barn Owl) Silver Proof	—	£60
British Flora (Oak Leaves and Acorn) Silver Proof	—	£60
Weather Vane Silver Proof	—	£60
2010 Olympic Celebration of Britain "The Spirit" series (incl. blue logo):		
Churchill Silver Proof	—	£60
— CuNi Proof	—	£20
Spirit of London (Kind Hearts etc.) Silver Proof	—	£60
— CuNi Proof	—	£20
Humour Silver Proof	—	£60
Unity (Floral emblems of Britain) Silver Proof	—	£60
Music Silver Proof	—	£60
Anti-slavery Silver Proof	—	£60
2011 90th Birthday of the Duke of Edinburgh BU	—	£12
2011 — Silver Proof	4,599	£60
2011 — — — Piedfort	2,659	£115
2011 — Gold Proof	—	£1250
2011 — Platinum Proof Piedfort	—	£6000
2011 Royal Wedding of Prince William and Catherine Middleton		
BU	—	£12
2011 — Silver Proof	26,069	£60
2011 — Gold-plated Silver Proof	—	£80
2011 — Silver Proof Piedfort	2,991	£95
2011 — Gold Proof.	—	£1250
2011 — Platinum Proof Piedfort	—	£5500
2011 Olympic Countdown (1 year) BU	—	£12
2011 — Silver Proof	25,877	£55
2011 — — Piedfort	4,000	£100
2011 — Gold Proof.	—	£1250
2012 Diamond Jubilee BU	—	£15
2012 — Proof	—	£25
2012 — Silver Proof	—	£65
2012 — Gold-plated silver proof	—	£85
2012 — Silver Piedfort Proof	—	£100
2012 — Gold proof	—	£1250
2012 — Platinum Piedford Proof	—	£5500
2012 Olympic Countdown (Games Time) BU	—	£13
2012 — Silver Proof	—	£65
2012 — Silver Piedfort Proof	—	£120
2012 — Gold proof	—	£1450
2012 Official Olympic BU	—	£15
2012 — Silver Proof	—	£70
2012 — Gold Plated Silver Proof	—	£90
2012 — Silver Piedfort Proof	—	£125
2012 — Gold proof	—	£1450
2012 Official Paralympic BU	—	£15

DATE	Mintage	UNC
2012 — Silver Proof	—	£70
2012 — Silver Piedfort Proof...	—	£125
2012 — Gold proof..	—	£1750
2013 60th Anniversary of the Queen's Coronation BU	—	£15
2013 — Proof	—	£35
2013 — Silver Proof	—	£80
2013 — Silver Piedfort Proof..	—	£125
2013 — Gold-plated silver proof...	—	£100
2013 — Gold proof..	—	£1750
2013 — Platinum Piedfort Proof..	100	£6000
2013 Queen's Portraits, 4 coins each with one of the four portraits, paired with James Butler's Royal Arms. Issued only as sets of 4 in precious metals (see under Proof and Specimen Set section).............................	—	£300
2013 Royal Birth of Prince George (St George & Dragon), Silver Proof..	—	£80
2013 Christening of Prince George BU	—	£15
2013 — Silver Proof	—	£80
2013 — — — Piedfort	—	£160
2013 — Gold proof..	—	£1750
2013 — Platinum Proof Piedfort..	—	£6000
2014 300th Anniversary of the death of Queen Anne BU	—	£15
2014 — Proof	—	£35
2014 — Silver Proof	—	£80
2014 — — — Piedfort	—	£160
2014 — Gold-plated Silver Proof	—	£100
2014 — Gold proof..	—	£1800
2014 First Birthday of Prince George Silver Proof	—	£80
2014 100th Anniversary of the First World War Outbreak, issued only as sets of the 6 Coins (see under Proof and Specimen Sets section)	—	—
2014 Portrait of Britain, issued only as sets of the 4 coins, incorporating trichromatic colour-printing (see under Proof and Specimen Sets section)	—	—
2015 50th Anniversary of death of Sir Winston Churchill BU....	—	£13
2015 — Silver Proof	—	£80
2015 — — Piedfort	—	£160
2015 — Gold Proof..	—	£1800
2015 — Platinum Proof Piedfort..	65	£5000
2015 200th Anniversary of the Battle of Waterloo, BU..............	—	£13
2015 — Gold Proof..	100	—
2015 First World War 100th Anniversary, continued, issued only as sets of 6 coins	—	—
2015 New Portrait, Second Birthday of Prince George, Silver Proof —		£80
2015 — Birth of Second Child to the Duke & Duchess of Cambridge, BU	—	£13
2015 — — Silver Proof..	—	£80
2015 — — Gold Proof..	500	£1800
2015 — Christening of Princess Charlotte, Silver Proof	—	£80
2015 — 200th Anniversary of the Battle of Waterloo, Silver Proof	—	£160
2015 — — Silver Proof Piedfort	—	£160
2015 — — Gold Proof..	—	£1650

DOUBLE SOVEREIGN

As with the Sovereign series Five Pound coins, those listed under this heading bear the Pistrucci St George and Dragon reverse, except where otherwise stated, and are minted in gold. They are, and always have been, legal tender at £2, and have a diameter indentical to that of the base metal Two Pound coins listed further below under a different heading. The denomination does not appear on Double Sovereigns.

DATE	Mintage	UNC
1980 Proof	10,000	£450
1982 Proof	2,500	£450
1983 Proof	12,500	£400
1985 New Portrait Proof	5,849	£500
1987 Proof	14,301	£475
1988 Proof	12,743	£475
1989 500th Anniversary of the Sovereign. Enthroned portrayal obverse and Crowned shield reverse Proof	14,936	£800
1990 Proof	4,374	£500
1991 Proof	3,108	£500
1992 Proof	2,608	£500
1993 Proof	2,155	£500
1996 Proof	3,167	£500
1998 New Portrait Proof	4,500	£500
2000 Proof	2,250	£500
2002 Shield reverse Proof	8,000	£500
2003 Proof	2,250	£500
2004 Proof	—	£500
2005 Noad's heraldic St George and Dragon Proof	—	£650
2006 Proof	—	£500
2007 Proof	—	£500
2008 Proof	—	£500
2009 Proof	—	£500
2010 Proof	—	£500
2011 Proof	—	£500
2012 Day's St George and Dragon BU	—	£650
2012 — Proof	—	£750
2013 BU	—	£650
2013 Proof	—	£750
2014 BU	—	£650
2014 Proof	—	£850
2015 Proof	—	—
2015 New Portrait Proof	—	—

ABBREVIATIONS COMMONLY USED TO DENOTE METALLIC COMPOSITION	
Cu	Copper
Cu/Steel	Copper plated steel
Ag/Cu	Silver plated copper
Ae	Bronze
Cu-Ni	Cupro-nickel
Ni-Ag	Nickel silver (note—does not contain silver)
Brass/Cu-Ni	Brass outer, cupro-nickel inner
Ni-Brass	Nickel-brass
Ag	Silver
Au/Ag	Gold plated silver
Au	Gold
Pl	Platinum

TWO POUNDS AND BELOW
(including Britannia Silver Series)

This series commenced in 1997, and, as with the Gold Britannia series, sets of the coins are listed in the "Proof and Specimen Sets" section. Coins contain one Troy ounce of fine silver (£2) alloyed to Britannia standard, i.e. 95.8 per cent fine silver, or fractions of one ounce as follows: half ounce (£1), quarter ounce (50 pence) and one tenth of an ounce (20 pence). Reverses change anually, all four coins of any particular date being of the same design. The reverses by Philip Nathan appear as follows:
1997 Chariot, 1998 Standing Britannia, 1999 Chariot, 2000 Standing Britannia, 2001 Una and the Lion, 2002 Standing Britannia, 2003 Britannia's Helmeted Head, 2004 Standing Britannia, 2005 Britannia Seated, 2006 Standing Britannia, 2009 Chariot.
  The 2007 design is by Christopher Le Brun, and features a seated Britannia with Lion at her feet. The 2008 is by John Bergdahl, and features a standing Britannia facing left.
  Two pounds Britannia coins to BU or "bullion" standard have been issued as individual coins for each year from 1998 onwards. 2010 features Suzie Zamit's Britannia with a portrait with a Corinthian style helmet.
  The 2011 coins feature a seated Britannia and Union Flag, as described in the Britannia gold series above.
  2012 saw the 15th anniversary of the Silver Series, but the reverse chosen was that of the Standing Britannia by Philip Nathan, which also marked the 25th Gold series. In addition, there is a 9-coin proof set of Half-Ounce silver coins dated 2012 featuring each of the Reverses used in the past, a 25th Anniversary collection. The story of the 2013 silver Britannia coins closely parallels that of the gold coins. The silver one-twentieth of an ounce has the logical face value of 10 pence.
  The 2014 Silver Britannias closely follow the pattern of the three designs of 2014 Gold. This included the introduction of the silver one-fortieth of an ounce, with a face value of 5 pence. The Nathan Britannia has crenellated borders on both the obverse and the reverse, while the Year of the Horse has plain borders on both. Examples exist, however, of both One ounce silver bullion coins having the Other's obverse, thus producing two error coins, or "mules". 2014 also saw the SS Gairsoppa Quarter-ounce silver Britannia bullion coin with the edge inscription SS GAIRSOPPA. These coins have the Nathan Britannia reverse, and are struck from metal recovered from the vessel which was sunk by enemy action in 1941.
  Both 2013 and 2014 one-ounce BU bullion Nathan Britannia coins exists with snakes or horses (respectively) on a plain edge. These were the result of a contract between the Royal Mint and the bullion dealers A-mark of Santa Monica, California, and commemorate Chinese Lunar years.
  A new metal combination was the Gold-plated Silver Proof One-ounce coin for the Year of the Sheep.
  NOTE: As the BRITANNIA series of coins are essentially bullion pieces, their values are usually related to the current price of gold and silver, therefore no attempt has been made in this publication to give values for the series. To ascertain the value of a piece it is necessary to check with the prevailing price of precious metals.

TWO POUNDS

This series commenced in 1986 with nickel-brass commemorative coins, with their associated base metal and precious metal BU and proof coins. From 1997 (actually issued in 1998) a thinner bi-metal version commenced with a reverse theme of the advance of technology, and from this date the coin was specifically intended to circulate. This is true also for the parallel issues of anniversary and commemorative Two Pound issues in 1999 and onwards. All have their BU and proof versions, as listed below.

In the case of Gold Proofs, a few have Certificates of Authenticity and/or green boxes of issue describing the coin as a Double Sovereign. All Gold Proofs since 1997 are of bi-metallic gold except for 2001 (red gold with the inner circle coated in yellow gold) and 2002 (Technology issue, uncoated red gold).

A new definitive design was introduced during 2015 incorporating the Jody Clark portrait and Britannia by Antony Dufort

NOTE: The counterfeiting of circulation £2 coins has been around for several years but 2015 saw the introduction of proof-like base metal designs. Five types are known at present: 2011 (Mary Rose) and 2015 (all four designs).

DATE	Mintage	UNC
1986 Commonwealth Games	8,212,184	£4
1986 — BU	—	£8
1986 — Proof	59,779	£15
1986 — Silver BU	—	£25
1986 — — Proof	—	£35
1986 — Gold Proof	—	£450
1989 Tercentenary of Bill of Rights.	4,392,825	£8
1989 — BU (issued in folder with Claim of Right)	—	£25
1989 — BU folder	—	£8
1989 — Proof	—	£15
1989 — Silver Proof	—	£35
1989 — — — Piedfort	—	£50
1989 Tercentenary of Claim of Right (issued in Scotland)	381,400	£12
1989 — BU (see above)	—	£12
1989 — Proof	—	£25
1989 — Silver Proof	—	£35
1989 — — — Piedfort	—	£50
1994 Tercentenary of the Bank of England	1,443,116	£5
1994 — BU	—	£8
1994 — Proof	—	£12
1994 — Silver Proof	27,957	£35
1994 — — — Piedfort	9,569	£60
1994 — Gold Proof	—	£400
1994 — — — with Double Sovereign obverse (no denomination)	—	£475
1995 50th Anniversary of End of WWII.	4,394,566	£5
1995 — BU	—	£8
1995 — Proof	—	£12
1995 — Silver Proof	35,751	£35
1995 — — — Piedfort	—	£60
1995 — Gold Proof	—	£450
1995 50th Anniversary of The United Nations	1,668,575	£6
1995 — BU	—	£9
1995 — Proof	—	£12
1995 — Silver Proof	—	£40
1995 — — — Piedfort	—	£60
1995 — Gold Proof	—	£450
1996 European Football Championships.	5,195,350	£6
1996 — BU	—	£8
1996 — Proof	—	£10
1996 — Silver Proof	25,163	£40
1996 — — Piedfort	7,634	£60
1996 — Gold Proof	—	£450
1997	13,734,625	£4
1997 BU	—	£8
1997 Proof	—	£12
1997 Silver Proof	29,910	£35
1997 — — Piedfort	16,000	£60
1997 Gold Proof (red (outer) and yellow (inner) 22ct)	—	£400

DATE	Mintage	UNC
1998 *New Portrait*	—	£3
1998 BU	91,110,375	£8
1998 Proof	—	£12
1998 Silver Proof	19,978	£35
1998 — — Piedfort	7,646	£60
1999	33,719,000	£3
1999 Rugby World Cup	4,933,000	£6
1999 — BU	—	£10
1999 — Silver Proof (gold plated ring)	9,665	£45
1999 — — — Piedfort (Hologram)	10,000	£85
1999 — Gold Proof	—	£450
2000	25,770,000	£3
2000 BU	—	£6
2000 Proof	—	£10
2000 Silver Proof	—	£40
2001	34,984,750	£3
2001 BU	—	£4
2001 Proof	—	£10
2001 Marconi	4,558,000	£4
2001 — BU	—	£8
2001 — Proof	—	£10
2001 — Silver Proof (gold plated ring)	11,488	£40
2001 — — — Reverse Frosting (issued in set with Canada $5)	—	£65
2001 — — — Piedfort	6,759	£60
2001 — Gold Proof	—	£450
2002	13,024,750	£3
2002 BU	—	£6
2002 Proof	—	£10
2002 Gold Proof (red 22ct)		£450
2002 Commonwealth Games, Scotland	771,750	£8
2002 — Wales	558,500	£8
2002 — Northern Ireland	485,500	£8
2002 — England	650,500	£8
2002 — BU (issued in set of 4)	—	£40
2002 — Proof (issued in set of 4)	—	£50
2002 — Silver Proof (issued in set of 4)	—	£150
2002 — — — Piedfort (painted) (issued in set of 4)	—	£275
2002 — Gold Proof (issued in set of 4)	—	£450
2003	17,531,250	£4
2003 BU	—	£8
2003 Proof	—	£12
2003 DNA Double Helix	4,299,000	£3
2003 — BU	—	£6
2003 — Proof	—	£10
2003 — Silver Proof (Gold-plated ring)	11,204	£40
2003 — — Piedfort	8,728	£60
2003 — Gold Proof	—	£450
2004	11,981,500	£3
2004 BU	—	£6
2004 Proof	—	£12
2004 Trevithick Steam Locomotive	5,004,500	£4
2004 — BU	—	£8
2004 — Proof	—	£30
2004 — Silver BU	—	£25
2004 — — Proof (Gold-plated ring)	10,233	£45
2004 — — — Piedfort	5,303	£60
2004 — Gold Proof	—	£450
2005	3,837,250	£3
2005 BU	—	£6
2005 Proof	—	£8
2005 Gunpowder Plot	5,140,500	£4
2005 — BU	—	£8
2005 — Proof	—	£6
2005 — Silver Proof	4,394	£40
2005 — — — Piedfort	4,585	£65
2005 — Gold Proof	—	£450

DATE	Mintage	UNC
2005 End of World War II	10,191,000	£4
2005 — BU	—	£8
2005 — Silver Proof	21,734	£40
2005 — — — Piedfort	4,798	£65
2005 — Gold Proof	—	£450
2006	16,715,000	£3
2006 Proof	—	£6
2006 Brunel, The Man (Portrait)	7,928,250	£4
2006 — BU	—	£6
2006 — Proof	—	£10
2006 — Silver Proof	—	£40
2006 — — — Piedfort	—	£65
2006 —Gold Proof	—	£450
2006 Brunel, His Achievements (Paddington Station)	7,452,250	£4
2006 — BU	—	£6
2006 — Proof	—	£10
2006 — Silver Proof	—	£40
2006 — — — Piedfort	—	£65
2006 —Gold Proof	—	£450
2007	10,270,000	£3
2007 Proof	—	£8
2007 Tercentenary of the Act of Union	7,545,000	£4
2007 BU	—	£6
2007 — Proof	—	£8
2007 — Silver Proof	8,310	£40
2007 — — — Piedfort	4,000	£65
2007 — Gold Proof	—	£450
2007 Bicentenary of the Abolition of the Slave Trade	8,445,000	£4
2007 — BU	—	£6
2007 — Proof	—	£10
2007 — Silver Proof	7,095	£40
2007 — — — Piedfort	3,990	£65
2007 — Gold Proof	—	£450
2008	15,346,000	£3
2008 BU	—	£6
2008 Proof	—	£12
2008 Centenary of 4th Olympiad, London	910,000	£4
2008 — BU	—	£6
2008 — Proof	—	£12
2008 — Silver Proof	8,023	£40
2008 — — — Piedfort	2,000	£70
2008 — Gold Proof	—	£450
2008 Olympic Games Handover Ceremony	853,000	£4
2008 — BU	—	£7
2008 — Silver Proof	30,000	£45
2008 — — — Piedfort	3,000	£75
2008 — Gold Proof	—	£450
2009	8,775,000	£3
2009 BU	—	£4
2009 Proof	—	£10
2009 Silver Proof	—	£45
2009 250th Anniversary of birth of Robert Burns	3,253,000	£3
2009 — BU	—	£8
2009 — Proof	—	£12
2009 — Silver Proof	9,188	£40
2009 — — — Piedfort	3,500	£70
2009 — Gold Proof	—	£450
2009 200th Anniversary of birth of Charles Darwin	3,903,000	£3
2009 — BU	—	£8
2009 — Proof	—	£12
2009 — Silver Proof	9,357	£40
2009 — — — Piedfort	3,282	£70
2009 Gold Proof	—	£450
2010	6,890,000	£3
2010 BU	—	£8
2010 Proof	—	£12

DATE	Mintage	UNC
2010 Silver Proof	—	£40
2010 Florence Nightingale 150 Years of Nursing	6,175,000	£4
2010 — BU	—	£10
2010 — Proof	—	£12
2010 — Silver Proof	5,117	£40
2010 – — – Piedfort	2,770	£70
2010 — Gold Proof	—	£450
2011	24,375,000	£4
2011 BU	—	£5
2011 Proof	—	£12
2011 Silver Proof	—	£35
2011 500th Anniversary of the Mary Rose	1,040,000	£4
2011 — BU	—	£9
2011 — Proof	—	£12
2011 — Silver Proof	6,618	£40
2011 — — — Piedfort	2,680	£75
2011 — Gold Proof	—	£450
2011 400th Anniversary of the King James Bible	975,000	£4
2011 — BU	—	£9
2011 — Proof	—	£15
2011 — Silver Proof	4,494	£45
2011 — — — Piedfort	2,394	£75
2011 — Gold Proof	—	£500
2012	3,900,000	£3
2012 BU	—	£6
2012 Proof	—	£12
2012 Silver Proof	—	£30
2012 Gold Proof	—	£450
2012 200th Anniversary of birth of Charles Dickens	8,190,000	£4
2012 — BU	—	£9
2012 — Proof	—	£12
2012 — Silver Proof	—	£45
2012 — — — Piedfort	—	£75
2012 — Gold Proof	—	£500
2012 Olympic Handover to Rio	845,000	£5
2012 — BU	—	£12
2012 — Silver Proof	—	£50
2012 — — — Piedfort	—	£100
2012 — Gold Proof	—	£500
2013	—	£3
2013 BU	—	£6
2013 Proof	—	£12
2013 Silver Proof	—	£65
2013 Gold Proof	—	£500
2013 150th Anniversary of the London Underground, Roundel design	—	£4
2013 — BU	—	£12
2013 — Proof	—	£18
2013 — Silver Proof	—	£50
2013 — — — Piedfort	—	£100
2013 — Gold Proof	—	£550
2013 150th Anniversary of the London Underground, Train design	—	£4
2013 — BU	—	£10
2013 — Proof	—	£15
2013 — Silver Proof	—	£50
2013 — — — Piedfort	—	£100
2013 — Gold Proof	—	£550
2013 350th Anniversary of the Guinea	—	£4
2013 — BU	—	£10
2013 — Proof	—	£15
2013 — Silver Proof	—	£50
2013 — — — Piedfort	—	£100
2013 — Gold Proof	—	£600
2014	—	—
2014 BU	—	—

DATE	Mintage	UNC
2014 Proof..	—	—
2014 Silver Proof..............................	—	—
2014 100th Anniversary of First World War Outbreak.	—	£3
2014 — BU.......................................	—	£10
2014 — Proof...................................	—	£20
2014 — Silver Proof...........................	—	£50
2014 — — Piedfort............................	—	£100
2014 — Gold Proof............................	—	£750
2014 500th Anniversary of Trinity House..........	—	£3
2014 — BU.......................................	—	£10
2014 — Proof...................................	—	£20
2014 — Silver Proof...........................	—	£50
2014 — — Piedfort............................	—	£100
2014 — Gold Proof............................	—	£750
2015	—	£3
2015 BU..	—	£10
2015 Proof......................................	—	£20
2015 Silver Proof..............................	—	£50
2015 Gold Proof................................	—	£750
2015 Royal Navy First World War................	—	£3
2015 — BU.......................................	—	£10
2015 — Proof...................................	—	£20
2015 — Silver Proof...........................	—	£50
2015 — — Piedfort............................	—	£100
2015 — Gold Proof............................	—	£750
2015 800th Anniversary of Magna Carta...........	—	£3
2015 — BU.......................................	—	£10
2015 — Proof...................................	—	£20
2015 — Silver Proof...........................	—	£50
2015 — — Piedfort............................	—	£100
2015 — Gold Proof............................	—	£695
2015 New Portrait, new Reverse................	—	£3
2015 — BU.......................................	—	£10
2015 — Proof...................................	—	£20
2015 — Silver Proof...........................	—	£50
2015 — Gold Proof............................	—	£750
2015 — Platinum Proof.......................	—	—
2015 — 800th Anniversary of Magna Carta..............	—	£3
2015 — — BU..................................	—	£10
2015 — — Silver Proof.......................	—	£50
2015 — — — Piedfort.......................	—	£100
2015 — — Gold Proof........................	—	£695

SOVEREIGN

All are minted in gold, bear the Pistrucci St George and Dragon reverse except where stated, and are legal tender at one pound. From 2009 there is no streamer behind St George's Helmet in the Pistrucci design.

DATE	Mintage	UNC
1974...	5,002,566	£200
1976...	4,150,000	£200
1978...	6,550,000	£200
1979...	9,100,000	£200
1979 Proof....................................	50,000	£250
1980...	5,100,000	£200
1980 Proof....................................	91,200	£250
1981...	5,000,000	£250
1981 Proof....................................	32,960	£250
1982...	2,950,000	£200
1982 Proof....................................	22,500	£250
1983 Proof	21,250	£250

DATE	Mintage	UNC
1984 Proof	19,975	£250
1985 New portrait Proof	17,242	£250
1986 Proof	17,579	£250
1987 Proof	22,479	£250
1988 Proof	18,862	£250
1989 500th Anniversary of the Sovereign—details as Five Pounds (Sov. Series). Proof	23,471	£750
1990 Proof	8,425	£250
1991 Proof	7,201	£250
1992 Proof	6,854	£250
1993 Proof	6,090	£250
1994 Proof	7,165	£250
1995 Proof	9,500	£250
1996 Proof	9,110	£250
1997 Proof	9,177	£250
1998 New Portrait Proof	11,349	£250
1999 Proof	11,903	£275
2000 (first Unc issue since 1982)	129,069	£225
2000 Proof	12,159	£250
2001	49,462	£200
2001 Proof	10,000	£250
2002 Shield Rev. ("bullion")	74,263	£200
2002 Proof	20,500	£250
2003 ("bullion")	43,208	£200
2003 Proof	—	£250
2004 ("bullion")	28,821	£200
2004 Proof	—	£250
2005 Noad heraldic St George and Dragon	—	£300
2005 — Proof	—	£350
2006 ("bullion")	—	£200
2006 Proof	—	£300
2007 ("bullion")	—	£200
2007 Proof	—	£250
2008 ("bullion")	—	£200
2008 Proof	—	£250
2009 ("bullion")	—	£200
2009 Proof	—	£250
2010 ("bullion")	—	£200
2010 Proof	—	£250
2011 ("bullion")	—	£200
2011 Proof	—	£300
2012 Day's St George and Dragon BU "bullion"	—	£250
2012 — Proof	—	£300
2013 BU "bullion"	—	£200
2013 — with "I" mintmark, minted by MMTC-PAMP, Haryana, India, under Licence from, and the supervision of, the Royal Mint	—	£250
2013 Proof	—	£350
2014 BU "bullion"	—	£225
2014 Proof	—	£300
2014 BU "bullion" with "I" mintmark	—	£250
2015 BU "bullion"	—	£325
2015 Proof	—	£360
2015 New Portrait, Proof	—	£360

IMPORTANT NOTE:
The prices quoted in this guide are set at August 2015 with the price of gold at £726 per ounce and silver £9 per ounce—market fluctuations can have a marked effect on the values of modern precious metal coins.

The Sovereign's war effort

At the outbreak of the First World War, Britain needed money to finance her war effort by any means possible. Posters were produced appealing to the patriotism of the great British public urging them to donate their gold coins for the war effort. Production of the sovereign as a circulation coin stopped completely in 1917.

HALF SOVEREIGN

Legal Tender at 50 pence, otherwise the notes for the Sovereign apply. From 2009 the exergue in the Pistrucci design is larger in area, and the initials B.P. are absent. From 2011, however, the initials were restored.

DATE	Mintage	UNC
1980 Proof only	86,700	£125
1982	2,500,000	£120
1982 Proof	21,590	£125
1983 Proof	19,710	£135
1984 Proof	19,505	£135
1985 New portrait Proof	15,800	£135
1986 Proof	17,075	£135
1987 Proof	20,687	£135
1988 Proof	18,266	£135
1989 500th Anniversary of the Sovereign—details as Five Pounds (Sov. Series) Proof	21,824	£400
1990 Proof	7,889	£135
1991 Proof	6,076	£135
1992 Proof	5,915	£135
1993 Proof	4,651	£135
1994 Proof	7,167	£135
1995 Proof	7,500	£135
1996 New Portrait Proof	7,340	£150
1997 Proof	9,177	£135
1998 Proof	7,496	£135
1999 Proof	9,403	£135
2000	146,822	£120
2000 Proof	9,708	£135
2001	98,763	£120
2001 Proof	7,500	£135
2002 Shield reverse ("bullion")	61,347	£120
2002 Proof	—	£135
2003 ("bullion")	47,805	£120
2003 Proof	—	£135
2004 ("bullion")	32,479	£120
2004 Proof	—	£135
2005 Noad heraldic St George and Dragon	—	£185
2005 — Proof	—	£200
2006 ("bullion")	—	£125
2006 Proof	—	£150
2006 ("bullion")	—	£125
2007 Proof	—	£150
2008 ("bullion")	—	£125
2008 Proof	—	£150
2009 ("bullion")	—	£125
2009 Proof	—	£150
2010 ("bullion")	—	£125
2010 Proof	—	£150
2011 ("bullion")	—	£125
2011 Proof	—	£175
2012 Day's St George and Dragon "bullion" or BU	—	£125
2012 — Proof	—	£175
2013 BU "bullion"	—	£125
2013 Proof	—	£170
2014 BU "bullion"	—	£150
2014 Proof	—	£175
2014 BU "bullion" with "I" mintmark	—	£200
2015 BU "bullion"	—	£170
2015 Proof	—	£190
2015 New Portrait, Proof	—	£190

QUARTER SOVEREIGN

Minted in 22ct Gold, this new denomination was introduced in 2009, and follows on from two different patterns of 1853.

DATE	Mintage	UNC
2009 ("bullion")	—	£65
2009 Proof	—	£85
2010 ("bullion")	—	£65
2010 Proof	—	£85
2011 ("bullion")	—	£65
2011 Proof	—	£85
2012 Day's St George and Dragon BU "bullion"	—	£75
2012 — Proof	—	£85
2013 ("bullion")	—	£65
2013 Proof	—	£85
2014 ("bullion")	—	£75
2015 Proof	—	£110
2015 New Portrait, Proof	—	£110

ONE POUND

Introduced into circulation in 1983 to replace the £1 note, all are minted in nickel-brass unless otherwise stated. The reverse changed yearly until 2008, and until 2008 the Royal Arms was the "definitive" version. 2008 also saw the introduction of the Matthew Dent Uncrowned Shield of the Royal Arms, a new "definitive", and this reverse appeared in 2008 and every year since then. A Capital Cities Series of two coins each year for two years commenced in 2010. From 2013 a further 4-coin series over two years was issued, portraying two floral emblems associated with each of the four countries making up the United Kingdom. Collectors and others should be aware of the many different counterfeit £1 coin versions in circulation, a high proportion of which do not have matching obverses and reverses although many do.

A 12-sided bi-metallic coin will replace the current £1 coin in 2017, and will incorporate several security features to help defeat the counterfeiters.

DATE	Mintage	UNC
1983 Royal Arms	443,053,510	£3
1983 — BU	1,134,000	£5
1983 — Proof	107,800	£8
1983 — Silver Proof	50,000	£32
1983 — — Piedfort	10,000	£85
1984 Scottish Thistle	146,256,501	£3
1984 — BU	199,430	£6
1984 — Proof	106,520	£8
1984 — Silver Proof	44,855	£35
1984 — — Piedfort	15,000	£50
1985 **New portrait.** Welsh Leek	228,430,749	£3
1985 — BU	213,679	£5
1985 — Proof	102,015	£6
1985 — Silver Proof	50,000	£35
1985 — — Piedfort	15,000	£50
1986 Northern Ireland Flax	10,409,501	£3
1986 — BU	—	£6
1986 — Proof	—	£7
1986 — Silver Proof	37,958	£35
1986 — — Piedfort	15,000	£50
1987 English Oak	39,298,502	£3
1987 — BU	—	£5
1987 — Proof	—	£8
1987 — Silver Proof	50,000	£35
1987 — — Piedfort	15,000	£50

1983, 1993, 1998, 2003
EDGE: *DECUS ET TUTAMEN*

1984, 1989
NEMO ME IMPUNE LACESSIT

1985, 1990
PLEIDIOL WYF I'M GWLAD

DATE	Mintage	UNC
1988 Crowned Shield Of The Royal Arms..................	7,118,825	£4
1988 — BU...	—	£6
1988 — Proof	—	£8
1988 — Silver Proof	50,000	£35
1988 — — Piedfort	10,000	£60
1989 Scottish Thistle	70,580,501	£4
1989 — BU...	—	£6
1989 — Proof	—	£9
1989 — Silver Proof	22,275	£35
1989 — — — Piedfort	10,000	£50
1990 Welsh Leek	—	£4
1990 — BU...	97,269,302	£6
1990 — Proof	—	£7
1990 — Silver Proof	23,277	£35
1991 Northern Ireland Flax	38,443,575	£3
1991 — BU...	—	£6
1991 — Proof	—	£9
1991 — Silver Proof	22,922	£35
1992 English Oak	36,320,487	£2
1992 — BU...	—	£6
1992 — Proof	—	£7
1992 — Silver Proof	13,065	£35
1993 Royal Arms	114,744,500	£3
1993 — BU...	—	£6
1993 — Proof	—	£7
1993 — Silver Proof	16,526	£35
1993 — — — Piedfort	12,500	£55
1994 Scottish Lion	29,752,525	£4
1994 — BU...	—	£6
1994 — Proof	—	£8
1994 — Silver Proof	25,000	£35
1994 — — — Piedfort	11,722	£55
1995 Welsh Dragon	34,503,501	£3
1995 — BU...	—	£6
1995 — — (Welsh)	—	£7
1995 — Proof	—	£10
1995 — Silver Proof	27,445	£35
1995 — — Piedfort	8,458	£65
1996 Northern Ireland Celtic Cross	89,886,000	£4
1996 — BU...	—	£6
1996 — Proof	—	£7
1996 — Silver Proof	25,000	£35
1996 — — Piedfort	10,000	£55
1997 English Lions	57,117,450	£4
1997 — BU...	—	£6
1997 — Proof	—	£7
1997 — Silver Proof	20,137	£35
1997 — — Piedfort	10,000	£55
1998 *New portrait*. Royal Arms. BU........................	—	£12
1998 — Proof	—	£15
1998 — Silver Proof	13,863	£35
1998 — — Piedfort	7,894	£50
1999 Scottish Lion. BU	—	£12
1999 — Proof	—	£15
1999 — Silver Proof	16,328	£35
1999 — — — Reverse Frosting.................................	—	£45
1999 — — — Piedfort	9,975	£60
2000 Welsh Dragon	109,496,500	£3
2000 — BU...	—	£6
2000 — Proof	—	£8
2000 — Silver Proof	15,913	£35
2000 — — — Reverse Frosting.................................	—	£45
2000 — — — Piedfort	9,994	£55
2001 Northern Ireland Celtic Cross.	63,968,065	£3
2001 — BU...	58,093,731	£6
2001 — Proof	—	£8
2001 — Silver Proof	11,697	£35
2001 — — — Reverse Frosting.................................	—	£45

1986, 1991
DECUS ET TUTAMEN

1987, 1992
DECUS ET TUTAMEN

1988
DECUS ET TUTAMEN

1994, 1999
NEMO ME IMPUNE LACESSIT

1995, 2000
PLEIDIOL WYF I'M GWLAD

1996, 2001
DECUS ET TUTAMEN

DATE	Mintage	UNC
2001 — — — Piedfort	8,464	£50
2002 English Lions	77,818,000	£3
2002 — BU	—	£5
2002 — Proof	—	£8
2002 — Silver Proof	17,693	£35
2002 — — Reverse Frosting	—	£45
2002 — — — Piedfort	6,599	£50
2002 — Gold Proof	—	£425
2003 Royal Arms	61,596,500	£4
2003 — BU	—	£6
2003 — Proof	—	£10
2003 — Silver Proof	15,830	£35
2003 — — — Piedfort	9,871	£50
2004 Forth Railway Bridge	39,162,000	£4
2004 — BU	—	£6
2004 — Proof	—	£10
2004 — Silver Proof	11,470	£35
2004 — — — Piedfort	7,013	£50
2004 — Gold Proof	—	£425
2005 Menai Bridge	99,429,500	£4
2005 — BU	—	£6
2005 — Proof	—	£10
2005 — Silver Proof	8,371	£35
2005 — — — Piedfort	6,007	£50
2005 — Gold Proof	—	£425
2006 Egyptian Arch	38,938,000	£4
2006 — BU	—	£6
2006 — Proof	—	£10
2006 — Silver Proof	14,765	£35
2006 — — — Piedfort	5,129	£50
2006 — Gold Proof	—	£425
2007 Gateshead Millennium Bridge	26,180,160	£4
2007 — BU	—	£6
2007 — Proof	—	£10
2007 — Silver Proof	10,110	£40
2007 — — — Piedfort	5,739	£50
2007 — Gold Proof	—	£425
2008 Royal Arms	3,910,000	£4
2008 — BU	—	£6
2008 — Proof	—	£8
2008 — Silver Proof	8,441	£35
2008 — Gold Proof	—	£425
2008 — Platinum Proof	—	£500
2008 A series of 14 different reverses, the 25th Anniversary of the modern £1 coin, Silver Proof with selected gold highlighting on the reverses. the latter being all those used since 1983, the coins being with appropriate edge lettering		£400
2008 The same as above, Gold Proof (the 2008 Royal Arms being already listed above)	—	£5800
2008 **New Rev.,** Shield of the Royal Arms, no border beads on Obv.	29,518,000	£3
2008 BU	—	£5
2008 Proof	—	£6
2008 Silver Proof	5,000	£35
2008 Silver Proof Piedfort	4,202	£55
2008 Gold Proof	—	£450
2008 Platinum Proof	—	£575
2009	7,820,000	£4
2009 BU	—	£5
2009 Proof	—	£6
2009 Silver Proof	8,508	£35
2009 Gold Proof	—	£595
2010	38,505,000	£4

1997, 2002
DECUS ET TUTAMEN

2004
PATTERNED EDGE

2005
PATTERNED EDGE

2006
PATTERNED EDGE

2007
PATTERNED EDGE

2008 (proof sets — silver and gold
DECUS ET TUTAMEN

DATE	Mintage	UNC
2010 BU	—	£5
2010 Proof...	—	£6
2010 Silver BU	—	£30
2010 — Proof	—	£40
2010 City Series (London)	2,635,000	£4
2010 — BU	—	£5
2010 — Proof	—	£6
2010 — Silver Proof	7,693	£40
2010 — — — Piedfort............................	3,682	£55
2010 — Gold Proof...............................	—	£450
2010 City Series (Belfast)	6,205,000	£3
2010 — BU	—	£5
2010 — Proof	—	£6
2010 — Silver Proof	5,805	£35
2010 — — — Piedfort............................	3,503	£55
2010 — Gold Proof...............................	—	£500
2011..	39,550,000	£2
2011 BU	—	£3
2011 Proof...	—	£8
2011 Silver BU (in 21st and 18th Birthday cards)	—	£45
2011 — Proof	—	£55
2011 City Series (Cardiff).......................	1,615,000	£4
2011 — BU	—	£5
2011 — Proof	—	£7
2011 — Silver Proof	5,553	£40
2011 — — — Piedfort............................	1,615	£60
2011 — Gold Proof...............................	—	£500
2011 City Series (Edinburgh)	—	£4
2011 — BU	—	£5
2011 — Proof	—	£8
2011 — Silver Proof	4,973	£45
2011 — — — Piedfort............................	2,696	£60
2011 — Gold Proof...............................	—	£500
2012..	—	£3
2012 BU	—	£5
2012 Proof...	—	£8
2012 Silver BU (in Silver Baby Gift)	—	£75
2012 Silver Proof	—	£50
2012 — with selective gold plating	—	£35
2012 Gold Proof	—	£450
2013..	—	£3
2013 BU	—	£6
2013 Proof...	—	£8
2013 Silver BU.....................................	—	£60
2013 Silver Proof	—	£45
2013 Gold Proof	—	£450
2013 Floral Series (England)...................	—	£3
2013 — BU	—	£6
2013 — Proof	—	£10
2013 — Silver Proof	—	£45
2013 — — — Piedfort............................	—	£60
2013 — Gold Proof...............................	—	£500
2013 Floral Series (Wales)	—	£3
2013 — BU	—	£6
2013 — Proof	—	£10
2013 — Silver Proof	—	£45
2013 — — — Piedfort............................	—	£60
2013 — Gold Proof...............................	—	£500
2013 Royal Coat of Arms (Sewell), Gold Proof	—	£500
2013 Crowned Royal Arms (Gorringe), Gold Proof	—	£500

(The above two coins are part of a set of three, along with the 2013 gold
proof, with definitive reverse with Uncrowned Royal Arms (Dent)).

2008, 2009, 2010, 2011
DECUS ET TUTAMEN

2011
**Y DDRAIG GOCH
DDYRY CYCHWYN**

2011
**NISI DOMINUS
FRUSTRA**

*2013 Wales £1 Floral
gold proof.*

*Most £1 coins are
also available in
precious metals.*

DATE	Mintage	UNC
2014..	—	£3
2014 BU	—	£6
2014 Proof..	—	£10
2014 Silver BU	—	£50
2014 Silver Proof..	—	£55
2014 Floral Series (Scotland).......................................	—	£3
2014 — BU	—	£6
2014 — Proof	—	£10
2014 — Silver Proof	—	£45
2014 — — — Piedfort	—	£60
2014 — Gold Proof...	—	£850
2014 Floral Series (Northern Ireland)............................	—	£3
2014 — BU	—	£6
2014 — Proof	—	£10
2014 — Silver Proof	—	£45
2014 — — — Piedfort	—	£60
2014 — Gold Proof...	—	£850
2015..	—	£3
2015 BU	—	£6
2015 Proof..	—	£10
2015 Silver Proof..	—	£50
2015 Gold Proof..	—	£450
2015 Platinum Proof	—	—
2015 New Portrait..	—	£3
2015 — BU	—	£6
2015 — Proof	—	£10
2015 — Silver Proof	—	£50
2015 — Gold Proof...	—	£450
2015 — Platinum Proof	—	—
2015 — Heraldic Royal Arms	—	£3
2015 — — BU	—	£6
2015 — — Silver Proof	—	£50
2015 — — — —Piedfort..	—	£100
2015 — — Gold Proof..	—	£450

*2014 Scotland
£1 Floral gold proof.*

2015

FIFTY PENCE

Introduced as legal tender for 10 shillings to replace the banknote of that value prior to decimalisation, coins of the original size are no longer legal tender. Unless otherwise stated, i.e. for commemoratives, the reverse design is of Britannia. The reverse legend of NEW PENCE became FIFTY PENCE from 1982.

The description of "Unc" has been used against some 50 pence pieces dated 2009 and 2011 (for Olympic and Paralympic sports) to distinguish them from coins minted to circulation standard and BU standard, being a standard between the latter two. The uncirculated standard coins have a more even rim than the circulation standard examples, particularly observable on the obverse.

All 29 sports coins dated 2011 have now been issued to circulation, a million or more of each (below). There is no limit to each of the uncirculated versions, while there is a 30,000 limit to each silver BU version.

DATE	Mintage	UNC
1969..	188,400,000	£6
1970..	19,461,500	£5
1971 Proof...	—	£8
1972 Proof...	—	£7
1973 Accession to EEC	89,775,000	£3
1973 — Proof	—	£5
1973 — Silver Proof Piedfort.....................................	—	£3000
1974 Proof...	—	£7
1975 Proof	—	£8
1976..	43,746,500	£5
1976 Proof	—	£7
1977..	49,536,000	£5
1977 Proof	—	£6
1978..	72,005,000	£5
1978 Proof	—	£6
1979..	58,680,000	£5

DATE	Mintage	UNC
1979 Proof	—	£6
1980	89,086,000	£5
1980 Proof	—	£6
1981	74,002,000	£6
1981 Proof	—	£8
1982	51,312,000	£5
1982 Unc	—	£6
1982 Proof	—	£8
1983	62,824,000	£5
1983 Unc	—	£6
1983 Proof	—	£8
1984 BU	—	£6
1984 Proof	—	£8
1985 ***New portrait*** estimated approx	3,400,000	£3
1985 BU	—	£5
1985 Proof	—	£6
1986 BU	—	£5
1986 Proof	—	£12
1987 BU	—	£4
1987 Proof	—	£12
1988 BU	—	£4
1988 Proof	—	£12
1989 BU	—	£4
1989 Proof	—	£12
1990 BU	—	£4
1990 Proof	—	£12
1991 BU	—	£5
1991 Proof	—	£12
1992 BU	—	£7
1992 Proof	—	£12
1992 Presidency of EC Council and EC accession 20th anniversary (includes 1993 date)	109,000	£12
1992 — BU	—	£12
1992 — Proof	—	£14
1992 — Silver Proof	26,890	£35
1992 — — — Piedfort	10,993	£55
1992 — Gold Proof	—	£500
1993 BU	—	£5
1993 Proof	—	£12
1994 50th Anniversary of the Normandy Landings	6,705,520	£3
1994 — BU (also in presentation folder)	—	£5
1994 — Proof	—	£12
1994 — Silver Proof	40,000	£35
1994 — — — Piedfort	10,000	£60
1994 — Gold Proof	—	£500
1995 BU	—	£8
1995 Proof	—	£12
1996 BU	—	£8
1996 Proof	—	£12
1996 Silver Proof	—	£25
1997 BU	—	£8
1997 Proof	—	£10
1997 Silver Proof	—	£25
1997 ***New reduced size***	456,364,100	£4
1997 BU	—	£5
1997 Proof	—	£6
1997 Silver Proof	—	£25
1997 — — Piedfort	—	£35
1998 ***New portrait***	64,306,500	£3
1998 BU	—	£5
1998 Proof	—	£8
1998 Presidency and 25th anniversary of EU entry	5,043,000	£4
1998 — BU	—	£5
1998 — Proof	—	£8
1998 — Silver Proof	8,859	£30
1998 — — — Piedfort	8,440	£45
1998 — Gold Proof	—	£450
1998 50th Anniversary of the National Health Service	5,001,000	£3
1998 — BU	—	£5

New reverses.

Accession to the EEC 1973.

Presidency of the EC Council 1992.

1994

1998

DATE	Mintage	UNC
1998 — Silver Proof	9,032	£30
1998 — — — Piedfort	5,117	£45
1998 — Gold Proof	—	£450
1999	24,905,000	£2
1999 BU	—	£5
1999 Proof	—	£10
2000	27,915,500	£2
2000 BU	—	£5
2000 Proof	—	£7
2000 150th Anniversary of Public Libraries	11,263,000	£5
2000 — BU	—	£6
2000 — Proof	—	£9
2000 — Silver Proof	7,634	£30
2000 — — — Piedfort	5,721	£45
2000 — Gold proof	—	£400
2001	84,998,500	£2
2001 BU	—	£5
2001 Proof	—	£7
2002	23,907,500	£2
2002 BU	—	£5
2002 Proof	—	£7
2002 Gold Proof	—	£375
2003	23,583,000	£2
2003 BU	—	£5
2003 Proof	—	£6
2003 Suffragette	3,124,030	£2
2003 — BU	—	£6
2003 — Proof	—	£7
2003 — Silver Proof	6,267	£30
2003 — — — Piedfort	6,795	£45
2003 — Gold Proof	—	£350
2004	35,315,500	£1
2004 BU	—	£5
2004 Proof	—	£8
2004 Roger Bannister	9,032,500	£5
2004 — BU	—	£6
2004 — Proof	—	£8
2004 — Silver Proof	4,924	£30
2004 — — — Piedfort	4,054	£45
2004 — Gold Proof	—	£350
2005	25,363,500	£3
2005 BU	—	£6
2005 Proof	—	£8
2005 Samuel Johnson	17,649,000	£3
2005 — BU	—	£5
2005 — Proof	—	£8
2005 — Silver Proof	4,029	£30
2005 — — — Piedfort	3,808	£45
2005 — Gold Proof	—	£350
2006	24,567,000	£2
2006 Proof	—	£8
2006 Silver Proof	—	£30
2006 Victoria Cross, The Award	12,087,000	£3
2006 — BU	—	£5
2006 — Proof	—	£8
2006 — Silver Proof	6,310	£30
2006 — — — Piedfort	3,532	£50
2006 — Gold Proof	—	£350
2006 Victoria Cross, Heroic Acts	10,000,500	£2
2006 — BU	—	£5
2006 — Proof	—	£8
2006 — Silver Proof	6,872	£30
2006 — — — Piedfort	3,415	£50
2006 — Gold Proof	—	£350
2007	5,300,000	£2
2007 BU	—	£6
2007 Proof	—	£8
2007 Centenary of Scout Movement	7,710,750	£5
2007 — BU	—	£8

DATE	Mintage	UNC
2007 — Proof	—	£12
2007 — Silver Proof	10,895	£30
2007 — — Piedfort	1,555	£65
2007 — Gold Proof	—	£400
2008	700,000	£2
2008 — BU	—	£5
2008 — Proof	—	£6
2008 — Silver Proof	—	£25
2008 — Gold Proof	—	£400
2008 — Platinum Proof	—	£1550
2008 *New Shield Rev.* Obv. rotated by approx. 26 degrees	12,320,000	£5
2008 BU	—	£6
2008 Proof	—	£8
2008 Silver Proof	—	£25
2008 Silver Proof Piedfort	—	£45
2008 Gold Proof	—	£400
2008 Platinum Proof	—	£1550
2009 BU	—	£4
2009 Proof	—	£6
2009 Silver Proof	—	£20
2009 250th Anniversary of Kew Gardens	210,000	£30
2009 — BU	—	£75
2009 — Proof	—	£85
2009 — Silver Proof	7,575	£125
2009 — — Piedfort	2,967	£150
2009 — Gold Proof	—	£500
2009 Olympic and Paralympic Sports (Track & Field Athletics) Unc (Blue Peter Pack)	—	£10
2009 16 different reverses from the past marking the 40th Anniversary of the 50p coin. Proof	1,039	£300
2009 — Silver Proof	1,163	£650
2009 — Gold Proof	125	£8000
2009 — — Piedfort	40	£20,950
2010 BU	—	£4
2010 Proof	—	£25
2010 Silver Proof	—	£35
2010 100 years of Girl Guiding UK	7,410,090	£2
2010 — BU	—	£7
2010 — Proof	—	£20
2010 — Silver Proof	5,271	£35
2010 — — Piedfort	2,879	£55
2010 — Gold Proof	—	£575
2011 BU	—	£2
2011 Proof	—	£8
2011 Silver Proof	—	£45
2011 50th Anniversary of the WWF	3,400,000	£2
2011 — BU	—	£5
2011 — Proof	—	£25
2011 — Silver Proof	24,870	£45
2011 — — Piedfort	2,244	£65
2011 — Gold Proof	—	£675

DATE	Mintage	UNC
2011 Olympic & Paralympic Sports Issues:		
Aquatics Unc, head clear of lines	2,179,000	£2
— Head with lines BU (as illustrated top right) ..	—	£750
— Head clear of lines. BU...................................	—	£4
— Silver BU..	30,000	£25
Archery Unc	3,345,000	£2
— BU...	—	£3
— Silver BU..	30,000	£25
Athletics Unc..	2,224,000	£2
— BU...	—	£3
— Silver BU..	30,000	£25
Badminton Unc	2,133,000	£2
— BU...	—	£3
— Silver BU..	30,000	£25
Basketball Unc	1,748,000	£2
— BU...	—	£3
— Silver BU..	30,000	£25
Boccia Unc...	2,166,000	£2
— BU...	—	£3
— Silver BU..	30,000	£25
Boxing Unc...	2,148,000	£2
— BU...	—	£3
— Silver BU..	30,000	£25
Canoeing Unc	2,166,000	£2
— BU...	—	£3
— Silver BU..	30,000	£25
Cycling Unc	2,090,000	£2
— BU...	—	£3
— Silver BU..	30,000	£25
Equestrian Unc...	2,142,000	£2
— BU...	—	£3
— Silver BU..	30,000	£25
Fencing Unc	2,115,000	£2
— BU...	—	£3
— Silver BU..	30,000	£25
Football Unc	1,125,000	£2
— BU...	—	£3
— Silver Bu..	30,000	£25
Goalball Und	1,615,000	£2
— BU...	—	£3
— Silver BU..	30,000	£25
Gymnastics Unc..	1,720,000	£1
— BU...	—	£3
— Silver BU..	30,000	£25
Handball Unc	1,676,000	£2
— BU...	—	£3
— Silver BU..	30,000	£25
Hockey Unc...	1,773,000	£2
— BU...	—	£3
— Silver BU..	30,000	£25
Judo Unc..	1,161,000	£2
— BU...	—	£3
— Silver BU..	30,000	£25
Modern Pentathlon Unc	1,689,000	£2
— BU...	—	£3
— Silver BU..	30,000	£25
Rowing Unc...	1,717,000	£2
— BU...	—	£3
— Silver BU..	30,000	£25
Sailing Unc	1,749,000	£2
— BU...	—	£3
— Silver BU..	30,000	£25
Shooting Unc	1,656,000	£2
— BU...	—	£3
— Silver BU..	30,000	£25
Table Tennis Unc	1,737,000	£2
— BU...	—	£3
— Silver BU..	30,000	£25

DATE	Mintage	UNC
2011 Olympic & Paralympic issues continued		
Taekwondo Unc	1,664,000	£2
— BU..	—	£3
— Silver BU...	30,000	£25
Tennis Unc...	1,454,000	£2
— BU..	—	£3
— Silver BU...	30,000	£25
Triathlon Unc	1,163,000	£2
— BU..	—	£3
— Silver BU...	30,000	£25
Volleyball Unc	2,133,000	£2
— BU..	—	£3
— Silver BU...	30,000	£25
Weightlifting Unc	1,879,000	£2
— BU..	—	£3
— Silver BU...	30,000	£25
Wheelchair Rugby Unc	1,765,000	£2
— BU..	—	£3
— Silver BU...	30,000	£25
Wrestling Unc...	1,129,000	£2
— BU..	—	£3
— Silver BU...	30,000	£25

Note—Each of the artists of the 29 Olympic sports above was presented with a gold proof coin with their own design. The Track & Field Athletics design coin was dated 2009, the Cycling was dated 2010, and the remaining 2011. No other examples of these coins were issued.

2012	32,300,000	£2
2012 BU	—	£5
2012 Proof...	—	£10
2012 Silver Proof with selective gold plating	—	£20
2012 Gold Proof	—	£500
2012 Gold Proof Piedfort. The 11 Olympic sports in which the United Kingdom Team GB achieved a Gold Medal was celebrated with an issue of 29 Piedfort coins for each sport, some in sets, some as individual coins (see under Proof and Specimen sets)	—	—
2013	—	£2
2013 BU	—	£5
2013 Proof...	—	£10
2013 Silver Proof	—	£55
2013 Gold Proof	—	£450
2013 100th anniversary of birth of Christopher Ironside	—	£2
2013 — BU	—	£5
2013 — Proof	—	£12
2013 — Silver Proof	—	£45
2013 — — Piedfort......................................	—	£90
2013 — Gold Proof......................................	—	£450
2013 Centenary of the Birth of Benjamin Britten	—	£2
2013 — BU	—	£5
2013 — Silver Proof	—	£55
2013 — — Piedfort	—	£90
2013 — Gold Proof......................................	—	£450
2014	—	£2
2014 BU	—	£5
2014 Proof...	—	£12
2014 Silver Proof	—	£55
2014 XX Commonwealth Games	—	£2
2014 — BU	—	£5
2014 — Proof	—	£12
2014 — Silver Proof	—	£45
2014 — — Piedfort......................................	—	£100
2014 — Gold Proof......................................	—	£450
2015	—	£2
2015 BU	—	£5
2015 Proof...	—	£10
2015 Silver Proof	—	£30

DATE	Mintage	UNC
2015 Gold Proof	—	£350
2015 Platinum Proof	—	—
2015 Battle of Britain 75th Anniversary	—	£2
2015 — BU	—	£5
2015 — Proof	—	£12
2015 — Silver Proof	—	£30
2015 — — Piedfort	—	£80
2015 — Gold Proof	—	£350
2015 New Portrait	—	£2
2015 — BU	—	£5
2015 — Proof	—	£12
2015 — Silver Proof	—	£30
2015 — Gold Proof	—	£350
2015 — Platinum Proof	—	—
2015 — Battle of Britain 75th Anniversary	—	£3
2015 — — Silver Proof	—	£30
2015 — — — Piedfort	—	£75
2015 — — Gold Proof	—	£350

TWENTY-FIVE PENCE (CROWN)

This series is a continuation of the pre-decimal series, there having been four crowns to the pound. The coins below have a legal tender face value of 25p to this day, and are minted in cupro-nickel except where stated otherwise.

DATE	Mintage	UNC
1972 Royal Silver Wedding	7,452,100	£2
1972 — Proof	150,000	£8
1972 — Silver Proof	100,000	£30
1977 Silver Jubilee	37,061,160	£2
1977 — in Presentation folder	Incl. above	£3
1977 — Proof	193,000	£8
1977 — Silver Proof	377,000	£25
1980 Queen Mother 80th Birthday	9,306,000	£2
1980 — in Presentation folder	Incl. above	£3
1980 — Silver Proof	83,670	£30
1981 Royal Wedding	26,773,600	£2
1981 — in Presentation folder	Incl. above	£3
1981 — Silver Proof	218,140	£30

TWENTY PENCE

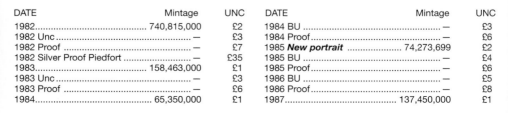

The series commenced in 1982, some 11 years after the introduction of decimal coinage. Its presence from introduction date meant that there was no requirement for ten pence circulation—standard coins until the latter's size was reduced in 1992. Its alloy is uniquely 84% copper and 16% nickel, unlike the 75/25 of the fifty pence.

DATE	Mintage	UNC	DATE	Mintage	UNC
1982	740,815,000	£2	1984 BU	—	£3
1982 Unc	—	£3	1984 Proof	—	£6
1982 Proof	—	£7	1985 *New portrait*	74,273,699	£2
1982 Silver Proof Piedfort	—	£35	1985 BU	—	£4
1983	158,463,000	£1	1985 Proof	—	£6
1983 Unc	—	£3	1986 BU	—	£5
1983 Proof	—	£6	1986 Proof	—	£8
1984	65,350,000	£1	1987	137,450,000	£1

DATE	Mintage	UNC
1987 BU	—	£3
1987 Proof	—	£5
1988	38,038,344	£1
1988 BU	—	£3
1988 Proof	—	£5
1989	132,013,890	£1
1989 BU	—	£3
1989 Proof	—	£5
1990	88,097,500	£1
1990 BU	—	£3
1990 Proof	—	£6
1991	35,901,250	£1
1991 BU	—	£3
1991 Proof	—	£6
1992	Est. approx. 1,500,000	£4
1992 BU	—	£5
1992 **Enhanced effigy** .... Est. approx. 29,705,000		£4
1992 — BU	—	£5
1992 — Proof	—	£8
1993	123,123,750	£1
1993 BU	—	£3
1993 Proof	—	£5
1994	67,131,250	£1
1994 BU	—	£3
1994 Proof	—	£5
1995	102,005,000	£1
1995 BU	—	£3
1995 Proof	—	£5
1996	83,163,750	£2
1996 BU	—	£3
1996 Proof	—	£5
1996 Silver Proof	—	£25
1997	89,518,750	£2
1997 BU	—	£3
1997 Proof	—	£5
1998 **New portrait**	76,965,000	£2
1998 BU	—	£4
1998 Proof	—	£5
1999	73,478,750	£2
1999 BU	—	£3
1999 Proof	—	£5
2000	136,428,750	£2
2000 BU	—	£3
2000 Proof	—	£5
2000 Silver Proof	—	£25
2001	148,122,500	£2
2001 BU	—	£3
2001 Proof	—	£5
2002	93,360,000	£2
2002 BU	—	£3
2002 Proof	—	£5
2002 Gold Proof	—	£225
2003	153,383,750	£2
2003 BU	—	£4
2003 Proof	—	£6
2004	120,212,500	£2
2004 BU	—	£4
2004 Proof	—	£6
2005	124,488,750	£2
2005 BU	—	£4
2005 Proof	—	£6

DATE	Mintage	UNC
2006	114,800,000	£2
2006 BU	—	£6
2006 Proof	—	£7
2006 Silver Proof	—	£25
2007	117,075,000	£2
2007 BU	—	£4
2007 Proof	—	£6
2008	11,900,000	£2
2008 BU	—	£4
2008 Proof	—	£7
2008 Silver Proof	—	£25
2008 Gold Proof	—	£250
2008 Platinum Proof	—	£750
2008 **New Rev.,** date on Obv.	81,920,000	£2
2008 — paired with old Obv. (thus no date).. Est. approx. 120,000 (?) .		£50
2008 BU	—	£3
2008 Proof	—	£6
2008 Silver Proof	—	£25
2008 — — Piedfort	—	£30
2008 Gold Proof	—	£250
2008 Platinum Proof	—	£750
2009	94,500,300	£2
2009 BU	—	£5
2009 Proof	—	£7
2009 Silver Proof	—	£25
2010	91,700,500	£2
2010 BU	—	£5
2010 Proof	—	£7
2010 Silver Proof	—	£25
2011	39,550,000	£2
2011 BU	—	£5
2011 Proof	—	£8
2011 Silver Proof	—	£25
2012	—	£2
2012 BU	—	£5
2012 Proof	—	£8
2012 Silver Proof (issued in set with Victorian 4 Shilling piece)	—	£25
2012 — — with selective gold plating	—	£35
2012 Gold Proof	—	£300
2013	—	£2
2013 BU	—	£5
2013 Proof	—	£20
2013 Silver Proof	—	£20
2013 Gold Proof	—	£300
2014	—	£2
2014 BU	—	£5
2014 Proof	—	£10
2014 Silver Proof	—	£25
2015	—	—
2015 BU	—	—
2015 Proof	—	—
2015 Silver Proof	—	—
2015 Gold Proof	—	—
2015 Platinum Proof	—	—
2015 New Portrait	—	—
2015 — BU	—	—
2015 — Proof	—	—
2015 — Silver Proof	—	—
2015 — Gold Proof	—	—
2015 — Platinum Proof	—	—

TEN PENCE

*The series commenced before decimalisation with the
legend NEW PENCE, this changed to TEN PENCE from 1982.
These "florin-sized" coins up to 1992 are no longer legal tender.
Cupro-nickel was replaced by nickel-plated steel from 2011.*

DATE	Mintage	UNC	DATE	Mintage	UNC
1968	336,143,250	£3	1995 BU	—	£5
1969	314,008,000	£4	1995 Proof	—	£7
1970	133,571,000	£3	1996	118,738,000	£2
1971	63,205,000	£3	1996 BU	—	£4
1971 Proof	—	£4	1996 Proof	—	£7
1972 Proof only	—	£5	1996 Silver Proof	—	£25
1973	152,174,000	£3	1997	99,196,000	£2
1973 Proof	—	£4	1997 BU	—	£4
1974	92,741,000	£3	1997 Proof	—	£4
1974 Proof	—	£4	1998 *New portrait* BU	—	£8
1975	181,559,000	£3	1998 Proof	—	£10
1975 Proof	—	£4	1999 BU	—	£4
1976	228,220,000	£3	1999 Proof	—	£11
1976 Proof	—	£4	2000	134,733,000	£1
1977	59,323,000	£6	2000 BU	—	£4
1977 Proof	—	£8	2000 Proof	—	£7
1978 Proof	—	£6	2000 Silver Proof	—	£15
1979	115,457,000	£2	2001	129,281,000	£1
1979 Proof	—	£4	2001 BU	—	£3
1980	88,650,000	£3	2001 Proof	—	£4
1980 Proof	—	£4	2002	80,934,000	£2
1981	3,487,000	£8	2002 BU	—	£3
1981 Proof	—	£15	2002 Proof	—	£5
1982 BU	—	£4	2002 Gold Proof	—	£250
1982 Proof	—	£6	2003	88,118,000	£2
1983 BU	—	£3	2003 BU	—	£3
1983 Proof	—	£4	2003 Proof	—	£5
1984 BU	—	£4	2004	99,602,000	£1
1984 Proof	—	£6	2004 BU	—	£3
1985 *New portrait* BU	—	£5	2004 Proof	—	£5
1985 Proof	—	£7	2005	69,604,000	£1
1986 BU	—	£4	2005 BU	—	£2
1986 Proof	—	£6	2005 Proof	—	£4
1987 BU	—	£4	2006	118,803,000	£1
1987 Proof	—	£7	2006 BU	—	£3
1988 BU	—	£5	2006 Proof	—	£7
1988 Proof	—	£7	2006 Silver Proof	—	£25
1989 BU	—	£6	2007	72,720,000	£1
1989 Proof	—	£9	2007 BU	—	£4
1990 BU	—	£6	2007 Proof	—	£7
1990 Proof	—	£9	2008	9,720,000	£1
1991 BU	—	£6	2008 BU	—	£4
1991 Proof	—	£9	2008 Proof	—	£5
1992 BU	—	£5	2008 Silver Proof	—	£25
1992 Proof	—	£7	2008 Gold Proof	—	£250
1992 Silver Proof	—	£12	2008 Platinum Proof	—	£450
1992 *Size reduced (24.5mm)*	1,413,455,170	£3	2008 *New Rev.*, no border beads on Obv.	53,900,000	£1
1992 BU	—	£4	2008 BU	—	£4
1992 Proof	—	£5	2008 Proof	—	£5
1992 Silver Proof	—	£12	2008 Silver Proof	—	£25
1992 — — Piedfort	—	£35	2008 — — Piedfort	—	£45
1993 BU	—	£2	2008 Gold Proof	—	£250
1993 Proof	—	£7	2008 Platinum Proof	—	£450
1994 BU	—	£2	2009	60,000,000	£1
1994 Proof	—	£7	2009 BU	—	£3
1995	43,259,000	£1			

DATE	Mintage	UNC	DATE	Mintage	UNC
2009 Proof	—	£5	2013 Silver Proof	—	£25
2009 Silver Proof	—	£25	2013 Gold Proof	—	£250
2010	25,320,500	£1	2014	—	£1
2010 BU	—	£5	2014 BU	—	£5
2010 Proof	—	£7	2014 Proof	—	£12
2010 Silver Proof	—	£25	2014 Silver Proof	—	£25
2011 Nickel-plated steel	40,601,850	£1	2015	—	—
2011 — BU	—	£5	2015 BU	—	—
2011 — Proof	—	£10	2015 Proof	—	—
2011 Silver Proof	—	£25	2015 Silver Proof	—	—
2012	—	£1	2015 Gold Proof	—	—
2012 BU	—	£5	2015 Platinum Proof	—	—
2012 Proof	—	£10	2015 New Portrait	—	—
2012 Silver proof with selective gold plating	—	£30	2015 — BU	—	—
2012 Gold Proof	—	£250	2015 — Proof	—	—
2013	—	£1	2015 — Silver Proof	—	—
2013 BU	—	£5	2015 — Gold Proof	—	—
2013 Proof	—	£10	2015 — Platinum Proof	—	—

FIVE PENCE

This series commenced simultaneously with the Ten Pence (qv). They were the same size and weight as their predecessor, the shilling, and such coins up to 1990 are no longer legal tender. As with the Ten Pence, cupro-nickel was replaced by nickel-plated steel from 2011.

DATE	Mintage	UNC	DATE	Mintage	UNC
1968	98,868,250	£3	1989	101,406,000	£1
1969	120,270,000	£3	1989 BU	—	£4
1970	225,948,525	£3	1989 Proof	—	£5
1971	81,783,475	£3	1990 BU	—	£2
1971 Proof	—	£3	1990 Proof	—	£5
1972 Proof	—	£7	1990 Silver Proof	—	£15
1973 Proof	—	£8	1990 *Size reduced (18mm)*	1,634,976,005	£2
1974 Proof	—	£8	1990 BU	—	£3
1975	141,539,000	£3	1990 Proof	—	£4
1975 Proof	—	£6	1990 Silver Proof	—	£20
1976 Proof	—	£7	1990 — — Piedfort	—	£25
1977	24,308,000	£8	1991	724,979000	£1
1977 Proof	—	£9	1991 BU	—	£3
1978	61,094,000	£4	1991 Proof	—	£5
1978 Proof	—	£4	1992	453,173,500	£1
1979	155,456,000	£4	1992 BU	—	£3
1979 Proof	—	£4	1992 Proof	—	£7
1980	220,566,000	£3	1993 BU	—	£3
1980 Proof	—	£4	1993 Proof	—	£5
1981 Proof	—	£7	1994	93,602,000	£1
1982 BU	—	£7	1994 BU	—	£5
1982 Proof	—	£9	1994 Proof	—	£7
1983 BU	—	£5	1995	183,384,000	£1
1983 Proof	—	£6	1995 BU	—	£5
1984 BU	—	£4	1995 Proof	—	£7
1984 Proof	—	£6	1996	302,902,000	£1
1985 *New Portrait*. BU	—	£2	1996 BU	—	£4
1985 Proof	—	£7	1996 Proof	—	£7
1986 BU	—	£2	1996 Silver proof	—	£25
1986 Proof	—	£7	1997	236,596,000	£1
1987	48,220,000	£1	1997 BU	—	£4
1987 BU	—	£3	1997 Proof	—	£7
1987 Proof	—	£5	1998 *New portrait*	217,376,000	£1
1988	120,744,610	£1	1998 BU	—	£4
1988 BU	—	£3	1998 Proof	—	£7
1988 Proof	—	£5	1999	195,490,000	£1

DATE	Mintage	UNC
1999 BU	—	£4
1999 Proof	—	£7
2000	388,512,000	£1
2000 BU	—	£4
2000 Proof	—	£7
2000 Silver Proof	—	£25
2001	337,930,000	£1
2001 BU	—	£3
2001 Proof	—	£5
2002	219,258,000	£1
2002 BU	—	£3
2002 Proof	—	£5
2002 Gold Proof	—	£150
2003	333,230,000	£1
2003 BU	—	£3
2003 Proof	—	£5
2004	271,810,000	£1
2004 BU	—	£3
2004 Proof	—	£5
2005	236,212,000	£1
2005 BU	—	£3
2005 Proof	—	£5
2006	317,697,000	£1
2006 BU	—	£3
2006 Proof	—	£7
2006 Silver Proof	—	£25
2007	246,720,000	£1
2007 BU	—	£5
2007 Proof	—	£7
2008	86,400,000	£1
2008 BU	—	£3
2008 Proof	—	£5
2008 Silver Proof	—	£20
2008 Gold Proof	—	£150
2008 Platinum Proof	—	£250
2008 **New Rev.,** no border beads on Obv	109,460,000	£1
2008 BU	—	£4
2008 Proof	—	£5
2008 Silver Proof	—	£15
2008 — — Piedfort	—	£35

DATE	Mintage	UNC
2008 Gold Proof	—	£150
2008 Platinum Proof	—	£250
2009	125,520,300	£1
2009 BU	—	£6
2009 Proof	—	£7
2009 Silver Proof	—	£15
2010	180,250,500	£1
2010 BU	—	£4
2010 Proof	—	£5
2010 Silver Proof	—	£15
2011 Nickel-plated steel	50,400,000	£1
2011 — BU	—	£4
2011 — Proof	—	£6
2011 Silver Proof	—	£15
2012	—	£1
2012 BU	—	£5
2012 Proof	—	£8
2012 Silver Proof with selective gold plating	—	£15
2012 Gold Proof	—	£150
2013	—	£1
2013 BU	—	£5
2013 Proof	—	£8
2013 Silver Proof	—	£20
2013 Gold Proof	—	£150
2014	—	£1
2014 BU	—	£5
2014 Proof	—	£8
2014 Silver Proof	—	£20
2015	—	—
2015 BU	—	—
2015 Proof	—	—
2015 Silver Proof	—	—
2015 Gold Proof	—	—
2015 Platinum Proof	—	—
2015 New Portrait	—	—
2015 — BU	—	—
2015 — Proof	—	—
2015 — Silver Proof	—	—
2015 — Gold Proof	—	—
2015 — Platinum Proof	—	—

TWO PENCE

Dated from 1971, and legal tender from Decimal Day that year, early examples are found in the blue Specimen decimal set wallets of 1968. They were minted in bronze up to 1991, and mainly in copper-plated steel from 1992. However details of where this rule does not totally apply (1992, 1996, 1998–2000 and 2002, 2006, 2008 and 2009) are given below. As with other denominations, "NEW" was replaced by the quantity of pence in word from 1982.

DATE	Mintage	UNC
1971	1,454,856,250	£2
1971 Proof	—	£3
1972 Proof	—	£5
1973 Proof	—	£6
1974 Proof	—	£6
1975	Est. approx. 273,145,000	£2
1975 Proof	—	£2
1976	Est. approx. 53,779,000	£2
1976 Proof	—	£2
1977	109,281,000	£2
1977 Proof	—	£2

DATE	Mintage	UNC
1978	189,658,000	£3
1978 Proof	—	£2
1979	260,200,000	£2
1979 Proof	408,527,000	£2
1980	—	£1
1980 Proof	—	£2
1981	353,191,000	£4
1981 Proof	—	£4
1982 Legend changed to TWO PENCE	—	£4
1982 Proof	—	£5
1983	—	£2

DATE	Mintage	UNC
1983 Error NEW instead of TWO	—	£850
1983 Proof	—	£4
1984	—	£2
1984 Proof	—	£4
1985 *New portrait*	107,113,000	£2
1985 BU	—	£2
1985 Proof	—	£4
1986	168,967,500	£1
1986 BU	—	£2
1986 Proof	—	£4
1987	218,100,750	£1
1987 BU	—	£2
1987 Proof	—	£4
1988	419,889,000	£1
1988 BU	—	£2
1988 Proof	—	£4
1989	359,226,000	£1
1989 BU	—	£2
1989 Proof	—	£4
1990	204,499,700	£1
1990 BU	—	£2
1990 Proof	—	£3
1991	86,625,250	£1
1991 BU	—	£2
1991 Proof	—	£5
1992 Copper plated steel	102,247,000	£1
1992 Bronze BU	—	£2
1992 — Proof	—	£5
1993	235,674,000	£1
1993 BU	—	£2
1993 Proof	—	£3
1994	531,628,000	£1
1994 BU	—	£2
1994 Proof	—	£5
1995	124,482,000	£1
1995 BU	—	£2
1995 Proof	—	£5
1996	296,278,000	£1
1996 BU	—	£2
1996 Proof	—	£5
1996 Silver Proof	—	£25
1997	496,116,000	£1
1997 BU	—	£2
1997 Proof	—	£5
1998 *New portrait*	Est. approx. 120,243,000	£1
1998 BU	—	£2
1998 Proof	—	£4
1998 Bronze	Est. approx. 93,587,000	£1
1999	353,816,000	£1
1999 Bronze BU	—	£2
1999 — Proof	—	£4
2000	536,659,000	£1
2000 BU	—	£3
2000 Proof	—	£5
2000 Silver Proof	—	£22
2001	551,880,000	£1
2001 BU	—	£2
2001 Proof	—	£4
2002	168,556,000	£1
2002 BU	—	£3
2002 Proof	—	£4
2002 Gold Proof	—	£275
2003	260,225,000	£1
2003 BU	—	£2
2003 Proof	—	£4

DATE	Mintage	UNC
2004	356,396,000	£1
2004 BU	—	£2
2004 Proof	—	£4
2005	280,396,000	£1
2005 BU	—	£2
2005 Proof	—	£3
2006	170,637,000	£1
2006 BU	—	£3
2006 Proof	—	£4
2006 Silver Proof	—	£15
2007	254,500,000	£2
2007 BU	—	£3
2007 Proof	—	£5
2008	10,600,000	£2
2008 BU	—	£3
2008 Proof	—	£5
2008 Silver Proof	—	£25
2008 Gold Proof	—	£275
2008 Platinum Proof	—	£450
2008 New Rev., no border beads on Obv.	129,530,000	£2
2008 — BU	—	£3
2008 — Proof	—	£5
2008 — Silver Proof	—	£20
2008 — Silver Proof Piedfort	—	£45
2008 — Gold Proof	—	£300
2008 — Platinum Proof	—	£500
2009	65,200,000	£2
2009 BU	—	£3
2009 Proof	—	£5
2009 Silver Proof	—	£25
2010	38,000,000	£2
2010 BU	—	£3
2010 Proof	—	£6
2010 Silver Proof	—	£25
2011	93,900,000	£2
2011 BU	—	£3
2011 Proof	—	£6
2011 Silver Proof	—	£25
2012	—	£2
2012 BU	—	£3
2012 Proof	—	£8
2012 Silver Proof with selective gold plating	—	£45
2012 Gold Proof	—	£250
2013	—	£2
2013 BU	—	£3
2013 Proof	—	£8
2013 Silver Proof	—	£25
2013 Gold Proof	—	£250
2014	—	£2
2014 BU	—	£3
2014 Proof	—	£8
2014 Silver Proof	—	£45
2015	—	—
2015 BU	—	—
2015 Proof	—	—
2015 Silver Proof	—	—
2015 Gold Proof	—	—
2015 Platinum Proof	—	—
2015 New Portrait	—	—
2015 — BU	—	—
2015 — Proof	—	—
2015 — Silver Proof	—	—
2015 — Gold Proof	—	—
2015 — Platinum Proof	—	—

ONE PENNY

The history of this coin is very similar to that of the Two Pence coin (qv) except that all 1998 examples were of copper-plated steel.

DATE	Mintage	UNC
1971	1,521,666,250	£1
1971 Proof	—	£2
1972 Proof	—	£5
1973	280,196,000	£2
1973 Proof	—	£5
1974	330,892,000	£2
1974 Proof	—	£3
1975	221,604,000	£2
1975 Proof	—	£4
1976	300,160,000	£2
1976 Proof	—	£3
1977	285,430,000	£2
1977 Proof	—	£3
1978	292,770,000	£3
1978 Proof	—	£3
1979	459,000,000	£3
1979 Proof	—	£3
1980	416,304,000	£2
1980 Proof	—	£3
1981	301,800,000	£2
1981 Proof	—	£3
1982 Legend changed to ONE PENNY	100,292,000	£1
1982 Unc	—	£2
1982 Proof	—	£3
1983	243,002,000	£1
1983 Unc	—	£2
1983 Proof	—	£4
1984	154,759,625	£1
1984 BU	—	£2
1984 Proof	—	£3
1985 New portrait	200,605,245	£1
1985 BU	—	£2
1985 Proof	—	£3
1986	369,989,130	£1
1986 BU	—	£2
1986 Proof	—	£3
1987	4999,946,000	£1
1987 BU	—	£2
1987 Proof	—	£3
1988	793,492,000	£1
1988 BU	—	£2
1988 Proof	—	£3
1989	658,142,000	£1
1989 BU	—	£2
1989 Proof	—	£3
1990	529,047,500	£2
1990 BU	—	£3
1990 Proof	—	£4
1991	206,457,000	£1
1991 BU	—	£2
1991 Proof	—	£4
1992 Copper-plated steel	253,867,000	£3
1992 Bronze BU	—	£6

DATE	Mintage	UNC
1992 — Proof	—	£4
1993	602,590,000	£1
1993 BU	—	£2
1993 Proof	—	£5
1994	843,834,000	£1
1994 BU	—	£2
1994 Proof	—	£5
1995	303,314,000	£1
1995 BU	—	£3
1995 Proof	—	£5
1996	723,840,060	£1
1996 BU	—	£2
1996 Proof	—	£5
1996 Silver Proof	—	£28
1997	396,874,000	£1
1997 BU	—	£2
1997 Proof	—	£4
1998 New portrait	739,770,000	£1
1998 — BU	—	£3
1998 Proof	—	£4
1999	891,392,000	£2
1999 Bronze BU	—	£4
1999 Bronze Proof	—	£8
2000	1,060,420,000	£1
2000 BU	—	£2
2000 Proof	—	£4
2000 Silver Proof	—	£25
2001	928,698,000	£1
2001 BU	—	£2
2001 Proof	—	£4
2002	601,446,000	£1
2002 BU	—	£2
2002 Proof	—	£4
2002 Gold Proof	—	£175
2003	539,436,000	£1
2003 BU	—	£2
2003 Proof	—	£3
2004	739,764,000	£1
2004 BU	—	£2
2004 Proof	—	£4
2005	536,318,000	£1
2005 BU	—	£2
2005 Proof	—	£3
2006	524,605,000	£1
2006 BU	—	£2
2006 Proof	—	£4
2006 Silver Proof	—	£15
2007	548,002,000	£1
2007 BU	—	£4
2007 Proof	—	£7
2008	180,600,000	£1
2008 BU	—	£3
2008 Proof	—	£5
2008 Silver Proof	—	£15

DATE	Mintage	UNC
2008 Gold Proof	—	£150
2008 Platinum Proof	—	£200
2008 New Rev, no border beads on Obv	386,830,000	£1
2008 — BU	—	£2
2008 — Proof	—	£3
2008 — Silver Proof	—	£15
2008 — Silver Proof Piedfort	—	£25
2008 — Gold Proof	—	£150
2008 — Platinum Proof	—	£200
2009	469,207,800	£1
2009 BU	—	£3
2009 Proof	—	£4
2009 Silver BU, in "Lucky Baby Gift Pack"	—	£15
2009 — Proof	—	£15
2010	402,602,000	£1
2010 BU	—	£3
2010 Proof	—	£4
2010 Silver BU, in "Lucky Baby Gift Card"	—	£15
2010 — Proof	—	£15
2011	210,404,000	£1
2011 BU	—	£2
2011 Proof	—	£3
2011 Silver BU in "Lucky Baby Pack"	—	£18
2011 – Proof	—	£15
2012	—	£1
2012 BU	—	£2
2012 Proof	—	£4

DATE	Mintage	UNC
2012 Silver BU (three different packagings)	—	£15
2012 Silver Proof with selective gold plating	—	£18
2012 Gold Proof	—	£175
2013	—	£1
2013 BU	—	£2
2013 Proof	—	£5
2013 Silver BU	—	£25
2013 — Proof	—	£30
2013 Gold Proof	—	£175
2014	—	£1
2014 BU	—	£2
2014 Proof	—	£5
2014 Silver BU	—	£20
2014 Silver Proof	—	£25
2015	—	—
2015 BU	—	—
2015 Proof	—	—
2015 Silver BU	—	—
2015 — Proof	—	—
2015 Gold Proof	—	—
2015 Platinum Proof	—	—
2015 New Portrait	—	—
2015 — BU	—	—
2015 — Proof	—	—
2015 — Silver Proof	—	—
2015 — Gold Proof	—	—
2015 — Platinum Proof	—	—

HALF PENNY

No longer legal tender, its history tracks that of the Two Pence and One Penny.

DATE	Mintage	UNC
1971	1,394,188,250	£2
1971 Proof	—	£3
1972 Proof	—	£15
1973	365,680,000	£2
1973 Proof	—	£3
1974	365,448,000	£2
1974 Proof	—	£3
1975	197,600,000	£2
1975 Proof	—	£3
1976	412,172,000	£2
1976 Proof	—	£3
1977	66,368,000	£1
1977 Proof	—	£3
1978	59,532,000	£1
1978 Proof	—	£4
1979	219,1322,000	£2

DATE	Mintage	UNC
1979 Proof	—	£4
1980	202,788,000	£2
1980 Proof	—	£3
1981	46,748,000	£2
1981 Proof	—	£4
1982 Legend changed to HALF PENNY	190,752,000	50p
1982 Unc	—	£2
1982 Proof	—	£3
1983	7,600,000	50p
1983 Unc	—	£1
1983 Proof	—	£4
1984	40,000	£4
1984 BU	—	£5
1984 Proof	—	£6

PROOF AND SPECIMEN SETS

NOTE: The prices quoted in this guide were set at August *2015* with the price of gold around £726 per ounce and silver £9 per ounce—market fluctuations will have a marked effect on the values of modern precious metal coins. However, the prices quoted here for the *recently issued* sets are the original Royal Mint retail prices.

The following listings are an attempt to include all officially marketed products from the Royal Mint of two coins or more, but excluding those which included non-UK coins. It is appreciated that not all have been advertised as new to the public, but it is assumed that at some time they have been, or will be, available. In a few cases, therefore, the prices may be conjectural but are, nevertheless, attempts at listing realistic values, in some instances based on an original retail price. In the case of Elizabeth II sets, if no metal is stated in the listing, the coins in the sets are of the same metal as the circulation coin equivalent. In addition to the above we have excluded historical gold coin sets, such as sets of sovereigns from different mints, where the dates of the coins vary from one set to another.

DATE   FDC

GEORGE IV
1826 £5–farthing (11 coins) ....From £45,000

WILLIAM IV
1831 Coronation £2–farthing (14 coins) ....From £35,000

VICTORIA
1839 "Una and the Lion" £5–farthing (15 coins)..From £75,000
1853 Sovereign–quarter farthing, including "Gothic"crown (16 coins) £50,000
1887 Golden Jubilee £5–3d (11 coins)...£30,000
1887 Golden Jubilee Crown–3d (7 coins)..£3000
1893 £5–3d (10 coins)..£28,000
1893 Crown–3d (6 coins)...£5000

EDWARD VII
1902 Coronation £5–Maundy penny, matt proofs (13 coins) £6500
1902 Coronation Sovereign–Maundy penny, matt proofs (11 coins) £3500

GEORGE V
1911 Coronation £5–Maundy penny (12 coins)..£8000
1911 Sovereign–Maundy penny (10 coins) £3500
1911 Coronation Halfcrown–Maundy penny (8 coins) £1500
1927 New types Crown–3d (6 coins)..£850

GEORGE VI
1937 Coronation £5–half sovereign (4 coins) £6500
1937 Coronation Crown–farthing including Maundy money (15 coins) £550
1950 Mid-century Halfcrown–farthing (9 coins) £200
1951 Festival of Britain, Crown–farthing (10 coins)..£250

ELIZABETH II
1953 Proof Coronation Crown–farthing (10 coins) £125
1953 Currency (plastic) set halfcrown–farthing (9 coins)..£15
1968 Specimen decimal set 10p, 5p and 1971-dated bronze in blue wallet (5 coins)...............................£3
1970 Proof Last £sd coins (issued from 1972) Halfcrown–halfpenny (8 coins)..£20
1971 Proof (issued 1973) 50p–half penny (6 coins)..£18
1972 Proof (issued 1976) 50p–half penny (7 coins including Silver Wedding crown) £24
1973 Proof (issued 1976) 50p–half penny (6 coins) £16
1974 Proof (issued 1976) 50p–half penny (6 coins) £18
1975 Proof (issued 1976) 50p–half penny (6 coins) £18
1976 Proof 50p–half penny (6 coins)...£18
1977 Proof 50p–half penny (7 coins including Silver Jubilee crown) £22
1978 Proof 50p–half penny (6 coins)..£16

DATE   FDC

1979 Proof 50p–half penny (6 coins)..£18
1980 Proof gold sovereign series (4 coins) £2500
1980 — 50p–half penny (6 coins)..£16
1981 Proof £5, sovereign, Royal Wedding Silver crown, 50p–half penny (9 coins) £800
1981 — 50p–half penny (6 coins)..£18
1982 Proof gold sovereign series (4 coins) £2500
1982 — 50p–half penny (7 coins)..£20
1982 Uncirculated 50p–half penny (7 coins) £15
1983 Proof gold double-sovereign to half sovereign (3 coins) £1000
1983 — £1–half penny (8 coins) (includes H. J. Heinz sets)..£25
1983 Uncirculated £1–half penny (8 coins) (includes Benson & Hedges and Martini sets) £30
1983 — — (8 coins) (only Benson & Hedges and Martini sets) with "2 NEW PENCE" legend £1000
1983 — 50p–half penny (7 coins) (H. J. Heinz sets)..£16
1983 — — (7 coins) (H. J. Heinz set) with "2 NEW PENCE" legend £1000
1984 Proof gold five pounds, sovereign and half-sovereigns (3 coins).......................£1000
1984 — £1 (Scottish rev.)–half penny (8 coins) £20
1984 BU £1 (Scottish rev.)–half penny (8 coins) £16
1985 New portrait proof gold sovereign series (4 coins)...£1250
1985 Proof £1–1p in de luxe case (7 coins) £25
1985 — in standard case £20
1985 BU £1–1p (7 coins) in folder £15
1986 Proof gold Commonwealth Games £2, sovereign and half sovereign (3 coins)........£1000
1986 — Commonwealth Games £2–1p, de luxe case (8 coins) £30
1986 — — in standard case (8 coins) £25
1986 BU £2–1p in folder (8 coins) £20
1987 Proof gold Britannia set (4 coins) £2000
1987 — — — £25 and £10 (2 coins) £450
1987 — — double- to half sovereign (3 coins) £1000
1987 — £1–1p in de luxe case (7 coins)..£35
1987 — £1–1p in standard case (7 coins) £25
1987 BU £1–1p in folder (7 coins) £20
1988 Proof gold Britannia set (4 coins) £2000
1988 — — — £25 and £10 (2 coins) £450
1988 — — double- to half sovereign (3 coins) £1000
1988 — £1–1p in de luxe case (7 coins) £35
1988 — £1–1p in standard case (7 coins) £30
1988 BU £1–1p in folder (7 coins) (includes Bradford & Bingley sets)........................£18
1989 Proof gold Britannia set (4 coins) £2000
1989 — — — £25 and £10 (2 coins) £450
1989 — — 500th anniversary of the sovereign series set (4 coins) £4000
1989 — — — double- to half sovereign (3 coins) £2000
1989 — Silver Bill of Rights £2, Claim of Right £2 (2 coins)......................................£65
1989 — — Piedfort as above (2 coins)...£100
1989 BU £2 in folder (2 coins)...£25
1989 Proof £2 (both)–1p in de luxe case (9 coins) £35
1989 — in standard case (9 coins) £30
1989 BU £1–1p in folder (7 coins) £25
1990 Proof gold Britannia set (4 coins) £2000
1990 — — sovereign series set (4 coins) £2000
1990— — double- to half sovereign (3 coins)...£1000
1990 — silver 5p, 2 sizes (2 coins) £28
1990 — £1–1p in de luxe case (8 coins)...£35
1990 — £1–1p standard case (8 coins) £30
1990 BU £1–1p in folder (8 coins) £20
1991 Proof gold Britannia set (4 coins) £2000
1991 — — sovereign series set (4 coins) £2000
1991 — — double- to half sovereign (3 coins) £1000
1991 — £1–1p in de luxe case (7 coins) £35
1991 — £1–1p in standard case (7 coins) £28
1991 BU £1–1p in folder (7 coins) £18
1992 Proof gold Britannia set (4 coins) £2000
1992 — — sovereign series set (4 coins) £2000
1992 — — double- to half sovereign (3 coins) £1000

DATE	FDC
1992 — £1–1p including two each 50p and 10p in de luxe case (9 coins)	£38
1992 — £1–1p as above in standard case (9 coins)	£32
1992 BU £1–1p as above in folder (9 coins)	£16
1992 — with Enhanced Effigy on obverse of 20p	£25
1992 Proof silver 10p, two sizes (2 coins)	£25
1993 Proof gold Britannia set (4 coins)	£2000
1993 — — sovereign series set (4 coins plus silver Pistrucci medal)	£2000
1993 — — double- to half sovereign (3 coins)	£1000
1993 — Coronation anniversary £5–1p in de luxe case (8 coins)	£38
1993 — — in standard case (8 coins)	£35
1993 BU £1–1p including 1992 EU 50p (8 coins)	£15
1994 Proof gold Britannia set (4 coins)	£2000
1994 — — sovereign series set (4 coins)	£2000
1994 — — £2 to half sovereign (3 coins)	£1000
1994 — Bank of England Tercentenary £2–1p in de luxe case (8 coins)	£38
1994 — — in standard case (8 coins)	£35
1994 BU £1–1p in folder (7 coins)	£18
1994 Proof gold 1992 and 1994 50p (2 coins)	£350
1994 — "Family silver" set £2–50p (3 coins)	£65
1995 Proof gold Britannia set (4 coins)	£2000
1995 — — sovereign series (4 coins)	£2000
1995 — — £2 to half sovereign (3 coins)	£850
1995 — 50th Anniversary of WWII £2–1p in de luxe case (8 coins)	£40
1995 — — as above in standard case (8 coins)	£35
1995 BU as above in folder (8 coins)	£16
1995 Proof "Family Silver" set £2 (two) and £1 (3 coins)	£90
1996 Proof gold Britannia set (4 coins)	£2000
1996 — — sovereign series set (4 coins)	£2000
1996 — — double- to half sovereign (3 coins)	£1000
1996 — Royal 70th Birthday £5–1p in de luxe case (9 coins)	£50
1996 — — as above in standard case (9 coins)	£45
1996 BU Football £2–1p in folder (8 coins)	£20
1996 Proof gold Britannia £10 and half-sovereign (2 coins)	£550
1996 — — sovereign and silver £1 (2 coins)	£250
1996 — "Family silver" set £5–£1 (3 coins)	£85
1996 — silver 25th Anniversary of Decimal currency £1–1p (7 coins)	£150
1996 Circulation and BU 25th Anniversary of Decimalisation 2s 6d–halfpenny (misc.) and £1–1p in folder (14 coins)	£25
1997 Proof gold Britannia set (4 coins)	£2000
1997 — — sovereign series set (4 coins)	£2000
1997 — — — £2 to half sovereign (3 coins)	£1000
1997 — — Silver Britannia set (4 coins)	£150
1997 — Golden Wedding £5–1p in red leather case	£45
1997 — — as above in standard case (10 coins)	£35
1997 BU £2 to 1p in folder (9 coins)	£25
1997 Proof silver 50p set, two sizes (2 coins)	£45
1997/1998 Proof silver £2 set, both dates (2 coins)	£70
1998 Proof gold Britannia set (4 coins)	£2000
1998 — — sovereign series set (4 coins)	£2000
1998 — — — double- to half sovereign (3 coins)	£1000
1998 Proof silver Britannia set (4 coins)	£185
1998 — Prince of Wales £5–1p (10 coins) in red leather case	£45
1998 — — as above in standard case (10 coins)	£38
1998 BU £2–1p in folder (9 coins)	£16
1998 Proof silver European/NHS 50p set (2 coins)	£60
1998 BU Britannia/EU 50p set (2 coins)	£8
1999 Proof gold Britannia set (4 coins)	£2000
1999 — — Sovereign series set (4 coins)	£2000
1999 — — — £2 to half sovereign (3 coins)	£1000
1999 — Princess Diana £5–1p in red leather case (9 coins)	£65
1999 — — as above in standard case (9 coins)	£45
1999 BU £2–1p (8 coins) in folder	£20
1999 Proof "Family Silver" set. Both £5, £2 and £1 (4 coins)	£150

DATE	FDC
1999 Britannia Millennium set. Bullion £2 and BU £5 (2 coins)	£30
1999/2000 Reverse frosted proof set, two x £1 (2 coins)	£75
2000 Proof gold Britannia set (4 coins)	£2000
2000 — — Sovereign series set (4 coins)	£2000
2000 — — — double- to half sovereign (3 coins)	£1000
2000 Millennium £5–1p in de luxe case (10 coins)	£50
2000 — — as above in standard case (10 coins)	£45
2000 — Silver set Millennium £5 to 1p plus Maundy (13 coins)	£225
2000 BU £2–1p set in folder (9 coins)	£20
2000 Millennium "Time Capsule" BU £5 to 1p (9 coins)	£30
2001 Proof gold Britannia set (4 coins)	£2000
2001 — — Sovereign series set (4 coins)	£2000
2001 — — — £2–half sovereign (3 coins)	£1000
2001 — Silver Britannia set (4 coins)	£150
2001 — Victoria £5–1p in Executive case (10 coins)	£100
2001 — — as above in red leather case (10 coins)	£75
2001 — — as above in "Gift" case (10 coins)	£48
2001 — — as above in standard case (10 coins)	£40
2001 BU £2–1p in folder (9 coins)	£18
2002 Proof gold Britannia set (4 coins)	£2000
2002 — — Sovereign series set, all Shield rev. (4 coins)	£2000
2002 — — — double- to half sovereign (3 coins)	£1000
2002 — — Golden Jubilee set £5–1p plus Maundy (13 coins)	£4500
2002 — Golden Jubilee £5–1p in Executive case (9 coins)	£75
2002 — — as above in red leather de luxe case (9 coins)	£50
2002 — — as above in "Gift" case (9 coins)	£42
2002 — — as above in standard case (9 coins)	£40
2002 BU £2–1p (8 coins) in folder	£16
2002 Proof Gold Commonwealth Games £2 set (4 coins)	£2000
2002 — Silver Piedfort Commonwealth Games £2 set (4 coins)	£250
2002 — — Commonwealth Games £2 set (4 coins)	£125
2002 — Commonwealth Games £2 set (4 coins)	£30
2002 BU Commonwealth Games £2 set (4 coins) in folder	£25
2003 Proof gold Britannia set (4 coins)	£2000
2003 — — £50–£10 (3 coins)	£1000
2003 — — — type set, one of each £100 reverse (4 coins)	£2500
2003 — — Sovereign series set (4 coins)	£2000
2003 — — — series £2–half sovereign (3 coins)	£1000
2003 — Silver Britannia set (4 coins)	£45
2003 — — — type set (one of each £2 reverse) (4 coins)	£85
2003 — £5 to 1p, two of each £2 and 50p in Executive case (11 coins)	£80
2003 — — as above in red leather case (11 coins)	£55
2003 — — as above in standard case (11 coins)	£48
2003 BU £2 (two)–1p in folder (10 coins)	£22
2003 Proof silver Piedfort set. DNA £2, £1 and Suffragette 50p (3 coins)	£150
2003 Proof "Family Silver" set £5, Britannia and DNA £2, £1 and Suffragette 50p (5 coins)	£175
2003 Circ & BU "God Save the Queen" Coronation anniversary set 5s/0d to farthing (1953) and £5 to 1p (2003) in folder (19 coins)	£55
2003 Circulation or bullion "Royal Sovereign" collection, example of each Elizabeth II date (21 coins)	£3500
2004 Proof gold Britannia set (4 coins)	£2000
2004 — — — £50 to £10 (3 coins)	£1000
2004 — — Sovereign series set (4 coins)	£2000
2004 — — — Series £2-half sovereign (3 coins)	£1000
2004 (Issue date) Royal Portrait gold sovereign set, all proof except the first: Gillick, Machin, Maklouf and Rank-Broadley sovereigns, and the 2nd, 3rd and 4th of above half-sovereigns, various dates (7 coins)	£1500
2004 Proof silver Britannia set (4 coins)	£150
2004 — "Family Silver" set £5, Britannia and Trevithick £2, £1 and Bannister 50p (5 coins)	£165
2004 — Silver Piedfort set, Trevithick £2, £1 and Bannister 50p (3 coins)	£175
2004 — £2 to 1p, two each of £2 and 50p in Executive case (10 coins)	£75
2004 — — as above in red leather case (10 coins)	£45
2004 — — as above in standard case (10 coins)	£40

DATE	FDC
2004 BU £2 to 1p in folder (10 coins)	£22
2004 — "New Coinage" set, Trevithick £2, £1 and Bannister 50p (3 coins)	£10
2004 BU "Season's Greetings" £2 to 1p and Royal Mint Christmas medal in folder (8 coins)	£18
2005 Proof Gold Britannia set (4 coins)	£2000
2005 — — — £50 to £10 (3 coins)	£1000
2005 — — Sovereign series set (4 coins)	£2000
2005 — — — series, double to half sovereign (3 coins)	£1000
2005 — Silver Britannia (4 coins)	£135
2005 — Gold Trafalgar and Nelson £5 crowns (2 coins)	£2000
2005 — Silver, as above (2 coins)	£85
2005 — — Piedfort, as above (2 coins)	£135
2005 — Silver Piedfort set, Gunpowder Plot and World War II £2, £1 and Johnson 50p (4 coins)	£200
2005 — £5 to 1p, two of each of £5, £2 and 50p in Executive case (12 coins)	£80
2005 — — as above in red leather case (12 coins)	£60
2005 — — as above in standard case (12 coins)	£45
2005 BU Trafalgar and Nelson £5 crowns in pack (2 coins)	£25
2005 — £2 (two) to 1p in folder (10 coins)	£25
2005 — "New Coinage" set, Gunpowder Plot £2, £1 and Johnson 50p (3 coins)	£10
2005 — "Merry Xmas" £2 to 1p and Royal Mint Christmas medal in folder (8 coins)	£20
2006 Proof Gold Britannia set (4 coins)	£2000
2006 — — Sovereign Series set (4 coins)	£2000
2006 — — — series, double to half sovereign (3 coins)	£1000
2006 — Silver Britannia (4 coins)	£145
2006 — Silver Brunel £2 coin set (2 coins)	£75
2006 — — Piedfort Brunel £2 coin set (2 coins)	£125
2006 — Gold Brunel £2 coin set (2 coins)	£950
2006 — Silver VC 50p coin set (2 coins)	£58
2006 — Silver Piedfort VC 50p coin set (2 coins)	£115
2006 — Gold VC 50p coin set (2 coins)	£675
2006 — Silver proof set, £5 to 1p plus Maundy coins (13 coins)	£325
2006 — — — Piedfort collection £5, with trumpets enhanced with 23 carat gold, both Brunel £2, £1, both VC 50p (6 coins)	£350
2006 — — Britannia £2 "Golden Silhouette" collection, five different reverses, all dated 2006 (5 coins)	£350
2006 — Britannia £25 Gold "Portrait" collection, five different reverses, all dated 2006 (5 coins)	£1550
2006 — £5 to 1p, three of each £2 and 50p in Executive case (13 coins)	£80
2006 — as above in red leather case (13 coins)	£55
2006 — as above in standard case (13 coins)	£45
2006 BU £2 (two), £1, 50p (two) and to 1p in folder (10 coins)	£18
2006 Proof Brunel £2 in folder (2 coins)	£15
2006 — VC 50p in folder (2 coins)	£15
2006 — Gold Half-Sovereign set dated 2005 Noad and 2006 Pistrucci St George and the Dragon (2 coins)	£250
2007 — Gold Britannia set (4 coins)	£2500
2007 — — Sovereign Series set (4 coins)	£2000
2007 — — — series, double to half sovereign (3 coins)	£1000
2007 — — Sovereign and half-sovereign (2 coins)	£375
2007 — "Family Silver" set, Britannia, £5 crown, Union and Slavery £2, Gateshead £1 and Scouting 50p (6 coins)	£225
2007 Proof Silver Piedfort Collection, as "Family Silver" above but excluding a Britannia (5 coins)	£300
2007 — Silver £1 Bridge series coins, dated 2004 to 2007 (4 coins)	£135
2007 — Silver Proof Piedfort £1 Bridge Series, dated 2004 to 2007 (4 coins)	£275
2007 — Gold £1 Bridge series coins, dated as above (4 coins)	£2000
2007 — £5 to 1p, three £2 and two 50p in Executive case (12 coins)	£85
2007 — as above, Deluxe in red leather case (12 coins)	£65
2007 — as above, in standard case (12 coins)	£50
2007 BU £2 (two) to 1p (9 coins)	£18
2007 Proof Silver Britannia (four coins)	£145
2007 — Platinum Britannia (4 coins)	£5000
2007 Satin Proof Silver Britannia, 20th Anniversary Collection, six different reverses, all dated 2007 (6 coins)	£300
2007 50th Anniversary Sovereign set, 1957 circulation standard and 2007 Proof (2 coins)	£450
2008 Proof Gold Britannia set (4 coins)	£2000
2008 — Platinum Britannia set (4 coins)	£5000
2008 — Silver Britannia set (4 coins)	£150
2008 — Gold Sovereign series set (4 coins)	£2000
2008 — — double to half-sovereign (3 coins)	£1000
2008 — — Sovereign and half-sovereign (2 coins)	£500
2008 — "Family silver" set, 2x £5, Britannia £2, Olympiad £2 and Royal Arms £1 (5 coins)	£200
2008 — Silver Piedfort Collection, 2x £5, Olympiad £2 and Shield of Royal Arms £1 (4 coins)	£285

DATE   FDC

2008 — 2 x £5, 2 x £2, £1 to 1p in Executive case (11 coins) £85
2008 — as above, Deluxe in black leather case (11 coins) £55
2008 — as above, in standard back case (11 coins) £60
2008 BU 2 x £2, Royal Arms £1 to 1p (9 coins) £20
2008 — "Emblems of Britain" ("old" Revs) Royal Arms £1 to 1p (7 coins) £15
2008 — "Royal Shield of Arms" ("new" Revs) Royal Shield of Arms £1 to 1p (7 coins) £15
2008 — Above two sets housed in one sleeve £28
2008 Proof Base Metal "Royal Shield of Arms" set, £1 to 1p (7 coins) £40
2008 — Silver "Emblems of Britain" set, £1 to 1p (7 coins) £160
2008 — — "Royal Shield of Arms" set, £1 to 1p (7 coins) £160
2008 — — Above two sets in one black case £325
2008 — Gold "Emblems of Britain" set, £1 to 1p (7 coins) £3500
2008 — — "Royal Shield of Arms" set, £1 to 1p (7 coins) £3500
2008 — — Above two sets in one oak-veneer case £6750
2008 — Platinum "Emblems of Britain" set, £1 to 1p (7 coins) £8500
2008 — — "Royal Shield of Arms" set, £1 to 1p (7 coins) £8500
2008 — — Above two sets in one walnut veneer case £15,750
2008 — Silver Piedfort "Royal Shield of Arms" set, £1 to 1p (7 coins) £325
2008 — Gold set of 14 £1 coins, one of each Rev used since 1983,
   all dated 2008 (25th anniversary)   (14 coins) £9500
2008 — Silver with gold Rev highlighting as above (14 coins) £500
2008 — 2 x £2, Royal Arms £1 to 1p (9 coins) Christmas Coin Sets,
   two different outer sleeves, Father Christmas or Three Wise men £20
2009 Proof Gold Britannia set (4 coins) £2200
2009 — Platinum Britannia set (4 coins) £4000
2009 — Silver Britannia set (4 coins) £150
2009 — Gold Sovereign series set (5 coins) £2700
2009 — — double to half-sovereign (3 coins) £1000
2009 — — sovereign and half-sovereign (2 coins) £450
2009 — "Family Silver" set, Henry VIII £5, Britannia £2, Darwin and Burns £2,
   £1 and Kew 50p (6 coins) £225
2009 — Silver Piedfort collection, Henry VIII £5, Darwin and Burns £2
   and Kew Gardens 50p (4 coins) £275
2009 — Silver Set, £5 to 1p (12 coins) £275
2009 — Base metal Executive set, £5 to 1p (12 coins) £80
2009 — — Deluxe set, £5 to 1p (12 coins) £55
2009 — — Standard set, £5 to 1p (12 coins) £45
2009 BU Base metal set, £2 to 1p (11 coins) £22
2009 — — —, £1 to 1p "Royal Shield of Arms" set (7 coins) £12
2009 — — —, £2 to 1p (8 coins) £15
2009 Proof set of 50p coins as detailed in FIFTY PENCE section, CuNi (16 coins) £195
2009 — Silver (16 coins) £425
2009 — Gold (16 coins) £8500
2009 — Gold Piedfort (16 coins) £20,000
2009 "Mind" set of £5 coins, silver (6 coins) £350
2010 Gold Britannia set (4 coins) £2750
2010 — —, £50 to £10 (3 coins) £1500
2010 — Silver Britannia set (4 coins) £140
2010 — Gold Olympic Series "Faster", £100 and £25 (2), (3 coins) £2000
2010 — — Sovereign series set (5 coins) £2750
2010 — — double to half (3 coins) £1250
2010 — — sovereign to quarter (3 coins) £550
2010 — "Silver Celebration" set, Restoration £5, Nightingale £2, London and Belfast £1
   and Girlguiding 50p (5 coins) £185
2010 Silver Piedfort set, coins as in "Silver Celebration" set (5 coins) £300
2010 — Silver Collection, £5 to 1p (13 coins) £300
2010 — Base Metal Executive Set, £5 to 1p (13 coins) £80
2010 — — Deluxe set £50
2010 — — Standard set £40
2010 BU — Capital Cities £1 (2 coins) £15
2010 — — Set, £2 to 1p (12 coins) £35
2010 — — Definitive pack, £2 to 1p (8 coins) £20
2010 Proof "Body" Collection of £5 coins, silver (6 coins) £300
2010 Proof "Spirit" Collection of £5 coins, silver (6 coins) £300
2011 Proof Gold Britannia set (4 coins) £2750
2011 — — Premium set (3 coins) £1500

DATE	FDC
2011 — Sovereign set (5 coins)	£3000
2011 — — double to half (3 coins)	£1200
2011 — — sovereign to quarter (3 coins)	£650
2011 — Silver Britannia set (4 coins)	£180
2011 — Olympic gold "Higher" set (3 coins)	£2650
2011 — — — "Faster" (2010) and "Higher" set (6 coins) in 9-coin case	£5300
2011 — Silver Collection, £5 to 1p (14 coins)	£400
2011 — — Celebration set, Duke of Edinburgh £5, Mary Rose and King James bible Cardiff and Edinburgh £1 and WWF 50p (6 coins)	£250
2011 — — — Piedfort, as above (6 coins)	£395
2011 Executive Proof Base metal set (14 coins)	£85
2011 De-luxe Proof Base metal set (14 coins)	£50
2011 Standard Proof Base metal set (14 coins)	£40
2011 BU set including £2, £1 and 50p commemoratives (13 coins)	£26
2011 BU set of Definitives (8 coins)	£25
2012 Proof Gold Britannia Set (4 coins)	£3600
2012 — — — £50 down (3 coins)	£1900
2012 — — — Half-ounce anniversary(9coins)	£9500
2012 — Sovereign set (5 coins)	£4000
2012 — — Double to Half (3 coins)	£1650
2012 — — Sovereign to Quarter (3 coins)	£825
2012 — Silver Britannia set (4 coins)	£195
2012 — Silver Britannia Half-Ounce Anniversary (9 coins)	£500
2012 BU Sovereign set Double to Half (3 coins)	£1550
2012 Proof Olympic gold Stronger set (3 coins)	£3500
2012 — — — 2x £25 (2 coins)	£1200
2010, 2011, 2012 Proof Olympic gold complete set (9 coins)	£10,500
2009, 2010, 2011, 2012 Complete Countdown sets:	
Gold Proof (4 coins)	£11,500
Silver Proof Piedport (4 coins)	£850
Silver Proof (4 coins)	£325
CuNi BU (4 coins)	£45
2012 Proof Gold set, Diamond Jubilee £5, Dickens & Technology £2, £1 to 1p (10 coins)	£8500
2012 — Silver set, as above with Selective Gold plating on £1 to 1p coins (10 coins)	£490
2012 — set (Premium) (10 coins)	£100
2012 — set (Collector) (10 coins)	£55
2012 BU set, include Diamond Jubilee £5 (10 coins)	£40
2012 — set, Technology £2 to 1p (8 coins)	£21
2012 Proof Gold, Diamond Jubilee £5 and Double Sovereign (2 coins)	£3200
2012 — Olympic and Paralympic £5 (2 coins)	£5500
2012 — Gold Piedfort 50p set, one each of the coins of Olympic sports in which Team GB gained gold medals (11 coins)	£25,000
2013 Proof Gold Britannia set, £100 to £1 (5 coins)	£3100
2013 — — — £50 to £10 (3 coins)	£1375
2013 — — — .£25 to £1 (3 coins)	£675
2013 — Silver Britannia set, £2 to 10p (5 coins)	£195
2013 — — — 20p and 10p (2 coins)	£39
2013 — Sovereign set (5 coins)	£4000
2013 — — Double to Half (3 coins)	£1650
2013 — — One to Quarter (3 coins)	£825
2013 — Gold £5 Portraits set (4 coins)	£9500
2013 — Silver Portraits set (4 coins)	£400
2013 — Silver Piedfort Portraits set (4 coins)	£800
2013 — Gold set, £5 Coronation anniversary to 1p (15 coins)	£12,500
2013 — Gold set of both London Underground £2 (2 coins)	£2000
2013 — Silver Piedfort set, as above (2 coins)	£200
2013 — Silver set, as above (2 coins)	£100
2013 BU set, as above (2 coins)	£20
2013 — Gold set, 30th anniversary of the One Pound coin, reverses from 1983 (Sewell), 1988 (Gorringe) and 2013 (Dent). (3 coins)	£3600
2013 — Silver, as above (3 coins)	£150
2013 BU Sovereign set, Double to Half (3 coins), struck June 2, 2013	£1550
2013 Proof Silver annual set, £5 Coronation anniv to 1p (15 coins)	£600
2013 — Piedfort commemorative set (7 coins)	£650
2013 — "Premium" set (15 coins plus a "Latent Image" item)	£150
2013 — "Collector" set (15 coins)	£110
2013 — Commemorative set (7 coins)	£65

2013 BU annual set (15 coins)..£50
2013 — Definitive Set (8 coins) £25
2014 Proof Gold Britannia (Clark) set £100 to 50p (6 coins) £2600
2014 — — — £50 to £10 (3 coins) £1175
2014 — — — £25 to £1 (3 coins) £595
2014 — Silver Britannia (Clark) set £2 to 5p (6 coins) £200
2014 — — — 20p to 5p (3 coins) £45
2014 — Sovereign set (5 coins) £3300
2014 — — Double to half (3 coins) £1300
2014 — — One to quarter (3 coins)...£625
2014 — Gold Commemorative set, £5 Queen Anne, 2 x £2, 2 x £1, 50p (6 coins)....................£5500
2014 — Silver Piedfort set, as above (6 coins)...£570
2014 — — set as above (6 coins) £295
2014 — — all major coins of 2014 (14 coins)..£560
2014 — Premium set (14 coins and a premium medal) £155
2014 — Collector set (14 coins) £110
2014 — Commemorative set (6 coins) £65
2014 BU annual set (14 coins)...£50
2014 — definitive set (8 coins) £25
2014 — Floral £1 set, Scotland and Northern Ireland (2 coins) £18
2014 Proof Silver Outbreak of First World War set of £5 (6 coins) £450
2014 — Gold set as above (6 coins) .... —
2014 — Silver Portrait of Britain £5 Silver collection (4 coins) £36
2015 Proof Gold Britannia (Dufort) set £100 to 50p, Clark portrait (6 coins) £2,600
2015 — — — — £50 to £10 (3 coins) £1,175
2015 — — — — £10 to 50p (3 coins) £350
2015 — Silver Britannia (Dufort) set £2 to 5p, Clark portrait (6 coins) £200
2015 — Sovereign set, Rank-Broadley portrait (5 coins) £2700
2015 — — Double to half, Rank-Broadley portrait (3 coins) £1300
2015 — — One to quarter, Rank-Broadley portrait (3 coins) £625
2015 — Gold Commemorative set, 2 x £5, 2 x £2, 2 x £1, 50p, Rank-Broadley portrait (5 coins) £5500
2015 — Silver Piedfort set, as above (5 coins)...£570
2015 — — set as above (5 coins) £295
2015 — Base metal set as above (5 coins) £65
2015 — Platinum definitive set £2 to 1p, Rank-Broadley portrait plus £2 to 1p Clark portrait (16 coins) £12,500
2015 — Gold ditto £7,600
2015 — Silver ditto..£480
2015 — Base metal ditto £120
2015 BU definitive set as per Platinum set above (16 coins) £50
The above four entries are also available as 8-coin sets with either the Rank-Broadley ("Final Edition") or the Clark ("First Edition" portrait. These are issued at half the prices quoted above.
2015 Proof Silver set of definitive and commemorative coins, Rank-Broadley portrait (13 coins) £560
2015 — Premium set as above (13 coins and a Premium medal)..£155
2015 BU Collector set as above (13 coins and medal) £110
2015 — Sovereign set, Clark portrait (5 coins)..£2,700
2015 — — Double to half sovereign, Clark portrait (3 coins) £1200
2015 Proof Silver commemorative set, Anniversary of First World War (6 coins) £450

In addition to the above the Royal Mint produce the BU sets detailed above in Wedding and in Baby gift packs each year. Also the following patterns have been made available:

1999 (dated 1994) Bi-metal £2, plus three unprocessed or part-processed elements....................... —
2003 Set of patterns of £1 coins with bridges designs, in gold, hall-marked on edges (4 coins) .... —
2003 — silver £1 as above (4 coins)..£150
2004 — gold £1 featuring heraldic animal heads, hall-marked on edge (4 coins) £1000
2004 — silver £1 featuring heraldic animal heads, hall-marked on edge (4 coins)......................£350

IMPORTANT NOTE:

In this section the prices quoted were set at August 2015 with the price of gold at around £726 per ounce and silver £9 per ounce. As the market for precious metals is notoriously volatile and unpredictable any price fluctuations have a marked effect on the values of modern precious metal coins, therefore it is important to seek professional advice when requiring a valuation for any of the precious metal sets listed. The prices quoted here are for guidance only whereas the prices quoted for the *recently issued* sets are the original Royal Mint retail prices.

SCOTLAND

The coins illustrated are pennies representative of the reign, unless otherwise stated.

	F	VF

DAVID I (1124–53)
Berwick, Carlisle, Edinburgh and Roxburgh Mints

	F	VF
Penny in the name of David	£1500	£5500
Penny in name of Stephen	£1000	£4000

David I

HENRY (1136–52)
Bamborough, Carlisle and Corbridge Mints for the Earl of Huntingdon and Northumberland

	F	VF
Penny	£2000	£7500

Henry

MALCOLM IV (1153–65)
Berwick and Roxburgh Mints

Penny (5 different types)	Extremely rare	

WILLIAM THE LION (1165–1214)
Berwick, Edinburgh, Dun (Dunbar?), Perth and Roxburgh Mints

	F	VF
Penny - cross pattee early issue ...... from	£2500	£7000
Penny – pellet & crescent ...... from	£175	£500
Penny – short cross & stars – mint & moneyer ...... from	£150	£450
Penny – short cross & stars HVE WALTER & var ...... from	£100	£225

William the Lion

ALEXANDER II (1214–49)
Berwick and Roxburgh Mints

	F	VF
Penny – in the name of William the Lion ...... from	£450	£1250
Penny – in own name ...... from	£550	£1500

Alexander II

ALEXANDER III (1249–86)

FIRST COINAGE (1250–80)
Pennies struck at the Mints at

	F	VF
Aberdeen ...... from	£150	£350
Ayr ...... from	£225	£600
Berwick ...... from	£85	£200
Dun (Dumfries / Dunfermline? / Dundee?) ...... from	£200	£550
Edinburgh ...... from	£150	£350
Forfar ...... from	£295	£800
Fres (Dumfries) ...... from	£300	£700
Glasgow ...... from	£300	£750
Inverness ...... from	£275	£600
Kinghorn ...... from	£295	£775
Lanark ...... from	£260	£665
Montrose ...... from	£550	£1000
Perth ...... from	£110	£285
Roxburgh ...... from	£120	£310
St Andrews ...... from	£275	£600
Stirling ...... from	£200	£550

Alexander III First Coinage

SECOND COINAGE (1280–86)

	F	VF
Penny	£70	£160
Halfpenny	£90	£325
Farthing	£275	£825

Alexander III Second Coinage

275

F   VF

JOHN BALIOL (1292–1306)

FIRST COINAGE *(Rough Surface issue)*

	F	VF
Penny .... from	£125	£275
Halfpenny .... from	£650	Ex. rare
Penny – St. Andrews .... from	£175	£475
Halfpenny – St. Andrews .... from	£800	Ex. rare

SECOND COINAGE *(Smooth Surface issue)*

	F	VF
Penny .... from	£200	£475
Halfpenny .... from	£150	£425
Farthing	Extremely rare	
Penny – St. Andrews .... from	£350	£950
Halfpenny – St. Andrews	Extremely rare	

John Baliol

ROBERT BRUCE (1306–29)

Berwick Mint

	F	VF
Penny .... from	£650	£1750
Halfpenny .... from	£750	£2000
Farthing .... from	£850	£2250

Robert Bruce

DAVID II (1329–71)

Aberdeen and Edinburgh Mints

	F	VF
Noble	Extremely Rare	
Groat (Edinburgh) .... from	£115	£300
Groat (Aberdeen) .... from	£375	£1000
Halfgroat (Edinburgh) .... from	£110	£325
Halfgroat (Aberdeen) .... from	£525	£1250
Penny 1st Coinage 2nd Issue .... from	£75	£220
Penny 2nd Coinage (Edinburgh) .... from	£95	£225
Penny 2nd Coinage (Aberdeen) .... from	£450	£1100
Halfpenny .... from	£250	£725
Farthing .... from	£450	£1250

David II

ROBERT II (1371–90)

Dundee, Edinburgh and Perth Mints

	F	VF
Groat .... from	£100	£275
Halfgroat .... from	£135	£395
Penny .... from	£85	£215
Halfpenny .... from	£95	£275

Robert II

ROBERT III (1390–1406)

Aberdeen, Dumbarton, Edinburgh, Perth Mints

	F	VF
Lion or crown .... from	£1750	£5750
Demy lion or halfcrown .... from	£1250	£4500
Groat .... from	£90	£225
Halfgroat .... from	£175	£350
Penny .... from	£250	£725
Halfpenny .... from	£275	£850

JAMES I (1406–37)

Aberdeen, Edinburgh, Inverness, Linlithgow, Perth, Stirling Mints

	F	VF
Demy .... from	£850	£2500
Half demy .... from	£750	£2250
Groat .... from	£125	£350
Penny .... from	£250	£650
Halfpenny	Extremely rare	

JAMES II (1437–60)

Aberdeen, Edinburgh, Linlithgow, Perth, Roxburgh, Stirling Mints

	F	VF
Demy .... from	£1050	£2950
Lion .... from	£1250	£4500

Robert III Lion

	F	VF
Half lion	Extremely rare	
Early groats (fleur-de-lis) .... from	£195	£550
Later groats (crown) .... from	£225	£650
Halfgroat .... from	£500	£1000
Penny (billon) .... from	£250	£650

JAMES III (1460–88)

Aberdeen, Berwick and Edinburgh Mints

	F	VF
Rider	£1750	£4500
Half rider	£1750	£4500
Quarter rider	£2500	£7000
Unicorn	£2750	£7500
Groat .... from	£130	£375
Halfgroat .... from	£225	£625
Penny (silver) .... from	£500	Ex. rare
Plack (billon) .... from	£175	£450
Half plack) .... from	£195	£525
Penny (billon) .... from	£175	£500
Farthing (copper)	£200	£650
Penny – ecclesiastical issue .... from	£70	£185
Farthing – ecclesiastical issue .... from	£125	£350

James III Groat, Berwick Mint

JAMES IV (1488–1513)

Edinburgh Mint

	F	VF
Unicorn	£1500	£4250
Half unicorn	£1250	£3500
Lion or crown	Extremely rare	
Half lion	Extremely rare	
Groat .... from	£400	£1375
Halfgroat .... from	£650	£1750
Penny (silver) .... from	£150	£400
Plack .... from	£40	£100
Half plack	Extremely rare	
Penny (billon) .... from	£55	£135

JAMES V (1513–42)

Edinburgh Mint

	F	VF
Unicorn	£2050	£5125
Half Unicorn	Extremely rare	
Crown	£1350	£4250
Ducat or Bonnet piece .... from	£1250	£5000
Two-thirds ducat	£2500	£6500
One-third ducat	£3500	£9500
Groat .... from	£175	£500
One-third groat .... from	£275	£775
Plack .... from	£50	£125
Bawbee .... from	£60	£165
Half bawbee .... from	£140	£325
Quarter bawbee	Extremely rare	

James IV Unicorn

MARY (1542–67)

Edinburgh and Stirling Mints
FIRST PERIOD (1542–58)

	F	VF
Crown	£1325	£3500
Twenty shillings	Extremely rare	
Lion (Forty-four shillings)	£1350	£4000
Half lion (Twenty-two shillings)	£1000	£2750
Ryals (Three pounds	£3500	£9500
Half ryal	£4500	£12500
Portrait testoon	£5000	£13500

James V Ducat or Bonnet Piece

		F	VF
Non-portrait testoon	from	£275	£800
Half testoon	from	£250	£750
Bawbee	from	£65	£180
Half bawbee	from	£125	£325
Bawbee - Stirling		£150	£425
Penny (facing bust)	from	£325	£900
Penny (no bust)	from	£225	£650
Lion	from	£50	£145
Plack	from	£70	£195

SECOND PERIOD (Francis and Mary, 1558–60)

		F	VF
Ducat (Sixty shillings)		Extremely rare	
Non-portrait testoon	from	£350	£1000
Half testoon	from	£400	£1150
12 penny groat	from	£80	£225
Lion	from	£55	£135

THIRD PERIOD (Widowhood, 1560–65)

	F	VF
Portrait testoon	£3250	£9500
Half testoon.	£3000	£8500

Mary Lion or Forty-Four Shillings

FOURTH PERIOD (Henry and Mary, 1565–67)

		F	VF
Portrait ryal.		£45000	£125000
Non-portrait ryal	from	£900	£2250
Two-third ryal	from	£650	£1750
One-third ryal	from	£850	£2550

FIFTH PERIOD (Second widowhood, 1567)

		F	VF
Non-portrait ryal	from	£850	£2250
Two thirds ryal	from	£475	£1350
One-third ryal	from	£650	£1550

JAMES VI (1567–1603)

(Before accession to the English throne)

FIRST COINAGE (1567–71)

		F	VF
Ryal	from	£500	£1250
Two-thirds ryal	from	£350	£900
One-third ryal	from	£350	£900

SECOND COINAGE (1571–80)

		F	VF
Twenty pounds		£25,000	£75,000
Noble (or half merk)	from	£125	£300
Half noble (or quarter merk)	from	£125	£300
Two merks or Thistle dollar	from	£1500	£3750
Merk	from	£2500	£7250

THIRD COINAGE (1580–81)

	F	VF
Ducat	£5000	£14500
Sixteen shillings	£2500	£7250
Eight shillings	£1950	£5750
Four shillings	£4000	£9500
Two shillings	Extremely rare	

FOURTH COINAGE (1582–88)

	F	VF
Lion noble	£5500	£15000
Two-third lion noble	£4750	£13500
One-third lion noble	Extremely rare	
Forty shillings	£5000	£14500
Thirty shillings	£800	£2500
Twenty shillings	£425	£1250
Ten shillings	£425	£1250

James VI Fourth coinage
Ten Shillings

	F	VF

FIFTH COINAGE (1588)
Thistle noble £1700 £5250

SIXTH COINAGE (1591–93)
"Hat" piece £3500 £10000
"Balance" half merk .... from £300 £895
"Balance" quarter merk £725 £2000

SEVENTH COINAGE (1594–1601)
Rider £850 £2750
Half rider £1000 £3500
Ten shillings .... from £150 £425
Five shillings .... from £125 £375
Thirty pence .... from £225 £625
Twelve pence .... from £130 £375

EIGHTH COINAGE (1601–04)
Sword and sceptre piece .... from £650 £1750
Half sword and sceptre piece .... from £425 £1250
Thistle-merk .... from £110 £295
Half thistle-merk .... from £65 £175
Quarter thistle-merk .... from £55 £135
Eighth thistle-merk .... from £50 £110

BILLON AND COPPER ISSUES
Eightpenny groat .... from £40 £110
Fourpenny groat .... from £350 £1000
Twopenny plack .... from £130 £375
Hardhead .... from £35 £95
Twopence .... from £80 £230
Penny plack .... from £160 £750
Penny .... from £500 £1250

James VI Seventh Coinage Rider

*James VI Seventh Coinage
10 Shillings*

JAMES VI (1603–25)
(After accession to the English throne)

Unit .... from £850 £2350
Double crown .... from £1100 £3250
British crown .... from £550 £1550
Halfcrown .... from £750 £2150
Thistle crown .... from £650 £2050
Sixty shillings .... from £350 £1000
Thirty shillings .... from £175 £500
Twelve shillings .... from £175 £575
Six shillings .... from £500 Ex. rare
Two shillings .... from £50 £140
One shilling .... from £125 £350
Copper twopence .... from £25 £70
Copper penny .... from £85 £250

CHARLES I (1625–49)
FIRST COINAGE (1625–36)
Unit £1250 £3500
Double crown £1000 £3150
British crown .... Extremely rare
Sixty shillings £800 £2500
Thirty shillings £150 £425
Twelve shillings £150 £425
Six shillings .... from £350 £1000
Two shillings £45 £110
One shilling £150 £495

*James VI after accession thirty
shillings*

		F	VF

SECOND COINAGE (1636)

		F	VF
Half merk		£90	£260
Forty penny piece		£75	£210
Twenty penny piece		£70	£200

THIRD COINAGE (1637–42)

		F	VF
Unit	from	£1250	£4250
Half unit	from	£950	£2950
British crown	from	£600	£1750
British half crown	from	£525	£1500
Sixty shillings		£575	£1500
Thirty shillings	from	£110	£350
Twelve shillings	from	£100	£325
Six shillings	from	£80	£225
Half merk	from	£120	£395
Forty pence	from	£40	£110
Twenty pence	from	£25	£70

*Charles I Third Coinage
Sixty Shillings*

FOURTH COINAGE (1642)

		F	VF
Three shillings thistle		£60	£150
Two shillings large II		£40	£110
Two shillings small II		£60	£155
Two shillings no value		£80	£225

COPPER ISSUES
(1629 Issue)

		F	VF
Twopence (triple thistle		£25	£70
Penny		£175	£500

(1632–?9 Issue)

		F	VF
Twopence (Stirling turner	from	£25	£70

(1642-50 ISSUE)

		F	VF
Twopence (CR crowned		£20	£55

*Charles I Fourth Coinage
Two Shillings*

CHARLES II (1660–85)

FIRST COINAGE

Four merks

		F	VF
1664 Thistle above bust		£950	£2750
1664 Thistle below bust		£1500	£4250
1665		Extremely rare	
1670	varieties from	£1150	£3350
1673		£1150	£3350
1674 F below bust	varieties from	£950	£2750
1675		£950	£2750

Two merks

		F	VF
1664 Thistle above bust		£650	£1750
1664 Thistle below bust		£850	£2250
1670		£850	£2250
1673		£550	£1650
1673 F below bust		£750	£1950
1674		£850	£2250
1674 F below bust		£850	£2250
1675		£550	£1550

Merk

		F	VF
1664	varieties from	£250	£715
1665		£275	£780
1666		£325	£850
1668		£185	£520

Charles II two merks

	F	VF

1669.................................... varieties from	£90	£250
1670..	£130	£375
1671..	£115	£325
1672.................................... varieties from	£100	£290
1673.................................... varieties from	£125	£350
1674..	£230	£650
1674 F below bust................................	£210	£585
1675 F below bust................................	£175	£475
1675..	£210	£585

Half merk

1664..	£250	£650
1665.................................... varieties from	£200	£520
1666.................................... varieties from	£225	£585
1667..	£200	£520
1668..	£115	£325
1669.................................... varieties from	£90	£250
1670.................................... varieties from	£115	£325
1671.................................... varieties from	£90	£250
1672..	£115	£325
1673..	£150	£425
1675 F below bust................................	£150	£390
1675..	£175	£455

Charles II Dollar

SECOND COINAGE
Dollar

1676..	£700	£1950
1679..	£650	£1625
1680..	£850	£1950
1681..	£650	£1625
1682..	£575	£1550

Half Dollar

1675..	£330	£950
1676..	£530	£1525
1681..	£330	£950

Quarter Dollar

1675..	£195	£550
1676.................................... varieties from	£100	£275
1677.................................... varieties from	£100	£275
1678..	£165	£450
1679..	£185	£500
1680..	£150	£375
1681..	£120	£295
1682.................................... varieties from	£120	£295

Charles II Sixteenth Dollar

Eighth Dollar

1676.................................... varieties from	£85	£195
1677..	£125	£300
1678/7	£195	£495
1679..	Extremely rare	
1680.................................... varieties from	£150	£345
1682.................................... varieties from	£225	£495

Sixteenth Dollar

1677..	£75	£200
1678/7 .... varieties from	£120	£320
1679/7	£135	£360
1680.................................... varieties from	£135	£360
1681..	£75	£200

Charles II Bawbee

	F	VF

Copper Issues

		F	VF
Twopence CR crowned .... varieties from		£25	£70
Bawbees 1677-79 .... varieties from		£65	£195
Turners 1677-79 .... varieties from		£45	£125

JAMES VII (1685–89)

Sixty shillings

	F	VF
1688 proof only .... varieties from	—	£3250

Forty shillings

	F	VF
1687... varieties from	£400	£950
1688... varieties from	£400	£950

Ten shillings

	F	VF
1687...	£150	£425
1688... varieties from	£250	£700

WILLIAM & MARY (1689–94)

Sixty shillings

	F	VF
1691...	£295	£1100
1692...	£395	£1000

Forty shillings

	F	VF
1689... varieties from	£295	£850
1690... varieties from	£185	£525
1691... varieties from	£195	£550
1692... varieties from	£225	£600
1693... varieties from	£195	£550
1694... varieties from	£225	£775

James VII ten shillings

Twenty shillings

	F	VF
1693...	£450	£1500
1694...	Extremely rare	

Ten shillings

	F	VF
1689...	Extremely rare	
1690... varieties from	£295	£750
1691... varieties from	£195	£600
1692... varieties from	£195	£600
1694... varieties from	£250	£700

Five shillings

	F	VF
1691...	£200	£575
1694... varieties from	£120	£350

Copper Issues

	F	VF
Bawbees 1691–94... varieties from	£100	£275
Bodle (Turners) 1691–94.................................. varieties from	£55	£180

William & Mary ten shillings

WILLIAM II (1694–1702)

	F	VF
Pistole	£3000	£7500
Half pistole	£3750	£8500

Forty shillings

	F	VF
1695... varieties from	£175	£450
1696...	£200	£495
1697...	£250	£550
1698...	£200	£495
1699...	£325	£650
1700...	Extremely rare	

	F	VF
Twenty shillings		
1695	£200	£550
1696	£200	£550
1697 .... varieties from	£250	£700
1698 .... varieties from	£175	£650
1699	£225	£625
Ten shillings		
1695	£150	£375
1696	£150	£375
1697 .... varieties from	£150	£375
1698 .... varieties from	£150	£375
1699	£295	£750
Five shillings		
1695	£70	£195
1696	£65	£180
1697 .... varieties from	£65	£180
1699	£95	£275
1700	£85	£230
1701	£125	£350
1702	£125	£350
Copper Issues		
Bawbee 1695–97 .... varieties from	£85	£325
Bodle (Turners) 1695–97 .... varieties from	£50	£150

William II ten shillings

ANNE (1702–14)

Pre -Union 1702-7
Ten shillings

	F	VF
1705	£175	£450
1706 .... varieties from	£225	£650
Five shillings		
1705 .... varieties from	£85	£225
1706	£85	£225

POST-UNION 1707–14
See listing in English section.

Anne five shillings

JAMES VIII (The Old Pretender) (1688–1766)

A number of Guineas and Crowns in various metals were struck in 1828 using original dies prepared by Norbert Roettiers, all bearing the date 1716. These coins are extremely rare and are keenly sought after.

Our grateful thanks go to David Stuart of ABC Coins & Tokens who has spent many hours updating the Scottish section for 2016.

www.coinsofbritain.com

ISLE OF MAN

DATE	F	VF	EF	UNC

PENNY

1709 Cast	£45	£150	£300	—	
1709 Silver cast Proof	—	—	—	£2000	
1709 Brass	£45	£150	£300	—	
1733 "Quocunque"	£40	£75	£250	£400	
1733 "Ouocunoue"	£40	£75	£260	£750	
1733 Bath metal "Quocunque"	£30	£65	£260	—	
1733 Silver Proof	—	—	—	£850	
1733 Bronze Proof	—	—	—	£500	
1733 Proof	—	—	—	£675	
1733 Cap frosted	£35	£75	£275	£500	
1733 Brass, cap frosted	£40	£75	£300	£650	
1733 Silver Proof cap frosted	—	—	—	£650	
1733 Bronze annulets instead of pellets	£50	£100	£400	£300	
1758	£30	£50	£250	£450	
1758 Proof	—	—	—	£650	
1758 Silver Proof	—	—	—	£1000	
1786 Engrailed edge	£35	£65	£275	£450	
1786 Engrailed edge Proof	—	—	—	£500	
1786 Plain edge Proof	—	—	—	£1000	
1786 Pellet below bust	£35	£65	£275	£550	
1798	£35	£65	£250	£500	
1798 Proof	—	—	—	£450	
1798 Bronze Proof	—	—	—	£450	
1798 Copper-gilt Proof	—	—	—	£2000	
1798 Silver Proof	—	—	—	£2500	
1813	£40	£75	£250	£500	
1813 Proof	—	—	—	£650	
1813 Bronze Proof	—	—	—	£650	
1813 Copper-gilt Proof	—	—	—	£2500	
1839	£35	£75	£175	£400	
1839 Proof	—	—	—	£500	

HALF PENCE

1709 Cast	£50	£125	£250	—	
1709 Brass	£55	£185	£490	—	
1723 Silver	£725	£1250	£3500	—	
1723 Copper	£300	£600	£1750	£2500	
1733 Copper	£35	£55	£225	£450	
1733 Bronze	£35	£55	£225	£450	
1733 Silver Proof plain cap	—	—	—	£675	
1733 Silver Proof frosted cap	—	—	—	—	
1733 Bronze Proof	—	—	—	£475	
1733 Bath metal plain cap	£40	£50	£215	—	
1733 Bath metal frosted cap	£40	£50	£215	—	
1758	£40	£50	£215	£450	
1758 Proof	—	—	—	£800	
1786 Engrailed edge	£30	£45	£120	£350	
1786 Proof engrailed edge	—	—	—	£450	
1786 Plain edge	£40	£65	£250	£350	
1786 Proof plain edge	—	—	—	£650	
1786 Bronze Proof	—	—	—	£450	
1798	£35	£45	£150	£350	
1798 Proof	—	—	—	£450	
1798 Bronze Proof	—	—	—	£400	

DATE	F	VF	EF	UNC
1798 Copper-gilt Proof	—	—	—	£1500
1798 Silver Proof	—	—	—	£1500
1813	£30	£45	£150	£300
1813 Proof	—	—	—	£375
1813 Bronze Proof....................................	—	—	—	£350
1813 Copper-gilt Proof	—	—	—	£1250
1839	£30	£45	£150	£300
1839 Bronze Proof....................................	—	—	—	£450

FARTHING

	F	VF	EF	UNC
1839 Copper	£30	£45	£125	£250
1839 Bronze Proof	—	—	—	£450
1839 Copper-gilt Proof	—	—	—	£2500

The last issue of coins made in the Isle of Man had been in 1839 but in 1970 Spink & Son Ltd was commissioned to produce a modern coinage for the Isle of Man Government which was struck at the Royal Mint. From 1973 onwards the Pobjoy Mint took over the contract and has been a very prolific producer of definitive and commemorative issues. It is not proposed to give a complete listing of all these coins but the Crown and 25p, which from the collector's point of view are the most interesting in the series, have been selected. Additionally a special 50p coin is issued to celebrate Christmas each year.
   The listings that follow are of the ordinary uncirculated cupro-nickel crown-size coins. The Island has also issued most of the coins listed in other metals, including silver, gold and platinum in non proof and proof form and in 1984 some were also issued in silver clad cupro-nickel in proof form.

DATE	UNC
1970 Manx Cat	£15
1972 Royal Silver Wedding	£15
1974 Centenary of Churchill's birth	£15
1975 Manx Cat	£25
1976 Bi-Centenary of American Independence	£15
1976 Centenary of the Horse Drawn Tram	£10
1977 Silver Jubilee	£10
1977 Silver Jubilee Appeal	£10
1978 25th Anniversary of the Coronation............................	£10
1979 300th Anniversary of Manx Coinage	£10
1979 Millennium of Tynwald (5 coins).................................	£20
1980 Winter Olympics	£15
1980 Derby Bicentennial	£15
1980 22nd Olympics (3 coins)...	£20
1980 80th Birthday of Queen Mother..................................	£15
1981 Duke of Edinburgh Award Scheme (4 coins)............................	£15
1981 Year of Disabled (4 coins)..	£15
1981 Prince of Wales' Wedding (2 coins)............................	£15
1982 12th World Cup—Spain (4 coins)	£20
1982 Maritime Heritage (4 coins)......................................	£20
1983 Manned Flight (4 coins)...	£20
1984 23rd Olympics (4 coins)...	£20
1984 Quincentenary of College of Arms (4 coins)............................	£20
1984 Commonwealth Parliamentary Conference (4 coins).................	£20
1985 Queen Mother (6 coins)	£20
1986 13th World Cup—Mexico (6 coins).............................	£15
1986 Prince Andrew Wedding (2 coins)	£15
1987 200th Anniversary of the United States Constitution	£20

DATE	UNC
1987 America's Cup Races (5 coins)...	£25
1988 Bicentenary of Steam Navigation (6 coins)	£30
1988 Australia Bicentennial (6 coins)	£30
1988 Manx Cat	£15
1989 Royal Visit	£10
1989 Bicentenary of the Mutiny on the Bounty (4 coins)	£20
1989 Persian Cat...	£20
1989 Bicentenary of Washington's Inauguration (4 coins)	£20
1990 150th Anniversary of the Penny Black	£15
1990 World Cup—Italy (4 coins)..	£20
1990 25th Anniversary of Churchill's Death (2 coins)..........................	£15
1990 Alley Cat	£15
1990 Queen Mother's 90th Birthday	£10
1991 Norwegian Forest Cat	£10
1991 Centenary of the American Numismatic Association.................	£10
1991 1992 America's Cup	£15
1991 10th Anniversary of Prince of Wales' Wedding (2 coins)............	£15
1992 Discovery of America (4 coins)...	£20
1992 Siamese Cat..	£20
1992 1992 America's Cup	£10
1993 Maine Coon Cat	£10
1993 Preserve Planet Earth—Dinosaurs (2 coins)..............................	£15
1994 Preserve Planet Earth—Mammoth..	£15
1994 Year of the Dog...	£15
1994 World Football Cup (6 coins)	£30
1994 Japanese Bobtail Cat	£10
1994 Normandy Landings (8 coins)...	£40
1994 Preserve Planet Earth—Endangered Animals (3 coins)..............	£20
1995 Man in Flight—Series i (8 coins)	£60
1995 Man in Flight—Series ii (8 coins)	£60
1995 Queen Mother's 95th Birthday	£15
1995 Year of the Pig	£25
1995 Turkish Cat	£15
1995 Preserve Planet Earth—Egret and Otter....................................	£15
1995 America's Cup	£15
1995 Aircraft of World War II (19 coins)..	£130
1995 Famous World Inventions—Series i (12 coins)	£120
1996 Year of the Rat	£15
1996 70th Birthday of HM the Queen	£20
1996 The Flower Fairies—Series i (4 coins)	£40
1996 Famous World Inventions—Series ii (6 coins)	£40
1996 Olympic Games (6 coins)	£35
1996 Preserve Planet Earth—Killer Whale and Razorbill	£15
1996 Burmese Cat..	£20
1996 Robert Burns (4 coins)...	£30
1996 King Arthur & the Knights of the Round Table (5 coins)	£35
1996 European Football Championships (8 coins)...............................	£50
1996 Football Championships Winner	£15
1996 Explorers (2 coins)..	£20
1997 Year of the Ox	£20
1997 The Flower Fairies—Series ii (4 coins).......................................	£25
1997 Royal Golden Wedding (2 coins)	£25
1997 Explorers—Eriksson and Nansen (2 coins)	£15
1997 Long-haired Smoke Cat	£15
1997 10th Anniversary of the "Cats on Coins" series (silver only)	£45
1997 90th Anniversary of the TT Races (4 coins)................................	£40
1998 The Millennium (16 coins issued over 3 years)...........................	£96
1998 Year of the Tiger	£20
1998 FIFA World Cup (4 coins)..	£35
1998 Birman Cat	£20
1998 The Flower Fairies—Series iii (4 coins)	£30
1998 18th Winter Olympics, Nagano (4 coins).....................................	£30
1998 Explorers—Vasco da Gama and Marco Polo (2 coins)	£25
1998 125th Anniversary of Steam Railway (8 coins)	£65
1998 International Year of the Oceans (4 coins)...................................	£33
1999 50th Birthday of HRH the Prince of Wales	£15
1999 Year of the Rabbit..	£15

286

DATE	UNC
1999 27th Olympics in Sydney (5 coins)	£40
1999 Rugby World Cup (6 coins)	£40
1999 Wedding of HRH Prince Edward and Sophie Rhys-Jones	£15
1999 Queen Mother's 100th Birthday (4 coins)	£45
1999 The Millennium (4 coins)	£35
1999 Titanium Millennium crown	£15
2000 Year of the Dragon	£15
2000 Scottish Fold cat	£15
2000 Millennium—own a piece of time	£15
2000 Explorers, Francisco Piarro and Wilem Brents (2 coins)	£15
2000 Life and times of the Queen Mother (4 coins)	£30
2000 Queen Mother's 100th Birthday	£20
2000 60th Anniversary of the Battle of Britain	£15
2000 BT Global Challenge	£15
2000 18th Birthday of HRH Prince William	£15
2001 Year of the Snake	£15
2001 The Somali cat	£15
2001 Life and times of the Queen Mother (2 coins)	£15
2001 Explorers, Martin Frobisher and Roald Amundsen (2 coins)	£15
2001 75th Birthday of HM the Queen	£15
2001 Joey Dunlop	£15
2001 Harry Potter (6 coins)	£80
2002 Year of the Horse	£15
2002 The XIX Winter Olympiad, Salt Lake City (2 coins)	£20
2002 World Cup 2002 in Japan/Korea (4 coins)	£35
2002 The Bengal Cat	£15
2002 The Queen's Golden Jubilee—i (1 coin)	£25
2002 Introduction of the Euro	£15
2002 The Queen's Golden Jubilee—ii (4 coins)	£60
2002 A Tribute to Diana Princess of Wales—5 years on	£30
2003 Year of the Goat	£15
2003 The Balinese Cat	£15
2003 Anniversary of the "Star of India"	£15
2003 Lord of the Rings (5 coins)	£60
2004 Olympics (4 coins)	£50
2004 100 Years of Powered Flight (2 coins)	£30
2005 Lord of the Rings: The Return of the King	£30
2005 Manx Hero Lt. John Quilliam and the Battle of Trafalgar (2 coins)	£30
2005 The Himalayan Cat with kittens	£20
2005 Bicentenary of the Battle of Trafalgar (6 coins)	£55
2005 60th Anniversary of D-Day (6 coins)	£65
2005 60th Anniversary of Victory in Europe	£30
2005 200th Anniversary of the Battle of Trafalgar	£30
2005 400th Anniversary of the Gun Powder Plot (2 coins)	£30
2005 Bicentenary of the Battle of Trafalgar and Death of Nelson	£30
2005 Italy and the Isle of Man TT races (2 coins)	£35
2005 Harry Potter and the Goblet of Fire (4 coins)	£35
2006 100 Years of Norwegian Independence	£25
2006 80th Birthday of Her Majesty the Queen (4 coins)	£35
2006 The Battles that Changed the World—Part II (6 coins)	£55
2006 150th Anniversary of the Victoria Cross (2 coins)	£30
2006 30th Anniversary of the first Translantic Flight	£25
2007 The Ragdoll Cat	£15
2007 Fairy Tales—Sleeping Beauty, The Three Little Pigs (2 coins)	£25
2007 The Graceful Swan	£15
2007 The Royal Diamond Wedding Anniversary	£15
2007 The Centenary of the TT races	£15
2007 The Centenary of the Scouting	£15
2008 50th Anniversary of Paddington Bear	£15
2008 Prince Charles 60th Birthday	£15
2008 Centenary of the Olympics	£15
2008 Burmilla Cat	£15
2008 Year of Planet Earth	£15
2008 The Adorable Snowman	£15
2008 UEFA European Football Championships	£15
2008 The Return of Tutankhamun	£30

DATE	UNC
2008 The Olympic Collection—The Olympics coming to London	£15
2009 Winter Olympics (2 coins)..	£30
2009 The Chinchilla Cat	£15
2009 40th Anniversary of the 1st Concorde Test Flight	£20
2009 50 Years of Championship Racing	£15
2009 Fifa World Cup South Africa 2010..	£15
2010 50 Years of racing by the Suzuki Racing Team	£15
2010 Abyssinian Cat and her Kitten...	£15
2010 Celebrating 15 Years of the Gold Noble......................................	£25
2010 25th Anniversary of the Gold Angel coin....................................	£15
2011 Year of the Rabbit coloured coin...	£25
2011 Engagement of HRH Prince William to Catherine Middleton.....	£15
2011 Royal Wedding of HRH Prince William and Catherine Middleton	£15
2011 Buckingham Palace..	£15
2011 A Lifetime of Service—Queen Elizabeth II and Prince Philip......	£15
2011 The Turkish Angora Cat..	£15
2011 Donatello's famous Chellini Madonna..	£15
2011 TT Races	£15
2012 European Football Championships (4 coins)...............................	£15
2012 Manx Cat Coin...	£15
2012 Centenary of RMS *Titanic*	£15
2012 Juno Moneta Coin	£15
2012 Petra Coin	£15
2012 River Thames Diamond Jubilee Pageant	£15
2012 Olympics (6 coins)	£72.50
2013 St. Patrick Commemorative	£15
2013 Kermode Bear	£15
2013 Anniversary of Queen Victoria and Queen Elizabeth II Coronations	£15
2013 Siberian Cat..	£15
2013 Winter Olympic (4 coins)	£50
2013 Lifetime of Service—Queen Elizabeth II and Prince Philip........	£15
2014 Centenary of WWI	£15
2014 200th Anniversary of Matthew Flinders.......................................	£15
2014 Snowshoe Cat..	£15
2014 The Snowman & Snowdog Christmas crown (+coloured issue)	£10
2014 70th Anniversary of D-Day (poppies picked out in red)	£15
2015 75th Anniversary of the Battle of Britain (search lights in yellow)	£12
2015 200th Anniversary of the Battle of Waterloo—Napoleon	£10
2015 200th Anniversary of the Battle of Waterloo—Wellington	£10
2015 Sir Winston Churchill	£12
2015 Selkirk Rex Cat...	£12
2015 175th Anniversary of the Penny Black Stamp (issued in a pack)	£20
2015 Paddington Bear	£15
2015 Her Majesty the Queen Elizabeth II longest reigning Monarch .	£12

The regular attractive issues from the Isle of Man are popular with many thematic collectors and can make a superb display.

GUERNSEY

DATE	F	VF	EF	UNC
TEN SHILLINGS				
1966..	—	£5	£9	£15
1966 Proof..	—	—	—	£25
THREEPENCE				
1956..	£1	£4	£8	£10
1956 Proof..	—	—	—	£15
1959..	£1	£4	£8	£15
1966 Proof..	—	—	—	£15
EIGHT DOUBLES				
1834..	£10	£15	£50	£175
1858 5 berries..................................	£6	£10	£50	£150
1858 4 berries..................................	£6	£10	£50	£160
1864 1 stalk......................................	£6	£10	£40	£70
1864 3 stalks....................................	£6	£10	£30	£65
1868..	£6	£10	£30	£65
1874..	£4	£6	£15	£50
1885H..	£4	£6	£15	£45
1889H..	£3	£4	£15	£40
1893H small date	£3	£4	£15	£40
1893H large date	£3	£4	£15	£40
1902H..	£3	£4	£15	£40
1903H..	£3	£4	£15	£40
1910..	£3	£4	£15	£40
1911H..	£3	£4	£15	£45
1914H..	£1	£3	£10	£30
1918H..	£1	£3	£8	£25
1920H..	£1	£3	£8	£25
1934H..	£1	£3	£10	£35
1934H Proof	—	—	—	£185
1938H..	£1	£3	£10	£25
1945H..	£1	£2	£8	£15
1947H..	£1	£2	£8	£15
1949H..	—	£2	£9	£15
1956..	—	£1	£7	£15
1956..	—	£1	£5	£15
1959..	—	£1	£5	£15
1966 Proof..	—	—	—	£35
FOUR DOUBLES				
1830..	£4	£9	£50	£125
1830 Mule with obv. St Helena 1/2d	—	£850	—	—
1858..	£6	£12	£50	£135
1864 Single stalk	£2	£6	£20	£60
1864 3 stalks....................................	£2	£6	£25	£65
1868..	£3	£7	£22	£75
1874..	£2	£6	£22	£75
1885H..	£2	£6	£20	£45
1889H..	£2	£3	£15	£35
1893H..	£2	£3	£15	£35
1902H..	£2	£3	£10	£30
1903H..	£2	£3	£13	£30
1906H..	£2	£3	£10	£25
1908H..	£2	£3	£10	£25
1910H..	£2	£3	£10	£25
1911H..	£2	£3	£8	£25
1914H..	£2	£3	£13	£45
1918H..	£2	£3	£12	£35
1920H..	£2	£3	£10	£35
1945H..	£2	£3	£10	£35
1949H..	£2	£3	£12	£35
1956..	£1	£2	£8	£15
1966 Proof..	—	—	—	£20

DATE	F	VF	EF	UNC
TWO DOUBLES				
1858..	£6	£10	£50	£200
1868 Single stick	£6	£12	£55	£200
1868 3 stalks	£7	£15	£85	£225
1874..	£4	£10	£50	£150
1885H...	£3	£6	£20	£35
1889H...	£3	£5	£20	£35
1899H...	£3	£5	£25	£50
1902H...	£3	£5	£20	£35
1903H...	£3	£5	£20	£35
1906H...	£3	£5	£20	£35
1908H...	£3	£5	£20	£35
1911H...	£3	£5	£25	£45
1914H...	£3	£5	£25	£45
1917H...	£7	£20	£85	£225
1918H...	£3	£5	£15	£30
1920H...	£3	£5	£15	£30
1929H...	£2	£3	£12	£20

	F	VF	EF	UNC
ONE DOUBLE				
1830..	£3	£4	£22	£45
1868..	£4	£10	£35	£120
1868/30	£5	£7	£27	£85
1885H...	£2	£3	£8	£20
1889H...	£1	£2	£6	£20
1893H...	£1	£2	£6	£20
1899H...	£1	£2	£6	£20
1902..	£1	£2	£6	£20
1903H...	£1	£2	£6	£20
1911H...	£1	£2	£8	£20
1911 (new shield)	£1	£2	£6	£20
1914H	£1	£2	£8	£20
1929H...	£1	£2	£6	£20
1933H...	£1	£2	£6	£20
1938H...	£1	£2	£6	£20

DECIMAL COINAGE
Ordinary circulating coinage from 1986 onwards is usually available in uncirculated condition at a small premium above face value thus it is not listed here. The coins listed are cupro-nickel unless otherwise stated.

	UNC
ONE HUNDRED POUNDS	
1994 50th Anniversary of Normandy Landings. Gold Proof....................	£1500
1995 Anniversary of the Liberation. Gold Proof	£1500
FIFTY POUNDS	
1994 50th Anniversary of Normandy Landings. Gold Proof....................	£950
1995 Anniversary of the Liberation. Gold Proof	£950
1998 Queen Elizabeth and Queen Mother Gold Proof............................	£1000
1999 Queen Elizabeth and Queen Mother Gold	£900
2004 Anniversary of D-Day. Gold	£1100
2013 70th Anniversary of the Dambuster Raid. Silver Proof 10oz	£600
TWENTY-FIVE POUNDS	
1994 50th Anniversary of Normandy Landings. Gold	£400
1994 — Gold Proof...	£400
1995 Anniversary of the Liberation. Gold Proof	£400
1995 Queen Mothers 95th Birthday. Gold...	£400
1996 European Football Championships. Gold Proof.............................	£400
1997 Royal Golden Wedding. Gold Proof	£400
1998 Royal Air Force. Gold Proof..	£400
2000 Queen Mother 100th Birthday. Gold Proof.....................................	£400
2001 Queen Victoria centennial Gold Proof	£400
2001 Queen Victoria gold proof	£400
2001 HM the Queen's 75th Birthday. Gold Proof....................................	£425
2002 Princess Diana memorial. Gold Proof	£400
2002 Duke of Wellington. Gold Proof..	£400

DATE	UNC
2002 Golden Jubilee. Gold Proof	£400
2002 Queen Mother. Gold Proof	£400
2003 Golden Jubilee. Gold Proof	£400
2004 Anniversary of D-Day. Gold Proof	£400
2006 FIFA World Cup. Gold Proof	£400

TEN POUNDS

1994 50th Anniversary of Normandy Landings. Gold proof	£200
1995 Anniversary of the Liberation. Gold proof	£200
2000 Century of Monarchy. Silver proof	£150
2000 Guernsey Gold Proof 'Nugget'	£200
2001 19th Century Monarchy. Silver proof	£150
2002 18th Century Monarchy. Silver proof	£150
2004 Anniversary of D-Day. Silver proof	£195
2012 Diamond Jubilee. 5 oz Silver proof	£250
2013 Coronation Jubilee 5 oz Silver proof	£250

FIVE POUNDS

1995 Queen Mother's 95th birthday	£25
1995 — Silver proof	£55
1995 — Small size gold	£225
1996 HM the Queen's 70th birthday	£18
1996 — Silver proof	£55
1996 European Football Championships	£35
1996 — Silver proof	£55
1997 Royal Golden Wedding	£25
1997 — Silver proof	£55
1997 — Small size gold. BU	£175
1997 Castles of the British Isles—Castle Cornet, Guernsey	£18
1997 — Silver proof	£65
1997 Castles of the British Isles—Caernarfon Castle. Silver proof	£75
1997 Castles of the British Isles—Leeds Castle. Silver proof	£75
1998 Royal Air Force.	£15
1998 Royal Air Force. Silver proof	£70
1999 Millennium. Brass	£25
1999 — Silver proof	£55
1999 Wedding of HRH Prince Edward and Sophie Rhys-Jones	£25
1999 — Silver proof	£55
1999 Queen Mother	£25
1999 — Silver proof	£80
1999 Winston Churchill	£15
1999 — Gold	£1000
2000 Queen Mother's 100th Birthday	£10
2000 — Silver proof	£85
2000 — Small size gold. Proof	£165
2000 Centuries of the British Monarchy	£45
2000 — Silver proof	£85
2000 — Small size gold. Proof	£180
2001 The Reign of Queen Victoria	£20
2001 — Gold proof	£360
2001 — Proof	£60
2001 — Silver proof	£60
2001 HM the Queen's 75th Birthday	£15
2001 — Silver proof	£60
2001 — Small size gold. Proof	£180
2001 19th Century Monarchy	£20
2001 — Silver proof	£60
2001 — Small size gold. Proof	£180
2002 Golden Jubilee (two types)	£15
2002 — Silver proof	£65
2002 Princess Diana Memorial	£15
2002 — Proof	£60
2002 — Gold proof	£1000
2002 Century of Monarchy	£15
2002 — Silver proof	£60
2002 — Small size gold. Proof	£180
2002 Queen Mother Memoriam	£20
2002 — Proof	£25

DATE	UNC
2002 — Silver proof	£65
2002 — Small size gold proof	£175
2002 — Large size gold proof	£1000
2003 Duke of Wellington	£15
2003 — Silver proof	£50
2003 — Small size gold proof	£160
2003 — Large size gold proof	£1000
2003 Prince William	£20
2003 — Silver proof	£60
2003 — Gold proof	£1000
2003 Golden Hind	£20
2003 17th Century Monarchy	£25
2003 History of the Royal Navy, Nelson	£20
2003 — Nelson with coloured flag. Proof	£30
2004 — Invincible. Silver proof	£50
2004 16th Century monarchs	£15
2004 History of the Railways, Mallard	£12
2004 — City of Truro	£15
2004 — The Boat Train	£12
2004 — The Train Spotter	£15
2004 History of the Royal Navy, Henry VIII	£15
2004 — Invincible	£15
2004 Anniversary of D-Day	£12
2004 — Silver proof	£50
2004 — Gold proof	£1000
2004 Anniversary of the Crimean War. Plain	£12
2004 — with colour	£15
2004 — Silver proof	£55
2004 — Gold proof with colour	£1250
2005 200th Anniversary of the Battle of Trafalgar	£25
2005 60th Anniversary of the Liberation of the Channel Islands	£25
2005 End of World War II. Silver proof	£55
2005 — Gold proof	£1250
2005 Anniversary of Liberation. Gold proof	£1250
2006 Royal 80th Birthday. Silver proof	£55
2006 FIFA World Cup. Silver proof	£55
2006 Great Britons—Sir Winston Churchill Silver. Issued as part of set.	£60
2006 80th Birthday of Her Majesty the Queen	£25
2007 History of the Royal Navy—Henry VIII, The Golden Hind (2 coins)	£65
2007 Royal Diamond Wedding	£25
2008 90th Anniversary of the RAF (10 different designs in silver proof) ea.	£35
2009 British warships (6 different designs in silver proof) .... ea.	£35
2009 Anniversary of Apollo Moon landings. Cu-ni	£5
2009 — Silver proof	£35
2010 Charles II Unite. Gold proof	£1500
2010 Florence Nightingale. Gold proof	£1500
2011 350th Anniversary of the Crown Jewels. Silver proof	£95
2011 90th Anniversary of the British Legion (gold-plated copper)	£45
2011 — Silver proof	£95
2011 40th Anniversary of decimalisation, proof	£20
2011 Anniversary of the sinking of the *Titanic*	£20
2011 — Silver proof	£55
2011 30th Birthday of Duke of Cambridge	£20
2011 — Silver proof	£55
2011 Wedding of Prince William and Kate Middleton	£25
2011 — Silver proof	£55
2011 400th Anniversary of the King James Bible	£25
2012 Diamond Jubilee £5	£25
2012 — Gold proof	£1500
2012 The Tribute to the British Army. Gold Proof	£2000
2013 70th Anniversary of the Dambuster Raid.	£20
2013 — Silver Proof	£65
2013 — Gold Proof	£2000
2013 Coronation Jubilee	£25
2013 — Silver proof	£55
2013 — Gold Proof	£2000
2013 200th Guinea Anniv.	£25
2013 — Silver Proof	£55
2013 — Gold Proof	£2000

DATE	F	VF	EF	UNC
2014 Centenary of the First World War. Silver Proof				£85
2014 — 5oz Silver Proof				£450
2014 — Gold Proof				£2500

TWO POUNDS

	F	VF	EF	UNC
1985 40th anniversary of Liberation				£10
1985 — Proof				£30
1985 — Silver proof				£55
1986 Commonwealth Games, in plastic case				£12
1986 — in special folder				£12
1986 — .500 Silver				£45
1986 — .925 Silver proof				£55
1987 900th Anniv. of death of William the Conqueror, in folder				£15
1987 — Silver proof				£55
1987 — Gold proof				£1300
1988 William II, in presentation folder				£15
1988 — Silver proof				£55
1989 Henry I, in presentation folder				£15
1989 — Silver proof				£55
1989 Royal Visit				£15
1989 — Silver proof				£55
1990 Queen Mother's 90th birthday				£15
1990 — Silver proof				£55
1991 Henry II, in presentation folder				£15
1991 — Silver proof				£55
1993 40th Anniversary of the Coronation				£15
1993 — Silver proof				£60
1994 Anniversary of the Normandy Landings				£15
1994 — Silver proof				£55
1995 50th Anniversary of Liberation				£154
1995 — Silver proof				£55
1995 — Silver Piedfort proof				£100
1997 Conserving Nature i				£12
1997 — Silver proof				£55
1997 Bimetallic Latent image				£8
1997 — Proof				£10
1998 Conserving Nature ii				£10
1998 Bimetallic Latent image				£6
2003 —				£6
2006 —				£8
2011 Prince Philip's 90th Birthday (conjoined portraits)				£6
2011 — Silver proof				£50

ONE POUND

	F	VF	EF	UNC
1981				£10
1981 Gold proof				£145
1981 Gold piedfort				£345
1983 New specification, new reverse				£10
1985 New design (in folder)				£10
1995 Queen Mother's 95th Birthday. Silver proof				£50
1996 Queen's 70th Birthday. Silver proof				£55
1997 Royal Golden Wedding. Silver BU				£20
1997 — Silver proof				£55
1997 Castles of the British Isles—Tower of London. Silver proof only				£35
1998 Royal Air Force. Silver proof				£45
1999 Wedding of Prince Edward. Silver proof				£55
1999 Queen Mother. Silver proof				£55
1999 Winston Churchill. Silver proof				£55
2000 Millennium. Silver proof (gold plated)				£65
2000 Queen Mother's 100th Birthday. Silver proof				£45
2001				£2
2001 HM the Queen's 75th Birthday. Silver proof				£45
2002 William of Normandy. Silver				£20
2003				£2
2006				£2

FIFTY PENCE

	F	VF	EF	UNC
1969				£4
1970				£6
1971 Proof				£9

DATE	UNC
1981...	£4
1982...	£4
1985 New design...	£4
2000 60th Anniversary of the Battle of Britain.	£4
2000 — Silver proof...	£55
2000 — Silver piedfort...	£55
2000 — Gold proof..	£365
2003...	£2
2006...	£2
2008...	£2
2012 The Diamond Jubilee (coloured portrait)	£10
2013 The RAF 617 Squadron Gold-Plated Coin	£25
2013 50th Anniversary of the Flying Scotsman's retirement in 1963......	£25
2014 New Queen Elizabeth II	£45

TWENTY-FIVE PENCE

1972 Royal Silver Wedding	£12
1972 — Silver proof	£45
1977 Royal Silver Jubilee	£10
1977 — Silver proof	£45
1978 Royal Visit	£10
1978 — Silver proof	£45
1980 Queen Mother's 80th birthday	£10
1980 — Silver proof	£45
1981 Royal Wedding	£10
1981 — Silver proof...	£45

JERSEY

DATE	F	VF	EF	UNC

FIVE SHILLINGS

1966	—	£3	£7	£15
1966 Proof	—	£3	£9	£25

ONE QUARTER OF A SHILLING

1957	—	£2	£5	£10
1960 Proof	—	—	£5	£15
1964	—	—	£4	£10
1966	—	—	£4	£10

ONE TWELFTH OF A SHILLING

1877H	£2	£3	£18	£60
1877H Proof in nickel	—	—	—	£1275
1877 Proof only	—	—	—	£475
1877 Proof in nickel	—	—	—	£1275
1881	£3	£3	£15	£60
1888	£2	£3	£15	£50
1894	£2	£3	£20	£50
1909	£2	£3	£15	£35
1911	£2	£3	£10	£30
1913	£2	£3	£10	£30
1923 Spade shield	£2	£3	£10	£30
1923 Square shield	£2	£3	£10	£30
1926	£2	£3	£12	£45
1931	£2	£3	£8	£15
1933	£2	£3	£8	£15
1935	£2	£3	£8	£15
1937	£2	£3	£8	£15
1946	£2	£3	£8	£15
1947	—	£3	£8	£15
"1945" GVI	—	—	£2	£10
"1945" QE2	—	—	£2	£8
1957	—	—	£2	£7
1960 1660–1960 300th anniversary	—	—	£2	£7
1960 Mule	—	—	—	£150
1964	—	£2	£3	£10
1966 "1066–1966"	—	—	£1	£8

ONE THIRTEENTH OF A SHILLING

1841	£4	£8	£40	£200
1844	£4	£9	£40	£200
1851	£5	£12	£60	£250
1858	£4	£9	£45	£200
1861	£5	£13	£60	£175
1865 Proof only	—	—	—	£750
1866 with LCW	£2	£5	£95	£150
1866 without LCW Proof only	—	—	—	£400
1870	£4	£8	£40	£125
1871	£4	£8	£42	£125

ONE TWENTY-FOURTH OF A SHILLING

1877H	£3	£4	£15	£60
1877 Proof only	—	—	—	£300
1888	£3	£4	£15	£45
1894	£3	£4	£15	£45
1909	£3	£4	£15	£45
1911	£2	£3	£10	£45

DATE	F	VF	EF	UNC
1913..	£2	£3	£10	£45
1923 Spade shield..	£2	£3	£10	£35
1923 Square shield.......................................	£2	£3	£8	£35
1926..	£2	£3	£10	£25
1931..	£2	£3	£10	£25
1933..	£2	£3	£10	£25
1935..	£2	£3	£10	£25
1937..	£1	£2	£6	£20
1946..	£1	£2	£6	£20
1947..	£1	£2	£6	£20

ONE TWENTY-SIXTH OF A SHILLING

	F	VF	EF	UNC
1841..	£4	£7	£30	£100
1844..	£4	£7	£25	£100
1851..	£3	£6	£25	£100
1858..	£4	£11	£50	£200
1861..	£3	£6	£25	£65
1866..	£3	£6	£30	£85
1870..	£3	£6	£20	£55
1871..	£3	£6	£20	£55

ONE FORTY-EIGHTH OF A SHILLING

	F	VF	EF	UNC
1877H..	£6	£12	£60	£150
1877 Proof only	—	—	—	£450

ONE FIFTY-SECOND OF A SHILLING

	F	VF	EF	UNC
1841..	£9	£25	£60	£200
1861 Proof only	—	—	—	£650

DECIMAL COINAGE

**Ordinary circulating coinage from 1986 onwards is usually available in
uncirculated condition at a small premium above face value thus it is not
listed here.**

ONE HUNDRED POUNDS

1990 50th Anniversary of the Battle of Britain. Gold Proof.	£1000
1995 50th Anniversary of Liberation. Gold proof	£1000

FIFTY POUNDS

1972 Silver Wedding. Gold proof	£850
1990 50th Anniversary of the Battle of Britain. Gold proof	£850
1995 50th Anniversary of Liberation. Gold proof	£850
2003 Golden Jubilee. Silver Proof (100mm)..	£650
2013 RMS Titanic Centenary. 10oz Silver Proof	£600

TWENTY-FIVE POUNDS

1972 25th Royal Wedding anniversary. Gold	£300
1972 — Gold proof...	£375
1990 50th Anniversary of Battle of Britain. Gold proof	£350
1995 50th Anniversary of Liberation. Gold proof	£350
2002 Princess Diana memorial. Gold proof..	£350
2002 Queen Mother. Gold proof...	£350
2002 Golden Jubilee. Gold proof	£350
2002 Duke of Wellington. Gold proof	£350
2003 Golden Jubilee. Gold proof	£350
2003 History of the Royal Navy. Naval Commanders	£350
2003 — Francis Drake..	£350
2003 — Sovereign of the Seas...	£350
2004 60th Anniversary of D-Day. Gold proof	£350
2004 Charge of the Light Brigade. Gold proof	£350
2004 HMS Victory. Gold proof..	£350
2004 John Fisher 1841–1920 Gold proof......................................	£350
2004 The Coronation Scot. Gold proof	£350
2004 The Flying Scotsman. Gold proof...	£350
2004 Golden Arrow. Gold proof	£350

DATE	UNC
2004 Rocket and Evening Star. Gold proof	£350
2005 Andrew Cunningham. Gold proof	£350
2005 HMS Conqueror. Gold Proof	£350
2005 200th Anniversary of Nelson. Gold proof	£350
2009 500th Anniversary of Accession. Gold proof	£350

TWENTY POUNDS

1972 Royal Wedding. The Ormer. Gold	£300
1972 — Gold proof	£300

TEN POUNDS

1972 25th Royal Wedding anniversary. Gold	£75
1972 — Gold proof	£180
1990 50th Anniversary of the Battle of Britain. Gold proof	£180
1995 50th Anniversary of Liberation. Gold proof	£140
2003 Coronation Anniversary. Gold/silver proof	£50
2004 Crimea. Silver proof	£20
2205 Trafalgar. Silver proof	£20
2005 — Silver/gold proof	£110
2005 End of World War II. Silver proof	£25
2007 Diamond Wedding. Platinum proof	£280
2008 History of RAF. Silver proof	£25
2008 — Silver/Gold proof	£110
2011 Royal Wedding of HRH Prince William & Catherine Middleton, silver (65mm)	£395
2012 Poppy. 5oz Silver Proof	£350
2013 Flying Scotsman. 5oz Silver Proof	£350

(Enlarged)

(Reduced)

FIVE POUNDS

1972 Gold proof	£65
1990 50th Anniversary of the Battle of Britain. Silver Proof (5 ounces)	£180
1997 Royal Golden Wedding	£10
1997 — Silver proof	£25
2000 Millennium. Silver proof	£35
2002 Princess Diana memorial	£12
2002 — Silver proof	£30
2002 — Gold proof	£800
2002 Royal Golden Jubilee	£25
2003 Golden Jubilee	£20
2003 — Silver proof	£55
2003 — Gold proof	£1000
2003 Prince William 21st Birthday	£15
2003 — Silver Proof	£55
2003 —Gold proof	£1000
2003 Naval Commanders	£15
2003 — Silver proof	£55
2003 — Gold proof	£1000
2003 Francis Drake	£15
2003 — Silver proof	£55
2003 — Gold proof	£1000
2003 Sovereign of the Seas	£15
2003 — Silver proof	£55
2003 — Gold proof	£1000
2004 60th Anniversary of 'D' Day	£15
2004 — Silver proof	£55
2004 — Gold proof	£1000
2004 Charge of the Light Brigade	£15
2004 — Silver proof	£50
2004 — Gold proof	£1000
2004 HMS Victory	£15
2004 — Silver proof	£55
2004 — Gold proof	£1000
2004 John Fisher 1841–1920	£15
2004 — Silver proof	£55

(Enlarged)

DATE UNC

2004 —Gold proof.. £1000
2004 The Coronation Scot £15
2004 — Silver proof... £55
2004 — Gold proof.. £1000
2004 The Flying Scotsman.. £15
2004 — Silver proof... £55
2004 — Silver/Gold proof... £500
2004 — Gold proof £1000
2004 Golden Arrow £15
2004 — Silver proof... £55
2004 — Gold proof.. £1000
2005 Driver and Fireman £15
2005 — Silver proof... £45
2005 — Gold proof.. £1000
2005 Box Tunnel and King Loco £15
2005 — Silver Proof £45
2005 — Gold Proof.. £1000
2005 Rocket and Evening Star... £15
2005 — Silver proof... £45
2005 — Silver/Gold proof... £500
2005 — Gold proof £1000
2005 200th Anniversary of the Battle of Trafalgar £30
2005 Andrew Cunningham... £20
2005 — Silver proof... £65
2005 — Gold proof.. £1000
2005 HMS Conqueror £15
2005 — Silver proof... £20
2005 — Gold proof.. £1000
2005 Battle of Trafalgar £15
2005 — Silver proof... £45
2005 — Gold proof (9mm)... £500
2005 — Gold proof (38.6mm)... £1000
2005 Returning Evacuees £15
2005 — Silver proof... £45
2005 — Gold proof... £1000
2005 Searchlights and Big Ben.. £15
2005 — Silver proof... £45
2005 — Gold proof.. £1000
2006 60th Anniversary of the Liberation of the Channel Islands............... £30
2006 80th Birthday of Her Majesty the Queen (3-coin set)...................... —
2006 Sir Winston Churchill £15
2006 — Silver proof... £45
2006 — Gold proof.. £1000
2006 Charles Darwin £15
2006 — Silver proof... £45
2006 — Gold proof.. £1000
2006 Bobby Moore... £20
2006 — Silver Proof £55
2006 — Gold Proof.. £1150
2006 Florence Nightingale.. £20
2006 — Silver proof... £55
2006 — Gold proof.. £1000
2006 Queen Mother £20
2006 — Silver proof... £55
2006 — Gold proof.. £1000
2006 Henry VIII £15
2006 — Silver proof... £55
2006 — Gold proof.. £1000
2006 Princess Diana.. £20
2006 — Silver Proof £60
2006 — Gold Proof.. £1250
2006 Sir Christopher Wren £15
2006 — Silver proof... £55
2006 — Gold proof.. £1000
2006 HM the Queen's 80th Birthday—Streamers........................... £15
2006 — Silver proof... £60

DATE	UNC
2006 — Gold proof	£1000
2006 HM the Queen's 80th Birthday—Trooping colour	£25
2006 — Proof	£60
2006 — Silver proof	£1000
2006 — Silver/Gold proof	£650
2006 — Gold proof	£1150
2006 HM the Queen's 80th Birthday—Wembley Stadium	£20
2006 — Silver proof	£55
2006 — Gold proof	£1150
2006 Guy Gibson	£15
2006 — Silver proof	£55
2006 — Gold proof	£1150
2006 Eric James Nicholson	£15
2006 — Silver proof	£55
2006 — Gold proof	£1150
2006 Hook, Chard and Bromhead	£15
2006 — Silver proof	£55
2006 — Gold proof	£1150
2006 1st Lancs Fusiliers	£15
2006 — Silver proof	£55
2006 — Gold proof	£1150
2006 Noel Chavasse	£15
2006 — Silver proof	£55
2006 — Gold proof	£1150
2006 David Mackay	£15
2006 — Silver proof	£55
2006 — Gold proof	£1150
2006 Coronation Scot. Silver proof	£60
2006 Flying Scotsman. Silver proof	£60
2006 Fireman and Driver. Silver proof	£60
2006 Box Tunnel. Silver proof	£60
2007 Diamond Wedding balcony scene waving	£15
2007 — Silver proof	£60
2007 Diamond Wedding cake	£15
2007 — Silver proof	£60
2007 Diamond Wedding balcony scene waving	£15
2007 —Silver proof	£60
2007 Diamond Wedding HM the Queen and Prince Philip	£20
2007 — Silver proof	£60
2007 Diamond Wedding arrival at Abbey	£20
2007 — Silver proof	£55
2007 — Gold proof	£1150
2008 George & Dragon	£20
2008 Dambusters, Wallis, Chadwick, Gibson	£15
2008 — Silver/Copper proof	£30
2008 — Silver proof	£55
2008 Frank Whittle	£15
2008 — Silver proof	£55
2008 — Gold proof	£1150
2008 R. J. Mitchell	£15
2008 — Silver proof	£55
2008 — Gold proof	£1150
2008 Maj. Gen. Sir Hugh Trenchard	£15
2008 — Silver proof	£55
2008 — Gold proof	£1150
2008 Bomber Command	£15
2008 — Silver proof	£55
2008 — Gold proof	£1150
2008 Coastal Command	£20
2008 — Silver proof	£60
2008 — Gold proof	£1200
2008 Fighter Command	£20
2008 — Silver proof	£60
2008 — Gold proof	£1200
2008 Battle of Britain	£20
2008 — Silver proof	£60
2008 — Gold proof	£1200

DATE	UNC
2008 RBL Poppy	£20
2008 — Silver proof	£60
2008 — Gold proof	£1200
2008 Flying Legends	£15
2008 — Silver proof	£55
2008 — Gold proof	£1150
2009 George & Dragon. Silver proof	£50
2009 Battle of Agincourt. Silver proof	£55
2009 Battle of the Somme. Silver proof	£55
2009 Capt. Cook and *Endeavour*. Silver proof	£55
2009 500th Anniversary of Accession of Henry VIII. Silver proof	£55
2011 Landmark birthdays of HM the Queen & Prince Philip	£15
2011 90th Anniversary of the British Legion (poppy-shaped)	£40
2011 — Silver proof	£95
2011 — 5oz silver	£500
2011 — Gold proof	£2500
2011 30th Birthday of the Duke of Cambridge. Silver proof	£50
2011 Wedding of Prince William and Kate Middleton. Silver proof	£50
2011 —Gold proof	£1500
2011 Spirit of the Nation (4 coins). Silver proof, each	£50
2012 HM the Queen's Diamond Jubilee. Gold proof	£2000
2012 Poppy. Silver Proof	£65
2012 — Gold Proof	£2000
2012 RMS *Titanic* Centenary	£15
2012 — Silver Proof	£65
2013 Coronation Jubilee. Silver proof	£65
2013 — Gold Proof	£2000
2013 The Flying Scotsman. Silver proof	£65
2013 350th Guinea Anniversary. Silver proof	£55
2013 — Gold Proof	£2000
2013 Poppy Coin. Silver proof	£95
2014 70th Anniversary of D-Day. Silver proof	£85
2014 — Gold Proof	£2500
2014 The Red Arrows 50th Display Season. Silver proof	£95
2014 William Shakespeare—450th Birthday. Silver proof	£80

TWO POUNDS FIFTY PENCE

1972 Royal Silver Wedding	£25
1972 — Silver proof	£35

TWO POUNDS

(note all modern Proof coins have frosted relief)

1972 Royal Silver Wedding. Silver	£25
1972 — Silver proof	£35
1981 Royal Wedding, nickel silver (crown size)	£5
1981 — in presentation pack	£7
1981 — Silver proof	£20
1981 — Gold proof	£450
1985 40th Anniversary of Liberation (crown size)	£5
1985 — in presentation pack	£12
1985 — Silver proof	£20
1985 — Gold proof	£1150
1986 Commonwealth Games	£6
1986 — in presentation case	£8
1986 — .500 silver	£12
1986 — .925 silver proof	£20
1987 World Wildlife Fund 25th Anniversary	£80
1987 — Silver proof	£25
1989 Royal Visit	£15
1989 — Silver proof	£25
1990 Queen Mother's 90th Birthday	£15
1990 — Silver proof	£25
1990 — Gold proof	£600

DATE	UNC
1990 50th Anniversary of the Battle of Britain, silver proof	£30
1993 40th Anniversary of the Coronation	£15
1993 — Silver proof	£20
1993 — Gold proof	£600
1995 50th Anniversary of Liberation	£15
1995 — Silver Proof	£25
1995 — — Piedfort	£75
1996 HM the Queen's 70th Birthday	£15
1996 — Silver proof	£25
1997 Bi-metal	£5
1997 — Silver proof	£50
1997 — new portrait	£5
1998 —	£5
2003 —	£5
2005 —	£5
2006 —	£5
2007 —	£5
2011 Prince Philip's 90th Birthday	£12
2012 HM the Queen's Diamond Jubilee. Gold proof	£1000

ONE POUND

1972 Royal Silver Wedding	£15
1972 — Silver proof	£20
1981	£15
1981 Silver proof	£15
1981 Gold proof	£320
1983 New designs and specifications on presentation card (St Helier)	£5
1983 — Silver proof	£18
1983 — Gold proof	£395
1984 Presentation wallet (St Saviour)	£21
1984 — Silver proof	£45
1984 — Gold proof	£450
1984 Presentation wallet (St Brelade)	£20
1984 — Silver proof	£45
1984 — Gold proof	£495
1985 Presentation wallet (St Clement)	£25
1985 — Silver proof	£45
1985 — Gold proof	£490
1985 Presentation wallet (St Lawrence)	£25
1985 — Silver proof	£40
1985 — Gold proof	£490
1986 Presentation wallet (St Peter)	£15
1986 — Silver proof	£35
1986 — Gold proof	£495
1986 Presentation wallet (Grouville)	£18
1986 — Silver proof	£40
1986 — Gold proof	£490
1987 Presentation wallet (St Martin)	£18
1987 — Silver proof	£40
1987 — Gold proof	£490
1987 Presentation wallet (St Ouen)	£12
1987 — Silver proof	£40
1987 — Gold proof	£495
1988 Presentation wallet (Trinity)	£15
1988 — Silver proof	£40
1988 — Gold proof	£495
1988 Presentation wallet (St John)	£15
1988 — Silver proof	£40
1988 — Gold proof	£490
1989 Presentation wallet (St Mary)	£15
1989 — Silver proof	£40
1989 — Gold proof	£490

DATE		UNC

1991 Ship Building in Jersey Series

1991 "Tickler". Nickel-brass		£5
1991 "Tickler". Silver proof		£25
1991 — Gold proof Piedfort		£495
1991 "Percy Douglas". Nickel-brass		£5
1991 "Percy Douglas". Silver proof		£25
1991 — Gold proof Piedfort		£450
1992 "The Hebe". Nickel-brass		£5
1992 "The Hebe". Silver proof		£25
1992 — Gold proof Piedfort		£490
1992 "Coat of Arms". Nickel-brass		£5
1992 "Coat of Arms". Silver proof		£25
1992 — Gold proof Piedfort		£450
1993 "The Gemini". Nickel-brass		£5
1993 "The Gemini". Silver proof		£25
1993 — Gold proof Piedfort		£490
1993 "The Century". Nickel-brass		£5
1993 "The Century". Silver proof		£25
1993 — Gold proof Piedfort		£495
1994 "Resolute". Nickel-brass		£5
1994 "Resolute". Silver proof		£25
1994 — Gold proof Piedfort		£495
1997 — Nickel-brass		£5
1998 — — Nickel-brass		£5
2003 — — Nickel-brass		£5
2005 — — Nickel-brass		£5
2006 — — Nickel-brass		£5
2007 Diana Commem. Gold proof		£280
2012 Diamond Jubilee. Gold Proof £1		£400
2012 Anniversary of the *Titanic*		—
2013 Coronation Jubilee. Gold Proof		£600

FIFTY PENCE

1969		£10
1972 Royal Silver Wedding. Silver		£12
1972 — Silver proof		£12
1980 —		£1
1980 Arms		£2
1980 — Proof		£5
1981 —		£1
1981 —		£5
1981 — Proof		£5
1983 Grosnez Castle		£10
1983 — Silver proof		£12
1984 —		£2
1985 40th Anniversary of Liberation		£3
1986		£5
1986		£5
1987		£5
1988		£5
1989		£5
1990		£5
1992		£5
1994		£5
1997		£5
1997 Smaller size		£4
1998 —		£3
2003		£3
2003 Coronation Anniversary (4 types)		£4
2003 — 4 types. Silver proof		£15
2005		£4
2006		£4

DATE	UNC
2009	£5
2011 Diamond Jubilee (full colour reverse, gold-plated)...........................	£15
2013 Coronation Jubilee	£25

TWENTY-FIVE PENCE

1977 Royal Jubilee...	£3
1977 — Silver proof...	£20

TWENTY PENCE

1982 Corbiere Lighthouse (cased)	£8
1982 — Silver proof piedfort	£35
1983 — Obv. with date, rev. no date on rocks	£5
1983 — — Silver proof...	£15
1984 —	£1
1986 —	£1
1987 —	£1
1989 —	£1
1992 —	£1
1994 —	£1
1996 —	£1
1997 —	£1
1998 —	£1
2002 —	£1
2003 —	£1
2005 —	£1
2006 —	£1
2007 —	£1
2009 —	£1

SOVEREIGN—Gold sovereign size

1999 The Millennium. King William on Throne	£250
1999 — Gold proof..	£300

TEN PENCE

1968 Arms..	£1
1975 Arms..	£1
1979 (dated 1975 on thick flan)...	£2
1980 —	£1
1980 — Proof	£5
1981 -	£1
1981 — Proof	£5
1983 L'Hermitage	£1
1983 — Silver proof..	£5
1984 —	£1
1985 —	£1
1986 —	£1
1987 —	£1
1988 —	£1
1989 —	£1
1990 —	£1
1992 —	£1
1997 —	£1
2002 —	£1
2003 —	£1
2005 —	£1
2006 —	£1
2007 —	£1

FIVE PENCE

1968 Arms..	£1
1980 —	£1
1981 —	£1

DATE	UNC
1981 — Proof	£2
1983 Seymour Towers	£1
1983 — Silver proof	£5
1984 —	£1
1985 —	£1
1986 —	£1
1987 —	£2
1988 —	£1
1990 —	£1
1991 —	£1
1992 —	£5
1993 —	£1
1997 —	£4
1998 —	£1
2002 —	£1
2003 —	£1
2005 —	£5
2006 —	£1
2008 —	£1

Other denominations are generally available at face value or a small premium above.

ALDERNEY

DATE	UNC

ONE THOUSAND POUNDS
2003 Concorde. Gold proof.. —
2004 D-Day Anniversary. Gold proof.. —
2011 Royal Wedding of Prince William and Catherine Middleton.............. —

ONE HUNDRED POUNDS
1994 50th Anniversary of D-Day Landings. Gold proof £285
2003 Prince Wiliam. Gold proof (100mm) .... —
2005 Trafalgar Anniversary. Gold proof (100mm).................................... —

FIFTY POUNDS
1994 50th Anniversary of D–Day Landing. Gold proof............................. £500
2003 Anniversay of Coronation (4 types). Silver proof ea. (100mm) £500
2003 Prince William. Silver proof (100mm).. £500
2004 Anniversary of D-Day. Silver proof (100mm) £500
2005 200th Anniversary of the Battle of Trafalgar. Silver proof (100mm) ... £500

TWENTY FIVE POUNDS
1993 40th Anniversary of Coronation. Gold proof.................................... £200
1994 50th Anniversary of D-Day Landings. Gold proof £200
1997 Royal Golden Wedding. Gold proof £295
1997 — Silver proof.. £40
1999 Winston Churchill. Gold proof £350
2000 Queen Mother. Gold proof.. £325
2000 60th Anniversary of the Battle of Britain. Gold proof £275
2001 Royal Birthday. Gold proof £300
2002 Golden Jubilee. Gold proof £295
2002 Princess Diana. Gold proof £295
2002 Duke of Wellington. Gold proof £300
2003 Prince William. Gold proof.. £300
2003 HMS Mary Rose. Gold proof £300
2004 D-Day Anniversary. Gold proof... £395
2004 The Rocket. Gold proof... £295
2004 Merchant Navy Class Locomotive. Gold proof £295
2005 Battle of Saints Passage. Gold proof £295
2006 World Cup 2006 (4 Coins). Gold ea... £350

TEN POUNDS
1994 50th Anniversary of D–Day Landing. Gold proof............................. £150
2003 Concorde. Silver proof (65mm) £280
2005 60th Anniversary of the Liberation of the Channel Islands (65mm)... £250
2007 80th Birthday of Her Majesty the Queen (65mm)............................ £180
2008 Concorde. Silver proof £180
2008 90th Anniversary of the end of WWI. Silver Proof £180
2009 50th Anniversary of the Mini—Silver with colour............................. £180
2012 Prince William's 30th Birthday .... —

FIVE POUNDS
1995 Queen Mother £15
1995 — Silver proof... £50
1995 — Silver piedfort... £155
1995 — Gold proof... £900
1996 HM the Queen's 70th Birthday £20
1996 — Silver proof... £60
1996 — Silver piedfort... £150
1996 — Gold proof... £1000
1999 Eclipse of the Sun £25
1999 — Silver proof with colour centre £55
1999 Winston Churchill. Gold proof £1000
2000 60th Anniversary of the Battle of Britain... £25
2000 — Silver proof... £55

DATE	UNC
2000 Queen Mother. 100th Birthday. Silver proof	£50
2000 Millennium. Silver proof	£35
2001 HM Queen's 75th Birthday.	£15
2001 — Silver proof	£45
2002 Golden Jubilee. Silver proof	£50
2002 50 Years of Reign.	£15
2002 —Silver proof	£50
2002 Diana memorial	£15
2002 — Silver proof	£45
2002 — Gold proof	£900
2002 Duke of Wellington	£20
2002 — Silver proof	£50
2002 — Gold proof	£900
2003 Prince William	£20
2003 — Silver proof	£50
2003 — Gold proof	£900
2003 Mary Rose	£20
2003 — Silver proof	£120
2003 Alfred the Great. Silver proof	£150
2003 —Gold proof	£1000
2003 Last Flight of Concorde	£25
2003 — Silver proof	£150
2003 — Gold proof	£1000
2004 Anniversary of D-Day	£20
2004 — Silver proof	£75
2004 — Gold proof	£1000
2004 Florence Nightingale	320
2004 — Silver proof	£45
2004 150th Anniversary of the Crimean War	£20
2004 — Silver proof	£45
2004 — Gold proof	£1000
2004 The Rocket	£20
2004 — Silver proof	£45
2004 — Gold proof	£900
2004 Royal Scot	£20
2004 — Silver proof	£45
2004 Merchant Navy Class Locomotive	£20
2004 — Silver proof	£45
2005 End of WWII. Silver proof	£45
2005 — Gold proof	£900
2005 200th Anniversary of the Battle of Trafalgar	£16
2005 — Silver proof	£50
2005 History of the Royal Navy. John Woodward. Silver proof	£30
2005 Anniversary of Liberation. Gold proof	£1000
2005 Anniversary of the Battle of Saints Passage	£15
2005 — Silver proof	£45
2005 HMS Revenge 1591	£15
2005 — Silver proof	£45
2006 80th Birthday of Her Majesty the Queen (3-coin set) ea	£20
2006 Gold plated portraits of Her Majesty the Queen	—
2006 80th Birthday of Her Majesty the Queen (3-coin set) ea	£16
2007 History of the Royal Navy—*Mary Rose* (2 coins) ea	£16
2007 150th Anniversary of the Victoria Cross (18 coin set). Silver proof	£250
2007 Monarchs of England (12 coin set). Gold plated	£150
2008 90th Anniversary of the end of WWI (3 coins). Gold proof	£2500
2008 Classic British Motorcars (18 coin set). Silver proof.	£250
2008 Concorde. Gold proof	£1000
2009 50th Anniversary of the Mini (4 coins). Silver proof ea.	£50
2011 Royal Engagement gold proof	£1000
2011 — Gold plated silver proof	£150
2011 — Silver proof	£55
2011 — Cupro Nickel	£15
2011 John Lennon Silver proof	£55
2011 Battle of Britain 70th Anniversary silver proof	£55
2012 RMS *Titanic*	£15

DATE	UNC
2012 Remembrance Day (Re-issued 2013)..	£25
2014 70th Anniversary of D-Day	£15
2014 — Silver proof..	£25
2014 — Gold proof..	£1000
2014 Destiny to Dynasty. Silver proof	£25
2014 300th Anniversary of the Coronation of King George I.....................	£20
2014 — Silver proof..	£25
2014 — Gold proof..	£1000
2014 Centenary of the birth of poet Dylan Thomas	£15
2014 — Silver proof..	£45
2014 — Gold proof..	£1000
2015 Churchill Quotations (4-coin set)	£40
2015 — Silver proof (4-coin)...	£250
2015 70th Anniversary of VE Day Platinum proof Piedfort.....................	—
2015 150th Anniversary of the Salvation Army	£10
2015 — Silver proof..	£45

TWO POUNDS

1989 Royal Visit	£12
1989 — Silver proof..	£25
1989 — Silver piedfort...	£45
1989 — Gold proof..	£1000
1990 Queen Mother's 90th Birthday	£12
1990 — Silver proof..	£25
1990 — Silver piedfort...	£45
1990 — Gold proof..	£1000
1992 40th Anniversary of Accession...	£15
1992 — Silver proof..	£35
1992 — Silver piedfort...	£50
1992 — Gold proof..	£1000
1993 40th Anniversary of Coronation..	£15
1993 — Silver proof..	£35
1993 — Silver piedfort...	£50
1994 50th Anniversary of D-Day Landings...	£15
1994 — Silver proof..	£35
1994 — Silver piedfort...	£50
1995 50th Anniversary of Return of Islanders	£15
1995 — Silver proof..	£35
1995 — Silver piedfort...	£50
1995 — Gold proof	£1000
1997 WWF Puffin..	£18
1997 — Silver proof..	£35
1997 Royal Golden Wedding..	£20
1997 — Silver proof..	£50
1999 Eclipse of the Sun. Silver..	£20
1999 — Silver proof..	£50
1999 — Gold proof..	£1250
2000 Millennium. Silver proof...	£50

ONE POUND

1993 40th Anniversary of Coronation Silver proof	£50
1995 50th Anniversary of VE Day Silver proof......................................	£45
1995 — Gold proof..	£500
2008 Concorde. Gold proof...	£275
2009 50th Anniversary of the Mini. Gold proof.....................................	£375

IRELAND

As in the English hammered section (q.v.) the prices given here are for the most common coins in the series. For a more specialised listing the reader is referred to Coincraft's *Standard Catalogue of Scotland, Ireland, Channel Islands & Isle of Man*, or other specialised publications. Collectors should be aware that with most of the coins of the Irish series there are many varieties struck at different mints. The coins listed are all silver unless mentioned otherwise. Another important factor to consider when collecting early Irish coins is that few examples exist in high grades.

	F	VF

HIBERNO-NORSE ISSUES (995–1155)
Penny, imitating English silver pennies,
many various types .... £250 — £550

JOHN, Lord of Ireland (1185–99)
Halfpenny, profile		Extremely rare
Halfpenny, facing	£100	£350
Farthing	£350	£1200

Hiberno-Norse phase II example.

JOHN de COURCY, Lord of Ulster (1177–1205)
| Halfpenny .... | | Extremely rare |
| Farthing .... | £700 | £3000 |

JOHN as King of England and Lord of Ireland (c. 1199–1216)
Penny	£70	£300
Halfpenny	£160	£450
Farthing	£650	£2300

John Lord of Ireland penny.

HENRY III (1216–72)
| Penny .... | £70 | £150 |

EDWARD I (1272–1307)
Penny	£70	£150
Halfpenny	£70	£150
Farthing	£150	£400

No Irish coins were struck for Edward II (1307–27).

Henry III penny.

EDWARD III (1327–77)
| Halfpenny .... | | Extremely rare |

No Irish coins were struck for Richard II (1377–99), Henry IV (1399–1413) or Henry V (1413–22).

HENRY VI (1422–61)
| Penny .... | | Extremely rare |

Edward I penny.

	F	VF

EDWARD IV (1461–83)

	F	VF
"Anonymous crown" groat	£650	£13000
— penny	£1200	—
"Titled crown" groat	£1600	—
— halfgroat............................		Extremely rare
— penny		Extremely rare
Cross on rose/Sun groat	£1850	—
Bust/Rose on sun double groat	£2250	£7000
— groat...............................	£2250	—
— halfgroat............................		Extremely rare
— penny		Extremely rare
Bust/Cross & pellets groat—First issue	£150	£550
— halfgroat............................	£600	£1500
— penny	£90	£350
— halfpenny		Extremely rare
— Second (light) issue.......................	£120	£450
— halfgroat............................	£650	£1650
— penny	£100	
£250— halfpenny		Extremely rare
Bust/Rose on cross groat.....................	£570	£1400
— penny	£80	£225
Billon/Copper issues		
Small crown/Cross farthing (1460–61) ..	£1700	—
— half farthing ("Patrick")................	£1100	—
Large crown/Cross farthing (1462)........		Extremely rare
Patricius/Salvator farthing (1463–65)	£350	£2000
— half farthing		Extremely rare
Shield/Rose on sun farthing	£200	£900

*Edward IV groat.
"Anonymous crown" issue.*

Edward IV penny struck in Dublin.

RICHARD III (1483–85)

	F	VF
Bust/Rose on cross groat.....................	£1100	£3850
— halfgroat.............................		Unique
— penny		Unique
Bust/Cross and pellets penny	£100	£3000
Shield/Three-crowns groat...................	£650	£2850

HENRY VII (1485–1509)

Early issues (1483–90)

	F	VF
Shield/Three crowns groat	£170	£500
— halfgroat.............................	£250	£550
— penny	£650	£2500
— halfpenny		Extremely rare

Later issues (1488–90)

	F	VF
Shield/Three crowns groat	£100	£370
— halfgroat.............................	£200	£600
— penny	£500	£1300
Facing bust groat (1496–1505).............	£150	£400
— halfgroat.............................	£1100	—
— penny	£950	—

Richard III bust/rose on cross groat.

LAMBERT SIMNEL
(as EDWARD VI, Pretender, 1487)

	F	VF
Shield/Three crowns groat	£1250	£4250

Henry VII groat.

	F	VF

HENRY VIII (1509–47)

"Harp" groat	£100	£350
— halfgroat..	£500	£2500

*The "Harp" coins have crowned initials either side of the reverse harp,
e.g. HR (Henricus Rex), HA (Henry and Anne Boleyn), HI (Henry and Jane
Seymour), HK (Henry and Katherine Howard).*

Posthumous (Portrait) issues

Sixpence	£150	£500
Threepence	£150	£550
Threehalfpence......................................	£500	£1750
Threefarthings	£650	£2000

*Henry VIII Posthumous portrait
issues threepence.*

EDWARD VI (1547–53)

Shilling (base silver) 1552 (MDLII)..........	£1000	£3500
Brass contemporary copy.....................	£100	£350

MARY (1553–54)

Shilling 1553 (MDLIII)............................	£850	£3300
Shilling 1554 (MDLIIII)...........................		Extremely rare
Groat..		Extremely rare
Halfgroat..		Extremely rare
Penny		Extremely rare

PHILIP & MARY (1554–58)

Shilling..	£350	£1400
Groat..	£100	£400
Penny		Extremely rare

ELIZABETH I (1558–1603)

Base silver portrait coinage

Shilling..	£350	£1500
Groat..	£180	£700

Philip & Mary shilling

Fine silver, portrait coinage (1561)

Shilling..	£300	£1000
Groat..	£350	£1100

Third (base silver) shield coinage

Shilling	£200	£700
Sixpence...	£150	£500

Copper

Threepence...	£250	£700
Penny	£50	£200
Halfpenny	£100	£300

JAMES I (1603–25)

Shilling..	£100	£400
Sixpence...	£100	£250

Coins struck under Royal Licence
from 1613

"Harrington" farthing (small size)...........	£50	£250
"Harrington" farthing (large size)	£50	£200
"Lennox" farthing	£50	£200

*Elizabeth I "fine" shilling of
1561.*

CHARLES I (1625–49)

During the reign of Charles I and the Great Rebellion many coins were struck under unusual circumstances, making the series a difficult but fascinating area for study. Many of the "coins" were simply made from odd-shaped pieces of plate struck with the weight or value.

	F	VF
Coins struck under Royal Licence from 1625		
"Richmond" farthing	£50	£200
"Maltravers" farthing	£50	£200
"Rose" farthing	£50	£200

Siege money of the Irish Rebellion, 1642–49

"Inchiquin" Money (1642)

	F	VF
Crown	£2200	£6000
Halfcrown	£2000	£5000
Shilling		Extremely rare
Ninepence		Extremely rare
Sixpence		Extremely rare
Groat		Extremely rare

"Dublin" Money (1643)

	F	VF
Crown	£900	£3500
Halfcrown	£600	£2500

"Ormonde" Money (1643–44)

	F	VF
Crown	£500	£1500
Halfcrown	£350	£1000
Shilling	£150	£450
Sixpence	£150	£450
Groat	£120	£350
Threepence	£110	£300
Twopence	£500	£1500

Charles I "Ormonde" crown.

"Ormonde" gold coinage (1646)

Double pistole. 2 known (both in museums)		Extremely rare
Pistole. 10 known (only 1 in private ownership		Extremely rare

"Ormonde" Money (1649)

	F	VF
Crown		Extremely rare
Halfcrown	£1200	£3750

Dublin Money 1649

	F	VF
Crown	£2800	£7850
Halfcrown	£2200	£4750

Issues of the Confederated Catholics

Kilkenny issues (1642–43)

	F	VF
Halfpenny	£300	£900
Farthing	£400	£1100

Rebel Money (1643–44)

	F	VF
Crown	£2500	£5500
Halfcrown	£3000	£5500

"Blacksmith's" Money (16??)

	F	VF
Imitation of English Tower halfcrown	£700	£3000

A rare Charles I "Rebel" halfcrown.

	F	VF

Local Town issues of "Cities of Refuge"

Bandon

	F	VF
Farthing (copper)		Extremely rare

Cork

	F	VF
Shilling......................................		Extremely rare
Sixpence..	£750	£1300
Halfpenny (copper)..............................		Extremely rare
Farthing (copper)	£600	—

Kinsale

	F	VF
Farthing (copper)	£400	—

Youghal

	F	VF
Farthing (copper)	£500	£2000

Halfpenny of Charles I.

CHARLES II (1660–85)

	Fair	F	VF	EF
"Armstrong" coinage				
Farthing (1660–61)................................	£65	£250	—	—
"St Patrick's" coinage				
Halfpenny	£225	£475	—	—
Farthing	£75	£200	£500	£1500
Legg's Regal coinage				
Halfpennies				
1680 large lettering................................	£35	£100	£275	—
1681 large lettering................................	—	£200	£675	—
1681 small lettering			Extremely rare	
1682 small lettering	—	£200	£650	—
1683 small lettering	£30	£45	£400	
1684 small lettering	£40	£125	£650	—

JAMES II (1685–88)

REGAL COINAGE

Halfpennies

	Fair	F	VF	EF
1685...	£25	£75	£300	£700
1686...	£25	£60	£200	£600
1687...			Extremely rare	
1688...	£25	£100	£300	£1300

"St Patrick" farthing of Charles II.

Our grateful thanks to Del Parker, specialist in Irish rarities, for supplying the images for this section. An impressive and extensive range of Irish coins can be viewed and purchased at his website at www.irishcoins.com.

	Fair	F	VF	EF

EMERGENCY COINAGE

GUN MONEY
Most of these coins were struck in gun metal but a few rare specimens are also known struck in gold and in silver

Crowns
1690 (many varieties).....................from	£45	£60	£600	—

Large halfcrowns
Dated July 1689–May 1690
....................................from	£35	£65	£200	—

Small halfcrowns
Dated April–October1690
....................................from	£35	£60	£220	—

Large shillings
Dated from July 1689–April 1690
....................................from	£35	£65	£120	£485

Small shillings
Dated from April–September 1690
....................................from	£25	£35	£120	£400

Sixpences
Dated from June 1689–October 1690
....................................from	£35	£60	£275	—

"Gun Money" crown.

PEWTER MONEY (1689–90)
	Fair	F	VF	EF
Crown	£700	£1100	£3000	—
Groat......................................		Extremely rare		
Penny large bust..................................	£230	£650	—	—
— small bust	£165	£485	£1350	—
Halfpenny large bust	£130	£325	£795	—
— small bust	£110	£235	£675	—

LIMERICK MONEY (1690–91)
	Fair	F	VF	EF
Halfpenny, reversed N in HIBERNIA......	£35	£75	£250	—
Farthing, reversed N in HIBERNIA........	£35	£75	£250	—
— normal N	£45	£125	£300	—

WILLIAM & MARY (1689–94)

Halfpennies
	Fair	F	VF	EF
1692..	£15	£50	£100	£650
1693..	£15	£50	£85	£650
1694..	£20	£75	£125	£700

William & Mary halfpenny of 1693.

WILLIAM III (1694–1702)
	Fair	F	VF	EF
1696 Halfpenny draped bust.................	£35	£75	£250	—
1696 — crude undraped bust	£45	£275	£875	—

No Irish coins were struck during the reign of Queen Anne (1706–11).

DATE	F	VF	EF	UNC

GEORGE I (1714–27)

Farthings

	F	VF	EF	UNC
1722 D.G. REX Harp to left (Pattern)	£650	£1550	£2350	—
1723 D.G. REX Harp to right	£120	£225	£500	—
1723 DEI GRATIA REX Harp to right	£35	£65	£250	£600
1723 — Silver Proof	—	—	—	£2500
1724 DEI GRATIA REX Harp to right	£60	£150	£350	£850

Halfpennies

	F	VF	EF	UNC
1722 Holding Harp left	£55	£130	£385	£1000
1722 Holding Harp right	£45	£110	£350	£795
1723/2 Harp right	£50	£150	£350	£795
1723 Harp right	£25	£65	£200	£550
1723 Silver Proof	—	—	—	£3500
1723 Obv. Rs altered from Bs	£35	£100	£275	—
1723 No stop after date	£25	£80	£275	£500
1724 Rev. legend divided	£40	£100	£300	—
1724 Rev. legend continuous	£40	£110	£385	—

GEORGE II (1727–60)

Farthings

	F	VF	EF	UNC
1737	£35	£60	£175	£475
1737 Proof	—	—	—	£500
1737 Silver Proof	—	—	—	£1200
1738	£35	£65	£165	£475
1744	£35	£65	£165	£475
1760	£30	£50	£100	£375

Halfpenny of George II

Halfpennies

	F	VF	EF	UNC
1736	£25	£60	£225	£600
1736 Proof	—	—	—	£650
1736 Silver Proof	—	—	—	£1350
1737	£25	£50	£200	—
1738	£30	£60	£200	—
1741	£30	£60	£200	—
1742	£30	£60	£200	—
1743	£30	£60	£180	—
1744/3	£30	£60	£185	—
1744	£30	£60	£350	—
1746	£30	£60	£250	—
1747	£30	£60	£225	—
1748	£30	£60	£225	—
1749	£30	£60	£225	—
1750	£30	£60	£225	—
1751	£30	£60	£225	—
1752	£30	£60	£225	—
1753	£30	£60	£250	—
1755	£30	£100	£350	—
*1760	£30	£60	£250	—

GEORGE III (1760–1820)

All copper unless otherwise stated

Pennies

	F	VF	EF	UNC
1805	£20	£40	£190	£475
1805 Proof	—	—	—	£575
1805 in Bronze Proof	—	—	—	£575
1805 in Copper Gilt Proof	—	—	—	£575
1805 in Silver Proof (restrike)	—	—	—	£3250
1822	£20	£40	£180	£400

George III proof penny 1805

DATE	F	VF	EF	UNC
1822 Proof	—	—	—	£575
1823	£12	£25	£150	£400
1823 Proof	—	—	—	£600

Halfpennies

	F	VF	EF	UNC
1766	£30	£55	£165	—
1769	£30	£55	£165	—
1769 Longer bust	£40	£75	£250	£650
1774 Pattern only Proof	—	—	—	£2000
1775	£30	£55	£200	£450
1775 Proof	—	—	—	£650
1776	£55	£140	£400	—
1781	£45	£60	£165	£400
1782	£45	£60	£165	£400
1805	£18	£45	£120	£400
1805 Copper Proof	—	—	—	£400
1805 in Bronze	—	—	—	£295
1805 in Gilt Copper	—	—	—	£450
1805 in Silver (restrike)	—	—	—	£1800
1822	£20	£40	£120	£400
1822 Proof	—	—	—	£600
1823	£20	£40	£120	£400
1823 Proof	—	—	—	£650

One of the scarcer dates, a 1776 George III halfpenny.

NB Prooflike Uncirculated Pennies and Halfpennies of 1822/23 are often misdescribed as Proofs. The true Proofs are rare. Some are on heavier, thicker flans.

DATE	F	VF	EF	UNC
Farthings				
1806	£20	£35	£100	£200
1806 Copper Proof	—	—	—	£375
1806 Bronzed Copper Proof	—	—	—	£265
1806 Copper Gilt Proof	—	—	—	£350
1806 Silver Proof (restrike)	—	—	—	£1150
1822 George IV (Pattern) Proof	—	—	—	£1800

TOKEN ISSUES BY THE BANK OF IRELAND

Five Pence in Silver				
1805	£30	£45	£75	£350
1806	£30	£65	£150	£375
1806/5	£60	£145	£450	£1400

Ten Pence in Silver				
1805	£20	£35	£95	£250
1806	£20	£65	£150	£275
1813	£20	£35	£90	£300
1813 Proof	—	—	—	£450

Thirty Pence in Silver				
1808	£45	£100	£250	£650

Six Shillings				
1804 in Silver	£100	£250	£450	£1850
1804 Proof	—	—	—	£1775
1804 in Copper (restrike)	—	—	—	£750
1804 Copper Gilt	—	—	—	£1700
1804 in Gilt Silver	—	—	—	£3000

In this series fully struck specimens, with sharp hair curls, etc., are worth appreciably more than the prices quoted.

1804 six shillings.

IRISH FREE STATE/EIRE

DATE	F	VF	EF	UNC
TEN SHILLINGS				
1966 Easter Rising	—	£12	£18	£40
1966 Cased Proof	—	—	—	£42
1966 special double case	—	—	—	£75
HALF CROWNS				
Silver				
1928	£7	£12	£40	£75
1928 Proof	—	—	—	£85
1930	£12	£35	£175	£550
1931	£12	£35	£175	£525
1933	£12	£25	£175	£550
1934	£12	£12	£55	£255
1937	£60	£200	£650	£1850
Modified obverse: Eire				
1938				Unique
1939	£7	£17	£30	£75
1939 Proof	—	—	—	£645
1940	£8	£18	£35	£90
1941	£7	£17	£35	£90
1942	£7	£20	£35	£85
1943	£85	£300	£975	£3350
Cupro-nickel				
1951	£2	£3	£20	£55
1951 Proof	—	—	—	£500
1954	£2	£3	£15	£85
1954 Proof	—	—	—	£520
1955	£2	£3	£15	£45
1955	—	—	—	£595
1959	£2	£3	£12	£45
1961	£2	£3	£25	£55
1961 Obv as 1928, rev. as 1951	£30	£75	£325	£750
1962	£2	£3	£6	£35
1963	£2	£3	£6	£35
1964	£2	£3	£6	£35
1966	£2	£3	£6	£35
1967	£2	£3	£6	£35
FLORINS				
Silver				
1928	£3	£6	£25	£60
1928 Proof	—	—	—	£75
1930	£5	£20	£150	£450
1930 Proof				Unique
1931	£5	£20	£175	£450
1933	£5	£18	£140	£450
1934	£15	£125	£275	£750
1934 Proof	—	—	—	£3000
1935	£5	£18	£65	£195
1937	£6	£25	£140	£410
Modified obverse: Eire				
1939	£2	£6	£35	£80
1939 Proof	—	—	—	£675
1940	£3	£6	£30	£80
1941	£3	£6	£35	£75
1941 Proof	—	—	—	£850
1942	£6	£15	£30	£75
1943	£3000	£5500	£10000	£22500

Beware of fake 1943 florins.

319

DATE	F	VF	EF	UNC
Cupro-nickel				
1951..	60p	£2	£12	£45
1951 Proof...	—	—	—	£480
1954..	60p	£2	£10	£42
1954 Proof...	—	—	—	£400
1955..	—	£2	£6	£45
1955 Proof...	—	—	—	£550
1959..	40p	£2	£6	£40
1961..	60p	£3	£15	£55
1962..	40p	£2	£6	£30
1963..	30p	£2	£6	£30
1964..	30p	£2	£6	£30
1965..	30p	£2	£6	£30
1966..	30p	£2	£6	£30
1968..	30p	£2	£6	£30

SHILLINGS
Silver

1928..	£2	£6	£18	£45
1928 Proof...	—	—	—	£75
1930..	£6	£25	£100	£455
1930 Proof...	—	—	—	£855
1931..	£3	£17	£95	£450
1933..	£3	£17	£95	£450
1935..	£3	£13	£50	£150
1937..	£10	£75	£250	£1250
1939..	£2	£6	£25	£65
1939 Proof...	—	—	—	£750
1940..	£2	£6	£17	£55
1941..	£2	£5	£17	£55
1942..	£2	£5	£12	£50
Cupro-nickel				
1951..	£1	£2	£6	£25
1951 Proof...	—	—	—	£450
1954..	£1	£2	£6	£25
1954 Proof...	—	—	—	£500
1955..	£1	£2	£6	£25
1959..	£1	£2	£6	£35
1962..	50p	£2	£3	£22
1963..	50p	£2	£3	£15
1964..	50p	£2	£3	£15
1966..	50p	£2	£3	£15
1968..	50p	£2	£3	£15

SIXPENCES
Nickel

1928..	£1	£5	£15	£50
1928 Proof...	—	—	—	£65
1934..	£1	£3	£18	£100
1935..	£1	£3	£25	£130
Modified obverse: Eire				
1939..	£1	£2	£10	£55
1939 Proof...	—	—	—	£650
1940..	£1	£2	£6	£55
Cupro-nickel				
1942..	£1	£2	£9	£65
1945..	£3	£12	£35	£100
1946..	£5	£10	£100	£400
1947..	£2	£2	£25	£90
1948..	£1	£3	£15	£75
1949..	£1	£2	£10	£50
1950..	£2	£3	£25	£100
1952..	£1	£2	£5	£25

DATE	F	VF	EF	UNC
1953	£1	£2	£5	£25
1953 Proof	—	—	—	£120
1955	£1	£2	£4	£25
1956	£1	£2	£3	£25
1956 Proof	—	—	—	£168
1958	£2	£3	£12	£68
1958 Proof	—	—	—	£380
1959	50p	60p	£3	£20
1960	50p	60p	£2	£20
1961	—	£2	£3	£25
1962	£2	£6	£35	£75
1963	£1	£3	£6	£20
1964	£1	£2	£5	£12
1966	£1	£2	£5	£12
1967	£1	£2	£2	£10
1968	£1	£2	£2	£10
1969	£2	£3	£6	£20

THREEPENCES
Nickel

	F	VF	EF	UNC
1928	£2	£3	£10	£35
1928 Proof	—	—	—	£42
1933	£3	£13	£75	£375
1934	£1	£3	£15	£80

Modified obverse: Eire
	F	VF	EF	UNC
1935	£2	£4	£30	£230
1939	£3	£7	£60	£375
1939 Proof	—	—	—	£1000
1940	£2	£3	£13	£65

Cupro-nickel
	F	VF	EF	UNC
1942	—	£2	£6	£50
1942 Proof	—	—	—	£500
1943	£2	£3	£15	£78
1946	£2	£5	£10	£50
1946 Proof	—	—	—	£500
1948	£2	£3	£25	£80
1949	—	£2	£6	£40
1950	—	£2	£6	£25
1950 Proof	—	—	—	£550
1953	—	£2	£4	£18
1956	—	£2	£3	£10
1961	—	60p	£2	£5
1962	—	60p	£2	£10
1963	—	60p	£2	£10
1964	—	60p	£2	£5
1965	—	60p	£2	£5
1966	—	60p	£2	£5
1967	—	60p	£2	£5
1968	—	—	£2	£5

PENNIES

	F	VF	EF	UNC
1928	£2	£3	£12	£50
1928 Proof	—	—	—	£60
1931	£2	£4	£35	£120
1931 Proof	—	—	—	£1000
1933	£2	£5	£50	£250
1935	£1	£2	£25	£75
1937	£1	£2	£35	£125
1937 Proof	—	—	—	£1000

Modified obverse: Eire
	F	VF	EF	UNC
1938		Only two known		
1940	£10	£50	£175	£750
1941	£1	£2	£10	£35
1942	—	£1	£5	£20
1943	—	£2	£6	£35

DATE	F	VF	EF	UNC
1946	—	£2	£4	£20
1948	—	£2	£4	£20
1949	—	£2	£4	£20
1949 Proof	—	—	—	£500
1950	—	£2	£6	£32
1952	—	£2	£4	£12
1962	—	£2	£4	£15
1962 Proof	—	—	—	£200
1963	—	—	£2	£12
1963 Proof	—	—	—	£200
1964	—	—	£2	£10
1964 Proof	—	—	—	£500
1965	—	—	£1	£5
1966	—	—	£1	£5
1967	—	—	£1	£5
1968	—	—	£1	£5
1968 Proof	—	—	—	£300

HALFPENNIES

	F	VF	EF	UNC
1928	£2	£3	£12	£35
1928 Proof	—	—	—	£45
1933	£6	£20	£100	£500
1935	£5	£10	£50	£200
1937	£2	£5	£15	£50

Modified obverse: Eire

	F	VF	EF	UNC
1939	£5	£10	£50	£200
1939 Proof	—	—	—	£875
1940	£2	£4	£50	£185
1941	£1	£2	£6	£25
1942	£1	£2	£6	£25
1943	£1	£2	£8	£35
1946	£2	£5	£20	£100
1949	£1	£2	£6	£25
1953	—	£2	£3	£12
1953 Proof	—	—	—	£500
1964	—	—	£1	£5
1965	—	—	£1	£6
1966	—	—	£1	£4
1967	—	—	£1	£4

FARTHINGS

	F	VF	EF	UNC
1928	£3	£4	£10	£20
1928 Proof	—	—	—	£45
1930	£3	£4	£10	£32
1931	£4	£6	£15	£35
1931 Proof	—	—	—	£850
1932	£4	£6	£18	£45
1933	£3	£4	£12	£32
1935	£4	£6	£18	£35
1936	£4	£6	£18	£35
1937	£3	£4	£12	£32

Modified obverse: Eire

	F	VF	EF	UNC
1939	£3	£4	£10	£18
1939 Proof	—	—	—	£600
1940	£4	£5	£10	£25
1941	£3	£4	£6	£12
1943	£3	£4	£6	£12
1944	£3	£4	£6	£12
1946	£3	£4	£6	£12
1949	£4	£6	£8	£25
1949 Proof	—	—	—	£465
1953	£3	£4	£5	10
1953 Proof	—	—	—	£320
1959	£3	£4	£5	£13
1966	£3	£4	£5	£13

For the 1928–50 copper issues it is worth noting that UNC means UNC with some lustre. BU examples with full lustre are extremely elusive and are worth much more than the quoted prices.

IRISH DECIMAL COINAGE

DATE	MINTAGE	BU

HALF PENCE
1971	100,500,000	£5
1975	10,500,000	£6
1976	5,500,000	£6
1978	20,300,000	£5
1980	20,600,000	£4
1982	9,700,000	£4
1985	2,800,000	Rare
1986. Only issued in the 1986 set	19,750,000	£100

ONE PENNY

1971	100,500,000	£3
1974	10,000,000	£10
1975	10,000,000	£15
1976	38,200,000	£5
1978	25,700,000	£8
1979	21,800,000	£12
1980	86,700,000	£3
1982	54,200,000	£5
1985	19,200,000	£8
1986	36,600,000	£5
1988	56,800,000	£5
1990	65,100,000	£5
1992	25,600,000	£6
1993	10,000,000	£6
1994	45,800,000	£5
1995	70,800,000	£3
1996	190,100,000	£1
1998	40,700,000	£1
2000	Unknown	£1

TWO PENCE

1971	75,500,000	£3
1975	20,000,000	£8
1976	5400,000	£12
1978	12,000,000	£12
1979	32,400,000	£8
1980	59,800,000	£6
1982	30,400,000	£5
1985	14,500,000	£6
1986	23,900,000	£6
1988	35,900,000	£5
1990	34,300,000	£5
1992	10,200,000	£8

1995	55,500,000	£5
1996	69,300,000	£2
1998	33,700,000	£2
2000	Unknown	£1

FIVE PENCE

1969 Toned	5,000,000	£5
1970	10,000,000	£5
1971	8,000,000	£6
1974	7,000,000	£10
1975	10,000,000	£10
1976	20,600,000	£5
1978	28,500,000	£5
1980	22,200,000	£5
1982	24,400,000	£4
1985	4,200,000	£8
1986	15,300,000	£5
1990	7,500,000	£5
Size reduced to 18.4mm		
1992	74,500,000	£5
1993	89,100,000	£5
1994	31,100,000	£5
1995	12,000,000	£5
1996	14,700,000	£2
1998	158,500,000	£1
2000	Unknown	£1

TEN PENCE

1969	27,000,000	£10
1971	4,000,000	£10
1973	2,500,000	£16
1974	7,500,000	£12
1975	15,000,000	£12
1976	9,400,000	£12
1978	30,900,000	£10
1980	44,600,000	£7
1982	7,400,000	£7
1985	4,100,000	£8
1986. Only issued in the 1986 set	11,280	£275
Size reduced to 22mm		
1992	2 known	—
1993	80,100,000	£5
1994	58,500,000	£5

DATE	MINTAGE	BU	DATE	MINTAGE	BU

1995	16,100,000	£5
1996	18,400,000	£3
1997	10,000,000	£3
1998	10,000,000	£3
1999	24,500,000	£3
2000	Unknown	£2

TWENTY PENCE

1985. Only 600 minted and 556 melted down, only 3 known	Extremely rare	
1986	50,400,000	£6
1988	20,700,000	£6
1992	14,800,000	£5
1994	11,100,000	£5
1995	18,200,000	£5
1996	29,300,000	£5
1998	25,000,000	£3
1999	11,000,000	£3
2000	Unknown	£2

FIFTY PENCE

1970	9,000,000	£8
1971	650,000	£7
1974	1,000,000	£55
1975	2,000,000	£55
1976	3,000,000	£45
1977	4,800,000	£55
1978	4,500,000	£45
1979	4,000,000	£45
1981	6,000,000	£25
1982	2,000,000	£25
1983	7,000,000	£25
1986. Only issued in the 1986 set	10,000	£300
1988	7,000,000	£5
1988 Dublin Millennium	5,000,000	£5
1988 — Proof	50,000	£25
1996	6,000,000	£7
1997	6,000,000	£7
1998	13,800,000	£5
1999	7,000,000	£4
2000	Unknown	£4

ONE POUND

1990	42,300,000	£5
1990 Proof	50,000	£25
1994	14,900,000	£5
1995	9,200,000	£5
1995 UN silver proof in case of issue	2,850	£175
1996	9,200,000	£5
1998	22,960,000	£4
1999	10,000,000	£5
2000	4,000,000	£5

2000 Millennium	5,000,000	£5
2000 – Silver Proof Piedfort	90,000	£35

OFFICIAL COIN SETS ISSUED BY THE CENTRAL BANK

1971 Specimen set in green wallet. 6 coins	£20
1975 6 coin set	£55
1978 6 coin set	£55
1978 6 coin set. Black cover, scarce	£75
1982 6 coin set. Black cover	£75
1986 Specimen set in card folder 1/2p to 50p, 7 coins. Very scarce. Most sets have glue problems	£650
1996 7 coin set	£60
1998 7 coin set	£50
2000 Millennium set. Last decimal set	£125
2000 — With 1999 instead of the 2000 £1 coin	£250

Dublin Millennium 50p

It is probably a strong love of history, rather than the strict disciplines of coin collecting that make collectors turn to commemorative medals. The link between the two is intertwined, and it is to be hoped that collectors will be encouraged to venture into the wider world of medallions, encouraged by this brief guide, originally supplied by Daniel Fearon (author of the *Catalogue of British Commemorative Medals*) and kindly updated again this year by Charles Riley.

DATE	VF	EF

JAMES I

1603 Coronation (possibly by C. Anthony), 29mm, Silver	£1200	£1800

QUEEN ANNE

1603 Coronation, 29mm, AR	£800	£1500

CHARLES I

1626 Coronation (by N. Briot), 30mm, Silver	£650	£1000
1633 Scottish Coronation (by N. Briot), 28mm, Silver	£450	£750
1649 Memorial (by J. Roettier). Struck after the Restoration, 50mm, Bronze	£120	£250

CROMWELL

1653 Lord Protector (by T. Simon), 38mm, Silver	£700	£1700
— Cast examples	£350	£600

CHARLES II

1651 Scottish Coronation, in exile (from design by Sir J. Balfour), 32mm, Silver	£1300	£2200

CHARLES II

1661 Coronation (by T. Simon), 29mm		
— Gold	£1800	£3200
— Silver	£350	£550
1685 Death (by N. Roettier), 39mm, Bronze	£150	£325

James I Coronation, 1603

Charles II Coronation, 1661

DATE	VF	EF

JAMES II
1685 Coronation (by J. Roettier), 34mm
— Gold £1900 £3600
— Silver £350 £800

MARY
1685 Coronation (by J. Roettier), 34mm
— Gold £1500 £3000
— Silver £300 £600

WILLIAM & MARY
1689 Coronation (by J. Roettier), 32mm
— Gold £1750 £3000
— Silver £350 £525
1689 Coronation, "Perseus" (by G. Bower),
   38mm, Gold £1750 £3000

MARY
1694 Death (by N. Roettier), 39mm, Bronze........ £95 £230

WILLIAM III
1697 "The State of Britain" (by J. Croker), 69mm,
   Silver £850 £1400

Queen Anne, 1702–1713.

ANNE
1702 Accession, "Entirely English" (by J. Croker), 34mm
— Gold £1500 £2600
— Silver £150 £295
1702 Coronation (by J. Croker), 36mm
— Gold £1800 £3200
— Silver £225 £300
1707 Union with Scotland (by J. Croker, rev. by S. Bull), 34mm
— Gold £1500 £2800
— Silver £200 £300
1713 Peace of Utrecht (by J. Croker—issued in gold to Members
of Parliament), 34mm
— Gold £800 £1500
— Silver £150 £275

GEORGE I
1714 Coronation (by J. Croker), 34mm
— Gold £1250 £1750
— Silver £150 £250
1727 Death (by J. Dassier), 31mm, Silver £150 £275

GEORGE II
1727 Coronation (by J. Croker), 34mm
— Gold £1500 £3000
— Silver £175 £350

QUEEN CAROLINE
1727 Coronation (by J. Croker), 34mm
— Gold £1750 £3000
— Silver £185 £350
1732 The Royal Family (by J. Croker), 70mm
— Silver £1500 £3000
— Bronze... £400 £700

George I Coronation, 1714.

327

DATE	VF	EF

GEORGE III
1761 Coronation (by L. Natter), 34mm

	VF	EF
— Gold	£2250	£3500
— Silver	£350	£550
— Bronze	£150	£250

QUEEN CHARLOTTE
1761 Coronation (by L. Natter), 34mm

	VF	EF
— Gold	£1750	£3500
— Silver	£375	£600
— Bronze	£150	£295
1810 Golden Jubilee, "Frogmore", 48mm, Silver	£130	£275
— Bronze	£95	£175

GEORGE IV
1821 Coronation (by B. Pistrucci), 35mm

	VF	EF
— Gold	£900	£1600
— Silver	£200	£325
— Bronze	£60	£110

WILLIAM IV
1831 Coronation (by W. Wyon; rev.shows
Queen Adelaide), 33mm

	VF	EF
— Gold	£1150	£2250
— Silver	£175	£325
— Bronze	£65	£100

QUEEN VICTORIA
1838 Coronation (by B. Pistrucci), 37mm

	VF	EF
— Gold	£950	£1500
— Silver	£185	£320
— Bronze	£45	£95

George III, Coronation, 1761

Queen Victoria Coronation, 1838

Queen Victoria Diamond Jubilee 1897

DATE	VF	EF
1887 Golden Jubilee (by J. E. Boehm, rev. by Lord Leighton)		
— Gold, 58mm	£2800	£3750
— Silver, 78mm	£250	£500
— Bronze, 78mm	£95	£180
1897 Diamond Jubilee (by G. de Saulles),		
— Gold, 56mm	£3000	£4000
— Silver, 56mm	£95	£125
— Bronze, 56mm	£35	£60
— Gold, 25mm	£450	£600
— Silver, 25mm	£20	£35

EDWARD VII
1902 Coronation (August 9) (by G. W. de Saulles)

	VF	EF
— Gold, 56mm	£3000	£3600
— Silver, 56mm	£95	£135
— Bronze, 56mm	£30	£55
— Gold, 31mm	£450	£600
— Silver, 31mm	£20	£30

Some rare examples of the official medal show the date as June 26, the original date set for the Coronation which was postponed because the King developed appendicitis.

GEORGE V
1911 Coronation (by B. Mackennal)

	VF	EF
— Gold, 51mm	£3000	£3500
— Silver, 51mm	£95	£250
— Bronze, 51mm	£30	£65
— Gold, 31mm	£450	£600
— Silver, 31mm	£20	£35

1935 Silver Jubilee (by P. Metcalfe)

	VF	EF
— Gold, 58mm	£3500	£4200
— Silver, 58mm	£100	£150
— Gold, 32mm	£450	£650
— Silver, 32mm	£20	£30

PRINCE EDWARD
1911 Investiture as Prince of Wales (by W. Goscombe John)

	VF	EF
— Gold, 31mm	£1000	£1950
— Silver, 31mm	£45	£75

EDWARD VIII
1936 Abdication (by L. E. Pinches), 35mm

	VF	EF
— Gold	£750	£1200
— Silver	£45	£65
— Bronze...	£20	£35

GEORGE VI
1937 Coronation (by P. Metcalfe)

	VF	EF
— Gold, 58mm	£3500	£4000
— Silver, 58mm	£65	£95
— Gold, 32mm	£550	£650
— Silver, 32mm	£25	£35
— Bronze, 32mm	£12	£15

George V Silver Jubilee, 1935

Edward, Prince of Wales, 1911

Edward VIII, Abdication, 1936.

DATE	VF	EF

ELIZABETH II
1953 Coronation (by Spink & Son)—illustrated
— Gold, 57mm	£3000	£3500
— Silver, 57mm	£65	£125
— Bronze, 57mm	£35	£65
— Gold, 32mm	£300	£400
— Silver, 32mm	£20	£35
— Bronze, 32mm	£12	£15

1977 Silver Jubilee (by A. Machin)
— Silver, 57mm	—	£70
— Silver, 44mm	—	£40

The gold medals are priced for 18ct—they can also be found as 22ct and 9ct, and prices should be adjusted accordingly.

PRINCE CHARLES
1969 Investiture as Prince of Wales (by M. Rizello)
— Silver, 57mm	—	£65
— Bronze gilt, 57mm...	—	£40
— Silver, 45mm	—	£35
— Gold, 32mm	—	£450
— Silver, 32mm	—	£35
— Bronze, 32mm	—	£8

QUEEN ELIZABETH THE QUEEN MOTHER
1980 80th Birthday (by L. Durbin)
— Silver, 57mm	—	£55
— Silver, 38mm	—	£38
— Bronze, 38mm	—	£25

N.B.—Official Medals usually command a premium when still in their original case of issue.

Prince Charles, Prince of Wales 1969.

The Royal Mint Museum contains a charming group of medallic portraits of seven of the children of Queen Victoria and Prince Albert. They appear to have been made in 1850 and therefore do not include the two children who were born after that date. The skilfully-executed portraits are the work of Leonard Wyon, a member of the extremely talented family of engravers whose name is so well known to numismatists. The son of William Wyon, he was actually born in the Royal Mint in 1826. These particular portraits were not commissioned by the Mint and little is known about the circumstances in which they were prepared, but for some reason the dies have survived in the Royal Mint Museum, along with single-sided bronze impressions roughly the size of a half-crown.

Images and information courtesy of Dr Kevin Clancy, The Royal Mint.

DIRECTORY *section*

O N the following pages will be found the most useful names and addresses needed by the coin collector.

At the time of going to press with this edition of the YEARBOOK the information is correct, as far as we have been able to ascertain. However, people move and establishments change, so it is always advisable to make contact with the person or organisation listed before travelling any distance, to ensure that the journey is not wasted.

Should any of the information in this section not be correct we would very much appreciate being advised in good time for the preparation of the next edition of the COIN YEARBOOK.

Dealers who display this symbol are Members of the

British Numismatic Trade Association

The primary purpose of the Association is to promote and safeguard the highest standards of professionalism in dealings between its Members and the public. In official consultations it is the recognised representative of commercial numismatics in Britain.

For a free Membership Directory please send a stamped addressed envelope to:

**General Secretary, BNTA, PO Box 2, Rye, East Sussex TN31 7WE
Telephone: 01797 229988 Email: secretary@bnta.net**

The BNTA will be organising the following events:

**COINEX 2015—25 & 26 September, COINEX 2016—30 September & 1 October
at The Ballroom, Millennium Hotel, London Mayfair,
44 Grosvenor Square, London W1K 2HP**

BNTA MEMBERS IN COUNTY ORDER

LONDON AREA

*A.H. Baldwin & Sons Ltd
www.baldwin.co.uk
ATS Bullion Ltd
www.atsbullion.com
Beaver Coin Room
www.beaverhotel.co.uk
Jon Blyth
www.jonblyth.com
Bonhams incorporating
Glendining's
www.bonhams.com
Arthur Bryant Coins Ltd
www.bryantcoins.com
Keith Chapman
www.anglosaxoncoins.com
*Classical Numismatic Group Inc
/ Seaby Coins
www.cngcoins.com

*Philip Cohen Numismatics
www.coinheritage.co.uk
Coin Invest Direct.com
www.coininvestdirect.com
Andre de Clermont
www.declermont.com
*Dix Noonan Webb
www.dnw.co.uk
Christopher Eimer
www.christophereimer.co.uk
Harrow Coin & Stamp Centre
*Knightsbridge Coins
C. J. Martin (Coins) Ltd
www.antiquities.co.uk
Nigel Mills
www.nigelmills.net
Morton & Eden Ltd
www.mortonandeden.com

Moruzzi Ltd
www.moruzzi.co.uk
Numismatica Ars Classica
www.arsclassicacoins.com
Physical Gold Ltd
www.physicalgold.co.uk
Predecimal.com incorporating
Rotographic Publications
www.predecimal.com
Roma Numismatics Ltd
www.romanumismatics.com
Simmons Gallery
www.simmonsgallery.co.uk
*Spink & Son Ltd
www.spink.com
Surena Ancient Art & Numismatic
The London Coin Company Ltd
www.thelondoncoincompany.com

(Those members with a retail premises are indicated with an *

The BNTA is a member of the International Numismatic Commission.

AVON
Saltford Coins
www.saltfordcoins.com

BEDFORDSHIRE
Simon Monks
www.simonmonks.co.uk

BERKSHIRE
*Douglas Saville Numismatic Books
www.douglassaville.com

BUCKINGHAMSHIRE
Charles Riley
www.charlesriley.co.uk

CAMBRIDGESHIRE
*Dave Allen Collectables
www.daveallencollectables.co.uk
Den of Antiquity International Ltd
www.denofantiquity.co.uk
ArtAncient Ltd
www.artancient.com

CHESHIRE
Colin Cooke
www.colincooke.com

CORNWALL
Richard W Jeffery

DEVON
Glenn S Ogden
www.glennogdencoins.com

DORSET
*Dorset Coin Co. Ltd
www.dorsetcoincompany.co.uk

ESSEX
Time Line Originals
www.time-lines.co.uk

GLOUCESTERSHIRE
Silbury Coins Ltd
www.silburycoins.com

HAMPSHIRE
*SPM Jewellers
www.spmjewellers.co.uk
Studio Coins
www.studiocoins.net
*Victory Coins
West Essex Coin Investments

HERTFORDSHIRE
Michael Dickinson
DRG Coins and Antiquities
www.drgcoinsantiquities.com
K B Coins
www.kbcoins.com
David Miller
David Seaman
www.davidseamancoins.co.uk

KENT
London Coins
www.londoncoins.co.uk
*Peter Morris
www.petermorris.co.uk
Wilkes & Curtis Ltd
www.wilkesandcurtis.com

LANCASHIRE
*Colin de Rouffignac

MONMOUTHSHIRE
Anthony M. Halse
www.coinsandtokens.com

NORFOLK
BucksCoins
www.westminsterauctions.com
*Roderick Richardson
www.roderickrichardson.com
Chris Rudd
www.celticcoins.com

NOTTINGHAMSHIRE
History in Coins
www.historyincoins.com

OXFORDSHIRE
*Richard Gladdle
Gladdle@plumpudding.org

SUFFOLK
*Lockdale Coins Ltd
www.lockdales.com
Mike R. Vosper Coins
www.vosper4coins.co.uk

SURREY
Daniel Fearon
www.danielfearon.com
M. J. Hughes
www.gbgoldcoins.co.uk
KMCC Ltd
Mark Rasmussen Numismatist
www.rascoins.com

SUSSEX
John Newman Coins
www.johnnewmancoins.com

TYNE AND WEAR
*Corbitts Ltd
www.corbitts.com

WARWICKSHIRE
*Peter Viola
*Warwick & Warwick Ltd
www.warwickandwarwick.com

WEST MIDLANDS
*Atkinsons Coins and Bullion
www.atkinsonsbullion.com
*Birmingham Coins
David Craddock
Paul Davis Birmingham Ltd
*Format of Birmingham Ltd
Mint Coins Ltd

WORCESTERSHIRE
J. Whitmore
www.whitmorectm.co.uk

YORKSHIRE
Airedale Coins
www.airedalecoins.co.uk
AMR Coins
www.amrcoins.com
Paul Clayton
Paul Davies Ltd
*Paul Dawson York Ltd
*Weighton Coin Wonders
www.weightoncoin.co.uk

WALES
Lloyd Bennett
www.coinsofbritain.com
Goulborn Collections Ltd
*North Wales Coins Ltd
Colin Rumney

SCOTLAND
*Scotmint Ltd
www.scotmint.com

IRELAND
Ormonde Coins
www.ormondecoins.com

www.bnta.net

MUSEUMS *& libraries*

Listed below are the Museums and Libraries in the UK which have coins or items of numismatic interest on display or available to the general public.

A

• Anthropological Museum, University of Aberdeen, Broad Street, **Aberdeen,** AB9 1AS (01224 272014).

• Curtis Museum (1855), High Street, **Alton,** Hants (01420 82802). *General collection of British coins.*

• Ashburton Museum, 1 West Street, **Ashburton,** Devon, TQ13 7DT (01364 653595) *Ancient British and Roman antiquities including local coin finds.*

• Ashwell Village Museum (1930), Swan Street, **Ashwell,** Baldock, Herts. SG7 5NY (01462 742956) *Roman coins from local finds, local trade tokens, Anglo-Gallic coins and jetons.*

• Buckinghamshire County Museum (1862), Church Street, **Aylesbury,** Bucks HP20 2QP (01296 331441). *Roman and medieval English coins found locally, 17th/18th century Buckinghamshire tokens, commemorative medals.*

B

• Banbury Museum, Spiceball Park Road, **Banbury,** Oxon OX16 2PQ (01295 753752). *Wrexlin Hoard of Roman coins.*

• Museum of North Devon (1931), The Square, **Barnstaple,** EX32 8LN (01271 346747). *General coin and medal collection, including local finds. Medals of the Royal Devonshire Yeomanry.*

• Roman Baths Museum, Abbey Church Yard, Stall St, **Bath,** Avon BA1 1LZ (01225 477785). *Comprehensive collection of Roman coins from local finds.*

• Bagshaw Museum and Art Gallery (1911), Wilton Park, **Batley,** West Yorkshire WF17 0AS (01924 326155). *Roman, Scottish, Irish, English hammered, British and foreign coins, local traders' tokens, political medalets, campaign medals and decorations.*

• Bedford Museum (1961), Castle Lane, **Bedford** MK40 3XD (01234 718618). *Collections of the Bedford Library and Scientific Institute, the Beds Archaeological Society and Bedford Modern School (Pritchard Memorial) Museum.*

• Ulster Museum (1928), Botanic Gardens, **Belfast** BT9 5AB (0845 608 0000). *Irish, English and British coins and commemorative medals.*

• Berwick Borough Museum (1867), The Clock Block, Berwick Barracks, Ravensdowne, **Berwick**. TD15 1DQ (01289 301869). *Roman, Scottish and medievial coins.*

• Public Library, Art Gallery and Museum (1910), Champney Road, **Beverley,** Humberside (01482 393939). *Beverley trade tokens, Roman, English, British and foreign coins.*

• Bignor Roman Villa (1811), **Bignor,** nr Pulborough, West Sussex RH20 1PH (01798 869259). *Roman coins found locally.*

• City Museum and Art Gallery (1861), Chamberlain Square, **Birmingham** B3 3DH (0121 303 2834). *Coins, medals and tokens (special emphasis on the products of the Soho, Heaton, Birmingham and Watt mints.*

• Blackburn Museum, Museum Street, **Blackburn,** Lancs BB1 7AJ (01254 667130). *Incorporates the Hart (5,000 Greek, Roman and early English) and Hornby (500 English coins) collections, as well as the museum's own collection of British and Commonwealth coins.*

• Museum Collection, 25 – 27 West Street, **Bognor Regis,** West Sussex PO21 1XA (01243 865636) *Roman, English and British coins and trade tokens.*

• Museum and Art Gallery,(1893), Le Mans Crescent, **Bolton,** Lancashire BL1 1SE (01204 332211). *General collection of about 3000 British and foreign coins, and over 500 British medals. Numismatic library.*

• Art Gallery and Museum, Central Library, Oriel Road, **Bootle,** Lancs. *Greek, Roman, English, British and some foreign coins, local trade tokens.*

• Roman Town and Museum (1949) Main Street, **Boroughbridge,** N. Yorks. YO2 3PH (01423 322768). *Roman coins.*

• The Museum (1929), South Street, **Boston,** Lincs PE21 6HT (01205 365954). *Small collection of English coins.*

• Natural Science Society Museum (1903), 39 Christchurch Road, **Bournemouth,** Dorset BH1 3NS (01202 553525). *Greek, Roman and English hammered coins (including the Hengistbury Hoard), local trade tokens.*

• Bolling Hall Museum (1915), Bolling Hall Road, **Bradford,** West Yorkshire BD4 7LP (01274 431814). *Some 2,000 coins and tokens, mostly 18th–20th centuries.*

• Cartwright Hall Museum and Art Gallery (1904), Lister Park, **Bradford,** West Yorkshire BD9 4NS (01274 431212). *Roman coins found locally.*

• Museum and Art Gallery (1932), South Street, **Bridport,** Dorset (01308 458703). *Roman coins, mainly from excavations at Claudian Fort.*

• The City Museum (1820), Queen's Road, **Bristol** BS8 1RL (0117 922 3571). *Ancient British, Roman (mainly from local hoards), English hammered coins, especially from the Bristol mint, and several hundred local trade tokens.*

• District Library and Museum (1891), Terrace Road, **Buxton,** Derbyshire SK17 6DA (01629 533540). *English and British coins, tokens and commemorative medals. Numismatic library.*

C

• Segontium Museum (1928), Beddgelert Road, **Caernarfon,** Gwynedd (01286 675625) *Roman coins and artifacts excavated from the fort.*

• Fitzwilliam Museum (1816), Department of Coins and Medals, Trumpington Street, **Cambridge** CB2 1RB (01223 332900). *Ancient, English, medieval European, oriental coins, medals, plaques, seals and cameos.*

• National Museum & Galleries of Wales, Cathays Park, **Cardiff** CF10 3NP (029 2057 3000). *Greek, Celtic, Roman and British coins and tokens with the emphasis on Welsh interest. Also military, civilian and comm. medals.*

• Guildhall Museum (1979), Market Street, **Carlisle,** Cumbria CA3 8JE (01228 618718). *General collection of coins and medals.*

• Tullie House (1877), Castle Street, **Carlisle,** Cumbria CA3 8TP (01228 618718). *Roman, medieval and later coins from local finds, including medieval counterfeiter's coin-moulds.*

• Gough's Caves Museum (1934), The Cliffs, **Cheddar,** Somerset BS27 3QF (01934 742343). *Roman coins.*

• Chelmsford and Essex Museum (1835), Oaklands Park, Moulsham Street, **Chelmsford,** Essex CM2 9AQ (01245 605700). *Ancient British, Roman, medieval and later coins mainly from local finds, local medals.*

• Town Gate Museum (1949), **Chepstow,** Gwent. (01291) 625981 *Local coins and trade tokens.*

• Grosvenor Museum (1886), Grosvenor Street, **Chester** CH1 2DD (01244 972197). *Roman coins from the fortress site, Anglo-Saxon, English medieval and post-medieval coins of the Chester and Rhuddlan mints, trade tokens of Chester and Cheshire, English and British milled coins.*

• Public Library (1879), Corporation Street, **Chesterfield,** Derbyshire (01246 2047). *Roman coins from local finds, Derbyshire trade tokens, medals, seals and railway passes. Numismatic library and publications.*

• Red House Museum (1919), Quay Road, **Christchurch,** Dorset (01202 482860). *Coins of archaeological significance from Hampshire and Dorset, notably the South Hants Hoard, ancient British, Armorican, Gallo-Belgic, Celtic and Roman coins, local trade tokens and medals.*

• Corinium Museum (1856), Park Street, **Cirencester,** Glos (01285 655611). *Roman coins.*

• Colchester and Essex Museum (1860), The Castle, **Colchester,** Essex (01206 712931/2). *Ancient British and Roman coins from local finds, medieval coins (especially the Colchester Hoard), later English coins and Essex trade tokens, commemorative medals.*

D

• Public Library, Museum and Art Gallery (1921), Crown Street, **Darlington,** Co Durham DL1 1ND (01325 462034). *Coins, medals and tokens.*

• Borough Museum (1908), Central Park, **Dartford,** Kent (01322 224739). *Roman, medieval and later English hammered coins, trade tokens and commemorative medals.*

• Dartmouth Museum (1953), The Butterwalk, **Dartmouth,** Devon TQ6 9PZ (01803 832923). *Coins and medals of a historical and maritime nature.*

• Museum and Art Gallery (1878), The Strand, **Derby** DE1 1BS (01332 641901). *Roman coins, English silver and copper regal coins, Derbyshire tradesmen's tokens, British campaign medals and decorations of the Derbyshire Yeomanry and the 9/12 Royal Lancers.*

• Museum and Art Gallery (1909), Chequer Road, **Doncaster,** South Yorkshire DN1 2AE (01302 734293). *General collection of English and foreign silver and bronze coins. Representative collection of Roman imperial silver and bronze coins, including a number from local hoards. English trade tokens, principally of local issues, medals.*

• Dorset County Museum (1846), High West Street, **Dorchester,** Dorset DT1 1XA (01305 262735). *British, Roman, medieval and later coins of local interest.*

• Central Museum (1884), Central Library, St James's Road, **Dudley,** West Midlands DY1 1HU (01384 815575). *Small general collection of coins, medals and tokens.*

• Burgh Museum (1835), The Observatory, Corberry Hill, **Dumfries** (01387 53374). *Greek, Roman, Anglo-Saxon, medieval English and Scottish coins, especially from local hoards. Numismatic library.*

• Dundee Art Galleries and Museums (1873). Albert Square, **Dundee** DD1 1DA ()1382 307200). *Coins and medals of local interest.*

• The Cathedral Treasury (995 AD), The College, **Durham** DH1 3EH (0191 386 4266). *Greek and Roman coins bequeathed by Canon Sir George Wheeler (1724), Renaissance to modern medals, medieval English coins, especially those struck at the Durham ecclesiastical mint.*

• Durham Heritage Centre, St Mary le Bow, North Bailey, **Durham** DH1 3ET (0191 384 5589). *Roman, medieval and later coins, mainly from local finds.*

E

• National Museum of Scotland (1781), Chambers Street, **Edinburgh** EH1 1JF (0300 123 6789). *Roman, Anglo-Saxon, English and Scottish coins, trade tokens, commemorative medals and communion tokens. Numismatic library. Publications.*

• Royal Albert Memorial Museum (1868), Queen Street, **Exeter** EX4 3RX (01392 265858). *Roman and medieval. Coins of the Exeter Mint.*

G

• Hunterian Museum (1807), Gilbert Scott Building, University Of Glasgow, University Avenue, **Glasgow** G12 8QQ (0141 330 4221). *Greek, Roman, Byzantine, Scottish, English and Irish coins, Papal and other European medals, Indian and Oriental coins, trade and communion tokens.*

• Art Gallery and Museum (1888), Kelvingrove, **Glasgow** G3 (0141 357 3929). *General collection of coins, trade tokens, communion tokens, commemorative and military medals.*

• Museum of Transport (1974), Riverside Museum, 100 Pointhouse Place **Glasgow** G3 8RS (0141 357 3929). *Transport tokens and passes, commemorative medals, badges and insignia of railway companies and shipping lines.*

• City Museum and Art Gallery (1859), Brunswick Road, **Gloucester** (01452 524131). *Ancient British, Roman, Anglo-Saxon (from local finds), early medieval (from local mints), Gloucestershire trade tokens.*

• Guernsey Museum and Art Gallery, St Peter Port, **Guernsey** (01481 726518). *Armorican, Roman, medieval and later coins, including the coins, medals, tokens and paper money of Guernsey.*

• Guildford Museum (1898), Castle Arch, **Guildford,** Surrey GU1 3SX (01483 444750). *Roman and medieval coins and later medals.*

H

• Gray Museum and Art Gallery, Clarence Road, **Hartlepool,** Cleveland (01429 268916). *General collection, including coins from local finds.*

• Public Museum and Art Gallery (1890), John's Place, Cambridge Road, **Hastings,** East Sussex (01424 721952). *General collection of English coins, collection of Anglo-Saxon coins from Sussex mints.*

• City Museum (1874), Broad Street, **Hereford** (01432 268121 ext 207). *Coins from the Hereford mint and local finds, Herefordshire trade tokens, general collection of later coins and medals.*

• Hertford Museum (1902), 18 Bull Plain, **Hertford** (01992 582686). *British, Roman, medieval and later English coins and medals.*

• Honiton and Allhallows Public Museum (1946), High Street, **Honiton,** Devon (01404 44966). *Small general collection, including coins from local finds.*

• Museum and Art Gallery (1891), 19 New Church Road, **Hove,** East Sussex (01273 779410). *English coins, Sussex trade tokens and hop tallies, campaign medals, orders and decorations, comm. medals.*

• Tolson Memorial Museum (1920), Ravensknowle Park, **Huddersfield,** West Yorkshire (01484 541455). *Representative collection of British coins and tokens, Roman and medieval coins, mainly from local finds.*

• Hull and East Riding Museum (1928), 36 High Street, **Hull** (01482 593902). *Celtic, Roman and medieval coins and artifacts from local finds. Some later coins including tradesmen's tokens.*

I

• The Manx Museum, Douglas, **Isle of Man** (01624 675522). *Roman, Celtic, Hiberno-Norse, Viking, medieval English and Scottish coins, mainly from local finds, Manx traders' tokens from the 17th to 19th centuries, Manx coins from 1709 to the present day.*

J

• Jersey Museum, Weighbridge, St Helier, **Jersey** (01534 30511). *Armorican, Gallo-Belgic, Roman, medieval English and French coins, coins, paper money and tokens of Jersey.*

K

• Dick Institute Museum and Art Gallery (1893), Elmbank Avenue, **Kilmarnock,** Ayrshire (01563 26401). *General collection of coins and medals, and the Hunter-Selkirk collection of communion tokens.*

L

• City Museum (1923), Old Town Hall, Market Square, **Lancaster** (01524 64637). *Roman, Anglo-Saxon, medieval English coins, provincial trade tokens, medals of the King's Own Royal Lancashire Regiment.*

• City Museum (1820), Municipal Buildings, The Headrow, **Leeds,** West Yorkshire (01532 478279). *Greek, Roman, Anglo-Saxon, English medieval, Scottish, Irish, British, Commonwealth and foreign coins. Several Roman and Saxon hoards. The Backhouse collection of Yorkshire banknotes, the Thornton collection of Yorkshire tokens, British and foreign commemorative medals.*

• Leicester Museum and Art Gallery (1849), New Walk, **Leicester** (01533 554100). *Roman, medieval and later coins, mainly from local finds, tokens, commemorative medals, campaign medals and decorations.*

• Pennington Hall Museum and Art Gallery, **Leigh,** Lancashire. *Roman and British coins and medals.*

• Museum and Art Gallery (1914), Broadway, **Letchworth,** Herts (01462 65647). *Ancient British coins minted at Camulodunum, Roman, medieval and English coins, Hertfordshire trade tokens, commemorative and campaign medals.*

• City Library, Art Gallery and Museum (1859), Bird Street, **Lichfield,** Staffs (01543 2177). *Roman, medieval and later English coins, Staffordshire trade tokens and commemorative medals.*

• Liverpool Museum(1851), William Brown Street, **Liverpool** L3 8EN (0151 207 0001). *General collection of Roman, medievaland later British coins, tokens.*

• Bank of England Museum, Threadneedle Street, **London** EC2 (020-7601 5545). *Exhibits relating to gold bullion, coins, tokens and medals, the design and manufacture of banknotes, and a comprehensive collection of bank notes dating from the 17th century to the present day.*

• British Museum(1752), HSBC Coin Gallery, Great Russell Street, **London** WC1 (020-7636 1555). *Almost a million coins, medals, tokens and badges of all period from Lydia, 7th century BC to the present time. Extensive library of books and periodicals.*

• British Numismatic Society (1903), Warburg Institute, Woburn Square, **London** WC1. *Library containing over 5,000 volumes, including sale catalogues, periodicals and pamphlets. Open to members only.*

• Cuming Museum (1906), Walworth Road, **London** SE17 (020-7703 3324/5529). *Some 8,000 items, including Greek, Roman, medieval English and modern British coins, English tokens and commemorative medals.*

• Gunnersbury Park Museum (1927), Acton, **London** W3. *Ancient British, Greek, Roman, medieval English, British and some foreign coins, tradesmen's tokens and commemorative medals, including local finds.*

• Horniman Museum and Library (1890), London Road, Forest Hill, **London** SE23 (020-7699 2339). *General collection, primitive currency, some tokens.*

• Imperial War Museum, Lambeth Road, **London** SE1 6HZ (020-7416 5000). *Emergency coinage of two world wars, occupation and invasion money, extensive collection of German Notgeld, commemorative, propaganda and military medals, badges and insignia.*

• Sir John Soane's Museum (1833), 13 Lincoln's Inn Fields, **London** WC2 (020-7405 2107). *Napoleonic medals and medallic series of the late 18th and early 19th centuries.*

• National Maritime Museum, Romney Road, Greenwich, **London** SE10 (020-8858 4422). *Commemorative medals with a nautical or maritime theme, naval medals and decorations.*

• Victoria and Albert Museum (1852), South Kensington, **London** SW7 (020-7938 8441). *Byzantine gold and medieval Hispano-Mauresque coins (Department of Metalwork), large collection of Renaissance and later medals (Department of Architecture and Sculpture). Numismatic books.*

• Ludlow Museum (1833). The Assembly Rooms. Castle Square, **Ludlow** (01584 873857). *Roman and medieval coins from local finds.*

• Luton Museum and Art Gallery (1927), Wardown Park, **Luton**, Beds (01582 36941). *Coins, tokens and medals.*

M

• Museum and Art Gallery (1858), **Maidstone**, Kent (01622 754497). *Ancient British, Roman, Anglo-Saxon and medieval coins found in Kent, modern British coins, Kent trade tokens, banknotes, hop tallies and tokens, primitive currency, collections of Kent Numismatic Society.*

• The Manchester Museum (1868), The University, **Manchester** M13 (0161-275 2634). *Very fine collections of Greek and Roman coins, comprehensive collections of English, European and Oriental coins, over 30,000 in all.*

• Margate Museum (1923), The Old Town Hall, Market Place, **Margate**, Kent (01843 225511 ext 2520). *Small collection of coins, including Roman from local finds.*

• Montrose Museum and Art Gallery (1836). Panmure Place, **Montrose**, Angus DD10 8HE (01674 73232). *Scottish and British coins.*

N

• Newark-on-Trent Museum (1912), Appleton Gate, **Newark**, Notts (01636 702358). *Siege pieces, trade tokens and coins from local finds and hoards.*

• Newbury District Museum, The Wharf, **Newbury**, Berkshire (01635 30511). *Ancient British, Roman and medieval coins and artifacts, later coins and tokens.*

• The Greek Museum, Percy Building, **Newcastle-upon-Tyne** (0191 2226000 ext 7966). *Ancient coins.*

O

• Heberden Coin Room, Ashmolean Museum (1683), **Oxford** (01865 278000). *Extensive collections of all periods, notably Greek, Roman, English and Oriental coins, Renaissance portrait and later medals, tokens and paper money. Large library. Numerous publications.*

Þ

• Peterborough Museum (1881), Priestgate, **Peterborough**, Cambs (01733 340 3329). *Roman (mainly from local hoards and finds), Anglo-Saxon, medieval English, British and modern European coins, English and British commemorative medals and tokens.*

• City Museum and Art Gallery (1897), Drake Circus, **Plymouth**, Devon (01752 264878). *General collections of British and Commonwealth coins and tokens, Devon trade tokens and Plymouth tradesmen's checks, Ancient British and Roman coins from local sites.*

• Waterfront Museum, 4 High Street, **Poole**, Dorset (01202 683138). *General collection of British and foreign coins, medals and tokens (view by appointment).*

• City Museum (1972), Museum Road, Old **Portsmouth** PO1 (023 80827261). *Roman, medieval and later coins mainly from local finds and archaeological excavation, British coins, trade tokens of Hampshire, commemorative medals.*

• Harris Museum and Art Gallery (1893), Market Square, **Preston**, Lancashire (01772 58248). *English and British coins, tokens and medals.*

R

• The Museum of Reading (1883), Blagrave Street, **Reading**, Berks (0118 939 9800). *British, Roman and medieval English coins, many from local finds, tradesmen's tokens and commemorative medals.*

• Rochdale Museum (1905), Sparrow Hill, **Rochdale**, Lancs (01706 41085). *Roman and medieval coins from local finds, Rochdale trade tokens, miscellaneous British and foreign coins and medals.*

• Municipal Museum and Art Gallery (1893), Clifton Park, **Rotherham** (01709 382121). *Collection includes Roman coins from Templeborough Forts, medieval English coins from local hoards and a general collection of British coins.*

S

• Saffron Walden Museum (1832) (1939), Museum Street, **Saffron** Walden, Essex (01799 522494). *Ancient British, Roman, medieval and later coins, mainly from local finds and archaeological excavation, trade tokens and commemorative medals.*

• Verulamium Museum, St Michael's, **St Albans**, Herts (01727 819339). *Coins and artifacts excavated from the Roman town.*

• Salisbury and South Wiltshire Museum (1861), The Cathedral Close, **Salisbury,** Wilts (01722 332151). *Collection of coins minted or found locally, including finds of Iron Age, Roman, Saxon and medieval coins, as well as 18th and 19th century tradesmen's tokens.*

• Richborough Castle Museum (1930), **Sandwich,** Kent (0304 612013). *Roman coins of 1st–5th centuries from excavations of the Richborough site.*

• Scarborough Museum (1829), The Rotunda, Vernon Road, **Scarborough**, North Yorkshire (01723 374839). Collection of *over 4,000 Roman coins, 1,500 English and 600 coins from local finds, siege pieces and trade tokens.*

• Shaftesbury and Dorset Local History Museum (1946), 1 Gold Hill, **Shaftesbury**, Dorset (01747 52157). *Hoard of Saxon coins.*

• City Museum (1875), Weston Park, **Sheffield** (0114 2 768588). *Over 5,000 coins of all periods, but mainly English and modern British. European coins, imperial Roman (including three hoards of about 500 coins each), Yorkshire trade tokens, British historical medals, campaign medals. Library.*

• Rowley's House Museum, Barker Street, **Shrewsbury**, Salop (01743 361196). *Coins minted at Shrewsbury 925-1180, Civil War coinage of 1642, Shropshire tradesmen's tokens, English coins and medals.*

• Museum of Archaeology (1951), God's House Tower, Town Quay, **Southampton**, Hants (023 8022 0007). *Main emphasis lies in Ancient British, Roman and medieval English coins from local archaeological excavations. General collection of later coins and medals.*

• Atkinson Art Gallery (1878), Lord Street, **Southport,** Lancs (01704 533133). *Roman coins.*

• Botanic Gardens Museum, Churchtown, **Southport,** Lancs (01704 87547). *English and British coins and medals, military medals and decorations.*

• Southwold Museum (1933), St Bartholomew's Green, **Southwold**, Suffolk (01502 722375). *General collection of coins, specialised Suffolk trade tokens.*

• Stamford Museum (1961), Broad Street, **Stamford,** Lincs (01780 66317). *General collection of coins, medals and tokens, including a selection from the Stamford mint.*

• Municipal Museum (1860), Vernon Park, Turncroft Lane, **Stockport**, Cheshire (0161 474 4460) *Miscellaneous collection of coins, tokens and medals.*

• Stroud Museum (1899), Lansdown, **Stroud**, Glos (01453 376394). *Ancient British, Roman, Saxon, Norman, later medieval English, British coins and Gloucestershire trade tokens.*

• Museum and Art Gallery (1846), Borough Road, **Sunderland,** Tyne & Wear (0191 514 1235). *Roman imperial, medieval and later English, including examples of the pennies minted at Durham, modern British and foreign coins, 17th-19th century tradesmen's tokens, local medallions and campaign medals.*

• Swansea Museum (1835), Victoria Road, **Swansea**, W. Glamorgan, SA1 1SN (0792 653765). *Coins and medals of local interest.*

T

• Tamworth Castle and Museum (1899), The Holloway, **Tamworth**, Staffs (01827 63563). *Anglo-Saxon coins, medieval English including coins of the Tamworth mint, later English and British coins, tokens, commemorative medallions and medals.*

• Somerset County Museum, Taunton Castle, **Taunton**, Somerset (01823 255510/320200). *Celtic, Roman, Anglo-Saxon, early Medieval, tokens, medallions and banknotes. Strong emphasis on locally-found items.*

• Thurrock Local History Museum (1956), Civic Square, **Tilbury**, Essex (01375 390000 ext 2414). *Roman coins.*

• Royal Cornwall Museum (1818), River Street, **Truro,** Cornwall (01872 72205). *Coins, tokens and medals pertaining principally to the county of Cornwall.*

W

• Wakefield Museum (1919), Wood Street, **Wakefield**, West Yorkshire (01924 295351). *Roman and medieval English silver and copper coins.*

• Epping Forest District Museum, 39/41 Sun Street, **Waltham Abbey**, Essex EN 9. *Ancient British, Roman and medieval coins, Essex tradesmen's tokens of local interest.*

• Warrington Museum and Art Gallery (1848). Bold Street, **Warrington**, Cheshire, WA1 1JG (01925 30550). *Coins, medals and tokens.*

• Worcester City Museum (1833), Foregate Street, **Worcester** (01905 25371). *Roman, medieval and later coins and tokens. Coins of the Worcester mint.*

• Wells Museum (18903), 8 Cathedral Green, **Wells,** Somerset (01749 3477). *Ancient and modern British and world coins, local trade tokens and medals.*

• Municipal Museum and Art Gallery (1878), Station Road, **Wigan**, Lancashire. *British, Commonwealth and foreign coins from about 1660 to the present. Roman coins from local sites, medals and tokens.*

• City Museum (1851), The Square, **Winchester**, Hants (01962 848269). *Roman and medieval coins chiefly from local hoards and finds. Hampshire tradesmen's tokens and commemorative medals. Small reference library.*

• Wisbech and Fenland Museum (1835), Museum Square, **Wisbech,** Cambridgeshire (01945 583817), *British Roman, medieval and later coins, medals and tokens.*

Y

• The Museum of South Somerset (1928), Hendford, **Yeovil,** Somerset (01935 24774). *Roman coins from local sites, medieval English, modern British coins and medals and a fine collection of tokens (particularly 17th century Somerset).*

• Castle Museum (1938), **York** (01904 653611). *English and British coins, campaign medals, orders and decorations, commemorative medals.*

• Jorvik Viking Centre (1984), Coppergate, **York** (01904 643211). *Coins and artefacts pertaining to the Viking occupation of York.*

• The Yorkshire Museum (1823), **York** (01904 629745). *Roman imperial, medieval English and later coins, about 12,000 in all.*

CLUB *directory*

Details given here are the names of Numismatic Clubs and Societies, their date of foundation, and their usual venues, days and times of meetings. Meetings are monthly unless otherwise stated. Finally, the telephone number of the club secretary is given; the names and addresses of club secretaries are withheld for security reasons, but full details may be obtained by writing to the Secretary of the British Association of Numismatic Societies, Keith Sugden, Honorary Curatorial Assistant, Department of Numismatics, Manchester Museum, Oxford Road, Manchester M13 9PL or visiting the website at www.coinclubs.freeserve.co.uk.

Banbury & District NS (1967). St John's Social Club, St John's Church, Oxford Road, Banbury 2nd Mon (exc Jul & Aug), 19.45. (01295 275128).

Bath & Bristol Numismatic Society (1950). Fry's Club, Keynsham, Bristol. 2nd Thu, 19.30. (0117 968 7259).

Bedfordshire Numismatic Society (1966). 2nd Thu. Dave Allen, Secretary (01234 870645).

Bexley Coin Club (1968). St Martin's Church Hall, Erith Road, Barnehurst, Bexleyheath, Kent. 1st Mon (exc Jan & Aug), 19.30. (020 8303 0510).

Birmingham Numismatic Society (1964). Friend's Meeting House, Bull Street. (0121 308 1616).

Matthew Boulton Society (1994). PO Box 395, Bir-mingham B31 2TB (0121 781 6558 fax 0121 781 6574).

Bradford & District Numismatic Society (1967). East Bowling Unity Club, Leicester Street, Bradford, West Yorkshire. 3rd Mon, 19.00. (01532 677151).

British Cheque Collectors' Society (1980). John Purser, 71 Mile Lane, Cheylesmore, Coventry, West Midlands CV3 5GB.

British Numismatic Society (1903). Warburg Institute, Woburn Square, London WC1H 0AB. Monthly meetings (exc Aug & Dec), 18.00. (020 7323 8585)

Cambridgeshire Numismatic Society (1946). Friends' Meeting House, 12 Jesus Lane (entrance in Park Street), Cambridge, CB5 8BA. 3rd Mon, Sept–June, 19.30. (01480 210992).

Chester & North Wales Coin & Banknote Society (1996). Liver Hotel, 110 Brook Street, Chester. 4th Tue, 20.00. (0151 478 4293)

Crewe & District NS. Memorial Hall, Church Lane, Wistaston, Crewe. 2nd Tue, 19.30 (exc Jan & July). (01270 569836)

Derbyshire NS The Friends Meeting House, St Helen's Street, Derby. (01283 223893)

Devon & Exeter NS, Courtenay Room, The St James Centre, Stadium Way, Exeter. 3rd Wed. (01395 568830)

Essex Numismatic Society (1966). Chelmsford Museum, Moulsham Street, Chelmsford, Essex. 4th Fri (exc Dec), 20.00. (01277 656627).

Glasgow & West of Scotland NS (1947). Woodside Halls, 26 Glenfarg Street, Glasgow, G3. 2nd Thu, Oct–May, 19.30. (0141 9424776).

Harrow Coin Club (1968). The Scout Building, off Walton Road, Wealdstone, Harrow. 2nd and 4th Mon, 19.30. (01923 826392).

Havering Numismatic Society (1967). Fairkytes Arts Centre, Billet Lane, Hornchurch, Essex. 1st Tue, 19.30. (07910 124549).

Horncastle & District Coin Club (1963). Bull Hotel, Bull Ring, Horncastle, Lincs. 2nd Thu (exc Aug), 19.30. (01754 2706).

Huddersfield Numismatic Society (1947). The Albert Hotel, Victoria Lane, Huddersfield. 1st Mon (exc Jul & Aug), 19.30. (01484 866814).

Hull & District Numismatic Society (1967). The Young People's Institute, George Street, Hull. Monthly (exc Aug & Dec), 19.30. (01482 441933).

International Bank Note Society (1961). Victory Services Club, 63–79 Seymour Street, London W1. Website: www.ibns.org.uk. Last Thu (exc Dec), 18.00. (www.ibnslondon.org.uk).

Ipswich NS, Citizens Advice Bureau, 19 Tower Street, Ipswich. (01473 728653)

International Bank Note Society (East Midlands Branch), Wollaton Park Community Association, Wollaton Park, Nottingham. (0115 928 9720).

International Bank Note Society, Scottish Chapter (1995). West End Hotel, Palmerston Place, Edinburgh. Last Sat (exc Dec), 14.30.

Ireland, Numismatic Society of (Northern Branch). Denman International, Clandeboye Road, Bangor or Shaws Bridge Sports Assoc.123 Milltown Road, Belfast. 1st Fri 19.30. (028 9146 6743)

Ireland, Numismatic Society of. (Southern Branch). Ely House, 8 Ely Place, Dublin. Third Fri, 20.00. (0035 3 283 2027).

Ipswich Numismatic Society (1966). Ipswich Citizens Advice Bureau, 19 Tower Street, Ipswich, Suffolk. Monthly meetings, 19.30. (01473 728653).

Kent Towns Numismatic Society (1913). (Mr. R. Josland, 01634 721187).

Kingston Numismatic Society (1966). St Paul's Parish Hall, 280 Hook Road, Chessington, Surrey. Meetings 3rd Thu (exc Dec & Jan), 19.30. (020-8397 6944).

Lancashire & Cheshire Numismatic Society (1933). Reception Room, 2nd Floor, Manchester Central Library, St Peter's Square, Manchester. Monthly, Sep-June, Sat (14.00). Manchester Museum (May & Dec only). (0161 275 2661).

Lincolnshire Numismatic Society (1932). Grimsby Bridge Club, Bargate, Grimsby, South Humberside. 4th Wed (exc Aug), 19.30.

London Numismatic Club (1947). Warburg Institute, Woburn Square, London WC1H 0AB. First Tuesday of month (except January and August), 1830. (01223 332918).

Loughborough Coin & Search Society (1964). Wallace Humphry Room, Shelthorpe Community Centre, Loughborough, Leics. 1st Thu, 19.30. (01509 261352).

Mid Lanark Coin Circle (1969). Hospitality Room, The Civic Centre, Motherwell, Lanarkshire. 4th Thu, Sep–Apr (exc Dec), 19.30. (0141-552 2083).

Newbury Coin & Medal Club (1971). Monthly, 20.00. (01635 41233).

Northampton Numismatic Society (1969). Old Scouts RFC, Rushmere Road, Northampton.
Norwich Coin & Medal Society, The White Horse, Trowse, Norwich. (01603 408393).

Norwich Numismatic Society (1967). Assembly House, Theatre Street, Norwich, Norfolk. 3rd Mon, 19.30. (01603 408393).

NS of Nottinghamshire (1948). Highfields Fire Station, Hassocks Lane, Beeston, Nottingham. 2nd Tue (Sep-Apr), 18.45. (0115 9257674).

Nuneaton & District Coin Club (1968). United Reformed Church Room, Coton Road, opposite Council House, Nuneaton, Warwickshire. 2nd Tue, 19.30. (01203 371556).

Orders & Medals Research Society (1942). National Army Museum, Royal Hospital Road, Chelsea, London SW3. Monthly, 14.30 (020-8680 2701).

Ormskirk & West Lancashire Numismatic Society (1970). The Eagle & Child, Maltkiln Lane, Bispham Green L40 1SN. 1st Thu, 20.15. (01704 531266).

Peterborough & District Numismatic Society (1967). Belsize Community Centre, Celta Road Peter-borough, Cambs. 4th Tue (exc July & Aug), 19.30. (01733 562768 or 567763).

Plymouth Numismatics Society (1970). Mutley Conservative Club, Mutley Plain, Plymouth, Devon. Meetings on second Wed (exc Dec), 19.30. (01752 490 394).

Reading Coin Club (1964). Abbey Baptist Church, Abbey Square, Reading. 1st Mon, 20.00. (01753 516390).

Romsey Numismatic Society (1969). Romsey WM Conservative Club, Market Place, Romsey, Hants SO5 8NA. 4th Fri (exc Dec), 19.30. (01703 253921).

Rotherham & District Coin Club (1982). Rotherham Art Centre, Rotherham, South Yorkshire. 1st Wed, 19.00. (01709 528179).

Royal Mint Coin Club, PO Box 500, Cardiff CF1 1HA (01443 222111).

Royal Numismatic Society (1836). Warburg Institute, Woburn Square, London, WC1H 0AB. (some meetings held at British Museum). Third Thursday of monthly (Oct-June), 18.00. Joe Cribb, Coins and Medals, British Museum, London WC1B 3DG (020-7323 8175).

Rye Coin Club (1955). Rye Further Education Centre, Lion Street, Rye, East Sussex. 2nd Thu (Oct-Dec, Feb-May), 19.30. (01424 422974).

St Albans & Hertfordshire Numismatic Society (1948). St Michael's Parish Centre, Museum Entrance, Verulamium Park, St Albans, Herts AL3 4SL. 2nd Tue (exc Aug), 19.30. (01727 824434).

Southampton and District Numismatic Society (1953). Central Baptist Church, Devonshire Road, Polygon, Southampton SO15 2GY. Contact T. Winsborough, (02380 556648).

South East Hants Numismatic Society. The Langstone Conservative Club, Havant. Second Fri. Contact: Tony Matthews, (01292 389419)

South Manchester Numismatic Society (1967). Nursery Inn, Green Lane, Heaton Mersey, Stockport. 1st & 3rd Mondays of each month (excl. Public hols), 20.15. (0161-476 3184).

South Wales & Monmouthshire Numismatic Society (1958). 1st Mon (except Bank Holidays when 2nd Mon, 19.30. (For location tel: 029 20561564).

Thurrock Numismatic Society (1970). Stanley Lazell Hall, Dell Road, Grays, Essex. 3rd Wed, 19.00.

Tyneside Numismatic Society (1954). RAFA Club, Eric Nelson House, 16 Berwick Road, Gateshead, Tyne & Wear. Meetings on second Wed, 19.30. (01661 825824).

Wessex NS (1948). Edward Wright Room, Beaufort Community Centre, Southbourne, Bournemouth, Dorset. 2nd Thurs (exc Aug), 20.00. (020 7731 1702).

Wiltshire Numismatic Society (1965). The Raven Inn, Poulshot, Nr. Devizes, Wiltshire. 3rd Wednesday, March–Dec, 20.00. (01380 828453).

Worthing & District Numismatic Society (1967). The Beechwood Hall Hotel, Wykeham Road, Worthing, BN11 4JD. 3rd Thu, 20.00. (01634 260114).

Yorkshire Numismatic Society (1909). Swarthmore Institute, Woodhouse Square, Leeds. 1st Sat (exc Jan, Aug & Dec) (0113 3910848).

Important Notice to Club Secretaries:

If your details as listed are incorrect please let us know in time for the next edition of the **COIN YEARBOOK**. Amendments can be sent via post or email to: fiona@tokenpublishing.com

IMPORTANT ORGANISATIONS

ADA
The Antiquities
Dealers Association

Secretary: Susan Hadida, Duke's Court, 32 Duke Street, London SW1Y 6DU

ANA
The American
Numismatic Association

818 North Cascade Avenue, Colorado Springs, CO 80903-3279, USA

BNTA
The British Numismatic
Trade Association

Secretary: Mrs R. Cooke, General Secretary, BNTA, PO Box 2, Rye, East Sussex TN31 7WE

IAPN
International Association of
Professional Numismatists

Secretary: Jean-Luc Van der Schueren, 14 Rue de la Bourse, B–1000, Brussels.

IBNS
International
Bank Note Society

Membership Secretary:
David Hunt, PO Box 412, Halifax
W. Yorks HX3 5YD

RNS
Royal Numismatic Society

Dept of Coins & Medals, British Museum, London WC1B 3DG.

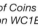

BAMS
British Art Medal Society

Philip Attwood, Dept of Coins & Medals, British Museum, London WC1B 3DG.

BNS
British Numismatic Society

Dr K. Clancy, The Royal Mint,
Llantrisant, Pontyclun,
Mid Glamorgan CF72 8YT

Society activities are featured every month in the "Diary Section" of COIN NEWS— available from all good newsagents or on subscription.
Telephone 01404 44166 for more details or log onto www.tokenpublishing.com

DIRECTORY
of auctioneers

Listed here are the major auction houses which handle coins, medals, banknotes and other items of numismatic interest. Many of them hold regular public auctions, whilst others handle numismatic material infrequently. A number of coin companies also hold regular Postal Auctions—these are marked with a **℗**

Art Coins Roma
Via Del Babuino 89, 00187 Rome, Italy.
(+39 0632609795, wwwartcoinsroma.it)

Baldwin's Auctions Ltd
399 The Strand, London WC2R 0LX.
(020 7930 6879, fax 020 7930 9450,
coins@baldwin.co.uk, www.baldwin.co.uk).

Banking Memorabilia
(016974 76465) memorabilia74@btinternet.com.
In association with Thomson Roddick & Medcalf,
Carlisle.

Biddle & Webb
Ladywood, Middleway, Birmingham, B16 0PP.
(0121 455 8042, www.biddleandwebb.com)

Blyth & Co
7/9 Market Square, Ely, Cambs, CB7 4NP.
(01353 668320, auctions@fenlord.com).

Bonhams (incorporating Glendinings)
Montpelier Street, Knightsbridge, London
SW7 1HH. (020 7393 3914, www.bonhams.com).

BSA Auctions
Units 1/2, Cantilupe Court, Cantilupe Road, Ross
on Wye, Herefordshire HR9 7AN . (01989 769529,
bids@birmauctions.co.uk,
www.birmauctions.co.uk).

Bushey Auctions
(020 8386 2552, enquiries@busheyauctions.
com, www.busheyauctions.com).

cgb.fr
(contact@cgb.fr, www.cgbfr.com)

Christie, Manson & Wood Ltd
8 King Street, St James's, London SW1Y 6QT.
(020 7839 9060).

Classical Numismatic Group Inc (Seaby Coins)
14 Old Bond Street, London W1X 4JL.
(020 7495 1888 fax 020 7499 5916,
cng@historicalcoins.com,
www.historicalcoins.com). **℗**

Corbitts
5 Moseley Sreet, Newcastle upon Tyne NE11YE.
(0191-232 7268, fax 0191-261 4130).

Croydon Coin Auctions
PO Box 201, Croydon, CR9 7AQ. (020 8656 4583,
www.croydoncoinauctions.co.uk).

Davissons Ltd.
PO Box 323, Cold Spring, MN 56320 USA.
((001) 320 6853835, info@davcoin.com,
www.davcoin.com).

Dix Noonan Webb (IAPN)
16 Bolton Street, Piccadilly, London.
(020 7016 1700, auctions@dnw.co.uk,
www.dnw.co.uk).

Dublin Coin Auction
5 St. Assam's Park, Raheny, Dublin 5.
(00 353 868 714 880).

Duke's
Brewery Square, Dorchester, Dorset DT1 1GA.
(01305 265080, www.dukes-auctions.com)

Edinburgh Coin Shop
11 West Crosscauseway, Edinburgh EH8 9JW.
(0131 668 2928 fax 0131 668 2926). **℗**

English Coin Auctions
West Court Lodge, West Street,
Scarborough YO11 2QL. (01723 364760,
www.englishcoinauctions.com)

Jean Elsen & ses Fils s.a.
Avenue de Tervueren 65, B–1040, Brussels.
(0032 2 7346356, www.elsen.eu).

Fellows & Sons
Augusta House, 19 Augusta Street, Hockley,
Birmingham B18 6JA. (0121-212 2131,
www.fellows.co.uk).

B. Frank & Son
3 South Avenue, Ryton, Tyne & Wear NE40 3LD.
(0191 413 8749 fax 0191 413 2957,
bfrankandson@aol.com).

Goldberg Coins & Collectibles
350 South Beverly Drive, Ste. 350, Beverly Hills CA 90212. (001 310.432.6688, fax: 001 310.551.2626, www.goldbergcoins.com).

Heritage World Coin Auctions
3500 Maple Avenue, 17th Floor, Dallas, Texas 75219–3941, USA. (001 214 528 3500, fax 001 214 443 8425, www.heritagecoins.com).

International Coin Exchange
Charter House, 5 Pembroke Row, Dublin 2. (+353 (1) 6768775, email: auctionice@gmail.com, www.ice-auction.com).

Kleeford Coin Auctions
22 Peak Avenue, Riddings, Alfreton, Derbyshire, DE55 4AR. (01773 528743 or 07969 645952, www.kleefordcoins.webs.com, kleeford@btinternet.com). **Ⓟ**

Fritz Rudolf Künker
Nobbenburger, Strasse 4A, 49076, Osnabrüeck, Germany. (0049 541 9620224, fax: 0049 541 96 20222, www.kuenker.com).

Lawrence Fine Art Auctioneers
South Street, Crewkerne, Somerset TA18 8AB. (01460 73041).

Lockdale Coins
52 Barrack Square, Martlesham Heath, Ipswich, Suffolk, IP5 3RF37. (01473 627110, www.lockdales.com).

London Coins
4–6 Upper Street South, New Ash Green, Kent DA3 8JJ. (01474 871464, email: info@londoncoins.co.uk, www.londoncoins.co.uk).

Morton & Eden Ltd
45 Maddox Street, London W1S 2PE. (020 7493 5344 fax 020 7495 6325, info@mortonandeden.com, www.mortonandeden.com).

Mowbray Collectables
Private Bag 63000, Wellington New Zealand. (+64 6 364 8270, www.mowbraycollectables.co.nz).

Noble Numismatics
169 Macquire Street, Sydney, Australia. (+61 2 9223 4578, www.noble.com.au).

Numismatica Ars Classica NAC AG
3rd Floor, Genavco House, 17 Waterloo Place, London SW1Y 4AR (020 783 97270, email: info@arsclassicacoins.com).

Pacific Rim Online Auction
P O Box 847, North Sydney, NSW 2060, Australia. (+61 2 9588 7111, www.pacificrimonlineauctions.com) Online coin auction.

Penrith, Farmers' & Kids PLC
Skirsgill Saleroom, Penrith, Cumbria, CA11 0DN. (01768 890781, www.pfkauctions.co.uk)

Simmons Gallery
PO Box 104, Leytonstone, London. (Tel: 0207 8989 8097. info@simmonsgallery.co.uk, www.simmonsgallery.co.uk). **Ⓟ**

Smiths of Newent
The Old Chapel, Culver Street, Newent, GL18 1DB. (Tel: 01531 821776. info@smithsauctionroom.co.uk, www.smithsnewentauctions.co.uk.

Spink & Son Ltd
69 Southampton Row, Bloomsbury, London WC1B 4ET. (020 7563 4000, fax 020 7563 4066, info@spink.com, www.spink.com).

Stacks, Bowers and Ponterio
118061 Fitch, Irvine, California 92614, USA. (001 949 253 0916, www.stacksbowers.com

St James's Auctions
10 Charles II Street, London SW1Y 4AA. (020 7930 7888, www.sixbid.com).

Tennants Auctioneers
The Auction Centre, Leyburn, North Yorkshire DL8 5SG. (01969 623780, www.tennants.co.uk).

The-saleroom.com
115 Shaftesbury Avenue, London WC2H 8AF. Live bidding in real-time auctions from around the world. (www.the-saleroom.com).

Thomson Roddick & Metcalf
Coleridge House, Shaddongate, Carlisle CA2 5TU. (01228 528939, www.thomsonroddick.com).

Timeline Auctions
PO Box 193, Upminster RM14 3WH. (01708 222824, www.timelineauctions.com).

Mavin International
20 Kramat Lane, #01-04/05 United House, Singapore 228773. (+65 6238 7177) mail@mavininternational.com).

Warwick & Warwick
Chalon House, Scarbank, Millers Road, Warwick CV34 5DB. (01926 499031 fax 01926 491906, richard.beale@warwickandwarwick.com, www.warwickandwarwick.com). www.wilkesandcurtis.com).

Whyte's Auctions
38 Molesworth Street, Dublin2, Ireland. (+00 3531 676 2888, www.whytes.com).

Wilkes & Curtis
PO Box 566, Tonbridge, Kent TN9 9LR (07535 383321)

Woolley & Wallis
51-61 Castle Street, Salisbury, Wiltshire SP1 3SU. (01722 424594, www.woolleyandwallis.co.uk)

DIRECTORY *of fair*

Listed below are the names of the fair organisers, their venue details where known along with contact telephone numbers. Please call the organisers direct for information on dates etc.

Aberdeen
Jarvis Amatola Hotel, Great Western Road, also venues in **Glenrothes** and **Glasgow.** *Cornucopia Collectors Fairs (01382 224946).*

Birmingham
National Motor Cycle Museum, Bickenhill, Birmingham. *Midland Stamp & Coin Fair (01694 731781, www.midlandfair.co.uk).*

Birmingham
Collingwood Centre, Collingwood Drive, Great Barr, Birmingham. *Dave Burnett Fairs (0776 5792998).*

Bristol
Patchway Community College, Hempton Lane, Almondsbury, Bristol. *Minster Stamps (01522 857343, minsterstamps@ntlworld.com).*

Britannia Medal Fair
Carisbrooke Hall, The Victory Services Club, 63/79 Seymour Street, London W2 2HF. *Coin & Medal Fairs Ltd (01694 731781).*

Colchester
Stanway Football Club, New Farm Road, Colchester. *ClickCollect Fairs (01485 578117).*

Cardiff
City Hall, Cardiff. *M. J. Promotions. (01792 415293).*

Dublin
Serpentine Hall, RDS, Ballsbridge, Dublin 4. *Mike Kelly (00353 86 87 14 880).*

Eastleigh
The Pavilion, Southampton University, Wide Lane Sports GroundEastleigh, Hants. *South Coast Coin Fair (07890 764452).*

East Grinstead
Sackville School, Bourg-De-Peague Avenue, East Grinstead, RH19 3TY. *John Terry Fairs (01342 326317).*

Ely
The Maltings, Ship Lane, Ely. *ClickCollect (01485 578117).*

Exeter
The America Hall, De La Rue Way, Pinhoe, Exeter. *Michael Hale Collectors Fairs (01761 414304).*

Harrogate
Old Swan Hotel, Swan Road, Harrogate HG1 2SR. *Simon Monks (01234 270260).*

Lichfield
Civic Hall, Castle Dyke, City Centre. *C. S. Fairs (01562 710424).*

London
Holiday Inn, Coram St., Bloomsbury, London WC1. *London Coin Fair. (01694 731781).*

London
Jury's Hotel, 16-22 Great Russell Street, London WC1 3NN. *Bloomsbury Fairs (01694 731781).*

Plymouth
Lower Guildhall. *Bruce Stamps (01749 813324).*

Stowmarket
Stowmarket Football Club, Bury Road, Stowmarket. *ClickCollect (01485 578117).*

Suttton Coldfield
Fellowship Hall, South Parade. *C. S. Fairs (01562 710424).*

Newcastle upon Tyne
The Park Hotel, Tynemouth, Newcastle upon Tyne. *B. Frank & Son (0191 413 8749).*

Wakefield
Cedar Court Hotel, Denby Dale Road, Calder Grove, Wakefield *Eddie Smith (01552 684681).*

West Bromwich
Town Hall, High Street. *C. S. Fairs (01562 710424).*

York
The Grandstand, York Race Course. *York Coin Fair (01793 513431, 020 8946 4489 or 01425 656459).*

Information correct at time of going to press

Important annual events — The B.N.T.A. (Coinex), Tel: 01797 229 988 for details
The I.B.N.S. (World Paper Money Fair), Email: enquiries@wpmf.info for details

COIN, MEDAL & BANKNOTE FAIRS

THE LONDON COIN FAIR
HOLIDAY INN
London, Bloomsbury, Coram Street, WC1N 1HT
2015 dates: 7th November
2016 dates: 6th February, 4th June, 3rd September, 5th November

THE MIDLAND COIN FAIR
NATIONAL MOTORCYCLE MUSEUM
Bickenhill, Birmingham, B92 0EJ
(Opposite the NEC on the M42/A45 junction)
2015 dates: 11th October, 8th November, 13th December
2016 dates: 10th January, 14th February, 13th March, 10th April,
8th May, 12th June, 10th July, 14th August, 11th September,
9th October, 13th November, 11th December

BRITANNIA MEDAL FAIR
CARISBROOKE HALL
The Victory Service Club,
63/79 Seymour Street, London W2 2HF
2015 dates: 15th November
2016 dates: 20th March, 20th November

For more information please contact:
Lu Veissid, Hobsley House, Frodesley, Shrewsbury SY5 7HD
Tel: 01694 731781   Email: l.veissid@btinternet.com

www.coinfairs.co.uk

Like us on facebook **f** @ coin and medal fairs
Follow us on twitter 🐦@coinmedalfairs

DEALERS *directory*

The dealers listed below have comprehensive stocks of coins and medals, unless otherwise stated. Specialities, where known, are noted. Many of those listed are postal dealers only, so to avoid disappointment always make contact by telephone or mail in the first instance, particularly before travelling any distance.

Abbreviations:
ADA— — Antiquities Dealers Association
ANA — American Numismatic Association
BADA — British Antique Dealers Association
BNTA — British Numismatic Trade Association
IAPN — International Association of Professional Numismatists
IBNS — International Bank Note Society
P — — Postal only
L — — Publishes regular lists

ABC Coins & Tokens
PO Box 52, Alnwick, Northumberland NE66 1YE. (01665 603851, email: d–stuart@d–stuart.demon. co.uk, www.abccoinsandtokens.com).

A. Ackroyd (IBNS)
62 Albert Road, Parkstone, Poole, Dorset BH12 2DB. (Tel/fax 01202 739039, www.AAnotes.com). **P L** *Banknotes and cheques*

Airedale Coins (ANA, BNTA)
PO Box 392, Guiseley, Leeds LS19 9JG. (01943 876221, email: info@airedalecoins.com, www.airedalecoins.co.uk). **P L** *British and modern coins of the world.*

Joan Allen Electronics Ltd
190 Main Road, Biggin Hill, Kent TN16 3BB. (01959 571255). Mon–Sat 09.00–17.00. *Metal detectors.*

Allgold of Sevenoaks
P.O Box 260, Wallington, SM5 4H. (0844 5447952, email: sales@allgoldcoins.co.uk, www.allgoldcoins. co.uk). *Quality Sovereigns.*

A. J. W. Coins
Taunton, Somerset. (0845 680 7087, email: andrewwide@ajw-coins.co.uk, www.ajw-coins. co.uk). **P** *Sovereigns and CGS-UK specialist.*

Dave Allen Collectables
Shop 1: 52 High Street, Biggleswade SG18 0LJ. Shop 2: Antiques Emporium, 13 Fishers Yard, St NEOTS, PE19 2AG. (07541 461021. Email: coinsandmedals@outlook.com, www.daveallencollectables.co.uk). *Coins, medals, banknotes, bullion and jewellery.*

AMR COINS
(07527 569308, www.amrcoins.com). *Quality English coins specialising in rare hammered and milled coins.*

Ancient & Gothic
PO Box 5390, Bournemouth, BH7 6XR. (01202 431721). **P L** *Greek, Roman, Celtic and Biblical coins. English hammered coins & antiquities.*

Otavio Anze
Avenida Oaula Ferreira, 2159 Vila Bonilha. Pirtuba. Sao Paulo. SP. Brazil.
Coins, Antiques and collectables.

Argentum Coins
PO Box 130, Peterlee, Co Durham SR8 9BE (07720769005, email: john.stephenson815@sky. com, www.argentumandcoins.co.uk). *British milled coins from 1662 to date.*

Arghans
Unit 9, Callington Business Park, Tinners Way Moss side, Callington PL17 7SH. (01579 382405, email: keithp44@waitrose.com). *British banknotes.*

ARL Collectables
(www.litherlandcollectables.com).
Coins, banknotes, medallions and paper emphemera.

S P Asimi
Cabinet at The Emporium, 112 High Street, Hungerford, Berkshire RG17 0NB. (01488 686959) *British milled coins.*

Atlas Numismatics
10 Jay Street, Suite 706, Brooklyn, NY 11201 USA. (www.atlasnumismatics.com)
Ancient, world and US coinage

ATS Bullion (BNTA)
2, Savoy Court, Strand. London WC2R 0EZ. (020 7240 4040, email: bullion@atslimited.fsnet. co.uk). *Bullion and modern coins.*

Keith Austin (IBNS)
10A-12-2 Pearl View Condo, Jalan Bunga Pudak, 1200, Tanjang Bunga, Penang, Malaysia. (0060 84890 7830 email: kaustin2368@gmail.com). **L** *Banknotes.*

Mark Bailey
120 Sterte Court, Sterte Close, Poole, Dorset
BH15 2AY. (01202 674936). **P L** *Ancient,
modern, world coins and antiquities.*

A. H. Baldwin & Sons Ltd (ANA, BADA, BNTA, IAPN)
399 The Strand, London WC2R 0LX.
09.00–17.00 weekdays.
(email: coins@baldwin.co.uk) *Coins, tokens,
commemorative medals, war medals and
decorations, numismatic books.*

Bath Stamp and Coin Shop
Pulteney Bridge, Bath, Avon BA2 4AY.
(01225 463073). Mon–Sat 09.30–17.30. *British.*

Michael Beaumont
PO Box 8, Carlton, Notts NG4 4QZ. (0115 9878361).
P *Gold & Silver English/Foreign Coins.*

Beaver Coin Room (BNTA)
57 Philbeach Gardens, London SW5 9ED.
(020 7373 4553). **P** *European coins and medals.*

R. P. & P. J. Beckett
Maesyderw, Capel Dewi, Llandyssul, Dyfed
SA44 4PJ. (Fax only 01559 395631, email:
becket@xin.co.uk). **P** *Coin sets and banknotes.*

Lloyd Bennett (BNTA)
PO Box 2, Monmouth, Gwent NP5 3YE. (01600
890634). Abergavenny Market (Tue), Monmouth
Market (Fri–Sat) 09.00–16.00. *English hammered,
milled and coins of the world.*

Berkshire Coin Centre
35 Castle Street, Reading, Berkshire RG1 7SB.
(0118 957 5593). 0630–15.00 W, Th, Fri & Sat.
Sat. *British British and world coins and militaria.*

Stephen J. Betts
4 Victoria Street, Narborough, Leics LE9 5DP.
(0116 2864434). **P L** *Medieval and modern coins,
counters, jetons and tokens, countermarks and
medals.*

Bigbury Mint
River Park, Ermington Mill, Ivybridge, Devon
PL21 9NT. (01548 830717. *Specialists in
reproduction hammered coins*

Jon Blyth
Office 63, 2 Lansdowne Row, Mayfair, London
W1J 6HL . (07919 307645. *Specialists in
quality British coins*

Barry Boswell and Kate Bouvier
24 Townsend Lane, Upper Boddington, Daventry,
Northants NN11 6DR. (01327 261877, fax 01327
261391, email: Barry.Boswell@btinternet.com).
P L *British and world banknotes.*

James & C. Brett
17 Dale Road, Lewes, East Sussex BN7 1LH.
P L *British and world coins.*

J. Bridgeman Coins
129a Blackburn Road, Accrington, Lancs
(01254 384757). 09.30–17.00 (closed Wednesday).
British & World coins.

Arthur Bryant Coins
PO Box 67499, London, NW3 3SN (07768 645686
email: abcoins@live.co.uk, website: www.bryancoins.
com). *British Coins and Medals.*

BRM Coins
3 Minshull Street, Knutsford, Cheshire WA16 6HG.
(01565 651480 and 0606 74522). Mon–Fri 11.00–
15.00, Sat 11.00–1.00 or by appt. *British coins.*

Bucks Coins
P O Box 199, Dereham, Norfolk (01392 638045,
07825 440085). *English milled coins, celtic and Roman.*

Iain Burn
2 Compton Gardens, 53 Park Road, Camberley,
Surrey GU15 2SP. (01276 23304).
Bank of England & Treasury notes.

BBM Coins
8–9 Lion Street, Kidderminster, Hereford &
Worcester, DY10 1PT. (01562 515007). Wed, Th, Fri.
10.00–14.00 or by appointment. *World coins.*

Cambridgeshire Coins
355 Newmarket Road, Cambridge CB5 8JG.
(01223 503073, info@cambridgeshirecoins.com,
www.cambridgeshirecoins.com).
Coins, banknotes and accessories.

Cambridge Stamp Centre Ltd
9 Sussex Street, Cambridge CB4 4HU.
(01223 63980). Mon–Sat 09.00–17.30.
British coins.

Castle Galleries
81 Castle Street, Salisbury, Wiltshire SP1 3SP.
(01722 333734). Tue, Thu Fri 09.00–17.00,
Sat 09.30–16.00. *British coins, medals and tokens.*

Cathedral Coins
23 Kirkgate, Ripon, North Yorkshire HG4 1PB.
(01765 701400). Mon–Sat 10.00–17.00.

Cathedral Court Medals
First Floor Office, 30A Market Place, West Ripon,
North Yorks HG4 1BN. (01765 601400). *Coin and
medal sales. Medal mounting and framing.*

Central Bank of Ireland
Currency Centre, Sandyford Road, Dublin 16,
Ireland. *Issuer of new coin and banknote issues of
Ireland.*

C. G. S.
4-6 Upper Street South, New Ash Green, Longfield,
Kent DA3 8JJ. (01474 874895, email: info@cgs-uk.
biz). *Coin grading service.*

Lance Chaplin
17 Wanstead Lane, Ilford, Essex IG1 3SB.
(020 8554 7154. www.shaftesburycoins.com).
P L *Roman, Greek, Celtic, hammered coins and
antiquities.*

Chard (BNTA)
Gold & Foreign Exchange: 521 Lytham Road,
Blackpool, Lancs FY4 1RJ. (01253 473931)
Main Showroom: 32-36 Harrowside, Blackpool,
FY4 1RJ. (01253 843525). (www.chards.co.uk,
info@chards.co.uk). Mon–Sat 09.00–17.00.
British and world coins.

Jeremy Cheek Coins Ltd
(01923 450385/07773 872686,
jeremycoins@aol.com). *Advice, valuation and
representation at auctions.*

Nigel A. Clark
28 Ulundi Road, Blackheath, London SE3 7UG. (020
8858 4020, email: nigel.a.clark@btinternet.com). **P L**
Tokens (Mainly 17th century) and British Farthings.

Classical Numismatic Group (IAPN)
20 Bloomsbury Street, London, WC1B 3QA.
(020 7495 1888, email cng@cngcoins.com,
www.cngcoins.com). **P** *Ancient and world coins.*
Publishers of the Classical Numismatic Review.
Regular high quality auctions of ancient coins.

Paul Clayton (BNTA)
PO Box 21, Wetherby, West Yorkshire LS22 5JY.
(01937 72441). *Modern gold coins.*

André de Clermont (BNTA)
PO Box 3615, London, SW10 0YD. (020 7351 5727,
Fax 020 7352 8127). *World coins, especially Islamic.*

M. Coeshaw
PO Box 115, Leicester LE3 8JJ. (0116 287 3808). **P**
Coins, banknotes, coin albums and cases.

Philip Cohen Numismatics (ANA, BNTA)
20 Cecil Court, Charing Cross Road, London
WC2N 4HE. (020 7379 0615). Mon–Sat 11.00–17.30.

Coin & Collectors Centre
PO Box 22, Pontefract, West Yorkshire WF8
1YT. (01977 704112, email sales@coincentre.co.uk,
www.coincentre.co.uk). **P***British coins.*

Coinage of England
51 Arnhem Wharf, 2 Arnhem Place, Canary Wharf,
London, E1 3RU. (020 7538 5686,
www.coinageofengland.co.uk). *Fine and rare English
Coins.*

Coincraft (ANA, IBNS)
44/45 Great Russell Street, London, WC1B 3JL.
(020 7636 1188 and 020 7637 8785 fax 020
7323 2860, email: info@coincraft.com). Mon–
Fri 09.30–17.00, Sat 10.00–14.30. **L**(newspaper
format). *Coins and banknotes.*

Coinote
74 Elwick Road, Hartlepool TS26 9AP. Tel: 01429
890894. www.coinnote.co.uk. Coins, Medals, ,
Banknotes and accessories.

Coinswap.co.uk
Swap, sell or trade coins.

Coins of Beeston
PO Box 19, Beeston, Notts BG9 2NE.**P L**
Tokens, medals and paranumismatics.

Coins of Canterbury
PO Box 47, Faversham, Kent ME13 7HX.
(01795 531980). **P** *English coins.*

Collectors' World (Mark Ray)
188 Wollaton Road, Wollaton, Nottingham NG8 1HJ.
(01159 280347). *Coins, Banknotes, Accessories.*

Constantia CB
15 Church Road, Northwood, Middlesex
HA6 1AR. **P** *Roman and medieval hammered coins.*

Colin Cooke
P.O. Box 602, Altrincham, WA14 5UN. (0161
927 9524 fax 0161 927 9540, email coins@colin
cooke.com, www.colincooke.com).
L*British coins.*

Colonial Coins & Medals
218 Adelaide Street, Brisbane, QLD 4001.
(Email:coinshop@bigpond.net.au).
Auctions of World coins

Corbitts (BNTA)
5 Mosley Street, Newcastle Upon Tyne NE1 1YE.
(0191 232 7268 fax: 0191 261 4130). *Dealers and
auctioneers of all coins and medals.*

David Craddock
PO Box 3785, Camp Hill, Birmingham B11 2NF.
(0121 733 2259) **L***Crown to farthings. Copper and
bronze specialist. Some foreign.*

Roy Cudworth
8 Park Avenue, Clayton West, Huddersfield HD8
9PT. *British and world coins.*

Paul Dawson
47 The Shambles, York, YO1 7XL, (01904 654769
email: pauldawsonyork@hotmail.com, www.
historycoin.com. *Ancient and British coins.*

Mark Davidson
PO Box 197, South Croydon, Surrey, CR3 0ZD.
(020 8651 3890). *Ancient, hammered coinage.*

Paul Davis
PO Box 418, Birmingham, B17 0RZ.
(0121 427 7179). *British and World Coins.*

R. Davis
(01332 862755 days/740828 evenings). *Maker of
traditional coin cabinets.*

Paul Davies Ltd (ANA, BNTA, IAPN)
PO Box 17, Ilkley, West Yorkshire LS29 8TZ.
(01943 603116 fax 01943 816326). **P**
World coins.

Ian Davison
PO Box 256, Durham DH1 2GW (0191 3750808).**L**
English hammered and milled coins 1066–1910.

Dei Gratia
PO Box 3568, Buckingham MK18 4ZS (01280
848000).**P L** *Pre–Roman to modern coins,
antiquities, banknotes.*

Den of Antiquity
(01223 863002, www.denof antiquity.co.uk.)
Ancient and medieval coins.

Clive Dennett (BNTA)
66 St Benedicts Street, Norwich, Norfolk NR2 4AR.
(01603 624315). Mon–Fri 09.00–17.30, Sat 09.00–
16.00 (closed 1.00–2.00 & Thu).**L** *Specialising in
paper money.*

C. J. Denton (ANA, BNTA, FRNS)
PO Box 25, Orpington, Kent BR6 8PU (01689
873690).**P** *Irish coins.*

Detecnicks
3 Orchard Crescent, Arundel Road, Fontwell. West
Sussex BN18 0SA. (01243 545060 fax 01243
545922) *Retail shop.*
Wide range of detectors.

Michael Dickinson (ANA, BNTA)
Ramsay House, 825 High Road Finchley, London
N12 8UB. (0181 441 7175).**P**
British and world coins.

Douglassaville.com
(0118 918 7628). *Out of print, second-hand and rare
coin and medal books.*

Eagle Coins
Winterhaven, Mourneabbey, Mallow, Co. Cork,
Ireland. (010 35322 29385).**P L** *Irish coins.*

Early World Coins
7–9 Clifford Street, York, YO1 9RA. (08454 900724).

Edinburgh Coin Shop (ANA)
11 West Crosscauseway, Edinburgh EH8 9JW.
(0131 668 2928 fax 0131 668 2926). Mon–Sat
10.00–17.30. **L** *World coins and medals. Regular
Postal auctions of coins and collectables.*

Educational Coin Company
Box 892, Highland, New York 12528, USA.
(+ 845 691 6100.) *World banknotes.*

Christopher Eimer (ANA, BNTA, IAPN)
PO Box 352 London NW11 7RF. (020 8458 9933
fax 020 8455 3535, email: art@christophereimer.
co.uk). ⓟ *Commemorative medals.*

Malcolm Ellis Coins
Petworth Road, Witley, Surrey, GU8 5LX. (01428
685566, email: malcolm.ellis@wizardvideo.co.uk,
www.malcolmelliscoins.co.uk). *Collectors
and dealers of British and foreign coins*

Elm Hill Stamps & Coins
27 Elm Hill, Norwich, Norfolk NR3 1HN. (01603
627413). Mon. 09.00–17.00, Tues–Wed. 09.00–
17.00, Thur. 0900–13.00, Sat. 09.30–15.00. *Mainly
stamps, occasionally coins.*

Europa Numismatics (ANA, BNTA)
PO Box 119, High Wycombe, Bucks HP11 1QL.
(01494 437307). ⓟ *European coins.*

Evesham Stamp & Coin Centre
Magpie Antiques, Paris House, 61 High Street,
Evesham, Worcs WR11 4DA (01386 41631).
Mon–Sat 09.00–17.30. *British coins.*

Michael E. Ewins
Meyrick Heights, 20 Meyrick Park Crescent,
Bournemouth, Dorset BH3 7AQ. (01202 290674).ⓟ
World coins.

Robin Finnegan Stamp Shop
83 Skinnergate, Darlington, Co Durham DL3 7LX.
(01325 489820/357674). Mon–Sat 10.00–17.30
(closed Wed). *World coins.*

David Fletcher (Mint Coins) (ANA, BNTA)
PO Box 64, Coventry, Warwickshire CV1 5YR.
(024 7671 5425, Fax 024 7601 0300). ⓟ
World new issues.

Format of Birmingham Ltd (ANA, BNTA, IAPN, IBNS)
2nd Floor, Burlington Court, Lower Temple Street,
Birmingham, B2 4JD. (0121 643 2058 fax 0121 643
2210). Mon–Fri 09.30–7.00. Ⓛ *Coins, tokens
and medals.*

B. Frank & Son (ANA, IBNS)
3 South Avenue, Ryton, Tyne & Wear NE40 3LD.
(0191 413 8749. www.b–frank–and–son.
co.uk). ⓟ Ⓛ*Banknotes and cheques.*

Galata Coins Ltd (ANA)
The Old White Lion, Market Street, Llanfylin,
Powys SY22 5BX. (01691 648 765).ⓟ*British and
world coins.*

G. Gant
Glazenwood, 37 Augustus Way, Witham, Essex
CM8 1HH. ⓟ*British and Commonwealth coins.*

A. & S. Gillis
59 Roykilner Way, Wombwell, Barnsley,
South Yorkshire S73 8DY. (01226 750371,
email: catalogues@gilliscoins.com. www.gilliscoins.
com). ⓟ Ⓛ*Ancient coins and antiquities.*

G. K. Coins
(Mob: 07956 838 572, email: info@gkcoins.co.uk).
Rare & common sovereigns. British & world coins.

Richard Gladdle – Northamptonshire
(01327 858511, email: gladdle@plumpudding.org).
Tokens. ⓟ Ⓛ

Glance Back Books
17 Upper Street, Chepstow, Gwent NP6 5EX.
(01291 626562). 10.30–17.30. *Coins, banknotes.*

Glendining's (Bonhams) (ANA, BNTA)
101 New Bond Street, London W1Y 9LG (020 7493
2445). Mon–Fri 08.30–17.00, Sat 08.30–13.00.
Auctioneers.

GM Coins
(01242 701144, email: gmcoins@blueyonder.co.uk,
www.gmonlinecoins.co.uk/gmcoins). *Hammered
and milled coins.*

Adrian Gorka Bond
(email: sales@ 1stsovereign.co.uk, website
www.1stsovereign.co.uk). *Coins bought and sold.*

Goulborn
4 Sussex Street, Rhyl LL18 1SG. (Tel: 01745
338112). *English Coins and Medallions.*

Ian Gradon
PO Box 359, Durham DH7 6WZ. (0191 3719 700,
email: igradon960@aol.com, www.worldnotes.
co.uk). Ⓛ *World banknotes.*

Eric Green—Agent in UK for Ronald J. Gillio Inc
1013 State Street, Santa Barbara, California, USA
93101. (020 8907 0015, Mobile 0468 454948).
Gold coins, medals and paper money of the world.

Philip Green
Suite 207, 792 Wilmslow Road, Didsbury,
Manchester M20 6UG. (0161 440 0685). *Gold coins.*

Gurnhills of Leicester
8 Nothampton Street, Leicester, LE1 1PA (0116
2556633). *British and World Coins and Banknotes.*

Hallmark Coins Ltd
PO Box 69991, I Canada Square, Canary Warf,
London (0800 612 7327 email: info@hallmarkcoins.
co.uk, www.hallmarkcoins.co.uk). British *Coins.*

Anthony Halse
PO Box 1856, Newport, Gwent NP6 2JN. (01633
413238).ⓟ Ⓛ*English and foreign coins and tokens.*

A. D. Hamilton & Co (ANA)
7 St Vincent Place, Glasgow G1 5JA. (0141 2215423,
email: jefffineman@hotmail.com, www.adhamilton.
co.uk). Mon, Wed & Fri 10am–5pm; Tues, Thurs &
Sat 10am–4pm. *British and World coins.*

Peter Hancock
40–41 West Street, Chichester, West Sussex
PO19 1RP. (01243 786173). Tues–Sat. *World coins,
medals and banknotes.*

Munthandel G. Henzen
PO Box 42, NL – 3958ZT, Amerogngen, Netherlands.
(0031 343 430564 fax 0031 343 430542,
email: info@henzen.org, www.henzen.org).
Ⓛ*Ancients, Dutch and foreign coins.*

History In Coins.com
(01949 836988, www.historyincoins.com).
World coins.

Craig Holmes
6 Marlborough Drive, Bangor, Co Down BT19 1HB.
P **L** *Low cost banknotes of the world.*

R. G. Holmes
11 Cross Park, Ilfracombe, Devon EX34 8BJ. (01271 864474). **P** **L**
Coins, world crowns and banknotes.

Homeland Holding Ltd (IBNS)
Homeland, St John, Jersey, Channel Islands
JE3 4AB. (01534 65339). Mon–Fri 09.00–2.00.
World coins.

HTSM Coins
26 Dosk Avenue, Glasgow G13 4LQ. **P** **L**
British and foreign coins and banknotes.

M. J. Hughes Coins
27 Market Place, Alton, Hampshire, GU34 1HA.
(07917 160308). *World coins specialising in
sovereigns and krugerands.*

T. A. Hull
15 Tangmere Crescent, Hornchurch, Essex RM12
5PL. **P** **L** *British coins, farthings to crowns, tokens.*

J. Hume
107 Halsbury Road East, Northolt, Middlesex UB5
4PY. (020 8864 1731). **P** **L** *Chinese coins.*

D. A. Hunter
(Email: coins@dahunter.co.uk, www.dahunter.co.uk/
coins). **P** **L** *UK and World Coins.*

D. D. & A. Ingle
380 Carlton Hill, Nottingham. (0115 9873325).
Mon–Sat 09.30–17.00. *World coins.*

R. Ingram Coins
206 Honeysuckle Road, Bassett, Southampton,
Hants SO16 3BU. (023 8032 4258, email: info@
ringramcoins.com, www.ringramcoins.com). **P** **L**
Dealers in UK coins.

Isle of Wight Mint
PO Box 195, Cowes, Isle of Wight, PO30 9DP.
(www.iowmint.org). *Producer of Isle of Wight bullion.*

J. B. J. Coins
(www.jbjcoins.dk). *World coins and banknotes.*

F. J. Jeffery & Son Ltd
Haines Croft, Corsham Road, Whitley,
Melksham, Wilts SN12 8QF. (01225 703143). **P**
British, Commonwealth and foreign coins.

Richard W. Jeffery
Trebehor, Porthcurno, Penzance, Cornwall TR19
6LS. (01736 871263). **P** *British and world coins.
Banknotes.*

Jersey Coin Co Ltd
26 Halkett Street, St Helier, Jersey, Channel Islands.
(01534 25743). Mon–Sat 09.00–17.00. *World coins.*

JN Coins
(07916 145038): ,
www.jncoins.co.uk).
British coins from Celtic to modern.

Kates Paper Money
Kate Gibson, PO Box 819, Camberley, Surrey,
GU16 6ZU. email: kate@katespapemoney.co.uk,
www.katespapermoney.co.uk). *Banknotes.*

KB Coins (BNTA)
PO BOX 499, Stevenage, Herts, SG1 9JT.
(01438 312661, fax 01438 311990).
09.00–18.00 by appointment only. www.kbcoins.com
L *Mainly British coins.*

Kleeford Coins
22 Peak Avenue, Riddings, Alfreton, Derbyshire,
DE55 4AR. (01773 528743 or 07969 645952,
www.kleefordcoins.webs.com, kleeford@
btinternet.com). **P** *Monthly Auctions of coins,
banknotes, tokens & medals.*

K&M Coins
PO Box 3662, Wolverhampton WV10 6ZW.
(0771 2381880/079719 50246,
email: M_Bagguley@hotmail.com). *English milled coins.*

Knightsbridge Coins (ANA, BNTA, IAPN, PNG)
43 Duke Street, St James's, London SW1Y 6DD.
(020 7930 8215/7597 Fax 020 7930 8214). Mon–Fri
10.00–17.30. *Quality coins of the world.*

Lancashire Coin & Medal Co
31 Adelaide Street, Fleetwood, Lancs FY7 6AD .
(01253 779308). **P** *British coins and medals.*

Lighthouse Publications (Duncannon Partnership)
4 Beaufort Road, Reigate, Surrey RH2 9DJ (01737
244222 Fax 01737 224743. www.duncannnon.
co.uk). **L** *Manufacturers and stockists of coin
albums, cabinets and numismatic accessories.*

Liberty Coins and Bullion
17g Vyse Street, Birmingham, B18 6LE.
(0121 554 4432, wwwlibertycoinsbullion.co.uk)
Coins and precious metals.

Lindner Publications Ltd
3a Hayle Industrial Park, Hayle, Cornwall TR27 5JR.
(01736 751914 fax: 01736 751911, email
lindner@prinz.co.uk). Mon–Fri 09.00–13.00.
L *Manufacturers of coin albums, cabinets and
accessories.*

Jan Lis (BNTA)
Beaver Coin Room, 57 Philbeach Gardens, London
SW5 9ED. (020 7373 4553 fax 020 7373 4555).
By appointment only. *European coins.*

Keith Lloyd
45 Bramblewood, The Beeches, Ipswich, Suffolk
IP8 3RS. (01473 603067). **P** **L** *Ancient coins.*

Lockdale Coins (BNTA)
52 Barrack Square, Martlesham Heath, Ipswich,
Suffolk, IP5 3RF. (01473 627110) (www.lockdales.
com). **L** *World coins, medals and banknotes*

Stephen Lockett (BNTA)
4–6 Upper Street, New Ash Green, Kent, DA3 8JJ.
(01474 871464). *British and world coins.*

The London Coin Company
PO Box 495, Stanmore, Greater London, HA7 9HS
(0800 085 2933, 020 8343 2231, email:
sales@thelondoncoincompany.com,
www.thelondoncoincomany.com).
Modern gold and silver coins.

Mike Longfield Detectors
83 Station Road, Balsall Common, nr Coventry,
Warwickshire CV7 7FN. (01676 533274).
Mon–Sat 09.30–17.00. *Metal detectors.*

MA Shops
(www.mashops.com). On-line coin mall. *Coins,
medals, banknotes and accessories.*

Mannin Collections Ltd
5 Castle Street, Peel, Isle of Man, IM5 1AN. (01624
843897, email: manncoll@advsys.co.uk). Mon–Sat
10.00–16.00. Closed Thu. *IOM coins, tokens, etc.*

Manston Coins of Bath
8 Bartletts St. Antique Centre, Bath. (01225 487888).
Coins, tokens and medals.

I. Markovits
1–3 Cobbold Mews, London W12 9LB.
(020 8749 3000). *Enamelled coins.*

C. J. Martin Coins (BNTA)
The Gallery, Trent Park Equestrian Centre, Eastpole
Farm House, Bramley Road, Oakwood, N14 4UW.
(020 8364 4565, www.ancientart.co.uk).**P L**Bi–
monthly catalogue. *Greek, Roman & English hammered coins.*

Maverick Numismatics
(07403 111843, www.mavericknumismatics.com).
Coin and currency design.

M. G. Coins & Antiquities
12 Mansfield, High Wych, Herts CM21 0JT. (01279
721719). **L***Ancient and hammered coins, antiquities.*

M&H Coins
PO Box 10985, Brentwood, CM14 9JB. (07504
804019, www.mhcoins.co.uk). **L** *British hammered
and milled coins.*

Michael Coins
6 Hillgate Street, London W8 7SR. (020 7727 1518).
Mon–Fri 10.00–17.00. *World coins and banknotes.*

David Miller Coins & Antiquities (ANA, BNTA)
PO Box 711, Hemel Hempstead, HP2 4UH. (Tel/fax
01442 251492). *Ancient,hammered English coins.*

Timothy Millett
PO Box 20851, London SE22 0YN.
(Tel: 020 8693 1111, fax: 020 8299 3733,
www.historicmedals.com). **L**
Historical medals.

Nigelmills.net
(020 8504 2569. email: nigelmills@onetel.com,
www.nigelmills.net). *Coins and antiquities.*

Graeme & Linda Monk (ANA, BNTA)
PO Box 201, Croydon, Surrey, CR9 7AQ.
(020 8656 4583 fax 020 8656 4583). **P** .

Moore Antiquities
Unit 12, Ford Lane Industrial Estate, Ford, nr.
Arundel, West Sussex BN18 0AA. (01243 824 232,
email moore.antiquities@virgin.net).
Coins and artefacts up to the 18th Century.

Mike Morey
19 Elmtrees, Long Crendon, Bucks HP18 9DG.**P L**
British coins, halfcrowns to farthings.

Peter Morris (BNTA, IBNS)
1 Station Concourse, Bromley North Station,
Bromley, BR1 1NN or PO Box 223, Bromley,
BR1 4EQ (020 8313 3410 fax 020 8466 8502,
email: info@petermorris.co.uk, www.petermorris.
co.uk). Mon–Fri 10.00–18.00, Sat 0900–14.00 or
by appointment. **L** *British and world coins, proof
sets and numismatic books.*

N3 Coins—London
(07768 795575, email: mail@n3coins.com,
www.n3coins.com). *Roman and Ancient coins.*

Colin Narbeth & Son Ltd (ANA, IBNS)
20 Cecil Court, Leicester Square, London WC2N.
4HE (020 7379 6975 fax 01727 811 244,
www.colin–narbeth.com). Mon–Sat 10.30–17.00.
World banknotes.

John Newman Coins
(01903 239867, email: john@newmancoins.co.uk,
www.johnnewmancoins.co.uk)**.** *English hammered
coins, British milled coins and British tokens.*

Peter Nichols Cabinet Makers
(0115 922 4149, email: orders@coincabinets.com,
www.coincabinets.com). *Manufacturers of bespoke
mahogany coin and medal cabinets.*

Wayne Nicholls
PO Box 44, Bilston, West Midlands. (01543 45476).
L *Choice English coins.*

Northeast Numismatics (BNTA)
10 Concord Crossing Suite 220, Concord MA 01742,
USA (001 978 369 9155, fax: 001 978 369 9619,
www.northeastcoin.com).
British and world coins.

North Wales Coins Ltd (BNTA)
1b Penrhyn Road, Colwyn Bay, Clwyd. (01492
533023/532129). Mon–Sat (closed Wed) 09.30–
17.30. *British coins.*

NP Collectables
9 Main Street, Gedney Dyke, Spalding, Lincs PE12
0AJ. (01406 365211Ireland (010 35322 29385).**P L**
English Hammered and Milled coins.

Notability Notes (IBNS)
(Email: info@notability-banknotes.com,
www.notability-banknotes.com). *British,
Commonwealth and world notes.*

Oddysey Antiquities
PO Box 61, Southport PR9 0PZ.(01704 232494).
Classical antiquities, ancient and hammered coins.

Glenn S. Ogden
(01626 859350 or 07971 709427,
www.glennogdencoins.com).
P L *English milled coinage.*

John Ogden Coins
Hodge Clough Cottage, Moorside, Oldham OL1
4JW. (0161 678 0709)**P L***Ancient and hammered.*

Don Oliver Gold Coins
Stanford House, 23 Market Street, Stourbridge,
West Midlands DY8 1AB. (01384 877901).
Mon–Fri 10.00–17.00. *British gold coins.*

Ongar Coins
14 Longfields, Marden Ash, Ongar, Essex IG7 6DS.
P *World coins.*

Roger Outing
PO Box 123, Huddersfield HD8 9WY. (01484
60415, email: rogerandlizbanknotes4u.co.uk,
www.chequemate4collectors.co.uk). *World
banknotes.*

Tim Owen Coins
63 Allerton Grange Rise, Leeds 17, West Yorkshire.
P L *Quality hammered coins.*

P&D Medallions
PO Box 269, Berkhampstead, Herts HP4 3FT.
(01442 865127, www.pdmedallions.co.uk). **P**
Historical and Commemorative medals.

Del Parker
PO Box 7568, Dallas, TX 75209, USA.
(+ 1 214 352 1475. Email: Irishcoins2000@
hotmail.com, www.irishcoins.com). *Irish, American
Coins. Irish Art medals and banknotes.* **L**

www.paulspapermoney.com
Selling and buying high quality UK banknotes.

Pavlos S. Pavlou
Stand L17, Grays Antique Market, 1–7 Davies Mews, Mayfair, London W1Y 2LP. (020 7629 9449, email: pspavlou@hotmail.com). *Ancient to Modern*

PCGS
(+33 (0) 140200994, email:info@pcgsglobal.com, www.pcgs.com). *Coin grading and authentication.*

www.pennycrowncoins.co.uk
Specialising in British milled coins 1662–1970.

Penrith Coin & Stamp Centre
37 King Street, Penrith, Cumbria CA11 7AY. (01768 64185). Mon–Sat 09.00–17.30. *World coins.*

Pentland Coins (IBNS)
Pentland House, 92 High Street, Wick, Caithness KW14 L5. Ⓟ *British and world coins and banknotes.*

John Phillimore
The Old Post Office, Northwood, Shropshire SY4 5NN. Ⓛ *Foreign coins 1600–1950.*

Philip. P. Phipps
PO Box 139, Tiverton, Devon EX16 0AU. (07850 864554, email p.p.phipps@tesco.net).ⓅⓁ *World and German banknotes.*

B. C. Pickard
1 Treeside, Christchurch, Dorset BH23 4PF. (01425 275763, email: bcpickard@fsmail.net). Ⓟ *Stone Age, Greek, Roman items (inc. coins) for sale.*

Pobjoy Mint Ltd (ANA)
Millennium House, Kingswood Park, Bonsor Drive, Kingswood, Surrey KT20 6AY. (01737 818181 fax 01737 818199). Mon–Fri 09.00–17.00. *Europe's largest private mint. New issues.*

David Pratchett
UCCE, PO Box 57648, Mill Hill, London NW7 0FE. (07831 662594, fax 020 7930 1152, email: uccedcp@aol.com, www.coinsonline.co.uk). Mon–Fri 10.00–7.30. *Gold and silver world coins.*

Benjamin Prince
(07788 253345, benjamin.prince2@gmail.com). *Ancient Greek, Roman, English hammered coins, antiquities & shipwreck treasure.*

Pykerleys Collectables
PO Box 649, Whitley Bay NE26 9AF. (Email: pykereley@yahoo.co.uk, www.pykerley.worldonline.co.uk). *Western European and US coins.*

George Rankin Coin Co Ltd (ANA)
325 Bethnal Green Road, London E2 6AH. (020 7729 1280 fax 020 7729 5023). Mon–Sat 10.00–18.00 (half-day Thu). *World coins.*

Mark Rasmussen (BNTA, IAPN)
PO Box 42, Betchworth RH3 7YR. (01737 84100, Email: mark.rasmussen@rascoins.com, www.rascoins.com). Ⓛ *Quality hammered, milled coins.*

Mark T. Ray (see Collectors World)

Rhyl Coin Shop
12 Sussex Street, Rhyl, Clwyd. (01745 338112). Mon–Sat 10.00–17.30. *World coins and banknotes.*

Chris Rigby
PO Box 181, Worcester WR1 1YE. (01905 28028). ⓅⓁ*Modern British coins.*

Roderick Richardson (BNTA)
The Old Granary Antiques Centre, King's Staithe Lane, King's Lynn, Norfolk. (01553 670833, www.roderickrichardson.com) Ⓛ *English, Hammered and early milled coins.*

Charles Riley (BNTA)
PO Box 733, Aylesbury HP22 9AX. (01296747598, charles.riley@virgin.net, www.charlesriley.co.uk). *Coins, medals and medallions.*

Robin–on–Acle Coins
Parkeston House, Parkeston Quay, Harwich, Essex CO12 4PJ. (01255 554440, email: enquiries@robin-on–acle–coins.co.uk). *Ancient to modern coins and paper money.*

Roma Numismatics
20 Hanover Square, London, W1S 1JY. (020 3178 2874, www.romanumismatics.com). *Dealers and Auctioneers of fine ancient coins.*

S. J. Rood & Co Ltd
52–53 Burlington Arcade, London W1V 9AE. (0171 493 0739). Mon–Sat 09.30–17.00. *World gold coins.*

Royal Australian Mint
(www.ramint.gov.au). *New coin issues.*

Royal Gold
PO Box 123, Saxonwold, 2132, South Africa, (+27 11 483 0161, email: royalg@iafrica.com, www.royalgold.co.za). *Gold coins.*

Royal Mint Coin Club
PO Box 500, Cardiff CF1 1YY. (01443 623456).Ⓟ *Updates and special offers of new issues struck by the Royal Mint.*

Colin de Rouffignac (BNTA)
57, Wigan Lane, Wigan, Lancs WN1 2LF. (01942 237927). *P. English and Scottish hammered.*

R. P. Coins
PO Box 367, Prestwich, Manchester, M25 9ZH. (07802 713444, www.rpcoins.co.uk). *Coins, books, catalogues and accessories.*

Chris A. Rudd (IAPN, BNTA)
PO Box 222, Aylsham, Norfolk, NR11 6TY. (01263 735007 fax 01263 731777, www.celticcoins.com).ⓅⓁ *Celtic coins.*

Colin Rumney (BNTA)
PO Box 34, Denbighshire, North Wales, LL16 4YQ. (01745 890621). *All world including ancients.*

R & J Coins
21b Alexandra Street, Southend-on-Sea, Essex, SS1 1DA. (01702 345995). *World coins.*

Safe Albums (UK) Ltd
16 Falcon Business Park, 38 Ivanhoe Road, Finchampstead, Berkshire RG40 4QQ. (0118 932 8976 fax 0118 932 8612). *Accessories.*

Saltford Coins
Harcourt, Bath Road, Saltford, Bristol, Avon BS31 3DQ. (01225 873512, email: info@saltfordcoins.com, www.saltfordcoins.com). Ⓟ*British, Commonwealth and world coins.*

Satin Coins
PO Box 63, Stockport, Cheshire SK4 5BU. (07940 393583 answer machine).

Scotmint Ltd
68 Sandgate, Ayr, Scotland KA7 1BX (01292 268244), email: rob@scotmint.com, www.scotmint.com. *Coins, medals and banknotes.*

David Seaman
PO Box 449, Waltham Cross EN9 3WZ. (01992 719723, email: davidseamancoins@outlook.com). ⓅⓁ *Hammered, Milled, Maundy.*

Patrick Semmens
3 Hospital Road, Half Key, Malvern, Worcs WR14
1UZ. (0886 33123). **P** *European and British coins.*

Mark Senior
553 Falmer Road, Woodingdean, Brighton, Sussex
(01273 309359). By appointment only.
P L *Saxon, Norman and English hammered.*

S. E. Sewell
Cronin, Westhorpe Road, Finningham, Stowmarket,
Suffolk, IP14 4TN. (01449 782185 or 07739 071822,
email: sewellmedals@hotmail.com,
www.sewellmedals.co.uk). *Mainly British milled.*

Shepshed Coins & Jewellery
24 Charnwood Road, Shepshed, Leics LE12 9QF.
(01509 502511). Mon, Wed–Sat 09.15–16.30. *British
coins.*

Silbury Coins
PO Box 281, Cirencester, Gloucs GL7 9ET (info@
silburycoins.com, www.silburycoins.com). *Iron Age,
Roman, Saxon, Viking, medieval coins and later.*

Simmons Gallery (ANA, BNTA, IBNS)
PO Box 104, Leytonstone, London E11 1ND (020
8989 8097, www.simmonsgallery.co.uk). **L** *Coins,
tokens and medals.*

E. Smith (ANA, IBNS)
PO Box 348, Lincoln LN6 0TX (01522 684681 fax
01522 689528). Organiser of the Wakefield (formally
known as Leeds) monthly coin fair. **P** *World coins
and paper money.*

Neil Smith
PO Box 774, Lincoln LN4 2WX. (01522 522772 fax
01522 689528). *GB and World Gold coins 1816 to
date, including modern proof issues.*

Jim Smythe
PO Box 6970, Birmingham B23 7WD. (Email:
Jimdens@aol.com).**P L** *19th/20th century British
and world coins.*

Spink & Son Ltd (ANA, BNTA, IAPN, IBNS)
69 Southampton Row, Bloomsbury, London.
WC1B 4ET. (020 7563 4000, fax 020 7563 4066,
email: info@spinkandson.com, www.spink.com).
Ancient to modern world coins, medals, banknotes.

SPM Jewellers (BNTA)
112 East Street, Southampton, Hants SO14 3HD.
(023 80 223255/020 80 227923, fax 023 80 335634,
email: user@spm.in2home.co.uk, www.spm
goldcoins.co.uk). Tue–Sat 09.15–17.00,
Sat 09.15–16.00. *World coins and medals.*

Stamford Coins
65–67 Stamford Street, Bradford, West Yorkshire
BD4 8SD. (07791 873595, email: stamfordcoins@
hotmail.co.uk).

Stamp & Collectors Centre
404 York Town Road, College Town, Camberley,
Surrey GU15 4PR. (01276 32587 fax 01276 32505).
World coins and medals.

St Edmunds Coins & Banknotes
PO Box 118, Bury St Edmunds IP33 2NE.
(01284 761894).

Sterling Coins & Medals
2 Somerset Road, Boscombe, Bournemouth, Dorset
BH7 6JH. (01202 423881). Mon–Sat 09.30–16.30
(closed Wed). *World coins and medals.*

Studio Coins (ANA, BNTA)
Studio 111, 80 High Street, Winchester, Hants SO23
9AT. (01962 853156 email: stephenmitchell13@
bttconnect.com). **P** *English coins.*

Jeremy Tenniswood
2 Temple Road, Colchester, CO2 9JN. (Tel: 01206
368787, fax: 01206 367836, www.militaria.co.uk).
Orders, medals, decorations, militaria and related
books.

The Coin House
01935 824 878), email: thecoinhouse@
btinternet.com. *Quality investment coins and silver
bars.*

Time Line Originals
PO Box 193, Upminster, RM14 3WH. (01708
222384/ 07775 651218, email: sales@time–lines.
co.uk).

Stuart J. Timmins
Smallwood Lodge Bookshop, Newport, Salop.
(01952 813232). *Numismatic literature.*

R. Tims
39 Villiers Road, Watford, Herts WD1 4AL.**P L**
Uncirculated world banknotes.

Token Publishing Ltd
Orchard House, Duchy Road, Heathpark, Honiton,
Devon EX14 1YD (01404 46972, email info@
tokenpublishing.com, www.tokenpublishing.com)
Publishers of COIN NEWS etc.

Michael Trenerry
PO Box 55, Truro, Cornwall TR1 2YQ. (01872
277977, email veryfinecoins@aol.
com). By appointment only. **L** *Roman, Celtic and
English hammered coins and tokens.*

Vera Trinder Ltd
Unit 3a, Hayle Ind Park, Hayle, Cornwall TR27 5JR.
(01736 751 910, email: richardvtrinder@aol.com
www.veratrinder.co.uk). **L** *Coin accessories.*

Robert Tye
7–9 Clifford Street, York, YO1 9RA. (0845 4 900 724,
email: orders@earlyworlscoins.com. **P** *European
and Oriental hammered coins.*

Universal Currency Coin Exhange
PO Box 57648, Mill Hill, London, NW7 0FE.
(07831 662594, email: uccedcp@aol.com.)
*German, Canadian and American Coins.
Accumulations.*

Vale (ADA)
21 Tranquil Vale, Blackheath, London SE3 0BU.
(020 8852 9817. *British coins and medals.*

Van der Schueren, John-Luc (IAPN)
14 Rue de la Borse, 1,000 Bussels, Belgium. (Email:
iapnsecret@compuserve.com, www.coins.be.) Mon–
Fri 1100–1800 hrs. Coins and tokens of the world
and of the low countries.

Tony Vaughan Collectables
PO Box 364, Wolverhampton, WV3 9PW. (01902
27351). **P L** *World coins and medals.*

Victory Coins (BNTA)
184 Chichester Road, North End, Portsmouth,
Hants PO2 0AX. (023 92 751908/663450). Thurs–Sat
09.00–17.00. *British and world coins.*

Mark J. Vincenzi (BNTA)
Rylands, Earls Colne, Essex CO6 2LE. (01787
222555). **P** *Greek, Roman, Hammered.*

Mike Vosper
PO Box 32, Hockwold, Brandon IP26 4HX. (01842 828292, email: mikevosper@vosper4coins.co.uk, www.vosper4coins.co.uk). *Roman, Hammered.*

Weighton Collectables
50 Market Place, Market Weighton, York, Y043 3AL, (01430 879740, www.weightoncoin.co.uk). *Modern gold, silver proofs and sets.*

John Welsh
PO Box 150, Burton–on–Trent, Staffs DE13 7LB. (01543 73073 fax 0543 473234). **P L** *British coins.*

Pam West (IBNS, BNTA)
PO Box 257, Sutton, Surrey SM3 9WW. (020 8641 3224, email: pamwestbritnotes@aol.com, www. brishnotes.co.uk,). **P L** *English banknotes*

West Essex Coin Investments (BNTA, IBNS)
Croft Cottage, Station Road, Alderholt, Fordingbridge, Hants SP6 3AZ. (01425 656 459). *British and World coins and paper money.*

West Wicklow Coins
Blessington, Co Wicklow, Ireland. (00353 45 858767, email: westwicklowcoins@hotmail.com). *Irish and World coins.*

Whitmore (BNTA)
Teynham Lodge, Chase Road, Upper Colwall, Malvern, Worcs WR13 6DT. (01684 50651). **P** *World coins, tokens and medals.*

Simon Willis Coins
(07908 240978, swcoins@simonwilliscoins.com, www.simonwilliscoins.com). *Quality hammered and early milled British coins.*

Worldwide Coins (IBNS)
PO Box 11, Wavertree, Liverpool L15 0FG. (Email: sales@worldwidecoins.co.uk,www.worldwidecoins. co.uk. *World coins and paper money.*

World Treasure Books
PO Box 5, Newport, Isle of Wight PO30 5QE. (01983 740712). **L** *Coins, books, metal detectors.*

Barry Wright
54 Dooley Drive, Bootle, Merseyside. L3O 8RT. **P L** *World banknotes.*

I. S. Wright (Australia Numismatic Co)
208 Sturt Street, Ballarat, Vic. Australia 3350. (0061 3 5332 3856 fax 0061 3 5331 6426, email: ausnumis@netconnect.comau). **P** *Coins, banknotes, medallions, tokens.*

D. Yapp
PO Box 4718, Shrewsbury Mail Centre SY1 9EA. (01743 232557, www.david-yapp.com). **L** *World and British Banknotes.*

York Coins
PO Box 160, Red Hook, New York 12571. (Tel/fax: (718) 544 0120 email: antony@yorkcoins.com). *Ancient coins.*

York Coin and Stamp Centre
Cavendish Antique & Collectors Centre, 44 Stone gate, York, YO1 8AS. *Retail shop. Coins and medals.*

Coin fairs can be an unrivalled source of new material for the collector.

Banks, Mints and Numismatic
BUREAUX *of the* World

Many national banks and mints operate numismatic bureaux and sales agencies from which coins, medals and other numismatic products may be obtained direct. The conditions under which purchases may be made vary considerably. In many cases at the present time bureaux will accept orders from overseas customers quoting their credit card number and its expiry date; but in others payment can only be made by certified bank cheque, or international money order, or by girobank. Cash is seldom, if ever, acceptable. It is best to write in the first instance to enquire about methods of payment.

A

National Mint, Baghe Arg, Kabul, Afghanistan

Bank Mille Afghan, Kabul, Afghanistan

Banque d'Algerie, Sucursale d'Alger, 8 Boulevard Carnot, Alger, Algeria

Banco de Angola, Luanda, Daroal, Angola

Casa de Moneda de la Nacion, Avenida Antartica, Buenos Aires, BA, Argentina

Royal Australian Mint, Department of the Treasury, Canberra, ACT, Australia

GoldCorp Australia, Perth Mint Buildings, GPO Box M924, Perth, Western Australia 6001

Oesterreichsiches Hauptmunzamt, Am Heumarkt 1, A-1031 Wien, Postfach 225, Austria

Oesterreichische Nationalbank, A-1090 Wien, Otto Wagner-platz 3, Austria

B

Treasury Department, PO Box 557, Nassau, Bahamas (*coins*)

Ministry of Finance, PO Box 300, Nassau, Bahamas (*banknotes*)

Bank of Bahrain, PO Box 106, Manama, Bahrain

Eastern Bank, PO Box 29, Manama, Bahrain

Monnaie Royale de Belgique, Avenue de Pacheco 32, B-1000 Bruxelles, Belgium

Banque Nationale de Belgique SA, Caisse Centrale, Bruxelles, Belgium

Banque de Bruxelles SA, 2 Rue de la Regence, Bruxelles 1, Belgium

Casa de la Moneda, Potosi, BoliviaBanco Central de Bolivia, La Paz, Bolivia

Casa da Moeda, Praca da Republica 173, Rio de Janeiro, Brazil

Hemus FTO, 7 Vasil Levski Street, Sofia C-1, Bulgaria

Banque de la Republique, Bujumbura, Burundi

C

Banque Centrale, Douala, Boite Postale 5.445, Cameroun

Royal Canadian Mint, 320 Sussex Drive, Ottawa 2, Ontario, Canada K1A 0G8

Casa de Moneda, Quinta Normal, Santiago, Chile

Casa de Moneda, Calle 11 no 4-93, Bogota, Colombia

Numismatic Section, The Treasury, Avarua, Rarotonga, Cook Islands

Banco Centrale de Costa Rica, Departamento de Contabilidad, San Jose, Costa Rica, CA

Central Bank of Cyprus, PO Box 1087, Nicosia, Cyprus

Artia, Ve Smekach 30, PO Box 790, Praha 1, Czech Republic

D

Den Kongelige Mønt, Amager Boulevard 115, København S, Denmark

Danmarks Nationalbank, Holmens Kanal 17, 1060 København K, Denmark

Banco Central de Santo Domingo, Santo Domingo, Dominican Republic

E

Banco Central, Quito, Ecuador

Mint House, Abbassia, Cairo, Egyptian Arab Republic

Exchange Control Department, National Bank of Egypt, Cairo, Egyptian Arab Republic

Banco Central de la Republica, Santa Isabel, Equatorial Guinea

Commercial Bank of Ethiopia, Foreign Branch, PO Box 255, Addis Ababa, Ethiopia

F

Currency Board, Victoria Parade, Suva, Fiji

Suomen Rahapaja, Katajanokanlaituri 3, Helsinki 16, Finland

Suomen Pankki, PO Box 10160, Helsinki 10, Finland

Hotel de Monnaie, 11 Quai de Conti, 75-Paris 6e, France

G

Banque Centrale Libreville, Boite Postale 112, Gabon

Verkaufstelle fur Sammlermunzen, D-638 Bad Homburg vdH, Bahnhofstrasse 16–18, Germany

Staatliche Munze Karlsruhe, Stephanienstrasse 28a, 75 Karlsruhe, Germany

Staatliche Munze Cannstatt, Taubenheimerstrasse 77, 7 Stuttgart-Bad, Germany

Bayerisches Hauptmunzamt, Hofgraben 4, 8 Munich, Germany

Hamburgische Munze, Norderstrasse 66, 2 Hamburg 1, Germany

Bank of Ghana, PO Box 2674, Accra, Ghana

Pobjoy Mint, Millennia House, Kingswood Park, Bonsor Drive, Kingswood, Surrey KT20 6AY

Royal Mint, Llantrisant, Mid Glamorgan, Wales, CF7 8YT

Royal Mint Coin Club, PO Box 500, Cardiff, CF1 1HA

Bank of Greece, Treasury Department, Cash, Delivery & Despatch Division, PO Box 105, Athens, Greece

Casa Nacional de Moneda, 6a Calle 4-28, Zona 1, Ciudad Guatemala, Republica de Guatemala CA

States Treasury, St Peter Port, Guernsey, Channel Islands

Bank of Guyana, PO Box 658, Georgetown, Guyana

H

Banque Nationale de la Republique d'Haiti, Rue Americaine et Rue Fereu, Port-au-Prince, Haiti

Banco Central de Honduras, Tegucigalpa DC, Honduras CA

State Mint, Ulloi utca 102, Budapest VIII, Hungary

Artex, PO Box 167, Budapest 62, Hungary

Magyar Nemzeti Bank, Board of Exchange, Budapest 54, Hungary

I

Sedlabanki Islands, Reykjavik, Iceland

Indian Government Mint, Bombay 1, India

Arthie Vasa, Keabajoran Baru, Djakarta, Indonesia

Perum Peruri, Djakarta, Indonesia

National Mint, Tehran, Iran

Bank Markazi Iran, Tehran, IranCentral Bank of Iraq, PO Box 64, Baghdad, Iraq

Central Bank of Ireland, Dublin 2, Republic of Ireland

The Treasury, Government Buildings, Prospect Hill, Douglas, Isle of Man

Israel Stamp and Coin Gallery, 4 Maze Street, Tel Aviv, Israel

Istituto Poligraphico e Zecca dello Stato, Via Principe Umberto, Roma, Italy

J

Decimal Currency Board, PO Box 8000, Kingston, Jamaica

Mint Bureau, 1 Shinkawasakicho, Kita-ku, Osaka 530, Japan

Numismatic Section, Treasury Department, St Helier, Jersey

Central Bank of Jordan, Amman, Jordan

Banque Nationale du Liban, Rue Masraf Loubnan, Beirut, Lebanon

K

Central Bank, PO Box 526, Kuwait

L

Bank of LatviaK. Valdemara iela 2A, LV-1050, Riga, Latvia

Bank of Lithuania, Cash Department, Gedimino av. 6, 2001 Vilius, Lithuania

Caisse Generale de l'Etat, 5 Rue Goethe, Luxembourg-Ville, Grande Duche de Luxembourg

M

Institut d'Emission Malgache, Boite Postale 205, Tananarive, Madagascar

Central Bank of Malta, Valletta 1, Malta

Casa de Moneda, Calle del Apartado no 13, Mexico 1, DF, Mexico

Le Tresorier General des Finances, Monte Carlo, Principaute de Monaco

Banque de l'Etat du Maroc, Rabat, Morocco

Banco Nacional Ultramarino, Maputo, Republica de Mocambique

British Bank of the Middle East, Muscat

N

Royal Mint, Dharahara, Katmandu, Nepal

Nepal Rastra Bank, Katmandu, Nepal

Rijks Munt, Leidseweg 90, Utrecht, Netherlands

Hollandsche Bank-Unie NV, Willemstad, Breedestraat 1, Curacao, Netherlands Antilles

Central Bank of Curacao, Willemstad, Curacao, Netherlands Antilles

New Zealand Post Stamps Centre, Private Bag 3001, Wanganui 4540, New Zealand

Banco de Nicaragua, Departamento de Emison, La Tresoria, Apartada 2252, Managua, Nicaragua

Nigerian Security Printing and Minting Corporation, Ahmadu Bello Road, Victoria Island, Lagos, Nigeria

Central Bank of Nigeria, Tinubu Square LB, Lagos, Nigeria

Norges Bank, Oslo, Norway

Den Kongelige Mynt, Hyttegaten, Konigsberg, Norway

P

Pakistan State Mint, Baghban Pura, Lahore 9, Pakistan

National Development Bank, Asuncion, Paraguay

Casa Nacional de Moneda, Calle Junin 791, Lima, Peru

Central Bank of the Philippines, Manila, Philippines

Bank Handlowy w Warszawie, Ul. Romuald Traugutta 7, Warsaw, Poland

Desa Foreign Trade Department, Al. Jerozolimskie 2, Warszawa, Poland

Casa da Moeda, Avenida Dr Antonio Jose de Almeida, Lisbon 1, Portugal

R

Cartimex, 14-18 Aristide Briand St, PO Box 134-135, Bucharest, Roumania

Bank of Foreign Trade, Commercial Department, Moscow K 16, Neglinnaja 12, Russian Federation

Banque Nationale du Rwanda, Boite Postale 351, Kigali, Republique Rwandaise

S

Numismatic Section, Box 194, GPO, Apia, Samoa

Azienda Autonoma di Stato Filatelica-Numismatica, Casalla Postale 1, 47031 Repubblica di San Marino

Banque Internationale pour le Commerce, 2 Avenue Roume, Dakar, Senegal

Bank of Yugoslavia, PO Box 1010, Belgrade, Serbia

The Treasury, PO Box 59, Victoria, Seychelles

Bank of Sierra Leone, PO Box 30, Freetown, Sierra Leone

The Singapore Mint, 20 Teban Gardens Crescent, Singapore 608928

South African Mint, PO Box 464, Pretoria, South Africa

Government Printing Agency, 93 Bukchang Dong, Chungku, Seoul, Republic of South Korea

Fabrica Nacional de Moneda y Timbre, Jorge Juan 106, Madrid 9, Spain

Bank of Sri Lanka, PO Box 241, Colombo, Sri Lanka

Hong Kong and Shanghai Banking Corporation, PO Box 73, Colombo 1, Sri Lanka

Sudan Mint, PO Box 43, Khartoum, Sudan

Bank of Sudan, PO Box 313, Khartoum, Sudan

Bank of Paramaribo, Paramaribo, Suriname

Kungelige Mynt och Justeringsverket, Box 22055, Stockholm 22, Sweden

Eidgenossische Staatskasse, Bundesgasse 14, CH-3003, Berne, Switzerland

Central Bank of Syria, Damascus, Syrian Arab Republic

T

Central Mint of China, 44 Chiu Chuan Street, Taipei, Taiwan, ROC

Royal Thai Mint, 4 Chao Fah Road, Bangkok, Thailand

Numismatic Section, The Treasury, Nuku'alofa, Tonga

Central Bank of Trinidad and Tobago, PO Box 1250, Port of Spain, Trinidad

Banque Centrale de Tunisie, Tunis, Tunisia

State Mint, Maliye Bakanligi Darphane Mudurlugu, Istanbul, Turkey

U

Bank of Uganda, PO Box 7120, Kampala, Uganda

Numismatic Service, US Assay Office, 350 Duboce Avenue, San Francisco, CA, 94102, USA

Office of the Director of the Mint, Treasury Department, Washington, DC, 20220, USA

Philadelphia Mint, 16th and Spring Garden Streets, Philadelphia, PA, 19130, USA

Franklin Mint, Franklin Center, Pennsylvania, 19063, USA

Banco Central del Uruguay, Cerrito 351, Montevideo, RO del Uruguay

V

Ufficio Numismatico, Governatorato dello Stato della Citta de Vaticano, Italy

Banco Central de Venezuela, Caracas, Venezuela

Y

Yemen Bank, Sana'a, Yemen.

Z

Bank of Zambia, PO Box 80, Lusaka, Zambia

Chief Cashier, Reserve Bank, PO Box 1283, Harare, Zimbabwe

TREASURE *and the law*

Until the introduction of the new Treasure Act, the legal position regarding articles of gold, silver or bullion, found long after they were hidden or abandoned, was not as simple and straightforward as it might be supposed. Furthermore, this was a case where the law in England and Wales differed fundamentally from that in Scotland.

Treasure Trove was one of the most ancient rights of the Crown, deriving from the age-old right of the monarch to gold, silver or bullion treasure whose owner was not known. In England and Wales, the law applied only to objects made of, or containing, gold or silver, whether in the form of coin, jewellery, plate or bullion. Moreover, the object had to be shown to have been deliberately hidden with intent to retrieve and the owner could not be readily found. The English law therefore excluded precious stones and jewels set in base metals or alloys such as bronze or pewter. It also took no account of artifacts in pottery, stone, bone, wood or glass which might be of immense antiquarian value.

In recent years, as a result of the rise in metal-detecting as a hobby, the archaeological lobby brought pressure to bear on Parliament to change the law and bring it into line with Scotland where the rules on Treasure Trove were far more rigorously interpreted. In Scotland the Crown is entitled to *all* abandoned property, even if it has not been hidden and is of little value. This applies even to objects dumped in skips on the pavement. Strictly speaking you would be committing a criminal offence if you removed an old chair from a skip without the owner's permission, although in practice such helping oneself rarely proceeds to a prosecution. In 1958 an archaeological expedition from Aberdeen University found several valuable

It's not only British coins that get unearthed by detectorists. Enthusiast John Stoner discovered a small silver coin in a Nottinghamshire field one summer day which turned out to be a rare Massachusetts threepence—one of only a small number minted in the middle of the 17th century in what was the new colony of New England!

In March 2014, near Winchester, a small but exceedingly rare gold coin (minted c. 50–30 BC) and weighing no more than a gram was discovered by one lucky metal detectorist. This Ancient British gold quarter stater shows two snakelike corded crescents on one side and a lanky belted horse on the other side. Only one other example is known.

artifacts on St Ninian's Isle, Shetland. These included silver vessels and ornaments, as well as a porpoise bone which had incised decoration on it. The archaeologists challenged the rights of the Crown to this treasure, arguing that the Crown would have to prove that the articles had been deliberately hidden, and that a porpoise bone was in any case not valuable enough to count as treasure. The High Court, however, decided that as long as the property had been abandoned, it belonged automatically to the Crown. Its value, intrinsic or otherwise, or whether or not it was hidden, did not make any difference. Since then, as a result of this decision in case law, the criteria for Treasure Trove have been very strictly applied in Scotland. It would have only required a similar test case in England or Wales to result in a similar tightening of the rules. This has been resisted, mainly by the detectorist lobby, but inevitably the government considered legislation to control the use of metal detectors, if not to ban them altogether.

In England and Wales a find of gold or silver coins, artifacts or ornaments, or objects which contain some of these metals, which appears to have been concealed by the original owner, was deemed to be Treasure Trove. It was not even necessary for the articles to be buried in the ground; objects concealed in thatched roofs or under the floorboards of buildings have been judged to be Treasure Trove. Such finds had to be notified immediately to the police who then informed the district coroner. He then convened an inquest which decided whether all or part of the find was Treasure Trove. Establishing the gold or silver content was straightforward, but

the coroner's inquest had to decide whether the material was hidden deliberately and not just lost or abandoned, and that the owner could not be located. A gold coin found on or near a country footpath might reasonably have been dropped by the original possessor through a hole in pocket or purse and in such cases it was very unlikely that it would be deemed Treasure Trove, even if the coin turned out to be very rare. In this instance the coroner would then have had to determine who was the lawful owner of the find: the actual finder, the owner of the land where it was found or even the tenant of the land. As a rule, however, it was left to the finder and landowner to decide between them who the owner of the coin should be, and in some cases the matter could only be resolved by referring to a civil court. For this reason it was vital that metal detectorists should secure permission *in writing* from landowners before going on to their land, defining rights and obligations on both sides, in order to determine the disposal or share-out of any finds or proceeds from the sale of finds, *beforehand*.

If the coroner decided that the articles were deliberately concealed, and declared them to be Treasure Trove, the find automatically reverted to the Crown. In practice the find was considered by the Treasure Trove Reviewing Committee of the Treasury. They might decide that although the articles, *invariably coins,* were gold or silver, they were so common that they were not required by the British Museum or one of the other great national collections, and would return them to the finder to dispose of at their discretion. If some or all of the coins were deemed vital for inclusion in a national collection the finder was recompensed with the full market value of the material. On the other hand, if someone found gold or silver which might be Treasure Trove and failed to declare it at the time, that person was liable to prosecution under the Theft Act 1968 should the find subsequently come to light. Not only could they face a heavy fine but the articles would be forfeit to the Crown, and of course no reward or recompense was then payable either.

The anomalies and inconsistencies of existing law on Treasure Trove were eliminated and the position considerably tightened up by the passage, on July 5, 1996, of the Treasure Act.

Announcing that the Treasure Act had received the Royal Assent, Lord Inglewood, National Heritage Minister, said, "This represents the first legislation on Treasure Trove to be passed in England and Wales and will replace Common Law precedents and practices dating back to the Middle Ages. The Act, which offers a clearer definition of treasure and simplified procedures for dealing with finds, will come into force after a code of practice has been drawn up and agreed by both Houses of Parliament". The Act came into force in England, Wales and Northern Ireland on September 24, 1997, replacing the Common Law of Treasure Trove.

The act was introduced as a Private Member's Bill by Sir Anthony Grant, after the failure of an earlier attempt by Lord Perth. For the first time, it would be a criminal offence to fail to report within 14 days the discovery of an item which could be declared Treasure Trove. Finders will continue to be rewarded for reporting their discoveries promptly, while landowners and occupiers will also be eligible for rewards for the first time.

The Treasure Act covers man-made objects and defines treasure as objects other than coins which are at least 300 years old and contain at least 10 per cent by weight of gold or silver; coins more than 300 years old which are found in hoards (a minimum of two coins if the precious metal content is more than 10 per cent, and a minimum of 10 coins if the precious metal content is below 10 per cent). The act also embraces all objects found in clear archaeological association with items which are treasure under the above definitions. It also covers any object which would have been Treasure Trove under the previous definitions (e.g. hoards of 19th century gold or silver coins).

An extension to The Act from January 1992 provides that groups of prehistoric bronze implements are also deemed to be Treasure.

The maximum penalty for failing to report the discovery of treasure within 14 days will be a fine of £5,000 or three months imprisonment, or both.

In Scotland the police pass the goods on to the procurator fiscal who acts as the local representative of the Queen's and Lord Treasurer's Remembrancer. If the articles are of little value, historically or intrinsically, the finder will usually be allowed to keep them. If they are retained for the appropriate national collection then a reward equal to the market value is payable.

A favourite haunt of metal-detectorists these days is the beach, and many hobbyists make quite a lucrative living by sweeping the beaches especially just after a Bank Holiday. It's surprising how much loose change gets lost from pockets and

One of the largest and best preserved 4th century collections of copper-alloy Roman coins ever to have been found in Britain was unearthed near the popular seaside town of Seaton in East Devon in November 2013.

handbags over a holiday weekend. Technically the coins recovered from the beach are lost property, in which case they ought to be surrendered to the police, otherwise the finder may be guilty of theft. In practice, however, the law turns a blind eye to coins, on the sensible grounds that it would be impossible to prove ownership. On the other hand, banknotes are treated as lost property since someone could in theory at least identify a note as his by citing the serial number.

In the case of other objects, such as watches and jewellery, of course the law governing lost property is enforced, and the old adage of "finders keepers" does not apply. Any object of value, identifiable as belonging to someone, that is washed up on the foreshore or found in territorial waters is known technically as "wreck". This includes not just a wrecked ship, but any cargo that was being carried by a ship.

If wreck is not claimed by its owner, it falls to the Crown. In this case it is not necessary to prove deliberate concealment, as in the case of Treasure Trove. This law has a specific numismatic application in the case of the gold and silver coins washed up after storms around our shores, from Shetland to the Scillies. Such coins, emanating from wrecks of Spanish treasure ships and Dutch East Indiamen in particular, are well documented, and any such finds ought to be reported immediately to the police.

Stray finds of coins, as well as other objects of value, on public places, such as the street, a public park or a sports ground, are also subject to law. In this case the finder must take all reasonable steps to locate the owner. Anyone who keeps a coin without making reasonable effort to find the owner could be prosecuted for theft. As with the beach, however, such "reasonable effort" would clearly be impractical. Finding coins on private premises is another matter. In this case large bodies, such as the Post Office, British Rail, the British Airports Authority, bus companies, municipal authorities, hospitals, the owners of department stores, theatre and cinema proprietors and the like, may have bye-laws, rules and regulations for dealing with lost property found within their precincts, or in their vehicles. If you found a purse or wallet on a bus or train, or in a telephone kiosk or a shop, common sense (and your conscience) would tell you to hand it over to the driver, conductor, shopkeeper or official in charge. As a rule, unclaimed lost property reverts eventually to the finder, but not always; British Rail and some other organisations have a rule that in such cases the property reverts to the organisation. In any event, failure to disclose the find immediately might render you liable to prosecution for stealing by finding.

Paul Coleman with his amazing find (courtesy Paul Coleman). One of the largest hoards of Anglo Saxon coins ever discovered in England. For the full story see COIN NEWS March 2015.

ADVERTISERS *Directory*

See our website at tokenpublishing.com for up-to-date dealer entries, with hyperlinks taking you directly to their websites.